MOTOR LEARNING
CONCEPTS AND APPLICATIONS

MOTOR LEARNING
CONCEPTS AND APPLICATIONS

■

FOURTH EDITION

RICHARD A. MAGILL

Louisiana State University

WCB Brown & Benchmark
PUBLISHERS

Madison, Wisconsin•Indianapolis, Indiana
Melbourne, Australia•Oxford, England

Book Team

Editor *Chris Rogers*
Developmental Editor *Scott Spoolman*
Production Editor *Deborah J. Donner*
Photo Editor *Shirley Charley*
Permissions Editor *Mavis M. Oeth*
Visuals/Design Freelance Specialist *Sherry Padden*
Visuals/Design Developmental Consultant *Marilyn A. Phelps*
Visuals/Design Developmental Associate *Mary L. Christianson*

 Brown &
Benchmark

A Division of Wm. C. Brown Communications, Inc.

Vice President and General Manager *Thomas E. Doran*
Editor in Chief *Edgar J. Laube*
Executive Editor *Ed Bartell*
Executive Editor *Stan Stoga*
National Sales Manager *Eric Ziegler*
Marketing Manager *Pamela S. Cooper*
Director of CourseResource *Kathy Law Laube*
Director of CourseSystems *Chris Rogers*

Director of Marketing *Sue Simon*
Director of Production *Vickie Putman Caughron*
Imaging Group Manager *Chuck Carpenter*
Manager of Visuals and Design *Faye M. Schilling*
Design Manager *Jac Tilton*
Art Manager *Janice Roerig*
Permissions/Records Manager *Connie Allendorf*

Wm. C. Brown Communications, Inc.

Chairman Emeritus *Wm. C. Brown*
Chairman and Chief Executive Officer *Mark C. Falb*
President and Chief Operating Officer *G. Franklin Lewis*
Corporate Vice President, President of WCB Manufacturing *Roger Meyer*

Cover photograph © Michael Stuckey/Comstock, Inc.

Part Opener photographs: 1, 3: © Jean-Claude Lejeune; 2: © Bruce Ayres/Tony Stone Worldwide.

Interior and cover design by **Tara Bazata**

The following illustrations by **Burmar Technical Corporation:** Figures 1.2-1, 1.2-8, 1.2-9, 2.2-4, 3.2-1, 3.2-4, 3.2-5, 3.2-7, 3.2-8, 3.3-4, 3.3-6, 3.4-2, 4.1-1, 4.2-2, 5.2-4, 7.1-1, 7.2-1, 7.3-1, 7.3-5, 7.4-2, 7.4-3, 7.4-7, 7.4-8, 7.5-2, 7.5-4, 8.1-5 and 8.4-1.

The credits section for this book begins on page 445 and is considered an extension of the copyright page.

In Memory of Susan

CONTENTS

UNIT 2

The Learner   83

UNIT 3

The Learning Environment 280

PREFACE

☐ This fourth edition continues the approach to the study of motor learning established in the first edition and carried on in the second and third editions. This approach views motor learning as an important component of the foundation needed to understand human behavior as it relates to learning and performing motor skills. And it sees motor learning as an essential body of knowledge underlying the development of successful instruction and training strategies critical for skill acquisition. The orientation of this text is also the same as in previous editions. The text examines motor learning issues from a behavioral perspective, as opposed to a physiological one.

The emphasis remains on those issues that are particularly relevant for application to human motor skill learning and performance situations in a variety of contexts. In fact, this fourth edition has been developed with the idea to enhance its application focus by expanding the number and type of skill performance situations described in the Application and Discussion sections of each concept. This is in response to a criticism of previous editions that the applications were too sport-

or physical education-context oriented. This criticism is an important concern because increasing numbers of users of this text are going into occupations other than teaching and coaching. Prominent has been the physical and occupational therapy professions in which motor learning is taking a more pronounced role in professional preparation. Accordingly, effort has been directed in this edition to include more applications relevant to rehabilitation settings.

While the overall orientation of this textbook remains consistent with previous editions, specific changes have been made in the organization and content of this edition. In terms of content, the entire book has been updated to include the latest research evidence related to each concept. Determining what research to include and how much is always a difficult process. However, as in the previous editions, the guiding principle has been to describe research that illustrates the empirical basis for the concept being discussed.

Because this is an introductory test designed with the undergraduate student in mind, discussion of controversial theoretical and empirical issues again have been kept to a minimum. This approach is in keeping with the overall goal to provide the student with fundamental information indicating "what we know," even though that knowledge may include arguable or controversial points. Providing this level of information has a twofold benefit. One, it establishes for the student a sufficient motor learning foundation for developing effective and efficient teaching, training, or rehabilitation strategies. Two, it gives the student who goes on to advanced study in motor learning a base on which to build a more complex knowledge structure.

One of the organizational changes in this edition has been to move some concepts from where they were located in the third edition. The most prominent is the relocation of two concepts that were previously in a chapter titled "Transfer of Learning." That chapter has been eliminated and one of the transfer concepts moved to Chapter 2 (Concept 2.3), another moved to Chapter 3 (Concept 3.4), and the third deleted altogether. The purpose of this change was to place the study of transfer in a more appropriate light. Throughout most of the history of the study of human learning and performance, transfer has been viewed as an entity in its own right rather than as one of the several processes involved in learning and performance. Because transfer of skill performance capability results from skill learning, transfer is better seen as an essential element in learning and performance. Accordingly, an introduction to the notion of transfer is provided as a concept in Chapter 2, which is an introduction to motor skill learning. And bilateral transfer is included in Chapter 3, which examines specific motor control issues. Reference to various transfer issues can be seen in chapters throughout this edition.

Another change has been to restructure what were chapters on knowledge of results (KR) and practice in previous editions. In this fourth edition, concepts related to KR are included in the chapter on instruction and augmented feedback (Chapter 7). Also in this chapter, two concepts, one related to modeling and the other to whole vs. part practice, have been added. Both of these were previously in the chapter on practice. The remaining concepts from the chapter on practice from the third edition have been kept intact, but the chapter title has been changed to "Practice Organization" (Chapter 8), to reflect the specific practice component to which the present set of concepts refers.

It will be apparent to users of previous editions that the approach to discussing KR has been changed. KR is now presented more specifically as one of several types of augmented feedback. This change was made to reflect what has become increasingly more apparent about the previous approach to discussing KR, which was too restrictive and needed to be expanded to include more information about other types of augmented feedback.

The chapter on attention (Chapter 4) has been reorganized from the previous edition. In the present edition, the concept on attention as limited processing capacity is the first rather than the second concept. This change reflects what is seen as providing a more appropriate arrangement of concepts with the most foundational one presented first. Because selective attention (Concept 4.2) and movement preparation (Concept 4.3) demands and characteristics are in large part due to attention capacity limits, presenting a discussion on attention capacity limits first is seen as a more logical organization for this chapter.

The chapter in this edition titled "Motivating Achievement" (Chapter 9) is a change in both organization and content from the third edition. A title change (from "Motivation") was done to reflect a more appropriate perspective on how motivation is being considered in this text. That is, only issues related to achievement motivation are at issue. As a result, the concept on motivation from the third edition has been deleted, and the concept on arousal and anxiety from the third edition has been incorporated into the concept on alertness and movement preparation (Concept 43). This latter change reflects the general approach taken in this book that psychological constructs are presented in the context of their relationship to motor skill learning and performance. Finally, the concept related to goal setting has been expanded to more adequately reflect the increased amount of theory and research efforts commonly neglected in the study of motor learning.

Three notable content changes from previous editions reflect changing research capabilities and directions in the study of motor learning. One of these is seen in Concept 1.2 where motor performance measurement is discussed. Added to this discussion has been an expanded discussion of kinematic measures. Becoming familiar with these types of performance measures is important for all students of motor learning because these measures are being seen with increasing regularity in the motor skills literature. As laboratories expand their levels of sophistication and gain access to computer-based movement analysis systems, this type of skill performance measurement will become the norm for motor learning research.

The two content changes that reflect new directions in the study of motor learning can be seen in the chapter titled "Controlling Movement" (Chapter 3). One is that an entire Concept (3.2) is now devoted to issues related to the role of vision in motor skill performance. In the third edition, a discussion of the role of vision was included for the first time to reflect the critical nature of this issue. Since that time, research activity has increased tremendously in both amount and direction. This new concept reflects those characteristics as they relate to learning and performing motor skills. The second content change in Chapter 3 has been to include information about a theoretical view of motor learning and performance known as "dynamic systems theory." This information was not included in previous editions and is now incorporated into Chapter 3 to show the increase in prominence attained by this view, which is an alternative approach to the theoretical orientation of this chapter in previous editions.

For the many users who indicated that the concept on the anatomy and physiology of the motor control system presented in the previous three editions seemed to be an out-of-place appendage in this book, note that it is not included in this fourth edition. Rather than expand that concept, which some had recommended, the decision was to delete it altogether, which was also recommended by some users. This decision was made on the basis of determining which option would be more in keeping with the overall orientation of the book. Because the emphasis is to look at motor learning and performance from a behavioral perspective and to emphasize an applied orientation, there was little doubt that including rudimentary information about the anatomy and physiology of the motor control system was not needed.

Pedagogically, the format of the previous editions has been maintained in this edition. Each chapter is subdivided into several distinct concepts developed to succinctly state information considered important to establish a fundamental level of understanding of the chapter topic. Each concept is presented first to give the student a focal point to guide his or her study of the discussion of that concept. And, before that discussion, there is an application section designed to give the concept relevance and meaning to the student. Also, related readings are recommended at the end of the discussion of each concept to provide the instructor and/or student with more in-depth information related to the concept. Study questions are again provided at the end of each chapter to direct the instructor and student to the key information contained in the chapter. Key terms for each concept and a glossary for those words have been added as important new pedagogical aids to assist students in acquiring the "language" of motor learning. Finally, the Subject Index has been expanded with particular attention given to including specific examples of motor skills.

It is important to acknowledge and thank the people who have contributed in various ways to this fourth edition. Chief among these is Tim Lee, who has provided critical comments and content suggestions throughout the revision process. His continued friendship and willingness to serve as a vital sounding board and source of criticism and reinforcement are deeply appreciated. I would also like to thank those anonymous individuals, my editors at Brown and Benchmark. I would also like to thank those individuals asked to provide reviews of the previous edition to provide me with direction for developing the present edition: Professor Bill Vogler, Arizona State University; Dr. Richard Engelhorn, Iowa State University; Professor Roger Simmons, San Diego State University; Professor Bill Kozar, Boise State University. The reviewers' comments and suggestions provided a good foundation from which to develop revision plans. Special thanks are due to Kathy Mueller, one of my doctoral students. She helped immeasurably in putting together this edition by assisting with developing the glossary, references, and the two indexes, and by providing editorial and critical comments on various drafts of the manuscript. Also, thanks to Marie Bernard for her assistance with typing the first draft of the glossary. As in previous editions, I cannot overlook the contributions to this book made by the students in my undergraduate and graduate motor learning classes who have contributed in immeasurable ways to this book. Their input needs to be acknowledged even though they are largely unaware of their influence. I would also like to acknowledge the important contribution of colleagues who have used this book in their classes and who have reported errors and have offered many helpful suggestions.

Richard A. Magill
Baton Rouge, Louisiana

MOTOR LEARNING
CONCEPTS AND APPLICATIONS

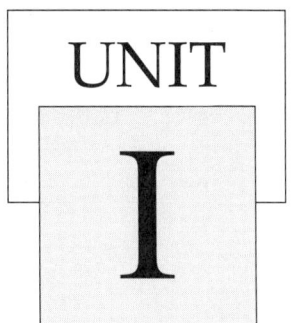

UNIT

I

INTRODUCTION TO MOTOR LEARNING

INTRODUCTION TO MOTOR SKILLS AND MOTOR LEARNING RESEARCH

CONCEPT 1.1
Motor skills can be classified into general categories.

CONCEPT 1.2
The measurement of motor performance is a critical part of understanding motor learning.

CONCEPT 1.3
The scientific method, or research, is an important tool
in understanding motor skill learning and performance.

□

CONCEPT 1.1

Motor skills can be classified into general categories

――――

Key Terms

skill	fine motor skill	continuous motor skill
action		
ability	discrete motor skill	closed motor skill
gross motor skill	serial motor skill	open motor skills

Application

Playing a piano, dancing, walking with an artificial limb, throwing a baseball, hitting a squash ball, operating a wood lathe, and piloting an airplane are all rather diverse and unique skills. However, each of these is a motor skill. In this text you will be presented with information that will help you understand how we learn and perform motor skills such as these, as well as how we can teach motor skills.

As you venture through this study you will find that it will be helpful to be able to draw general conclusions and make applications that can be related to a broad range of motor skills. You will inevitably find that this is preferable to being limited to making specific statements about each skill.

The discussion section of this concept presents a starting point for making these kinds of general statements. That starting point involves knowing what motor skills are and how they can be classified into broad categories that emphasize the similarities rather than the distinctions among skills.

For example, piloting an airplane and playing the piano seem quite distinct from each other. However, based on at least one of their underlying components, some similarity can be seen between these skills; and this is important for designing instruction. Both tasks involve serial movements. That is, in order for these tasks to be performed correctly, a certain number of distinct movements must occur in a very specific order. If any part of the series of movements is forgotten, or if the order is improperly arranged, the probability for successful performance of these skills is diminished. In this way, then, generalizations can be made concerning the learning of skills involving serial movements. Therefore, two seemingly diverse skills such as piano playing and piloting an airplane become related when those generalizations are applied to specific motor skills.

――――――― □ ―――――――

Discussion

As you begin your study of motor learning, it is important to discover some essential information about the skills that are the focus of this book. In this discussion we will address two aspects of this information. First, we will consider what motor skills are and what distinguishes them from other skills. Second, we will discuss how motor skills can be classified into categories that identify common characteristics of various skills. We will discuss three different methods that have been developed

to classify motor skills. As you have just read, the benefit of this classification process is to provide us with a better understanding of what motor skills are as well as a basis for establishing generalizations, or principles, about how we perform and learn motor skills. These generalizations enable us to develop theories about how we perform and learn skills. Additionally, they help establish guidelines for developing effective instructional strategies to enhance motor skill learning and rehabilitation.

Skill

Before specifically defining what is meant by the term *motor skill,* it will be helpful to first consider the "skill" part of that term, a term that is often misunderstood. The word *skill* can be used in different ways in different contexts. For instance, its meaning when used as "That tennis player is a tremendously skilled performer," is rather distinct from its meaning when the term is used as "Serving is a skill essential to playing tennis." Each of these distinct uses of the term skill is appropriate and will be used throughout this text.

Skill as an act or task. When the term *skill* is used in connection with the example of serving in tennis as a skill, it denotes an action or a task that has a specific goal to achieve. Piano playing, welding, swimming, picking up a cup, and leaping are other examples of skills in the motor domain. The use of the term *skill* in this manner is quite straightforward and causes little confusion regarding its meaning. In this text, when the term **skill** is used to refer to a *motor skill,* it denotes *an action or a task that has a goal and that requires voluntary body and/or limb movement to achieve the goal.* Thus, the skill of piano playing has a goal of striking the correct keys in the proper sequence and at the approriate time, and it requires finger and hand movement to achieve that goal.

The way in which we will use the term *skill* indicates that there are several characteristics common to motor skills. First, there is a goal to achieve, which means that skills have a purpose. You may see the term "action goal" used in motor learning and control literature when the goal of a motor skill is discussed. Second, skills are performed voluntarily, which indicates that we are not considering reflexes as skills. Although an eye blink may have a purpose and can be classified as an action involving movement, it occurs involuntarily and is therefore not a skill in the sense that we are using the term. Third, a motor skill requires body and/or limb movement to accomplish the goal of the action or task. This characteristic indicates that when we use the term skill, we are referring to a specific type of skill. Although

reading and calculating math problems are skills, they do not require body and/or limb movement to achieve their goals. Thus, these types of skills are not motor skills, but are commonly referred to as cognitive skills.

One additional point needs to be mentioned here. In this text our interest is in motor skills that have in common the property of needing to be learned in order for the goal of the skill to be successfully achieved. For example, while walking may seem to be something that humans do "naturally," it requires learning by the child who is attempting to move in his or her environment by this new and exciting means of locomotion. Also, walking is a skill that must be re-learned by a person who has had hip or knee joint replacement surgery, or by a person who must learn to walk with an artificial leg.

An important characteristic of motor skills, when viewed from the perspective or motor learning and control theory, is that skill is synonymous with the term *action.* That is, an **action** is viewed as a goal-directed response that consists of body and/or limb movements. What is important here is that a variety of movements or movement patterns can produce the same action. For example, if we consider hitting a baseball with a bat as an action, it is easy to see that no one pattern of movement must be produced to achieve the goal of this action, which is to hit the ball with the bat. A person can achieve this goal by using a variety of movement patterns, even though some may be better than others. It should be noted, however, that there are some exceptions. In some cases an action goal can only be achieved by a very limited set of specific movement patterns. These exceptions involve skills where performance criteria are established and must be met in order for the goal to be achieved. Some examples include skills such as those involved in gymnastics and diving.

Skill as an indicator of quality performance.
Probably a more confusing and ambiguous use of the term *skill* occurs when it is used to refer to a skilled performer. In this use, **skill** is a *qualitative*

expression of performance. Here the word connotes a degree of proficiency that is often subjectively determined. That proficiency can be expressed in different ways. One way is to establish a degree of *productivity* that would characterize a skilled performer. For example, we would most likely agree that a basketball player is a skilled free throw shooter if he or she can make 80% of free throws attempted. We likewise would consider a tennis player a skilled server if 60% to 70% of their first serves are good. These examples indicate that skill is judged by productivity of performance. An important characteristic of the use of the term skill in relation to productivity is relative to the context of the performance. The "skilled" professional tennis player is judged by a much more stringent set of criteria to be acclaimed skilled than is the high school player. This seems especially apparent when the person's peers are the judges.

A second means of expressing that an individual is a skilled performer is on the basis of certain *characteristics of the person's performance.* These characteristics can include such things as the consistency of performance, the use of meaningful cues rather than being distracted by non-meaningful cues, and the anticipating in advance what should be done.

These characteristics can be illustrated with some examples in sports activities. If a golfer sinks several difficult putts during a round of golf, we would hesitate to say that he or she is a skilled putter until we have observed him or her for many rounds of golf. If this golfer continued to make many difficult putts, we would be more justified in labeling that person a skilled putter. Thus, the consistency of a high level of performance is critical to considering the golfer "skilled."

If we compare a skilled and an unskilled baseball or softball batter, one of the important differences we would observe would be the use of meaningful cues. The skilled batter has learned to ignore cues that are not important or are meaningless. While a pitcher who includes many irrelevant movements may confuse the unskilled batter, these same moves will have little disrupting effect on the skilled batter.

If a soccer player must wait until an opponent is on top of him or her before knowing whether to dribble or pass, we would not be justified in calling that person skilled. On the other hand, the player who successfully anticipates what to do on the basis of what he or she has observed in the opponents in advance of when he or she must actually carry out the decision to dribble or pass, the label "skilled" can be more aptly applied to that individual.

These three performance characteristics are some examples of the criteria we often use in the process of determining whether or not a person is a skilled performer. Other characteristics could also be considered. However, the use of these three should be sufficient to establish that we use the term *skill* to express a quality of performance and that the quality of performance is often based on certain characteristics. You will discover other characteristics of skilled performance as you progress through the chapters of this book.

The word *skill,* then, when designating the quality of performance is typically based on how well the individual accomplishes the goal of the task. This can be established by measuring the outcome of performing the task or by observing certain characteristics of the performance that lead to the successful outcome.

Ability

A term that is important to consider, and to distinguish from skill, is the term *ability,* a word used commonly in conversation about motor skill performance. Although we will be considering this term more specifically in Chapter 6 when individual differences are discussed, it will be beneficial to define the term here.

Edwin Fleishman (1972, 1978) has been responsible for developing much of the present understanding of the relationship between human abilities and the performance of motor skills. He has defined the term **ability** as a "general capacity of the individual" that is related to the performance of a variety of skills or tasks. For example, the ability that Fleishman has labeled "spatial visualization" has been found to be related to the performance of such diverse tasks as aerial navigation, blueprint reading, and dentistry. In a sport context, the ability "speed of movement" can be seen as an important component in performing a variety of skills in soccer, baseball, tennis, and track. A *motor ability* therefore, is a general trait or capacity of an individual that is related to the performance of a variety of motor skills.

As you will see in Chapter 6, there are many different motor abilities. The level of success a person can achieve for a motor skill is in large part dependent on how those abilities related to performing the skill are characterized in the individual. That is, a person with a high degree of all the abilities required to successfully play golf can be expected to have good potential to be an excellent player. You will learn more about the relationship between abilities and performance in Chapter 6.

The important point to remember here is that ability and skill should not be used interchangeably. We often hear a person described as having "a lot of ability" when in fact the intent is to indicate that the person is skilled. A skilled person may have a lot of ability, but, as you will learn from your study of individual differences, an unskilled person may also have a lot of ability.

Motor Skill Classification Systems

The general approach of this text is to present motor learning concepts that can be applied to a variety of motor skill contexts. However, as you have seen in the discussion thus far, there is an extremely large number of possible motor skills that can be performed. The task of applying these concepts to motor skill learning and performance situations would be much simpler if motor skills themselves could be organized in such a way to eliminate the need to apply concepts to specific skills. To address this problem, organizational schemes have been developed to classify motor skills into distinct groups. In this section we will consider three different skill classification systems

that have been developed and are used rather extensively, although each tends to be used in certain contexts.

Classifying motor skills into general categories is based on determining what components or elements of a skill are common or similar to components of another skill. Each of the methods of classification discussed will be considered as one of two categories, or dichotomous. Rather than considering these two categories as unique and unrelated, so that all motor skills must fit into one or the other category, consider each of the two categories as an extreme end of a continuum. This approach suggests that skills can be classified as being more closely allied with one category than with the other without having to fit into one category exclusively.

An analogy may be helpful in classifying skills. The concepts "hot" and "cold" are two categories of temperatures that we typically consider as distinct. However, it is more accurate to place these terms at the ends of a continuum since there are degrees of hot or cold that do not fit exclusively in one or the other category. By considering hot and cold as anchor points on a continuum you can maintain the distinction of these two concepts. At the same time you can more accurately classify various temperature levels that do not fit in only one or the other category.

As you can see from the analogy, the benefit of considering classification system categories as anchor points at opposite ends of a continuum allows the complex nature of motor skills to be accommodated. An emphasis on the common characteristics of the wide range of skills being classified can also be maintained. You will find it helpful to keep in mind that the primary purpose for developing classifications is to provide a convenient vehicle to aid in the process of making generalizations. If this point is understood, the problems that may appear in classifications will be less important.

Many approaches have been developed to classify motor skills. Each classification system is based on the general nature of motor skills relating to some specific *feature of the skills*. We will consider three systems in which motor skill classification is based on: (1) the precision of the movement; (2) defining the beginning and end points of the movement; and (3) the stability of the environment. As each of these is discussed, consider how the various examples fit along the continuum anchored by the two categories. Think of additional examples that would fit these categories. Remember that some motor skills will fit very easily into one or the other category. In other cases, you will find that a particular skill is more like one category than the other, even though it does not meet all the characteristics implied by that category.

In addition to discussing the two categories in each classification system, we will also consider the typical context in which the use of the system is popular. As you will see, the different classification systems seem to have appeal or relevance for a particular use. For example, one classification system is more common in elementary physical education while another is common in physical therapy and adapted physical education. Within these settings, specific classification systems provide a more convenient means of classifying the motor skills involved in the different instructional contexts.

Precision of Movement

Classifying motor skills on the basis of the precision of movement involved in the skills has led to the development of two categories: gross motor skills and fine motor skills. **Gross motor skills** are characterized as involving large musculature and a goal where the precision of movement is not as important to the successful execution of the skill as it is for fine motor skills. Fundamental motor skills, such as walking, jumping, throwing, leaping, etc., are considered to be gross motor skills. While precision of movement is not an important component, the smooth coordination of movement is essential to the skilled performance of these tasks.

Fine motor skills are skills that require control of the small muscles of the body to achieve the goal of the skill. Generally, these skills involve hand-eye coordination and require a high degree of precision of movement for the performance of the particular skill at a high level of accomplishment. Writing, drawing, sewing, and fastening a button are examples of fine motor skills.

Skills like the ones presented here are relatively easy to categorize. However, when skills such as pitching a baseball and riding a bicycle are considered, where do they belong? Here is where the continuum helps the categorization process. Obviously, skills such as these involve large musculature to a great extent, but a high degree of movement accuracy is also required. On the basis of the characteristics of skills classified as gross or fine, it would seem likely that pitching a baseball and riding a bicycle are more closely related to the gross end of the classification continuum.

Where this classification system is used. The use of the gross-fine distinction for motor skills is popular in a number of settings. One of these is special education or adapted physical education, where the training or rehabilitation of motor skills is typically related to working with gross or fine skills. This classification system is also commonly used in therapy settings. Physical therapists typically work with patients who need to rehabilitate gross motor skills such as walking; whereas occupational therapists more commonly deal with patients who need to learn fine motor skills. Finally, individuals who are involved in early childhood motor skills development research also find the gross-fine categorization useful. Thus, the classification of motor skills based on the type of musculature primarily involved in achieving the goal of the movement appears to be a popular and useful classification method.

Defining the Beginning and End Points

Another means of classifying motor skills is on the basis of how clearly defined the beginning and end of the skill are. If there are clearly defined beginning and end points, the skill is categorized as a

discrete motor skill. If the skill has rather arbitrary beginning and end points, it is *continuous.* Discrete motor skills include such movements as flipping a light switch, depressing the clutch of an automobile, and hitting a typewriter key. Each of these movements has beginning and end points defined by the object being manipulated. The performer must adhere to these beginning and end point boundaries if the task is to be performed successfully.

Discrete skills can be put together in a series. When this occurs, we consider the skill to be a **serial motor skill.** Starting a standard shift automobile is a good example because the performance of a series of discrete motor tasks is required. The clutch must be depressed, the key must be turned to start the engine, the gear shift must be put into first gear, and the accelerator must be properly depressed as the clutch is let out and the car finally begins to move. Playing the piano can also be considered a serial motor skill, because discrete movements of striking the piano keys must be accomplished in a definite, serial order. Performing a dance routine or a floor exercise routine in gymnastics, and shooting an arrow in archery are other examples where a specific series of discrete movements must be performed in a specific order for the proper execution of the skill.

Continuous motor skills have arbitrary beginning and end points. The performer, or some external agent, rather than the characteristics of the skill itself, determines the beginning and end points of the skill. In addition, continuous skills are repetitive in nature in that they require the person to repeat movements during the course of performing the skill. Skills required to perform what are known as "tracking tasks" are examples of continuous motor skills. These include such skills as steering an automobile, tracking a moving cursor on a computer monitor with a joystick, and following a revolving dot on a pursuit rotor. Sport skills such as swimming or running can be considered continuous in that the beginning and end points of the skill are determined by the performer and not specified by the skill itself.

Where this classification system is used. The use of this classification system has been especially prevalent in motor skills research literature. Researchers have found, for example, that certain phenomena about how we control movement is applicable to discrete skills but not to continuous skills, and vice versa. This distinction between discrete and continuous skills seems to be especially popular with researchers who view the performance of motor skills from a human engineering perspective, and with people interested in human factors.

Stability of the Environment

In 1957 British experimental psychologist E. C. Poulton presented a classification system for motor skills as they were related to the industrial setting. The basis for his classification was the stability of the environment in which the skill was performed. If the environment was stable, that is predictable, then Poulton classified the skill as *closed.* If, on the other hand, the skill involved an ever-changing, unpredictable environment, the skill was classified as *open.* Gentile (1972) expanded this classification system to make it applicable to instruction of sport skills.

Rather than considering open and closed skills as dichotomous, it is better to see these terms as anchor points of a continuum. **Closed motor skills** are at one end of the continuum. Included in this category are skills that take place under fixed, unchanging, environmental conditions. Some examples are bowling, shooting an arrow at a stationary target, picking up a cup, buttoning a shirt, stair climbing, and walking across an uncluttered floor. *The object or environment in each of these situations waits to be acted upon by the performer.* In bowling for example, the pins are the object of the action. Because the pins are not going to move from their location, the performer does not have to initiate action until he or she is ready to do so. The environment of an uncluttered floor contains nothing that will determine where or when you can begin walking. Thus, the environment is considered closed.

Conversely, **open motor skills,** at the other end of the continuum, include such skills as stroking a tennis ball, catching a ball, shooting a rifle at a moving target, driving a car, stepping onto a moving escalator, and walking through the woods. Each of these skills takes place in a temporally and/or spatially changing environment. For these skills to be performed successfully, *the performer must act according to the action of the object or the characteristics of the environment.* For example, during a rally a tennis player cannot stand in one spot and decide when he or she will respond to the ball. To be successful, the player must move and act in accordance with the ball's spatial location and speed characteristics. Sometimes an object is not being acted upon, rather an action takes place in what is called an "open environment" making the skill an open skill. Walking through the woods illustrates this situation. A person's walking characteristics will be determined by the characteristics of the woods, that is, where there are trees, stumps, stones, and holes in the ground. An open environment, then, is one that is "cluttered" with objects, which dictates the spatial and temporal characteristics of a person's actions.

Another set of terms used in conjunction with open and closed skills are *self-paced* and *externally-paced.* These terms refer to the timing characteristics of the initiation of action by a person. If the person can initiate the action at will, the term self-paced is used to characterize the skill. Typically, closed skills are self-paced because the object being acted upon and the environment do not determine when the action must begin. The term *externally-paced* applies to skills where the timing of the initiation of action is dictated by the object being acted upon, or by the environment. Open skills are typically externally-paced because the performer cannot initiate the action at will but must initiate action on the basis of the characteristics of an external source.

A four-category classification system. An extension of the two-category open and closed classification system developed by Gentile, Higgins, Miller, and Rosen (1975), is helpful in further identifying where a motor skill belongs on the

open-closed continuum. Rather than two categories of skills, this expanded classification system identifies four categories. These involve two types of variations from one response attempt to the next, change or no change; and two types of environmental conditions during execution of the movement, stationary and in motion. These are presented in a 2 × 2 diagram in Figure 1.1–1. As you can see from this diagram, the new category concerns "response-response variability." A skill is classified according to how it fits the intersections of any two of these types of movement conditions. Descriptions and examples of skills that fit each of the four categories are presented in Figure 1.1–1.

In keeping with our continuum approach, it is interesting to rearrange Gentile's 2 × 2 diagram by placing it on the closed-to-open skills continuum described in the preceding section. This rearrangement is presented in Figure 1.1–2. Note that now the "no-change/stationary conditions" category (Category 1) becomes the anchor point on the closed end of the continuum, while the "change/ in-motion condition" category (Category 4) is the anchor for the open end of the continuum. The "change/stationary conditions" category (Category 3) becomes an in-between point on the continuum that is closer to the closed- than to the open-skill end, and the "no-change/ in-motion conditions" category (Category 2) falls on the open side of the continuum. It should be noted that because the category numbers are in keeping with the Gentile designation, they do not follow a consecutive order on the continuum.

One potential benefit of this four-point continuum is that it can be used to establish how to modify an open skill for purposes of teaching the skill in a sequence of steps that increase the difficulty and complexity of the skill. Developing an instruction sequence for learning to hit a ball thrown by a pitcher is an example of using this approach. A suggested sequence is included in Figure 1.1–2. Notice that at the closed end of the continuum the ball is batted from a batting tee. In this situation the ball is stationary and remains in the same place on each practice attempt. The next level of modification keeps the ball stationary

Response-to-Response Variability

	No Change	**Change**
Stationary	Category 1 The object of the response remains stationary, and there is no change in response requirements from one response to the next.	Category 3 The object of the response remains stationary, and the response requirements change from one response to the next.
In Motion	Category 2 The object of the response is in motion, and there is no change in the response requirements from one response to the next.	Category 4 The object of the response is in motion, and the response requirements change from one response to the next.

(Left axis label: **Environmental Conditions**)

FIGURE 1.1-1   A 2 × 2 diagram representing the four-category classification system presented by Gentile, Higgins, Miller, and Rosen.

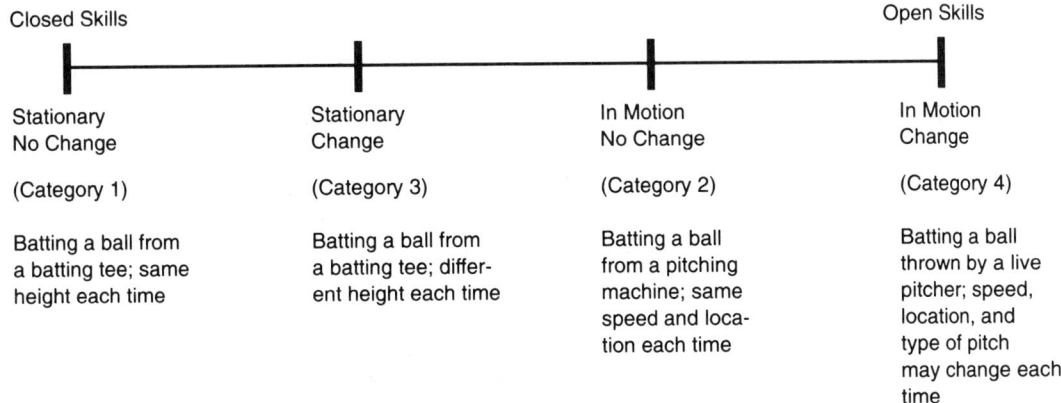

Closed Skills			Open Skills
Stationary No Change	Stationary Change	In Motion No Change	In Motion Change
(Category 1)	(Category 3)	(Category 2)	(Category 4)
Batting a ball from a batting tee; same height each time	Batting a ball from a batting tee; different height each time	Batting a ball from a pitching machine; same speed and location each time	Batting a ball thrown by a live pitcher; speed, location, and type of pitch may change each time

FIGURE 1.1-2   The four categories from the Gentile et al., system placed on a continuum having closed- and open-skill categories aŝ its extremes. Four different types of ball-batting tasks are presented to show how the categories are different.

but requires that it be batted from different heights on each practice attempt, thus presenting a varying situation from one attempt to the next. The third level of modification goes back to a no-change situation for each practice attempt but puts the ball in motion. This can be easily done by using a pitching machine, with which the speed and location of the pitch can be kept the same on each pitch. Finally, the open end of the continuum is reached by having a live pitcher pitching the ball with a different pitch on each practice attempt. A further discussion of the use of this approach to teaching open skills will be considered in Chapter 9, where specific practice-related issues are presented.

Where this classification system is used. The use of the open-closed classification system has found a large degree of popularity in instructional methodology contexts. It is not uncommon, for example, to find references to open and closed motor skills in textbooks related to teaching methods of physical education (e.g., Singer & Dick, 1980) or in research journal articles related to teaching motor skills (e.g., Del Rey, Wughalter, & Whitehurst, 1982). Gentile (1987) has applied this classification system to physical therapy situations. A likely reason for the popularity of the open-closed skills classification system by those involved in teaching motor skills is that these skill categories are readily adaptable to the types of skills that are taught in instructional settings. Also, skills in these categories have in common characteristics that follow principles of instruction that are based on motor learning research. As such you will find this classification system frequently referred to in various parts of this book. This system has become commonly used in the motor learning research literature because of its simplicity and its ability to accommodate complex "real-world" skills as well as laboratory skills.

Summary

Motor skills are defined as skills in which physical movement is required to accomplish the goal of the task. The word skill can be considered either a synonym for the word task or as an indicator of the quality of a performer's achievement in performing a particular motor skill. There is a wide variety of motor skills. Skills as diverse as throwing a ball, grasping a cup, dancing, and playing the piano are included under the general label of motor skills. One means of increasing the ease with which we can apply learning concepts and principles to instruction in motor skills is to develop general categories of such motor skills that are based on some common features of various motor aptitudes. Three categories or classification systems have been discussed, and each system is based on a general, common feature. One system, based on the precision of the movement required by the skill, classifies skills as either gross or fine. Second is a system that is based on the distinctiveness of the beginning and end points of a skill, and classifies skills as either discrete or continuous. The third system is based on the stability of the environment in which the skill is performed; this environment may be stable, or closed; or it may be very changeable, or open. An extension of this third system adds the characteristic of whether the skill involves change or no change in how the skill will be performed from one attempt to the next.

Related Readings

Adams, J. A. (1991). Historical review and appraisal of research on the learning, retention, and transfer of human motor skills. *Psychological Bulletin, 101*, 41–74. (Read section on Definition of Skill, pp. 41–42)

Gentile, A. M. (1975). Skill acquisition: Action, movement, and the neuromotor processes. In J. H. Carr, R. B. Shepherd, J. Gordon, A. M. Gentile, & J. M. Held (Eds.), *Movement science: Foundations for physical therapy in rehabilitation* (pp. 93–154). Rockville, MD: Aspen. (Read pp. 93–117)

Higgins, J. R. (1977). *Human movement: An integrated approach.* St. Louis: Mosby. (Read Chapter 2)

Holding, D. H. (1981). Skill research. In D. H. Holding (Ed.), *Human skills* (pp. 1–13). New York: John Wiley & Sons.

Newell, K. M. (1978). Some issues on action plans. In G. E. Stelmach (Ed.), *Information processing in motor control and learning* (pp. 41–54). New York: Academic Press. (Read pp. 41–43)

□

CONCEPT 1.2

The measurement of motor performance is a critical part of understanding motor learning

---

Key Terms

reaction time (RT)

movement time (MT)

response time

constant error (CE)

absolute error (AE)

variable error (VE)

absolute constant error (|CE| or ACE)

E

root-mean-squared error (RMSE)

kinematics

electromyography (EMG)

Application

When teaching motor skills, you must be able to determine whether or not the people you are teaching are learning the skills being taught. An important part of making that decision is based on the motor performance characteristics you measure and the tests you give. Consider the following two examples.

Suppose you are a physical educator teaching your students a tennis serve. What characteristic of performance will you measure to assess students' progress? Consider a few possibilities. You could count the number of serves that land in and out of the proper service court. Or you could mark the service court in some way so that the "better" serves, in terms of where they land, are scored higher than others. Or you could establish a measure that is concerned with the students' serving form. These are just three of many different performance measurements you could make.

Consider another motor skill instruction situation. Suppose that you are a physical therapist helping a stroke patient learning to walk again. How would you measure your patient's progress to determine if what you are doing is facilitating his or her rehabilitation? You would have several

possible walking characteristics to choose from as the basis for what you measure. For example, you could count the number of steps made on each walking attempt. You could devise a way to evaluate the balance and stability of the person as he or she walks. You could measure the distance walked. Or you could videotape the person as he or she walks and then later analyze the kinematic characteristics of the segments of the legs, trunk, and arms. Each of these measurements could be valuable and will tell you something different about the person's walking performance.

The important point is that to effectively assess skill learning, you must first establish a performance measure, or measures, on which you will base your assessment of learning. In the discussion that follows, we will focus on this issue of measuring motor performance. The discussion should be considered an essential first step in a two-step process of assessing learning. The first step is to establish the performance characteristics to be measured, and the second step is to use those measures in an appropriate test that evaluates the learning resulting from the students' practice. This second step will be the focus of the first concept of the next chapter, which introduces you to the concept of learning.

Because the goal of this book is to present motor learning concepts that have been derived from experimental research, the discussion of motor performance measures will be directed primarily to those measures that have been used in research where understanding motor skill learning and performance is the primary goal. Performance measures related to assessing motor performance in your particular area of application, such as physical education, physical therapy, dance, and so on, are the basis for tests and measurements courses, and, therefore, will not be discussed here.

The intent of this discussion is to provide you with a brief introduction to motor performance measurement, which should help you better understand the various concepts presented in this book. As you will see, however, although this discussion relates primarily to motor performance measurement concerns involved in motor learning research, much of this discussion is directly applicable to your own instruction and rehabilitation situations.

——— □ ———

Discussion

There are a variety of ways to measure motor performance, some of which have already been mentioned. It is helpful to organize the various types of motor performance measures into two categories. These categories relate to different levels of performance observation. The first category is called *response outcome measures*. The performance measures included in this category are measures that indicate the product or result of a motor performance. For example, you may want to measure how far a person ran in a certain amount of time, or how many points a person scored. To answer those questions, response outcome measures are used. However, notice that these measures do not tell you anything about how the limbs or body behaved in producing these results, or how the nervous system functioned while the response was being made. If we want to know something about these characteristics, we should use measures in the category called *response production measures*. These measures can tell us a number of different things about how the nervous system was functioning, how the muscular system was operating, or how the limbs or joints were acting before, during, or after a response was made. Although additional categories of measures could be developed, response outcome and response production measures represent the motor performance measures that will be found in this text. Examples of the two categories of motor performance measures are presented in Table 1.2–1.

Most of the measures in the response output category are well known to you and need no further explanation, although some may be new to you and will need to be explained. This is also likely the case for the response production measures category. In the remainder of this discussion, we will look more closely at some of those measures. In particular, we will discuss measures that are popular in motor learning research and frequently seen in the research literature. In the discussion of each measure, you will see how each is determined, how each is used in a motor learning research setting, and the problems that exist related to that measure.

Reaction Time

A popular measure of how long it takes a person to initiate a movement is **reaction time (RT)**. Figure 1.2–1 shows that RT is the interval of time between the onset of a signal (stimulus) and the *initiation* of a response. It is important to note that RT does not include the movement itself but only the time prior to when the movement begins. In Figure 1.2–1, the three events that typically occur when RT is measured are labeled "warning signal," "stimulus signal," and "initiation of the response." The first two are controlled by the experimenter, while the third depends on the person performing the skill.

The stimulus signal is the indication to respond, and can be a variety of indicators such as a light, buzzer, shock, or word on a screen. As such, the signal may be presented to any sensory source, i.e., vision, hearing, or touch. The response made by the person can be designated as any particular movement. For example, the subject may be required to lift a finger off a telegraph key, depress a keyboard key, speak a word, or kick a board. The response, then, may be required from any body part or even the entire body. It should be mentioned that the warning signal, which can be

TABLE 1.2-1   Two categories of motor skill performance measures

Category	Examples of Measures	Performance Examples
1. Response outcome measures	Time to complete a response e.g., sec., min., hr.	Amount of time to: Run a mile; Type a word
	Reaction time	Time between starter's gun and beginning of movement
	Amount of error in performing criterion movement e.g., AE, CE, VE	Number of cm away from the target in reproducing a criterion limb position
	Number or percentage of errors	Number of free throws missed
	Number of successful attempts	Number of times the beanbag hit the target
	Time on/off target	Number of seconds stylus in contact with target on pursuit rotor
	Time on/off balance	Number of seconds stood in stork stance
	Distance	Height of vertical jump
	Trials to completion	Number of trials it took until all responses correct
2. Response production measures	Displacement	Distance limb traveled to produce response
	Velocity	Speed limb moved while performing response
	Acceleration	Acceleration/deceleration pattern while moving
	Joint angle	Angle of each joint of arm at impact in hitting ball
	Electromyography (EMG)	Time at which the biceps initially fired during a rapid flexion response
	Electroencephalogram (EEG)	Characteristic of the P300 for a choice RT response

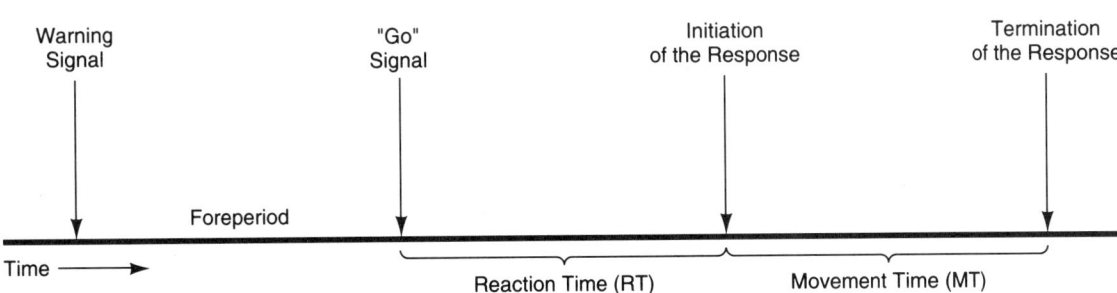

FIGURE 1.2-1   The events and time intervals related to the typical measurement of reaction time (RT) and movement time (MT).

FIGURE 1.2-2   Three different types of reaction time (RT) test situations: simple RT, choice RT, and discrimination RT.

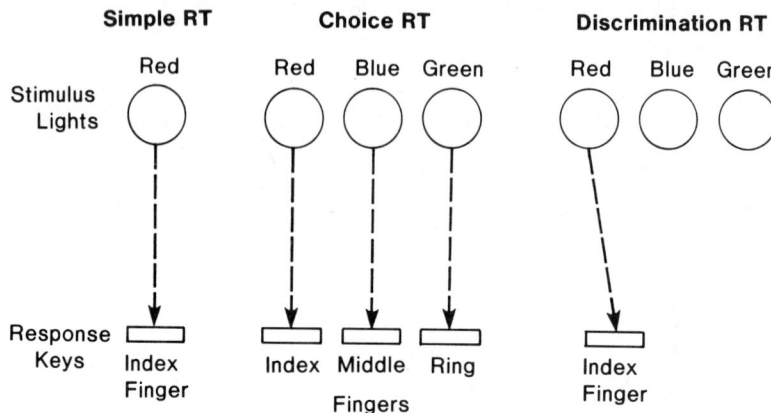

any type of indicator, may or may not be used when RT is measured, although there usually is some type of warning given to the person prior to the stimulus signal.

There are several types of RT situations. Three of the most common are depicted in Figure 1.2–2. Each of these situations is based on using a light as the stimulus signal and lifting a finger from a telegraph key as the required movement. One RT situation is known as *simple* RT; only one signal and one response are required. In the example presented in Figure 1.2–2, the subject must lift a finger from the telegraph key when a light comes on. Another type of RT situation is *choice* RT, where there is more than one signal to which the person must respond, and each signal has a specified response. The example in Figure 1.2–2 indicates that the person must respond to the red light by lifting the index finger from a telegraph key, the blue light by lifting the middle finger, and the green light by lifting the ring finger. If the specified response is not made, the attempt is considered an error and is typically redone. The third type of RT situation is *discrimination* RT, where there is also more than one signal, but only one response. In Figure 1.2–2 this is illustrated by requiring the subject to lift the finger from the telegraph key only when the red light comes on. If the blue or green light illuminates, no response is to be made.

An important point to keep in mind about RT is that it is a performance measure. When RT is

used in motor learning research it is typically used to indicate the time a person takes to process information to produce a required action. That is, the experimenter will look at how RT changes as a function of the influence of a particular variable so that a conclusion can be made about the influence of that variable on the cognitive or motor processing that occurred between the onset of the "go" signal and the beginning of the actual observed movement. A longer RT signifies that more information processing was required than for a shorter RT.

RT has been a very popular measure of human motor skill performance. Several examples of how RT has been used in motor skills research will be described in the discussion sections of the Concepts in Chapters 3 and 4. Researchers have long considered the understanding of how different variables influence RT as a means of gaining insight into how people interpret information in the environment and how they make decisions about what action should be taken in response to that information. These issues are of particular interest for understanding how the sensory and perceptual system interacts with the environment, and will be considered in the discussion of the roles of proprioception (Concept 3.1) and vision (Concept 3.2) in controlling movement, and how the movement control system prepares to produce an action, which will be discussed in Concept 3.3 and in all the concepts in Chapter 4.

Movement Time and Response Time

Two response measures closely related to RT are movement time (MT) and response time. These are both depicted in Figure 1.2–1. **Movement time (MT)** begins when RT ends and is defined as the interval of time between the initiation and completion of movement. Response time is the total time interval involving both RT and MT.

An example of how RT, MT, and response time intervals are involved in a common everyday situation will help you understand how these are measured and what intervals of time they involve. Suppose you were interested in knowing how long it took an individual to move his or her foot from the accelerator to the brake pedal of a car in response to the sudden appearance of an obstacle in the road. The total amount of time from the appearance of the obstacle until the person contacted the brake is the **response time.** This response time consists of the RT, the time from the appearance of the obstacle until the person's foot begins to move from the accelerator, and the MT, the time it takes to begin moving from the accelerator until contact with the brake is made.

As you will see in many of the research examples used throughout this text, the use and distinction of these measures is important. Response time should not be considered synonymous with reaction time, which, unfortunately is common in much of the popular literature. The need for distinction among these measures will become more apparent as you see how they provide useful dependent measures from which inferences can be made related to the learning and control of movement skills.

Error Measures

Measuring the amount of error made as a result of a movement has been one of the more prominent measures used in motor learning research. One reason for this is that many tasks used in motor learning research require subjects to make an accurate movement to a target or to move a certain distance in a specified amount of time. In each of these situations *accuracy* is the movement goal. In the first case spatial accuracy is the goal; in the latter case temporal accuracy is the goal. As a result, the amount of error the subject makes in relation to achieving the spatial or temporal goal becomes a meaningful performance measure.

Consider first the goal of *spatial accuracy,* which has been the goal of many experimental tasks used in motor learning research. Suppose that the task a person must do requires that he or she move an arm or leg to a specified position in space. For example, the subject could move a sliding handle along a trackway until the desired limb position is reached. This task, known as a linear positioning task, has been commonly used in motor learning research. The positioning movement made by the subject may involve reproducing a positioning movement previously performed or demonstrated, or it may be one that the subject must learn to produce. In these situations, error is recorded as the amount of distance between the subject's positioning response and the criterion or target position. While this experimental setting example illustrates a situation that you will see described in various experiments discussed in the chapters that follow, limb positioning is also a movement goal in practical settings. For example, the physical therapist who is working with a person needing to develop knee flexion or extension may flex the person's knee to a certain angle. The patient is then asked to reproduce that angle. Again, the accuracy of this positioning movement can be measured by comparing the goal angle with the angle achieved by the patient's attempt.

An illustration of how the limb-positioning accuracy measurement is made is presented in Figure 1.2–3, where a linear positioning task is diagramed. In this example suppose that the goal of the movement (known as the target, or criterion) is to position the sliding handle at the 60-cm mark on the trackway. Suppose that the subject moved the sliding handle to the 40-cm mark. As a result, the score is −20 cm (40 − 60 = −20). That is, the subject undershot the target, or criterion position, by 20 cm.

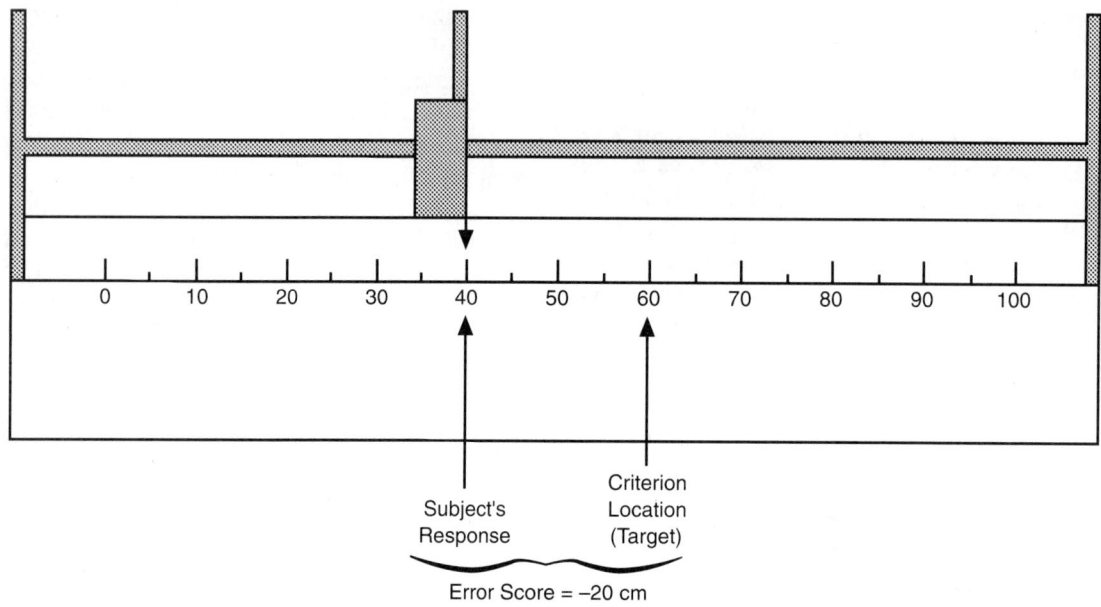

FIGURE 1.2-3 Drawing of a linear positioning apparatus showing the sliding handle that moves freely along the trackway. Scaled along the side facing the experimenter are the measurement values (typically in cm) used to score the response. In this example, the subject has moved the handle to the 40-cm mark.

The other type of movement accuracy situation is *temporal accuracy*. Here the goal is to move as accurately as possible in a specified amount of time. For example, a person could be required to move an object from one location to a new location in 500 msec (which is .5 seconds). To assess the accuracy of the person's timing movement, simply determine the difference between the person's movement time (MT) and the criterion, or target, time of 500 msec. If the person's MT was 750 msec, the amount of timing error is 750 (subject's time) − 500 (criterion time) = +250 msec. In other words, the subject moved too slowly by 250 msec.

Many of the motor skill performance situations you will study in this text involve determining the amount of error as a measure of performance. An important feature of using amount of error as a performance measure is that while it appears to be a rather simple measure, it is actually a complex one. That is, there are several different error scores that can be calculated in these situations. In the following section, these various error scores

will be described so that you will be able to more effectively understand how they are calculated and what each one means in terms of describing motor performance.

Reporting the amount of error scores. The amount of error made in responses such as in the examples just presented can be reported in five different ways, each indicating a different characteristic of the performance. And each of these error measures leads to a different interpretation of what may have caused the error observed in the person's performance.

Consider the following example. Suppose you are conducting an experiment in which subjects must perform a limb-positioning task on the apparatus illustrated in Figure 1.2–3. The movement goal is to learn to move the handle of this apparatus a distance of 20 cm in 300 msec. It should be noted that in an experiment like this subjects are typically not told in advance what the criterion movement time is. Subjects are instructed to reduce their error to 0, which would indicate they have moved in the exact amount of

TABLE 1.2-2   An example of calculations for five error measures for one subject performing six trials of a timing task where each trial has a movement time goal of 300 msec.

Subject 1		**Trial**							
		1	2	3	4	5	6	Total	$\overline{X}$
	Movement Time	75	596	104	243	411	216	—	—
	Criterion Time	300	300	300	300	300	300	—	—
	CE	−225	+296	−196	−57	+111	−84	−155	−25.8[a]
	AE	225	296	196	57	111	84	969	161.5[b]
	VE								180.4[c]
	E								182.2[d]
	ICEI								25.8

$$ {}^{a}\overline{CE} = \frac{\Sigma(X - \text{Criterion Value})}{k} \qquad {}^{b}\overline{AE} = \frac{\Sigma |X - \text{Criterion Value}|}{k} \qquad {}^{c}VE = \sqrt{\frac{\Sigma CE^2 - \frac{(\Sigma CE)^2}{k}}{k}} \qquad {}^{d}E = \sqrt{CE^2 + VE^2} $$

where: X = the subject's score for the trial (Movement Time in the above example)
       k = number of trials

time. To assist them in reaching this goal, the experimenter tells the subjects their error for an attempt after it is completed, which is commonly known as knowledge of results (KR). If the subject moved in 75 msec, he or she would be told, "You were 225 msec too fast."

Table 1.2–2 presents an example of how one subject did on six trials of practice. In this table, the five different error measures and how each measure is calculated are presented. Each measure is based on the six practice trials. In the first row under the trial numbers are the subject's movement times. The criterion time (300 msec) is in the second row. The third row presents the difference between those times for the six trials and is labeled **constant error (CE)**. This measure indicates the signed deviation from the target or criterion. As such, CE represents both the amount and direction of the error. The next row indicates another measure that can be derived from the subject's response. This is **absolute error (AE)** and is the unsigned deviation from the target or criterion. Here, the amount of error and not the direction of that error is represented. The average AE for the six trials is calculated by averaging the six CE scores without their algebraic signs. The next row presents the **variable error (VE)** measure. This score represents the variability, or consistency, of the subject's responses. The calculation of this score is simply the standard deviation of the subject's six CE scores.

These three scores, AE, CE, and VE, represent the three primary error measures describing performance in this situation. Note that CE and AE are actually mean scores, that is, they represent the average CE and AE for the trials. However, when CE and AE are reported in the research literature, the bar above the CE and AE labels (as shown in the formulas in Table 1.2–2), which designates a mean value, are dropped and not included as a part of the CE and AE error measures.

AE represents a general measure of the amount of error. It is a composite score that is mathematically derived from both CE and VE. As such, it does not permit interpretation about whether the error is due to a tendency to inaccurately undershoot or overshoot or due to a lack of consistency in the response from trial to trial. To provide this type of interpretation, CE and VE must be considered. CE is a measure of bias in the subject's movement. That is, did the subject tend to move too slow (a positive average CE) or too fast (a negative average CE)? Finally, VE is a measure of the consistency of the subject's performance for the set of practice trials being evaluated. VE is actually the standard deviation about a person's own CE. Thus, a large VE indicates inconsistency in the responses whereas a low VE indicates consistent responding for the trials being considered.

While these three error measures provide the essential kinds of information that describe performance for skills involving spatial or temporal accuracy, there has been some controversy concerning the validity of CE and AE. This controversy is especially pertinent to the use of these measures for research purposes where groups of subjects are involved and where interpretations of performance relate to causes of that performance. CE, while agreeably measuring bias, has problems when averaged across a group of subjects. The principal concern is that when several subjects are considered, it is possible that subjects' scores can cancel out each other. That is, if one subject had an average CE score of −13 cm and another subject had a +13 cm, the result would be 0, which would not be an accurate reflection of the amount of bias-related error. Clearly, there is no distinct direction of bias; one subject undershot the target and the other subject overshot it. However, 0 does not accurately reflect the amount of bias, because both subjects missed the target by an average 13 cm. To accommodate this problem, Henry (1974) and Schutz (1977) argued that after a CE score is calculated for an individual subject, the absolute value of that subject's CE score should be used for determining a group CE value. Thus,

the group's CE becomes an average of the **absolute CE (| CE |)** scores for the subjects in the group. |CE| is considered to be a more valid representation of the amount of bias for a group of subjects. To determine the average direction of that bias for a group, simply compare the number of +'s and −'s for the CE scores for each subject in the group.

AE also has been the focus of concern as a measure of performance in research applications. For example, Schutz and Roy (1973) identified several problems associated with using AE as the *only* error score reported to represent performance. The primary problem is that AE is actually a composite score that has CE and VE as components. Thus, using AE as the only performance measure causes difficulty for interpreting the results of an experiment.

The fifth error score, **E,** described in Table 1.2–2 came about as a result of the controversy about the use of AE as a sole measure of performance. In 1974 Franklin Henry, although agreeing with Schutz and Roy that AE was an inadequate performance measure, disagreed that CE and VE should be used. Rather, Henry suggested the use of another composite score which he called E. E, he argued, is a more appropriate measure of total error because it reflects the relative contributions of both components VE and CE. AE does not adequately reflect that contribution.

While it is important to acknowledge that there are theoretical disagreements associated with the use of error scores,[1] we will simplify matters for purposes of this book. We will consider AE, VE, CE, and |CE| as basic performance measures in experiments where groups of subjects are the basis for interpreting results. Each of these scores will refer to a specific aspect of performance. That is, AE is a measure of magnitude or amount of error, CE is a measure of the direction of response

---

1. For those interested in investigating that debate, the articles by Schutz and Roy (1973), Henry (1974), Schutz (1977), and Spray (1986) cited in the Related Readings section will be helpful.

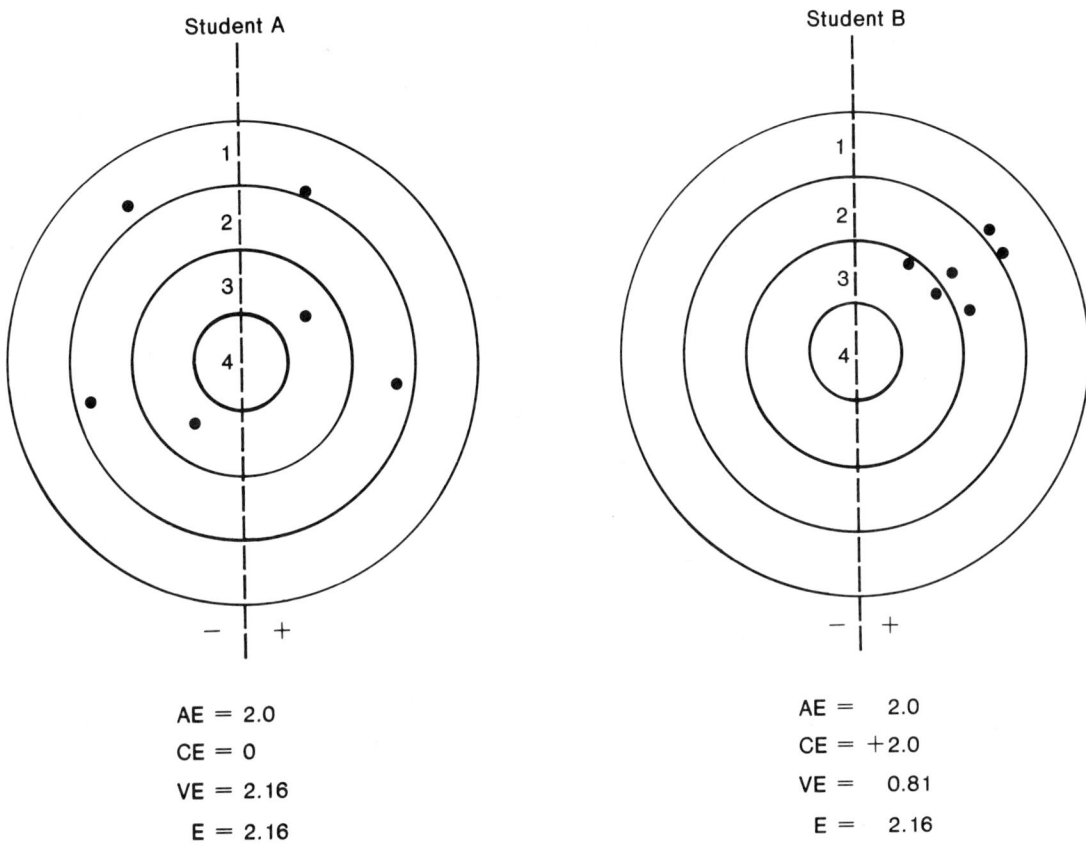

FIGURE 1.2-4   An example of two sets of scores from a target-accuracy task where the AE scores are the same but the CE, VE, and E scores are different.

biasing, | CE | is a measure of the amount of response biasing, and VE is a measure of response consistency. Thus, CE, | CE |, and VE should be seen as performance measures that help to interpret and explain AE. In other words, was the AE calculated for a group's performance the result of subjects being biased to overshoot or undershoot, or, due to moving inconsistently, or both? While the answer to this question has distinct theoretical implications, as will be seen in discussions in various chapters of this book, the relevance of this answer also has specific implications for motor skill instruction.

Relating error measures to skill instruction.
Suppose you are teaching an archery or riflery class, in which target accuracy is the critical measure of performance. Or suppose that you are a physical therapist helping a patient reproduce knee flexions. Next, suppose you have two students with target accuracy for six shots that look like those in Figure 1.2–4. It is important to note here that the target-accuracy example in Figure 1.2–4 is based on the actual value of the points for each target ring, rather than a calculated error score. Thus, the terms AE, VE, and CE as used in this example are analogous to the scores discussed in

the preceding section. The application to instruction remains the same whether error scores or number of points scored are used.

An interesting problem for instruction occurs when two students have identical total AE and E scores, as in Figure 1.2–4. Both students have AE and E scores of 2.0 and 2.16 respectively. However, if we arbitrarily cut the targets in half, we can actually evaluate these students' performances in terms of response bias and consistency. Let the right half of the target be the + side and the left half the − side. When you do this, it becomes apparent that each student's AE and E scores are due to very different reasons. This conclusion is reached by calculating the CE and VE scores for each student. As you can see, these two scores are distinctly different for each student. Student A has a CE score of 0, while Student B's CE score is +2.0, indicating that bias is a problem for Student B but not for Student A. On the other hand, VE for Student A is 2.16 while it is only 0.81 for Student B, indicating that Student A is much more inconsistent from shot to shot than Student B.

As the instructor, what would you do to help the students improve? If you had only AE as the measure of performance you would miss the important difference between the problems each student is having. Student A is having difficulty being consistent from one shot to the next. This could be caused by a variety of problems, such as not focusing on the target, or lack of steadiness before shooting. Student B, on the other hand, has a simpler problem that seems to be one of aim; the student needs to adjust his or her aim to the left a bit. Thus the information and assistance you would provide each of these students would be quite different.

Tracking Performance Error

The use of the error measures described in the preceding section is based on motor skills where the movements have a specific discrete goal, such as a limb position, distance to be moved, or movement time. Some motor skills, though, have movement goals that require accuracy, but the assessment of achieving the goals requires a measure of continuous movement. For example, if a person is in a car simulator and must steer the car along the road projected on a screen, assessment of performance would be based on how well the person kept the car on the road. This type of skill is called *tracking* in the motor skills literature.

In the laboratory tracking skills are commonly simulated by developing tasks that require a subject to make a joystick, steering wheel, or lever to follow a specified pathway. The pathway can be presented in various ways, such as in the car simulation situation, or as a moving cursor on a computer monitor. The pathway that must be followed, or tracked, can be described for analysis purposes kinematically as a displacement curve. An example is shown in Figure 1.2–5. The subject's tracking of this pathway can also be represented by a displacement curve. To determine how accurately the subject tracked the criterion pathway, an error score can be calculated.

An example of how an error score can be determined for tracking performance is illustrated in Figure 1.2–6. The error score is known as **root-mean-squared error (RMSE),** which can be thought of as AE for a continuous task. RMSE is calculated by determining the amount of error between the displacement curve produced by the subject's tracking performance and the displacement curve of the criterion pathway. An example of how RMSE is actually calculated is shown in Figure 1.2–6. Note that the solid line in this figure indicates the displacement curve of criterion pathway while the dashed lines represent an example of a subject's displacement curve produced on one trial. The actual calculation of RMSE is complex and requires a computer to be programmed to sample and record the subject's position in relation to the criterion pathway at specified intervals of time, such as every .100 sec (100 Hz). At each interval, the difference between the criterion pathway location and the subject's location is calculated. In effect, this yields 100 error scores each second. If the criterion pattern were 5 sec, a subject would have 500 error scores for a given trial. However, one score, RMSE, is calculated from these by determining an average error score for the total pathway.

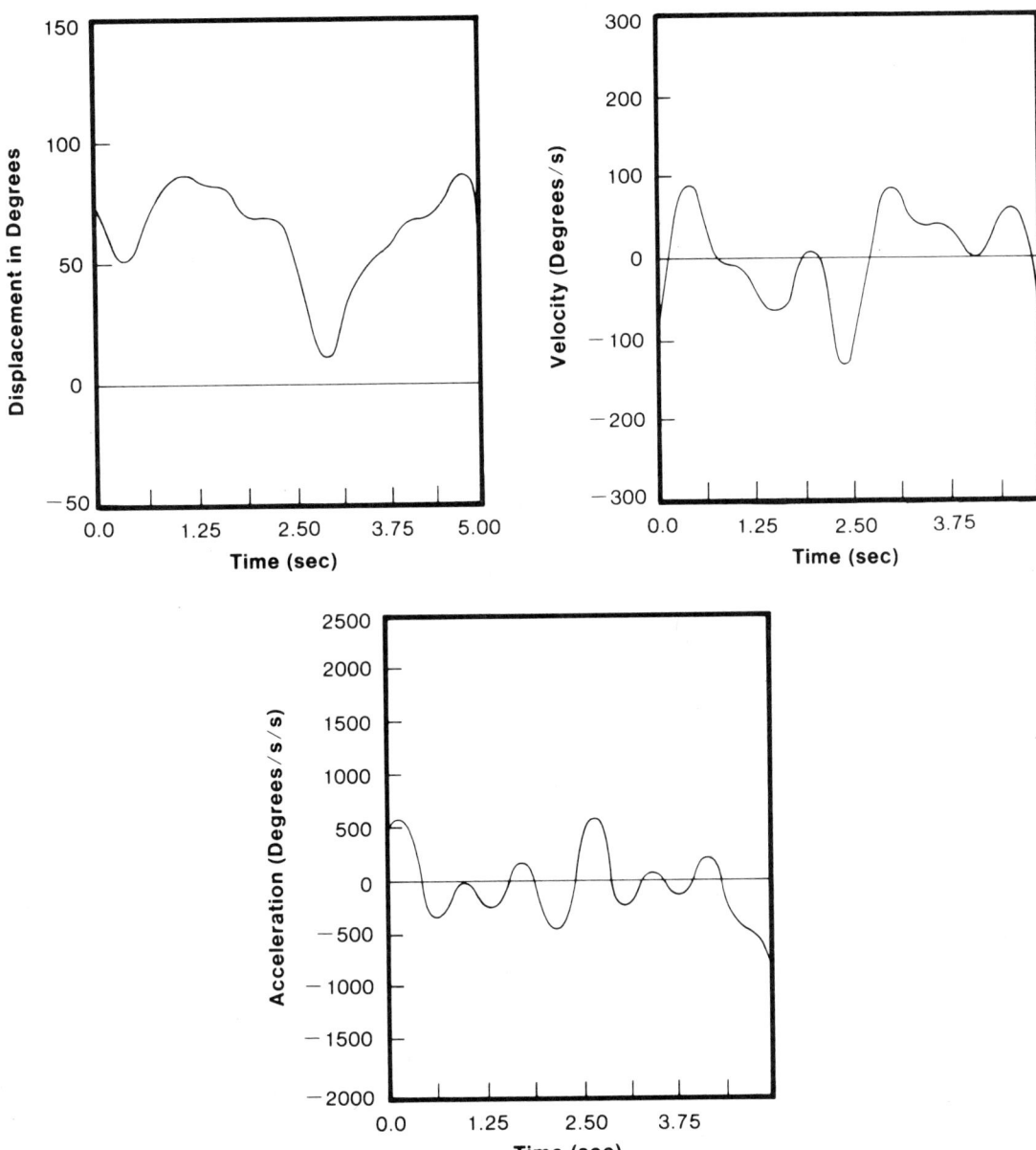

FIGURE 1.2-5   Recordings of displacement, velocity, and acceleration for a tracking task.

FIGURE 1.2-6 The difference between the subject's response and the stimulus at each specified time interval is used to calculate one root-mean-squared error (RMSE) score.

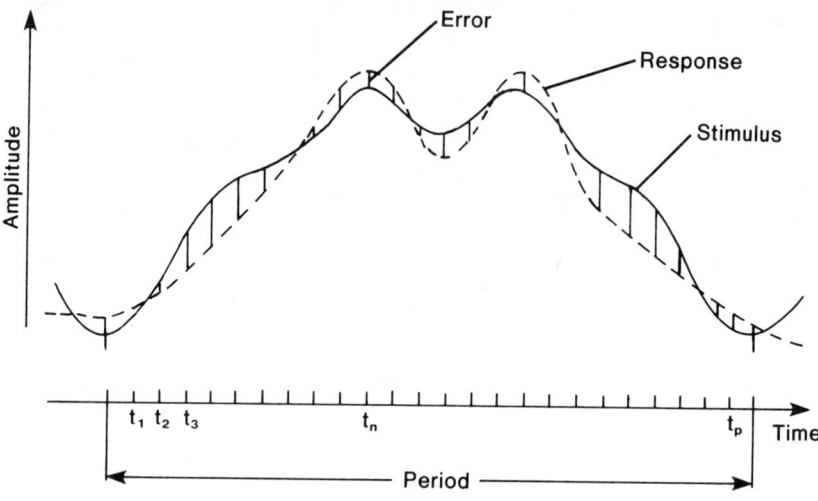

Kinematic Measures

In the preceding section, you were introduced to one example of a kinematic measure of motor performance, displacement. Kinematic measures are becoming more common as descriptors of motor skill performance as laboratories, clinics, and instructional settings are increasing their acquisition of equipment that has the capability to provide an analysis of movements where movement kinematics can be assessed. The term **kinematics** refers to descriptions of movement without regard to force or mass. Commonly used kinematic measures typically describe a movement's position in space, velocity, and acceleration.

These kinematic measures are usually based on recording the movement of particular body segments while a person is performing a skill. The typical procedure is first to mark the body segments in a distinctive way with a marking pen, tape, special light-reflecting balls, or light-emitting diodes (LEDs). The movement is then recorded on film or videotape, or by using special movement analysis system cameras. The recordings are then analyzed by computer software developed to calculate kinematic measures. This approach is used in commercially available movement analysis systems such as those produced by Peak Performance®, Motion Analysis Systems®, Selspot®,

and WATSMART®. Examples of kinematic measures derived from these types of systems are seen in Figures 1.2–7 and 1.2–8.

The recordings of movement needed to derive kinematic measures may also be made by a computer that samples the electrical voltage changes associated with the movement of a potentiometer. In the tracking example described in the preceding section and as seen in Figure 1.2–5, the potentiometer was attached to the axle of a lever that was moved by the subject. Similar samplings of movement can be made from the movement of a joystick, mouse, or rollerball.

The tracking example presented in Figure 1.2–5 will serve to illustrate how kinematic measures are derived. The first measure of interest is *displacement,* which is the spatial position of a limb or joint during the time course of the movement. The focus of displacement is in describing changes in spatial locations as a movement is carried out. Displacement is calculated by identifying where the marked limb or joint is in space (in terms of its X-Y coordinate in two-dimensional analysis or its X-Y-Z coordinate in three-dimensional analysis) at a given time and determining the change in that position for the next sampled time. These spatial positions are sampled (observed by the analysis system) at specific rates, which vary according to the analysis system used. For example, common videotape sampling rates

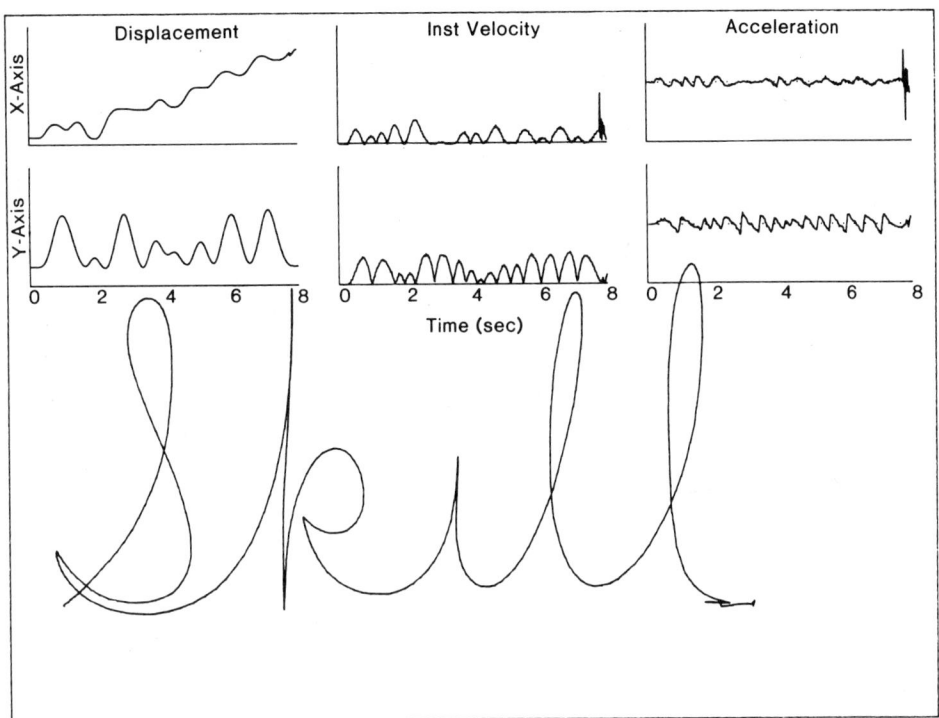

FIGURE 1.2-7   Handwriting described by attaching light-emitting diodes to the limb and using a computerized camera system to show the movement's pathway.

are 60 Hz, while other analysis systems allow 100 Hz, 200 Hz, or even 1000 Hz sampling rates (1 Hz = 1 time/sec). Thus, the spatial location of the marked joint or limb can be plotted for each sampled time (an example of this sampling procedure was presented in Figure 1.2–6). The graph of a displacement curve, then, always has a spatial location measure on the Y-axis and time on the X-axis. Examples of displacement curves can be seen in Figures 1.2–5, 1.2–6, and 1.2–7.

Velocity, the second measure of interest, is related to displacement in that velocity refers to the rate of change in a movement's position with respect to time. That is, how rapidly did this change in position occur and in what direction was this change? Velocity is typically derived in movement analysis systems from displacement. The calculation involves dividing a change in position (from time 1 to time 2) by the change in time from time 1 to time 2. Thus, as depicted in Figures 1.2–5 and 1.2–7, velocity is always presented on a graph as

a position by time curve and is referred to in terms of an amount of distance per an amount of time, such as the number of degrees per second in the tracking example in Figure 1.2–5, and as cm/sec in the handwriting example in Figure 1.2–7. As the slope of this curve steepens, it represents greater velocity, while negative velocity is represented by a slope that goes downward. Zero velocity is indicated by no change in the position of the curve.

The third kinematic measure to be discussed is *acceleration,* which describes change in velocity during movement. Acceleration is derived from velocity by dividing change in velocity by change in time. Acceleration curves are also shown as a function of time, as can be seen in Figures 1.2–5 and 1.2–7. Here, the speeding up and slowing down of the movements are recorded as the subject moves. Rapid acceleration means that a velocity change occurred quickly.

Skilled Runners

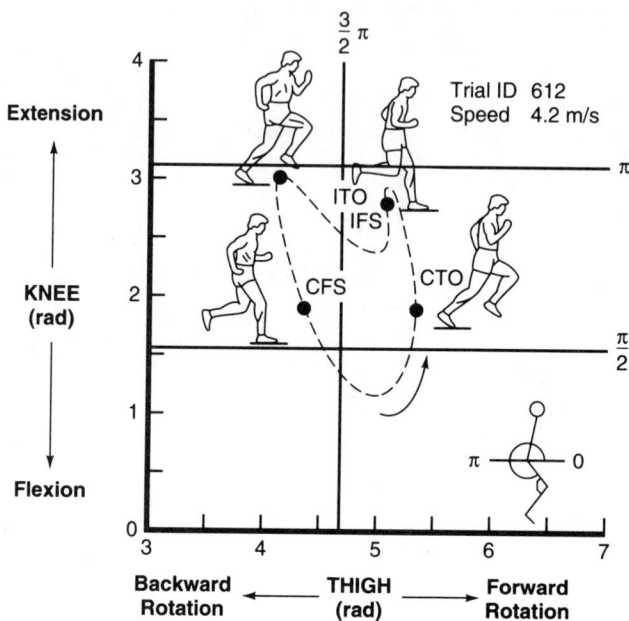

Three Below-Knee Amputees

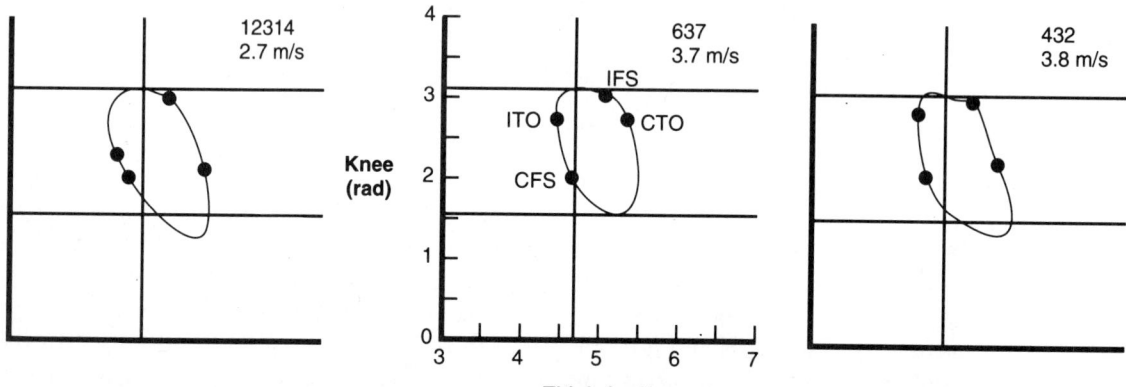

FIGURE 1.2-8 Angle-angle diagrams showing knee-thigh relationships during running by a skilled runner (top) and three below-knee amputees (bottom). The abbreviations indicate ipsilateral (left) footstrike (IFS), ipsilateral takeoff (ITO), contralateral (right) footstrike (CFS), and contralateral takeoff (CTO), which are the four components of a running stride.

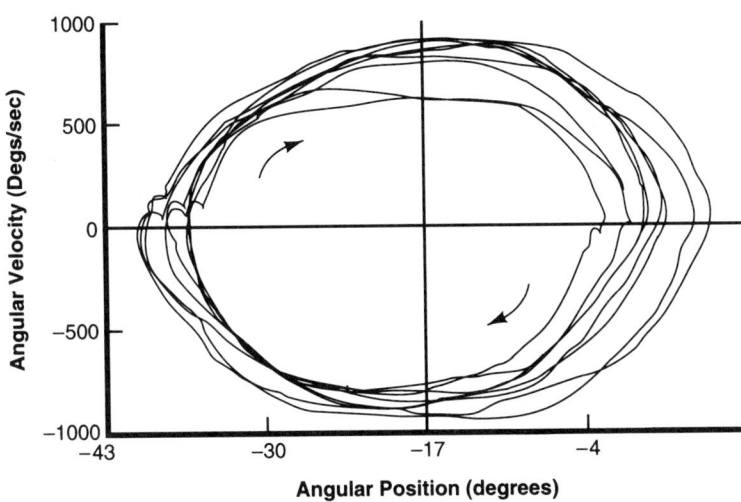

FIGURE 1.2-9 Phase-plane portrait for a person making rhythmic back and forth finger movement.

In kinematic descriptions of movement displacement, velocity, and acceleration can refer either to linear or angular motion. The distinction between these types of motion is important to understand and is a critical distinction for the analysis of movement. *Linear motion* describes the movement of all parts of the moving object while *angular motion* refers to movement that occurred for some parts of the object but not other parts. If you want to describe the kinematics of walking, for example, linear motion descriptions are appropriate for movement from one location to another; the whole body is moving linearly. However, if you want to describe the foot movement characteristics during walking, angular motion descriptions are more appropriate because the foot rotates about the ankle joint during walking.

The most common way angular motion is described is by comparing the motion of one joint to the limb segment as it rotates about while a movement is occurring. Two examples are shown in Figure 1.2–8. The top part of this figure shows an angle-angle diagram for a skilled runner where the displacement of the knee joint is compared to the thigh during the four phases of a running stride, footstrike, takeoff, opposite footstrike, and opposite foot takeoff. The bottom part of the figure shows a similar diagram for a person who has had an amputation below the knee. What is noticeable

here is that the amputee does not flex the knee joint at the beginning of the stance as the skilled runner does. Thus, an important benefit of kinematic measures is that the characteristics of critical components of a skill can be described during movement.

Another interesting approach to the use of kinematic measures has appeared recently in research focused on describing laws and principles of coordination. Rather than describing displacement, velocity, and acceleration alone, it is common in this work to show the relationship between two of these measures, especially velocity and displacement. The results of this procedure produce what are termed *phase-plane portraits*. For example, if a person moves an index finger back and forth according to a specified rhythm, the resulting phase portrait of the velocity of the finger plotted by displacement (presented in Figure 1.2–9) shows a closed band of oval-shaped lines called orbits. Each orbit represents one back and forth movement of the finger. This phase-plane portrait demonstrates two characteristics of the movements that cannot be described by any one of the kinematic measures themselves, which are also seen in Figure 1.2–9. First, the degree to which each of the movements are similar although slightly different is shown. Second, the regular oscillatory characteristic of these movements is demonstrated.

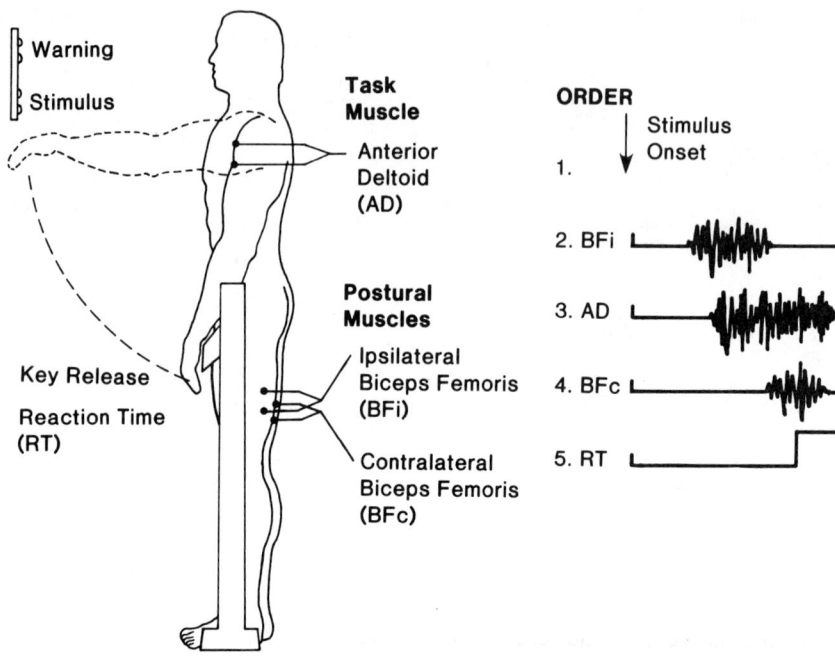

FIGURE 1.2-10 Using EMG recordings to measure a movement response. The figure on the left shows the reaction-time apparatus and where each electrode was placed to record the EMG for each muscle group of interest. The figures on the right show the EMG recordings for each of the three muscle groups and the reaction-time interval for the response.

EMG Measures

Movement involves electrical activity in the muscles, which can be measured by **electromyography (EMG)**. This is accomplished by attaching electrodes on the skin over muscles and recording electrical activity by means of a polygraph recorder or a computer. Each muscle can be recorded individually. Figure 1.2–10 shows some EMG recordings of electrical activity in the ipsilateral biceps femoris (BFi) and contralateral biceps femoris (BFc) of the legs and the anterior deltoid (AD) of the shoulder girdle for a task that required subjects to move their arm from the reaction-time key, on a signal, to a position directly in front of their shoulders. The EMG signals presented for these muscles show when electrical activity began in the muscles, and can be seen by the increase in the frequency and height of the traces for each muscle. The actual beginning of movement off the RT key is designated in the diagram by the vertical line at the end of the RT recording (line 5 of this figure).

An interesting use of the EMG is to relate it to RT. If an EMG recording is made when RT is measured, it is possible to *fractionate* RT into two component parts. The EMG recording will indicate the time at which the muscle shows increased activity after the stimulus occurred. Thus the first component part of RT is the period of time between the onset of the stimulus and the beginning of the increase in EMG activity, which is called the *premotor time*. The second component is the period of time beginning with the increase in EMG activity and the actual beginning of limb movement, which is called the *motor time*. In this way, the RT is fractionated into two parts. This measurement method has been popular because most researchers agree that the premotor time is a measure of the receipt and transmission of information from the environment, through the nervous system, and to the muscle itself (i.e., the "cognitive" component of RT). The motor time, on the other hand, indicates the lag in the muscle to overcome the inertia of the limb following receipt of the command to contract. We will refer to this in more detail in later sections.

The Speed-Accuracy Measurement Problem

One additional performance measure that needs to be highlighted involves a relatively common measurement problem. This measure of performance problem occurs in any skill that requires both speed and accuracy. These skills require the person to perform at a certain speed, which, for some skills means to be as fast as possible, while at the same time to be as accurate as possible. Examples include skills such as fencing, tennis serving, hitting a baseball, playing the piano, playing a xylophone, and dancing. To become skilled at fencing, tennis serving, and hitting a baseball requires a person to move an implement as quickly and accurately as possible. For other skills such as piano playing, xylophone playing, and dancing, speed, or tempo, is typically specified by the music. To perform successfully, the person must achieve the tempo and perform the notes or steps accurately. Suppose you were plotting the daily performance of a person learning any of these types of skills to determine the progress he or she was making in learning that skill. What feature of their performance would you measure to put on your graph? Would you measure the accuracy of each lunge, the speed of each lunge, or both? This example, then, points out the measurement problem associated with skills where one performance measure alone cannot be used to indicate performance achievement.

When only one measure of performance is desired so that recording of achievement progress can be simplified, several options are available in a speed-accuracy situation. The simplest is to choose one over the other, depending on which one is deemed more important for performing the skill successfully at a particular stage of learning. However, in this case valuable information is lost, and the measure, when considered alone, is generally not a valid one. A second option is to calculate a score that is based on a combination of the two measures. This second alternative is the preferred one and the one you will most often find reported in the research literature.

Two common methods of combining speed and accuracy measures are related to the type of task used. When the task involves speed for its completion but considers errors that are made, the suggestion is to add the number of errors and the time to complete the task and divide by two. If the task involves speed for completion but considers points scored, as with a target, then multiply the time to complete the task by the total points in order to obtain the speed-accuracy score.

Guidelines for Selecting Performance Measures

From the discussion thus far, it should be apparent that to determine the amount of learning that has taken place in any skill learning situation, an adequate performance measure is first required. The suggestions that have been made here should help you to understand why a particular measure is selected. Although most performance measures are simply selected because the task being learned can only be measured one way, there are certain cases where several measures can be used for one task. When the latter occurs, there are some guidelines that can be used to help make the appropriate selection.

There are four major criteria for judging the appropriateness of a task and/or performance measure for any learning situation. These four criteria are (1) objectivity, (2) reliability, (3) validity, and (4) novelty. The first three criteria are standard concerns that can be found in most tests and measurement textbooks. These three conditions are essential as criteria for performance measure selection in either the instructional setting or the experimental setting. The fourth criterion, however, is unique to the task selection process of the learning experiment.

Objectivity means simply that two different people should be able to arrive at a similar score for performance. In the examples presented in Table 1.2–1, objectivity is generally not difficult to achieve. It can become difficult when you measure a performance according to abstract and subjective terms such as "good," "bad," "fair," and "excellent," when no objective measuring criteria are available.

Reliability refers to the repeatability of the test and results, that is, the certainty of obtaining a similar performance score on the task if the subject is tested a second time. Control must be used to ensure that measures are as reliable as possible.

Validity indicates whether the task or performance score actually measures what you want it to measure. For motor learning experiments you must consider whether the task is motor; that is, does the task demand physical movement to be successfully accomplished? You must also consider whether the task you use accurately reflects the factor in question in the experiment, e.g., strength, coordination, or balance.

The fourth criterion is of particular importance in the learning experiment. The *novelty* of the task, that is, how familiar the task is to the subjects, is essential to the learning experiment to avoid the problem of using subjects who have had different amounts of experience with the task. A novel task, then, is one with which subjects have had no previous experience. The benefit of the novel task can be seen in an example of an experiment that is designed to assess or measure the effect of fatigue on learning a motor skill. If a basketball free throw is used, misleading results could occur if all subjects had varying prior experiences in free-throw shooting. It would be difficult to attribute any observed performance differences to the effects of fatigue. The differences could also be attributed to different skill levels of subjects at the beginning of the experiment. Using a novel task such as bouncing a basketball into the hoop with the non-preferred hand would help avoid such ambiguous results.

Summary

An essential element in understanding motor learning is the measurement of motor performance. All concepts presented in this text are based on research in which motor performance was observed and measured. Measuring motor performance is also important for a person who teaches motor skills because it is essential that the performance of students or patients is evaluated as they practice and perform the skills being taught. An important part of this evaluation process is measuring motor performance. In this concept, the discussion focused on considering different ways that motor performance can be measured, and some guidelines for selecting appropriate measures were presented. Because there are so many kinds of motor performance measures, they were organized into two categories. The response output measures category includes performance measures where time, error, and magnitude of a response are measured. The second category, response production measures, includes kinematic, EMG, and EEG measures that describe characteristics of limbs, joints, muscles, and brain activity during movement. Several measurement problems were discussed, with particular attention given to error measures and speed-accuracy measures. Finally, four criteria were discussed that should be considered when judging the appropriateness of a task to be used in a motor learning experiment or for selecting a performance measure to evaluate motor skills: objectivity, reliability, validity, and novelty.

Related Readings

Atha, J. (1984). Current techniques for measuring motion. *Applied Ergonomics, 15,* 245–257.

Clarys, J. P., Cabri, J., DeWitte, B., Toussaint, H., de Groot, G., Huying, P., & Hollander, P. (1988). Electromyography applied to sport ergonomics. *Ergonomics, 31,* 1605–1620.

Enoka, R. M. (1988). *Neuromechanical basis of kinesiology.* Champaign, IL: Human Kinetics. (Read Chapter 1, pp. 3–20)

Heatherington, R. (1973). Within-subject variation, measurement error, and selection of a criterion score. *Research Quarterly, 44,* 113–117.

Spray, J. A. (1986). Absolute error revisited: An accuracy indicator in disguise. *Journal of Motor Behavior, 18,* 225–238.

Thomas, J. R. & Nelson, J. K. (1985). *Introduction to research in health, physical education, recreation, and dance.* Champaign, IL: Human Kinetics. (Read Chapters 13 & 14)

CONCEPT 1.3

The scientific method, or research, is an important tool in understanding motor skill learning and performance

Key Terms

scientific method	dependent variable	applied research
independent variable	basic research	theory law

Application

As you progress through this book, you will find that each chapter includes a series of *concepts* related to the topic of that chapter. These concepts should be considered as generalized statements about a particular issue, statements that have been developed by synthesizing research findings. As such, these concepts can be thought of as similar to principles or general conclusions. The role of research is important in the development of these concepts. Information gained from research activity provides evidence from which a concept can be generated. In the discussion that follows, you will be introduced to the scientific method, the foundation upon which research in motor learning is based. By becoming familiar with this method of scientific inquiry, you will be better able to understand the process involved in obtaining the information on which the concepts in this book are based.

A further benefit of studying the scientific method can be seen in the following example. Suppose you were working in your teaching or rehabilitation setting and someone was observing you. After some time had passed, the observer asks you, "Why did you provide feedback to that person the way you did?" Suddenly you are required to consider the basis or rationale for decisions that you made as you performed your duties. Other similar questions could also be asked, such as, Why

was the instruction sequenced as it was? Why did the group practice like that? Why did you use that instructional aid? Why did you say what you did to them? The point is, how often do we really consider the reasons *why* we structure a setting as we do? This very basic question is at the heart of this book. The primary intent of the study of motor learning is to acquaint you with the learner, the learning environment, and the process of learning in such a way to provide you with a basis for your instructional decisions. Furthermore, it is also the intent of this study to provide you with a foundation for understanding how complex motor skills are performed and controlled and how various environmental variables influence that performance.

In order to answer effectively the types of questions we have here, we must first understand how such questions can be investigated. Throughout this book you will encounter many reports of research. The purpose of such encounters is to provide you with an opportunity to see for yourself how the very perplexing questions related to the hows and whys of motor behavior are investigated, so that the answers which we so urgently seek when confronted with the need for instructional decisions can be found. It is through careful use of research that we can begin to uncover the clues about the mysteries of motor behavior. Through the following discussion you will see what research is about, and you will feel more confident as you read about various research reports in the ensuing chapters of this book. This discussion should help you to better understand the processes involved in that research so that you can better determine for yourself the appropriateness of the generalizations about the processes of learning and performing motor skills, which are made in later chapters.

Discussion

When we are confronted with the "why" questions formulated in the previous section, we must depend on the knowledge we have in order to answer those questions. Knowledge is based on the gathering of reliable information. Unfortunately, we usually limit the acquisition of our knowledge to such means as intuition, common sense, tradition, or personal experience. For example, the teacher who uses a particular teaching method because that is the way he or she was taught is basing knowledge on personal experience or tradition. These means can be very powerful and beneficial. They are certainly not to be disparaged. These methods of obtaining information, however, are very subjective. The rationale for decisions or the understanding may be different for one teacher than for another. When knowledge is subjective it is difficult to apply to a variety of situations and individuals. It should be stated, though, that when subjective means are combined with the objective method, which we are about to discuss, a very useful approach to gaining and using information can be achieved.

The objective means for gathering information is termed the **scientific method,** the basis for research in the motor domain. It will become apparent that the application of the scientific method to the understanding of motor behavior is often difficult. It is necessary to understand that behavior provides a strong incentive to overcome such difficulties and to approach the study of human motor behavior as scientifically as possible.

The Method of Science

At the core of science is the need for *observation.* Because our focus is motor behavior, the initial point for understanding the method of science is to know that observation of motor behavior is the primary element in such study. Observation of behavior can be a rather elusive concept. What is meant by observation? How should it occur? How do we know what to look for? And so on. These questions are all important to the basic understanding of the scientific method; as you study this section, answers to these questions should become more apparent.

The primary goal of science is to help us understand our universe. To accomplish this primary goal, three subgoals of science are important: to *describe, explain,* and *predict.* These three goals are hierarchically listed and form the basis for the several possible forms of research in motor behavior. Describing motor behavior simply indicates that a statement can be made about what behavior has occurred. For example, a group of boys learned to walk through a maze in an average time of 10 minutes. The next level of understanding in science involves explaining why the observed behavior occurred. Here we are not only concerned with stating that the group of boys learned to walk through the maze in 10 minutes but we also want to know why. Perhaps they received a reward, while another group of boys who received no reward took an average of 20 minutes to learn the maze. Finally, we want to be able to predict motor behavior. From our example we would predict that when a reward is available, children will learn a complex task, such as walking through a maze, more quickly than when no reward is available. Successful prediction can be seen as achieving the primary goal of science, because to successfully predict demonstrates an understanding of a phenomenon. Prediction is the ability to generalize results of careful observation from one setting and to apply them to another setting. If the prediction or generalization is correct, results in the new setting should resemble the results from the previous setting. Prediction is based on the attainment of the goals of description and explanation. These goals can only be achieved through the careful observation of behavior and can occur in very natural settings, such as on the playground, in the gymnasium, or in the therapy room; or it can occur in a laboratory where the essential elements observed can be specifically controlled and manipulated.

The experiment. The primary means of observation employed in the motor behavior research throughout this book is the *experiment.* The primary purpose in the experiment is to control as many elements as possible, except for the ones that are the focus of observation in a particular experiment. The elements that need to be controlled or released to act naturally are called *variables.* In any experiment the experimenter must determine what variable he or she is interested in, and to observe its effects on some type of behavior. This variable is termed the **independent variable.**[2] The example of the boys' learning to walk a maze with or without a reward is a good example to consider here. The purpose of such an experiment is to determine the influence of rewards on the learning of a motor skill. The independent variable in this situation is the presence or absence of a reward. Thus the experimenter manipulates the variable by intentionally changing its use for different groups of subjects; that is, one group of subjects would get a reward following each trial while a second group, the control group, would not receive any reward at all. If the group receiving the reward learns to perform the task better than the other group, and if other possible influencing variables have been controlled by keeping them equal between the groups, the experimenter has answered his or her basic question concerning a particular variable that influences learning.

This simple example of an experiment illustrates how observation is used in a controlled experiment. The procedures to be followed, the task to be performed, the location of the experiment, and so on, are all decisions the experimenter must make. He or she will make those decisions on the basis of his or her own knowledge of the particular area of study the experiment is related to. The experimenter must be very careful in making decisions because they will have a great influence on what the results will be and what he or she can say about those results.

Relationships and experiments.　Every experiment includes a basic concern for relationships,

primarily between either the independent and dependent variable or two dependent variables. If the relationship of interest is between the independent and **dependent variables,** the experiment is primarily concerned with a *causal relationship.* The goal is to determine cause-and-effect. In our example of the rewards experiment, the goal was to determine the effect of rewards (the independent variable) on the learning of walking through a maze (the dependent variable). It is essential in experiments of this type that all dependent variables be similar between groups. Then if differences between groups do occur, you can be quite certain that the cause of the performance differences was due to the only variable that was different between the groups, the independent variable.

Sometimes it is not the experimenter's intention to determine a causal relationship between variables. Instead, the interest is in a *noncausal relationship,* that is, in how two dependent variables are related to each other. For example, the question might be raised that if a person reacts quickly to a sound will he or she also move very quickly? The problem being investigated is whether the reaction time and the speed of movement are related to each other. The cause-and-effect relationship between these two variables is not of interest here. The experimenter manipulates no variables. He or she simply tests subjects on two tasks, one measuring reaction time and the other measuring speed of movement. The two performance scores (the dependent variables) are then correlated; a high correlation indicates a strong relationship, while a low correlation shows little if any relationship.

Conclusions.　It is important to understand the distinction between causal and noncausal relationships, each of which can be investigated through controlled experimentation. You will encounter both types of experiments throughout this book. As you consider these types of relationships, you should become aware that understanding the difference between causal and noncausal relationships is related to the type of *conclusion* that can

2. *Dependent variables,* which were considered in Concept 1.2, are the performance measures used in an experiment. In the example experiment, the number of minutes required by a subject to learn to walk through the maze is the dependent variable.

be made on the basis of the results of an experiment. The conclusion that a fast reaction time *causes* fast speed of movement could *not* be made from the experiment described, even if the relationship between the two was found to be strong, because the experiment was designed to consider noncausal relationships. Thus, the conclusion about the relationship between the two variables must be always stated in a noncausal manner. For example, if the results show a high relationship, the conclusion could be that reaction time and speed of movement are highly related to each other, although we could not say anything about the cause of these results. However, in terms of prediction, it would be possible to say that if a person had a fast reaction time, he or she also had fast speed of movement.

Conclusions that suggest cause can only be validly made when the experiment has been designed as a cause-and-effect type of experiment. If the experimenter has manipulated a particular variable to observe the effects of that manipulation on some behavior, then a cause-and-effect experiment has been designed.

An example of a cause-and-effect experiment is the one described earlier where the boys were required to learn to walk through a maze. The variable manipulated in that experiment was availability of a reward. Suppose that one group of subjects is given a reward after each trial that is better than the previous best trial while the other group receives no rewards as they practice the skill. In this experiment, all conditions are the same except the availability of a reward. That is, all subjects practice the same skill, receive the same instructions, and so on. Therefore, if the results show that the reward group learned the skill faster than the no reward group, then a causal conclusion can be made about the benefit of rewards. We can have confidence in this conclusion because the availability of rewards is the only thing that differed about the conditions related to practice and performing the skill. Any observed difference in performance between the two groups must therefore be attributed to the reward availability variable.

Generalization.   Generalizations are important to science. A major goal of every experiment is that the conclusion can be taken beyond the specific experiment and applied to general situations involving similar variables. This book is filled with generalizations; in fact, each concept that is presented in every chapter is a generalization. These generalizations are made by synthesizing the research evidence that is available as a result of many experiments. The presentation of much consistent research evidence that has controlled and manipulated variables in a variety of ways and settings provides generalizations that become generally accepted. When the results are reliable or consistent, generalizations can be made with some degree of confidence. This is the ultimate goal of science, because generalizations permit prediction. However, further experiments based on the predictions may indicate that some modifications of the generalizations are necessary. Thus the process of science continues in the search for absolute prediction. When human behavior is of concern, however, such absolute prediction is very improbable. Nevertheless, generalizations in which we can be quite confident can be made; but it is only through careful observation by means of controlled experimentation that these generalizations can be developed.

Types of research.   An important aspect of the research process that is related to the issue of generalization concerns the type of research conducted. That is, does the research have generalization goals that are primarily theoretical or primarily applied? Put another way, does the researcher want the experiment to have impact on a theoretical issue or does the researcher want the experiment to have impact on solving a "real" problem? If the goal of the experiment is directed primarily to a theoretical generalization, the research is categorized as **basic research;** if the research is directed primarily toward answering an immediate problem that a practitioner faces, the research is classified as **applied research.** Both basic and applied research are valuable to furthering our knowledge of motor learning.

An example of a basic research experiment would be one that investigates how a learned motor skill is represented in human memory. As you will see in Chapters 3 and 5, this question has been the basis of much motor learning research. The answer to this question does not have direct application to the teaching of skills, but it does increase our understanding of processes responsible for motor performance. An example of an applied research experiment is one that attempts to solve a problem a teacher might confront during a class. For example, when teaching the tennis serve, should the serve be demonstrated to the class to help them learn it? The experiment designed to answer this question would provide an immediate answer about the efficacy of using demonstration as a teaching strategy for tennis serving.

There are two points to emphasize about the distinction between basic and applied research. First, these two types of research should be thought of as end points on a continuum, which allows for research to be classified as some combination of the two. Much of the research you will read about in this book falls somewhere along the continuum, rather than in either one category or the other. In this type of research it is possible to make a generalization to both theory and to real-world problems. The degree of generalization possible to either of these depends on where along the continuum between basic and applied the research falls. The second important point to remember about the basic-applied research distinction is that each type of research has strengths and weaknesses. One type should not be thought of as "better" than the other. Rather, one type may be preferable for a certain type of generalization goal than the other.

Theory Development

An issue closely related to developing effective research is developing theory. A theory of motor learning proposes to present the cause of performance effects that have been consistently observed in experiments. A **theory** addresses why we consistently observe a certain effect of an independent variable on a dependent variable in motor

learning. If we are to increase our understanding of how we learn motor skills and what influence specific variables will have on skill learning, as well as how we can effectively improve instructional methods for teaching motor skills, a theoretical base is essential. Accordingly, this need for viable motor learning theory is as important for researchers in motor skills who may not teach as it is for teachers of motor skills who may not be involved in research. As evidence for such a perspective, consider the views expressed by two individuals who developed two of the most influential motor learning theories that influence our understanding and research of motor learning, and from two highly respected scholars who study teacher behavior.

Jack Adams (1971) stated that in order for scientific productivity to develop, researchers must begin with laws and theory about movement and then find situations in which to test these laws and theories. The most productive means of accomplishing the development of a viable theory of motor learning is by research that will allow the steady building of scientific knowledge to enable us to "some day have power to answer all the problems" (p. 112). Whether this actually happens is secondary to the importance of developing research that provides the greatest potential for it to happen.

Another perspective was presented by Richard Schmidt (1975b) when he argued that without adequate theory to provide explanations for motor learning, a loss of interest in motor learning as a viable area for research could result. Interestingly, from a historical perspective, this is what occurred with motor learning research in the late 1950s and most of the 1960s. Immediately prior to that time, during and after World War II, there was a flurry of motor learning research activity. However, that research was not based on learning theory specific to motor skills learning, although Hull's popular theory of learning made several predictions about factors that influence the learning of motor skills (Hull, 1943). Nonetheless, the primary incentive for conducting motor learning research at that time was from the immediate needs of the military for developing effective methods for teaching military personnel various jobs involving motor skills, such as gunnery or piloting an airplane. In fact, it was not until the publication of the motor learning theory by Adams in 1971 that motor learning research once again increased.

The need for a solid theoretical base for teaching motor skills can be seen in statements made by theorists concerned with the process of effective teaching. It is interesting to note that these statements are similar to those made by motor learning theorists about the need for a theoretical base. For example, N. L. Gage (1972) published a book presenting the view that teaching is both a science and an art. The art aspect of teaching, he says, calls for "intuition, creativity, improvisation, and expressiveness" (p. 15). The science part of teaching involves the application of laws and theories on which teaching methods can be based. Along these same lines, Siedentop (1983) stated that teaching is not just applying the right method at the right time because you have been told to do so. Rather, the effective teacher must be able to *construct* the use of the right method to use according to the demands of the specific teaching situation, which may or may not have been confronted before.

In order for a theory to be developed, there must be a set of laws or principles on which it can be based. These laws and principles are the result of many experiments that provide evidence that dependable effects result from the influence of certain independent variables. For example, you will be introduced to Fitts' Law in Chapter 3 and Hick's Law in Chapter 4. Fitts' Law is specifically related to movement situations involving speed and accuracy and predicts movement time based on certain characteristics of the situation. Hick's Law is specific to choice reaction time situations and predicts RT characteristics for different RT situation characteristics. Many of the concepts discussed in this book are best described as principles rather than laws of motor learning.

They are not presented as laws because research has not been as consistent in showing reliable performance outcomes in situations to which they refer. However, they present useful guidelines for making such predictions. Guidelines about the use of augmented feedback, which will be discussed in Chapter 7, are examples of what in motor learning are described as principles rather than laws. In effect, a theory extends laws and principles by hypothesizing the causes of the effects predicted by these laws and principles. Thus, the theory should be able to predict the laws and principles on which it is based.

Laws and principles become the building blocks of a theory, as you will see in discussions in Chapter 3 of Adams's "closed-loop theory" and Schmidt's "schema theory" of motor learning. These theories are the result of a synthesis of many experiments. A theory is more general than a law because it is presented as a basis from which predictions can be made in related situations in which the conditions addressed by the theory have not yet been specifically tested. Additionally, a good theory establishes ways in which it can be tested in order to be further substantiated by new situations, or revised to accommodate new situations. Theories are constantly being tested and revised according to these tests. The tests come from well-conceived and designed experiments, which are critical to determining the validity of any theory. Thus the process of science in motor learning involves carrying out experiments that will increase our knowledge about the influence of certain variables on learning motor skills. This knowledge can in turn be used to establish laws of motor learning, which are then used to develop theories to explain why the effects predicted by these laws occur. Without this ongoing scientific process, our knowledge of factors influencing motor skill learning and how skill learning occurs would be severely limited.

Summary

When you are confronted with the need to provide a rationale to support your approach to teaching, you would like to have a more objective basis than intuition or tradition can provide. The scientific method provides a cogent means of obtaining information that can be used as a solid foundation for supporting instructional decisions. The scientific method is based on objective observation; through observation the goals of science, which are to describe, explain, and predict, may be attained. The primary means of observation in the scientific method is the experiment, which includes independent and dependent variables. Independent variables are those variables in which the experimenter is interested in determining the influence on the dependent variable. In a broad sense all experiments are concerned with relationships between variables. Causal relationships involve relationships between the independent and the dependent variables. Noncausal relationships are concerned with the relationship between dependent variables. These relationships determine the type of conclusion that can be made from any experiment. Generalizations are essential to the scientific method, because they are statements that go beyond the narrow limits of any one experiment. In this book, the concepts that are presented and discussed in each chapter are generalizations which have been made on the basis of information obtained through the scientific method. An important part of the method of science is the development of theory. Theories are important for advancing our knowledge because they propose causes of results of research. Theories are based on laws and principles and predict specific effects of independent variables on dependent variables. An essential part of the process of science is the development and testing of theory.

Finally, both basic and applied research will be found in the research literature related to motor learning. Basic research is designed to provide generalizations that can be related to theoretical issues, whereas applied research is designed to provide generalizations that can help answer specific problems a practitioner might face. Both types of research are valuable for furthering our understanding of motor learning.

Related Readings

Anderson, B. F. (1971). *The psychology experiment: An introduction to the scientific method.* Belmont, California: Brooks/Cole. (Read Chapter 2)

Arnold, R. K. (1982). Research on sport skill: Is it applicable to coaching? *Motor Skills: Theory into Practice, 6,* 93–102.

Christina, R. W. (1989). Whatever happened to applied research in motor learning? In J. Skinner (Ed.), *Future directions in exercise/sport research.* Champaign, IL: Human Kinetics. (Read pp. 413–424)

Prytula, R. E. (1975). The concept of organ use revisited in the gluteus maximus. *Perceptual and Motor Skills, 40,* 289–290.

Thomas, J. R., & Nelson, J. K. (1985). *Introduction to research in health, physical education, recreation, and dance.* Champaign, IL: Human Kinetics. (Read pp. 3–17)

Winstein, C. J., & Knecht, H. G. (1991). Movement science and its relevance to physical therapy. *Movement Science,* APTA Monograph, 7–10.

STUDY QUESTIONS FOR CHAPTER 1

1. What is the meaning of the term skill when it is used to refer to a motor skill? What is another use of the term skill?

2. What is the difference between a dichotomous classification system and a classification system that involves a continuum of categories?

3. What distinguishes (a) a gross from a fine motor skill? (b) a discrete from a continuous motor skill? (c) a closed from an open motor skill? Give three examples of motor skills for each category.

4. How does the Gentile 2 × 2 classification system differ from the two-category open and closed skills classification? Is the Gentile approach an improvement over the two-category system? Why or why not?

5. Cite three examples of different measures of motor performance that can be classified as response outcome measures. Cite three examples of response production measures.

6. Describe how simple RT, choice RT, and discrimination RT situations differ. How does MT differ from RT?

7. What different information can be obtained about a person's performance by calculating AE, CE, and VE when performance accuracy is the movement goal?

8. What information can kinematic measures of performance provide that other forms of performance measures cannot?

9. What information about a movement can be provided by using EMG?

10. Name three important criteria that should be considered when a performance measure must be selected. Explain why each is important.

11. What is meant by the scientific method of obtaining information? How does this method differ from other methods of obtaining information?

12. What is the difference between the *independent* and the *dependent* variables in an experiment?

13. What is the difference between a *causal* and a *noncausal* relationship? Why is this distinction an important one when doing motor learning research?

14. What is the difference between *applied* and *basic* research?

CHAPTER

2

INTRODUCTION TO MOTOR SKILL LEARNING

CONCEPT 2.1
Learning can be inferred from practice observations, retention tests, and transfer tests.

CONCEPT 2.2
The learning of a motor skill occurs in stages.

CONCEPT 2.3
Transfer of learning is an integral part of understanding motor skill learning and performance.

□

CONCEPT 2.1

Learning can be inferred from practice observations,
retention tests, and transfer tests

Key Terms

performance	transfer test	performance
learning	plateau	variable
retention test	ceiling effect	learning
	floor effect	variable

Application

A typical requirement in any profession involving motor skills instruction is an assessment to determine whether or not what is taught is learned. Consider the following two examples taken from physical education and rehabilitation settings. Suppose you are a physical educator teaching a tennis unit. If you are teaching your students to serve, what will you look for in their service that will help you assess their progress in learning? How can you be certain that what you are observing is the result of learning and not just luck? Or suppose you are a physical therapist helping a stroke patient to grasp a cup and drink from it. The same questions apply here as in the physical education teaching situation. That is, what evidence will you look for in the patient's performance to assess their progress in learning this skill? How will you know that the performance characteristics you observe are due to learning and not to other factors, such as luck or your assistance?

These questions relate to an important aspect of learning that must be considered when skill learning is assessed. That is, we must make an inference about learning. We do not directly observe learning. Instead, we directly observe behavior, which in this case is motor performance. It is from this performance observation that we must determine if the observed behavior reflects learning. Thus, the determination of whether or not a skill has been learned involves a two-part process. First, there must be observation of performance of the skill under conditions where an appropriate evaluation of learning can take place. Second, there must be a translation of that observation into a meaningful conclusion about learning.

In the discussion that follows, the problem of how to assess learning will be approached from two general directions. First, a definition of learning will be established. This is a critical step because it is important to know what learning is before attempting to determine how to evaluate whether or not it has taken place. Then, the focus will shift to considering different ways that the learning inference can be made. The primary concern will be to establish the appropriate conditions under which performance should be observed. As you will see, when inappropriate conditions are established, inappropriate conclusions about learning usually result. Three learning assessment methods will be discussed so that you will be able to make confident conclusions about learning.

The importance of making appropriate conclusions about learning can be illustrated in several different ways. For example, if you are a teacher, you will undoubtedly want to base a student's grade, at least in part, on how well he or she has learned the skills you taught in class. Also, as a teacher you want to know if a particular teaching strategy you use is more effective than an available alternative. The more desirable teaching strategy is the one that leads to more effective learning of the skill being taught. A similar situation exists in physical therapy settings. You would not want to release a patient from therapy without some assurance that the skills you have been working on have been learned by the patient to the degree that your assistance is no longer required. And it is important for you to know that the techniques used to help patients learn certain skills will lead to better learning than other available techniques. Thus, it is essential to keep in mind that unless you are able to confidently assess learning, it is difficult to derive valid conclusions that are applicable to any of these situations.

──────── □ ────────

Discussion

Two important terms are important for you to keep distinct in this discussion and throughout this book: *performance* and *learning*. **Performance** can be thought of most simply as observable behavior. In terms of motor skills, observable behaviors are what we see a person do when a skill is attempted. Thus, such things as hitting a baseball, running a mile, tracing through a maze, drinking from a cup, dancing a waltz, or operating a lathe are examples of observable motor behaviors. Each attempt to do any of these skills is a performance. We discussed how we can quantify performances such as these for evaluation purposes in Concept 1.2, where several different motor performance measures were described. Additionally, a performance may include behaviors of greater magnitude than these examples. For example, playing an entire game of basketball may be considered a performance. Again, measures of how a person performed in these situations are available. Thus, the term performance should be thought of as referring to executing a skill at a particular specific time and in a specific situation.

Learning, on the other hand, is an internal phenomenon that cannot be observed directly; it can only be inferred from the observation of a person's performance. It is common for us to make inferences about a person's internal states based on what we observe them doing. For example, when someone smiles (an observable behavior), we infer that he or she is happy. When someone cries, we infer that he or she is sad, or perhaps very happy. When a person's face gets red, we believe that person is embarrassed. Notice that in each of these situations, certain characteristics about the indi-

vidual's behavior are specifically identified as the basis for making a particular inference about some internal state we cannot directly observe. However, because we must make an inference based on observed behavior, it is possible to make an incorrect inference. If a student sitting beside you in class yawns during the lecture, you might infer from that observable behavior that person is bored. However, it may be that he or she is very interested and the yawning is due to being very tired because of lack of sleep the night before. In the same way, then, because we must infer on the basis of observed behavioral characteristics that learning is occurring or has occurred, we must select the most appropriate behavioral characteristics to observe and then observe those characteristics under appropriate circumstances. It is those circumstances that we will consider in this discussion.

Performance Changes during Learning

One of the first questions that must be answered in order to assess learning is, What performance characteristics should be identified in order to make an appropriate inference about learning? Because we expect that performance changes should occur as learning takes place, we can look for key indicators of learning in performance changes. This means that the performance measure, or measures, being observed should show certain distinct changes as the person practices the skill. Two performance characteristic changes are especially important to look for.

First, performance of the skill should show *improvement* over a period of time. This means that the person can exhibit a greater degree of skill at some later time than at some previous time during which performance of the skill was observed. However, note that we would expect this improvement should be marked by *persistence*. That is, the improvement we have observed should last for more than one performance, and should continue over an extended period of time. A person who is judged to have learned something should not only be able to demonstrate the improved performance today, but also tomorrow, next week, and so on. It is important to note that an improvement in performance may not always be directly observable. As will be discussed later, there can be extended periods of time where learning is occurring, but performances of the skill do not show any observable improvement. However, these periods are usually temporary and should end with notable improvements in performance. Finally, we must be careful not to limit learning to improvement in performance. There are cases when bad habits result from practice, which in turn results in the observed performance not showing improvement. In fact, performance may actually become worse as practice continues. Because this text is concerned with skill acquisition, though, we will focus on learning as involving improvement in performance.

The second characteristic of learning occurring is that performance becomes *increasingly more consistent*. This means that trial-to-trial, or attempt-to-attempt performances reveal decreasing variability. Early in practicing a new skill a person is likely to be very inconsistent in performing the skill. On one attempt the measured response may be better than the previous one, whereas on the next attempt it may be worse. Eventually, however, the performance becomes more consistent.

These two characteristics of performance changes during learning both are important in making inferences about learning, and are also closely interrelated. The first characteristic is concerned with the improvement in performance and the persistence of that improvement, whereas the second characteristic involves how consistent that change in performance becomes. To-

gether, these characteristics emphasize that motor learning is a process in which many physical and psychological changes are taking place.

Learning Defined

On the basis of the characteristics of performance related to learning just described, it is possible to develop a general definition for the term *learning*. This definition will be used as the basis for all that follows in this book. Accordingly, **learning** is defined as a change in the capability of a person to perform a skill that must be inferred from a relatively permanent improvement in performance as a result of practice or experience.

It is important to note that this definition indicates that the person has increased his or her capability, or potential, to perform that skill. Whether or not the skill is actually performed in a way that is consistent with this potential will depend on the presence of what are known as performance variables. These include such factors as the alertness of the person, the anxiety created by the situation, the uniqueness of the setting in which the skill is performed, fatigue, and so on. As a result, it is critical that the methods used to assess learning take factors such as these into account to allow an accurate inference about learning.

Assessing Learning

Now that you are familiar with some important performance characteristics that should be associated with learning a motor skill, it is important to establish the conditions under which these characteristics should be observed. Of interest are methods that can be used to assess learning so that an accurate inference can be made about learning. Three such methods will be discussed: *practice observations, retention tests, and transfer tests*. Consider the following examples of situations you may have experienced yourself.

Once again, suppose you are a physical educator teaching a tennis serve to your class. In Concept 1.2 several possible performance measures were discussed that could indicate tennis serving performance and provide a quantitative means for evaluating students' progress. For example, you could simply record the number of legal serves made by the students during class. Or you could establish an accuracy measure whereby you give different point values to balls landing in different locations in the service court. You might even develop a serving form measure that is concerned only with the form the students use as they serve. The selection of the performance measure is an important step in assessing learning. However, after that measure has been selected, you must determine the conditions in which the students will perform so that you can assess their progress.

One way to set up a learning assessment evaluation situation is to observe the students' performance each day for a specified period. The students could record the number of legal serves, if that is the performance measure you have selected, that they make each day out of 20 attempted serves. After several class periods, you can look at these records and determine if the expected performance improvement and consistency changes are occurring.

Another way to assess learning of the serve would be to give the students a serving test several days after serving practice has ceased. Then, a few days after that, test them again. Based on the record of serving performance your students have been keeping and on their scores on these tests, you can assess how well the performance scores they made during practice persisted after a period of limited or no practice. According to the definition of learning stated earlier, they should be able to serve better during these tests than they were able to before they began practicing the serve.

One additional means of determining how well the serve has been learned is by having the students use the serve in situations different from those in which they have been practicing. For example, during a game, can the student serve in a manner consistent with how he or she did during practice? For certain skills it is important they be learned in such a way that they can be performed in a variety of situations. A person who can serve effectively only in practice conditions that are unlike a game situation will not become a successful tennis player.

These three examples demonstrate that learning can be inferred from performance observations that take place in different circumstances. These three situations provide the basis for three different types of learning assessment methods. The first situation was an example of assessing learning by using practice observations. The second situation was an example of using a retention test, and the third situation described the use of a type of transfer test. Each of these methods is useful and is preferred for certain situations. The following sections will consider the important features of these three learning assessment methods and provide information that will enable you to select the appropriate method for the various situations you may encounter as you teach skills.

Practice Observations

A useful method to assess learning is to keep a performance record throughout the period during which the new skill is being practiced. The record should be of the performance measure you have chosen for the skill. There are several ways to graphically represent such a record so that performance changes resulting from practice are readily apparent. Two methods will be discussed here. The first is the performance curve, which is especially useful to graphically represent performance when the performance measure is one of the response outcome measures discussed in Concept 1.2. The second graphic presentation method is useful for more complex performance measures, such as the kinematic measures discussed in Concept 1.2.

Performance curves. Sometimes incorrectly referred to as a learning curve, the performance curve plots the progress made by a person or a group of persons during a certain period of time. It provides a graphic picture or illustration of the performance changes that have taken place. Both improvement in performance and in performance consistency can be observed on a performance curve.

Before discussing how to interpret a performance curve, it will be helpful to first consider how a performance curve is constructed. Figure 2.1–1

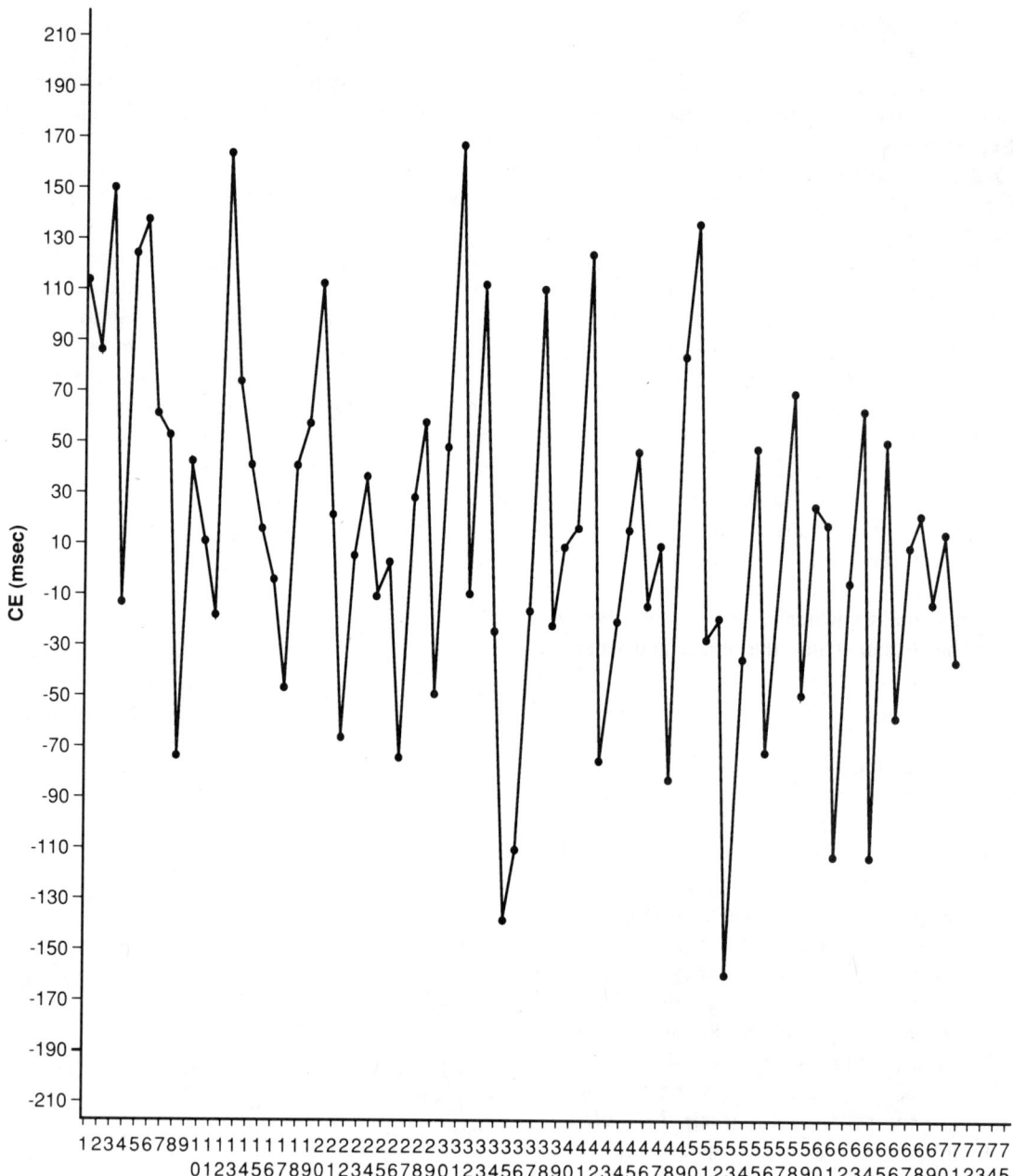

Trials

FIGURE 2.1-1 An example of the performance curve for one subject performing 75 trials on an anticipation timing task. The performance measure (CE) is the error made on each trial (a negative value means the subject responded too early; a positive value means the subject responded too late).

is an example of a performance curve for one person practicing a motor skill requiring a person to knock down a small wooden target with a hand-held bat while a moving light traveling along a long trackway reaches the target. This is known as an anticipation timing task and is designed to simulate in the laboratory the skill of striking an object moving toward the subject, such as hitting a baseball or tennis ball.

Three features of this person's performance curve need to be considered to understand how a performance curve is constructed. First, the vertical axis of the graph, which is commonly referred to as the *y-axis* or the *ordinate,* is the performance, or dependent, measure used to assess performance of the skill. In Figure 2.1–1, this measure is CE, or constant error, which was discussed in Concept 1.2. Because the task requires the person to make an accurate timing response, a useful performance measure is the timing error the person makes, which is the difference between when the person struck the object and when the light reached the target. A negative error value indicates the object was struck too early, whereas a positive error value indicates the object was struck too late. It is important to note that the vertical axis is always marked in equal units, which are determined by the person making the graph. Also notice that the bottom of this axis, where it intersects the horizontal axis, is always assumed to have the value of 0. Thus, performance measures should be represented on the vertical axis progressing from smaller to larger values.

Second, the horizontal axis of the graph, commonly referred to as the *x-axis* or the *abcissa,* typically represents the time over which the performance was observed. In the graph in Figure 2.1–1 this measure is trials. Each trial represents a new attempt at performing the skill. The person represented by this performance curve performed 75 trials. Again, notice that the units along this axis are of equal size. It is also important to notice that the point of intersection between this axis and the y-axis is assumed to be 0. The unit of time represented on the x-axis is always presented progressing from lower to higher values.

The third important part of the graph is the performance curve itself. The curve is formed by marking the error score for each trial at the appropriate intersection point on the graph, then connecting each of these points with a line. Although the line that results rarely looks like a "curve," it nevertheless is called a performance curve.

For many experiments you will read about in this text, graphs are presented with performance curves for groups of subjects rather than for just one individual. Figure 2.1–2 presents such a graph, which is based on performing the anticipation timing task used to produce Figure 2.1–1. Notice some differences between these two graphs. First, in Figure 2.1–2, there are two performance curves, one for each of two different experimental conditions used in the experiment. Each group is designated on the graph by its own symbol. In the experiment, one condition involved having subjects perform the anticipation timing task without verbal feedback about the accuracy of their responses. This verbal information is typically called knowledge of results, or KR. On the graph, this group is labeled "No KR." The other condition, labeled "KR" on the graph, involved providing verbal KR after every practice trial. The performance curves represent the mean, or average, performance of all subjects in each group. Second, note that the performance measure shown on the y-axis is absolute constant error (|CE|). |CE| was discussed in Concept 1.2 as being a more appropriate group performance measure of response bias than is constant error (CE), which was presented for the individual subject in Figure 2.1–1. Third, notice that the x-axis unit of measurement has changed in this graph to "blocks of trials." You will see this terminology in many experiments. It simply means that each unit is the average of a block or series of trials. In Figure 2.1–2, each block is the average of 5 trials, thus performance for only 15 blocks is represented. Blocking trials is a useful means of providing a less-variable representation of performance.

FIGURE 2.1-2 An example of performance curves for two groups of subjects performing an anticipation timing task. One group performed with knowledge of results (KR) after each trial whereas the other group performed without KR. Notice that although the two groups appear to differ from each other after seven blocks of trials, there is no statistical difference between the two groups.

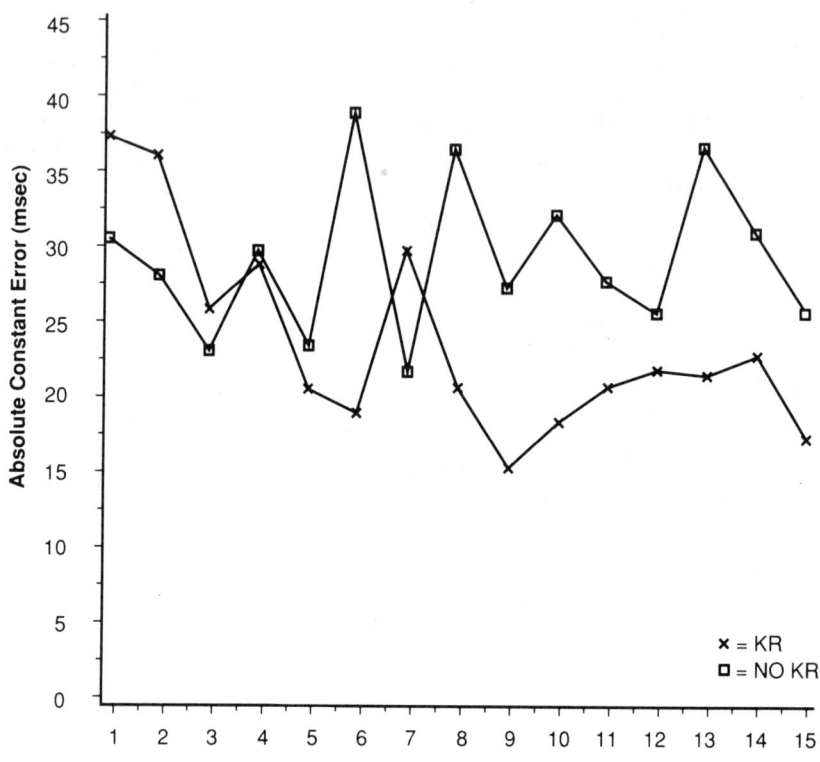

Blocks of 5 Trials

Interpreting the performance curve. Now that you have in mind the basic elements that make up a curve, the next step is to consider how to interpret a curve. In any performance curve an important characteristic that should be considered in order to make any inference about learning is that the curve should show an *improvement* in the performance score over the practice trials. Statistically, a significant improvement in the score should be expected. To more easily see this, it will be helpful to understand the types of curves typically presented. Four generalized performance curve types are commonly seen in motor learning research. Examples of these curves are presented in Figure 2.1–3.

Curve A is a *linear curve* or a straight line. This indicates proportional performance increases over time; that is, each unit of increase on the horizontal axis (e.g., one trial) results in a propor-

tional increase on the vertical axis (e.g., one second). Curve B is a *negatively accelerated curve,* which indicates that a large amount of improvement occurred early in practice and then leveled off to some extent. Although improvement is usually still occurring in the latter part of the curve, it is very slight. Curve C is the inverse of curve B and is called a *positively accelerated curve.* This curve indicates slight performance gain early in practice but a substantial increase later in practice. Curve D is a combination of all three curves, and is called an *ogive* or *S-shaped curve.*

Each of these curves shows better performance as the curve slopes upward. There are, however, instances in which improvement in performance is indicated when the slope of the curve is in a downward direction. That occurs when the performance, or dependent, measure is some aspect such as errors or time, where a decrease in the

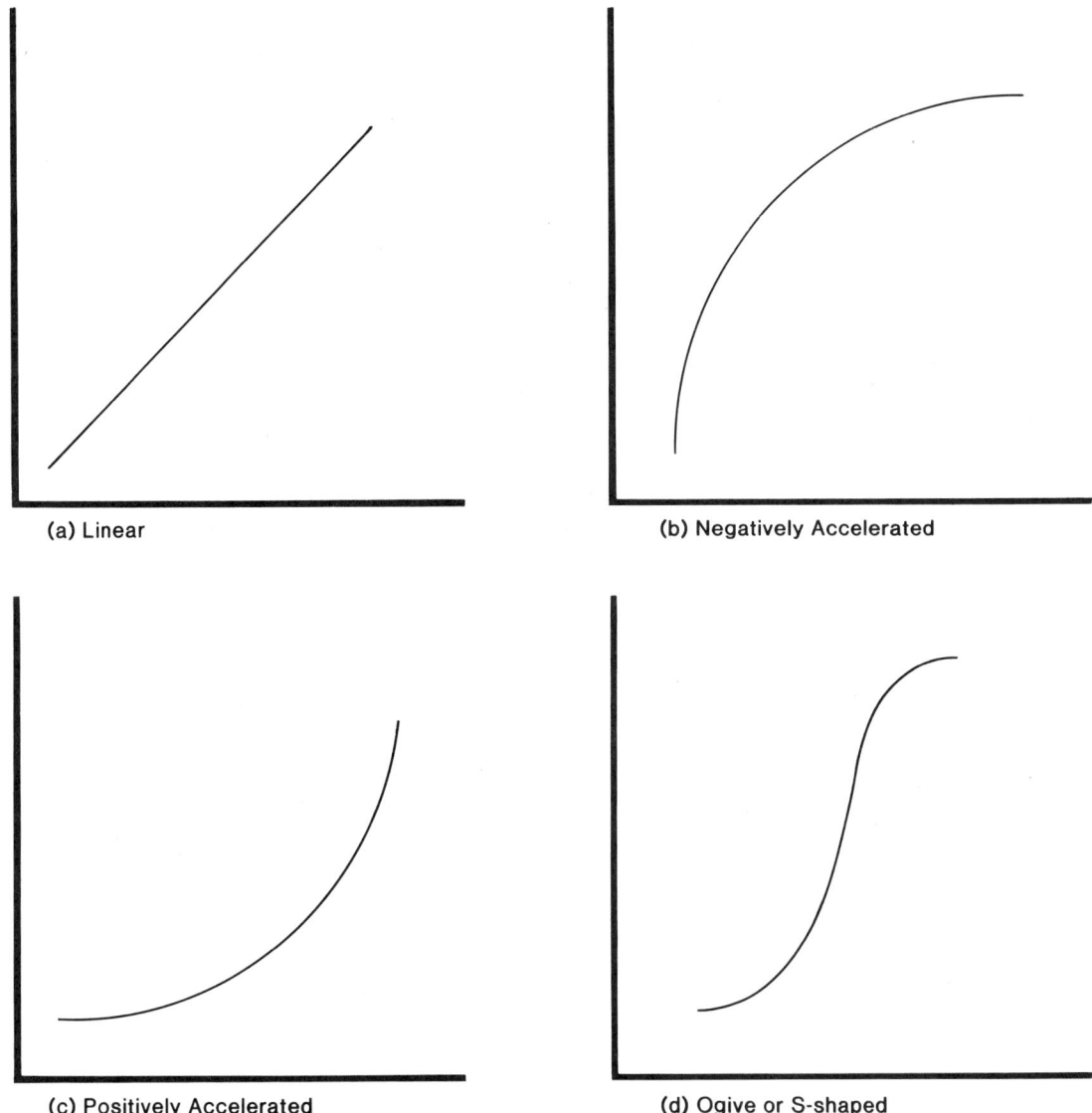

(a) Linear

(b) Negatively Accelerated

(c) Positively Accelerated

(d) Ogive or S-shaped

FIGURE 2.1-3   Four general types of performance curves.

performance measure means better performance. Some examples would be absolute error, reaction time, and running the mile. Performance improvement is noted when the amount of error or time for the performances decreases. In these cases, the performance curves would be in the direction opposite to those just described, although the types of curves would be the same.

One further point needs to be clarified concerning performance curves. The four curves presented in Figure 2.1–3 are termed smooth curves. Typical curves found in research studies are not smooth but erratic, as can be seen in Figure 2.1–3. However, when the curves are hypothetically smoothed, they appear as presented in this discussion of types of curves.

Although improvement in trial-to-trial consistency is an important characteristic of learning, this is not typically readily observable in most performance curves in most research articles for the following two reasons. First, the performance curves you typically see are for groups of subjects, such as the one in Figure 2.1–2. The individual subjects' scores have been averaged together to present a general picture of the group's performance. When this is done, the individual's trial-to-trial performances cannot be determined. Second, the trial performance scores are often grouped into blocks of trials, as in Figure 2.1–2 where they are in a block of five trials. The result of this is the reduction of the actual trial-to-trial variability, although it presents a more realistic picture of performance.

Graphically representing kinematic measures.

Another means of judging improvement in performance and a decrease in trial-to-trial variability can be seen in the graphs of movement displacement in Figure 2.1–4. These graphs are from the experiment by Marteniuk and Romanow (1983) that you were introduced to in the discussion of kinematic measures in Concept 1.2. Because of the complexity of the performance measures used in that experiment, it is not possible to develop a performance curve where the measure for every trial is represented by a point on a graph. The graphs in Figure 2.1–4 illustrate one way that these types of measures can be graphically presented for a series of practice trials, which in the Marteniuk and Romanow experiment involved 800 trials.

The graphs in Figure 2.1–4 represent the performance for one subject practicing a task that required the horizontal movement of a handle in such a way to produce the criterion pattern of movement that was shown as the displacement curve in Figure 1.2–6 in Concept 1.2. This criterion movement was shown to the subject on a computer monitor. The subject was required to move the handle in the proper direction and speed to produce the pattern. Each graph to the right of the criterion represents the subject's average pattern

drawn for a series of 10 trials, indicated by the solid line (mean) and the variability of the patterns drawn for those same 10 trials, as indicated by the dashed lines (s.d.). Notice two things about these graphs. First, the average pattern drawn becomes more like the criterion pattern as the subject gets more practice. In fact, by trials 751 through 760, the pattern made by the subject is almost identical to the criterion pattern in Figure 1.2–6. Second, notice how far from the mean pattern drawn are the lines for the standard deviation in trials 1 through 10. This shows a large amount of trial-to-trial variability. However, notice how close to the mean the standard deviation lines are during trials 751 through 760. The subject has become more consistent in producing the same pattern on each practice trial.

Retention Tests

Another means of inferring learning from performance is to administer a retention test. You have experienced this approach to assessing learning since you began school. Teachers are always giving tests that cover units of instruction. As you are well aware, **retention tests** are used to determine how much you know, or have retained from your study. However, what is more important is that the teacher makes an inference concerning how much you have learned about a particular unit of study on the basis of your test performance.

The usual way of administering a retention test in a motor skill situation is to develop an appropriate test of skills you were teaching your students. Administer the test to the students on their first day of practice for a particular skill. After a period of time, administer the test again. The difference between the two scores will be an indicator of performance increase. However, if you are interested in learning you should administer the test once again some time later, after no actual practice of the skill has occurred. If there is a statistically significant difference between that score and the score on the first practice day, you can be certain that learning has occurred. Thus, the inference of learning from performance can be made

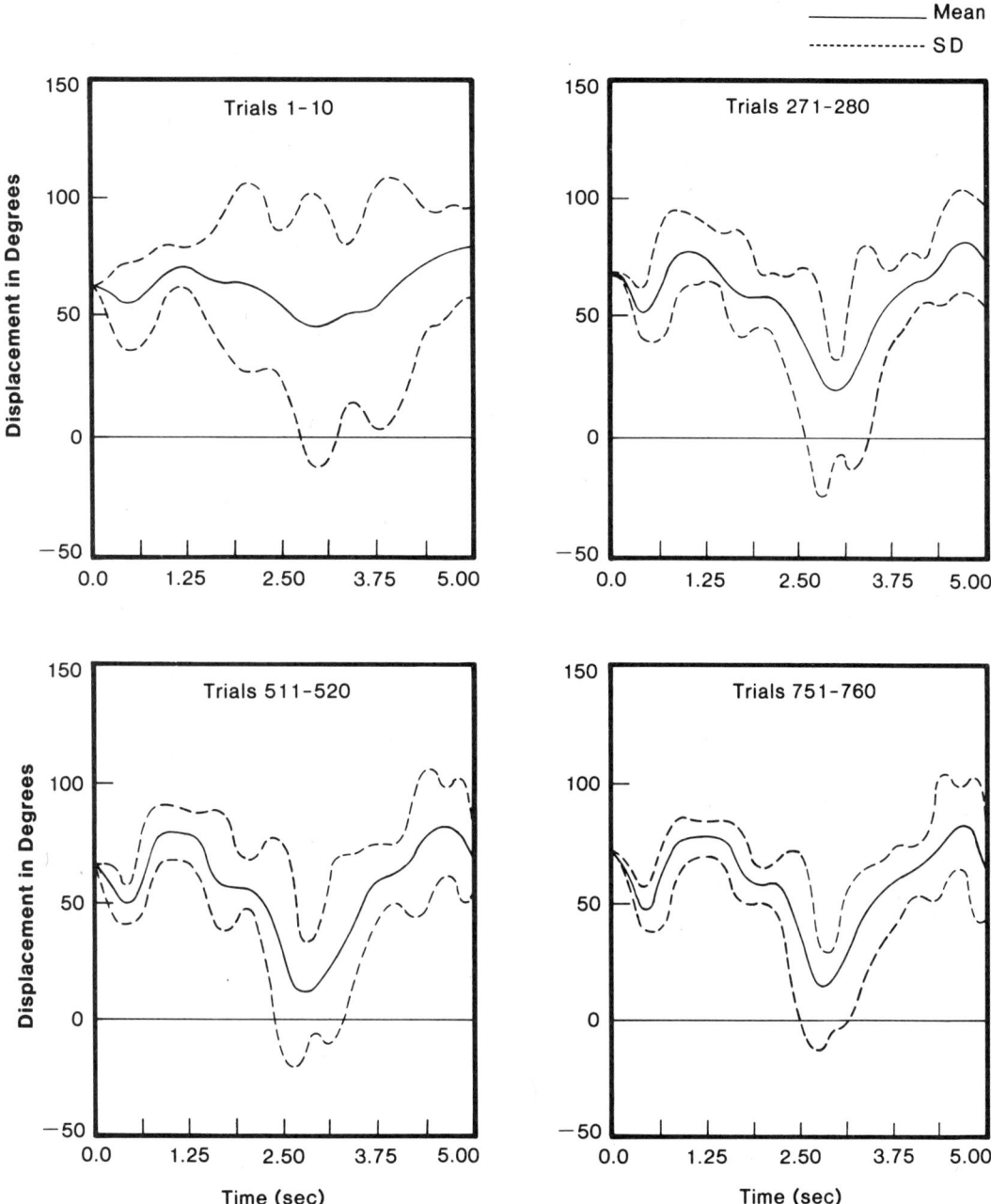

FIGURE 2.1-4 Results of an experiment by Marteniuk and Romanow showing changes in performance accuracy (displacement) on a tracking task at different practice trial blocks for one subject.

on the basis of a retention test. The decision concerning how much learning has occurred is a measurement problem. Our concern, however, will be to determine only that learning has occurred and that inferences about learning can have an objective basis. The inference based on retention test results that learning has occurred provides a very practical and useful tool for the teacher, who must objectively and quickly assess the learning that has occurred in students.

In the motor learning experiments you will read about in this text, retention tests are used rather frequently. The most common use of the retention test is to have the subjects perform the same skill they have been practicing some time after the practice period has been completed. The time interval may be any length. Usually, the retention test involves subjects performing the skill without receiving any verbal knowledge of results after each trial. The reason for this is that the experimenter wants to determine how well the subjects can perform the practiced skill on their own, without relying on any assistance from the experimenter.

Transfer Tests

The third means of inferring learning is by using what are known as **transfer tests.** This involves establishing a test situation where the subjects or students must use the skill they have been practicing, but in a new situation. In the tennis serve example presented earlier, the transfer test was serving in a game situation. If the students were learning the tennis serve during practice, then there should be an increase in the number of good serves in the games compared to good serves before they actually began practicing. In this example, the teacher uses the transfer test as a pretest, a test given before practice begins, and as a posttest, a test given after practice ends. The inference about learning is made on the basis of an observed, or statistical, increase in serving performance from the pretest to the posttest.

Transfer tests are especially important when the skill being learned will have to be performed under a variety of test conditions. Recall that open skills have this characteristic. For example, although you can practice receiving a variety of tennis serves, it is highly unlikely that in a game you will receive a serve that has every characteristic of a serve you practiced. These types of skills require the individual to adapt to the demands of each response situation. Closed skills may also require the person to be adaptable. For these skills, rather than having to adapt to new variations of the skill, the person must be able to perform the practiced skill in a variety of contexts. Shooting a free throw in basketball is such an example. During a game a variety of context factors will differ both from practice and on each shot. One way to test how capable a person is at adapting to unique situations is to use a transfer test. Learning can be inferred on the basis of how successful the person is at performing the skill in a new situation. An example of using a transfer test is when students are evaluated on their performances using the skill they have been practicing.

In motor learning experiments, transfer tests usually involve changing the context in which the practical skill must be performed, or changing the skill to be a new variation of the practiced skill. The performance context can be anything related to the condition of the subjects when they perform, such as being fatigued or stressed, or it can be related to the environment in which the skill is performed, such as in front of an audience, or in a game situation. Performing a new variation of the practiced skill involves performing the same skill, but under conditions where some characteristics of the skill are different. An example of variation of a skill that involves striking a moving object would be an object that moves at a faster rate of speed or that moves in a different spatial plane.

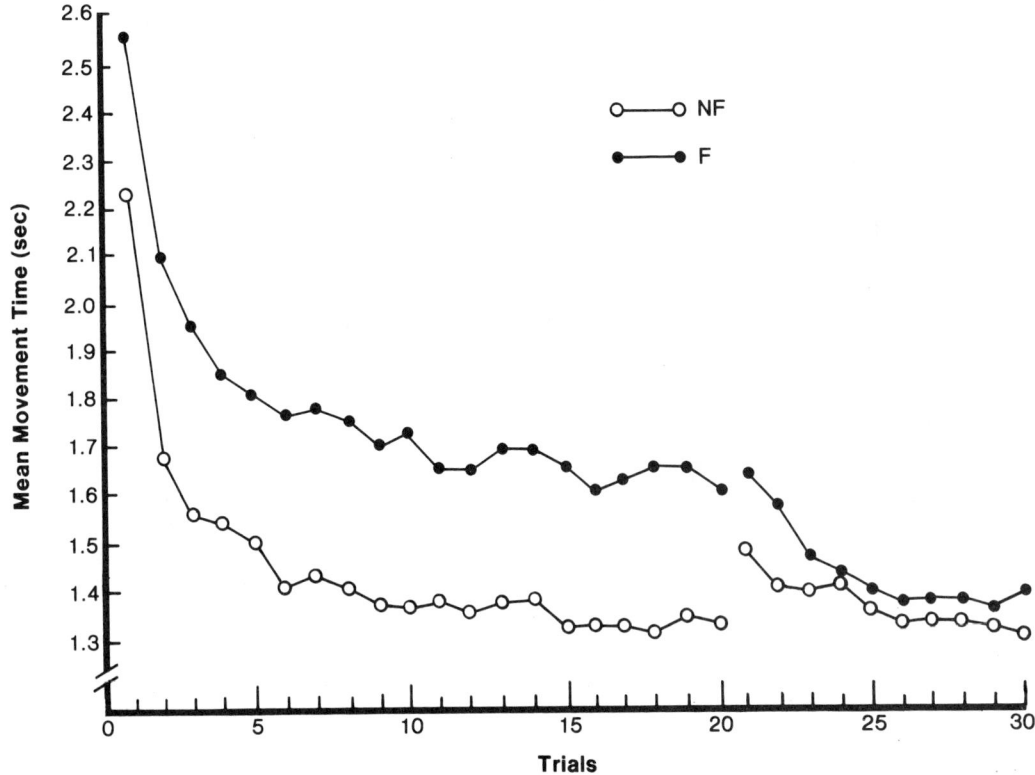

FIGURE 2.1-5 Results of the experiment by Godwin and Schmidt showing the performance curves for the fatigued (closed circles) and the nonfatigued (open circles) groups for the sigma task.

Practice Observations Can Be Misleading

One of the benefits of using retention tests or transfer tests to assess learning, rather than relying solely on practice performance observations, is that they can often lead to more reliable inferences about learning. To see this, consider an example from motor learning research where an incorrect learning inference would have resulted if a transfer test had *not* been used.

In an experiment by Godwin and Schmidt (1971), subjects were required to learn an arm-movement task called a sigma task. This task required subjects to move a handle as rapidly as possible in a complete circle in one direction, then reverse direction making another circle, let go of the handle, and knock down a small barrier a few inches from the handle. The performance measure was movement time, the amount of time it

took to begin moving the handle before the barrier was contacted. One group of subjects (the fatigued group) was required to engage in arm-cranking activity for 20 seconds between trials, while the other group (the nonfatigued group) rested for 20 seconds. Results of the 20 practice trials are presented in the left portion of the graph in Figure 2.1–5. From these results, it appears that the fatigued group did much worse than the nonfatigued group.

Before drawing any conclusions about the influence of fatigue on learning, notice the right-hand portion of the graph. This portion represents the results from a transfer test of 10 trials. In this test, all subjects performed the sigma task again, but with a 20-second rest between trials. Consider the nonfatigued group as a control condition and the fatigued group as an experimental condition.

As such, the control, nonfatigued group continues under the same performance conditions during the transfer trials as they did during the practice trials. However, the experimental, fatigued group are transferred to a new situation and rest between trials. The logic here is that if fatigue influences learning, removing the fatiguing situation during the transfer trials should lead to performance similar to that during the trials with fatiguing exercise between trials. However, the results in this experiment showed that there was a difference between the groups' performance during the common situation of the transfer trials only for the first two trials. After that, the groups did not differ. Thus, the conclusion should be that the between-trials exercise influenced practice performance but *not* learning.

The Godwin and Schmidt (1971) experiment illustrates how an incorrect inference about learning can be made if a transfer test is not used. Without the transfer test, the inference would have been that fatigue influences learning. However, when the transfer trials are taken into consideration, it becomes apparent that the fatigue influence was not on learning but on practice performance.

This example of the use of transfer tests is just one of many you will find in this book. You will also see retention tests used in similar ways. The important point is that you are aware of the problems that can arise when making inferences about learning. Retention and transfer tests are important for looking at the "performance" part of the learning definition. As such they are critical for making accurate inferences.

Performance Plateaus

Another point in support of the need for using retention and transfer tests for making inferences about learning can be seen in practice situations where **plateaus** in performance seem to occur. During plateaus, performance that had been steadily improving suddenly seems to reach a steady state where there appears to be little or no further improvement. Then, after further practice, performance begins to show improvement again.

The idea that plateaus exist as a normal phase of the learning experience has been debated since the end of last century. Plateaus seem to be something that people frequently experience in real life; but researchers have had difficulty finding plateaus in an experimental setting. The question that develops from the conflict is this: Are plateaus normal in learning, or are they merely concomitants of performance? As performance concomitants, plateaus may not be typical of learning but can be observed on occasion in practice performance.

The first research evidence that brought about discussion of the possible existence of plateaus appeared in 1897 in a classic article by Bryan and Harter. Telegraphers were learning Morse code over a period of 40 weeks. Steady improvement in the telegraphers' letters-per-minute speed was observed for the first 20 weeks. But then performance leveled off for the next 6 weeks before any improvement was again noted. The final 12 weeks were characterized by performance similar to that observed over the first 20 weeks. Those 6 weeks of no improvement were labeled a plateau. Whether this plateau was a real learning phenomenon or merely a temporary performance artifact was discussed with little resolve until 1958, when Keller wrote an article entitled "The Phantom Plateau," which attempted to clarify some problems concerning the interpretation of plateaus. (See Adams, 1987, for an excellent review of plateau research.) Keller maintained that plateaus are not general characteristics of learning but of performance. This interpretation takes us back to the learning inference. Plateaus may appear during the course of practice, but it appears that learning is still going on; performance has plateaued, but learning continues.

An example of a performance plateau. It is difficult to see evidence of performance plateaus in the motor learning research literature because experimenters rarely report performance curves for individual subjects. Because plateaus are individual performance characteristics, performance curves for individual subjects are necessary if plateaus are to be observed. An exception to this sit-

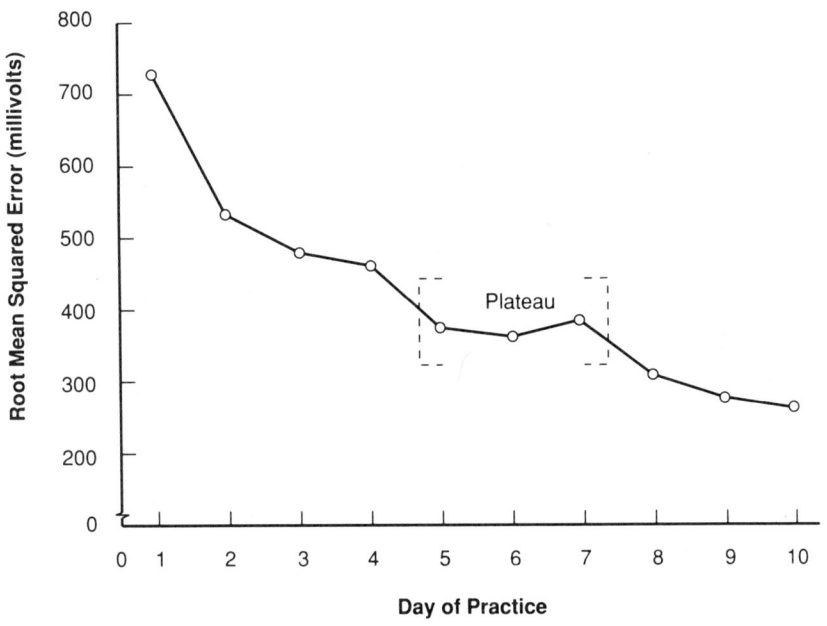

FIGURE 2.1-6 Results from the experiment by Franks and Wilberg showing the results of one subject performing the complex tracking task for 10 days, with 105 trials per day. Notice the performance plateau for 3 days (days 5, 6, and 7) where performance leveled off before showing improvement again.

uation, and one that provides a good illustration of a performance plateau, is an experiment reported by Ian Franks and Robert Wilberg (1982). One of the subjects in their experiment practiced a complex tracking task for 10 days, with 105 trials each day. The task involved moving a lever that was mounted on a tabletop in such a way to follow the movement of a target cursor on the computer screen. The pattern made by the target cursor can be seen in Figure 1.2–7 in the discussion of the root-mean-squared error (RMSE) performance measure (Concept 1.2). Only the moving target cursor, not the pattern, was seen by the subject. The subject was instructed to try to follow the target cursor as accurately as possible. One trial, which meant the pattern was presented one time, lasted just over 2.5 seconds.

Results of the 10 days of practice on this tracking task for one subject are presented in Figure 2.1–6. Notice that the trials along the x-axis are presented in blocks of 105 trials each, or one day of practice. As you can see from the performance curve for this subject, she showed consistent improvement in accurate tracking (as measured by RMSE) for the first four days of practice. Days 5 through 7 show a period when performance improvement stopped, and actually worsened slightly on one day. Those days of practice are a good example of a performance plateau. However, as is typical of most plateaus, the steady-state performance was temporary as the subject again showed improvement on day 8 and continued to improve each of the next two days of practice. If you removed the plateau section from this graph, and only plotted days 1 through 5 and 8 through 10, it would appear as if the subject showed steady improvement throughout practice. But this was not the case because there was a distinct period of no improvement that lasted several days.

The cause of plateaus. Now that we have described and illustrated performance plateaus, we will consider their causes. One of the most plausible explanations has been proposed by Singer (1980), who postulated that when a complex skill is learned a "hierarchy of habits" must be mastered by the learner. This means that when you are learning a skill, you first learn the fundamental phases of the skill and then begin to concentrate on learning the more advanced aspects of that skill. For example, you should learn to stroke the tennis ball while you are in a stationary position before you learn to hit the ball on the run. Singer's point is that between these two steps of learning the skill, you begin to try to apply what you already know to a new situation. It is during this time the plateau in performance may occur.

Other possible explanations for performance plateaus may be a period of poor motivation, or a time of fatigue, or a lack of attention directed to an important aspect of a skill. Furthermore, plateaus may also be the result of the performance measure that is being used. This would be the case when the performance measure involves what is known as *ceiling* or *floor effects*. These effects occur when the nature of the performance measure will not permit the score to go above or below a certain point. An example of a **ceiling effect** is when a performance score is a certain number of correct responses out of a possible total number of responses, and improvement in performance can be recorded only up to a certain point. If tennis serves are being scored on a number of good serves out of 20 each day, no further improvement can be observed as soon as the person reaches 20 out of 20. It is possible, however, that improvement was in fact occurring, though the performance measure included a ceiling effect that limited the amount of improvement that could be observed. The term **floor effect** would be applicable when a decrease in the performance score indicated improvement.

Plateaus seem to be common in motor skills practice. While there is limited information on which to base any conclusion about *why* they occur, it seems safe to conclude that they do not appear to be related to a lack of increase in learning. Plateaus should more accurately be considered performance "artifacts" that are caused by variables influencing performance. Teachers of motor skills would do well to determine what that cause is. The students may be tired or bored, or attending to the wrong cues in trying to learn a more complex part of the skill. Assessment of the cause of a performance plateau is often possible, and such investigation can aid the student in learning any motor skill.

Learning and Performance Variables

From the preceding discussion, it is possible to conclude that in any learning situation, some conditions, or variables, influence practice performance but not learning. Learning seemingly continues even though practice performance does not reveal it. These kinds of variables are considered to be **performance variables.** Such things as fatigue, boredom, certain practice organization routines, etc., are good candidates for this type of variable. You will confront more performance variables as you continue to study motor learning.

On the other hand, there are variables that when involved in practice conditions will influence both the observed practice performance and learning. These variables, called **learning variables,** yield transfer or retention performance that may be either similar to or different from performance at the end of the practice sessions. Again, you will become more acquainted with these variables as you study this text. For now, it is important that you realize the difference between performance and learning variables and prepare yourself to see them in a variety of topics covered in this text.

Summary

Three methods have been discussed that can be used to infer that learning has occurred. The first is the use of practice observations, typically seen in the form of performance curves plotted over practice trials or trial blocks and series of kinematic measures that are recorded for each trial. Because practice observations can sometimes be misleading, other methods are often necessary. One of these is the second method of making a learning inference. This is by using retention tests. Such are tests given after a specified time of no practice and are usually given under the same conditions in which a skill was practiced. Third, transfer tests also provide a powerful means of assessing the amount of learning that has occurred. They require the learners either to perform the skill that has been practiced in a new situation or to perform a new variation of the practiced skill. For both retention tests and transfer tests, learning can be inferred when performance is better than if no practice on the skill had occurred. Because learning must be inferred from performance, the use of these three methods can be valuable tools in developing appropriate conclusions about learning, a task that is required of all teachers.

Finally, an intriguing performance phenomenon known as a performance plateau was discussed. A plateau is actually a performance artifact, because it appears to represent a period of practice when, although performance seems to have stabilized, learning still occurs. Several causes of performance plateaus were considered.

Related Readings

Carron, A. V., & Marteniuk, R. G. (1970). An examination of the selection of criterion scores for the study of motor learning and retention. *Journal of Motor Behavior, 2,* 239–244.

Davis, F. B. (1964). *Educational measurements and their interpretations.* Belmont, CA: Wadsworth.

Dunham, P. (1971). Learning and performance. *Research Quarterly, 42,* 334–337.

Keller, F. S. (1958). The phantom plateau. *Journal of the Experimental Analysis of Behavior, 1,* 1–13.

CONCEPT 2.2

The learning of a motor skill occurs in stages

Key Terms

cognitive stage

associative stage

autonomous stage

"getting the idea of the movement"

relevant stimuli

non-relevant stimuli

fixation/ diversification

Application

Have you noticed when you are first learning a skill, such as the serve in tennis, the hook in bowling, or a jump in ballet, that you must think about some very specific aspects of the skill, which differ from what you think about after you have become rather proficient at performing that skill? When you are first learning the tennis serve, you are very concerned with how you are holding the racket, how high you are tossing the ball, whether you are transferring your weight properly at contact, and so on. These fundamental elements of the serve are very important when you are first learning the serve. However, when you practice the serve and improve, these concerns seem less important; you become more familiar with serving and you improve your own serving skill. After much practice, you notice that you concentrate on other aspects of serving. Although you still concentrate on looking at the ball while tossing it and during contact, you also find that you are thinking about where you are going to place this serve in your opponent's service court.

Consider novice basketball players. If you put them in a one-on-one situation, you will observe that most of what they are thinking about are the basic mechanics of the fundamental skills involved. They are probably very concerned with dribbling the ball properly because they do not want to lose it to the opponent. Or they attend to the basic mechanics of shooting a lay-up. This is quite different from highly skilled basketball players. Highly skilled performers do not direct attention to the mechanics of dribbling or shooting, because these skills are already mastered. Rather, concentration is centered on how to maneuver around the opponent. They may be watching for specific cues from the opponent's movements that will let them know exactly how to move to make a shot. Because skilled players do not have to concentrate on the dribbling or shooting mechanics of the task, they are free to direct attention to other concerns.

Both these situations typify phases that occur during the process of learning a motor skill. As practice continues, under proper conditions, certain changes take place in the learner. These modifications can be noted in terms of what the learner thinks about or concentrates on during the performance of the skill. The changes will also be evident in certain characteristics of the individual's performance. In the discussion that follows we will consider these developments more specifically by discussing the stages or phases of learning identified by certain theorists to describe the learning process.

Discussion

One characteristic of motor skill learning is that it is possible to identify distinct stages or phases that all learners seem to experience as they learn skills through practice. Several attempts have been made by researchers to identify these stages to assist us in better understanding the learning process. Three proposals to identify the stages of learning will be presented here. Each view purports that the earliest stage of learning is predominated by cognitive concerns about a skill although later the focus shifts to more automatic performance of the skill. The first approach we will consider was developed by Paul Fitts and Michael Posner in 1967 and is traditionally accepted as the classic stage of learning model. This model is commonly referred to in the motor learning literature when stages of learning are being addressed. The other two learning stages proposals have been published since the Fitts and Posner model was proposed and have some unique features that are interesting to consider. One model was developed by Jack Adams as a part of his theory of motor learning, which will be discussed in Chapter 3. The other model was proposed by Ann Gentile in a monograph in *Quest* in 1972 and, of the three, is the most closely related to motor skill instruction applications.

Fitts and Posner's Three-Stage Model

When learners begin to acquire a new skill, they are generally confronted with some very specific, cognitively oriented problems. What is the basic task? How do you score in this game? How do you know who wins? What is out of bounds? What is the best way to hold this racket, or bat, or club, etc.? Each of these questions indicates the basic and cognitive level at which the new learner is operating in the early part of learning a motor skill. To account for this cognitive activity, Fitts and Posner labeled the first stage of learning the **cognitive stage.** This stage is marked by a large number of errors in performance, and the nature of the errors being committed tends to be gross. For example, the beginning golf student gets the

ball in the air sometimes, while dribbling it on the ground at other times. The results are due to some very gross errors made by the student during the golf swing itself. The cognitive stage is also marked by performance that is highly variable. Although beginners may know that they are doing something wrong, they are generally not aware of exactly what should be done differently the next time to improve. As a result, they need specific information that will assist them in correcting what they have done wrong.

The second stage of learning in the Fitts and Posner model is called the **associative stage.** The nature of the cognitive activity that characterized the cognitive stage changes during the associative stage. Many of the basic fundamentals or mechanics of the skill have to some extent been learned. The errors are fewer and less gross in nature. The learners are now concentrating on refining their skill. They have developed an ability to detect some of their own errors in performing the task. While this ability to locate their errors is not perfect, they are able to identify some of the errors. This provides the learners with some specific guidelines about how to continue practice. The golfer may be getting the ball into the air rather consistently now, but often he or she still "slices" the ball. He or she does not always get maximum distance or height out of the shot. However, the student can notice that he or she did not transfer weight properly, grip the club correctly, and so on. Such types of detections are rather gross in nature but represent a definite change in the course of the learning process. At this stage variability of performance from one attempt to another also begins to decrease.

After much practice and experience with the skill, the learner moves into the final stage of learning, the **autonomous stage.** Here the skill has become almost automatic or habitual. The individual does not have to attend to the entire production of the skill but has learned to perform most of the skill without thinking about it at all. Highly skilled golfers concentrate on the ball and some of the specific adjustments that they must make in their normal swing to produce a particular shot.

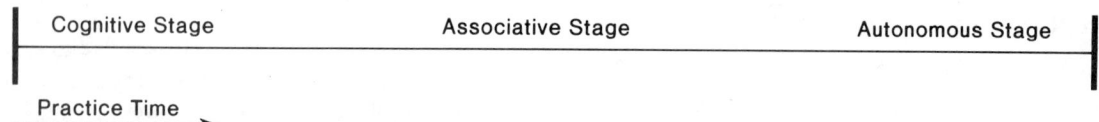

FIGURE 2.2-1   The stages of learning from the Fitts and Posner model placed on a time continuum.

Highly skilled dancers do not think about the individual steps of the routine, for they have become automatic. Instead, they have learned to concentrate on some of the more critical phases of the routine that are particularly difficult or that indicate that some major change in the routine is to begin.

In this autonomous phase skilled performers are able to not only detect their own errors but also make the proper adjustments to correct them. In this stage the variability of the day-to-day performance has become very small. The autonomous stage is the result of a tremendous amount of practice; it allows performers to produce a response without having to concentrate on the entire movement. Therefore, they are able to attend to other aspects that will permit optimal performance.

Fitts and Posner state that "there is a good deal of similarity between highly practiced skills and reflexes" (p. 15). This does not mean that learning stops or that the individual ceases to make errors but rather that there ceases to be the need for conscious attention to the motor act itself. Thus, the highly skilled tennis player is able to serve without having to concentrate on the particular fundamentals of the serve, on how to hold the racket, toss the ball, and so on, but can concentrate on what is needed to produce a serve that will land in a particular part of the service court.

It will help you to think of the three stages of the Fitts and Posner model as parts of a continuum of practice time, as depicted in Figure 2.2–1. The cognitive stage represents the first portion of this continuum. This is followed by the associative stage and then the autonomous stage. It is important to realize that learners do not make abrupt moves from one stage to the next. There is a gradual changing of the learner's characteristics

from stage to stage. It is often difficult to detect which stage best represents an individual at a particular moment, especially when that individual is in a transitional state, moving out of one stage and into the next. However, as we will discuss in more detail, the beginner and the skilled performer have distinct characteristics that need to be understood.

Adams' Two-Stage Model

In contrast to Fitts and Posner's three-stage model, Adams (1971) proposed a model of the stages of learning where there are only two stages. The first stage of learning is the *verbal-motor stage*. This stage is essentially the same as Fitts and Posner's cognitive and associative stages. Adams' second stage incorporates the autonomous stage and is called the *motor stage*. Adams' terminology implies that the first stage of learning a motor skill is not entirely cognitive, as might be erroneously concluded if one uses the Fitts and Posner label for this stage. However, the same connotation problem that Adams avoided with his label for the first stage of learning is not eliminated by his second stage label. There is also a cognitive component to the response even though this response can be produced almost automatically. Chapter 4 will deal with this problem more specifically. Here it will suffice to realize that learning does progress in stages that can be differentiated on the basis of the amount and nature of the cognitive activity associated with the production of the response.

Gentile's Two-Stage Model

Another model that proposes two stages of learning is one proposed by Gentile (1972). The first stage is identified by what Gentile sees as the goal of the learner in this stage, which is **getting**

the idea of the movement. The "idea" of the movement can be thought of as the general concept of what must be done in order to accomplish the goal of the skill. Gentile proposes that the learner must do two things during this stage of learning. First, the learner must establish the relevant and the non-relevant stimuli related to the skill. **Relevant stimuli** are those pieces of information in the environment that will regulate the movements produced as the skill is performed. For example, if the goal of the skill is to hit a pitched ball with a bat, the relevant stimuli include such information as the spin of the ball, the speed of the ball, the spatial trajectory of the ball, and so on. These pieces of information will determine specific characteristics of the batter's swing. If the person is to learn to hit the ball, these relevant stimuli must be given attention. On the other hand, there are other available pieces of information that also can attract the individual's attention but are in fact distracting and are called **non-relevant stimuli.** To give attention to those stimuli would not help the person accomplish the goal of the skill. For example, the motion used by the pitcher in the delivery is usually information not relevant for helping the batter know what the pitch will be like. Other non-relevant stimuli can be things such as the pitcher's eyes, which tend to attract the attention of novice batters, or talk by other players in the field during the pitch, such as "swing batter."

The second important thing the learner must do during this first stage is establish the most appropriate movement pattern for effectively attaining the goal of the skill. This aspect of learning involves coordinating the limbs correctly so that they work together properly. For example, hitting a baseball is a complex skill that requires much coordination among the limbs. It is during this first stage of learning that the individual concentrates on developing coordination by practicing the skill so that the coordinated movement pattern becomes characteristic of the response.

The second stage of learning in Gentile's model is called **fixation/diversification.** The learner must focus on accomplishing two things during this stage as well. First, he or she must develop the

capability of doing what is needed to accomplish the goal of the skill, regardless of the situation. Second, the learner must increase his or her consistency in achieving the goal of the skill. The two terms used to label this stage relate to what the learner must do with respect to whether the skill being learned is an open or a closed skill. The terms fixation and diversification are related specifically to what each of these types of skills requires in terms of the movement patterns that must be produced to accomplish the goals. *Fixation* refers to what is required of closed skills. That is, to be successful in performing a closed skill, the person must refine the movement pattern developed in the first stage of learning so that this pattern can be correctly produced at will. Practice during this stage must enable the learner to refine the movement pattern learned in the first stage so that the required movement pattern can be produced correctly, consistently, and efficiently from response to response. *Diversification,* on the other hand, relates to the needs of performing open skills. Because a critical characteristic of open skills is that the exact same movement pattern will not be required on successive responses, the movement pattern learned in the first stage must be practiced, but with the goal to diversify the variations of the pattern that can be produced. The focus in this stage, then, is on developing the capability of successfully adapting to the changing environmental demands that characterize open skills. To accomplish this, Gentile states that the learner must develop a larger repertoire of motor patterns that will provide the basis for adapting to the demands of open skill performance situations.

An important feature of Gentile's two-stage model is its suggested application to instruction. The goal of practice in the first stage is to develop the basic movement pattern that will achieve the goal of the skill, regardless of whether the skill is open or closed. But different conditions of practice must be established in the second stage according to the type of skill being practiced. Closed skills require a structure as similar as possible to the actual test or game they will be experiencing. For open skills the teacher must systematically vary the conditions under which the skill is to be performed. These are some of the practice-related suggestions Gentile made in connection with her learning stages model. We will consider these as well as other suggestions in more detail in the chapters concerned with practice issues.

Research Evidence Related to the Stages of Learning

One way to better understand the learning process is to look at what characterizes learners' performance at different points in time along the learning stages continuum. Different stages of learning are recognizable, and some insight can be gained into understanding why these stages occur. An additional benefit of studying learners in this way is to provide a basis for determining what teaching strategies will be optimally beneficial for people during the different learning stages. As you will see, teaching strategies that are effective for beginners are likely not to be successful in helping skilled performers, and vice versa. Because an important goal of motor skill instructors is to help people move along the learning continuum from beginner to highly skilled performer, understanding what characterizes the points along the continuum will enable the instructor or therapist to more effectively influence progress through the stages.

The remainder of this discussion, then, is a look at some of the characteristics that differentiate learners at different points along the learning stages continuum. Two different research approaches have been used to investigate these changes. One approach is to have novices practice a skill and have them continue to practice until they become skilled. This is usually a difficult approach to take for complex skills because there is a large amount of practice required to change from being a novice to being skilled. An alternative approach is to compare people who are novices with those who are experts at performing a particular skill. Although this approach allows comparison of performance and performer characteristics across the full learning continuum, it is limited in that comparisons must be made among individ-

uals rather than within one individual. Nonetheless, this approach to studying the learning process is a valuable one and has become increasingly popular during the past few years.

We will look at seven different performer- or performance-related changes that have been identified as related to progression through the learning stages. For each, one or two research examples will be described to illustrate how we know that the change actually occurs. The changes to be discussed are (1) changes in the person's knowledge structure of the skill, (2) changes in detecting and correcting errors, (3) changes in how the goal of the skill is achieved, (4) changes in coordination, (5) changes in movement efficiency, (6) changes in muscles used to perform the skill, and, (7) changes in visual attention. The intent here is to introduce you to the concept of performer and performance changes that result from learning. Some of the changes introduced to you here will be developed further in later chapters in this book. And you will find additional changes described in later chapters as well.

Changes in the person's knowledge structure of the skill. An interesting finding that has come primarily from research investigating novice-expert differences among a variety of skills is that there are some distinct commonalities among a variety of activities for experts. Among these are characteristics related to the knowledge structure a person has concerning the activity. (The concept of knowledge structure will be discussed more extensively in Concept 5.1.)

As might be expected, experts have more knowledge about an activity than novices. And this knowledge is structured quite differently as well. For example, experts who participate in diverse activities such as chess (Chase & Simon, 1973), computer programming (McKeithern, Reitman, Reuther, & Hirtle, 1981), bridge (Engle & Bukstel, 1978), and badminton (Housner, 1981) provide evidence that they have developed their knowledge about the activity into more concepts. Novices, on the other hand, have structured their knowledge primarily as independent facts or pieces of information. Experts have also organized concepts better than novices in that the expert is better able to interrelate the concepts. The expert's knowledge structure is also characterized by more decision rules, which they use for knowing how to perform a response in specific situations.

Two examples of this knowledge structure difference between novices and experts will provide a better understanding of what is meant by the term knowledge structure and how it changes as a person moves along the learning continuum. In an experiment reported by Housner (1981), a novice and an expert badminton player were asked to respond to a detailed set of questions related to the strategies they use in a game. Questions included "What do you think about during a game?" "Why do you choose to respond in a particular way in this situation?" and so on. After completing this questionnaire, the two subjects were put into actual badminton games against opponents of similar skill levels. The subjects were interviewed before, during, and after the games to determine what they planned to do, what they actually did and why, and how well they followed their game plans. Results showed that the expert player had more strategy concepts than did the novice and that the expert used the concepts in ways that resembled problem-solving approaches. The novice tended to operate on very specific rules that were not very adaptable to the changing conditions of the game.

Another example is an experiment by French and Thomas (1987). What is different in that experiment is the experts and novices were limited to 8 to 10-year-olds and 11 to 12-year-olds playing in youth basketball leagues. Players were assessed in terms of basketball skills and knowledge of the game. As expected, the child experts possessed more skill and knowledge than the novice players. Even more interesting was that children who possessed greater basketball knowledge about aspects such as rules of the game and positions of players exhibited greater decision-making capabilities during games. This finding has important implications for teaching sport skills. An inter-

esting additional feature of this study was the observation of changes that resulted from an entire season of practices and games. Again the results have important implications for instruction. The children in the basketball programs demonstrated a greater increase in their cognitive knowledge than in their motor skills. In particular, the players learned what to do in certain basketball situations faster than they learned the motor skills required to carry out the actions.

Changes in error detection and correction capability. One of the characteristics commonly cited for people in the final stage of learning is the capability to identify and correct their own movement errors. In slow movements, this correction process may occur during the performance of the skill itself, as when a person grasps a cup and brings it to their mouth to drink from it. During this action, some adjustments can be made so that the grasping, bringing the cup to the mouth, and drinking can be done successfully. However, in rapid movements, such as initiating and carrying out a swing at a baseball, the correction cannot usually be made in time during the execution of the swing. The awareness of what correction should be made will have to be used to correct future swings. However, regardless of when the correction of errors must be done, the important point is that the capability to make corrections develops as the individual progresses along the learning stages continuum.

An experiment that demonstrates the development of this capability to detect and correct errors was published by Schmidt and White (1972). Subjects were required to learn to move a lever along a linear trackway a distance of 9 inches in 150 msec. The goal was to move the lever so that it passed a marker at the 9-inch mark at exactly 150 msec. After each attempt, or trial, subjects were asked to estimate how accurate they thought their responses were and were then told their actual accuracy score. Following 140 practice trials, they were no longer told their accuracy score but were still required to estimate their error.

FIGURE 2.2-2   Results from the experiment by Schmidt and White showing the correlation between the subjects' estimates of their error (subjective error) and their actual error (objective error) when KR was given or withheld during 170 trials of practice over two days.

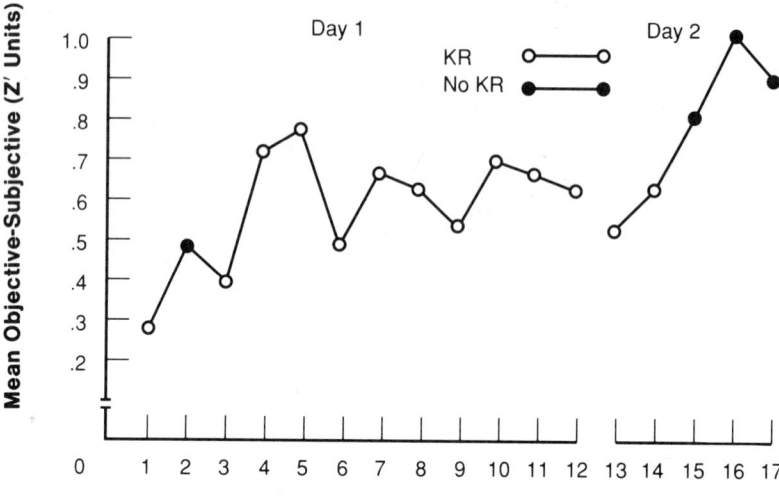

If learners increase their capability to detect and correct errors as they learn a skill, they should become increasingly able to match their estimates of their own responses (called subjective error) with the actual error score for that response (called objective error). The relationship between the subjective and objective error measures is shown correlated in Figure 2.2–2. A low correlation indicates the subjects demonstrated poor error estimation capability whereas a high correlation indicates they demonstrated good error estimation capability. As you can see from trial block 16, this correlation had risen from .30 on the first trial block to above .90. Even more convincing is that they continued to demonstrate this high degree of error estimation capability even after they were no longer told their actual error after each trial.

Changes in how the goal of the skill is achieved. Because every motor skill has a goal that must be achieved to successfully perform that skill, it is possible to investigate changes that occur during learning by looking at how people change the way in which they attempt to acheive the goal. That is, how do their movement characteristics differ early in practice compared with later in practice as they become more successful at achieving the

goal of the skill? A good example of an experiment that investigated this question was published by Marteniuk and Romanow (1983), and was briefly introduced in Concepts 1.2 and 2.1.

Subjects in that experiment practiced producing the complex waveform pattern shown in Figure 1.2–6 by moving a horizontal lever back and forth. The goal of the skill was to reproduce the waveform pattern as closely as possible, both spatially and temporally. To achieve that, subjects had to learn how often to move the lever back and forth, where to make each reversal of the lever, and how fast to move the lever at different times throughout the entire pattern. As you saw in Figure 2.1–3, the subjects became increasingly accurate and consistent at achieving the goal of the skill during 800 trials of practice.

On the basis of the kinematic performance measures that were analyzed, Marteniuk and Romanow concluded that early in practice subjects focused primarily on the spatial components of this task. This conclusion was based on results that showed that displacement characteristics became more accurate and consistent before acceleration and velocity characteristics, which are time-based features of the skill. Only after a significant amount of practice did the subjects show evidence

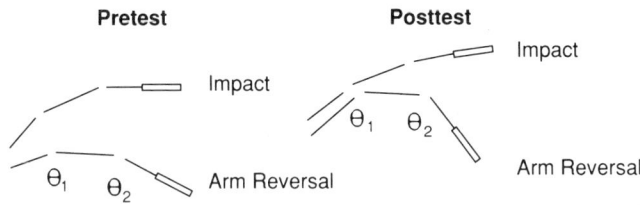

FIGURE 2.2-3 The pretest and posttest configurations of the arm segments at arm reversal and impact for hitting a racquetball forehand shot. From the experiment by Southard and Higgins. Note: θ_1 = joint angle at the elbow; θ_2 = joint angle at the wrist.

that they were refining their skills by increasing the accuracy and consistency of the acceleration and velocity components of the complex task. Also, even though the task was very complex, subjects always worked on improving the entire skill as a unit. Their performance characteristics during practice showed that they did not divide the task into smaller parts and try to improve each part independently and then put them together into larger and larger units until the entire pattern was performed correctly. Thus, the goal of the complex skill was achieved by systematically improving specific kinematic features of the movements required for this skill.

Changes in coordination. In the discussion of Concept 3.1, you will be introduced to the concept of coordination. You will find that an important characteristic of a skilled person is possessing the capability of controlling a group of limb segments so that they can attain the goal of an action. At the same time, however, their control is characterized by the capability to adapt to novel demands of a situation in which action takes place. One of the changes that occurs while progressing from being a novice to a skilled performer relates to the characteristics of the development of the control of coordination. The novice seems to "lock" joints of a limb so that instead of the limb being free to adapt as needed, it is restricted in its movement. Thus, goal achievement is sporadic. The skilled performer, however, develops a coordination characteristic where the limb segments operate as a flexible unit to enable goal achievement in various situations. Two research examples, one based on learning a sport skill and the other based on learning handwriting, will help illustrate what is meant by this change in coordination control.

In an experiment reported by Southard and Higgins (1987), subjects practiced a racquetball forehand shot 10 minutes a day for 10 days. The investigation of coordination in this experiment focused on three segments of the arm holding the racquet. One segment was the upper arm between the shoulder and elbow joints; the second segment was the forearm between the elbow and wrist joints; the third segment was the hand from the wrist joint to, and including, the racquet. The interrelationship of the segments was evaluated during the arm reversal part of hitting the ball and during the actual impact when the ball was hit. Figure 2.2–3 compares the interrelationships before practice began and after 10 days of practice, during which subjects were able to observe the appropriate swing action.

Before practice began, there was no significant change in elbow and wrist joint angles from the arm reversal to impact with the ball. This result shows that the novice locked the joints of the arm, essentially operating it like a single segment without joints. With practice, however, unitary control changed; the elbow and wrist joints functioned much differently during the arm reversal than they did at impact. The wrist joint angle during arm reversal at the pretest was 205° (with 180° being a straight line). After the 10 days of practice the wrist joint angle was 232°. The elbow joint angle also changed with practice and increased from 190° at the pretest to 225° after 10 days of practice. For the impact phase the elbow and wrist angles did not appreciably change as a result of practice. Finally, it is worth noting the increases in the velocities of each arm segment in relation to each of the other segments as the arm moved through space to hit the ball. Before practice, the forearm segment moved at a velocity of

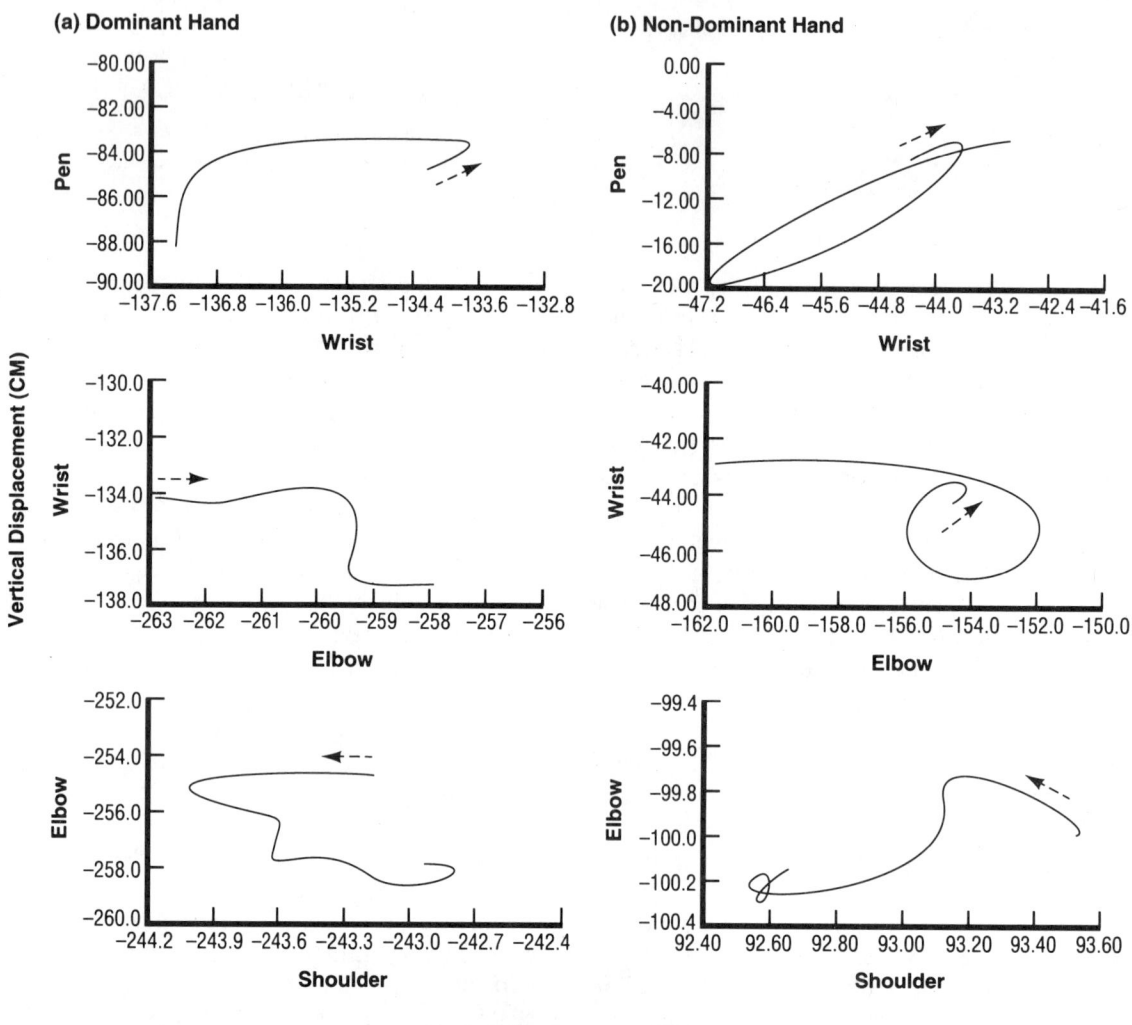

FIGURE 2.2-4   Results of the handwriting experiment by Newell and van Emmerik showing position-position plots of pairs of pen and joint movements for the same signature written with (a) the dominant and (b) non-dominant hands.

23.5 degrees/sec relative to the upper arm, whereas after 10 days of practice the segment velocity increased to 320.7 degrees/sec. The velocity of the hand-racquet segment relative to the forearm was 34.5 degrees/sec and increased to 596.5 degrees/sec after 10 days of practice.

An experiment reported by Newell and van Emmerik (1989) examined novice and expert handwriting coordination characteristics by com-

paring limb segments related to writing with the preferred and non-preferred hand. Using the Selspot movement analysis system, they analyzed the movement characteristics of the elbow and wrist joints and the pen while subjects wrote their names. Figure 2.2–4 shows position-position plots for pairs of three points while the signature was written by the dominant hand (panel A in the figure) and non-dominant hand (panel B) of one subject. These plots can be interpreted similar to a correlation, where a 1.0 correlation would be characterized by a diagonal straight line that passes through 0 of the X-Y axis intersection. Note that when the non-dominant hand was used the between joint relationships look very close to 1.0, especially the pen-wrist and the elbow-wrist relationships. These results indicated that the segments were operating like one segment rather than three. In contrast, writing with the dominant hand showed low correlations, indicating the independence of the three segments.

The results of these two experiments demonstrate that for both hitting a racquetball and handwriting, the control of coordination changes as a function of practice. At the beginning of practice, the various joints of the arm were controlled as if they were a single unit. With practice, however, a more segment-specific coordination control developed so that the goal of the action could more effectively be accomplished.

Changes in movement efficiency. Efficiency of movement refers to the amount of energy expended while producing a movement. It is a commonly accepted characteristic of skilled performers that skills are performed efficiently, that is, with a minimum expenditure of energy.[1] Skilled performers appear to perform effortlessly. A problem with this view, however, was brought to light by Sparrow (1983), who showed that although commonly accepted, there is little empirical evidence to support that view. As a result, he (Sparrow & Irizarry-Lopez, 1987) developed an experiment to look specifically at movement efficiency changes that occur as a person practices and learns a complex motor skill. Subjects were required to learn to crawl on their hands and feet on a motor-driven treadmill that was moving at a rate of .76 m/sec. They practiced the skill for 3 minutes per day for 20 days. Two common exercise physiology measures were used to determine if efficiency increased during practice. One mea-

sure was mechanical efficiency, which is the mechanical work rate divided by the metabolic rate of the individual. The other measure was caloric cost. Subjects showed a 13.7% improvement in mechanical efficiency from the beginning to the end of the practice period, along with a significant improvement in caloric cost. Thus, evidence appears to demonstrate that as we learn a skill, our performance efficiency increases so that the energy cost becomes more economical.

Changes in muscles used to perform the skill. If efficiency of movement in terms of energy expenditure improves with practice and if coordination of the various body parts involved in producing a movement improves with practice, we should see evidence of these changes at the muscular level. One way to see this is to look at changes in EMG patterns while a person practices a skill. The increases in movement efficiency and coordination imply that more muscles than necessary are involved in performing the skill early in practice and that as practice progresses, the amount of muscle involvement decreases. Two experiments will be described illustrating these changes for a person learning to throw a ball at a target and learning to move a lever a specified distance in a precise amount of time.

The experiment in which subjects learned to throw a ball at a target was reported by Vorro, Wilson, and Dainis (1978). The focus of that experiment was on the involvement of two arm muscle groups, the biceps brachii and the coracobrachialis, in the throwing action and how their involvement changed during practice. EMG recordings of the muscle groups were made for 103 practice trials. Results indicated that as practice progressed, the two muscle groups began to respond differently. For example, early in practice, the biceps began contracting 15 msec before the throwing movement began, and the coracobrachialis began contracting just 1 msec before the movement began. By trial 103, both muscles were contracting almost simultaneously, 40 msec after the movement began. Obviously, with practice, the functions of these muscles in the total throwing

---

[1]It should be noted that there are many who prefer the term "economy" rather than "efficiency"; see Cavanagh & Kram, 1985.

movement change. The article did not discuss precisely what those functions were and how other muscles involved in the movement changed. However, the results do illustrate how EMG measures can be used to observe performance-related changes across the stages of learning.

In an experiment by Moore and Marteniuk (1986), subjects were required to make a 45° horizontal forearm extension to a target in either 200 or 500 msec. The experimenters wanted to compare the actions of the agonist and antagonist pair of muscles as a function of practice. The results showed two distinct characteristic changes. One change that was noted for both the 200- and 500-msec movements was that at the beginning of practice, there were very inconsistent EMG patterns for the triceps (the agonist for this movement) and biceps (antagonist) from trial to trial. With practice, however, the patterns become more consistent from trial to trial, especially for the faster 200–msec movement. The second distinct change was that subjects typically showed a regular pattern of co-contraction of the two muscles early in practice but a more efficient pattern of distinct separate EMG bursts of activity for each muscle later in practice.

These two experiments demonstrate similar changes in the involvement of muscles as a person practices a skill. Early in practice, muscles that are not needed are used in the group of muscles performing the skill. With practice, however, only those muscles necessary for achieving the goal of the skill are involved. Also, early in practice muscles function at the same time when they should not, while later in practice, the muscles function at appropriate times.

Changes in visual attention.   A key characteristic that changes as a function of practice in skill learning is the use of vision. In performing many skills, attending visually to the appropriate cues in the environment determines the degree of performance success. For example, if a tennis player is not certain about what to look at while receiving a serve, his or her chances for hitting a successful return are greatly diminished. This plight is not uncommon for beginners because they typically look at too many things and therefore direct visual attention at many inappropriate cues. Skilled performers, on the other hand, direct visual attention more judiciously and spend more time looking at cues that are more appropriate for guiding their actions. Two research examples will illustrate this change for two different types of skills, badminton and gymnastics. In badminton, proper visual attention is necessary for directing the person's return of serve. In gymnastics the use of vision is not for guiding an action, but for determining how to correct errors.

A popular approach to studying visual attention has been to ask subjects to watch a film of a person performing an action and to make a decision about the appropriate response that should be made. This approach was used in an experiment by Abernethy and Russell (1987) in which they compared experts and novices in badminton. The subjects watched filmed sequences of a player making different fundamental badminton strokes. When the film was stopped, subjects were to indicate the landing position of the shuttle from the player's stroke. To assess novice-expert differences in the use of visual information, the film was stopped at different times during the stroke, 167 ms or 83 msec before racquet-shuttle contact, at contact, or 83 msec after contact. Sometimes the film was not stopped. The results indicated that the experts were correct more often when the film stopped before and at racquet-shuttle contact than were novices. Thus, the experts could make predictions about shuttle landing much earlier than novices. Another part of this study involved novice and expert badminton players observing a film of a player hitting different strokes. But certain body parts of the player and the racquet were occluded from view: the racquet and arm, the racquet only, the face and head, and the lower body. The results showed that novices primarily use racquet information to anticipate where the shuttle is going, whereas experts use the racquet and the arm holding the racquet to make a judgment. The benefit of observing the arm is that its location provides information earlier than the racquet. Thus, one of the performance characteristics that evolves during practice while learning badminton skills is where visual attention is directed so that reliable information used to make a response can be extracted as early as possible in the opponent's action.

Another method for studying the use of vision during motor skill learning is to assess eye movements by using computer-based equipment that tracks visual gaze. Vickers (1988) used this method to determine how novice and expert gymnasts differed in how they direct their visual attention to make specific judgments about the performance they observed. The gymnasts were shown sequences of slides of other gymnasts performing various skills. The results showed that novices tended to observe the performer's head and off-body features (such as equipment and anticipated direction of movement) more than experts did, whereas experts focused on the center of gravity of the performer more than did novices. The results indicate that as novices progress to the expert stage of learning, they learn to determine which part of the body provides the most useful information for evaluating a performance. This knowledge becomes an essential component of the capability to detect and correct their own performance errors.

Summary

Learning is a process that involves time and practice. As an individual progresses from being a beginner in an activity to being a highly skilled performer, he or she progresses through several distinct stages. These stages have been described in three different models. Fitts and Posner proposed that the learner progresses through three stages, which they identify as the cognitive, the associative, and the autonomous stages. Adams proposed only two stages, called the verbal-motor and the motor stages. Gentile proposed two stages that are identified on the basis of the goal of the learner in each stage. The first stage is known as "getting the idea of the movement," whereas the second stage is known as the fixation/diversifi-cation stage. The goals of the second stage are related specifically to closed and open skills, respectively. Evidence that learners show distinct characteristics as they progress through the different learning stages has been shown by research that typically follows one of two methods. One is to follow the progress of people learning a skill beginning as a novice until they attain a certain level of expertise. The other method is to compare performance characteristics of people who are novices with those who are experts in a skill. Some of the changes that occur as a result of progressing through the learning stages involved changes related to the person's knowledge structure of the skill; detecting and correcting errors; how the goal of the skill is achieved; coordination, movement efficiency, and the muscles used to perform the skill; and visual attention.

Related Readings

Abernethy, B. (1988). Visual search in sport and ergonomics: Its relation to selective attention and performer expertise. *Human Performance, 1,* 205–235.

Adler, J. (1981). Stages of skill acquisition: A guide for teachers. *Motor Skills: Theory into Practice, 5,* 75–80.

Allard, F., & Burnett, N. (1985). Skill in sport. *Canadian Journal of Psychology, 39,* 294–312.

Fitts, P. M., & Posner, M. I. (1967). *Human performance* (pp. 243–285). Belmont, CA: Brooks/Cole. (Read chapter 2)

Gentile, A. M. (1987). Skill acquisition: Action, movement, and neuromotor processes. In J. H. Carr, R. B. Shepard, J. Gordon, A. M. Gentile, & J. M. Held (Eds.), *Movement science: Foundations for physical therapy in rehabilitation* (pp. 93–154). Rockville, MD: Aspen. (Read pp. 117–141)

Starkes, J. L., & Deakin, J. (1984). Perception in sport: A cognitive approach to skilled performance. In W. Straub & J. Williams (Eds.). *Cognitive sport psychology* (pp. 115–128). Lansing, NY: Sport Science Associates.

Thomas, J. R., French, K. E., & Humphries, C. A. (1986). Knowledge development and sport skill performance: Directions for motor behavior research. *Journal of Sport Psychology, 8,* 259–272.

□

CONCEPT 2.3

Transfer of learning is an integral part of understanding
motor skill learning and performance

___

Key Terms

transfer of
    learning

positive
    transfer

negative
    transfer

intertask
    transfer

intratask
    transfer

percentage of
    transfer

savings score

identical
    elements
    theory

transfer-
    appropriate
    processing

Application

If you have never played squash before but have
had much experience playing handball, do you
think that you would learn to play squash more
easily than someone who has not played handball
before? Undoubtedly, you would. Why? Primarily because many aspects of both games are
very similar, even though the games themselves
are quite distinct. Both games are played in a
similar-sized, four-wall court. Both require that
the ball hit the front wall prior to hitting the floor.
Both games involve moving and positioning in
order to hit a moving ball. We could easily expand
this list of similarities. However, there are some
definite differences between the two games. The
most obvious is that squash involves a racquet
while handball does not. Another major difference is that the ball in squash must strike the front
wall at least 17 inches from the floor, whereas in
handball the ball may hit the front wall at any location. The balls are different in size and consistency in the two games; the squash ball is smaller
and harder than the handball. Even though dif-

ferences exist, it seems reasonable to expect that
a person with handball experience would learn to
play squash more readily than a person with no
previous handball experience.

In the elementary school much time is often
devoted to the game of kickball. The intent of this
game, other than providing fun, is to function as
a good lead-up game for baseball. The important
question is whether the child who has had previous experience playing kickball will more easily
adapt to learning to play baseball than the child
who has not had previous kickball experience.

When you learned to play tennis, undoubtedly
your teacher required you to spend a lot of time
hitting the ball off a back wall. You also probably
practiced hitting balls thrown to you either by another person or by a ball machine. The purpose of
that practice was to help you learn a particular
stroke without having to deal with the added requirements of rallying with another player. As in
the kickball-baseball example, the important instructional question is whether that type of practice is beneficial in helping a person successfully
perform the stroke in a rallying or a game situation.

In each of the previous three situations, a similar learning and instructional concern is highlighted. That is, what is the relationship between
previous experiences and learning a new motor
skill? In the squash-handball and kickball-baseball
examples, the interest is in a general relationship
between experiences in one sport activity and another new one. In the tennis example, the concern

is with the relationship between practice procedures and the eventual goal of that practice, which is to be able to successfully perform the practiced skill in a game. In all three situations the learning phenomenon focused on is called transfer of learning. The intent is to transfer what is learned in one experience to a new experience in order to facilitate learning the new skill. Although you have become acquainted with the concept of transfer of learning in previous chapters of this book, the discussion that follows will help you better understand what transfer of learning is and why it is an important learning phenomenon.

Discussion

One of the most universally applied principles of learning in systems of education and rehabilitation is the principle termed *transfer of learning*. It is the foundation of curriculum development in educational systems because it provides the basis for arranging in sequence the skills to be learned during a student's educational experience. This concept is also extensively used in the classroom, gymnasium, dance studio, skill training center, and rehabilitation clinic as the basis for developing and implementing methods for teaching skills. Because of its widespread importance, an understanding of this learning phenomenon is essential for developing a foundation for studying motor learning.

In this discussion, the goal will be to develop your knowledge of this critical learning principle. To achieve that goal, four questions will be presented and answered. These questions will be related to (1) defining transfer of learning, (2) determining why the understanding of transfer of learning is important, (3) discussing how we know transfer has occurred, and (4) presenting some of the various conditions that influence the transfer of learning phenomenon, including why transfer occurs.

What Is Transfer?

Transfer of learning is generally defined as the influence of having previously practiced a skill or skills on the learning of a new skill or on performing the skill in a new context. It appears that this influence may be either positive, negative, or neutral (zero). **Positive transfer** occurs when experience with a previous skill aids or facilitates the learning of a new skill. The handball-squash and the kickball-baseball examples are positive transfer situations. In fact, each of the three examples of transfer that were suggested in the application section shows some positive transfer.

Negative transfer occurs when experience with a previous skill hinders or interferes with the learning of a new skill. We must examine specific components of skills to find negative effects. For example, having learned the forehand in tennis before learning the forehand in badminton will generally result in negative transfer. The badminton forehand is a wrist snap, whereas the tennis forehand requires a relatively firm wrist. It must be emphasized that negative transfer effects will generally be seen only in specific aspects of an activity. This is because when we consider the overall transfer effects of the two activities, there is most likely a positive transfer effect from previous experience with tennis to the learning of badminton. Thus, in the handball-squash example the overall transfer effects are positive. However, certain aspects of one game would be negatively transferred to the other game, such as the distance you stand from the ball to hit it, because squash uses a long-handled racquet, but handball uses no racquet. Negative transfer effects are typically temporary and are usually overcome rather quickly with practice.

Zero transfer occurs when experience with a previous skill has *no effect* or influence on the learning of a new skill. Obviously, there is no transfer effect from learning to swim to learning to drive a car. Nor can it be assumed that experience with some motor skills will always have an influence on the learning of new motor skills.

Why Is Transfer of Learning Important?

Perhaps the answer to the question of the importance of transfer of learning as a learning principle is obvious by now. We have already pointed out that the principle of transfer of learning forms the basis for educational curriculum development as well as for instructional methodology. Actually, the two roles of the transfer principle are at the very core of the practical significance of transfer. The transfer principle also has theoretical significance for understanding processes underlying the learning and control of motor skills. In Concept 2.1 you studied the need for using transfer tests to determine the degree of learning that resulted from practice. Implicit in the need for such tests is the view that if learning has occurred, positive transfer should be observable when the practiced skill must be performed in a new context or when a variation of the practiced skill is performed. However, although this transfer expectation plays an important part in making the learning inference, there is much to be learned about control and learning processes by understanding *why* the transfer occurs. In the following sections, we will discuss the practical and theoretical significance of the transfer principle in more detail.

Sequencing skills to be learned. Mathematics provides a very useful example of how the transfer principle is applied in learning sequencing skills. The school curriculum from grades 1 through 12 is based on a simple to complex arrangement. Numeral identification, numeral writing, numeral value identification, addition, subtraction, multiplication, and division must be presented in this specific sequence, because each is based on the preceding concept. If a person were presented with a division problem before having learned addition, subtraction, or multiplication, he or she would have to learn those skills before completing the problem. Algebra is not taught before basic arithmetic. Trigonometry is not taught before geometry. We could go on, but the role played by transfer of learning in the development of mathematics curriculum should be apparent at this point.

The teaching of skills in a physical education program should also be based on a transfer of learning foundation. It is difficult to understand why baseball would be taught before students have had ample experiences in learning to throw, catch, or bat. To do so would be like having a person do a division problem before learning addition, subtraction, and multiplication.

The same point can be made about any situation involving the training of motor skills. The sequencing of skills should be designed to take advantage of the transfer of learning principle. Basic or foundational skills should be learned *before* more complex skills are introduced requiring mastery of certain basic skills. This means that there should be a logical progression of skill experiences where the decision of when to introduce a given skill should be made in terms of how it provides a basis for transfer to succeeding skills. If this approach is not used, time is wasted while people "go back" and learn prerequisite basic skills.

Instructional methods. The second important application of the transfer of learning principle to motor skill instruction is in the area of methods for providing instruction. When an instructor teaches students the basic swimming strokes by using dry land drills before letting students try the strokes in the water, the instructor is assuming that there will be a positive transfer effect from the dry land drills to performing the strokes in water. That is, the assumption is that the students will learn the strokes more effectively and more efficiently because of their dry land drill experience.

John Brady (1979) published an interesting illustration of the positive transfer that results from using dry land training for skills that must be performed in the water. Certified SCUBA divers were used in Brady's experiment in which the goal was to assemble a complex mechanical device underwater as fast as possible. Eight subtasks were involved in this assembly task, which required the use of a box-end wrench. One group of subjects, the low-practice condition, only watched and participated in a demonstration of how the assembly task should be performed. They then practiced assembling the device one time on dry land before attempting to perform the task underwater. The second group of subjects, the high-practice condition, not only viewed the demonstration of assembling the device, but also practiced assembling it eight times on dry land before entering the water. If the dry land training was not beneficial, that is, if it did not positively transfer to underwater performance, then both groups would be expected to perform the skill similarly underwater. However, the results indicated that the high-practice group performed the task underwater significantly faster than the low-practice group. Thus, dry land practice facilitated, or positively transferred to, the underwater performance of assembling the complex mechanical device. This finding has important implications for those who instruct persons who must perform skills underwater because it suggests that the generally safer and less expensive dry land practice will facilitate performance of the skill underwater, thus requiring less underwater training time.

The transfer principle is invaluable when the skill to be learned has a strong element of danger in it such as in diving or gymnastics. In those activities, body harnesses are used in practicing certain skills to aid the learner in developing confidence in his or her ability to perform without having fear of injury hinder the learning process.

Other examples of instruction methodology in which the transfer principle is used include activities such as using a pitching machine to teach hitting in baseball, hitting tennis balls from a ball machine, and rebounding basketballs from a rebounder. Each of these instructional procedures is based on the assumption that practice with the machines will positively transfer to the "real" situation. Batting practice with a pitching machine, for example, will aid batting performance when a live pitcher is throwing the ball. The batter can concentrate on his or her swing and on making consistent contact with the ball when the pitching machine is used rather than being concerned with where the ball will be, how fast it will be pitched, etc. Instructional situations can make the skill to be learned less difficult by not changing certain

conditions related to performing the skill. This instruction and practice strategy will also be discussed in Concept 7.2 when methods for implementing the practice of parts of a skill are considered.

Learning inferences. In Concept 2.1 you were introduced to the use of experimental designs incorporating the transfer of learning principle. These designs are structured to include a series of performance trials on a new task or under new performance conditions after practice trials have been performed under other conditions. The purpose of the transfer trials is to provide a means for observing performance under new conditions so that a valid inference can be made about the influence of the experimental conditions on learning. The use of this type of transfer design is especially important for making inferences concerning the influence of certain practice procedures and instructional techniques on learning a motor skill.

In an article by Bransford, Franks, Morris, and Stein (1979), an impressive argument is made for *only* considering the effectiveness of any acquisition activity on the basis of how the skill being practiced is performed in a "test" context. That is, if we want to know whether one form of practice procedure is superior to another for learning a motor skill, no conclusion should be made until the skill is observed in a test performance situation. The test may be a game, a specific test, or any condition that involves the expressed goal of the practice experience. Because this point has been emphasized in many portions of this text, it should be apparent that we cannot ignore it if we are to make valid inferences in motor learning research.

How Do We Know Transfer Has Occurred?

Transfer designs in learning research usually involve one of three different types of transfer situations. One situation involves performing the same skill that has been practiced in a novel situation. For example, the dry land practice and underwater test experiment by Brady (1979) discussed earlier is a good example of using this type of transfer test situation. A second transfer test situation involves performing a novel variation of the skill that has been practiced, such as performing the skill more rapidly or more slowly than practiced. Third, the transfer test may involve performing a different, although somewhat related, skill than was practiced. This approach is especially common when the researcher is interested in knowing how well a particular practice drill transfers to a particular skill, such as determining how well hitting a baseball off a batting tee transfers to hitting a ball thrown by a pitcher.

There are various ways of designing experiments to implement transfer situations and to make desired inferences about learning and learning conditions. You will see many examples of each type of experimental design in the research discussed throughout this book. In the following discussion, two common uses of transfer designs will be considered. This brief introduction to experimental designs in research will help you better understand the motor learning research in which transfer tests are an important component. Most transfer situations you will encounter in that research will involve one of the basic designs or a slight variation of them.

The two designs to be considered here differ on the basis of whether the transfer is between two different tasks or between two different practice or performance conditions for the same task. The term *task* is being used here in the same way that we have used the term *skill* throughout this text. Because task has traditionally been used in the transfer of learning literature when reference is made to experimental designs, this term will be used here as well. Thus, when two different tasks are considered, they may be related to the transfer between two completely different skills or between different variations of the same skill. Although there are theoretical reasons for keeping distinct the issue of transfer between different skills versus variations of the same skill, the experimental designs investigating these issues generally follow a similar approach.

The first experimental design to be considered is typically labeled an **intertask transfer** design, which focuses on the influence of experience with one skill on a new skill, the new one being either a different skill or a variation of the first one. Examples when this type of design (or a variation of it) would be used were discussed in the second and third transfer situations described at the beginning of this section. The second experimental design common in the transfer of learning research literature is called an *intratask transfer* design. The first transfer test situation described at the beginning of this section would use **intratask transfer,** which is typically related to comparing how different types of practice conditions affect learning a particular skill.

Intertask transfer.   The simplest and most frequently used experimental design for testing intertask transfer effects is the following:

Experimental Group	Practice Task A	Perform Task B
Control Group	Nothing	Perform Task B

For analysis purposes, the primary interest in the results of this experimental paradigm is in the performance by both groups of task B. If the experience with task A facilitated the learning of task B, then the experimental group would show more rapid improvement on task B than would the control group. On the other hand, if the learning of task A interfered with the learning of task B, then the experimental group would take longer to learn task B than would the control group.

A variation of this design will be presented in Concept 9.1 in the discussion of practice conditions leading to success in performing a novel variation of a previously practiced skill. Researchers varied the experimental design explained here by having the experimental group practice several different tasks, such as task A, B, and C, while the control group practices only task A. The transfer test condition is conducted as the design illustrated above indicates in that both groups transfer to the same novel task, which in this case could be labeled task D.

Various methods of quantifying the amount of transfer have been proposed for intertask transfer. Two of the more frequently used quantifications of transfer have been percentage of transfer and savings score. **Percentage of transfer** is simply the percent of improvement on task B that would be attributable to having learned task A. A high percentage of transfer would indicate a strong influence of task A on task B, while a low percentage would suggest a much less, though positive, influence.

Percentage of transfer can be calculated simply by subtracting the control group task B score from the experimental group task B score and then dividing that difference by the total of the task B scores for both groups. To obtain a percentage, multiply the result by 100. Note that the "task score" used in this calculation should be based on initial performance on task B. Expressed as a formula, this calculation is as follows:

$$\text{Percentage of Transfer} = \frac{\text{Experimental Grp} - \text{Control Grp}}{\text{Experimental Grp} + \text{Control Grp}} \times 100$$

Although many different formulas have been proposed in order to determine percentage of transfer, this formula, suggested by Murdock (1957), appears to avoid the theoretical problems found in other formulas.

The **savings score** is the amount of practice time saved in learning task B because of prior experience with task A. By using that score, it would be possible to show that the task A experience saved a quantity of practice trials on task B. Thus, if the experimental group reached a criterion of 100 points on task B in 20 trials while the control group took 30 trials, the savings score would be 10 trials. A question here is whether or not the savings score is actually a real savings. Remember, the experimental group practiced task A while the control group did nothing. If the experimental group practiced 20 trials on task A, we would have to question the "savings score," because the score refers only to the amount of practice time "saved" on task B.

For practical applications, use of the savings scores has particular merit. This is especially true when the question is whether or not a particular drill effectively aids the learning of a skill. The savings score would indicate how much practice time of the skill itself could be saved by using a particular drill. If no practice time is saved, there would be some concern about the continued use of the drill.

In experiments that use intertask transfer tests as the basis for inferring learning due to practice, the *amount* of transfer typically is not measured. Instead, the learning inference is based on comparisons of the performance of different experimental conditions in the transfer test common to all conditions. And there is often a control group that does not experience any prior practice. The advantage of using a control group is that while one of the practice conditions may lead to better learning, i.e., transfer, a comparison can be made to determine whether prior practice of the new skill was better than no practice.

Intratask transfer research. To consider the transfer effects for intratask transfer conditions, it will be helpful to recall some of what was presented in Concept 2.1. There, it was explained how transfer tests are used to make inferences in research about effective practice conditions and skill learning. The typical research paradigm used is as follows:

Group A	Practice Condition A	Perform Under Condition C
Group B	Practice Condition B	Perform Under Condition C

For analyzing this type of experimental design, three points must be considered. First, how did performance under practice conditions A and B compare? Second, how did the two groups compare when performing under condition C? Third, what characterized each group's performance when comparing the last practice trial with the first transfer trial? Did the group improve, get worse, or show no change in performance? This last point of analysis is often overlooked. Its importance becomes apparent when groups show different performance level results during the transfer trials than they did during the practice trials.

In terms of quantifying the amount of transfer in an intratask transfer experimental situation, both the percentage of transfer and savings score measures can be calculated. The savings score can be calculated in the same way it is calculated for intertask transfer. To calculate the percentage of transfer, use the same principle as expressed in the formula presented in the discussion of intertask transfer. To apply the formula to the intratask transfer situation, use the task scores for performance trials under condition C. That score should be based on initial performance trials under condition C. Two separate calculations will be required, one to determine the percentage of transfer from practicing under condition A, and one from practicing under condition B. To calculate the percentage of transfer to condition C due to condition A practice, subtract the transfer condition score of the condition B group from the transfer condition score of the condition A group. Then, divide this difference by the total of the conditions A and B scores. Again, remember to multiply by 100 to obtain a percentage value. To determine the percentage transfer due to practice under condition B, simply reverse the numerator of the formula and subtract the condition A score from the condition B score, and follow the same steps.

Why Does Transfer of Learning Occur?

As you study the many concepts discussed in this book, you will find that it is common to see different practice conditions yield dissimilar transfer of learning effects. However, such effects do not provide an answer to the question of why transfer occurs, although they do provide evidence that can be used to determine if hypotheses about why transfer occurs are valid. To give you a background for making such determinations, we will consider two hypotheses that have been proposed to account for why transfer of learning occurs: the similarities of the components of the skills and/or

the context in which skills are performed, and the amount and type of previous experiences.

Before discussing the hypotheses, it is necessary to point out that this discussion accounts for why *positive* transfer occurs. The question of why negative transfer occurs is a unique one. Thus, it will be helpful to consider negative transfer in a separate section.

Similarity of skill and context components.

The first and more traditional view of the two, argues that transfer is due to the similarity of components between two skills or between two performance situations. The expectation is that the higher the degree of similarity between the component parts of two skills or two performance situations, the greater the amount of positive transfer that can be expected between them. Thus, we would expect that the amount of transfer between the tennis serve and volleyball serve would be greater than between the tennis serve and racquetball serve. We would likewise expect that practice conditions that emphasized performance characteristics similar to those that are required in a game would lead to a high degree of transfer. Hitting a tennis ball from a ball machine should lead to a high degree of transfer to rallying with another player because the skills required to be successful in the two performance situations have in common many components.

This view has its roots in the early work of Thorndike (1914), who proposed his **identical elements theory** to account for transfer effects. Identical elements had a very broad meaning to Thorndike. "Elements" could refer to general characteristics such as the purpose of the response or the attitude related to the performance, or to specific characteristics such as particular components of the skill being performed. In fact, Thorndike considered identical elements to be mental processes that shared the same brain cell action as the physical action correlate.

Later work by Osgood (1949) modified Thorndike's view by proposing that the amount and direction of transfer is related to the similarity of the stimulus and the response aspects of two tasks.

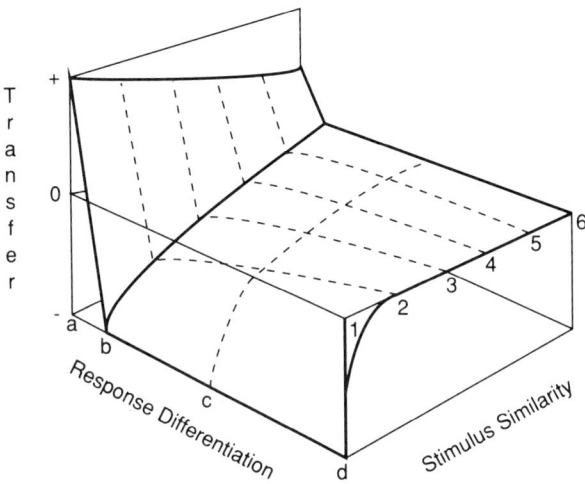

FIGURE 2.3-1 The transfer surface proposed by Holding showing the expected transfer between two tasks in terms of the similarity or difference of characteristics of stimulus and response aspects of the skills. Maximum positive transfer is predicted when the stimulus and response characteristics are identical, whereas negative transfer is predicted when the stimuli for the two tasks are identical but the two responses are completely different from each other.

To formalize this relationship, Osgood developed a "transfer surface" that provided a means for determining what type and amount of transfer to expect given the stimulus and response characteristics of two verbal tasks. Thus, the more similar both the stimuli and responses are, the more transfer will occur between the tasks. This "transfer surface" approach was extended to motor skills by Holding (1976) and is illustrated in Figure 2.3–1. Holding viewed this "surface" as a "loose predictive device" that could be suitably applied to instructional needs if broadly interpreted. Notice that maximum positive transfer is predicted when the stimulus (S) and the response (R) for one task is the same as for the second task, and that as the stimuli decrease in similarity, transfer progresses toward 0.

Similarity of processing requirements. The second hypothesized view proposing why positive transfer occurs argues that rather than focusing on the similarity of the physical components of a skill or the context characteristics of the two performance situations, the focus should be on the similarity of cognitive processing characteristics required by the two skills or two performance situations. Work by John Bransford and colleagues (Morris, Bransford, & Franks, 1977; Bransford, Franks, Morris, & Stein, 1979; see also, Lee, 1988)

has promoted what they have termed the **transfer-appropriate-processing** view of explaining transfer effects. They argued that although similarity of skill and context components may explain some transfer effects, many transfer effects cannot be explained by such a view. For example, if a novel response must be performed in a new context, a similarity view is weak because similarity is minimal; yet, certain previous experiences can yield better novel response transfer performance than other previous experiences. The prior beneficial experiences do not require that the skills involved be more similar to the transfer skill, but, more important, that the cognitive processes required by the two skills be similar. More recently, Kolers & Roediger (1984) have argued a similar view that what accounts for transfer between practice and test or between two skills is the similarity of the "procedures" required by the two situations or skills. In fact, they argued that many transfer effects in motor learning could be accounted for by invoking this "procedures" explanation.

An experiment by Damos and Wickens (1980) provides an example of this view. Two different cognitive training tasks were used. One was a classification task in which subjects were presented with two digits simultaneously that differed in either size or name. Subjects were required to determine the number of dimensions on which the two stimuli were alike. The second training task was a short-term memory task in which subjects were presented between one and four digits in a sequence. Subjects had to respond by recalling the next to the last digit in the sequence, thus they were required to hold that digit in memory and respond when the last digit appeared. Subjects never knew which digit was the next to the last or last until the last digit appeared. The transfer task was a motor task called a compensatory tracking task. Subjects saw a moving circle on the video screen. Their task was to keep the circle centered on a horizontal bar that was also on the screen by making left to right movements with a control stick. At the same time on the screen was a moving vertical bar that had to be moved up and down on the screen to keep it in contact with a constant horizontal line. This task was also controlled by a control stick. One control stick for each task was in each hand of the subjects.

Three groups of subjects were used in the experiment. One group received training with both the cognitive dual tasks. A second group received training on only one of the cognitive dual tasks, while a third group received no training on either cognitive dual task. All three groups performed the compensatory tracking task. Notice that in terms of task or context components, there is minimal to no similarity between the training and test tasks. The commonality is that both tasks require attention-capacity timesharing, which can be considered a cognitive process. Thus, if the similarity of skill and context components view more accurately explains transfer, the group that had no practice on the cognitive tasks should not be at a disadvantage when they begin performing the tracking task. Further, they should do as well at tracking as the other groups. On the other hand, if the similarity of processing view more adequately explains transfer, the group that had training with two of the cognitive dual tasks should do the best when transferred to the tracking task. Results supported the second view; the group that practiced both cognitive dual tasks performed the tracking task better than the other two training

groups. Thus, the transfer benefit was due to the transfer of the timesharing cognitive process.

Much is still unknown about what causes transfer of learning. There is evidence to support both views currently held of why transfer occurs. More than likely, the processing view may be an extension of the components view and may come into play only when skill components and context similarities are minimal, while processing activities are highly similar. But, as Schmidt and Young (1987) concluded in their extensive review of transfer in motor skills, we do not know very much about what accounts for the transfer phenomenon. Much more work is needed to answer the question of *why* transfer occurs.

Negative Transfer

While it has been argued that negative transfer effects are rare in motor learning (e.g., Annett & Sparrow, 1985; Schmidt, 1987), it is important to keep in mind what is involved in negative transfer. The essential argument that negative transfer is rare refers to the actual movement control parameters in motor performance. It is argued that what are typically observed as negative transfer effects are essentially cognitive rather than motor. The influence is not on the actual control parameters directing the movement. While this may be the case, and most research seems to support such a view, it does not diminish the need to consider negative transfer effects in motor learning. A person who teaches motor skills must be aware of what may influence negative transfer as well as determine how to deal with the phenomenon in the instructional setting.

How, then, do we account for negative transfer effects? The most plausible explanation appears to be that negative transfer effects occur when a new response is required for an old stimulus. Two response conditions seem to be especially susceptible to negative transfer effects. They involve the change in *spatial locations* of a response to the same stimulus and the change in *timing* characteristics of the response to the same stimulus. Two experiments illustrate this.

In an experiment reported many years ago by Siipola (1941) subjects were required to learn to move a lever into one of 10 slots in response to a stimulus numbered 1 through 10. After learning the task as criterion, the subjects were required to learn a new but similar task. The second task required the same type of response as the first, except that the response to stimulus number 3 was to move the lever to the slot that had been the response to number 7 in the first task. Also, the response to number 4 was to be the response that had been to number 8 in the first task. As expected, considerable negative transfer effects were noted in the learning of the second task. Thus, requiring a new spatial location response to an old stimulus produced negative transfer effects.

In an experiment demonstrating negative transfer effects for timing characteristics of a response, Summers (1975) required subjects to learn a sequential finger-tapping task. Subjects learned to execute a particular sequence of nine key presses. Each key press-to-key-press interval required a specified criterion time. Following many practice trials, subjects were able to produce the correct sequence and timing structure from memory. Then subjects were told to produce the same sequential response but to do it as quickly as possible, thus ignoring the just-learned timing structure. While subjects were able to perform the entire sequence more rapidly, they were not able to overcome the learned timing structure. That is, they could speed up the entire task but the key-press-to-key-press intervals showed a similar relationship structure as had been characteristic of the learned sequence. While these results have important implications for what motor programs are like (which will be discussed in Concept 3.3), they also show how timing components of a learned skill influence the performance of a modification of the response of that skill.

These experiments illustrate the essential point that if a subject must produce a new response to a familiar stimulus, negative transfer effects can be expected. First, negative transfer effects can be caused by *confusion*. In the Siipola experiment, the transfer task conditions undoubtedly led to subjects' confusion over which lever response went with which stimulus number. This is similar to the experience of having to type on a typewriter that is different from the one with which you are familiar. Typewriters often vary in their placement of certain keys, such as the backspace or margin release. When you first begin typing on a new machine, you have difficulty with those keys. The problem is not with your limb control, but with the confusion created by the novel position of the keys.

The second point is that negative transfer effects are typically *temporary*. Depending on the task itself, the negative transfer effects can be overcome rather quickly. In the typewriter example, you find that after just a little practice, you are no longer bothered by the different key locations.

People who teach motor skills need to be aware that when a person is required to make new responses to old stimuli, there will be some initial difficulty in performing the skill. In such cases, it is important for the instructor to direct the person's attention to the parts of the skill where the negative transfer effects are occurring. With their attention directed specifically at those parts of the skill, and with practice, overcoming negative transfer effects can be facilitated.

Summary

Transfer of learning is a concept that involves the influence of previous experiences on the learning of a new skill or on performing a practical skill in a new context. The influence of the previous experience may either facilitate, hinder, or have no effect on the learning of the new skill. The transfer of learning concept is an integral part of the development of curriculum in educational environment as well as for training and rehabilitation programs. The concept also forms the basis for many instruction, training, and rehabilitation methods decisions that must be made. And, the transfer of learning concept is an essential part of conducting research in motor learning because it is basic to the process of making inferences about the influence of practice conditions on learning motor skills. Several basic experimental paradigms were described and discussed that form the basis for investigating transfer issues related to intertask and intratask transfer. Also, methods to quantify the amount of transfer that occurs were described. The amount and direction of transfer can be influenced by many factors, of which three were discussed. Two hypotheses are commonly given to account for why positive transfer occurs. The first of these concern the similarities in the components of motor skills and in the contexts in which a skill will be performed. Generally, the greater the component similarity between two skills or between two performance situations, the greater the positive transfer from one skill to another. The second hypothesis argues that the similarity of the cognitive processing demands of the two situations accounts for transfer between two skills or two performance contexts. Negative transfer effects can occur when a new response is required for a familiar stimulus. These effects are typically cognitively based and are relatively temporary.

Related Readings

Annett, J., & Sparrow, J. (1985). Transfer of training: A review of research and practical implications. *Programmed Learning and Educational Technology, 22,* 116–124.

Fischman, M. G., Christina, R. W., & Vercruyssen, M. J. (1981). Retention and transfer of motor skills: A review for the practitioner. *Quest, 33,* 181–194.

Lee, T. D. (1988). Testing for motor learning: A focus on transfer-appropriate-processing. In O.G. Meijer & K. Roth (Eds.), *Complex motor behaviour: 'The' motor-action controversy* (pp. 210–215). Amsterdam: Elsevier Science Publishers.

Livesey, J. P., & Laszlo, J. I. (1979). Effect of task similarity on transfer performance. *Journal of Motor Behavior, 11,* 11–21.

Schmidt, R. A., & Young, D. E. (1987). Transfer of movement control in motor skill learning. In S. M. Cormier & J. D. Hagman (Eds.), *Transfer of learning,* pp. 47–79. Orlando, FL: Academic Press.

Singer, R. N. (1966). Transfer effects and ultimate success in archery due to degree of difficulty of the initial learning. *Research Quarterly, 37,* 532–539.

□

STUDY QUESTIONS FOR CHAPTER 2
(Introduction to Motor Learning)

1. Explain how the terms *performance* and *learning* differ.

2. Name two important performance characteristics that should change during learning a motor skill and how they should change. Give an example of the changes in a motor skill with which you are familiar.

3. Why must we *infer* learning from performance situations?

4. What are the advantages of using retention tests and transfer tests compared with observing practice performance for making a valid assessment of learning? Give an example of how an incorrect inference about learning a skill could be made from only observing practice performance and how the use of a retention or transfer test would permit a more appropriate inference.

5. What is a performance plateau? What seems to be the most likely reason why a performance plateau occurs in motor skill learning?

6. What are some characteristics of learners as they progress through the three stages of learning proposed by Fitts and Posner?

7. How does Gentile's stages of learning model differ from the Fitts and Posner model? How does her model relate specifically to differences in learning open and closed skills?

8. What are two research approaches used to determine changes that occur as people learn motor skills?

9. Describe four changes that research has shown occur as a person progresses through the stages of learning a motor skill.

10. What are two types of experimental designs used to assess transfer? How can the amount of transfer be quantified?

11. What are two reasons proposed to explain why transfer occurs? For each of these, give a motor skill example.

12. What type of situation characteristics predict negative transfer? Give two motor skill performance examples of these characteristics and indicate why negative transfer would occur.

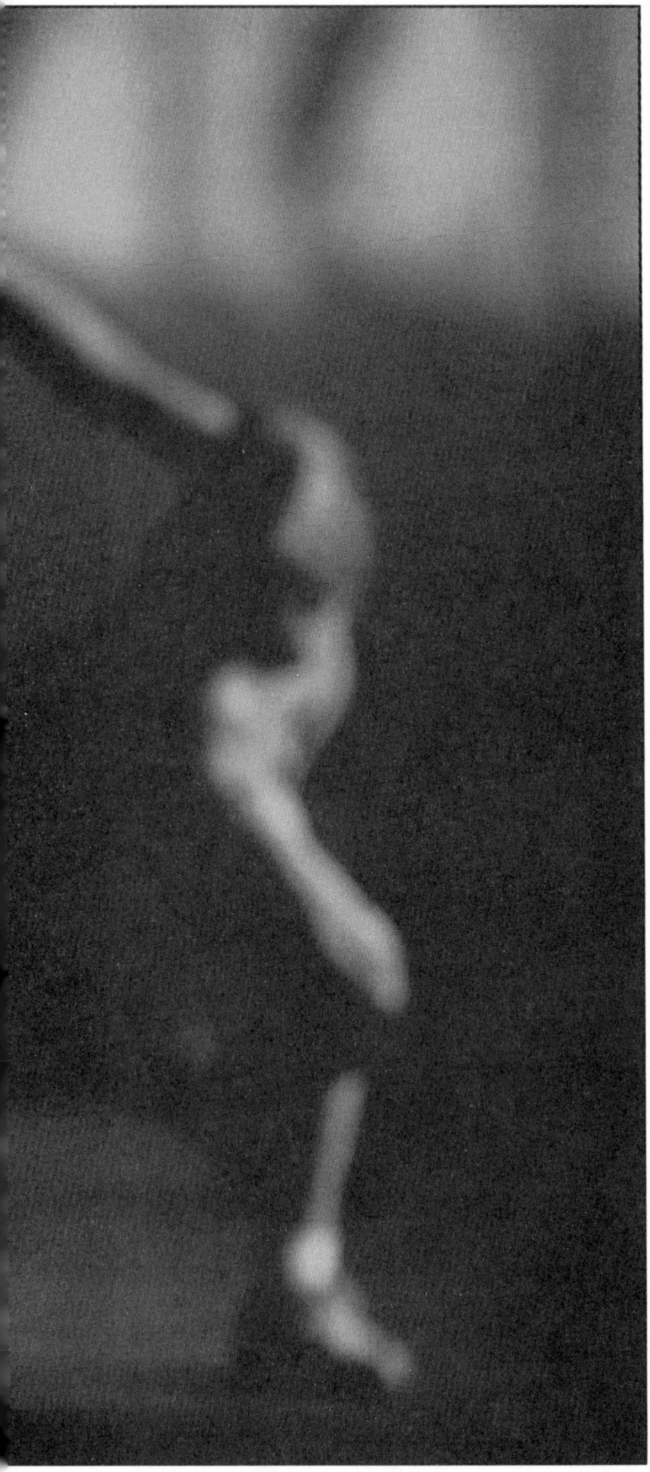

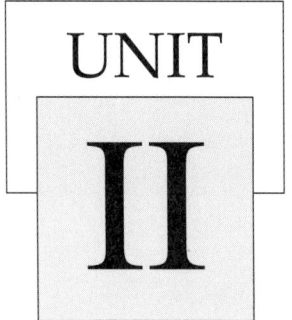

UNIT
II

THE
LEARNER

CHAPTER 3

CONTROLLING MOVEMENT

CONCEPT 3.1

The control of coordinated voluntary movement involves open-loop and closed-loop control systems.

CONCEPT 3.2

Vision plays an important role in the control of voluntary movement.

CONCEPT 3.3

Motor programs are important components in the process of controlling coordinated movement.

CONCEPT 3.4

Bilateral transfer of skills is a phenomenon that blends motor control and cognitive processes.

CONCEPT 3.1

The control of coordinated voluntary movement involves
open-loop and closed-loop control systems

Key Terms

coordination

degrees of
   freedom

open-loop
   system

closed-loop
   system

perceptual
   trace

memory trace

schema

generalized
   motor
   program

dynamic
   systems
   theory

coordinative
   structures

Application

To successfully perform the wide variety of motor
skills we experience in everyday life, various muscles and joints must be coordinated to function together. These muscle and joint combinations differ
for many skills. Some skills require coordinating
muscles and joints of the body and all the limbs,
such as a serve in tennis or volleyball. Some skills
involve the coordination of the arms, hands, and
fingers, as in playing the guitar or typing on a keyboard. Other skills demand the coordination of
fewer muscles and joints, as in manipulating a
joystick or a simple lever, where only one arm and
hand are involved.

   In addition to coordination characteristics,
there are other movement characteristics involved

in performing skills. Some skills are performed
with relatively slow movements, such as positioning a bow before releasing an arrow, or picking
up a cup to take a drink from it. Others require
fast, ballistic movements, such as throwing a ball
or jumping from a bench to the floor. Some motor
skills are relatively simple, such as moving a gear-
shift from first to second gear or buttoning a shirt,
while others are very complex, as in a dance routine or playing the piano.

   These different characteristics are important
to consider as we look at the control processes involved in carrying out voluntary, coordinated
movement to achieve a specific goal. The movements required for an action must be controlled
by the nervous system in such a manner to allow
the intended goal to be achieved. In the discussion
of this concept, you will be introduced to one
approach to describing the general components
involved in the control process and how the components interact. The approach involves describing movement control by two general models
of control systems called open-loop and closed-loop
control systems. As you will see as you progress
through the study of this chapter, the first concept
discussed forms the basis for more specific control
components and processes.

Discussion

The discussion of this concept is organized into
three parts. First, the term *coordination* is discussed to establish its meaning and why it is an
important consideration when studying the control of motor skills. Second, *open-loop* and *closed-
loop* control systems are presented as two general
models of control systems that are applicable to
describing the control of motor skills. Finally, we

will look more closely at proprioceptive feedback
as one type of feedback component essential to a
closed-loop control system.

Coordination

Defining coordination. When some of the
characteristics of skilled motor behavior of experts were described in Concept 2.2, coordination

was an important part of several of those characteristics. Skilled motor performance suggests that the performer organizes the muscles of the body in a way that enables him or her to accomplish the goal of the skill in an effective and efficient manner. It is this organizational aspect of the muscles that is at the heart of the definition of the term coordination. For this discussion then, we will define **coordination** as the patterning of body and limb motions relative to the patterning of environmental objects and events, which is a definition provided by Michael Turvey (1990) in an article in the *American Psychologist* about coordination.

You were introduced to the idea that coordination involves a pattern of body and limb motions in the various views of the stages of learning (Concept 2.2). Gentile (1972) emphasized the development of an appropriate pattern of movement as an important goal of the first stage. That is, in order to achieve the goal of a motor skill, a certain pattern of body and/or limb movements will allow for the achievement of that goal better than other patterns. For example, an experiment by Higgins and Spaeth (1972) looked at subjects learning to throw darts at either a stationary or moving target. A distinct pattern of movement emerged with the practice of these skills as described by the displacement characteristics of the three segments of the throwing arm (shoulder to elbow joints, elbow to wrist joints, and hand). Thus, the segments of the arm became organized in a way that established a pattern of motion for successfully performing the skill.

The second part of the definition of coordination may not be so obvious to you: The pattern of limb and body motion is relative to the pattern of environmental objects and events. This is a critical feature of our definition because it addresses the need to consider coordination of motor skill as it relates to the context in which the skill is performed. As discussed in Concept 1.1, motor skills are goal-directed actions. As a result, the movements that comprise these actions may vary according to the constraints imposed on them by the context in which the action is performed.

For example, to walk along a certain pathway people must adapt the pattern of body and limb movements to the characteristics of the surface on which they are walking and to the characteristics of where they are walking. That is, we walk somewhat differently on a concrete sidewalk than we do on a sandy beach. And we walk somewhat differently when walking into a strong head wind than when there is no wind at all. Thus, coordination of skill must be thought of not only in terms of the body and limb movements involved in the skill itself, but also in terms of the environment in which the skill is carried out.

The degrees of freedom problem. Because coordination involves a pattern of body and limb movements, a logical question to ask is, How do we control the many muscles and joints involved in producing that pattern as we perform a skill? To answer this question we must take into account an important problem. This problem has come to be known as the "degrees of freedom problem." The **degrees of freedom** a system has refers to the number of independent elements or components of the system. The degrees of freedom problem arises when the system needs to be controlled to act in one specific way. Thus, the control problem is, how can an effective yet efficient control system be designed to allow this complex system to be constrained to act in a particular way?

Consider the following mechanical system example of a control problem. A helicopter is designed so that it can fly up or down, left or right, forward or backward, and so on, and at a variety of speeds. There are many different features in the helicopter that need to be controlled to enable it to do all these things. The control problem for the helicopter designer is to make the job of the pilot as simple as possible. If there were one switch or lever for each component involved in the helicopter flying a certain way, the pilot's job would be overwhelming. The designer, therefore, reduces the complexity of the control by allowing the pilot to control all possible helicopter actions with control sticks and pedals the pilot can control simultaneously with his or her hands and feet. Thus, several functions can be controlled by one stick or pedal rather than requiring a stick or pedal for each function.

The human body presents a degrees of freedom control problem similar to that of the helicopter. We know that there are 792 muscles in the human body that can act to make the 100 joints behave in different ways. And each joint has mechanical characteristics that define its degrees of freedom for movement. Turvey (1990) put into perspective the control of coordination problem by indicating that if the joints were all only hinge joints like the elbow, there would be 100 mechanical degrees of freedom to be controlled at the joint level. But if two specific characteristics, such as position and velocity, needed to be defined for these joints to carry out a specific act, the degrees of freedom would increase to 200. As you can see, the control problem involved in coordination of body and limbs to accomplish a goal-directed action is an enormous one that must be accounted for by any control system model developed to describe motor control processes.

The degrees of freedom problem continues to pose a challenge for motor control theorists. At present, there is considerable debate how this problem is solved by the human motor control system. In the sections that follow, you will be introduced to two general control systems models that provide one of several approaches to dealing with the control problem. The models in themselves do not offer specific solutions to the problem. Instead, they establish the basic framework within which control components can be described that can provide a basis for solving the degrees of freedom problem. These more specific control components involved in these control systems will be described and discussed in the next two concepts of this chapter.

Open-Loop and Closed-Loop Control Systems

To help you better understand how coordinated voluntary movement is controlled, two systems of control can be described that are incorporated into most current theories of motor control. These two control systems, called **open-loop** and **closed-loop systems,** are based on mechanical engineering models of control. While these two control systems do not provide exact descriptions of control processes involved in controlling complex human movement, they do provide a useful guide for illustrating some of the basic components involved in the control process. Therefore, it will be helpful to view these two control models as elementary descriptions of how the central and peripheral nervous systems initiate action and control ongoing action so that the goal of that action can be achieved. These models will be referred to throughout the discussions in this chapter.

Diagrams illustrating simple open-loop and closed-loop control systems are presented in Figure 3.1–1. These are the typical diagrams you would see in any general presentation of these types of control systems. Notice that in each of these systems is a *control center*. The control center is sometimes referred to as an *executive*. An important part of its role is to generate and issue movement commands to the *effectors,* which are the muscles and joints involved in producing the desired movement. Both control systems also contain *movement commands* that come from the control center and go to the effectors.

These systems differ, however, in two essential ways. The first difference is evident in the diagrams. A closed-loop control system involves *feedback* while an open-loop system does not. In human movement, the feedback is afferent information sent by the various sensory receptors to the control center. The purpose of this feedback is to update the control center about the correctness of the movement while it is in progress.

As you look at the closed-loop control system diagrammed in Figure 3.1–1, it is important to be aware that the way the feedback loop is depicted can be misleading. The feedback in the diagram indicates that the source is the muscles producing the movement, because these are the "effectors" that enable the body and limbs to move. But that is only partially correct because feedback may come from *any* of the sensory receptors involved

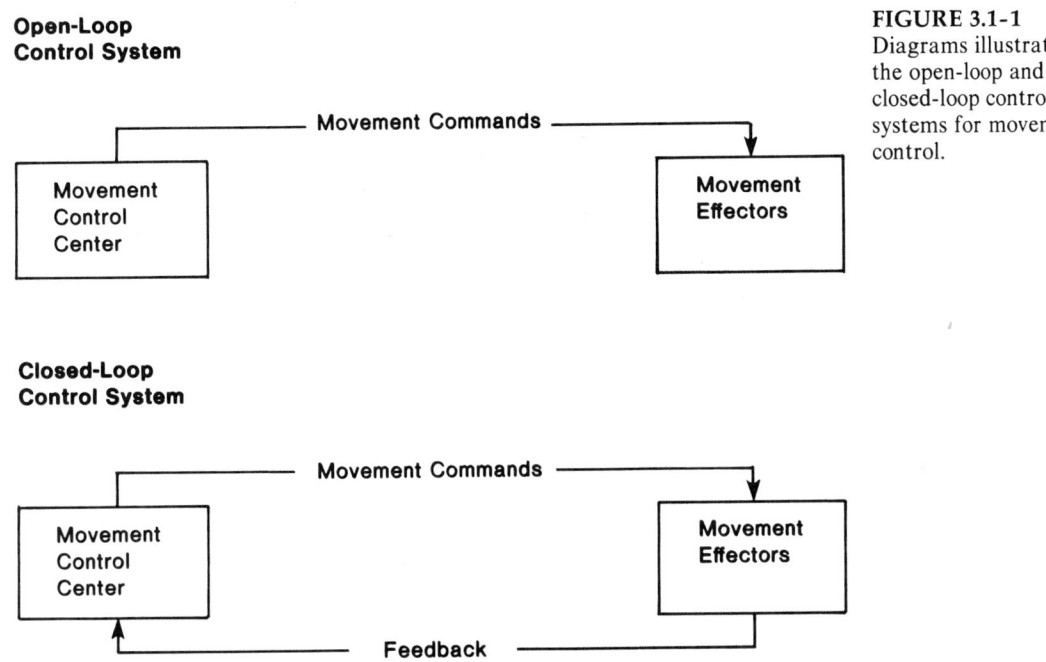

**Open-Loop
Control System**

**Closed-Loop
Control System**

FIGURE 3.1-1
Diagrams illustrating
the open-loop and
closed-loop control
systems for movement
control.

in the performance of the skill. Thus, visual, auditory, and tactile receptors, as well as proprioceptive receptors may be sources of feedback for the ongoing movement. We will discuss two feedback sources, proprioception and vision, in more detail later in this discussion and in the next concept.

The second important difference between open- and closed-loop control systems is the movement commands issued by the control center. In the open-loop system, the commands contain all the information necessary for the effectors to carry out the planned movement. While feedback is produced and available, it is not used to control the ongoing movement. This may be because feedback is not needed, or there is no time to use feedback to effectively control the movement after it is initiated. In either case, the feedback resulting from a movement may be used to help plan the next response after completing the present one. In the closed-loop system, the movement commands are quite different. First, there is an initial command to the effectors that is sufficient only to initiate the movement. The actual execution and

completion of the movement are dependent on feedback information reaching the control center. In this case, then, feedback is used to help control the ongoing movement as well as to help plan the next response using the same movement.

The question that is the focus of developing an appropriate solution to the control of coordination problems described earlier is, What characterizes the control center, its commands, and the feedback? To answer that question, several issues need to be resolved. For example, there is a need to determine what are the components in the control center and the responsibilities of each component. There is also a need to determine what information is needed by the control center to carry out its responsibilities, and to determine where that information comes from. And there is a need to characterize the movement commands forwarded to the effectors in terms of what information they need from the control center and what information they use from other sources, such as the environment. There is also a need to establish what feedback is needed to provide appropriate control and how that feedback is used and transmitted to the effectors. We will not attempt to resolve the theoretical conflict that currently exists about the answers to these questions. However, in the discussions of the next two concepts in this chapter, an overview will be provided of some of the solutions proposed to address these specific control problem issues.

Mechanical examples of open- and closed-loop control.   There are many machine-type examples of open-loop and closed-loop control all around us. For example, open-loop systems control traffic lights. Each light is programmed to go on at specific time intervals. Traffic conditions will not affect the intervals because the signals are impervious to that type of feedback. The alarm on your clock radio will turn on at the preset time regardless of whether or not you are asleep, want the radio to turn on, or are gone from the house. The only way you can stop this from occurring is by turning off the alarm. Similarly, you can program a videocassette recorder to tape certain programs from your television even when you are not home. What is common in each of these examples is that commands are programmed in advance. These commands will be carried out as specified without regard to environmental conditions that may actually indicate that it is not necessary to carry out the prepared commands.

A good example of a mechanical closed-loop control system is a thermostat that controls the air-conditioning system in a house. The desired room temperature is set on the thermostat. The setting becomes a reference against which varying room temperatures can be compared. If the temperature is higher than the reference, a command is sent to the air-conditioning unit to turn on and begin cooling the room. If the temperature is lower than this reference, the unit stays off. Thus, continuous "information" is sent from the room, to the thermostat, to the air-conditioning unit, to the room, and back to the thermostat, thereby establishing a constant "loop" of information flow to control the room's temperature in accordance to the specified thermostat temperature. Other examples of mechanical closed-loop control systems

include such things as speed-control sensors included in many stereo turntables and cruise-control systems in automobiles. In each of those examples, feedback is necessary for the mechanism to carry out the desired action.

Relating Open- and Closed-Loop Systems to Movement Control

Because current theories of movement control include both control systems, it will be helpful to consider some examples of how these systems have been incorporated into models or theories of movement control. In this section, we will briefly consider some current theories of movement control that incorporate some type of open- and closed-loop control and that shape current views of how we learn and control motor skills. The first is the closed-loop theory presented by Jack Adams in 1971. The second is the schema theory published by Richard Schmidt in 1975. The third is the dynamic systems view of motor control, which takes issue with both the Adams and Schmidt theories.

Adams' closed-loop theory.   The motivation behind Adams' development of a theory of motor learning was what he considered to be an unfortunate lack of a well-defined subject matter and a paradigm on which to base and pursue the study of motor learning. To overcome this problem, he presented his "closed-loop theory" of motor learning (Adams, 1971). Adams' frame of reference for his theory was simple, self-paced, limb-positioning movements. Although Adams felt that this theory could be generalized to include more complex movements, he argued that it was essential to begin the process of theory development for motor learning by focusing on simple skills. He also wanted to develop a theory around existing research literature, which primarily involved the use of simple, limb-positioning movements.

Every closed-loop control system must have a reference mechanism that can be used to assess the status of a movement being made. In Adams' theory, this reference mechanism is called the **perceptual trace,** which is the memory of past movements and is responsible for determining the status of a movement in progress. It is used by the performer to know where to stop the limb as well as how to adjust another attempt at the same movement. These functions are accomplished by the perceptual trace by comparing feedback about what the movement is currently like with what it is supposed to be like. If there is a perfect match, the command is issued to stop the movement. If error is detected in this comparison, commands are sent to make some adjustments in the movement. How well this comparison and correction process can be accomplished depends on how accurate and well-developed the perceptual trace is at the time.

Essential to the development of the perceptual trace is that it gets stronger, or better developed, as practice of the movement occurs. Adams' view was that an essential part of this development is the availability of knowledge of results (KR), or information about the correctness of a response provided by some external source, such as an experimenter, teacher, or coach. (KR will be discussed in Chapter 7.) As a part of practice, the individual combines KR information with the feedback information received through his or her own sensory system. Eventually, the perceptual trace becomes strong enough for the individual to be able to detect and correct his or her own errors when making the movement. When this occurs, Adams indicates that the individual has moved to a "motor stage" of learning where the movement can be made "automatically."

The open-loop component of Adams' theory is the *memory trace*. While the perceptual trace is used to determine how far the limb should move, the **memory trace** is responsible for getting the limb moving in the first place. Adams proposed that the essential role of the memory trace is to "select and initiate a response, preceding the use of the perceptual trace" (p. 125). This trace is also developed as a result of practice. Different from the perceptual trace, the memory trace was described by Adams as a "modest motor program." That is, it is from this trace that all the necessary information to *initiate* the movement is sent, requiring no feedback.

Thus, according to Adams' theory, controlling a limb-positioning movement involves both open- and closed-loop control processes, despite the theory being called a closed-loop theory. Open-loop control is involved in initiating the movement while closed-loop control is needed for terminating the movement. The degrees of freedom problem is not directly addressed in Adams' theory but it is apparent that the memory and perceptual traces provide necessary control characteristics.

Schmidt's schema theory. Richard Schmidt (1975b) identified limitations in Adams' theory he proposed to overcome by presenting an alternative theory of motor learning and control. Two limitations were that the theory was limited to simple, slow, limb-positioning movements and could therefore not be generalized to other types of motor skills. The theory also did not provide a logical way to establish how people could make a correct response for a movement they had not previously performed in exactly that way, as is common in open motor skills.

To accommodate the limitations in Adams' theory, Schmidt presented his schema theory. A **schema** can be defined as a rule or set of rules that serves to provide the basis for a decision. A schema is developed by abstracting important pieces of information from related experiences and combining them into a type of rule. For example, the formation of your concept of "dog" is the result of seeing many different types of dogs. As a result of your experiences, you have developed a set of rules that will allow you to produce the response "dog" when you are asked to identify the animal that is being shown to you. You may never have seen that particular type of dog before, yet you still can identify it as a dog.

Schmidt proposed two control components that are characterized as abstract-rule based. The first is the **generalized motor program,** which is the general memory representation of the action to be controlled. This program is responsible for controlling a class of actions, such as a throwing or kicking action, or a walking or running action. The second component is the *motor response schema,* which is responsible for providing the specific rules governing an action in a given situation. Thus, the motor response schema provides situation-specific characteristics to the action controlled by the generalized motor program.

The motor response schema is actually made up of two schemas, each with different responsibilities. First is the *recall schema,* which is responsible for adding specific response characteristics instructions to the motor program and initiating the execution of the intended action. The second schema, called the *recognition schema,* enables the performer to evaluate the correctness of the initiated action by comparing actual sensory feedback against the expected sensory feedback and make movement corrections.

Schmidt's theory did not address the question of how a generalized motor program is developed through learning. However, the theory proposes that for a given class of actions, such as the overhand throw, we abstract different pieces of information from every throwing experience we have that involves an overhand throwing pattern. We then construct schemas that will enable us to successfully use the overhand throw in a variety of situations and circumstances.

The recall and recognition schemas are constructed by abstracting four pieces of information from each movement experience. The first information concerns the *initial conditions* related to performing a skill, which includes things such as the position of the limbs and body, the environmental conditions in which the skill is performed, etc. Second, the performer stores information about the *response specifications.* These are the specific requirements of the action to be performed, such as the direction, speed, force, etc. These specifications must be applied to the motor program before the action can be carried out. Third, the *sensory consequences* of performing the skill are determined. These are acquired by the sensory feedback received from the various sensory systems during and after the movement is actually made. Finally, information is abstracted about the *response outcome,* which is information

related to the comparison of the actual outcome with the intended outcome. These four sources of information are stored to form the schemas responsible for controlling and evaluating movements.

One of the features of the schema theory that generated a great deal of research interest was the problem of accounting for success in performing a novel response within a movement class. That is, how can a person make a response that had not been made in exactly the same way before? Because the motor response schema is an abstract set of rules, Schmidt predicted that the performer can successfully perform a well learned skill in a novel situation. This is done by relating the response requirements of the novel situation to the general rules for performing that action available in the motor response schema. The probability of making a correct response in the novel response situation can be enhanced by increased amounts of practice and variety of practice experiences involving the skill. This practice prediction will be considered in more detail in Chapter 8.

According to Schmidt's schema theory, the degrees of freedom problem is solved by an executive control operation that organizes motor programs and schemas. An important emphasis in this approach is the abstract or general nature of what is stored in the control center. Both open- and closed-loop control systems are involved in controlling coordinated movement. The generalized motor program and recall schema work together to provide the specific movement characteristics needed to initiate an action in a given situation. The action initiation is an open-loop control process. However, once the action is initiated, feedback can influence its course if there is sufficient time to process the feedback. Thus, for the control of a skill where there is time to use feedback, control is open-loop to initiate it and closed-loop to continue it to completion. However, for rapid, ballistic actions, such as swinging a bat at a ball or throwing a ball, there usually is not sufficient time to use feedback to make necessary movement corrections while the movement is being executed. The movement is completed too quickly

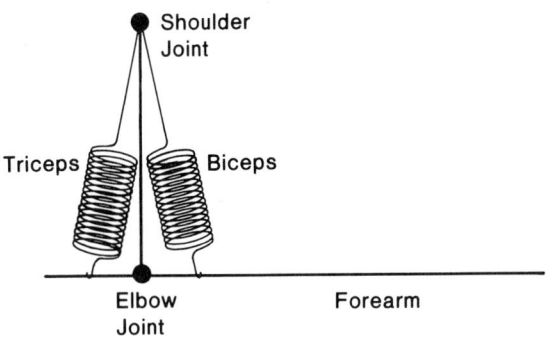

FIGURE 3.1-2 The mass-spring model illustrated by showing the biceps and triceps as springs attached to a mass at one end (forearm) and fixed at the other end (shoulder).

for the feedback-correction command loop to operate effectively. In such cases, Schmidt indicated that the entire movement is controlled by an open-loop system governed also by the motor program and recall schema. Feedback is used in the updating of the motor program and motor response schema.

Dynamic systems theory. An alternative to Adams' and Schmidt's theories of controlling coordinated movement is an approach commonly known as **dynamic systems theory.** Other terms used for this approach are "action theory" or "ecological theory." The key proponents of this view include Peter Kugler, Scott Kelso, Michael Turvey (e.g., Turvey, 1990). The dynamic systems theory approach to describing control of coordinated movement deemphasizes the role of the central command center and emphasizes the role of information in the environment and the dynamic properties of the body and limbs. The key characteristic of this approach to movement control is the interaction between the person and the environment. Perception and action are integrally linked so that control of action involves the setting in motion of specific actions according to the relationship between perceptual information and the motor system.

Rather than propose an executive command center and motor programs, the dynamic systems approach argues that skilled action is controlled by the nervous system constraining functionally-specific collectives of muscles and joints to act cooperatively so that an action can be carried out

according to the dictates of the situation. These functional collectives, called **coordinative structures** or action units, are developed through practice or experience, or may exist naturally. An example would be the muscles and joints (the degrees of freedom to be controlled) involved in the action of reaching and grasping an object. These muscles and joints are constrained to act together as a unit for the specific purpose of reaching and grasping an object. Thus, if a person has the intention to reach and grasp a cup, the coordinative structure involved in that action is organized to carry out that action in accordance to the dictates of the environmental constraints. Rather than the commands for this organization coming from a central executive, the coordinative structure is "self-organized" as a result of the person's intention to perform this action and of the characteristics of the environmental information related to the cup and its location.

An illustration of how this type of control can occur is seen in the mechanical example of a mass-spring system. If a mass is suspended by a spring it returns to an equilibrium point each time it is perturbed based on the mechanical properties of the spring, such as the stiffness, or length-tension ratio. The dynamic systems view argues that a person's arm is analogous to a mass-spring system. Because of this, it is possible to see how the arm could achieve a specific position in space, as is required in a reaching task, regardless of its starting point. As depicted in Figure 3.1–2, the forearm can be thought of as a lever that is attached to a pivot, the elbow. The agonist and antagonist muscles involved in flexion and extension of the forearm, the biceps and triceps, are represented as springs, attached at one end to the forearm lever (a mass) and fixed at the other end to the shoulder. If a specific limb position must be achieved, the limb will stop at the desired location, regardless of its starting point, because the stiffness of the springs, preset by the movement commands, dictates the final equilibrium, or stopping point for the springs. In this way, the limb moves to its prescribed location in space without the need for sensory feedback to indicate where it should stop.

In this view of movement control, open-loop type control systems are operating. Commands are forwarded from the nervous system to the coordinative structures, prompting the action to occur. However, these commands do not necessarily come from a central executive command center but can come from various sources within and external to the person. These commands also do not necessarily involve specific movement information, as in the mass-spring example. Closed-loop control systems operate in this type of control but their operation is different from that described by the Adams and Schmidt theories. In the dynamic systems view, feedback loops exist within components of the coordinative structures so that adaptations to unique situations can occur. For example, if a person has a pencil in his or her mouth and tries to speak, the coordinative structure related to articulatory control of speech adapts to this situation by providing compensation for the inability of certain muscles to operate normally. This adaptation can occur from short feedback loops within the coordinative structure indicating the need for certain muscles in the collective to compensate for what other muscles cannot do at the time. The feedback does not need to return to a central command center to be operated on so that new movement commands can be forwarded to the musculature.

Feedback and Sensory-Perceptual Systems

A key feature in the distinction between open- and closed-loop control systems is the role played by feedback in the control of an ongoing movement. Because of this, it is important to develop a better understanding of feedback as it relates to movement control. Accordingly, the remainder of this discussion as well as much of the discussion of the next concept are devoted to the role of feedback in controlling coordinated movement.

Feedback is provided by sensory receptors located in various parts of the human body. The process of detecting sensory information is typically termed *sensation*. However, when that information is used or interpreted, the process known as *perception* is involved. However, in this text these two processes are considered closely linked and cannot be logically separated. Thus, when the terms *vision* and *proprioception* are used to refer to feedback, it is important to think of both sensation and perception because both the reception and interpretation of sensory information are involved. Because of this interaction between sensation and perception, we will refer to feedback sources such as vision and proprioception as *sensory-perceptual systems*.

For most motor skills, the most critical sensory receptors for providing feedback are those related to providing proprioceptive and visual information to the central nervous system. In the remainder of this discussion we will focus on proprioceptive feedback and its role in this control process. The focus will shift to the role of vision in the next concept in this chapter. However, before getting into those discussions there is an issue common to the study of both visual and proprioceptive feedback that is important for understanding these feedback systems. This issue, which concerns how well these systems discriminate sensory information, is discussed next.

The sensitivity of vision and proprioception.

An important characteristic of any sensory-perceptual system is what we will call the sensitivity of the system. That is, how easily that system can discriminate one level of intensity of sensory information from another. This characteristic must be taken into account when establishing how feedback is used in the control of voluntary movements.

An example of how this sensitivity question is related to movement control can be seen in the following question. How sensitive, or keen, is vision for judging if two lights are different in their intensity? In perceptual terms, the question becomes: Is one light brighter than the other? This question becomes an important movement control question when a specific action is demanded by different light intensities. The answer to this question must be considered two ways. One is an objective answer to the question because the intensity of the two lights can be objectively measured. However, the other way to answer the question is from the point of view of the person observing the light. While two lights may be measurably different in terms of their intensity, it is possible that a person may not judge them as different. In this case, the concern is how accurately we can make these types of comparison judgments when perceiving sensory information. The same questions relate to the use of proprioception as feedback in making perceptual judgments. For example, consider the question: How much heavier or lighter does a baseball bat need to be before you can tell that it is different from the one you just used?

In the study of perception, these questions are investigated by researchers involved in *psychophysics,* which is the study of the relationship between our objective world and our perception of it. Of particular interest for this discussion is how precisely our visual and proprioceptive system can discriminate differences. The measure that has been developed to indicate the sensitivity of a perceptual system to make these discrimination judgments is called the *just noticeable difference (j.n.d.).* The j.n.d. is also referred to as the difference limen or difference threshold. The j.n.d. can be generally defined as the least amount of change in the intensity of a stimulus that can be correctly detected by the individual. For example, suppose you were given a tennis racket that was strung with 50 lbs. pressure. How much of an increase or decrease in that string weight would it take for you to detect that the new string weight was actually different from the 50 lb. one?

Research has shown that we have rather keen senses of vision and proprioception. For example, if a light has an intensity level of 1,000 photons, we can usually detect a change in intensity with only a 16 photon change in actual brightness (Woodworth & Schlosberg, 1954). For any luminance intensity level within that range, we would typically indicate that the two lights were the same. For proprioception, evidence indicates that people can discriminate between two arm positions if they are greater than 1.25 cm apart (Magill & Parks, 1983). Conversely, if the two positions are within 1.25 cm, it is unlikely that they will be detected as different.

Understanding the characteristics and limitations of proprioceptive feedback used for making perceptual judgments has implications for both movement control and motor skills instruction. For example, the fact that each sensory system has certain perceptual limitations suggests that any understanding of the roles of sensory feedback systems in the control of movement must take these limitations into account. In the Magill and Parks (1983) study, for example, it was demonstrated that we can more precisely discriminate differences between two limb positions in space than we can differences between two movement distances made by the same limb.

In terms of motor skill instruction, implications of understanding the perceptual limits of proprioception can most readily be seen in a situation where the teacher or therapist must help a person correct a movement error. For example, as the students are working on a gymnastics or dance routine you notice an error in the arm placement of a student in a critical part of the routine. After repeated efforts to correct this problem, the student states that he or she can't seem to correct the problem because it feels like the arm is exactly where you indicated it should be. The problem here may well be an inability to discriminate between the arm position you have shown the student and the actual position of the student's arm during the routine. In this case, your awareness of this possible perceptual limitation can help you realize that correcting the problem will simply require more time than you had thought. Continued practice in making the correction will alleviate the problem.

Proprioceptive Feedback and Controlling Movement

Because the role of feedback is the primary distinguishing feature between open- and closed-loop control systems, it is important to establish the need for feedback in controlling movement. In the following sections, we will consider different experimental approaches that have been followed in attempting to determine the extent to which movement control depends on or does not require proprioceptive feedback. As will become apparent from studying these approaches, the evidence indicates that this is not an either/or issue. While there are situations in which open-loop control can lead to a movement carried out as required, these situations have distinct limitations.

Deafferentation studies. One approach to determining the extent to which proprioceptive feedback is important in controlling movement has been to compare a movement performed under normal conditions with the same movement performed when the proprioceptive feedback is not available. One way to make proprioceptive feedback unavailable is to surgically sever or remove the afferent pathways involved in the movement,

a process called *deafferentation.* Typically, this procedure is used in experiments using monkeys to perform movements.

An early example of using this deafferentation procedure was provided in several experiments by Taub and Berman (1963, 1968). In these experiments, the researchers observed monkeys performing well-developed motor skills, such as climbing, reaching, and grasping, before and after deafferentation of the afferent pathways from the limbs to the CNS. Results of these experiments were consistent in showing that the deafferented monkeys were still capable of performing the skills.

The studies of Taub and Berman considered skills that were well developed in the animals. What would happen if the same deafferentation procedure were used with newly learned skills? This approach was taken by Emilio Bizzi and his colleagues at Massachusetts Institute of Technology (e.g., Bizzi & Polit, 1979; Polit & Bizzi, 1978). In these experiments, monkeys were placed in an apparatus as shown in Figure 3.1–3 and trained to point an arm at one of a series of lights when it came on. The lights were arranged in a semicircle in front of the monkey, who could see the lights but not the arm making the pointing movement. Following training, that is, after the monkeys had learned to accurately point to each light when required, the monkeys were deafferented so that no proprioceptive feedback information from the pointing arm was available during the movement. The monkeys were again placed in the positioning apparatus. Results from these experiments showed that the monkeys were able to accurately position their limbs in the deafferented state. In fact, they were even able to make accurate movements from starting positions that were different from the starting positions used during training. As you may recall, this was one of the predictions made by the mass-spring model discussed earlier.

Deafferenting human subjects for experimental purposes is not possible for obvious reasons. However, Kelso, Holt, and Flatt (1980) reported an experiment that used humans who had no joint

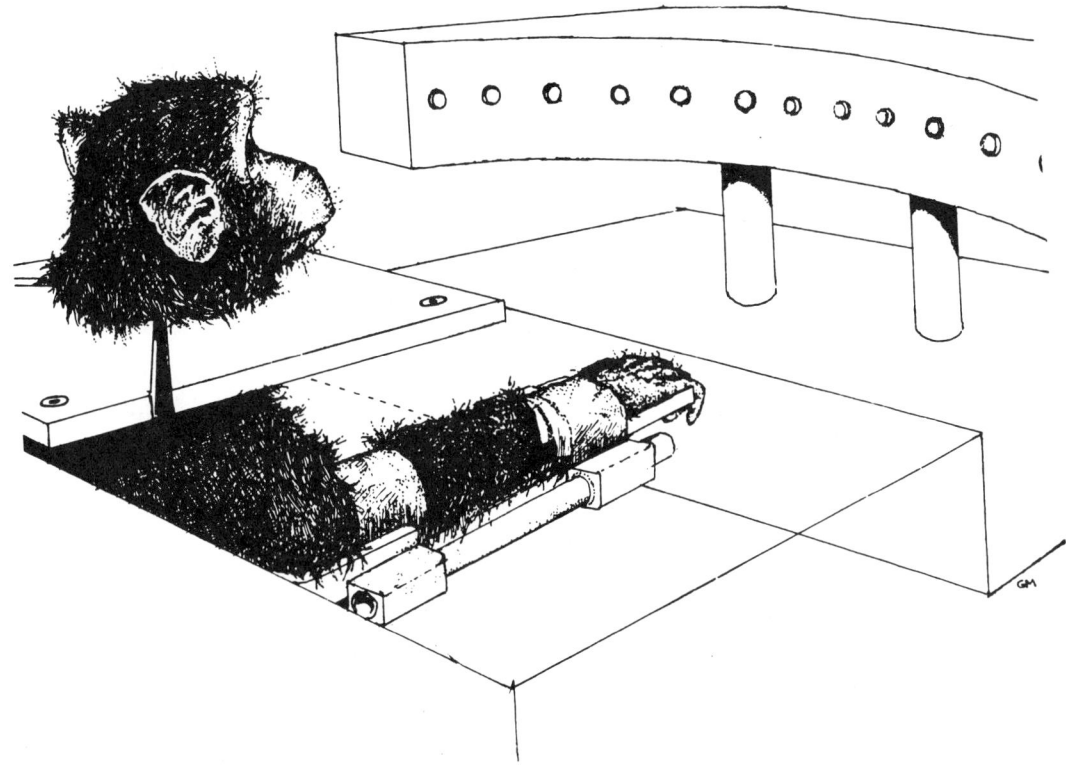

FIGURE 3.1-3   Monkey in the experimental apparatus used in the experiment by Polit and Bizzi. The monkey's arm is strapped to the splint that pivots at the elbow. Target lights are mounted at 5° intervals. During experimental sessions, the monkey could not see its arm and the room was darkened.

receptors available. The subjects in these experiments were rheumatoid arthritis patients who had recently had the metacarpophalangeal joints removed from their fingers. The joints were replaced with flexible silicone rubber implants to hold the bones together. As a result, joint receptors were not available as a source of proprioceptive information during movement. These patients performed positioning responses using a device that allowed only finger movement of a pointer over a protractor graduated in degrees. On each trial, the subjects moved to a specified finger position (the criterion location) or moved through a specified distance (the criterion distance), returned to a new starting point, and then attempted to reproduce the criterion location or

distance. Results, as shown in Figure 3.1–4, indicated the subjects had little difficulty in accurately reproducing the criterion location from a starting point that was either −5° or −15° from the original starting point. However, for reproduction of the movement distance, accuracy was severely influenced by how far the new starting point was from the original starting point.

Results of these studies suggest that limb movements, especially limb-positioning movements, *can* be carried out in the absence of proprioceptive feedback. The control of these movements must therefore be considered to follow an open-loop rather than a closed-loop system, because the lack of proprioceptive feedback did not disrupt the movements. However, this open-loop

FIGURE 3.1-4 Absolute error results from the experiment by Kelso, Holt, and Flatt where finger-joint-replacement patients were asked to reproduce location and distance movements. Recall movements were begun either 5° beyond (−5°) or 15° beyond (−15°) the starting point used for the presentation of the criterion movement.

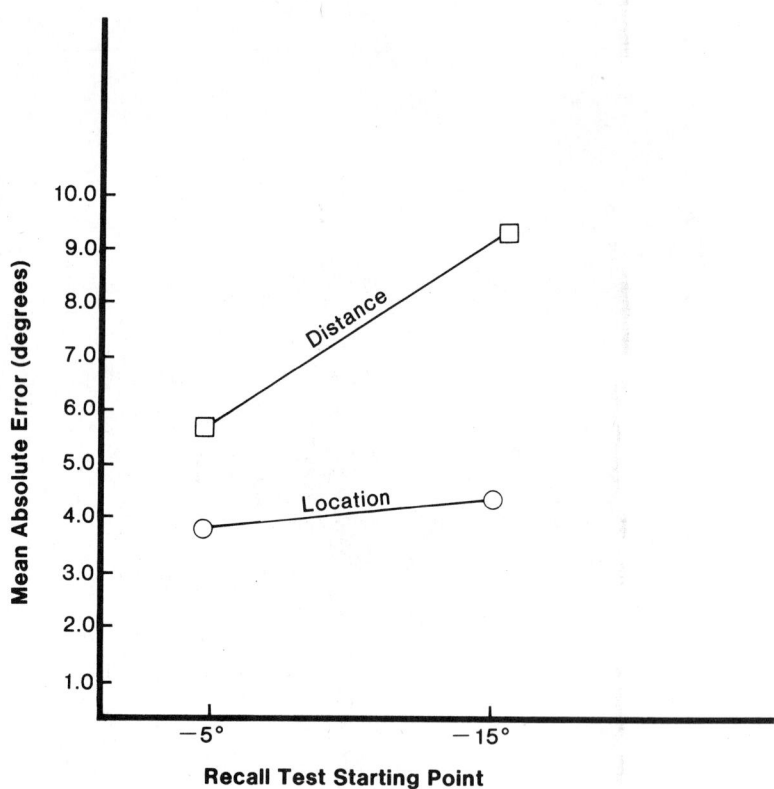

control was seen as subject to specific limitations. Primary among these is the degree of accuracy possible without feedback in the control process. For example, in the Taub and Berman studies, the monkeys, while portraying climbing, grasping, and reaching responses, were clumsier than they had been before deafferentation. In fact, it was difficult for them to grasp food with their hands in this condition. In the Bizzi experiments, a relatively wide target area was used to indicate a correct pointing response for the monkeys. It is difficult, then, to compare the *precision* of the accuracy responses under the normal and deafferented conditions. In the Kelso, Holt, and Flatt experiments, while a comparison was not made of positioning

accuracy before and after joint-capsule replacement, distance movements were severely disrupted by changing starting positions. Thus, while open-loop control processes could control these movements, movement precision appeared to be enhanced by having proprioceptive feedback available.

Nerve-block studies. An interesting approach was developed by Judith Laszlo and her associates in Australia to try to replicate the animal deafferentation studies using humans but without having to surgically deafferent them. In this procedure, known as a nerve block, a blood pressure cuff is placed just above the subject's elbow and then inflated until the subject can no longer feel anything with the fingers. Thus, afferent pathways are assumed to be blocked. However, it is important to note that while afferent pathways are inoperable, the efferent pathways remain unaffected. Following the nerve block, subjects were required to produce finger-tapping responses.

Results of several studies by Laszlo (e.g., 1966, 1967) indicated that motor skills could be performed in the absence of afferent sensory information from the muscles and joints of the fingers, hand, and forearm. However, some work by Kelso and others (e.g., Kelso, Stelmach, & Wanamaker, 1974; Kelso, Wallace, Stelmach, & Weitz, 1975) questioned the efficacy of Laszlo's procedures. A particular question has been the validity of the assumption concerning the unaffected condition of efferent pathways using these procedures. To overcome this problem, Kelso (1977) modified Laszlo's procedure by placing a child's blood pressure cuff on the subjects' wrists after the subjects felt no sensation in the fingers. The arm cuff was then removed and the positioning task was performed. Results of these experiments and others (Kelso & Holt, 1980) showed that subjects were able to position their fingers as accurately after the nerve block as they could prior to it. Again, evidence has been provided to show that certain kinds of voluntary movement can accurately be performed without proprioceptive feedback.

Switched-limb studies. Another way to examine the accuracy of limb movement and the involvement of proprioception is to have subjects reproduce a criterion location with the arm that was not used originally to experience or learn the movement. While the rationale behind this procedure was actually developed to test a question related to how we represent movement informa-

tion in memory (to be considered in Chapter 5), the switched-limb procedure can provide some insights into the role of proprioception in movement control.

An example of a study using this approach is by Wallace (1977). Subjects were blindfolded and required to move a lever to a specific location. The subjects were then required to reproduce the movement with either the same or opposite (switched) arm. If the same proprioceptive feedback available when the movement was first produced is not important, then the switched-arm movement should be as accurate as the same-arm movement reproduction. Wallace's results indicated that this was indeed the case as there was no difference between switched- and same-arm movement reproduction.

Recently, however, attempts to replicate Wallace's (1977) findings have not been successful. Reeve and Stelmach (1982), for example, found that reproduction of a series of six limb positions was more accurate when the subjects used the same rather than the opposite arm that was used for presentation of the movements. Magill and Goode (1982) found similar accuracy results when subjects were required to learn to position their arm to within 0.5 cm for three consecutive trials and then reproduce that position with either the practiced (same) or non-practiced (switched) arm (see Figure 3.1–5). However, when all subjects were then asked to move to specified positions and respond whether this position was or was not the learned position, they responded equally well with either limb, as shown in the bar graph on the right of Figure 3.1–5. These results suggest that reasonable or "ball park" accuracy of a learned limb position can be obtained without the same sensory feedback that was available during practice. However, limb-positioning accuracy can be increased when feedback is available.

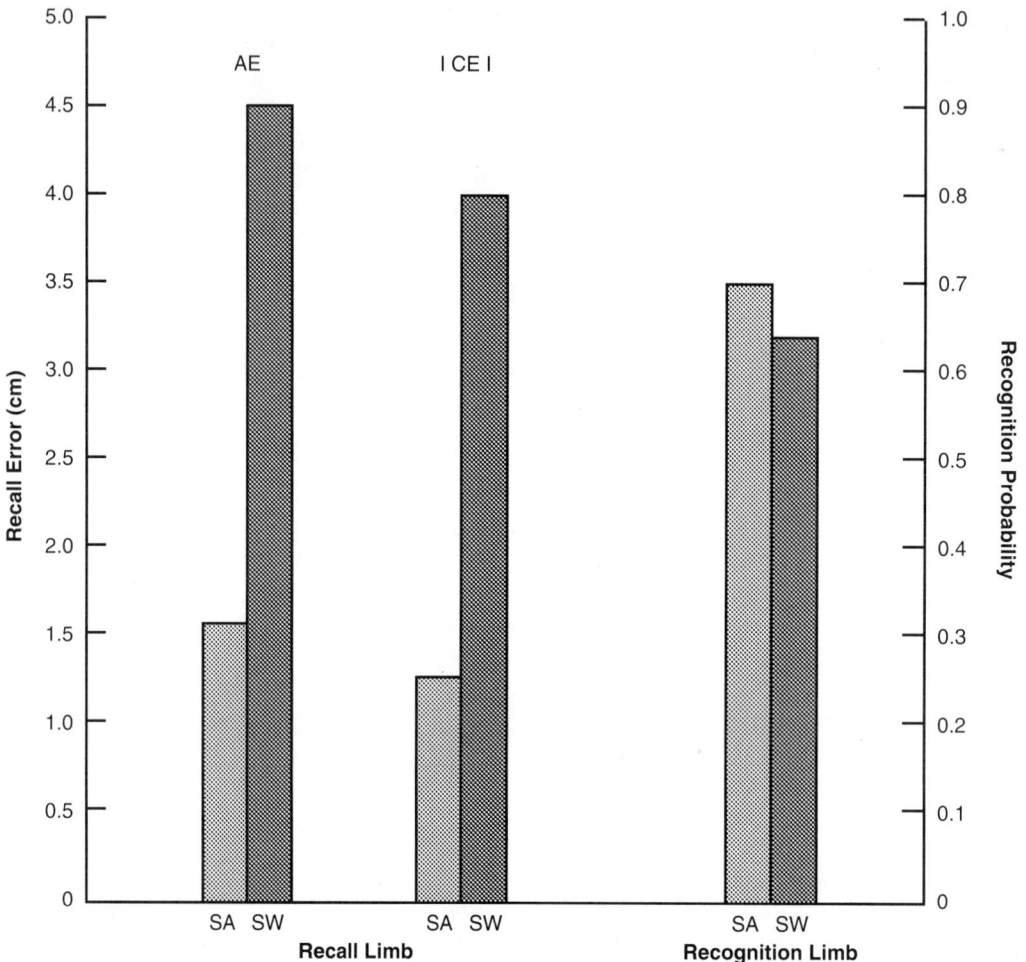

FIGURE 3.1-5 Results of the experiment by Magill and Goode showing absolute error (AE), absolute constant error (CE), and recognition probability for same (SA) and switched (SW) limb for the recall and recognition tests for a practiced limb-positioning movement.

Summary

Controlling movement should be thought of as a process in which coordinated body and limb movement is controlled. Coordination involves a pattern of body and limb movements that permit the person to achieve the goal of a skill in a specific situation. To achieve this goal, the degrees of freedom problem must be solved by the control system so that a specific pattern of movement occurs. Most present day theories of movement control incorporate two simple systems of control,

the open-loop and closed-loop systems. Both of these systems involve a command center, commands, and effectors. However, the closed-loop system operates on the basis of feedback from the different sensory-perceptual systems in the body.

When applied to the control of voluntary movement, these systems are involved in different ways in different theories of movement control. The Adams closed-loop theory views the memory trace as a type of motor program that initiates movement in an open-loop manner. However, the movement is continued and terminated on the basis of closed-loop control processes involving the perceptual trace as the reference mechanism in the system. Schmidt's schema theory proposes that a generalized motor program provides the basis for controlling an action but requires situation-specific information to be added before the action can be carried out as required. Once the program is prepared, it initiates the action in an open-loop way but soon involves feedback to continue the action. Information specific to initiating and evaluating an ongoing movement is provided by recall and recognition schemas. The dynamic systems view de-emphasizes the role of the central command center and places emphasis on the role of the environment and the dynamics of the limbs and joints. The control of coordinated movement involves controlling coordinative structures that respond to the constraints of the environmental characteristics related to the required action. Commands to these structures can be from various sources within and external to the person. Feedback is involved in controlling movement but does not need to go to a central command center.

Proprioceptive feedback is one of several important sources of feedback involved in movement control. Several different experimental approaches exist for investigating the degree of proprioceptive feedback needed to control movements. These include deafferentation, nerve blocks, and switching limbs. Results of these approaches have shown that certain movements can occur without proprioceptive feedback but the degree of precision in these movements appears to be negatively influenced when feedback is not available.

Related Readings

Adams, J. A. (1976). Issues for a closed-loop theory of motor learning. In G. E. Stelmach (Ed.), *Motor control: Issues and trends* (pp. 87–107). New York: Academic Press.

Marken, R. S. (1991). Degrees of freedom in behavior. *Psychological Science, 2,* 92–100.

Schmidt, R. A. (1977). Schema theory: Implications for movement education. *Motor Skills: Theory into Practice, 2,* 36–48.

Schmidt, R. A. (1982). The schema concept. In J. A. S. Kelso (Ed.), *Human motor behavior* (pp. 219–235). Hillsdale, NJ: Erlbaum.

Tuller, B., Turvey, M. T., & Fitch, H. L. (1982). The Bernstein perspective: II. The concept of muscle linkage or coordinative structure. In J. A. S. Kelso (Ed.), *Human motor behavior* (pp. 253–270). Hillsdale, NJ: Erlbaum.

Turvey, M. T. (1990). Coordination. *American Psychologist, 45,* 938–953.

CONCEPT 3.2

Vision plays an important role in the control of voluntary movement

Key Terms

visual search

movement
  preparation
  phase

initial impulse
  phase

error
  correction
  phase

prehension

tau

Application

Many of the motor skills we use to carry out our daily activities require the use of vision. For example, when you reach for a cup to drink the coffee in it, vision plays an important role in accomplishing your goal. Putting your door key into the keyhole of a lock can be done more quickly and accurately if you involve vision. Walking along a corridor requires you to maneuver around people and objects. To do this, vision is important. Driving your car requires you to use vision in several different ways so that you can get to where you are going safely.

Similarly, vision is an essential part of sport activities. Many sports require you to catch or hit a ball. Without vision, your success would be seriously impaired. Or, if you are trying to determine where to hit a return shot in tennis or racquetball, you involve vision in anticipating where the best place will be for that shot. Determining where to direct a pass in soccer or hockey, or which type of move to put on a defender in basketball or football, are all related to successfully applying the use of vision.

In each of these daily living and sport activities, vision plays a critical role. In some cases, information must be used to make a certain decision about what action to take. Visually searching the environment can provide this information. In other situations, visual information provides what is needed to specify how to carry out the actions you determined were required. Visual information also provides effective guidance information that allows you to make necessary movement adjustments so that you can move efficiently and accurately. The role of vision in controlling motor skills is the basis for the discussion that follows.

Discussion

In the discussion of Concept 3.1, you were introduced to how sensory feedback is seen as a component of movement control. And you saw examples of the role played by proprioceptive feedback in this control process. In this discussion, we will consider vision as another source of feedback that is involved in movement control. However, you will find that vision is not only used in a feedback role. It is also used to prepare the motor system to act and therefore can act as a type of feed-forward mechanism that sends information in advance to the effectors so that an action can be accurately performed.

Before considering the role of vision in controlling movement, it is important to be aware of two components of visual function. These components relate to the reception of information in the field of vision, which is said to extend up to 200 degrees horizontally and 160 degrees vertically. One component is *central vision,* sometimes referred to as foveal or focal vision. Central vision can only process information about a stimulus pattern in small areas, having a range of about 2 to 5 degrees. The detection information in the visual field outside these limits occurs by means of *peripheral vision.* As you study this discussion about vision and motor control, you will find that

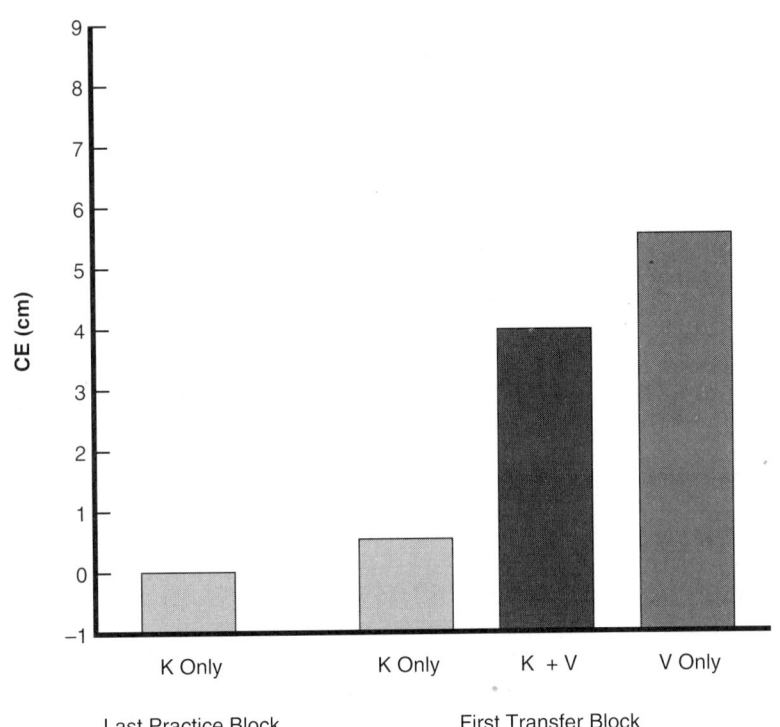

FIGURE 3.2-1 Results from the experiment by Reeve, Mackey, and Fober showing the CE results for practicing a limb position with kinesthetic feedback (K only) available and then performing under transfer conditions without KR and either kinesthetic (K) and/or vision (V) available.

one important issue concerns the relative functions of the components of vision.

Vision Predominates the Sensory Feedback Systems

When all sensory systems are available to us, we tend to use and trust vision the most. For example, when you first learned to type or play the piano, you undoubtedly felt that if you could not see your fingers hit each key, you could not perform accurately. Beginning dancers have a similar problem. Many times they feel that they cannot perform accurately if they cannot watch their feet. In other motor skills like these, we only feel comfortable when we can see our limbs carry out the required movement.

Research evidence demonstrates our tendency to allow vision to predominate over the other sensory systems. For example, in a study by Reeve, Mackey, and Fober (1986), blindfolded subjects

practiced a limb-positioning skill. After having practiced this skill, with KR provided about the error for each trial, the subjects performed 9 trials without KR in one of three transfer conditions. In the kinesthetic feedback-only condition, subjects continued to perform the positioning response without vision. In the kinesthetic plus visual feedback condition, subjects were allowed to perform the positioning response with vision available. The third group, the visual feedback-only condition, did not make a limb-positioning movement but watched the experimenter move the handle of the apparatus and verbally indicated where the experimenter should stop the handle as he moved it along the trackway. The results (see Figure 3.2–1) indicated that when vision was available, subjects greatly overshot the target. Thus, subjects relied on vision when it was available even though the appropriate source of information for performing the skill was proprioceptive feedback. And visual feedback provided inappropriate information that led them to performing more poorly than if they had not attended to it.

These results fit very well with the dominant role given vision by Posner, Nissen, and Klein (1976) in a general review of research about vision and its role in processing information. There seems to be little doubt that we assign vision a very special place in our daily activities. Unless we have learned to do otherwise, such as in touch typing or playing the piano, we will attend to visual information whenever possible to guide our movements.

The knowledge that vision tends to dominate the other sensory feedback systems does little to help us understand the role of vision in movement control, however. In the following sections, we will look specifically at some examples of research directed at uncovering how vision is involved in controlling movement.

Visual Search Strategies in Motor Skill Decision Making

In many daily activities as well as in many sport activities, visual search is an important part of making decisions about appropriate actions. **Visual search** is actively looking for information in the environment that will enable the performer to determine what to do in a situation. This search is especially critical in situations where there is a limited amount of time available for making an appropriate decision and response. In these situations, people gain an advantage by successfully anticipating what will occur and preparing an appropriate action accordingly. The success of this anticipation depends on being able to select critical environmental cues in advance so that the performer can anticipate action requirements. Thus, visual search is an important element in performing in "time pressure" situations.

An example of a time pressure situation occurs when driving a car in a busy street. To successfully drive the car, the driver must determine

where to steer, when to accelerate or decelerate, or when to brake. The cues that provide the advance information to allow the driver to perform these actions can come from a variety of places, such as from other cars, people, and so on. And within one of these cue sources, there are several locations for important cues, such as the driver's head or eyes, the movement of the steering wheel, the movement of the front wheels, and so on. The driver, therefore, must visually search these sources to find the appropriate cues that will give him or her enough time to perform whatever driving actions are necessary.

A similar need for visual search exists for decision-making in many sport performance situations where there are many sources providing possible cues and there is a limited amount of time for searching for and selecting the correct cues. For example, to return a serve in tennis, a serve traveling at 40 to 45 m/sec allows the receiver only 500 to 600 msec for determining how to respond. The player must search for the cues that will provide information about the direction, speed, landing point, and bounce characteristics of the ball so that an appropriate return stroke can be selected, organized, and executed. It is clearly to the player's advantage to determine this information about the serve as early as possible in the serving action or the ball flight.

These two examples of visual search situations illustrate how anticipatory decisions must be made so that a person can successfully perform the skill. As these examples have shown, the decisions will be determined in large part by the effectiveness of the visual search strategies used by the performer. Fortunately, our knowledge about effective search strategies is increasing; there is a growing body of research literature concerning visual search strategies in skill performance situations such as the ones just described. The evidence is consistent in showing that these strategies become more effective as skill level develops, a point that was discussed in Concept 2.2, in which performance changes during learning were considered.

Next we will look at some common research procedures used to answer questions about visual search strategies. Then some examples will be described to demonstrate visual search strategies employed by people performing in various contexts.

Procedures for investigating visual search in motor skills. To address questions about visual search strategies and the information used to make action decisions based on this search, researchers have developed three experimental procedures that are popular for addressing these questions. You were briefly introduced to these in Concept 2.2 when we discussed changes in visual attention that result from practice and becoming more expert at performing a motor skill.

Two of these procedures involve *film simulation* of a skill performance situation where a subject is asked to observe a film, video, or series of slides, in which the skill performance environment is presented. The person is asked to perform specific responses to what is observed as if he or she were actually in that situation. Consider the tennis serve situation as an example. The subject is asked to act as if he or she is actually receiving the serve of the tennis player in the film. The subject's response is to select as quickly as possible the ball landing position on the court of the serve. The two procedures used in this film simulation relate to determining two characteristics of making the response decision. One procedure addresses the amount of time required to select the information needed to make a correct response. The other addresses the characteristics of the observed performance that are critical for providing necessary information.

To address the time issue, a *temporal occlusion procedure* is used where the film is stopped at various time periods of the action. In the tennis serve example, the film would be stopped at different times prior to, during, and after ball contact. You saw an example of this procedure in Concept 2.2 in the discussion of the experiment by Abernethy and Russell (1987), ·in which novice and expert

badmintion players were compared. Based on when a person can consistently make a correct response, the experimenter can determine what visual information is important for making the decision.

To address the movement characteristics issue, an *event occlusion procedure* is used. Various parts of each frame of film are masked so that the observer cannot see selected parts of the action. This eliminates specific visual cues to assess responding without those cues. An example of this procedure is presented in Figure 3.2–2, which is taken from the Abernethy and Russell (1987) study. The logic of this approach is that if performance is worse without a particular cue than with it, then it can be concluded that the particular visual cue is important for successful performance.

The third experimental procedure used to investigate visual attention issues in motor skills is to produce *eye movement recordings*. This procedure requires the use of specialized equipment that will track the movement of the eye and record where the eye is "looking" at a particular time. A recording can be made of the displacement of central vision for a specific time interval as well as where and for how long the person fixated their gaze while tracking. One way this approach has been used is to have the subject observe a film simulation of an action, such as the tennis serve, and make the ball-landing decision. The movement of the eye is plotted as a function of the film scene so that spatial location of eye movements (displacement) can be determined along with gaze fixation characteristics related to observing the serving action. Another way to use eye movement recording is to have people actually perform a skill in the performance setting, such as recording the eye movements of a hockey goalie while a player prepares and executes a shot on goal. This latter use is not as common as the film observation setting because the eye tracking equipment presents limitations on the extent to which the person can move, and on the accuracy of recordings that can be made while a person is moving.

3.2-2 Examples of what subjects saw in the Abernethy and Russell experiment when they watched a film of a badminton serve where various parts of the serving action were masked and could not be seen.

For the remainder of this discussion on visual search, findings from research that employs these experimental procedures will be described for several different types of motor skill performance situations.

Visual search in badminton. Abernethy and Russell (1987), whose experiment was described earlier in this discussion and in Concept 2.2, used time and event occlusion procedures in a film simulation setting. They found that the time between the initiation of the server's backswing and the shuttle hitting the floor in the receiver's court is approximately 400 msec. There appears to be a critical time window of about 166 msec that occurs 83 msec before and after racquet shuttle contact for picking up critical cues predicting where the shuttle will land. This window provides the receiver with critical information about racquet movement and shuttle flight that seem to resolve uncertainty about where the served shuttle will land. Experts appear to more effectively use the 83 msec prior to racquet-shuttle contact than novices. Hence, they are able to gain a longer amount of time for preparing their return. In particular, experts search the racquet and arm as primary sources for providing the anticipatory cues needed to prepare their own response.

Visual search in batting in baseball. An example of investigating visual search patterns by batters in baseball is a study by Shank and Haywood (1987). College and novice players viewed a videotape of a right-handed pitcher as if they were right-handed batters. Eye movements were recorded as the subjects viewed 20 pitches, which included a random presentation of fastballs and curves from both the wind-up and stretch positions. The subjects' task was to verbally indicate if the pitch were a fastball or curve. The expert players correctly identified almost every pitch whereas the novices were correct only about 60% of the time. Both groups showed they did not begin to track the ball until about 150 msec after the ball left the pitcher's hand. During the wind-up, experts fixated on the release point wheras novices tended to shift fixations from release point to the pitcher's head. This shows that the expert batter knows that the most relevant information prior to the release of a pitch comes from the release point, and ignores other possible sources of information prior to the release.

Visual search in tennis. Two experiments by Goulet, Bard, and Fleury (1989) investigated visual search strategies involved in preparing to return a tennis serve. Expert and novice tennis players watched a film of a person serving and were asked to identify the type of serve as quickly as possible. The subjects' eye movements were recorded as they watched the film. Three phases of the serve were of particular interest. These were the "ritual phase" (the 3.5 sec preceding the initiation of the serve), the "preparatory phase" (the time between the elevation of the arm for the ball toss and the ball reaching the top of the toss), and the "execution phase" (from the ball toss to racquet-ball contact). During the ritual phase, the experts focused mainly on the head and the shoulder/trunk complex, where general body position cues could be found. During the preparatory phase, visual search was directed primarily around the racquet and ball, where it remained until ball contact. Interestingly, the experts also looked at the server's feet and knees during the

preparatory phase. These search patterns allowed the expert players to make more correct serve identification decisions sooner than novices.

Visual search in soccer. Characteristics of visual search patterns of expert and novice soccer players were investigated by Helsen and Pauwels (1990). Subjects observed slides of a typical attacking situation and then had to respond as quickly as possible whether the ball handler should shoot at the goal, dribble around the goalkeeper or opponent, or pass to a teammate. Eye movement recordings were used to describe the visual search patterns of the participants. Consistent with expectations, the experts took less time to make their decisions. The primary reason for this was that the experts determined critical cues for making their decision more quickly than novices. One way the experts did this was by fixating on fewer features of the scene and by spending less time at each fixation. This is especially important because there were no appreciable differences in visual search patterns for the experts and novices.

Visual search in volleyball. Ripoll (1988) used eye movement recordings of national volleyball coaches and players to determine visual search characteristics related to determining the information used to predict the kind of set that should be carried out in a particular situation. These subjects observed film sequences from a match between two world-class women's volleyball teams. The sequences all began 2 sec before a serve and ended with a freeze frame on the highest point of the pass to the setter. The coaches and the players, who were spikers and setters, had clearly distinct visual search characteristics. Coaches and setters were more closely aligned than were spikers with either coaches or setters.

Coaches tended not to watch the ball trajectory but rather viewed the defenders and block setup. And they typically ignored the receiver of the serve but observed events related to attackers' and defenders' movement and alignment. Setters showed similar visual search patterns although they watched the ball more than did the coaches.

Through their visual search strategies, spikers showed that they had less tactical comprehension than did the coaches and setters. Spikers typically only followed the path of the ball and neglected information about defensive and attack alignments of the receiving team. But the visual search characteristics differentiating setters and spikers specialized position requirements. Ripoll speculated that because spikers are primarily responsible for concluding the action, they do not develop tactical options that must be developed by setters. Ball trajectory provides spikers with the information needed to produce the appropriate coincident timing action required by the spike. Setters, on the other hand, need to make tactical decisions that require awareness of opposing team defensive and attacking patterns. Thus, the visual search patterns for spikers and setters reveal searches for the information specific to the unique requirements of each position.

Visual search in driving a car.   In a study of novice and experienced drivers, Mourant and Rockwell (1972) had subjects drive a 2.1 mi neighborhood route and a 4.3 mi freeway route. The novices were students in a driver education class. Students' eye movements were recorded while they drove. The results showed that novice drivers concentrated their eye fixations in a smaller area as they gained driving experience. The novices looked closer in front of the car and more to their right than the experienced drivers (note that this study was done in England). This indicates that novices have a smaller scanning range while driving than do experts, thus increasing the likelihood of not detecting important cues in the environment. And the novices made pursuit eye movements on the freeway whereas experienced drivers made specific eye fixations. That is, experts know what cues are important and specifically search for those cues. Experienced drivers looked into the rear and side view mirrors more frequently than the novices while the novices looked at the speedometer more than the experienced drivers.

This study by Mourant and Rockwell is consistent with other studies of driver visual search strategies. There is general agreement that environmental information must actively be searched by vision so that circumstances requiring emergency action can be detected. And visual search is needed so that regular driving activities, such as moving through an intersection, entering a freeway, and passing another vehicle, can be accomplished effectively and safely.

Training visual search.   One of the striking similarities in many of the experiments described in the preceding sections is that there are many examples of novices and experts showing no visual search pattern differences as they seek information to help them make an action decision. This indicates that in many situations, training the novice to look at the correct places for relevant cues is not necessary. But when experts have distinct visual search strategies, the question for instructors is, Can visual search strategies be taught so that novices can begin to pick up the same types of information as experts?

One approach to improving visual search has been to provide visual training to improve visual acuity, focal vision, and peripheral vision. However, there is little reason to expect this type of training to be effective. As Abernethy (1986) described, there is very little, if any, difference between novices and experts in terms of these "hardware" components of vision. And the evidence supporting training programs designed to enhance vision components appears to have limited research support indicating their effectiveness.

A training approach that appears to have merit for improving visual search in sport activities involves using film and video procedures where the links between early cues and eventual outcome can be shown. One way to accomplish this would be to use the same temporal occlusion technique described earlier. By having the film or video stop at specific times and by requiring the person to specify what will result from the action, links can be developed between what the person observes at different times and the action outcomes of those observed cues. An example of a beneficial video-based training program was reported by Christina, Barresi, and Shaffner (1990). They provided a case study of one football linebacker and showed that this player's response speed was improved as he developed better cue selection capabilities developed through video-based training. Similarly, Burroughs (1984) showed that film simulation training helped improve the batting performance of baseball players.

Another effective training procedure involves providing visual search drills that are based on simulating visual search demands of a situation in a simpler context. An example of this approach was provided in an experiment by Shapiro and Raymond (1989), in which they reported benefits of visual search training for enhancing performance on a video game. The training program was designed to minimize eye movements and optimize search characteristics, which was beneficial for performing the game because many visual stimuli were involved requiring detection so that appropriate action could be taken. The training program consisted of several drills that required subjects to perform simple tasks requiring visual search strategies that were similar to those they would use in the complex video game. One drill trained subjects not to make eye movements to peripherally appearing objects but to use peripheral vision to detect these objects. Thus, when the specific visual search demands of a situation are known, it is possible to provide training drills that simulate those demands and allow a person to effectively transfer skills acquired in the drills to an actual, more complex situation.

Finally, it is important to note that questions exist about the effectiveness of instructions to novices that emphasize "what to look for" as they carry out their search procedures. It appears that much of the specific information picked up by experts during their visual search is developed through years of practice, with little awareness of the specific cues being seen. We will address this awareness issue more specifically in Concept 4.2.

The Role of Vision in Controlling Movement

In addition to being involved in searching the environment for cues on which to base action decisions, vision is also involved in the control of the action itself. This control involvement may occur prior to the initiation of any movement as well as during the action. Because vision is a part of movement control for many different motor skills, it is best discussed in the context of different motor skill performance situations.

Vision and manual aiming tasks. A manual aiming task requires rapid movement of an arm over a prescribed distance to a target. In an experimental setting, a subject usually holds a stylus on a starting point and then, when told to move, lifts the stylus from that point and moves it to hit the target as accurately as possible. Some experiments require the subject to move as quickly as possible while others require the subject to move at a specific speed. These laboratory aiming tasks are designed to simulate motor skill situations that are a part of daily living activities as well as of sport, military, and industrial tasks. For example, an assembly line worker may be required to pick up an item from a conveyer belt and quickly place it in a carton in which the item just fits. Or a person may be walking along a pathway that requires accurate foot placement on stepping stones. In these situations vision plays an important role in the control of the action.

Based on a long history of research about manual aiming movements, Abrams, Meyer, and Kornblum (1990) described three generally accepted phases of an aimed limb movement. The first phase is the **movement preparation phase,** which begins as soon as the decision has been made to produce the movement to the target. Several types of information from vision appear to be involved here. One of these is determining information about the current position of the limb. Another is determining information about the target location and characteristics. The second phase is the **initial impulse phase,** in which the actual movement is begun as the limb is propelled in the general direction of the target. This phase is typically ballistic, where vision, if it plays any role, may provide some immediate limb movement information that can be used later for error correction purposes. The third phase is the **error correction phase** where attempts are made to minimize error between the current position of the limb and the target. This phase is very dependent on visual feedback about the position of the limb and its relation to the target.

Research investigating manual aiming tasks has shown that in order to fully understand the role of vision in controlling manual aiming skills, several factors need to be taken into account. These include the duration of the movement, the certainty of the availability of vision, and whether the preferred limb is used to perform the action. Each of these factors will be considered in the remainder of the discussion of this section.

There is strong evidence to indicate that the error correction phase of aimed limb movements occurs only when the *duration of the limb movement* is longer than a certain amount of time. The specific amount of time appears to be an arguable point, as you will see from the examples of research addressing this question. However, there is agreement that this amount of time is related to the amount of time required to use visual feedback to "home in" on the target and to make the movement adjustments needed to accurately hit the target. One of the benefits of investigating this issue is that we can gain insight into the amount of time visual feedback requires for processing.

The classic experiment showing the relationship of the duration of the aiming movement and the use of visual feedback was reported by Keele and Posner (1968). Subjects moved a stylus from a starting point to one of two targets one-quarter inch in diameter and 6 inches away. Subjects were trained to make their movements in as close as possible to 150, 250, 350, and 450 msec. On half of the trials, the lights were turned off as soon as the subjects left the starting point. On the other half of the trials, the lights remained on throughout. If visual feedback is needed to perform the final error corrections, having the lights turned off should seriously affect accuracy. The results showed that the lights-off condition did not affect movements that took approximately 190 msec or less to execute, but did impair accuracy for movements lasting longer than 260 msec. These results indicate that when aiming movements are of short duration, lasting less than 190 msec, the entire action is programmed in advance and is controlled on an open-loop basis. However, when aiming movements are of longer duration, the error correction phase can occur and the action is completed by using visual feedback.

From experiments such as the one by Keele and Posner, researchers have speculated about the amount of time required to use visual feedback. Based on the Keele and Posner results, the time needed for effectively using visual feedback is between 190 and 260 msec. However, this amount of time has been questioned. For example, a series of experiments by Zelaznik, Hawkins, and Kisselburgh (1983) showed that there were beneficial effects of using vision for movements lasting less than 200 msec. It seems safe to assume that for visual feedback to affect changes in arm movements, approximately 150 to 260 msec is required.

Another approach to the role of visual feedback in the control of aiming movements was reported by Smith and Bowen (1980). By using cameras and mirrors, they either distorted visual information about the movement to the right by 10° or delayed the visual information by 66 msec. This was accomplished by having the subjects see their hand movements only by watching a monitor. As can be seen in Figure 3.2–3, both forms of distortion decreased aiming accuracy. However, as in the studies we considered earlier, the distance moved or the length of time required to complete the movement had different effects on accuracy.

Based on what we have discussed so far, the evidence indicates that for longer duration movements, vision is primarily important during the preparation and termination of the movement. If this is so, then eliminating vision during the first

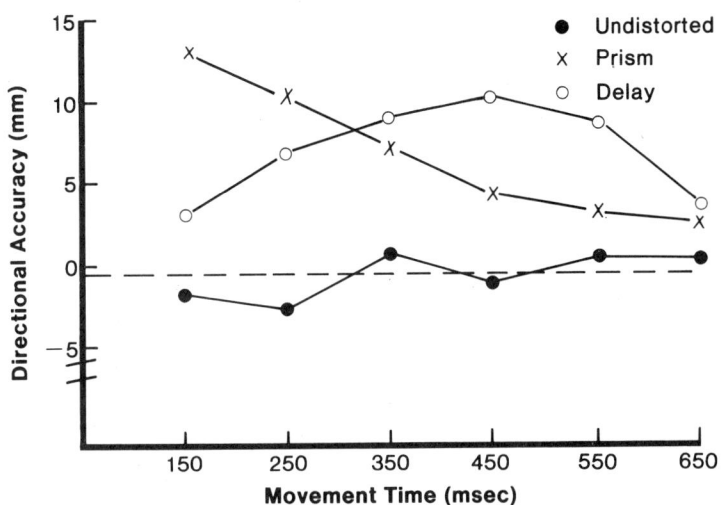

FIGURE 3.2-3 Directional accuracy (CE) results from the Smith and Bowen experiment where subjects practiced aiming movements of different movement times under three different vision conditions.

half of an aiming response should not alter accuracy, whereas eliminating it during the latter half should lead to increased inaccuracy. This hypothesis has been supported by several investigators. For example, Carlton (1981) found that when a movement lasted between 364 and 440 msec, seeing the initial 50% of the limb movement was not important for target accuracy. Further support can be seen in an experiment by Moore (1984) in which the availability of vision was systematically varied during the initial 25%, 50%, 55%, 60%, 65%, and 100% of a 400 msec aiming movement. Results showed that aiming error did not increase when vision was not available for the first 50% of the response, while for all other conditions accuracy decreased dramatically. Beaubaton and Hay (1986) reported an experiment in which they included a condition in which visual information about the termination of the response was blocked. As in Moore's, their results showed that vision of the initial phase of the movement was not crucial for aiming accuracy, whereas vision of the final phase was strongly related to accuracy.

Evidence that the *degree of certainty about the availability of vision* during the aiming movement is influential in the role of vision in controlling the aiming movement was demonstrated in a series of experiments by Elliott and Allard (1985). They showed that, similar to the results described

earlier from the experiment by Zelaznik, Hawkins, and Kisselburgh (1983), rapid use of visual feedback was most pronounced when subjects knew in advance that the lights would be on during the response. In the Elliott and Allard experiment, when subjects knew before a trial began that the lights would be on, movements of 225 msec benefited from having vision available. However, when subjects did not know if the lights would be on or off, their error increased when the lights were on and decreased when the lights were off. Thus, certainty about what the vision conditions will be during the aiming response influences the use of vision. If there is uncertainty, fast movements will typically be programmed in advance and performed in an open-loop manner, whereas slower movements will require visual feedback to terminate the movement.

Finally, a finding about the role of vision in the control of an aiming movement that deserves some consideration is the fact that there is a *performance advantage for the preferred hand* (Flowers, 1975; Roy, 1983). The important motor control question here is, Why does this hand advantage occur? With respect to our discussion on vision, one possible reason is that visual information during movement is processed more efficiently for the preferred hand. To test this possibility, Roy and Elliott (1986) had subjects perform rapid aiming movements (100–400 msec) with the lights on or off. For movements that were made very rapidly, that is, in less than 200 msec, there was no difference between the condition of lights on or off, although there was a preferred hand accuracy advantage. Because the presence or absence of visual information during movement did not influence the hand advantage, it seems likely that the handedness advantage explanation in these aiming tasks is inappropriate. However, a vision-based explanation is still a possibility. Turning the lights off after a movement has been initiated does not remove the possibility that visual information about the required response can be obtained *before* the response is initiated. Thus, the hand advantage could be due to more efficient processing of visual information related to that hand, but the processing may occur before movement initiation rather than during. However, research is needed in this area because the cause for the preferred hand advantage in aiming movements remains undetermined.

Vision and prehension.   **Prehension** is the reaching and grasping of an object that may be stationary or moving. Usually, we reach for and grasp an object in order to do something with it. For example, we reach for and grasp a cup in order to drink from it. Or, we reach for and grasp a pen to pick it up so we can put it in our pocket or write with it. It would be very difficult to get along in our everyday activities if we did not have control of prehension skills. Vision is clearly involved in these activities.

It appears that the action of reaching and grasping a stationary object is composed of four components. The first component is the *transport component,* in which the arm transports the hand toward the target object. Then, there is the *hand orienting component,* in which the hand is oriented in the correct position to grasp the object. Third is the *grasp component,* which involves the control of the fingers and thumb to grasp the object. Finally, there is the *lift component,* in which the grasped object is moved to accomplish the goal of the reach and grasp action. Research activity has focused primarily on variables that influence these components. Evidence has shown that object characteristics, such as size, shape, and texture; situation characteristics, such as object location and orientation; and task requirements, such as speed of the movement, and what the person needs to do with the object, all influence these components. Certain variables affect one component but not others. For example, the distance to the object affects the transport component but not the grasp component. On the other hand, the size of the object affects the grasp component but not the transport component. And, the texture of the object affects the lift component but not the other components (see Weir, Mackenzie, Marteniuk, & Cargoe, 1991, for further discussion of how different variables influence the components of prehension).

To reach for and grasp an object, a person lifts their arm and moves their hand toward the object and then begins to shape the hand according to the object characteristics, while the arm is moving. The initial grasping of the object involves fine tuning the finger and thumb opening and the force used to grip the object. According to a control model developed by Marc Jeannerod (1981) of France, vision is involved in the prehensile movement by assessing the observable object characteristics and then presetting the motor control system to initiate and move the arm and hand toward the object. Thus, an open-loop control process that is based on advance visual information establishes where the arm must go, how the hand must be shaped, and how much force should be applied to get to the object, grasp it, and pick it up. If there is sufficient time, vision can provide "homing-in" information to enable the hand to accurately get to the object and grasp it. Once the object is initially grasped, tactile feedback provides the necessary information to make needed adjustments to continue the course of action. Thus, the role of vision in prehension is very similar to what was described earlier for manual aiming skills.

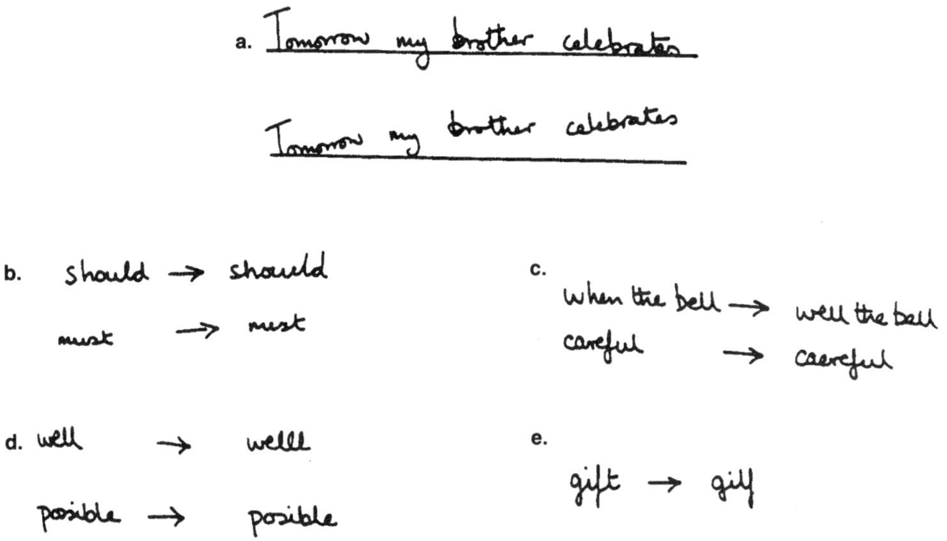

FIGURE 3.2-4 Handwriting examples from the experiment by Smyth and Silvers showing errors related to writing without vision available (bottom line in (a); right side of arrows in others) compared to writing with vision available. (a) shows errors as deviating from the horizontal; (b) shows errors as adding and deleting strokes; (c) shows adding and deleting letters; (d) shows adding or deleting repetitions of double letters; (e) shows reversing letters.

Vision and handwriting. While there has been a great deal of research activity directed toward understanding how the motor control system is involved in controlling handwriting, very little effort has been given to investigating the role of vision. Based on a review of available research evidence, Smyth and Silvers (1987) indicate that vision plays an important role in controlling handwriting actions. They cite evidence showing that when a person is asked to write with eyes closed, extra strokes are added to some letters, strokes are omitted from some letters, and some letters are duplicated. And if visual feedback is delayed while a person is writing, many errors occur, including repeating and adding letters. Based on their own research and that of others, Smyth and Silvers proposed that vision performs two distinct functions in the control of handwriting. One function is the overall spatial arrangement of words on a horizontal line. As you can see in Figure 3.2–4, when vision was not available, people deviated from a horizontal line. The second function for

vision is to help produce accurate handwriting patterns, such as the appropriate strokes and letters required for the written material. You can see evidence for this role of vision in Figure 3.2–4 where people who wrote without vision available added or omitted strokes, added extra letters, deleted letters, and reversed some letters. Thus, visual feedback is seen as an essential part of controlling handwriting.

Vision and manual tracking. If a person is trying to maintain a cursor contact with a target cursor by manipulating a joystick or lever, vision becomes an obvious part of the process. However, what is not so obvious is how vision operates in the performance of this manual tracking skill. One possibility is that vision acts as a *feedback* device by assessing the error between the two cursors and providing information necessary to correct that error. Another possibility is that visual information is used as a *feed-forward* device to predict target cursor position so that the person can anticipate where the cursor is going and move accordingly. A third possibility is that by observing the target movement over many practice trials, the person is able to memorize the pattern and therefore controls his or her own cursor on the basis of *memory*. Evidence exists supporting all three roles for vision in tracking situations. The distinguishing feature that determines which role is played by vision appears to lie in the characteristics of the tracking situation.

An experiment that compared several different manual tracking characteristics, and demonstrated how the role of vision was specific to certain characteristics was reported by Weir, Stein, and Miall (1989). When the target cursor followed unpredictable pathways, vision acted as a feedback device and followed the target cursor. When the cursor followed a predictable pathway that could be seen, vision was used in a feed-forward way by providing advance information about where the cursor was going. And if the cursor followed a very regular, predictable pattern, where the same pathway was repeated several times, subjects memorized the pattern and performed on that basis. The smallest amount of tracking error was found for this latter situation.

Vision and locomotion.   Although the study of locomotion has been popular in a variety of areas of science, the study of the role of vision in the control of locomotion does not have a long history. One of the first attempts to show that locomotion is controlled by information picked up by the visual system was made by David Lee at Edinburgh University in Scotland. Lee (1974, 1976) argued that locomotion is visually guided by what he called "time-to-contact" information on the retina of the eye. More specifically, Lee meant that as a person walks or runs closer to an object, the object becomes a larger image on the retina. When this retinal image reaches a certain size, it triggers specific action to produce the appropriate locomotor response so that the person can either avoid the object or step on the object. In fact, Lee showed that an optic variable could be described mathe-

matically by a function he termed **tau,** which specifies time to contact with an object (see Lee, 1980, for a further description of the derivation of tau).

With respect to controlling locomotion, Lee argued that the optic variable tau modifies one parameter of the gait action, the vertical impulse, to cause the appropriate locomotor response. This means that vision provides *time-based,* rather than distance-based, information to the motor control system to establish when a particular action should occur to allow accomplishment of the task goal.

An example of research evidence supporting this role of vision in controlling locomotion can be seen in an experiment by Lee, Lishman, and Thomson (1984). Skilled long jumpers were used in this study because they require regulated step lengths to be successful. In long jumping, the athlete runs down a long trackway and must accurately strike a takeoff board. The closer the jumper is to the edge of the board nearest the jumping pit, the better jumping distance can be attained. In this study, step length characteristics of three highly skilled female long jumpers were observed throughout their approaches to the takeoff board. These athletes used an 18–stride takeoff, a 19–stride takeoff, and a 21–stride takeoff. By filming and analyzing stride-length changes as each athlete approached and contacted the takeoff board for a series of 6 long jumps, certain observable characteristics suggested how the gait patterns required for the approach and takeoff were controlled.

Results obtained from one the these athletes (an Olympic level performer) are presented in Figure 3.2–5. There are several things to notice about her performance that are represented in the figure. First, notice that her stride length increased for the first five to six strides and then began to become similar for the next six strides. Also, although not included in this figure, these strides were relatively consistent across the six jumps. Then, on the final six strides, something different began to occur. The athlete began to make stride length adjustments so she could accurately hit the board. In fact, almost 50% of these adjustments were

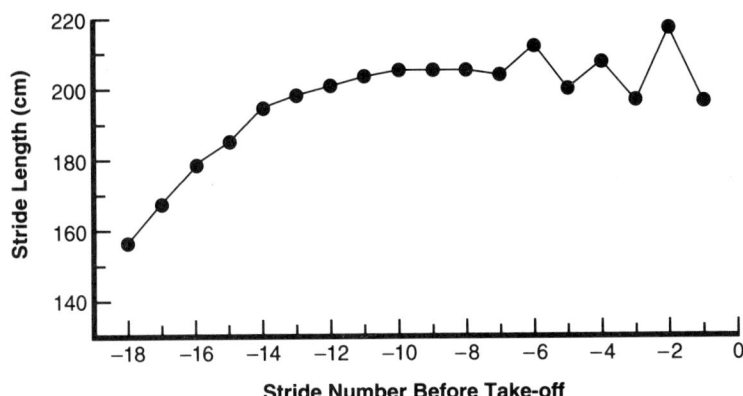

FIGURE 3.2-5 Results of the experiment by Lee, Lishman, and Thomson showing the stride length characteristics (top) and the standard errors for 6 long jumps by an Olympic class female long jumper.

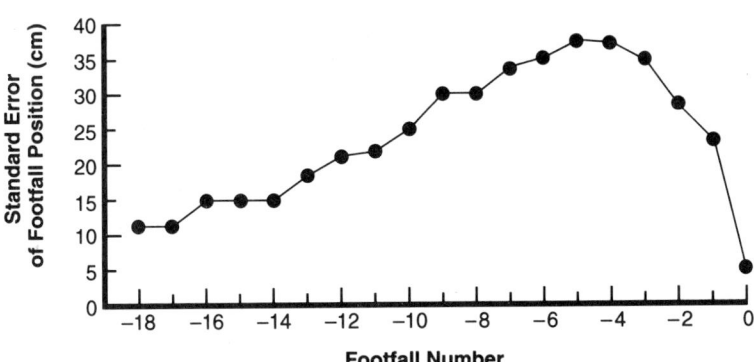

made on the last stride. A look at the bottom part of the figure indicates why these adjustments had to be made. As the athlete ran down the track, small inconsistencies in each stride had a cumulative effect so that by 5 strides from the board, the standard error had risen to 37 cm, which would have led to a large error in hitting the board had she not adjusted her stride lengths on the remaining strides before hitting the board. These characteristics led the authors to describe the long jump run-up as consisting of two phases, an initial accelerative phase where stereotypic stride patterns are produced, and a zeroing-in phase where stride patterns are adjusted to eliminate error that has accumulated, so that hitting the takeoff board as accurately as possible can occur.

The authors contend that the stride length adjustments in the second phase were made by the athlete adjusting the vertical component of her stride to make error corrections. This correction process was based on visual information obtained in advance of these strides. That is, to accommodate for the need to correct the future error at the take-off board, the visual system picked up information from the board about time-to-contact and directed the final adjustments needed to contact the board as accurately as possible. It is worth noting that similar stride-length adjustments occurring only close to the target have been found in walking, when the goal is to walk a given distance to a target line and to step on the target with a specified foot (Laurent & Thomson, 1988).

Other experiments have also demonstrated that gait action is adjusted during locomotion on the basis of time-to-contact visual information. For example, Warren, Young, and Lee (1986) simulated walking or running through a cluttered environment where the subject must step very precisely, as when crossing a creek on rocks or navigating along a wooded, rocky path. Here again, step lengths were adjusted so that each step could be correctly made.

The vault in women's gymnastics was demonstrated by Meeuwsen and Magill (1987) to be mediated by time-to-contact information in a way similar to what was shown for long jumping. To perform a vault, an additional accuracy demand is required because the gymnast must hit the spring board with the feet and hit the horse with the hands. Mark (1987) showed that visual information guides the required actions for stair climbing. And Warren (1987) reported evidence that vision guides walking through apertures, such as different-sized doorways. Instead of being time-to-contact related, the critical variable assessed by vision-guiding action in these last two activities was the ratio between the size of the door opening or the stair step height and the shoulder width or the leg length of the individual. (See Patla, 1989, for a good overview of issues related to the visual control of locomotion.)

One further issue that needs to be addressed is whether or not visual information must be continuous during locomotion to achieve accurate contact with a target. You saw earlier in this discussion that for rapid aiming tasks performed with the arm, continuous visual information was not necessary; the task could be performed just as accurately with the lights on as with the lights off. A similar conclusion was made by Thomson (1983) regarding walking to specific target locations in the environment. As in the manual-aiming tasks, Thomson showed that there is a time limit for which continuous visual information is not needed. In his experiments, subjects first observed and walked to a target point on a path. These target points were located 3, 6, 9, and 12 meters from the subjects' starting point. The subjects were

then asked to close their eyes and walk to the target point. Results showed that subjects were able to do this with little difficulty for distances as far away as 21 meters with fewer than 8 seconds required to reach the target. When more than 8 seconds elapsed, target accuracy diminished.

More recently, concern has been raised about the time limit established by Thomson's results. For example, Elliott (1986; Elliott, Calvert, Jaeger, & Jones, 1990) has conducted several experiments that have failed to find evidence for a critical 8-second time limit. He argues that error increases quickly after only 1 or 2 seconds. Thus, Elliott has argued that continuous visual information is required during locomotion when the goal is to make contact with a specific target a certain distance away. Clearly more research is needed to resolve this question, which is important in that it relates well to the work of David Lee discussed earlier and it provides information about the interaction of visually detected information and memory.

Vision and jumping from heights. Jumping from a platform to the floor is another skill in which evidence has been provided supporting the view that the optical variable tau triggers specific preparatory actions so that an action goal can be achieved. In an experiment by Sidaway, McNitt-Gray, and Davis (1989) subjects jumped from three different heights, .72 m, 1.04 m, and 1.59 m. The subjects were instructed to land with both feet on a force plate on the floor at which they were to direct their visual attention throughout the jump. A unique characteristic of this experiment is that the EMG activity of the rectus femoris was measured so that the onset of this prime mover muscle could be assessed in relation to the distance the person was from landing on the floor. The logic here was that according to Lee's view of the role of the optical variable tau as a triggering mechanism for a certain action, there should be a specific relationship between tau and the onset of the rectus femoris, regardless of the height of the jump. The results of this experiment support this prediction. Thus, the control of the onset of the

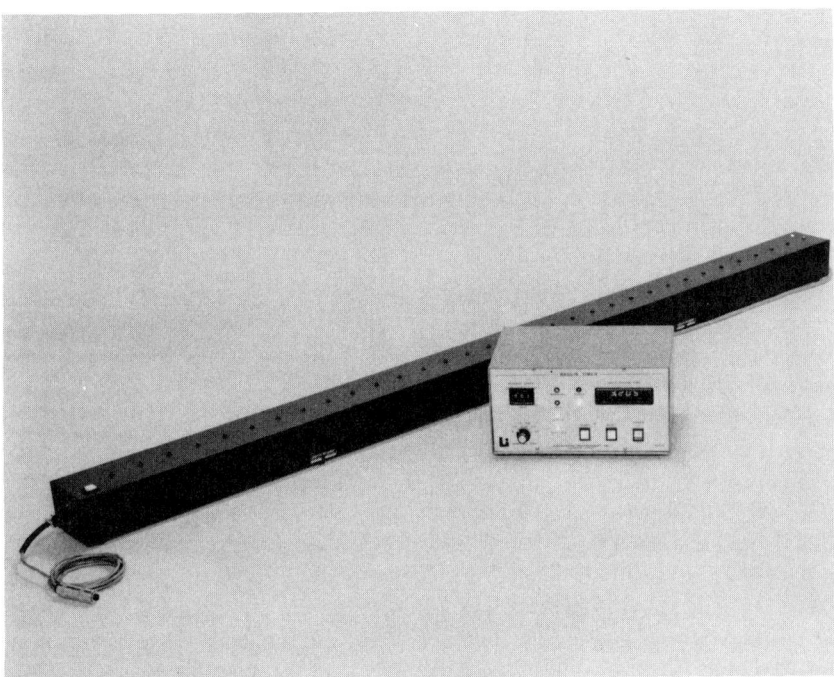

FIGURE 3.2-6 The Bassin anticipation timing apparatus.

muscle activity required for jumping from different heights was mediated by the optical variable tau, indicating a critical role for vision in the control of performing this skill.

Vision and laboratory anticipation timing tasks. An anticipation timing task involves common skills such as hitting a pitched baseball, catching a pitched ball, walking through a crowd, walking across a busy street, and passing another car while you are driving in traffic. In each of these situations, a person must accurately time his or her own movements with the action of another object. In an earlier section in this discussion, we considered several of these types of skills in terms of the visual search that is involved in making the anticipatory decisions about what to do and when to initiate the action. In this section and in several to follow, we will consider the role played by vision in the control of the action required in an anticipation timing skill. Before discussing this issue for specific "real world" motor skills, it will be helpful

to consider what is known about vision and anticipation timing skill control based on controlled laboratory studies.

In the laboratory, anticipation timing experiments involve having subjects perform laboratory simulations of real world anticipation timing skills. For example, Slater-Hammel (1960) used a clock on which one revolution of the sweep hand was one second. The stimulus was the sweep hand on the clock. The target was the *8* on the clock. The subject's task was to release a telegraph key to try to stop the sweep hand at the target. A more popular task has been the Bassin anticipation timer, which is shown in Figure 3.2–6, or some variation of this commercially available apparatus. To perform this task, a subject views a runway of lights that appear one after the other according to a preset time. As each light goes on in rapid succession, there is a simulation of motion. The subject is seated at the end of the runway of lights and is required to depress a button at the time he or she thinks the final

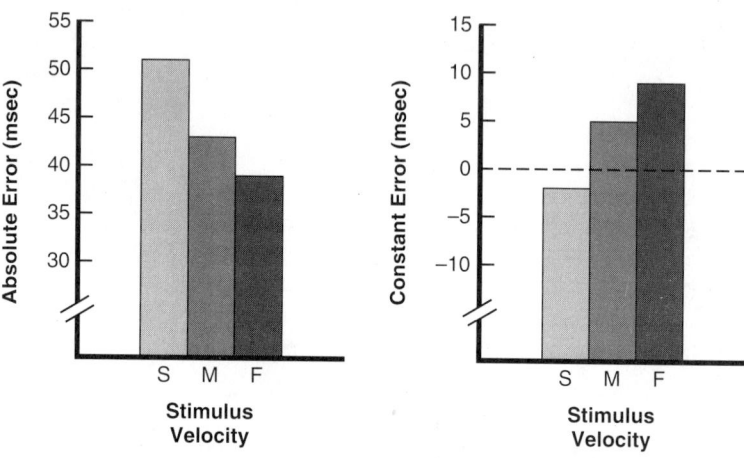

FIGURE 3.2-7 Results of the experiment by Wrisberg, Hardy, and Beitel showing effects of different stimulus velocities on anticipation timing errors. (*Velocity:* S = slow, 134.1 cm/sec; M = moderate, 223.5 cm/sec; F = fast, 312.9 cm/sec. *Distance:* S = short, 43 cm; M = medium, 73 cm; L = long, 103 cm.)

light of the runway will go on. A timer then records the difference between the time when the subject depressed the button and the time when the last runway light went on.

One consistent factor that influences anticipation timing accuracy is the *predictability of the stimulus.* Research results have typically shown that the more predictable characteristics are of the oncoming stimulus, the easier it is to make an accurate response (Christina, 1977). When used in this context, the term *predictability* refers to the consistency of the spatial and/or temporal pattern of the oncoming stimulus. A high degree of *spatial* consistency occurs when the oncoming object travels in a path that does not vary from the beginning of its flight until it reaches the target point, e.g., the point at which a ball must be hit or caught. It is easier to respond in a case such as this than when the object travels in an unpredictable flight pattern.

Temporal predictability is also involved in influencing anticipation timing accuracy. If a consistent rate of speed is maintained by the stimulus, it becomes easier to accurately time when the stimulus will arrive at the target. Finally, stimulus predictability can be related to a situation in which a number of different *stimulus events* occur in succession and require the responding individual to make a correct response to each one. In these situations, the spatial and/or temporal characteristics of the stimulus may change from one trial

to the next. The consistent effect here is that the more predictable these characteristics are from one trial to the next, the more accurate the person is in their anticipation timing response.

Another factor influencing anticipation timing success for laboratory tasks is the *rate of speed of the stimulus.* There appears to be somewhat of an inverted-U relationship between the rate of speed of an oncoming object and the response accuracy associated with intercepting that object. That is, very slow objects are more difficult to respond to accurately than are faster objects. And there is a point at which oncoming objects are moving so fast that an accurate response to them is impossible and only reaction time is involved in the response.

An example of evidence demonstrating that very slow speeds are difficult to accurately time can be seen in an experiment by Wrisberg, Hardy, and Beitel (1982) in which subjects had to respond to different runway light speeds on the Bassin anticipation timing apparatus. These speeds were 134.1 cm/sec, 223.5 cm/sec, and 312.9 cm/sec. These velocities translate into 2.2, 1.32, and 0.93 sec, respectively, of viewing time. As you can see in the results of this experiment in Figure 3.2–7, anticipation timing error became larger as the stimulus speed became slower. The slower speeds were typically undershot, i.e., early anticipation, whereas the faster speeds showed late anticipations.

In many respects, these laboratory-based results are not surprising. You have undoubtedly experienced a similar effect in performing an open skill. For example, you have probably found you have more difficulty returning a soft lob or easy, slow bound in racquetball or tennis than you have in returning a hard driving shot. The paradox of this situation seems to relate to the expectation that a person would have more time to predict the arrival of the stimulus and therefore have more opportunity to properly prepare a response for the slower moving stimulus than for the one moving more rapidly. Results of an experiment by Simon and Slaviero (1975) may provide some insight. Their results show that for performing a simple RT task involving a 2-sec foreperiod on every trial, RT was shorter when subjects were provided a series of six "countdown" lights going on every .28 sec during this interval than when no such aid was provided. Thus, the subjects did not seem to time 2 seconds very accurately. If that is indeed the case, then slower stimuli give us trouble because they lead to problems in internal timing accuracy.

Finally, *practice* has been shown to improve anticipation timing accuracy for laboratory tasks where the stimulus moves at the same rate of speed on every trial and when it moves at different rates. For example, Christina and Buffan (1976) instructed subjects to anticipate the arrival of a moving pointer on a V-belt at a target. The pointer moved at a consistent rate of 161.27 cm/sec on every trial. Absolute error averaged 63 msec on the first block of 10 trials. By the last block of the 150 trials, error had been reduced to only 30 msec. In the experiment by Wrisberg, Hardy, and Beitel (1982) discussed earlier, three different movement speeds were used across the 180 practice trials. While the actual improvement scores were not reported, it was reported that subjects showed a significant improvement in accuracy during the practice trials.

Now that we have considered laboratory anticipation timing tasks, we can shift our attention to anticipation timing tasks that occur in everyday skills and in sport skills. We will look at several of these skills to consider what the research evidence indicates about the role of vision in controlling these skills.

Vision and catching. Although researchers have investigated a number of questions concerning the role of vision when the action goal is to catch an object such as a ball, we will consider only two. (See articles by von Hofsten, 1987, and by Whiting, Savelsbergh, and Faber, 1988, for more elaborate discussions of these questions as well as other questions that have been considered.) The two questions that our discussion will focus on will provide you with a good foundation for understanding the involvement of vision in the coordination and control necessary to catch an object. These questions are: How long must a person watch an object to successfully catch it? Must the person be able to see his or her hands in addition to the object to successfully catch the object? As you can readily see, these questions are similar to those asked in regard to the role of vision in the control of other actions.

A good example of research related to *how long a person must watch an object* if it is to be successfully caught can be seen in what is considered a classic experiment on this question. Whiting, Gill, and Stephenson (1970) designed a special ball that could be illuminated for specific lengths of time during its flight. The subjects sat in a dark room and were required to catch the ball as often as possible. The ball was illuminated for 0.1, 0.15, 0.2, 0.25, 0.3, and 0.4 sec during its flight. As you can see from the results shown in Figure 3.2–8, the longer the ball was illuminated, the more catches were made. However, a closer look at these results indicates that there was little difference in the number of catches made between the 0.3- and 0.4-sec conditions. This finding suggests that after an initial period, which lasts for at least 0.3 sec (or 300 msec), visual information that can be obtained from the ball is no longer critical for catching it. This, of course, only relates to a ball that will not unexpectedly change its course of flight after that period.

FIGURE 3.2-8 Results from the experiment by Whiting, Gill, and Stephenson showing the number of balls caught (out of 20) under different periods of illumination.

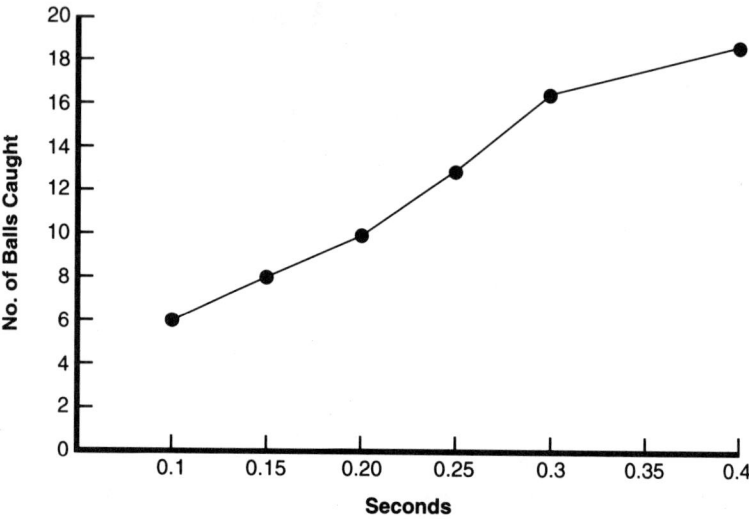

The second question to be considered related to vision and catching has generated an interesting debate in the research literature. The question is, *must a person's hands be seen throughout the flight of a ball* to successfully catch the ball? One of the first experiments developed to look at this question was reported by Smyth and Marriott (1982). They hypothesized that if the eyes are occupied with tracking the moving ball, thus preventing subjects from seeing their hands though still being able to see the ball, ball-catching accuracy should not be affected. In their experiment, a screen was designed and attached to the subjects so they could see the oncoming ball but not their hands. The results showed that when the subjects could see their hands, they averaged 17.5 catches out of 20 balls thrown. However, when they could *not* see their hands, subjects were able to catch an average of 9.2 balls out of 20. What characterized the differences in these two situations? When the hands could *not* be seen, the typical error was in positioning; that is, the subjects could not get their hands into the correct spatial position, which led to no contact between the hands and the ball. But when subjects could see their hands, the typical errors involved grasping, rather than not getting the hands into the correct spatial

position. Grasping errors occurred when subjects initiated the flexion of the fingers to grasp the ball too early and the ball hit the fingers after they had already begun to close.

Although there has been additional evidence showing that catching accuracy diminishes when a person cannot see his or her hands during the flight of a ball (e.g., Rosenberg, Pick, & von Hofsten, 1988), controversy exists concerning why this outcome occurs. For example, it could be argued that the subjects in the Smyth and Marriott experiment showed different types of errors when they could or could not see their hands because of the experience level of their subjects. This argument seems justified on the basis of evidence showing that developing the capability of effectively using peripheral vision information may be a function of age and experience (Davids, 1988). Persons with more ball-catching experience could have more accurately predicted ball arrival location and time and therefore not exhibit different types of errors under the two conditions.

An experiment by Fischman and Schneider (1985) investigated this experience argument by performing the same experimental procedures as used by Smyth and Marriott but using subjects who had at least five years experience in varsity

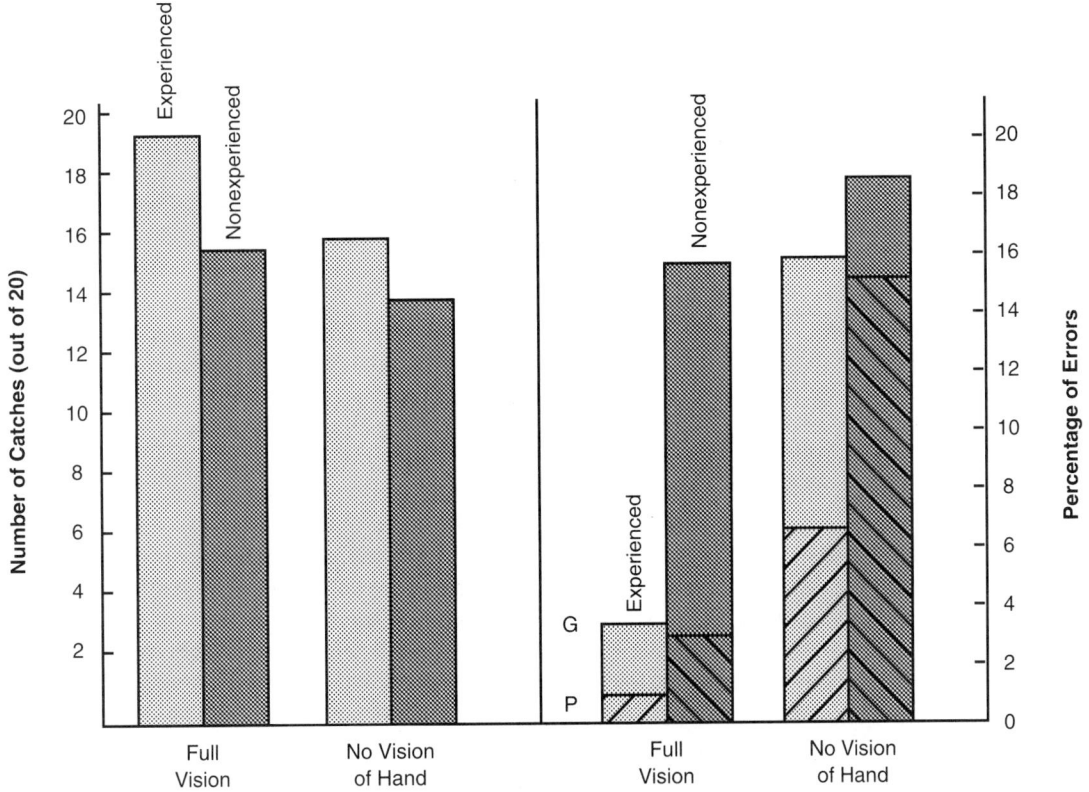

FIGURE 3.2-9 Results of the experiment by Fischman and Schneider showing the number of right-hand catches made (out of 20 chances) for experienced softball/baseball players and nonexperienced subjects, and the percentage of errors made (based on 360 attempts) by each group that were classified as positioning (P), or grasp (G) errors when subjects either could or could not see their hands.

baseball or softball. They hypothesized that these more-experienced subjects would not show diminished catching success under the condition where they could not see their hands. As you can see in the results of this experiment presented in Figure 3.2–9, while the number of catches decreased when the hands could not be seen, there was no interaction between the type of error and whether or not the hands could be seen. However, with the inexperienced subjects, positioning errors increased much more than grasp errors when the hands could not be seen.

The results of these experiments reveal features about catching an object that are similar to what was shown for prehension. First, there is an initial transport stage in which the arm and hand move toward an oncoming object. Then, there is a stage where the hand is shaped to catch the object. Finally, the fingers contact the object in a grasping stage. Evidence demonstrating these stages was shown by Williams and McCririe (1988) on the basis of movement analysis of the catching action of 11-year-old boys. These subjects attempted to catch a ball traveling 3.5 m in 850 msec with one hand. The movement analysis showed that there was no arm motion for the first 160 to 240 msec of ball flight. Then, gradual elbow flexion began, which continued slowly and uniformly for about 80% of the ball flight. The fingers began to extend at about the same time.

The hand began to withdraw from the oncoming ball until about one-half of the ball flight had elapsed. Then the upper arm accelerated about the shoulder, which resulted in the hand being transported to the spatial position required for intercepting the ball. In this study, Williams and McCririe observed that when the ball was caught, final positioning action began 80 msec earlier than when the ball was not caught. By the time 75% of the ball flight was complete (113 msec prior to contact), the hand and fingers were in a ready state for catching the ball.

There appears to be a minimum amount of object observation time necessary if each stage of catching an object is to be carried out successfully. According to work by Whiting and his associates (e.g., Whiting, Gill, & Stephenson, 1970; Sharp & Whiting, 1974, 1975) this amount of time is about 300 to 340 msec, with the 240 msec preceding the final 125 msec of object flight being the most critical time interval. This fits nicely with the findings from the Williams and McCririe experiment where catching errors increased when the hands were not in their final position to grasp the ball by approximately 113 msec prior to contact. This critical view time also fits well with results obtained by Alderson, Sully, and Sully (1974) with adults who were skilled at catching. They showed that the final stage of hand positioning begins about 150 to 200 msec before ball contact and that final finger grasping position is attained about 32 to 50 msec before contact. Thus, visual information about the ball flight must be fed forward to the musculature of the hand and fingers to prepare them to catch the ball. There must be sufficient time for this feed-forward process to occur. As a result, seeing the final portion of the ball flight will not influence catching success because there will not be sufficient time to use that information.

Thus, vision provides advance information to enable the motor control system to spatially and temporally set the arms, hands, and fingers *before* the ball arrives so that the ball can be caught. This is especially interesting with regard to the grasp phase because it shows that grasping a ball occurs

on the basis of information obtained before the ball actually makes contact with the hand, rather than on the basis of feedback obtained after the ball has hit the hand. Tactile and proprioceptive feedback become involved after contact because adjustments need to be made to the grasp. It is apparent, then, that both central and peripheral vision are operating in providing critical information necessary for catching an object.

Vision and batting in baseball and table tennis.
Just as precise time constraints are related to successful catching, so are there similar limits for successfully batting a ball. Batting in baseball and in table tennis share common characteristics with respect to the role of vision. Results from research that has investigated this skill in these two activities will provide insight into how vision interacts with the motor control system to allow successful striking of an oncoming object.

A classic experiment indicating the role of vision in successful batting in baseball was reported by Hubbard and Seng (1954). Using photographic techniques, they found that their subjects, including 25 professional baseball players, were able to track the ball only to a point at which the swing was made. This point did not seem to coincide with where contact of the ball was made. Hubbard and Seng also found that the batters tended to synchronize the start of their step forward with the release of the ball from the pitcher's hand. Additionally, the duration of the subjects' swings were remarkably consistent from swing to swing. These results were taken to indicate that all of the adjusting to the oncoming pitch was made during the 500 msec between the release of the ball from the pitcher's hand and the initiation of the swing. In this situation, then, vision provides the needed information to initiate and execute the correct bat swing. This information appears to be provided during the first one-half second of the pitch.

Some of the findings of Hubbard and Seng have been either verified or extended in research reported since their study. For example, Bahill and LaRitz (1984) closely monitored eye and head movements of a major league baseball player and several college baseball players in a laboratory situation that simulated players responding to a high-and-outside fastball thrown by a left-handed pitcher to a right-handed batter. The major league player visually tracked the ball longer than the college players. The college players tracked the ball to a point about 9 ft in front of the plate at which point their visual tracking began to fall behind the ball. The major league player kept up with the ball to a point about 5.5 ft in front of the plate before falling behind. Also, regardless of the pitch speed, the major league player followed the same visual tracking pattern and was very consistent in every stance taken to prepare for the pitch. His head position was within one degree on all pitches. Interestingly, he had slight head movements while tracking the ball but never moved his body.

In a study of five top table tennis players in The Netherlands, Bootsma and van Wieringen (1990) amplified the conclusion by Hubbard and Seng that batters are consistent in the movement time of their swing. They found, on the basis of more sophisticated movement analysis than Hubbard and Seng had available, that the table tennis players could not completely rely on consistent movement production. Players involved the visual system because evidence for tau operating in this batting skill was determined. More importantly, players seemed to compensate for differences in when they initiated their swing so that the ball could be hit as fast and as accurately as possible. For example, when time to contact was shorter at swing initiation, players compensated by applying more force during the stroke. And evidence suggests some of these players were making very fine adjustments to their swing while they were moving. Thus, while visual information may trigger the initiation of the swing and provide information about its essential characteristics, vision also provides information that can be used to make compensatory adjustments to the initiated swing, although these are very slight in terms of time and space quantities.

Finally, it is important to note that research evidence related to striking an oncoming ball indicates that batters probably never see the bat hit the ball. If they do, it is because they jumped their visual focus from some point in the ball flight to the bat contact point. Tracking the ball from pitcher's hand to bat contact or from the other racquet or paddle to contact is apparently physically impossible. However, it is worth noting that more-skilled batters watch the ball for a longer time than less-skilled players. From an instruction point of view, this suggests that the instruction to "watch the ball all the way to your bat" is a good one, even though it really can't be done. This instruction directs the individual's attention to visually tracking the ball for as long as physically possible.

Summary

Vision is involved in the control of coordinated, voluntary movement in significant ways. One way is by searching the environment for information to provide advance information to enable a person to anticipate the action required in a situation. In time pressure situations, the visual search is critical for successful performance. Examples of how visual search is carried out in motor skill situations has been discussed for badminton, baseball batting, tennis, soccer, volleyball, and driving a car. Other roles played by vision in the control of movement has been shown by discussing a variety of motor skills and describing how visual information is important for performing these skills. Skills discussed were manual aiming skills, prehensile skills, handwriting, manual tracking, locomotor skills, jumping from heights, laboratory anticipation timing skills, catching a ball, and hitting a baseball and table tennis ball. One of the consistent roles for vision in these skills involves presetting limb and body movement in accordance with the characteristics of initial limb and body position and with the characteristics of the performance environment. For skills requiring accurate limb movement, vision is involved in helping to ensure that the movement is made accurately by being the basis for providing error correction information to direct the limb to the target.

Related Readings

Abernethy, B. (1988). Visual search in sport and ergonomics: Its relation to selective attention and performer expertise. *Human Performance, 1,* 205–235.

Christina, R. W. (1977). Skilled motor performance: Anticipatory timing. In B. B. Wolman (Ed.), *International Encyclopedia of Psychiatry, Psychology, Psychoanalysis, and Neurology* (Vol. 10, pp. 241–245). New York: Van Nostrand Reinhold.

Lee, D. N. (1980). Visuo-motor coordination in space-time. In G. E. Stelmach & J. Requin (Eds.), *Tutorials in motor behavior* (pp. 281–295). Amsterdam: North-Holland.

Paillard, J. (1980). The multichanneling of visual cues and the organization of a visually guided response. In G. E. Stelmach & J. Requin (Eds.), *Tutorials in motor behavior* (pp. 259–279). Amsterdam: North-Holland.

Tyldesley, D. A. (1981). Motion prediction and movement control in fast ball games. In I. M. Cockerill & W. W. MacGillivary (Eds.), *Vision and sport* (pp. 91–115). Cheltenham, England: Stanley Thornes.

von Hofsten, C. (1987). Catching. In H. Heuer & A. F. Sanders (Eds.), *Perspectives on perception and action* (pp. 33–46). Hillsdale, NJ: Erlbaum.

CONCEPT 3.3

Motor programs are important components in the process of controlling coordinated movement

Key Terms

motor
 program
invariant
 characteristics
parameters
relative force

relative
 timing
speed-
 accuracy
 trade off

Fitts' Law
index of
 difficulty
 (ID)

Application

Several characteristics of motor skill performance continue to intrigue scholars who study the control of skills. One characteristic is that we can produce remarkably accurate and consistent movement patterns from one performance attempt to another. Another is that we are capable of performing well-learned skills with a remarkable degree of success in a variety of situations, even though we have never before been in similar situations. And it seems that we can perform many motor skills with little if any conscious thought to what we are doing during the performance of the skill.

Consider some examples illustrating these characteristics. If you have learned a dance routine very well, you are are quite capable of performing that routine many times. Each time you perform the routine, it is unlikely that an observer would detect much variation in your performance from one time to the next, unless, of course, you had purposely altered something.

If you are a skilled tennis player, you have learned the forehand stroke to a high degree of proficiency. In game situations, you will be confronted with many different situations in which you must use this stroke. What do you think are the chances that any two game situations will have every characteristic exactly the same? It can be

predicted with a high degree of certainty that this is very unlikely. Given a number of different characteristics in any situation, such as the ball flight pattern, speed, spin, bounce, location on the court, the opponent's position, your position, the wind, sun, and so on, there is little chance of any two situations being exactly alike. Yet, generally, you are quite capable of successfully hitting the ball using the forehand stroke.

Running is a relatively simple skill that most of us have performed for years. Do you really think about what you are doing as you run? Is not one of the suggestions for helping in long-distance running or jogging to run with a friend so that you can converse and keep your mind off your running? Even in the midst of intense conversation, you can keep on running until it is time to stop or until you notice something in your path that you think you must respond to by altering your running.

Each of these three examples points to a basic concept in current thinking about how we control coordinated movement. This concept is that the motor program, like a computer program, stores essential information needed to perform motor skills and provides the basis for giving commands to the motor system so that these skills can be performed in a way that will allow their action goals to be achieved. The motor program provides the basis for organizing the many degrees of freedom that must be controlled in coordinated movement and establishes a means for skills to be stored in memory in an efficient manner. The motor program will be considered in the following discussion by addressing what the motor program is like, what kinds of commands it gives, how these commands can be altered during movement, and how the program is involved in some specific examples of coordinated skill.

Discussion

The motor program is by no means a new idea; in fact, it has been known for many years. Indeed, it has appeared in various types of research literature since 1917, when Lashley used the motor program concept to describe the control of movement of one of his patients. This individual had suffered a gunshot wound in the back that destroyed the sensory neural pathways from his legs, although the motor pathways were apparently intact. Lashley found that the patient could still position his legs with "surprising accuracy" when commanded to do so, even though he could not receive any kinesthetic feedback from his legs. Previously it was thought that this peripheral feedback would be essential to control such a positioning task. However, the apparent ability to control movement in the absence of peripheral feedback led Lashley to conclude that the movement was being controlled centrally.

Lashley's demonstration provides anecdotal evidence that can be added to the empirical evidence discussed in Concept 3.1 to support claims that open-loop control of a movement is possible. What has not been discussed, however, is the means by which the movement was organized and specified by the central command center so that the movement could be controlled in an open-loop manner. In the present concept, we shall consider that organization to be a characteristic role of a motor program. And we will consider other motor program characteristics that allow complex skills to adapt features that suggest both open- and closed-loop control processes operating to control these skills.

In this discussion, rather than spend time trying to examine the theoretical arguments for and against the existence of the motor program, we shall take a less devious path. The approach we will take is to simply assume the existence of a motor program and work from there. However, such an assumption is not unfounded. As you will see, there is evidence to support the motor program notion; it is on this evidence that we acknowledge the validity of accepting the existence

of the motor program, and it is from that point that we shall move by defining it and providing some evidence for it. In doing so, we shall also try to describe how the motor program provides the basis for controlling voluntary coordinated movement. However, we should not be so closed-minded to consider that alternatives to motor program based control do not exist. In fact, one of these, the dynamic systems view, was described in Concept 3.1. This view will be considered in the present discussion by providing an alternative perspective on how coordinated movement can occur without requiring a motor program as the basis for control.

Defining the Motor Program

When a theoretical construct in science is difficult to support unequivocally on the basis of empirical research, the definition of that construct becomes critical to how the construct is viewed and investigated. The motor program appears to be one of those types of theoretical constructs. Because of this, investigating the motor program has been a perplexing problem. A big part of this problem has been that the definition of the motor program has gone through an evolution since the time Lashley presented his view. Because the definition of the motor program is such a critical part of how it is proposed to be involved in controlling coordinated movement and how it is investigated by researchers, a brief overview of the history of this definition is important for this discussion. It is worth noting that because this definition has gone through several modifications during its history, opponents of a motor program based view of motor control have often attacked definitions that have since been modified.

Earlier views. The notion of a motor program can be traced back as far as William James (1890), who argued that in order for an action to occur, all a person must do is form a clear "image" of that action. James called this an "idea-motor" action. Sir Frederick Bartlett (1932) alluded to a motor program concept when he used the term *schema* to describe internal representations and organizations of movements. However, it was K. S. Lashley (1917), who first used the term "motor program." During his career, he developed a view of the motor program as the "intention to act" that determines the sequence of events to produce a well-learned motor act (Lashley, 1951). Later, in a book that became an important turning point for investigating both cognitive and motor skill learning and control, Miller, Galanter, and Pribram (1960) presented a well-developed argument centering on the notion of a "Plan" as being responsible for controlling the sequence of events of an action. This Plan, they stated is "essentially the same as a program for a computer" (p. 16).

These examples indicate that the concept of the "programmed" control of voluntary movement has been with us for many years. However, it was not until Franklin Henry and his students at Berkeley developed a series of experiments directly related to exploring motor skill programming that the motor program concept gained a needed conceptual and empirical boost. Henry hypothesized that the "neural pattern for a specific and well-coordinated motor act is controlled by a stored program that is used to direct the neuromotor details of its performance" (Henry & Rogers, 1960, p. 449). Henry's concept of the motor program was that of a computer program, which when initiated, controls the exact movement details with essentially no modifications possible during the execution of the movement. What is significant here is not only the further development of the notion of a motor program, but the development of the concept of what the motor program is like and what it controls.

As research and theorizing about motor programs continued, the primary point of definitional change was related to the structural characteristics of the program. This issue was by no means a new one; Lashley had discussed the structure controversy in 1951. However, the development of perspectives on the structure of the motor program since the Henry and Rogers (1960) article marks the intensity of the formalized pursuit of coming to grips with an old problem. Perhaps the most formalized theorizing about the motor program following the Henry and Rogers article was by Steven Keele (1968). While his definition of the motor program did not significantly alter the view expressed by Henry, it did present a more formal version of that view which led to increased research activity directed at identifying the characteristics and operation of motor programs.

Keele (1968) defined the motor program as "a set of muscle commands that are structured before a movement sequence begins, and that allows the entire sequence to be carried out uninfluenced by peripheral feedback" (p. 387). In his discussion of this definition, Keele indicated that the motor program is *not* a movement but rather it acts to *control* movements. It should also be emphasized that the definition asserts that the movement will be *uninfluenced* by peripheral feedback. This does not mean that there is no peripheral feedback during the movement; it means that even in the presence of sensory feedback, the movement is carried out in accordance with the predetermined commands. The peripheral sensory feedback is not attended to by the performer and thus does not influence the movement sequence.

The current view. The current view of the **motor program** is best expressed by Richard Schmidt (1987, 1988). To overcome previous views limiting the motor program to specific movements or sequences of movements, Schmidt described a *generalized motor program*. The addition of the term "generalized" was intended to indicate that his definition of the motor program provided a broader scope of control for the program. Rather than being limited to controlling a specific movement or sequence, Schmidt proposed that it controls a "class of actions." A class of actions is defined as different actions having a common but unique set of features. He called these features **invariant characteristics.** These characteristics were proposed as being the "signature" of the program and as such formed the basis of the representation of the class of actions in memory. However, Schmidt also proposed that in order to produce a specific action in accordance with the demands of the performance context, the program requires other features. He called the features **parameters,** which give the generalized motor program the flexibility and adaptability that Schmidt proposed must be characteristic of an appropriate view of the motor program. We will discuss invariant characteristics and parameters in more detail later.

It is important to note how this view of the motor program differs from earlier views. The first important distinction is that this view presents that motor program as an *abstract representation of action.* That is, the motor program is not stored in memory with the specific details of a specific movement. Instead, it is stored in an abstract form of a class of actions having distinct common characteristics. This means, for example, that instead of having a motor program for every possible variation of an overhand throw to a target, the program contains certain characteristics of this action that enable one motor program to control throws of different objects, speeds, or by either arm on a windy or calm day. This feature of the motor program gives it a very flexible and adaptable quality that allows the same program to control a wide variety of movements.

Second, because the motor program is only an abstract representation of action, specific *muscles involved in an action are not an invariant feature of the motor program.* The specific muscles that need to be used to produce an intended action are a program parameter and are specified at the time the action is to be produced in accordance with the requirements of the performance situation. This means that an action can be carried out in a variety of ways and still be under the control of the same motor program. For example, you can write your name on a check, or on a blackboard, or in the sand with your foot. The current view of the motor program argues that underlying control of these actions is attributable to one program. What differs about these situations are the muscles that must be used to accomplish the goal of the action, which is to write your name.[1]

If you are interested in an in-depth discussion of this issue and evidence supporting the distinction between the sequence of events represented in the motor program and the effector system implementing that sequence, see the article by Keele, Cohen, and Ivry (1990).

A third important distinctive feature of the current view of the motor program is not included in the definition provided earlier. However, it is a critical characteristic that distinguishes the view of the motor program expressed by Schmidt from earlier definitions. The current view indicates that *feedback can influence the ongoing program.* This is a marked departure from the more restrictive views of Henry and Keele, which presented the motor program as controlling movement in a completely open-loop fashion so that the course of the movement was unaffected by sensory feedback. As you shall see later in this discussion, an action can be amended after it has been initiated. However, such modification appears to be possible only after a certain amount of time has elapsed in the progress of the movement. As a result, there are some actions where such modification is not possible because there would not be sufficient time remaining in the course of the movement for it to be amended.

Given this starting place, then, we can begin our investigation of what the motor program is like and how it functions in the control of coordinated movement. Before doing this, however, it will be helpful to backtrack and consider the kinds of research evidence that led to establishing the viability of a mechanism such as a motor program in the movement control system.

Evidence Suggesting Motor Program Control

Research findings that goal-oriented movement can be accomplished in the absence of sensory feedback, as you saw in the previous two concepts, led to the need for proposing a mechanism that could account for how the movement was controlled so that the goal was attained. While the open-loop control system model provided an elementary description of the control process, it did not accommodate the need for specifying the mechanism responsible for this control. With the advent of the computer, and because the open-loop control situation seemed analogous to the running of a computer program, the motor program metaphor seemed appropriate to handle this void. While it appears that the idea of motor programs came about primarily as a default argument, the point remains that there was a need to propose a mechanism that would accommodate the results of a wide range of movement control research. We will consider some of this research next.

Evidence of movement accuracy without feedback.   The most obvious research findings indicating the need for a control mechanism like the motor program came from studies such as those we considered in Concepts 3.1 and 3.2., where accurate limb control occurred in the absence of sensory feedback. As you may recall, those studies compared performance of motor skills with and without sensory feedback. In general, it was demonstrated that certain movements can be accurately carried out in the absence of peripheral feedback. For example, accurate limb positioning was shown to be possible without visual or proprioceptive feedback, and accurate manual aiming for short distances or durations occurred without visual feedback of the arm or target. These results indicated that motor commands could be generated that enabled the limb to achieve its intended goal in the absence of certain sensory feedback. Thus, the need developed to provide a reasonable explanation for why this could occur and a mechanism responsible for controlling the movement in these situations.

Evidence that we prepare certain movements in advance.   The motor program concept proposed by Franklin Henry was based on a number of experiments that provided evidence that we prepare movements *before* we physically initiate them. This evidence of advance preparation, or preplanning as it is sometimes called, seemed especially pertinent for rapid, ballistic movements. Because of this characteristic, there was a need to describe a control mechanism that was responsible for this advance preparation. To illustrate how this evidence developed, the classic experiment by Henry and Rogers (1960) demonstrating this preparation effect will be described.

Henry hypothesized that if advance preparation occurs, a complex movement should take longer to plan than a simple one. It is important

here to note that the term "complex" was viewed by Henry as being related to the number of component parts of a movement. The reasoning underlying Henry's hypothesis was that there would be increasingly larger amounts of stored information in memory as movements increased in complexity. Thus, it would take longer to prepare a more complex movement than a less complex one because the amount of information to be organized in the preparation process would be greater. For a movement where the goal was to move as fast as possible and as soon as possible after a signal to move, Henry argued that this increased preparation time would be reflected in a change in the amount of time from the signal to move until the person physically begins the response, which is reaction time (RT).

To test this hypothesis, Henry and Rogers (1960) compared RTs for three different rapid movement situations that varied in the complexity of the movement that was performed. The lowest level of complexity required subjects to release a telegraph key as quickly as possible after a gong (movement A). The next level of movement complexity required subjects to release the key at the sound of the gong and then to move their arm forward 30 cm as rapidly as possible and grasp a tennis ball hanging from a string (movement B). The most complex movement (movement C) required subjects to release the key at the gong, reach forward and strike the hanging tennis ball with the back of the hand, reverse directions and push a button, and then finally reverse directions again and grasp another tennis ball. All of these movements were to be done as quickly as possible. If Henry's hypothesis was correct that these types of movements are prepared prior to initiating movement, the RTs associated with each of these three movements should be increasingly larger. As you can see from the results of this experiment in Figure 3.3–1, this hypothesis was supported. The average RT for movement A was 165 msec, for movement B the average RT was 199 msec, for movement C the average RT was 212 msec.

Because reaction time increased as the complexity of the movement increased, Henry argued that this was evidence that these movements were

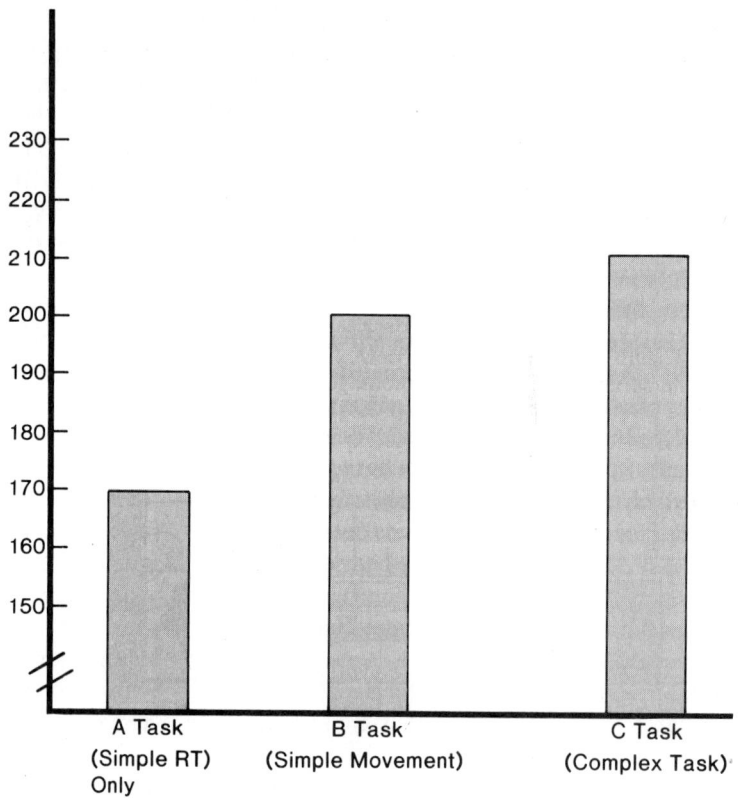

FIGURE 3.3-1 Results of the experiment by Henry and Rogers showing the changes in RT associated with performing rapid movements of different complexities.

prepared in advance. And the increase in RT was due to the increase in the amount of movement-related information that had to be prepared so that the movement could be made as rapidly as possible. The mechanism that Henry proposed handled this movement preparation was the motor program, which, as discussed earlier, he considered to be analagous to a computer program that controlled the details of the sequence of events required to perform a movement.

Evidence from EMG characteristics of unexpectedly blocked movements. An impressive type of evidence showing the need for a central control mechanism such as the motor program comes from research where a person prepares to make a practiced response, but then is unexpectedly blocked from moving. The expectation here would be that

if there is a central control mechanism that sends movement commands to the musculature in advance of the initiation of movement, and if those commands include the timing of agonist and antagonist muscle firing, then EMG patterns should be observed for a brief amount of time in the blocked limb that are similar to those when the movement can be performed. Research evidence supporting this expectation can be seen in an experiment by Wadman, Dernier van der Gon, Geuze, and Moll (1979).

In this experiment, subjects practiced a rapid arm flexion movement that involved moving a handle along a trackway 7.5, 15, 22.5, or 30 cm. After 20 practice trials, they performed 20 additional trials. On some of the trials, the subjects were unexpectedly mechanically blocked from making the movement. The EMG recordings from the biceps and the triceps indicated that for the first 100 msec after the signal to move occurred, there was strong EMG similarity between the situations in which movement actually occurred and in which no movement occurred. These results indicated that centrally forwarded movement commands were received by the muscles for the first 100 msec, during which time the motor control system could not make use of the proprioceptive feedback, indicating that no movement occurred. As soon as the control system could implement this feedback, the EMG patterns indicated that commands to move ceased to be forwarded.

More recently Young, Magill, Schmidt, and Shapiro (1988) presented evidence that replicated the results of Wadman et al. with a more complex movement. Subjects practiced making a two-part arm movement that required an initial flexion of a lever to a target area and then a quick reversal back to the starting area. Rather than practicing different movement distances, subjects moved the lever the same distance every trial but practiced making the movement in different movement times. Figure 3.2–2 presents the results of the EMG characteristics for the biceps and triceps for one subject performing this reversal movement at a 150–msec goal. As you can see, there is very little difference between EMG patterns for either muscle group when a normal, unblocked movement was carried out compared to when the planned movement was unexpectedly blocked. It is important to keep in mind that the EMG patterns for the blocked movement occur even though no movement was made. As in the experiment by Wadman et al., the first 100 msec showed very similar EMG patterns for blocked and normal movements.

These types of results, then, indicate that some central control mechanism prepares a movement in advance and executes that movement as planned until sensory feedback indicates that the planned response cannot be made. The current view of the motor program provides such a mechanism to accommodate this situation.

Evidence from the time needed to inhibit a movement prepared in advance.   If a central control mechanism prepares and initiates a rapid movement, then once planned, that movement should be initiated even if the movement *should not* be made. Note the difference between this situation and the one just described. Here, the person receives information indicating the movement should not be made whereas in the preceding section, information indicated the movement could not be made. Many of you may have experienced this "should not" situation when you are typing. For example, you see the word *there,* but for some reason you prepare, unconsciously, to type *their.* Even though you catch yourself by the time you type the *e* and begin the *i,* you probably type both the *i* and *r.* You are not able to inhibit your typing responses in the short period of time it takes to type the last two letters.

Research evidence exists indicating that this type of characteristic actually occurs when typing. In a series of experiments by Logan (1982), skilled typists were given a "stop" signal at different times after they had begun to type words or sentences. Results of the experiment indicated that the typists continued typing for at least one or two more letters before stopping. In some cases, as for a short word such as *the,* the entire word was typed before typing stopped. These results suggest that the typists prepared typing movements in such a way that the planned keystrokes could only be inhibited after the prepared action had taken place to the extent that feedback could intervene and stop the movement.

Another example showing the problem we have with inhibiting a prepared movement was provided many years earlier by A. T. Slater-Hammel (1960), one of the early physical educators involved in motor behavior research. In this experiment, subjects observed the sweep hand of a clock on which one revolution took one second. Their task was to lift a finger from a response key so that it coincided with the sweep hand reaching a target at the *8* on a clock face (i.e., 800 msec after the

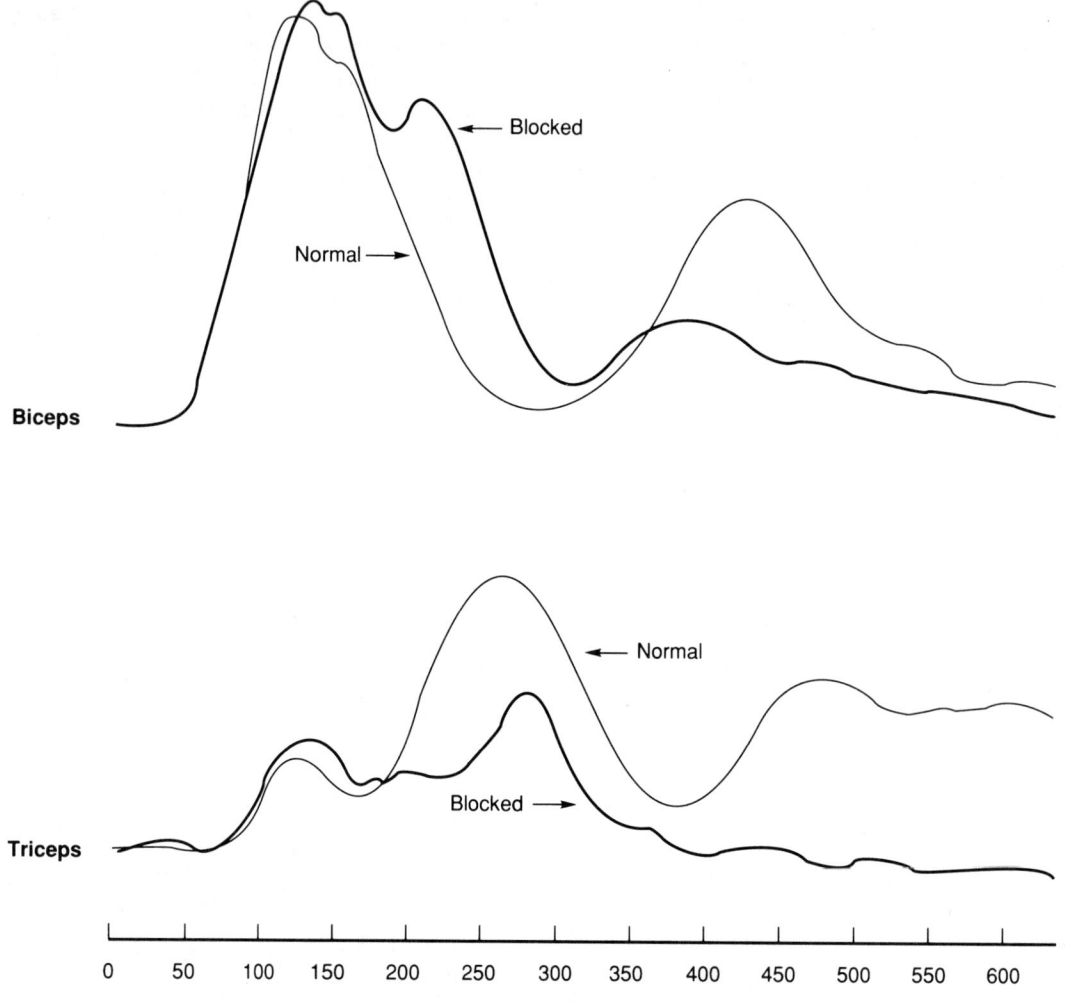

Biceps

Blocked

Normal →

Triceps

← Normal

Blocked →

0   50   100   150   200   250   300   350   400   450   500   550   600

Time (msec)

FIGURE 3.3-2   EMG results from one subject performing an arm flexion-extension reversal movement with a goal movement time of 150 msec to the reversal point. On some trials, the movement was unexpectedly blocked (the darker line on the figure). The 150-msec movement time to reversal occurred at the 350-msec point in time in the figure, as the horizontal axis marks time from the signal to begin the movement.

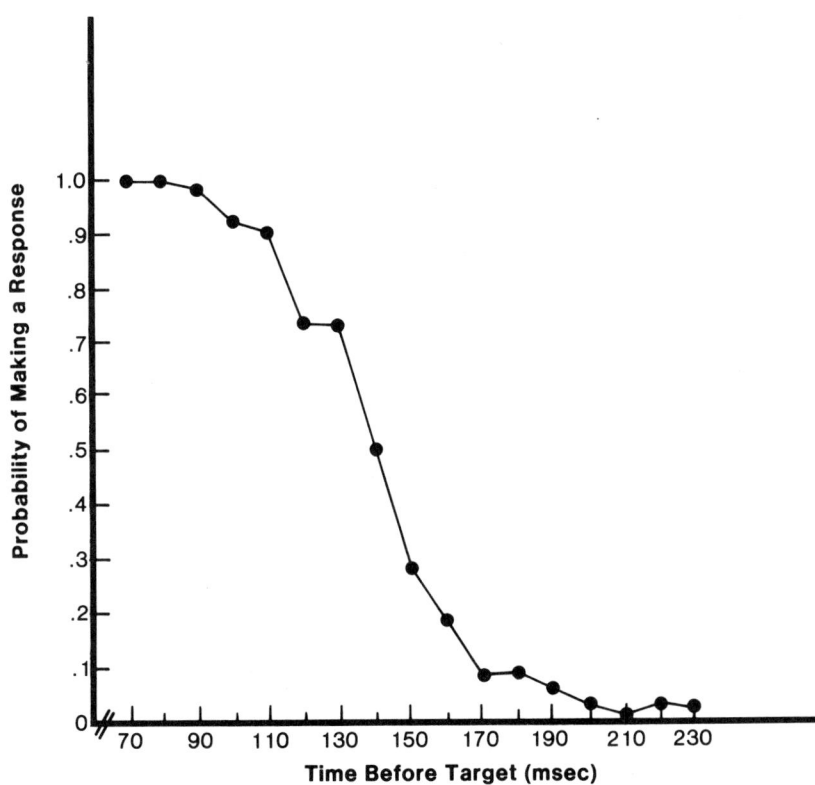

FIGURE 3.3-3 Results of the Slater-Hammel experiment showing the probability of subjects actually making a response when they were given a signal at different time intervals not to respond. The time intervals indicate when the clock hand stopped unexpectedly before it reached the target location on the clockface.

hand started). Obviously, in order to do this accurately, subjects would have to initiate the lifting movement *before* the hand reached the target. On some trials, the hand unexpectedly stopped before it reached the target. When this happened, subjects were told to do nothing and to keep their finger on the key. By having the hand stop unexpectedly at points between 200 and 750 msec (i.e., 600 to 50 msec before the target), Slater-Hammel could observe the length of time it took to inhibit a prepared movement. As you can see from the results of this experiment in Figure 3.3–3, subjects were correctly able *not* to move from the key only half of the time if the clock stopped approximately 140 msec before the target. If it stopped with less time than that before the target, then inhibiting the prepared key lift movement became increasingly difficult. In fact, when the hand stopped at 50 to 100 msec before the target, subjects almost always lifted their finger. It was not

unless the hand stopped 180 to 200 msec before the target that subjects could almost always inhibit the lifting movement.

These results indicate that there is a need to describe a mechanism that prepares and initiates a movement even after visual feedback tells the person that the movement should not be made. Again, the current view of the motor program concept accommodates this need.

Evidence from rapid serial movements. Many piano pieces contain sections that require a very rapid series of finger movements. This point was used by Lashley (1951) as an important part of his proposal for the need for a central mechanism to control the correct organization and movement of these responses. The alternative view, which states that sensory feedback from the response of one finger is the stimulus for the next finger's response, argues for the importance of feedback in the control of such movements. The problem with this response-chaining view is that many piano passages require faster finger movements than can be controlled by a feedback-dependent control system.

Support for the use of motor programming by highly skilled pianists has been provided by Shaffer (1976, 1980, 1981). Based primarily on the timing involved between key strokes, Shaffer argued that only a motor program view can accommodate these results. Similar arguments have been made on the basis of the rapid serial response skills exhibited by skilled typists (e.g., Rumelhart & Norman, 1982; Shaffer, 1978).

Characteristics of a Motor Program

Now that you have seen the need for a mechanism like a motor program, and a definition of the motor program has been established, the next step is to describe the characteristics of the motor program. An important point to establish here is that these characteristics must accommodate the need for the motor program to be flexible, in that several variations of an action can be controlled by the same program, and adaptable, in that the action can be performed in a variety of performance contexts. Because the definition of the motor program proposed by Schmidt (1987, 1988) is being used as the basis for this discussion, we will consider his views about the characteristics of the motor program.

Recall that it was because of the flexibility and adaptability requirement that Schmidt argued that a motor program should be thought of as a *generalized* motor program. That is, the motor program contains only an abstract representation of a class of actions that is defined by the invariant characteristics of the class. The specific requirements demanded by a particular action must be added as parameters before that required action can be successfully carried out. Thus, the two primary categories of characteristics of the motor program are its invariant characteristics and its parameters. Examples of characteristics within each of these categories will be dicussed in the following sections.

Invariant characteristics. The importance of identifying the invariant characteristics of the generalized motor program is that a program is defined by its own unique set of these characteristics. Undoutedly, there are many different possible candidates that could be invariant features of a motor program. However, based on research using diverse tasks such as handwriting, piano playing, typing, walking, running, rapid arm movements to targets, and tracking, three seem to be the most commonly proposed. These include the **relative force** used in performing the skill, the **relative timing** (which is analagous to rhythm) of the components of the skill, and the order, or sequence, of the components (Schmidt, 1987, 1988).

The term "relative" in relative timing and relative force indicates that what is invariant are the percentages of overall force and timing of the components of a skill. Figure 3.3–4 presents an illustration of relative time to help describe how to interpret the relative time (as well as relative force) characteristic of the motor program. Suppose you perform a skill that has four components, and that Component 1 takes up 30% of the total performance time; Component 2, 20%; Component 3, 40%; and; Component 4, 10%. If performing this skill under typical conditions has an overall duration of 10 sec (represented in A of the figure), then regardless of how much you speed up or slow down this overall duration, the actual amount of time characteristic of each component would change proportionately. In Figure 3.3–4, parts B and C represent this proportional component change for speeding up (part B) and slowing down (part C) the skill. Thus, if you typically perform this skill in 10 sec, then the amount of time spent performing each component would be 3, 2, 4, and 1 sec respectively. And, if you perform the skill twice as fast in 5 sec, then each

a. Normal Speed (10 sec)

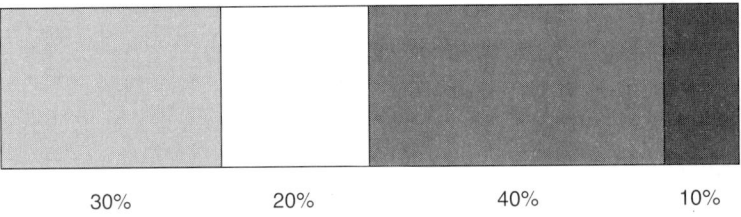

30%   20%   40%   10%

b. Faster (5 sec)

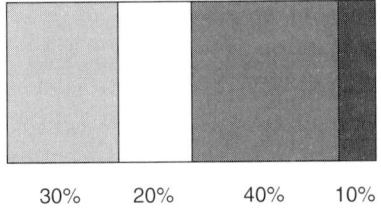

30%   20%   40%   10%

c. Slower (15 sec)

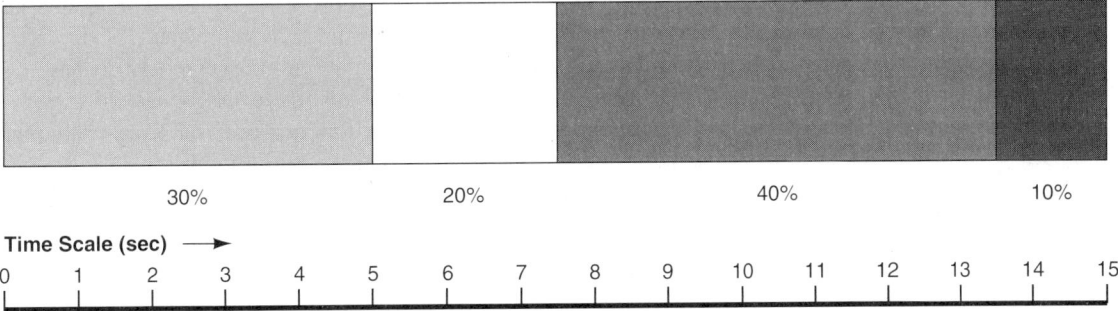

30%   20%   40%   10%

Time Scale (sec) ⟶
0   1   2   3   4   5   6   7   8   9   10   11   12   13   14   15

FIGURE 3.3-4 An illustration of changes in relative time for a hypothetical four-component motor skill when it is performed normally at a 10-second duration (a), increased to a 5-second duration (b), and slowed down to a 15-second duration (c).

component would change proportionally to be 1.5, 1, 2, and .5 sec respectively. Or, if you slow down your overall performance time to 15 sec, then each component would change to 4.5, 3, 6, and 1.5 sec, respectively.

Consider the tennis serve as an example for showing how the invariant characteristics would be identified. The tennis serve has several identifiable components, such as the ball toss, the backswing, the forward swing, ball contact, follow

through, etc. To produce a serve, there is a specific order for these events. If that order is disrupted, the serve will not be executed correctly. In carrying out this order of events, the body and limbs must be in relatively similar positions at relatively the same time from one serve to the next. If this does not occur, your serve will be inconsistent. But one may have been hit harder than another. However, a comparison of the two would reveal that the amount of force generated by each of the muscle groups producing each component of the serve remained proportionately similar between the two serves.

Parameters. While the relative timing, relative force, and order of components characteristics of a motor skill are proposed to be rather fixed characteristics of a motor program, there are other features of a skill that can be varied from one performance to the next. Examples of these parameters include the *overall force* and the *overall duration* characteristics of an action. These parameters are easily changed from one performance situation to another, and can be readily adapted to the specific requirements of each situation. This modification was illustrated in Figure 3.3–4 for overall duration and it was described in the tennis serve example. To hit one serve harder than another, the overall force applied must be greater and the overall time taken to carry out the events of the serve must be faster. Speeding up the sequence of movements and increasing the overall force can seemingly be done without altering the invariant characteristics of the motor program controlling the response.

Another parameter discussed earlier in the current definition of a motor program was the muscles that must be used to perform the action. Recall from that discussion that this characteristic makes it possible for the same motor program to control an action regardless of which limb or combination of limbs are used.

Investigating invariant characteristics and parameters. While several features have been identified as invariant characteristics of the generalized motor program, the one that has generated the most research interest has been relative timing. The result of this research has been to provide a great deal of empirical evidence supporting relative timing invariance. This support has been generated by experiments investigating skills such as typing, gait, handwriting, prehension, sequences of key presses among others (see Schmidt, 1985, 1988, for reviews of this evidence). The common approach to investigating the

invariance of relative timing, or of any potential invariant characteristic, has been to observe changes in relative timing across a range of parameter values, such as overall duration.

A good example of this research approach is a study by Shapiro, Zernicke, Gregor, and Diestal (1981) in which walking and running at different speeds on a treadmill were investigated. The researchers wanted to determine what percentage of the total step-cycle time (i.e., relative time) would be taken up by each of the four components, or phases, of the step cycle at each treadmill speed. If relative time is invariant for the generalized motor program involved in controlling walking and/or running gait patterns, then these percentages should remain constant across the different speeds. The results, which are presented in Figure 3.3–5, showed that as the subjects sped up or slowed down their gait, the percentage of time each component of the step cycle while walking remained essentially the same at each speed. Thus, the overall duration parameter of the motor program governing walking could be speeded up (at least to 6 km/hr) or slowed down while the relative timing among the components of the step-cycle was maintained. Notice what happened for treadmill speeds greater than 8 km/hr. At this speed, subjects were no longer walking but running. And it appears that a different motor program is operating because there is an obvious difference in the percentages of step-cycle time required for running than there was for walking.

It is important to point out that controversy exists over the indentity of invariant characteristics of the motor program. This is especially the case for relative timing. While evidence such as that provided by the experiment by Shapiro et al. (1981) strongly supports relative timing as an invariant feature of motor programs involved in the control of walking and running, evidence has been commonly reported in the past few years suggesting that perhaps gait patterns are unique in this respect. The most influential case developed against relative timing as an invariant characteristic was presented by Gentner (1987) in an article in which he re-analyzed data from several

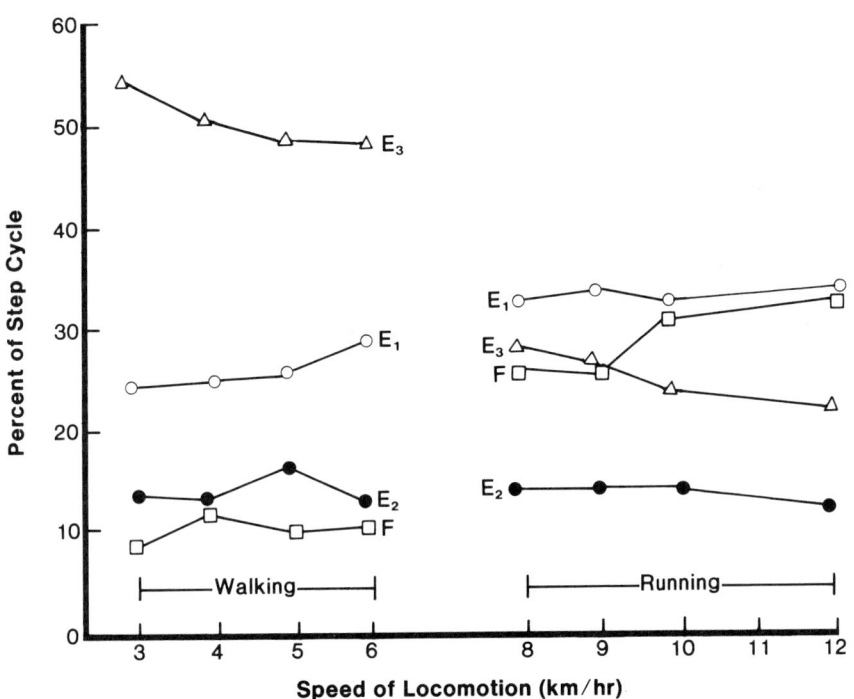

FIGURE 3.3-5
Results of the experiment by Shapiro, et al., showing the relative timing of the four step-cycle phases (mean values), determined by comparing percentages at the different locomotion speeds.

experiments that had supported relative timing invariance. He argued that the analyses were inappropriate because they were based on averages of groups of subjects. His view is that an issue such as identifying motor program invariant characteristics requires evidence based on individual data. That is, if relative timing is invariant, then all individual subjects in an experiment should show evidence of this invariance. When reanalyzed from this perspective, the results did not provide the broad base of support that had been given to the invariance of relative timing. Research since that article has similarly cast additional doubts on this invariance (e.g., Heuer & Schmidt, 1988; Wann & Nimmo-Smith, 1990).

However, the case about relative timing invariance is far from closed. Arguments have been presented, for example, indicating that Gentner's approach to testing invariance was too restrictive in that motor program characteristics refer to central nervous system constructs and that Gentner's strict analysis was done on the basis of be-

havioral evidence, which includes "noise" characteristics inherent in human performance. Thus, testing for invariance of any motor program characteristic is a difficult task. Expectations must be adjusted accordingly concerning what invariance means if it is investigated by observing the results of performing a skill. Heuer and Schmidt (1988) argued that while deviations in relative timing appear when analyzed by Gentner's method, those deviations are probably still acceptable discrepancies given that they occur at the performance end of the control process. And Schmidt and Young (1987) contended that while these re-analyses may detract from the idea of a simple model of relative timing invariance as the basis for organizing a motor program, they do not detract substantially from the idea that abstract structures such as motor programs are the basis for movement control.

One other issue is worth noting with respect to relative timing invariance. Those who argue against the existence of motor programs point out that while relative timing invariance may be observed in the performance of a variety of motor skills, this invariance may be the *result* of the performance situation rather than due to a program causing it to occur. For example, the relative timing invariance typically observed for keystroking a word (e.g., Terzuolo & Viviani, 1980) could be due to keyboard constraints rather than due to motor program characteristics. That is, between letter keystrokes relative timing occurs because of the relationship among keys on the keyboard. And, opponents of motor programs argue, just because relative time is observed in a performance of a skill does not mean that time is a feature of the control mechanism. As evidence supporting this point, an analogy is commonly provided. This analogy is that we can tell time by observing the burning characteristics of a candle but there is no time-based control mechanism in a candle. (See Schmidt, 1988, for a more in-depth discussion of both sides of these arguments.)

There is little doubt that the question of what are or what are not invariant characteristics of motor programs is far from resolved. Much more research is needed before definitive answers can be provided. For the present, then, we will operate on the basis that invariant characteristics do exist for motor programs and that features such as relative time, relative force, and the order of events are likely candidates. However, the degree to which these features actually mandate performance characteristics must be acknowledged as an issue that remains to be given further attention.

An Alternative to Motor Program Based Control

Based on the arguments described in the preceding section about relative timing as an invariant characteristic of the generalized motor program, it is obvious that there are people who study the control of motor skills who do not accept the motor program as a basis for this control. As you may recall, you have already been introduced to this type of alternative viewpoint when you were introduced to the *dynamic systems view* of motor

control in Concept 3.1. It was pointed out in that discussion that the dynamic systems view argues that there is no real need to propose a construct like the motor program to mediate the control of coordinated movement because coordination is primarily a self-organizational process that is driven by a person's intention to perform a certain skill and the environmental constraints characterizing the conditions in which the skill is to be performed. We will consider three lines of evidence often used to argue against the need for a control mechanism such as the generalized motor program.

First, consider the notion of coordinative structures, which were described in Concept 3.1. The argument against motor programs based on the existence of coordinative structures follows: Because inate and learned coordinative structures exist for various coordinated acts, no memory representation construct such as a motor prgram is needed. These structures become self-organized as needed. Modifications occur within the coordinative structure according to environmental conditions. Components of the structure adapt to compensate for each other according to constraints placed on each component.

An impressive form of evidence supporting the existence of coordinative structures comes from a study of speech control by Kelso, Tuller, Vatikiotis-Bateson, and Fowler (1984). They reported a series of experiments in which they observed what occurred in the various components of articulators when the jaw was perturbed during an utterance. In two experiments, subjects were asked to say the syllable "bab." On several utterances, an unexpected force load was applied to the jaw during the upward jaw motion for the final "b" sound of the syllable. According to the coordinative structure notion, such a perturbation should result in an immediate compensation by other parts of the articulation system involved in producing this sound, because all parts work as a functional unit to achieve the common goal of the intended sound. This is, in fact, what they found. As the jaw was forced upward, there was an almost immediate compensation in the upper and lower

a.

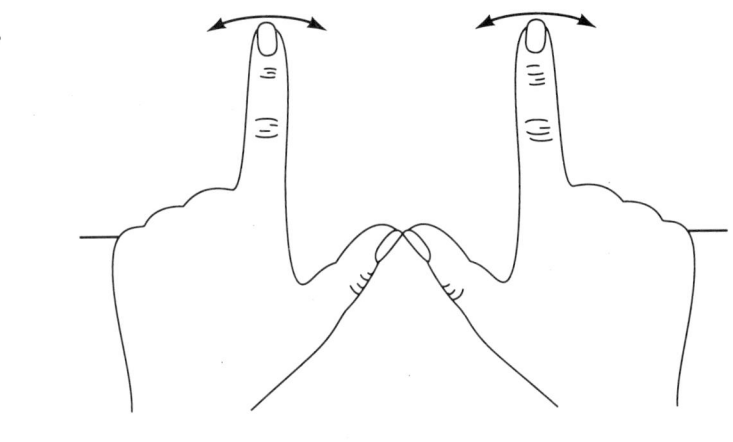

FIGURE 3.3-6 (a) Shows the hand and finger placement for performing the finger movement task used in the experiments by Kelso. (b) and (c) Show fingertip movement position as a function of time, during which movement frequency increased. (b) Shows fingertip positions for both index fingers as they moved from being out-of-phase to in-phase.
(c) Shows the relationship of the left index finger's peak extension to the right finger's peak extension as a different way to portray the phase transition shown in (b).

b.

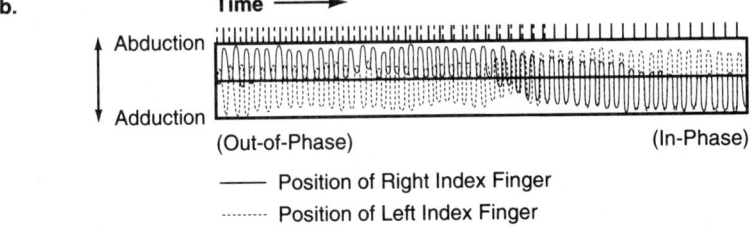

—— Position of Right Index Finger
------ Position of Left Index Finger

c.

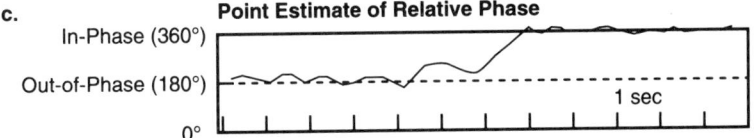

lips so that the sound was still produced in an understandable way. A similar perturbation was applied as the subjects uttered "baz." The result was an immediate tongue compensation. Thus, the articulators can be seen as working together as functional units to achieve specified goals. When one element of the unit is disturbed, other elements compensate in a way that allows the goal to be achieved. The elements involved in this compensation and how they achieve it depend on the goal of the action.

One of the strongest kinds of evidence arguing against the need for a motor program-based views of coordinated skill comes from research showing that certain parameter changes, such as overall speed of movement, can make dramatic changes in coordination characteristics. An example of this has been demonstrated in several experiments by Kelso and his colleagues (e.g, Kelso, 1984; Kelso & Scholz, 1985). The top panel in Figure 3.3–6 illustrates the type of task used in these experiments. Subjects began moving their right and left index fingers at a specified rate of speed so that they were out of phase, which meant that when the right finger was flexed, the left finger was extended (i.e, 180 degree relationship of fingertips). This is graphically illustrated in terms of finger position in panels B and C. Subjects were then required to systematically increase the speed of this bimanual rhythmical movement. As you can see in panels B and C, a transition occurred during which the fingers shifted from being out-of-phase to being in-phase, where both were flexed or extended at the same time (i.e., a 360 degree relation of fingertips). This transition was involuntary and coincided with a critical movement speed, where only out-of-phase movements occurred at slower speeds and only in-phase movements occurred at faster speeds.

The resulting argument has been that this coordination change does not indicate that a different motor program became involved in the control, but that the control system reorganized due to the influence of the speed change on the finger movement coordination. This type of dynamic change is consistent with many parameter-based changes seen in the physical world, such as the dramatic changes observed in the rolling characteristics of fluid in cylinders caused by changing only the amount of heat applied to the cylinders (See Gleick, 1987, for further discussions of physical world examples like this one.)

Finally, opponents of the motor program view argue that there are invariants in the environment that provide the basis for controlling action, which take away the need for control by an internal control mechanism like a motor program. You saw an example of one of these environmental invariants in the discussion of tau as an optical variable in Concept 3.2 as it related to locomotion and jumping from heights.

There seems to be little doubt that most discussions in the motor learning and control literature commonly do not take into account the dynamics of the control system and the characteristics of the environmental constraints placed on that system. However, at the same time, it does not seem necessary to completely replace a control system in which the motor program plays an important role with a system in which there is no program. The program provides a useful means of integrating and accounting for many complex skill learning and performance characteristics. What evidence presented by the dynamic systems perspective has indicated, however, is that there is a need to look at motor program based control in ways that are quite different than traditionally has been the case. It is apparent that much less in-

formation about coordinated skill needs to be represented in the motor program and that less needs to be controlled by the program than previously thought.

The Motor Program and the Control of Coordinated Movement

You have seen some examples of some of the characteristics of a motor program that have been proposed to be relatively fixed or changeable from one response to the next. What remains to be seen is how the motor program would be involved in the actual control of coordinated movement. The approach here will be to consider this control only as it relates to motor program involvement and not to try to present a detailed description of how the entire skill is controlled by the motor control system.

In general, it appears that there are several levels of control involved in producing an intended action. Following the selection of an appropriate action to perform and the motor program responsible for that action, events must occur that will allow the action to be performed as intended. Determining precisely what those events are and how they are carried out are issues that continue to be debated and investigated among motor control researchers. However, it seems that some type of hierarchical system operates to produce coordinated movement. Smyth and Wing (1984) describe this hierarchical control process as analogous to the managerial organization of a business. At the top level, there is a managing director who issues instructions to several lower level managers, such as production managers and sales managers. These managers control people working at lower levels, such as shop foremen and salespeople. Then there are the workers who produce the product or sell it to the customer. With the progression down the hierarchy of management comes an increase in specialization of knowledge and responsbilities. However, it is not essential for every level of management to know the details of this knowledge and responsibility, such as how to run a particular piece of machinery. But lines of communication going up as well as down the hierarchy need to exist. Thus, the goals of the system are decided at one level and are implemented as each level of the hierarchy adds its particular function to the process.

In the remainder of this discussion, several examples of coordinated movement will be discussed. For each, the role of the motor program will be considered to illustrate how the goal of an action can be achieved and what role the motor program plays in helping to implement that goal. As will become evident, the generalized motor program must be viewed as a high-level manager in the management hierarchy that specifies only certain details of the action. Where applicable, possible alternative control mechanisms will be pointed out.

Speed-accuracy tradeoff situations and Fitts' Law. One of the fascinating characteristics about motor skills in which successful performance is related to the speed and accuracy of the movements, is that there is a tradeoff between speed and accuracy. That is, when the person emphasizes speed, acccuracy is reduced. And, conversely, if accuracy is emphasized, speed is reduced. This situation is common in many skills. For example, a skilled fencer must move quickly yet accurately to score a touch. Similarly, a pianist must hit each key accurately but at the correct time in keeping with the rhythm and tempo of the music. By far, the most common motor skill that has been used used to investigate the speed-accuracy tradeoff has been the manual aiming task where a person must move a hand-held stylus as quickly as possible to a target some distance away from the starting point of the movement.

The **speed-accuracy tradeoff** is such a common characteristic for performing skills where speed and accuracy are essential components that a law specifying this tradeoff has been developed. This law, known as **Fitts' Law,** is based on the work of Paul Fitts (1954). It indicates that there are two essential components of a task in which the speed-accuracy tradeoff will occur. These are the *distance* to move and the *target size*. Fitts' Law spec-

ifies how these two components are related so that the movement time can be derived. Fitts' Law describes this relationship as:

$$MT = a + b \log_2(2D/W)$$

where MT is movement time
        a and b are constants
        D is the distance moved
        W is the target width, or size

That is, movement time will be equal to the $\log_2$ of two times the distance to move divided by the width of the target. As the target size gets smaller or as the distance gets greater, the movement speed will slow down in order to allow for an accurate movement. In other words, there is a speed-accuracy tradeoff. Because of this relationship, Fitts indicated that $\log_2(2D/W)$ provides an **index of difficulty (ID)** where the higher the ID, the more difficult the task, because more difficult tasks will require more movement time.

Fitts based his MT calculation on a reciprocal tapping task performance that involves repetitive moving back and forth between two targets as fast as possible for a specified period of time. Thus, the MT that results from this calculation is the average MT of each movement from one target to the other. However, this MT effect can be generalized for use in a wide range of motor skill performance situations where moving a limb to a target is required. For example, Fitts' Law has been shown to be applicable to single manual aiming tasks, moving pegs from one location to insert them into a hole, throwing darts at a target, reaching or grasping containers of different sizes, moving a cursor on a screen to a target, and so on.

While the demonstration of Fitts' Law is no longer a significant issue in motor control, the understanding of why the speed-accuracy tradeoff occurs, and explaining the control characteristics underlying it continues to intrigue researchers. From a movement control perspective, the interesting question here is how the control system operates in this movement situation. There have been several different proposals offered but three are most commonly addressed.

The traditionally held view is one that was developed by Crossman and Goodeve (1963). Their view was that that open-loop programmed control is involved in the initiation of the movement toward the target and that feedback intermittently provided information to allow corrections along the way until the target was contacted. Greater distance or narrower targets required more corrections, therefore leading to increased MT.

A second view is related to the impulse-timing model proposed by Schmidt, Zelaznik, Hawkins, Frank, and Quinn (1979). This view is primarily a prepared program view in which advance commands are programmed and forwarded to the musculature. These commands are translated into impulses, which are the forces produced over time and produce the actual movement.

Third, is a view developed by Meyer, Abrams, Kornblum, Wright, and Smith (1988) which they called the optimized initial impulse model, which is a combination of the previous two explanations. According to this model, an initial impulse directs the limb toward the target. Because movement as fast as possible is the goal, one optimal impulse, as in the Schmidt et al. model, is generated. But because spatial accuracy of movements is imperfect, the person produces the minimum number of sub-movements needed along the way, based on error feedback, to hit the target, as in the Crossman and Goodeve model. The number of sub-movements required can be predicted based on the distance to be moved, the target width, and the total MT. Which of these views most adequately explains performance in a speed-accuracy trade-off situation awaits further research.

Prehension.   The act of reaching and grasping was discussed in Concept 3.1 as it related to the role of vision in the control process. As was evident in that discussion, the role of the motor program has also played an important part in proposals describing how prehensile activities are controlled. The earliest control model, proposed by Jeannerod (1981, 1984) gave the motor program a critical role along with visual feedback. Jeannerod argued that the transport and grasp

phases of prehension are independent because only the grasp phase is influenced by the size of the object. While this grasp phase was proposed to be under feedback control, the transport phase, including the timing of the finger and thumb aperture opening, is centrally represented in a motor program.

Research by Wallace and Weeks (1988) has shown evidence that regardless of the speed of the movement or the size of the aperture, the relative timing of the maximum aperture remained invariant. These results would be consistent with the generalized motor program view of control where relative time of maximum aperture was a part of the central command issued to the musculature. However, Wallace and Weeks provide an alternative explanation for their results and indicate that those results can be explained without the need for a motor program. Following the arguments of the dynamic systems perspective, they proposed that the relative time observed in their experiment was not a part of any central command, but was evidence of a functional unit, or coordinative structure, and that relative time emerged from the performance of this unit due to the constraints of the task being performed.

It is clear that both a motor program based view and a dynamic systems view can provide an explanation for the timing and kinematic characteristics that typify the results of research on prehension. Which of these views, or whether a compromise view, best explains this control must wait for additional research.

Handwriting.   Investigating the control mechanisms responsible for handwriting is a prominent theme in the study of motor control. Evidence of this can be seen in a recent special issue of the journal *Human Movement Science* devoted exclusively to this topic (May, 1991, edited by van Galen, Thomassen, and Wing). Much of the research and theoretical knowledge about the control of handwriting has come from work at the University of Nijmegen in the Netherlands and at Cambridge University in England. There is general agreement that different control mechanisms are involved in controlling what is written (letters, words, numbers etc.) and how it is written (the writing strokes producing the letters, words, etc. on the writing surface).

A characteristic of handwriting samples from one person is that there is a large amount of similarity in characteristics of letter forms and writing slant, even when handwriting tasks are carried out with different implements and limbs. This characteristic clearly fits the flexibility and adaptability nature that was ascribed to a generalized motor program based control. And features such as relative force for stroke production and relative timing between strokes appear to be reasonably invariant across a wide range of writing parameter changes by an individual. Parameter variables have been described to include movement time and writing size, among others.[2] Thus, the control of handwriting appears to fit well within a generalized motor program based view of control in which invariant features and parameters are components of the program and in which achieving a specific handwriting task goal involves the hierarchical specification of characteristics in accordance with the demands and specifications of the task and writing surface.

Bimanual coordination skills.   There are many motor skills in which successful performance depends on the two arms performing simultaneously. From a control perspective the most intriguing performance situation is when each arm must do something different. For example, a guitar player holds strings with one hand to produce chords, while plucking or striking strings with the other hand to produce sound. A skilled drummer can produce one rhythm with one hand while producing another with the other hand. An airplane pilot controls a lever with one hand while steering the plane with the other. How does the motor control system control these skills?

See van Galen, 1991, for a more detailed description of a handwriting control model based on these and other characteristics, and Wann & Nimmo-Smith, 1990, for evidence arguing against relative timing invariance for handwriting.

Researchers investigating the control of bimanual coordination skills typically have looked at several types of performance situations, both laboratory and real world. In this section, three of these will be considered. The first bimanual coordination situation involves piano playing. The second and third examples come from laboratory tasks designed to simulate characteristics of real world bimanual coordination skills. One of these involves bimanual aiming movements where each arm must move a stylus to a target as quickly as possible. The other involves moving two levers simultaneously to produce two different patterns of motion or timing. A brief discussion of each of these will provide an overview of current notions of how such skills are controlled.

One of the attractions for investigating the control of piano playing is that pianos can easily be interfaced with a computer to record time and force information related to striking the keys. Much of the piano playing research has addressed the issue of timing. For example, how is the timing of the various events in playing a piano piece represented in the motor program? Timing is critical in this task because each hand has specifically timed responsibilities and the hands must work together to produce the notes at appropriate times. Shaffer (1980, 1981, 1982) has provided evidence and arguments favoring relative timing characteristics for performing a piano piece as being represented in the motor program. For a complex piano piece, a timing pattern is represented for a group of notes containing a rhythmic figure. The pianist adds certain specifications to this abstract plan that allow for variations in such things as tempo, rhythm, and intensity from one performance to another. For the skilled pianist, these specifications can be made differently for each hand as well as for the two hands together. In this view the motor program sends timing-based commands to the musculature to control the movements. These commands are based on abstract timing requirements for the task. These abstract requirements are made specific by the performer's adding specifications related to the needs of the performance being executed.

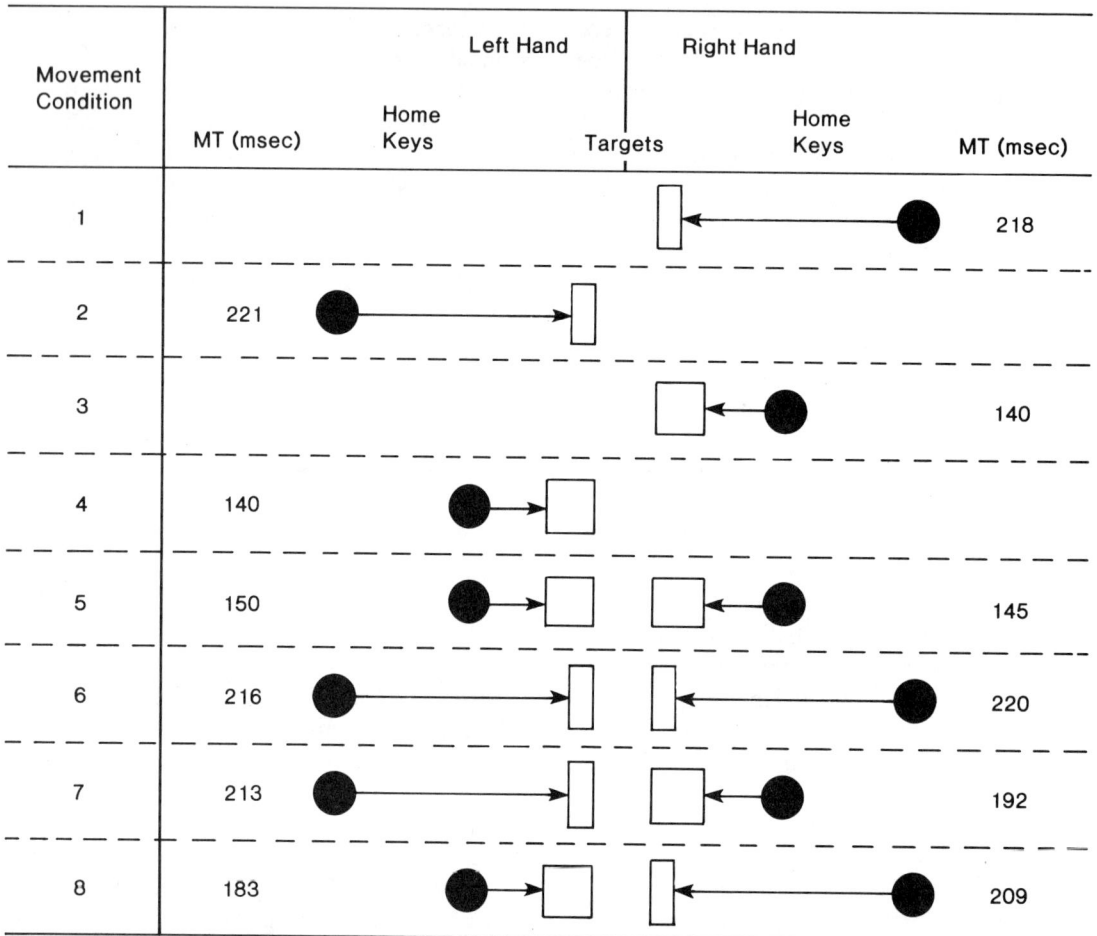

FIGURE 3.3-7 Movement time scores for one- and two-hand movements to targets of different distances and sizes reported in Kelso, Southard, and Goodman's second experiment.

A study by Kelso, Southard, and Goodman (1979) provides support not only for the existence of coordinative structures but also that bimanual skills are under a timing-based control system. In a series of experiments, subjects performed simple, rapid-aiming movements with the right, left, and both hands. One hand moved to a target that was different in size and distance from that of the other hand. According to Fitts' Law, the hand moving to the target with the smaller ID should move faster. As can be seen in Figure 3.3–7, when each hand moved alone to a target, the Fitts prediction was upheld. However, when the two hands moved together to the two targets, the movement times

became similar for the two hands. In this type of movement situation, the Fitts prediction was not upheld.

These results suggest that something constrained the two hands to act together as one unit. Kelso, Southard, and Goodman argued that this was due to the two limbs operating as a coordinative structure. As such, when the two hands were in a situation in which they had to act at the same time, although their two tasks were different, the system controlled them as though they both had the same task to perform. And time appears to have been the critical control variable because it seemed to regulate the action of the two hands by

slowing down the hand performing the less difficult task. Whether time actually is the critical
control feature here, or whether it is some other
element, such as force, is an issue of some debate
that awaits further research (note e.g., Corcos,
1984; Marteniuk & MacKenzie, 1980).

The control of asymmetrical bimanual lever
movements has been studied extensively by
Swinnen and Walter and their colleagues (e.g.,
Swinnen & Walter, 1988; Swinnen, Walter, Pauwels, Meugens, & Beirinckx, 1990). In these
studies, subjects typically are required to move a
horizontal lever with one arm so that a specific
movement pattern is produced, such as a simple
flexion and extension movement. And, at the same
time, the other arm must move another lever to
produce a second movement pattern, such as a
simple one-direction movement. Each of these
movements usually has specified goal movement
times. One typical finding is that when subjects
first attempt to produce these different movement
patterns simultaneously, the tendency is for the two
arms to make the same pattern. And it is usually
the more complex reversal movement that takes
the lead. Here again, then, is evidence for the
linkage of the two arms as described above in the
work of Kelso, Southard, and Goodman. Thus,
learning this task involves learning to unlink or
dissociate the natural tendency of the two arms to
work together as one unit. With practice, this un-
linking occurs and the asymmetrical lever movements can be performed.

The evidence from studies of two different types
of bimanual skills indicates that the two arms seem
to be functionally linked to act together as one unit.
This coordinative structure must be reorganized
if the two limbs need to perform different movements in which different spatial patterns or time
characteristics are needed. This process takes
much practice to achieve the amount of independence each limb requires to carry out its own distinct task. Timing and kinematic inaccuracies and
inconsistencies characterize practice experiences
as the person strives to achieve this interlimb independence goal. Exacty how the motor control
system is involved in this process is not known, although attempts continue to provide an adequate

explanation. Whether the coordinative structure
characteristics observed in this situation indicates
a useful means of organizing degrees of freedom
by the motor program or they provide evidence of
no need for control based on a motor program also
remains the topic of debate and further research.
Also, research continues to establish evidence on
which to base guidelines for developing practice
strategies to facilitate learning to dissociate the
two limbs in these types of skills.

Summary

The production of coordinated movement appears
to involve the motor program as an essential control mechanism. The motor program should be
defined as a generalized motor program that is an
abstract representation of action stored in memory
and retrieved when the action must be produced.
The generalized motor program consists of certain characteristics of an action that are invariant,
such as the order of events, relative time, and relative force. At the time a specific action must be
produced, this abstract program must be param-
eterized to accommodate the demands of the specific situation. The parameters that are applied
include features such as the overall duration and
the overall force of the movement, as well as the
musculature that will be used to perform the
movement. An alternative view to motor program
based control has been described that is based on
evidence indicating that things such as environmental invariants and limb dynamics can account
for much of the control ascribed to the motor program. Skills such as those involved in speed-
accuracy tradeoff situations, prehension, handwriting, and bimanual coordination, have been
discussed with consideration given to the role of
the motor program in controlling these skills. Particular emphasis was given to describing Fitts' Law
as it relates to the speed-accuracy tradeoff and to
explanations that have been proposed to explain
this tradeoff. Also, the problem with simultaneously performing different limb patterns of
motion and/or time were considered due to the
tendency for the two arms to work together as a
functional unit.

Related Readings

Gentner, D. R. (1987). Timing of skilled motor performance: Tests of the proportional duration model. *Psychological Review, 94,* 255–276.

Haggard, P. (1991). Task coordination in human prehension. *Journal of Motor Behavior, 23,* 25–37.

Keele, S. W. (1982). Behavioral analysis of movement. In V. B. Brooks (Ed.), *Handbook of physiology Sec. 1: The nervous system. Vol. II: Motor Control, part 2* (pp. 1391–1414). Baltimore: American Physiological Society.

Rosenbaum, D. A. (1991). *Human motor control.* San Diego: Academic Press. (Read chapters 4, 6, 7, and 8)

Schmidt, R. A. (1985). The search for invariance in skilled motor behavior. *Research Quarterly for Exercise and Sport, 56,* 188–200.

Schmidt, R. A. (1988). Motor and action perspectives on motor behavior. In O.G. Meijer and K. Roth (Eds.), *Complex motor behavior: 'The' motor-action controversy* (pp. 3–44). Amsterdam: Elsevier.

Scholz, J. P. (1991). Dynamic pattern theory—Some implications for therapeutics. *Movement Science,* Monograph pp. 75–91. American Physical Therapy Association.

Smyth, M. M., Morris, P. E., Levy, P., & Ellis, A. W. (1987). *Cognition in action.* London: Erlbaum. (Read Chapter 4)

CONCEPT 3.4

Bilateral transfer of skills is a phenomenon that
blends motor control and cognitive processes

Key Terms

| bilateral transfer | asymmetric transfer | symmetric transfer |

Application

Beginning basketball players are told that it will
be an advantage if they learn to dribble the ball
with either hand. Similarly, young soccer players
are encouraged to learn to shoot or kick the ball
with either foot. These examples seem to indicate
that in many sport activities, bilateral skill development is an important aspect of the training process. However, our own experiences tell us that we
seldom use both limbs in practice with equal emphasis. More often than not, the young basketball
player becomes very adept at dribbling with his
or her right or left hand and remains relatively
poor at dribbling with the other hand. The same
is too often the case with the beginning soccer
player.

Perhaps there are some reasons for this situation. The learning of motor skills is very often restricted by the amount of time available for
instruction or practice. Add to that the often strong
feeling by the novice of wanting to be successful
at the skill. Such factors combine to suggest that
the novice, when given a choice, will emphasize
the limb with which he or she feels most comfortable. Generally, that limb will be the one that
will provide the greatest opportunity for quick
success. The other limb remains largely ignored
until the player becomes involved in situations
where a lack of bilateral competence becomes a
distinct liability.

Obviously, the most reasonable way to solve the
problem would be to provide equal practice with
both limbs. But some practical problems that are
often overlooked intervene to make this solution
less than desirable or possible. One problem is the
availability of time for instruction and practice. If
time is limited, the beginner will generally attempt to attain as high a level of success as possible during the time available. Because success is
usually not measured by a criterion emphasizing
skill with both arms and feet, emphasis on practicing with only one limb seems quite reasonable.
A second problem relates to an unavoidable di-
lemma that the person does not want to devote an
equal amount of time to practice with each limb.

A possible alternative solution to situations such
as these will be considered by discussing an intriguing phenomenon known as bilateral transfer.
We will consider evidence that shows improvement is possible in a limb even though it has had
little if any practice. Then, we will investigate different views for why bilateral transfer occurs. And
we will address the issue of designing instruction
to promote optimal bilateral skill development
when equal practice of each limb does not seem
to be a practical alternative.

Discussion

The ability to learn a particular skill more easily with one hand or foot after the skill has been learned with the opposite hand or foot is related to what is known as **bilateral transfer.** Bilateral transfer is based on the principle discussed in Concept 2.3: Learning transfers in some degree from previously learned skills to new skills so that the new skill is in reality not totally new to the learner. The focus of bilateral transfer is the transfer of learning *between limbs rather than between tasks.* Here we will be generally involved with learning the same task but with different limbs, that is from arm to arm and from leg to leg.

It has been well documented in physiology that there can be a gain in strength in an unpracticed extremity or limb as a result of training of that limb's contralateral muscle group. Such evidence has existed as far back as the late nineteenth century. We want to know whether similar effects are found in the area of skill acquisition. Do these bilateral transfer effects that are so well documented in physiological situations occur also in motor skill learning situations? To answer that question, we will discuss some evidence indicating that bilateral transfer does indeed occur in the motor skill learning situation. Then we will consider some of the reasons why the bilateral transfer phenomenon occurs. Finally, in order to give this discussion practical significance, we will suggest how this information gives us a basis for providing instruction to promote bilateral skill development.

Evidence for Bilateral Transfer

Experiments that have been designed to determine whether bilateral transfer does indeed occur have followed similar experimental designs. The most typical design has been the following:

This design allows the experimenter to determine if bilateral transfer to the non-preferred limb, which had no practice, occurred because of practice with the preferred limb. If we are interested in the amount of bilateral transfer to the preferred limb because of practice with the non-preferred limb, the preferred limb/non-preferred limb arrangement in this design would be reversed. Thus, we need to determine the pretest to posttest gains for each limb, then compare those gains. It would be expected that the practiced limb should show the greatest gain or improvement. However, it should also be expected that a significant improvement in performance was made by the limb not used in practice. In that case, the obvious conclusion would be that bilateral transfer had occurred.

Research support for bilateral transfer. Investigation of the bilateral transfer phenomenon was very widespread during the 1930s through the 1950s. In fact, the bulk of evidence supporting the bilateral transfer of motor skills can be found in the psychology journals of that period. One of the more prominent investigators of the bilateral transfer phenomenon during the early part of that era was T. W. Cook. During the years from 1933 to 1936, Cook published a series of five articles relating to the various concerns of bilateral transfer, or cross education as he called it. He terminated this work by indicating that the evidence was sufficiently conclusive to support the notion that bilateral transfer does indeed occur for motor skills. Very few experiments published since those by Cook have investigated the question of the occurrence of the bilateral transfer phenomenon. That fact seems to be well accepted. The literature since the 1930s has been directed more toward other issues related to bilateral transfer, such as

	Pretest	Practice Trials	Posttest
Preferred Limb	X	X	X
Nonpreferred Limb	X		X

reminiscence, practice distribution, the overload principle, fatigue, the direction of the most transfer, as well as determining why bilateral transfer occurs and what this means in terms of underlying processes involved in the learning and control of skills.

Symmetry vs. asymmetry of bilateral transfer.
One of the more intriguing questions concerning the bilateral transfer effect concerns the direction of the transfer. The question is whether a greater amount of bilateral transfer occurs from one limb to the other (termed **asymmetric transfer**), or whether the amount of transfer is similar from one limb to the other (termed **symmetric transfer**). Reasons for investigating this question are theoretical as well as practical. From a theoretical perspective, knowing if bilateral transfer is symmetric or asymmetric would provide insight into the role of how the two cerebral hemispheres control movement. That is, do the two hemispheres play similar or different roles in movement control? A more practical reason for investigating this question relates to the issue of designing practice to facilitate optimal skill performance with either limb. If asymmetric transfer predominates, then this would suggest that training with one limb should always be done before training with the other, whereas if symmetric transfer predominates, it would not make any difference which limb was trained first.

The generally accepted view about the direction of bilateral transfer is that it is *asymmetric*. But there seems to be some controversy concerning whether this asymmetry favors initial preferred or non-preferred limb practice. Ammons (1958), in a comprehensive review of the bilateral transfer research completed prior to 1958, concluded that greater transfer can be expected to occur from the preferred limb to the non-preferred limb. However, more recently, evidence appears to favor the opposite direction for greater transfer. For example, Taylor and Heilman (1980) showed that for a complex finger-sequencing task, initial training with the non-preferred hand (the left hand for subjects in this experiment) led to greater transfer to the preferred hand than did the opposite practice and transfer schedule. Interestingly, subjects in this experiment were not permitted to see their hands while performing. When subjects were able to see their hands, the transfer was symmetric. Support for the asymmetric transfer direction of non-preferred to preferred limb, even with vision available, was provided more recently by Elliott (1985) using a sequential finger-tapping task similar to the one used by Taylor and Heilman.

While the direction of bilateral transfer appears to be asymmetric, we do not seem to know whether more transfer occurs following initial practice with the preferred or the non-preferred limb. Perhaps one way of rectifying this issue is to consider the types of tasks used when one direction was supported over the other. The one clear distinction is that when non-preferred to preferred limb transfer showed a greater amount of transfer, the tasks required a complex sequencing of events, or parts of a complex skill. In terms of applying this result to designing effective instruction, the suggestion is that if the skill being taught is a complex one that has several parts that must be sequenced in a specific order, more bilateral transfer will occur if initial training is with the non-preferred limb. However, it would appear that when other factors are taken into account, such as motivation related to initial process, this direction of transfer conclusion may not be as critical from a practical perspective as it is from a theoretical one.

The Causes of Bilateral Transfer

There are two likely reasons why bilateral transfer occurs. One of these is based on a cognitive explanation that postulates what is transferred is important cognitive information related to what to do to achieve the goal of the skill. The second reason for bilateral transfer proposes a motor control explanation that incorporates the generalized motor program and the transfer of motor output characteristics through the nervous system. The arguments supporting each of these viewpoints along with some evidence related to each will be considered next.

A cognitive explanation.   The traditional view of why bilateral transfer occurs is that the common elements of the tasks performed by the two limbs transfer (Ammons, 1958). This explanation must be considered as being based on the "identical elements" theory suggested by Thorndike, which was discussed in Concept 2.3. This view gives strong consideration to those elements of a skill that relate to knowing "what to do," which was described in Concept 2.2 as being primarily cognitive information about performing a skill.

For example, a skill being performed with one limb and then the other can be considered to be essentially two distinct skills. Throwing a ball at a target using the right arm is a different task from throwing a ball with the left arm. However, elements of these skills are common to both regardless of the hand being used. Examples would be the arm-leg opposition principle, the need to keep your eyes focused on the target, and the need to follow through. Each of these elements describe what to do to successfully throw the ball at a target and do not specifically relate to either arm. If you achieve proficiency at this task using the right arm, these common elements do not need to be relearned when you begin practicing with the left arm. You should begin at a higher level of proficiency with the left arm than you would have if you have never practiced using the right arm. Thus, the cognitive components of the task being learned, which involve much of the beginning learner's attention (recall the stages of learning discussion in Concept 2.2) have been learned *before* practice with the opposite limb begins.

Some support for a cognitive basis for bilateral transfer was provided in a series of experiments by Kohl and Roenker (1980). In the second experiment, which is representative of the overall findings, subjects were divided into three groups. The physical practice group practiced a pursuit rotor task (60 rpm for 30 seconds) with their right hand for 18 trials. The mental imagery group held the stylus with their right hand and, with eyes closed, imaged themselves tracking the target for 18 trials (they had observed the experimenter perform one trial prior to these imagery trials). The third group, the control group, had no right-hand practice or imagery practice and did not see the apparatus until the transfer trials. Following these practice conditions, all three groups practiced on the pursuit rotor with their left hand for 18 trials. As you can see in Figure 3.4–1, the physical practice and mental imagery practice groups performed similarly on the transfer trials. Both groups performed better than the control group. These results indicate the cognitive nature of bilateral transfer.

A motor control explanation.   The second possible basis for bilateral transfer is a *motor control* explanation. There are two ways of considering this explanation. The first is related to the generalized motor program discussed in Concept 3.3. Recall that this program is characterized as an abstract memory representation responsible for the control of a class of movements or actions. A key feature of the program is that the muscles required to produce an action are *not* represented in the motor program as an invariant characteristic. Rather, muscles are a *parameter* of the program that are added to the program according to what muscles are required to achieve the goal of the action. As was described in the discussion in Concept 3.3, such a view of the motor program provides a way to explain our capability to write our name with a pen in our preferred hand as well as with some other limb, or even with a pen held between our teeth. In fact, Raibert (1977) demonstrated movement pattern similarities for this type of handwriting regardless of the muscle group required to produce the movement. Thus, bilateral transfer as a motor control phenomenon is consistent with the view that the generalized motor program operates as a control mechanism by specifying time and space features of movement.

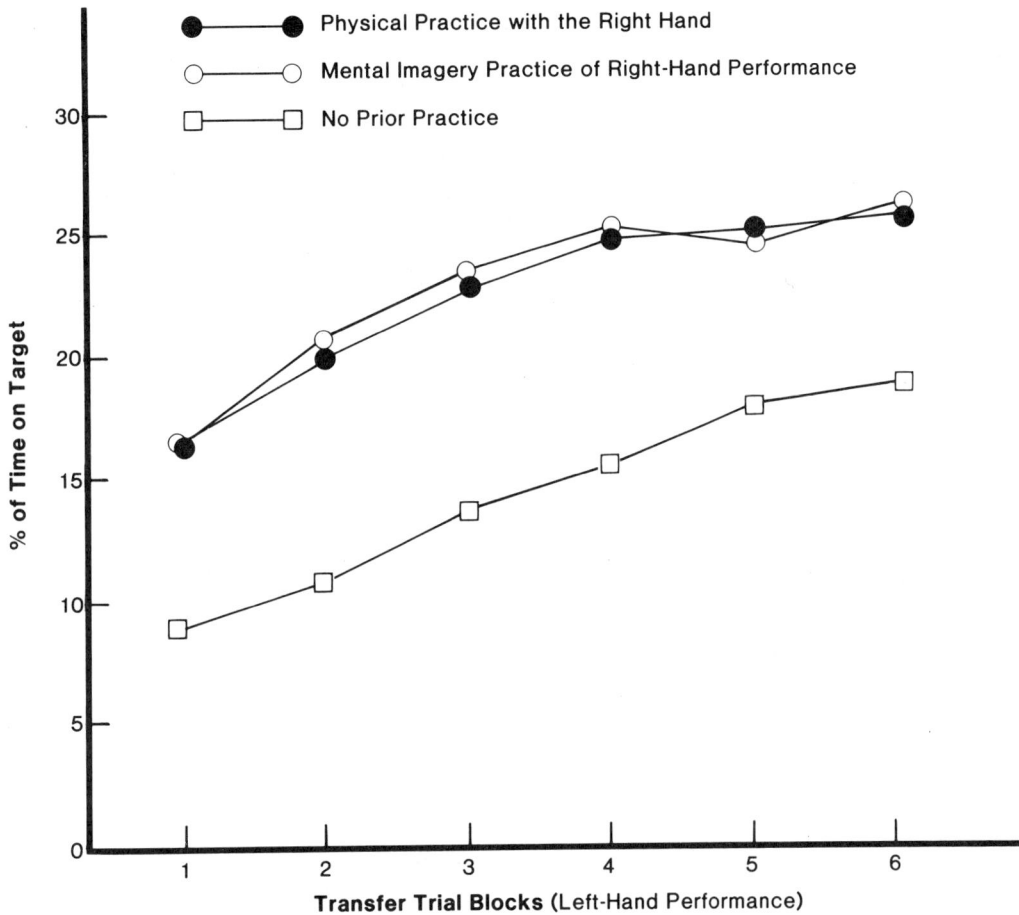

FIGURE 3.4-1 Transfer trial results from the experiments by Kohl and Roenker. Shown here are the performances of three groups experiencing different practice conditions during the preceding 18 trials.

And this program can be adapted to produce a goal-directed action for a muscle group that has not previously been involved in performing the skill.

Because the generalized motor program develops for a skill as a result of practice, and because effector system information is not an invariant feature of the program, it would be expected that if following sufficient program development through practice with one limb, a reasonable level of performance with a non-practiced limb would be possible. However, due to other factors, such as perceptual, biomechanical, and specificity of training problems, initial performance with the non-practiced limb would not be expected to be as good as performance with the practiced limb. But this initial performance can be expected to be better than if there had been no practice at all with the other limb.

The second way to establish a motor control explanation for bilateral transfer is based on evidence showing that at least some bilateral transfer of skill is meditated by interhemispheric transfer of the motor components of the task (Hicks, Gualtieri, & Schroeder, 1983). This mediation can be demonstrated by measuring the EMG activity in all four limbs when one limb performs a movement. Results from earlier research by Davis (1942) indicated that the greatest amount of EMG activity is for the contralateral limbs (i.e., the two arms), a lesser amount for the ipsilateral limbs (i.e., arm and leg on the same side), and the least amount for the diagonal limbs.

Additionally, Hicks, Frank, and Kinsbourne (1982) showed that when subjects practiced a typing task with one hand, there was bilateral transfer only when the other hand was free. When the nontyping hand grasped the table leg during typing, no bilateral transfer effects were observed. These results were interpreted to indicate that when the control centers for the muscles that will be involved in the test trials are otherwise engaged, as they were when the fingers were flexed to grasp the table leg, those centers are unavailable for the "central overflow of programming" that goes on during an action.

A two-part explanation conclusion. The evidence clearly points to an explanation of bilateral transfer that is based on *both* cognitive and motor factors. There is no doubt that much of what is transferred from practicing a skill with one limb are the cognitive components related to "what to do." This is quite consistent with the various models of the stages of skill learning described in Concept 2.2, in which this type of information was proposed to be critical for performing the skill in the first stage of learning. And there is likewise no doubt that motor components of a skill are transferred from one limb to the other. This is consistent with our view of the motor program presented in Concept 3.3, and with evidence that there is some motor outflow to other limbs when one limb performs a skill.

For the person involved in motor skill instruction or rehabilitation, the next important question concerns how to take advantage of the bilateral transfer phenomenon and implement it into the instructional or rehabilitation setting. This question is considered next.

Implementing Bilateral Transfer Training

Facilitating bilateral skill development for many motor skills is an important responsibility of the instructor. We discussed earlier several situations in which this type of development is essential. We concluded that equal amounts of practice with both limbs in a particular skill is not a practical means of achieving bilateral skill development. Furthermore, the evidence we have just discussed indicates that this equal practice approach is not a necessary solution.

Two key points provide the basis for developing guidelines for implementing effective practice conditions to enhance bilateral training in motor skills. To begin with, the first stage of learning a motor skill is oriented toward learning what to do and what movement pattern will allow achievement of the goal of a skill. Second, the control of coordinated movement is based on the operation of a generalized motor program in which actions are represented without regard to which muscles can produce the action. When these two points are taken together and applied to the question of what is an appropriate practice condition to develop effective bilateral training, a very specific conclusion results. That is, early practice sessions should concentrate on the development of a reasonable degree of skill performance proficiency with one limb before practice begins with the other limb. By achieving some level of proficiency, the individual will have answered most of the cognitive questions that need to be answered in early practice and will have developed a motor program for the practiced action to a point where skill refinement becomes the goal of practice.

Although there is some controversy about which limb should be practiced first, it seems that a reasonable argument can be made for initiating practice with the student's preferred limb. The basis for this argument comes from the importance of

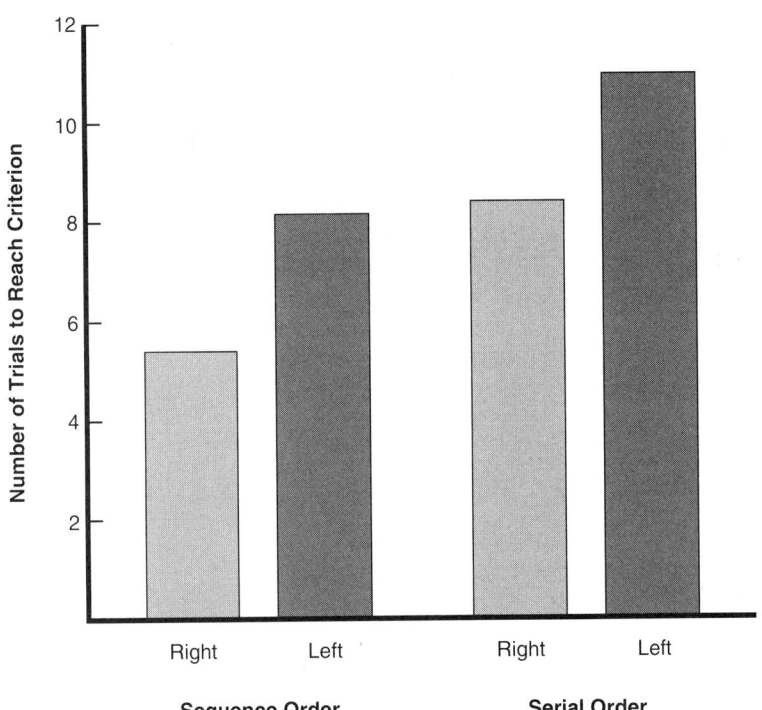

FIGURE 3.4-2 Results of the experiment by Dunham showing the number of trials needed to reach a performance criterion of 70% time on target on a pursuit rotor. Right-hand practice preceded left-hand practice.

initial success in motivating the student to continue trying to learn the skill (a point to be discussed further in Chapter 9), the benefit of establishing practice conditions in which the student can attain a degree of confidence in his or her capability of learning the skill, and the need to provide a practice environment where perceptual and cognitive confusion will be minimal. Each of these characteristics can be enhanced by initiating practice with the student's preferred limb. By adopting this approach to bilateral skill development, an effective as well as efficient means of learning should result.

There is, in fact, research evidence to support the practice schedule organizaton recommended here for bilateral skill training. For example, in an experiment by Dunham (1977), subjects practiced a pursuit rotor task (20 rpm for 20 seconds) according to either a "sequence" order of right and left hand practice, or a "serial" order of practice. In the sequence order, subjects practiced with the

preferred hand until a score of 70% on target (14 seconds out of 20) for two consecutive trials was achieved. When this criterion was reached, the subjects transferred to the opposite hand and practiced until they achieved the same 70% criterion with that hand. The serial order group alternated hands until each 70% criterion was achieved by each hand. The results, seen in Figure 3.4–2, show that the sequential order group achieved criterion performance with both hands in fewer trials than the serial order group. These results indicate that bilateral transfer occurs faster when one limb is practiced to a reasonable degree of proficiency before practice is begun with the opposite limb.

Summary

Bilateral transfer of learning involves the improvement in performance of one limb as a result of practice with the opposite limb. For many motor skills, performance is enhanced if the skill can be performed successfully with either arm or either leg. Bilateral transfer has been demonstrated for motor skills since the early part of this century. What remains the biggest mystery is why it occurs. Both cognitive and motor control characteristics are involved in explaining bilateral transfer. Cognitive elements related to what to do transfer to the non-practiced limb. Practice with one limb establishes a generalized motor program for a skill that is not muscle-specific. Thus, the program can be adapted to the control requirements of performing the skill with the non-practiced limb. Bilateral transfer can be facilitated by orienting early practice toward development of proficiency with the preferred limb. After a degree of proficiency has been developed with that limb, practice with the non-preferred limb can be included in the practice sessions.

Related Readings

Elliott, D. (1985). Manual asymmetries in the performance of sequential movements by adolescents and adults with Down's Syndrome. *American Journal of Mental Deficiency, 90,* 90–97.

Elliott, D., & Jaeger, M. (1988). Practice and the visual control of manual aiming movements. *Journal of Human Movement Studies, 14,* 279–291.

Laszlo, J. I., & Baguley, R. A. (1971). Motor memory and bilateral transfer. *Journal of Motor Behavior, 3,* 235–240.

Schmidt, R. A., and Young, D. E. (1987). Transfer of movement control in motor skill learning. In S. M. Cormier and J. D. Hagman (Eds.), *Transfer of learning* (pp. 47–79). Orlando, FL: Academic Press.

□

STUDY QUESTIONS FOR CHAPTER 3
(Controlling Movement)

1. Describe how a movement would be controlled by (a). a closed-loop system; (b). an open-loop system.

2. What is a j.n.d.? What implications does the j.n.d. have for aiding our understanding of how we control movement?

3. Describe three methods for investigating the role of proprioception in the control of movement and what the results of these investigations using these methods tell us about the role of proprioception in controlling movement?

4. What do we know about the length of time it takes to process visual information in performing a motor skill? How have researchers investigated this question?

5. What is visual search? Describe visual search characteristics for skilled performers in three different skills?

6. What two roles does vision play in controlling manual aiming movements? How is the duration of the movement a variable influencing these roles?

7. Define the term anticipation timing. Describe three variables that influence anticipation timing accuracy and indicate how each factor influences this accuracy.

8. Describe how vision is involved in controlling two of the following motor skills: prehension; locomotion; catching a ball; batting a ball.

9. Define a generalized motor program and describe two invariant characteristics and two parameters proposed to characterize this program?

10. How is Fitts' Law related to the speed-accuracy tradeoff phenomenon observed in many motor skills? What are two explanations of Fitts' Law?

11. What are two types of evidence given to argue against the motor program being involved in controlling coordinated movement?

12. Why is performing an asymmetrical bimanual limb skill so difficult to control? How does bimanual limb control provide evidence for coordinative structures?

13. What is bilateral transfer? What are two reasons why it occurs?

14. Describe how you would organize practice for a skill in which using either arm or either leg would be beneficial for performing that skill.

CHAPTER 4

ATTENTION

CONCEPT 4.1

Attention is related to the idea that we have a limited capacity to process information.

CONCEPT 4.2

Limited attention capacity requires selecting and attending to meaningful information in order to achieve skill performance success.

CONCEPT 4.3

Limited attention capacity requires alertness and preparation of the movement control system to produce voluntary, coordinated movement.

CONCEPT 4.1

Attention is related to the idea that we have
a limited capacity to process information

Key Terms

single-channel
theory

limited-
capacity
theories

capacity

pool of effort

arousal

enduring
dispositions

momentary
intentions

multiple-
resource
theories

dual-task
procedure

automaticity

Application

When you are driving your car on a road that has little traffic and few sharp curves, it is relatively easy to carry on a conversation with a passenger in the car at the same time, even if you have to shift gears. But what happens when you are driving on a congested city street? It is much more difficult to carry on a conversation with your passenger while driving under those conditions.

Why is it easy to do several things at the same time in one situation but difficult to do these same things in another situation? One answer to this question is an important aspect of Concept 4.1. That is, we can only consciously attend to, or think about, so much at one time. As long as what we are doing can be handled within the capacity limits of our information processing system, we can effectively carry out several activities at the same time. However, if what we are doing requires more of our attention than we can give to all the tasks being attempted at the same time, we either have to stop doing some things in order to do others well,

or we will do all of them poorly. In the example above, driving requires little attention on the open road so you can converse relatively easily at the same time. However, when traffic becomes heavy, your conversation suffers because driving requires all your attention.

Consider some other examples that incorporate this concept of attention, but in a slightly different way. Why, for example, is it easy for a skilled second baseman to effectively do all that is required in completing a double play when a beginner has so much difficulty in trying to complete all the parts of that skill at once? Or why can a skilled typist carry on a conversation with someone while continuing to type? Why does a physical therapy patient tell the therapist not to tell him or her so many things to think about at the same time? And why does a skilled gymnast or dancer show little difficulty in smoothly and effortlessly carrying out a complex routine, whereas the beginner typically performs in a rough, inefficient way. These examples are related to our capacity to attend to, or capability for attending to, what we are doing as we perform complex motor skills. Each example shows how there exists conditions under which several things can be done simultaneously, while there are other conditions under which these same things cannot be done simultaneously. In the following discussion, different performance conditions will be considered along with reasons explaining their effects.

Discussion

Since the earliest days of experimental psychology, the study of attention has interested people concerned with understanding human performance. In 1859, Sir William Hamilton conducted studies dealing with attention. Others, such as William Wundt, the "father of experimental psychology," were also interested in the concept of attention. William James provided an early definition of attention in 1890, describing attention as the "focalization, concentration, of consciousness." In 1908 Pillsbury wrote a classic work titled *Attention* in which he related attention to eight psychological concepts such as memory, perception, and the self. E. B. Titchener was also involved in the early investigation of attention, as noted by his book *Lectures on the Elementary Psychology of Feeling and Attention,* published in 1908.

This turn-of-the-century emphasis on attention was soon to wane as the influence of behaviorism became more insistent. The study of attention simply was considered no longer relevant to the understanding of human behavior. A renaissance of attention research occurred, however, when the practical requirements of World War II developed a need to understand human performance in a variety of military skills. Researchers were interested in several attention-related areas, such as performing more than one component of a skill or more than one skill at the same time, performing tasks where rapid decisions had to be made when there were several response choices, and performing tasks where attention had to be maintained over long periods of time. These, among other factors, created renewed interest in the study of attention as it relates to motor skill learning and performance. Several of these concerns are the focus of the concepts discussed in this chapter. We will begin the discussion of attention by considering the most basic concern, which is attention limits related to doing more than one thing simultaneously.

Interest in the problem of successfully doing more than one thing at a time can be traced back to 1886, when a French physiologist named

Jacques Loeb showed that the maximum amount of pressure that can be exerted on a hand dynamometer actually decreases when the operator is engaged in mental work. Unfortunately, prior to the 1950s very little was done to develop the implications of this result, which was the notion that humans have a limited information processing capacity. However, since that time, much research effort has been directed toward understanding human performance limitation. The result of this work has been the development of several different theoretical viewpoints that propose explanations for performance limitation. We will consider some of the more prominent of these theories of attention in the following section.

Theories of Attention

The Single-Channel Theory

The first formal theory addressing human performance limits related to engaging in more than one activity at a time was proposed and advanced by British psychologists A. T. Welford (1952, 1967, 1968) and Donald E. Broadbent (1958). The **single-channel theory** suggested that the human performer, or operator, constitutes a single limited processing capacity channel. This perspective of a human as a single channel processor of information viewed the individual as having difficulty doing several things at one time because the information processing system took time to perform its functions. Added to this was the idea that in performing its functions, the system only did one thing at a time. That is, the system contained a *bottleneck* so that only one activity could be performed at a time. Other activities were "put on hold" until one was completed. Much of the rationale behind this single-channel, or bottleneck, view came from research related to the psychological refractory period (PRP), which will be discussed in Concept 4.3.

It became apparent from research investigating this theory, however, that because it is often possible to respond appropriately to more than one stimulus at the same time, this single-channel

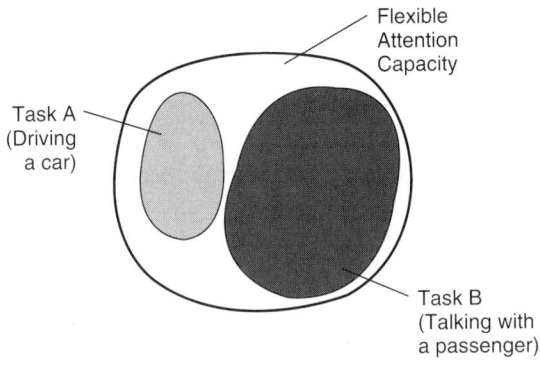

Task A
(Driving
a car)

Flexible
Attention
Capacity

Task B
(Talking with
a passenger)

FIGURE 4.1-1 Diagram showing that two tasks (A and B) can be performed simultaneously (e.g., driving a car while talking with a passenger) if the attention demanded by the tasks does not exceed the available attention capacity. Note that the amount of available capacity and the amount of attention demanded by each task to be performed may increase or decrease, which would be represented in this diagram by changing the sizes of the appropriate circles.

theory had to be modified. The most acceptable alternative proposed that not all mental operations require space in a single limited-capacity mechanism because some operate "automatically." This modification of the single-channel view, advanced by Posner and Boies (1969), argued that the only time it was difficult to do more than one mental operation at a time was when the tasks required more information processing space than was available. Otherwise, the tasks could easily be performed at the same time. Here, then, the limit for doing more than one thing simultaneously was not related to time limits but to *space* limits. Thus, the theoretical emphasis shifted from time-based theoretical accounts of attention to space-based accounts, in which the capacity of the system became the focus.

Limited-Capacity Theories

Limited-capacity theories, which were developed after single-channel notions were no longer considered valid, proposed it would be possible to do more than one task simultaneously as long as the "processing space" demands of these activities did not exceed the capacity limits of the system. If capacity limits were exceeded, however, interference would result and difficulty in performing one or more of these tasks would be experienced. One way of looking at this limited-capacity view is to represent the information processing system as a large circle, as depicted in Figure 4.1–1. In this figure, the driving and talking situation described in the Application section of this concept is used

to illustrate the limited-capacity notion. The different tasks of driving (Task A) and talking with a friend (Task B), which we try to do at the same time, are seen as small circles. As long as all of the small circles can fit into the large circle, we can effectively carry out the tasks. Problems arise, however, when we try to fit more small circles into the large circle than will fit.

It is worth noting that, in the development of the theories of attention that propose there is a limited capacity to process information, there have been attempts to overcome use of the rather difficult to define term **capacity.** Some have suggested that there is a limit to *resources* available to appropriately process the information. Others have proposed that there is a limit in the amount of *effort,* or mental activity, that can be devoted to processing the information. Regardless of the terminology, the underlying theme is similar. That is, humans are distinctly limited in being able to effectively process information. The continuing search by scholars is to ascertain *why* this limitation occurs. Limited-capacity theories reflect one approach to answering this question.

Three different types of limited-capacity theories have emerged over the years since general agreement was reached that a single-channel view could not acceptably account for attention limits. Two of these theories hold that the capacity limit is a global, central one. That is, all information that enters a person's processing system, regardless of its source, its characteristics, or its output requirements, must compete for space in a single processing mechanism. The first of these theories holds that this mechanism has a fixed capacity, whereas the second holds that the capacity has flexible limits. The third theory of processing capacity argues against a single, central mechanism and proposes that there are multiple sources of attention, with each source having its own capacity limits. We will look briefly at each of these three types of limited-capacity theories.

Fixed-capacity theories. The first limited-capacity model alternative to the single-channel, time-based models of attention proposed that there is a central mechanism of attention that has a fixed capacity for processing information. The limit of this mechanism is based on how much information can be handled simultaneously. Most of the early capacity theories of attention were of this type (e.g., Deutsch & Deutsch, 1973; Moray, 1967; Norman, 1969). According to these theories, because there is a fixed, limited attention capacity for processing information, it would not be possible to successfully perform simultaneously two difficult tasks, although two easy tasks would be possible. Whether an easy and a difficult task could be successfully performed together would depend on the demand on capacity of the difficult task (see Kantowitz & Knight, 1978, for more discussion of this point).

The most debated issue among the different fixed-capacity theories has been *where* in the stages of processing the limit exists for incoming information. Because there is a large amount of information coming into the system from the environment before and during task performance, and because there is a fixed limit to how much of that information can be processed at one time, the logical questions become, Where does the information that gets processed get selected? and How does this selection take place? These questions are difficult to answer and have led to a variety of conflicting views. We will address these questions in the next concept where selective attention is discussed.

Flexible-capacity theories. Some researchers have argued that a fixed-capacity view of attention capacity is not acceptable. Although these persons agree that the attention mechanism is a single, centrally located unit, they proposed that its capacity limits are flexible. This means that the capacity could be larger or smaller depending on certain conditions related to the individual and the situation. A good example of this type of theory was proposed by Daniel Kahneman (1973). We will consider this theory in some detail because it has many interesting practical implications for motor skill learning and performance.

Kahneman stated that the *available* attention that could be given an activity or activities should be thought of as a general **pool of effort,** which involves the mental resources necessary to carry out activities. This one pool can be subdivided so that attention can be distributed to several activities at the same time. This distribution, or allocation as Kahneman called it, is determined on the basis of the characteristics of the activities and the allocation policy of the individual, which is influenced by situations internal and external to the individual. Figure 4.1–2 illustrates Kahneman's capacity model by portraying the various conditions that influence how a person will allocate the mental resources that constitute the available attention capacity.

Notice first that the box containing the wavy line represents the available attention capacity. This represents the single pool of limited resources available for allocation to activities. The wavy line suggests that the arousal level (which will be discussed in Concept 4.3) of the individual influences the available capacity. **Arousal** refers to the general state of excitability of the person. If the arousal level is too low or too high, the result will be a decrease in available attention capacity. Kahneman further indicates that both the arousal level and the available capacity will increase or decrease according to the demands of the activities being performed. That is, some activities will demand more processing capacity, or mental re-

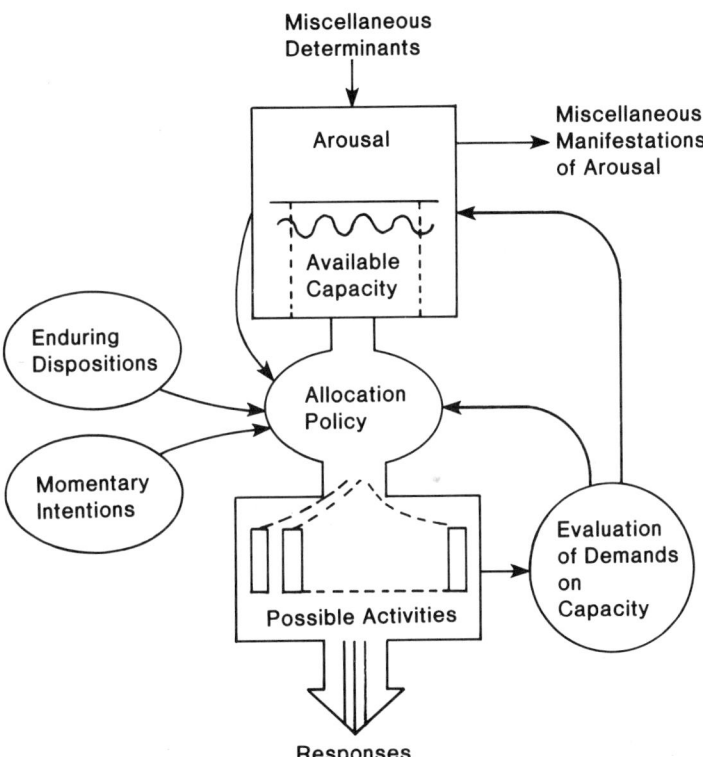

FIGURE 4.1-2 Kahneman's model of attention.
From David Kahneman, *Attention and Effort*, © 1973, p. 10. Reprinted by permission of Prentice-Hall, Inc., Englewood Cliffs, NJ.

sources, than will other activities. Thus, both individual and task characteristics play important roles in determining attention capacity allocation.

The *allocation policy* of the person will influence the distribution of the available attention capacity. This policy is controlled by four kinds of factors. The first are called **enduring dispositions** and are the basic rules of "involuntary" attention, such as attention given to a novel signal, to a sudden noise, or to one's name being called in a crowded room. Second are the **momentary intentions,** which are the instructions given to the individual or the individual's specific intentions for the situation. They include things such as being directed to watch a ball or the intention to listen to the coach while performing. The third factor is the *evaluation of demands*. That is, the demands of the activities to be engaged in are evaluated in terms of whether sufficient attention capacity is available. Kahneman suggests that there is a type of rule operating in this situation where the system will be directed to complete one activity if more capacity is needed than is available to do two activities. Finally, the *effects of arousal* will have a systematic influence on the allocation policy.

The benefit of this model is that it demonstrates the various processes involved in allocating the available attention to activities. If the activities to be performed simultaneously can be effectively handled within the available capacity, the result should be the effective performance of all activities. On the other hand, if performing these activities simultaneously will result in an "overload," this model indicates the basis on which the limited resources, or attention capacity, will be allocated. Thus, some activities may be performed better than others due to the way in which resources were distributed among the activities.

Multiple-resource theories. One of the problems faced by attention theories positing a central pool of attention is how to account for different performance effects for a task when it is performed simultaneously with one of two different tasks. The expectation of a central pool of attention theory is that performance of the task would be similarly influenced by either of the other tasks. However, research evidence has shown that this is not always the case. To account for these types of results, different types of attention theories have been developed. **Multiple-resource theories** propose that we do not have just one central information-processing mechanism with a limited capacity, but rather several mechanisms, each of which is limited in how much information can be processed simultaneously. The most prevalent of these multiple-resource theories were proposed by Navon and Gopher (1979), Allport (1980), and Wickens (1980, 1984).

Wickens proposed that resources for processing information are available from three different sources. These are the *input and output modalities* (e.g., vision, limbs, and speech system), the *stages of information processing* (e.g., perception, memory encoding, response output), and the *codes of processing information* (e.g., verbal codes, spatial codes). When two tasks must be performed simultaneously and they share a common resource, they will not be performed as well as when the two tasks must compete for different resources. An example of this situation would occur for performing a tracking task and a verbal memory task together compared to performing a tracking task and a verbal task requiring spatial decisions. The multiple-resource view would predict that the tracking task and verbal memory task would be more effectively performed simultaneously than the tracking task and verbal task requiring spatial decisions, because tracking and the spatial task would compete for the same resource because they each involve spatial coding of information. Further, when task difficulty is taken into account, two difficult tasks could be performed simultaneously if they require different resources, but could not if they competed for the same resources (see Wickens, Sandry, & Vidulich, 1983, for examples of experiments supporting the predictions of this model).

Thus, the focus of multiple-resource theories of attention is on the demands placed on various information processing and response outcome structures rather than on mental activity resource capacity. Two tasks, one involving a hand response and the other a vocal response, can be peformed simultaneously because they do not demand attention from the same resource structure. Conversely, two different hand responses are difficult to do simultaneously because they demand resources from the same structure. According to the multiple-resource view, whether or not attention limits are exceeded depends on the degree of structural interference created by the various activities performed simultaneously.

Dual-Task Procedures

As you saw throughout the discussion of the various theories of attention, the common interest was the simultaneous performance of two or more activities. Because of this, the most common experimental procedure used to investigate attention limitation issues has been the **dual-task procedure.** The general purpose of experiments using this technique is to determine the attention demands and characteristics of two different tasks when performed simultaneously. The general approach has been to determine the attention demands of one of the two tasks by noting the degree of interference caused on one task while being simultaneously performed with another task, called the secondary task. The *primary task* in the dual-task procedure is the task of interest in terms of assessing the attention demands to perform it. In some experiments using the dual-task procedure, it is important that performance on the primary task be as consistent as possible at all times. Performance of the primary task should be similar whether performed alone or simultaneously with the second task. In other experiments, instructions do not provide this restriction. The task that is performed simultaneously with the primary task is called the *secondary task*. If instructions in the experiment require the subject to pay attention to the primary task so that it is performed as well with the secondary task as alone, then performance on the secondary task is assessed as the basis for making inferences about the attention demands required of the primary task. On the other hand, the experiment may not direct the subject's attention to either task and ask him or her to perform both tasks the best they can. In this case, performance on both tasks is assessed and compared to when each task is performed alone.

The more common, and simpler to interpret, of these dual-task procedures has been when the instructions given are to maintain performance of the primary task while performing the secondary task. Two different approaches to the use of this procedure will be discussed in the following sections. One procedure involves having the secondary task performed continuously during performance of the primary task. The other procedure "probes" performance of the primary task with performance of the secondary task by having the secondary task being performed at different times during primary task performance.

Continuous secondary task technique. One approach to the use of the dual-task procedure where subjects were required to maintain performance on a primary task while performing a secondary task is exemplified in a study by Kantowitz and Knight (1976). The primary task was a reciprocal tapping task in which subjects had to maintain a specified rate of speed as they moved a stylus back and forth between two targets. The tapping speed was indicated by a metronome. The secondary task involved the continuous performance of some type of mental task, such as adding columns of digits. The subject was told to perform both tasks at the same time but to be certain to maintain the proper tapping speed at all times. The logic behind interpreting the results of this procedure was that if the tapping task and the adding task can be done together, the subject should be able to perform the secondary task as well while doing the primary task, as when doing the secondary task alone. In

other words, a type of "time-sharing" can go on in the processing system to enable both tasks to be done simultaneously.

Kantowitz and Knight have shown that two tasks can be done together with little difficulty if the secondary task is an easy one, such as simply naming digits presented to the subject. However, as the secondary task becomes more difficult, as in subtracting nine from a presented number, performance on the secondary task worsens. These results provide a clear demonstration of the limited-capacity concept. That is, whether two tasks can be performed simultaneously depends on the attention demanded by them. If both can be performed as well together as they can separately, then the attention capacity has not been exceeded. However, when performing the two tasks together leads to poor performance in one or both tasks, it seems reasonable to conclude that the available attention capacity has been exceeded.

Let's interpret the results of the Kantowitz and Knight research in terms of the circle analogy presented in Figure 4.1–1. If the Task A circle represents the primary task, then it should remain the same size when performed alone or with the secondary task, because the subjects were instructed to maintain constant performance on that task at all times. However, the size of the secondary task circle, which is the Task B circle, depended on the difficulty of that task. When the secondary task was an easy task, the Task B circle was small so that it and the primary task circles fit inside the large, attention capacity circle. However, when Task B was difficult, the Task B circle was too large for both it and the primary task circles to fit into the larger one representing the total available information-processing capacity. The attention demanded of the two types of secondary tasks differed to the extent that the easy one could be done simultaneously with the primary task while the difficult one could not be done simultaneously with the primary task.

Probe technique. The second approach followed in using the dual-task procedure involves the use of a discrete secondary task and has been called

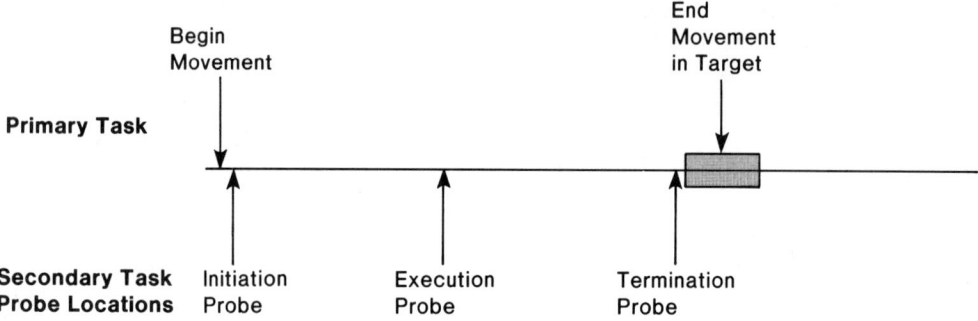

FIGURE 4.1-3 Diagram illustrating one form of probe technique to determine attention demands of primary task at three different phases of the primary task movement, which is depicted here as a rapid movement to a target area. The three probe locations represent points along the primary task movement where a reaction time signal occurs.

the *probe technique*. This approach is especially popular when the researcher is interested in the attention demands of the individual parts, or components, of a task. In the study of attention and motor skill performance, the typical primary task is a type of discrete movement, such as an aiming task or moving a sliding handle along a trackway at a specified rate of speed to a target area. For example, the subject may be told to "move the handle 40 cm in 2 seconds." Here, as in the tapping time-sharing technique, it is important that the subject maintain consistent performance on the primary task at all times.

The secondary task in the probe technique differs markedly from what was used in the continuous secondary task technique. Because the primary interest is in determining the attention demands required of certain components of the primary task, it is only necessary to "probe" that component with a secondary task. This is usually done by using a reaction time task in which the subject is required to depress a response button when a signal sounds while the primary task is being performed. Figure 4.1–3 illustrates a typical probe technique situation.

The subject is required to move the handle with one hand and respond to the RT stimulus, such as a buzzer, with the other hand. The buzzer is positioned so that it can be set to go off at different phases of the primary task movement, such as at the very beginning, in the middle, or at the end. The subject is told to concentrate on the primary task because it is the task of interest. But he or she is also instructed to respond to the buzzer as quickly as possible.

The rationale behind such a procedure is that any phase of the primary task that demands the performer's attention will diminish processing space required by the secondary task. Thus, performance of the secondary task should be much poorer than it would be if it were being carried out alone.

Results of experiments using the probe technique have revealed that all components of a simple, discrete movement do not require the same degree of attention. There has been general agreement that movements require attention or processing capacity to *begin* them. This was shown rather vividly by Ells in 1973. Using the secondary task technique just described, Ells demonstrated that attention demands were highest at the initiation of the response of moving a sliding handle to a stop, but that these demands decreased as the movement continued. There also seems to be agreement that the *actual movement* or *execution phase* of a well-learned movement does not require processing capacity. However, the *termination* or completion of a movement may or may not demand processing capacity, depending on the requirements or limitations of the comple-

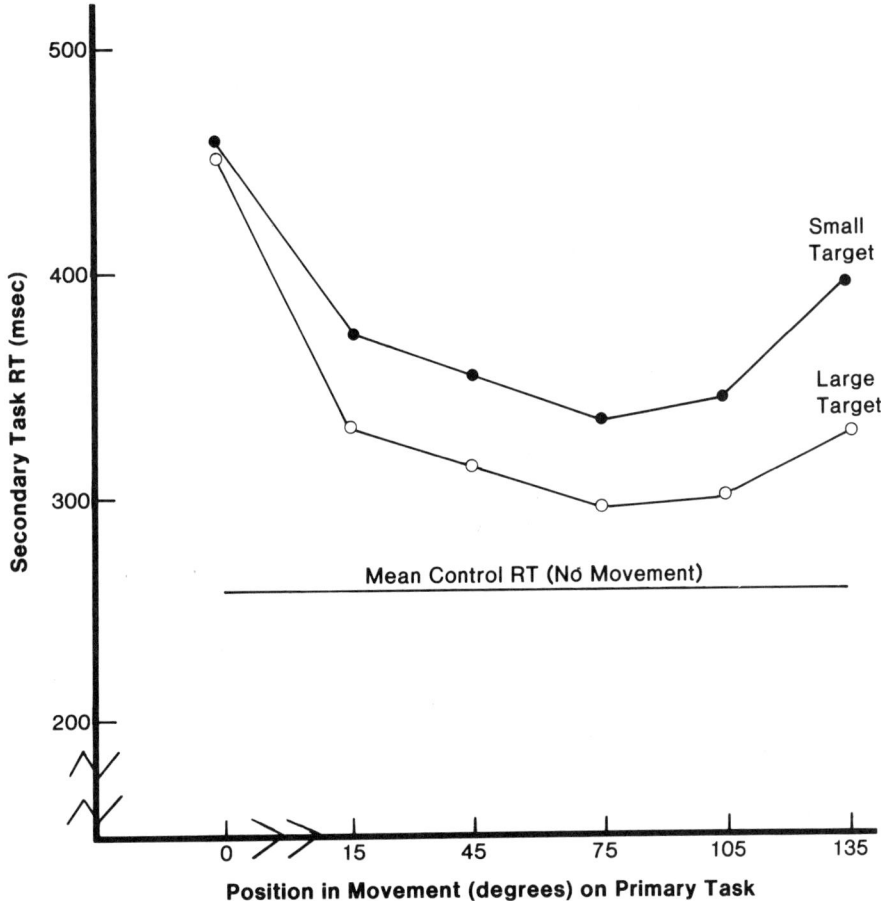

FIGURE 4.1-4 Results of the experiment by Posner and Keele showing differences in secondary task performance (RT) as a function of where the response was made during the 135° rapid primary task. RT effects are shown for primary task movements to large and small targets.

tion of the movement. When Ells' subjects completed their movement, they hit a stop, and processing capacity was not required. However, in an earlier experiment by Posner and Keele (1969), the subjects were to move to a target and to make a correction of their movement if they overshot the target. In this situation, attention demands were dependent on the characteristics of the target (see Figure 4.1–4). If the target was small and therefore required a precise termination, attention demand was high for that phase of the movement, a point more clearly substantiated by Salmoni,

Sullivan, and Starkes (1976). When the target was large, however, the attention required to stop the movement was much less.

Thus, it seems that when the termination of a movement can be corrected, the attention demanded by that action will depend on how precise the final position must be. If there is a relatively minimal demand for precision to terminate a movement, such as at the completion of the follow-through in tennis or golf, little or no attention is demanded during the termination phase of the movement. However, attention is required if the termination of the movement requires a precise placement of the hands or feet, such as a person grasping a cup with a small handle or a long jumper hitting a precise spot on the take-off board.

An important point to emphasize at this stage of our discussion concerns the use of the term *attention demands*. As it is typically used, and as we have been using it, the term implies "conscious" attention. This can be seen in the examples presented in the application section of this concept. Another example occurs when a child is learning to bounce a ball with one hand and run at the same time. This is difficult to do because bouncing the ball requires the child to be "thinking about" that aspect of the skill while doing it. As a result, there is little attention space left to think about running too. However, there do seem to be situations in which attention demand is not the same as "conscious" attention. An example of this was seen in the study of the long jumper by Lee, Lishman, and Thomson (1984), considered in Concept 3.2. Their results indicated that while visual attention was important for the precise hitting of the take-off board, skilled long jumpers and coaches were not aware of the corrections being made as the approach run was being completed. Here, then, attention is demanded of the visual system; however, it is not a conscious attention situation for the skilled athlete.

A word of caution about the probe technique.
Many of the conclusions and applications in this discussion of attention are based on studies using the probe technique. While this appears to be a valid approach, there is need for a word of caution. This need stems from certain research findings presented by Peter McLeod (1978, 1980). He argued that if the secondary task probe actually permitted an inference about capacity demands of attention, it should make little difference what physical structure was involved in performing the secondary task. However, if the typical probe technique was actually demonstrating a structural rather than a capacity interference, using some other physical structure for the RT task, such

as the voice, should lead to different results than were obtained when the other hand was used for the secondary task.

McLeod (1980) compared performance under conditions similar to those of Ells (1973). One group of subjects performed the secondary task using the hand RT probe used by Ells and other researchers. The other group performed the secondary task using a vocal RT, where speaking a word into a microphone stopped the RT clock. Results showed that the hand RT probe was higher than the vocal RT probe, indicating that the two probes were not assessing a central capacity of attention. Additionally, McLeod reported that no one phase of the movement showed a demand for more attention capacity than any other phase of the movement.

An interesting follow-up to McLeod's experiment was reported by Girouard, Laurencelle, and Proteau (1984). In their experiment, subjects performed a primary task that involved either moving the right arm from a home base to a small target 11 cm to the right, then back to the home base, or moving from the home base to a target 11 cm to the left, and then back to the home base. The target to be moved to was appropriately lighted. This task was performed for 50 continuous trials at a time. The secondary task was a two-choice RT task with a high or low tone as the stimulus. In experiment 1, a high tone indicated that the index finger should depress a key while the low tone signaled a middle finger response. In experiment 2, a high tone indicated that the word "quatre" should be said aloud while the low tone indicated that the word "quatorze" should be said aloud. (These are the French words for four and fourteen.) Five parts of the primary task were probed with the RT signal: (1) the interval between arrival at the home base and the onset of the next light signal; (2) the interval between the light onset and the departure from the home base; (3) during the movement to the target; (4) while on the target; and (5) during movement to return to the home base. The results of these experiments, presented in Figure 4.1–5, showed that

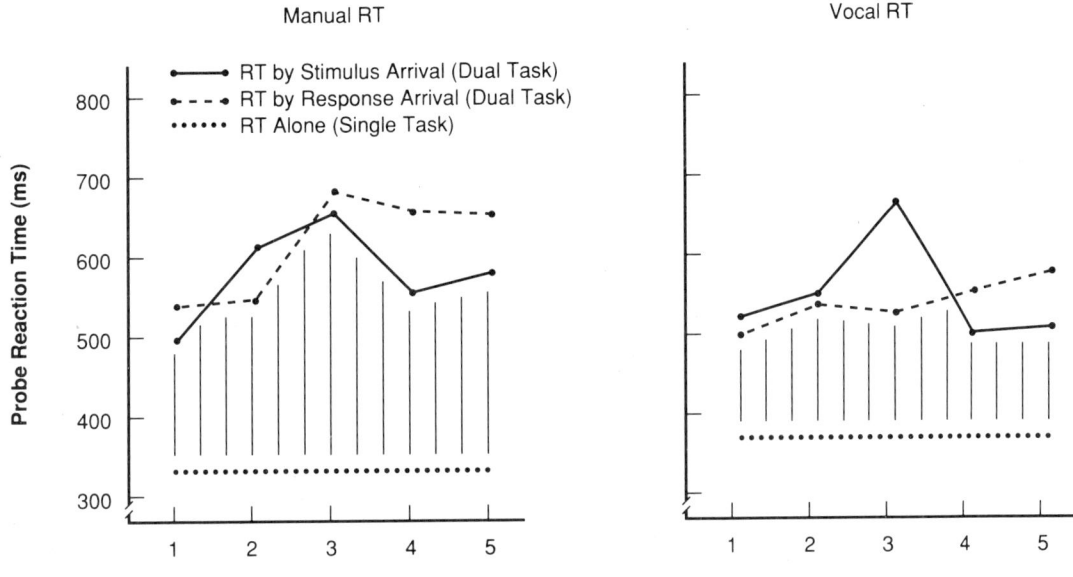

FIGURE 4.1-5 Vocal and manual RT results from the experiment by Girouard, Laurencelle, and Proteau. RTs are plotted for each of five phases of the primary movement (described in the text) and are plotted according to when the stimulus occurred during the primary movement and when the RT response was made during the primary movement.

probe RT was elevated in a different pattern for the manual response than for the vocal response and that plotting of RT on the basis of when the stimulus occurred versus when the response to that stimulus occurred also showed a different pattern of results for both the manual and vocal response.

What do these results mean? First, they indicate support for McLeod's findings regarding vocal RT as plotted for probe response that no particular phase of the primary task demands more attention than any other. However, these results also indicate that McLeod was not correct in contending that no central attention capacity is required by the primary movement. In the results shown in Figure 4.1-5, RT is elevated above its baseline level (which is determined by having the RT task performed alone) throughout the primary task for both RT response modes, regardless of when RT is plotted, although the manual re-

sponse created more of an RT deterioration. These results suggest that we should be cautious in how strictly we interpret results of experiments using probe RT as the basis for determining *when* attention is demanded in the course of preparing or performing a movement. And these results indicate that much research remains to be done to increase our knowledge of attention demands required by performing movements.

Attention Demands and Practice

In the discussion of Concept 2.2, you saw that one of the changes that characterizes performance of a skill from the early to later stages of practice is the amount of attention demanded by the task. Fitts and Posner (1967) actually called the final stage of learning the autonomous or automatic stage. The implication here is that movements become more automated and therefore demand less attention as they are practiced over long periods of time.

When a beginner practices a skill, practice "is carried out under conscious control, in an awkward, step-by-step, poorly coordinated manner" (Henry & Rogers, 1960, p. 449). In other words, the beginner consciously attends to, or thinks about, each step of a complex skill. It seems that for each component part of the skill, conscious attention is directed at what to do next as well as to the sensory feedback of that component. As a result, the fluid, effortless motion characteristic of a skilled individual is not evident in the beginner. However, with practice, the beginner moves along the learning stages continuum and finds that the components of the movement fit together in a more coordinated manner and that less and less conscious attention is needed to be directed to the actual mechanics of performing the skill. Eventually, the skill can be performed virtually automatically with little conscious attention directed toward the performance of the skill.

For example, suppose you are learning a serve in tennis. This is a complex task that has several identifiable parts, such as the stance, racquet grip, ball toss, backswing, forward swing, ball contact, and follow-through. As a beginner it is likely that you will try to think about each of these individual parts as you perform a skill. As a result, you will perform in a rather awkward manner, and your serve will not look like a skilled player's serve. However, as you practice, you stop "thinking about" the individual parts. You begin to put the individual parts together as larger parts so that the ball toss, backswing, etc., become one, fluid action. You find that you may attend only to the height of the ball toss, or its placement in relation to your body. You don't even think about the rest of the serve movements, you just "let them happen." Then as you become even more skilled, you may not think about any of the parts of the serve. Your conscious attention is directed to carrying out the type of serve you want to hit, while your visual attention is directed at the ball.

This example shows how attention demands change over extended periods of practice. The fine spatial-temporal relationships of each of the parts of the serve become automatically controlled. In fact, if you "think about" what you are doing as you serve, you may find that you won't serve well. This occurs because directing conscious attention to the various parts of the skill disrupts the established motor program controlling the task by adding extra time to the intervals of time between the components of the task. This results from the reliance on feedback to provide you with information to control the task. Consequently, you disrupt the programmed spatial-temporal relationships of the parts of the serve that you have developed through practice.

Automaticity

The preceding section about the change in attention demands for skills as a function of practice emphasized an important assumption that has characterized views of motor skill learning for many years. That is, as skills become practiced, and therefore well learned, they can be performed "automatically." **Automaticity** implies that skills can be performed without conscious attention demands. However, there exists in current thinking some concern about this concept of automaticity and how it relates to motor skills. What exactly is automaticity and what does it have to do with motor skill performance?

Some insight into the issues surrounding the concept of automaticity and its relationship to motor skill performance are shown in an important article by Gordon Logan (1985). Logan points out that the concept of skill, i.e., being a skilled performer of some activity, and the concept of automaticity are closely related, as we have alluded to in this text. Automaticity is an important component of skill in that skill consists of knowledge and procedures that can be called upon and carried out automatically. Both automaticity and skill can be acquired through practice. However, automaticity, like our concept of skill, should not be considered as a dichotomous category where some aspect of skill is or is not automatic. Automaticity should be thought of as a continuum of varying degrees. It is possible, for example, that some processing activity required in the performance of a skill may only be partially automatic. If this is so, then there is a need to restructure the dichotomous yes/no question that researchers have asked regarding attention demands when dual-task procedures are employed. One approach to addressing this need would be to assess dual-task performance at various stages of practice.

How automated do complex skills become?

Some skills are highly complex, such as performing a dance or gymnastics routine or playing a piano piece. Do these become automated all the way through the piece so that little, if any, attention is needed? The reasonable response to this question seems to be that the performer develops automated "chunks" of the entire piece (see Miller, 1956). These chunks are parts of the pieces that have been put together into groups and performed with little attention directed toward what is in the chunks. Attention is demanded, however, at the beginning or initiation of each chunk.

Anecdotal evidence for this view of attention demands for performing well-learned complex skills comes from discussions with skilled individuals. During performances, individuals indicate that they perform many parts of the routine automatically, that is, without directing conscious attention toward these parts. However, they also indicate that there are also places in the routine to which they must direct conscious attention. Those places seem to be identified by distinct characteristics. The dancer may attend to the place where the tempo changes or a partner must be contacted or lifted; the pianist may attend to tempo changes. The gymnast may direct attention to parts of the routine that would be dangerous if missed. All of these individuals indicate that they give attention to parts of the routine with which they have had difficulty.

There is, unfortunately, almost no research evidence supporting this view of attention and the performance of complex skills. One reason is that it is difficult to test. However, some studies concerned with simple movements have shown that attention demand changes as a result of practice. These studies (e.g., Reeve, 1976; Wrisberg & Shea, 1978) have shown that while attention may be reduced for some aspects of the movement, the movement does not reach what might be considered a completely automated state. Attention remains critical regardless of the amount of practice for some parts of the skill. What remains to be determined are the characteristics of the parts of a complex skill that will always demand the performer's conscious attention regardless of the stage of learning.

One example of a feature of skills that does not appear to permit the degree of automaticity we might expect as a result of practice is timing. According to Peters (1977), when two different motor activities must be performed at the same time, only one set of time commands will be issued at one time. Thus, it would be expected that there would be certain skills in which different timing activities must be performed simultaneously, and some degree of interference could always be expected. Peters (1985) reported evidence of this when he compared novice and skilled pianists performing rubato, which involves one hand temporarily departing from the common time base and playing another while the other hand continues playing the common time base. Novices were essentially unable to do this. While the skilled pianists were better than the novices, they also showed evidence of interference.

Attention Capacity and Instruction

While the portions of a movement demanding attention may vary according to the skill or action being performed and the stage of learning of the performer, it remains an important principle that the amount of attention demanded by a movement varies according to the critical nature or degree of importance of the part of the movement being performed.

For any task and at any level of performance, the initiation of the movement demands attention. We should give attention to how we begin to move in any skill. The golfer is taught to be sure to begin the movement properly by paying attention to body and hand position and to starting the club back properly. The tennis player attends to the initial phases of hitting a forehand by briefly attending to getting set properly in preparation to hit the ball. The archer attends to the beginning phases of drawing back the arrow. In each of these situations, attention, or processing capacity, is directed toward the initiation of the movement to be executed. Attention directed toward other aspects of the skill or game during this initiation phase will probably cause performance of the movement to be poorer than otherwise expected.

Another instructional point relates to the way in which a complex skill is sequenced in the instructional unit. Because one of the benefits of practice is to automate certain parts of a skill, it becomes an effective strategy to make certain that sufficient practice is given to those parts before adding additional parts of the skill. For example, suppose your goal is to teach a child to dribble a ball, one-handed, while running around a series of obstacles. For the beginner, this task demands more attention than is typically available. What must be done is to break the task into parts to allow each part to reduce its attention demands. Dribbling a ball while standing still may require all of a child's attention. If this is the case, provide sufficient instruction and practice to allow that part of the task to decrease in attention demand before having the child dribble and run at the same time. Then allow sufficient practice with dribbling and running before having the child run an obstacle course.

A similar approach can be taken to teaching almost any complex skill. You must first break the skill into parts that are meaningful and not just arbitrarily determined. Then determine which part should be practiced first. This will usually be a part that needs to become automated so that it can be performed without thought. Build on this by adding the other parts of the skill until finally all that remains is the part that will essentially always demand attention. For open skills, this part will typically be the actual response to the moving object. Thus, it would seem reasonable to make sure a person practices the basics of the tennis stroke and practices hitting a ball that was predictable in terms of speed and where it would bounce, before having the person rally with a partner.

If you go back to the discussion in Concept 1.1, you will find that this progression of practice follows the four parts of the Gentile 2×2 classification system. That is, the student first practices the skill as a completely closed, or Category 1 skill, and then progressively opens it by practicing the skill as a Category 3 then Category 2, and finally as a completely open Category 4 skill.

A research example. By changing certain characteristics of a skill, you can influence attention demands in such a way to facilitate learning of the skill. Reducing attention demands for one aspect of the skill allows the student to give additional attention to another part of the skill. An example of how this can benefit the learner was provided in a study by Jack Leavitt (1979) of the attention demands of skating and stickhandling in ice hockey. Subjects were from six age-group hockey programs, pre-novice through university varsity. (See Figure 4.1–6 for average age and prior experience for each age group.)

In the first experiment, the players were required to skate and/or stickhandle under four conditions: skating only, skating while identifying as many geometric figures shown on a screen as possible, skating while stickhandling a puck, and skating while stickhandling a puck and identifying geometric figures. Results for the skating speed times are shown in Figure 4.1–6 for these four conditions. Notice that it was not until the bantam group (age 14 with 8 years experience) that the skating and stickhandling or the skating

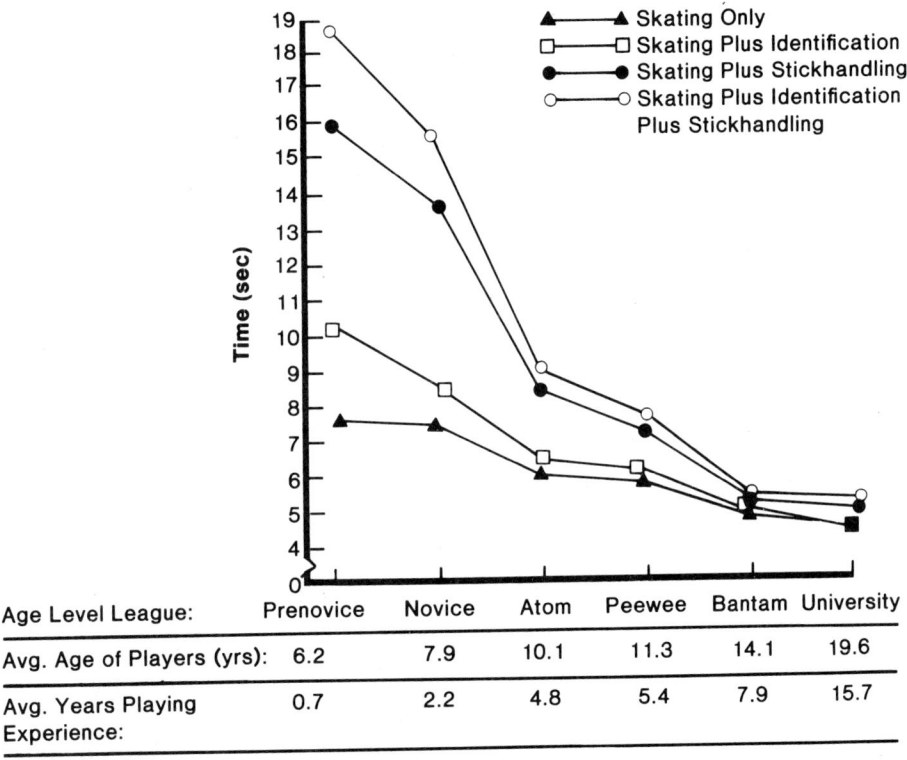

FIGURE 4.1-6 Skating speeds by the different ice hockey players in the experiment by Leavitt.

while stickhandling and identifying figures could be done without slowing down the skating speed. An obvious interpretation of these results is that skating was not "automated" enough in players with less than 8 years of experience to allow skating and stickhandling to be done simultaneously without negatively influencing skating speed.

To consider an attention demand interpretation, Leavitt conducted a second experiment in which the players were given a larger than regulation-sized puck to use. The idea was that a larger puck would be less attention demanding for the stickhandling. The results indicated that the larger puck did in fact lead to skating and stickhandling speeds that were comparable to when the players were only skating.

These experiments by Leavitt provide support for the suggestion that instruction of a complex skill needs to consider the attention demands of

the parts of the skill that must be performed simultaneously. Beginning instruction must emphasize those parts of the skill that must eventually become automated, such as skating in ice hockey. Additional tasks to be done simultaneously should be added after there has been sufficient practice as demonstrated by a reasonable degree of skill with the part of the task that should eventually become automated. When additional tasks are added, they should be added in such a way that will allow the entire skill to be performed without exceeding attention capacity limits. This procedure was exemplified in the Leavitt study when the larger puck was used for stickhandling.

Summary

Attention has been considered as indicating information-processing space. The individual is portrayed as having a limited capacity to process information. As a result, it is often difficult to perform more than one attention demanding task at a time. The most popular theories of attention limits propose that we have a limited capacity to process information. Some theories consider this limitation to be a central, fixed capacity while others consider it to be a central, flexible capacity. An example of a flexible limited-capacity view was presented by Kahneman. According to this view, attention is allocated from a single, central pool of resources that is influenced by several factors related to the individual and to the activities to be performed. Other limited-capacity models include the multiple-resource models, which propose that rather than a central capacity limitation, we have several resources from which attention can be allocated. The typical experimental procedures used to support a limited-capacity view are called dual-task procedures. Two of these, the continuous secondary task technique and the probe technique were discussed. Attention demands are determined according to how well the individual performs two tasks simultaneously. Results of these experiments indicate that different amounts of attention are required by different phases of a movement. Attention demands for performing a

motor skill decrease as a result of practice. Implications based on an understanding of attention demands and motor performance were suggested for providing effective instruction for complex motor skills.

Related Readings

Abernethy, B. (1988). Dual-task methodology and motor skills research: Some applications and methodological constraints. *Journal of Human Movement Studies, 14,* 101–132.

Allport, A. (1987). Selection for action: Some behavioral and neurophysiological considerations of attention and action. In H. Heuer & A. F. Sanders (Eds.), *Perspectives on perception and action* (pp. 395–419). Hillsdale, NJ: Erlbaum.

Kantowitz, B. H. (1985). Channels and stages in human information processing: A limited analysis of theory and methodology. *Journal of Mathematical Psychology, 29,* 135–174.

Logan, G. D. (1985). Skill and automaticity: Relations, implications, and future directions. *Canadian Journal of Psychology, 39,* 367–386.

Stelmach, G. E., & Hughes, B. (1983). Does motor skill automation require a theory of attention? In R. A. Magill (Ed.), *Memory and control of action* (pp. 67–92). Amsterdam: North-Holland.

□

CONCEPT 4.2

Limited attention capacity requires selecting and attending to meaningful information in order to achieve skill performance success

Key Terms

selective attention

feature integration theory

pertinence model

Application

As the tennis player prepares to return a ground stroke from an opponent, an obvious question comes to mind: What should the player be watching or concentrating on to provide the best opportunity for returning the ball? Consider the possibilities or choices that are available. The player could watch the opponent's eyes, or feet, or even body motions for the necessary information. The movements of the opponent's racquet or the ball could also be observed for needed indications. The list of possible cues could go on and on. However, the important fact is that a variety of cues are available to tennis players, cues that they should pay attention to in order to increase their chances of hitting a good return shot.

Consider this same tennis action situation from another perspective also related to the problem of selecting information to attend to. To return the serve, you not only must select and attend to relevant cues from the environment, but you must also select and attend to relevant information within your own information-processing system. For example, information must be selected to determine the appropriate response to make and what muscles should be activated to make that response. Specific kinematic and kinetic details of action must be applied to these muscles to carry

out the response. These examples indicate the volume of information that must be dealt with from within your own motor control system to allow the intended response to occur. Because you know from your study of the preceding concept that you have a limited capacity to process information, it seems only logical then, that you will need some means of selecting the appropriate information to generate and carry out a successful ground stroke.

The same problem occurs when a child is learning to catch a thrown ball. There are a number of possible choices of what to watch. While the skilled individual has learned to watch the ball, the child will watch any number of things, such as the thrower's eyes or hands or just about anything but the thrower and the ball. The child must also select and apply appropriate motor control–related information so that the ball can be caught. Even with the simple, fundamental skill of catching, then, the problem of selecting appropriate information from the environment to pay attention to is a significant one that must be addressed by the instructor in the process of teaching a child this skill.

These examples are critical problems for motor skill performance, especially because we realize that we have a limited capacity to process information. Because of our limitation, and a very short amount of time available to us for selecting a proper response, we are forced to select only certain cues or information from the environment and from within our own cognitive and motor control systems before responding, which is referred to as selective attention. We have already discussed why this is so, but a few questions remain relating specifically to *selective attention*. How can we select certain information or cues and ignore others? What kinds of cues do we pay attention to, and what cues *should* we observe? How does the kind of cue we select to attend to change as a result of our becoming more proficient at the skill? These and other important questions will be considered in the following discussion. It should become apparent that selection of correct cues from those available in the environment may be one of the most important procedures that an instructor of motor skills can include in the teaching process.

———— □ ————

Discussion

The study of selective attention deals with the way in which we select certain information for processing and ignore other information. The examples considered earlier of the tennis player hitting a ground stroke and the child catching a ball illustrate the selection of appropriate visual cues from the environment so that a catching action can be successfully executed. Because people have a limited amount of time to make decisions necessary to prepare and execute these actions, and they have a limited capacity to process the large amount of information associated with performing these actions, there seems to be little doubt about the importance of selecting meaningful information to perform the correct action. In the sections that follow, empirical evidence establishing the need for selective attention and factors that influence this selection process will be discussed along with various accounts of how this selection process occurs.

Cocktail Party Phenomenon

One of the earliest generalizations about selective attention was given the rather intriguing label of the "cocktail party phenomenon." Very simply, this deals with something we have all experienced in any large crowd, such as at a cocktail party. Much talking is going on all around you, and yet you are able to attend quite specifically, or selectively, to one person with whom you are engaged in conversation. Furthermore, if during that conversation someone nearby mentions your name, your attention is immediately diverted to that person.

Thus, in this cocktail party setting, two common experiences lead to two interesting questions that are at the heart of issues related to the study of selective attention. One concerns the capability we have to selectively attend to one message in the midst of many other competing messages. The second question concerns how we can be attending to one message and then suddenly be distracted by another message to which we were not specifically, or at least knowingly, attending.

Some rather significant experiments have investigated this phenomenon. The earliest research was reported in 1953 by E. Colin Cherry, a British experimental psychologist. He introduced an experimental technique called *shadowing*. In these experiments, a subject was presented messages or sounds through one or both sides of a set of earphones. The experimental procedure required the subject to repeat the message, or *shadow* the message. Thus, the subject was generally following or receiving one message and ignoring any others. In effect, this is the same situation that occurs at the cocktail party, but it is now present in a controlled, laboratory setting.

The first set of Cherry's experiments dealt specifically with how we recognize what one person is saying when others are speaking at the same time. The subject was presented with two mixed speeches that had been recorded on tape and was then asked to repeat one message, either word by word or phrase by phrase. The task was to separate one of the messages. While subjects often required the tape to be replayed many times, the task was always quite successfully accomplished. A further set of experiments fed one message into one ear while a different message was sent to the other. Again, the subjects experienced no difficulty in selecting one message and rejecting the other.

Other experiments involved changing the message or characteristics of the message that was being sent to the ear where the message was to be rejected. During transmission of the message to the "rejected" ear, certain changes occurred. These changes included modifications such as the message being presented in a different language, or a shift from a male to a female voice, or the speech being reversed, or the message becoming a pure tone. Following the test, subjects were asked if they could identify what had happened in the rejected ear during the test. In most cases, they could not report what had happened. However, the male to female voice change was always identified, as was the tone. Thus, it became obvious that subjects were able to attend to one message and completely reject another, unless the other message took on certain physical characteristics. In none of these cases could the subjects repeat the message that was sent to the "rejected" ear.

Other experiments, such as those of Moray (1959), showed that we are generally unaware of the content of a rejected message. Studies by Anne Treisman (1969, 1971), however, indicated that subjects could repeat some content of a rejected message when that content was relevant to the subject. Thus, as in the cocktail party situation, we may be attending to only one message, but we can be directed to notice a different one if it contains information that is very relevant, such as our name or a topic of more interest than the one presently being discussed.

Visual Selective Attention

Recall from the discussion of visual search in Concept 3.2 that people must select appropriate information or cues from the environment to determine what action to take and how that action should occur. When considered in its totality, the process of observing a scene relevant to producing an appropriate movement can be overwhelming. How, for example, can a person driving a car observe and interpret all the information that must be considered to make the decisions necessary to negotiate the car through a busy city street that is filled with cars, trucks, bicycles, motorcycles, and pedestrians? Yet, this complex perceptual process goes on rather effortlessly and very quickly. In Concept 3.2, you saw examples of research showing the search strategies people use to carry out this search process. Now, consider why these strategies are successful and what factors influence the degree of success that can be expected in these situations.

Eye movements and attention in visual search. Recall from the discussion of visual search strategies in Concept 3.2 that an increasingly popular method for investigating visual search is the use of eye movement recordings. These recordings track the displacement characteristics of focal vision while subjects observe a film, slides, or an actual skill performance situation. An important question that must be considered when results obtained from this procedure are used to assess visual selective attention is related to the logic behind the use of this procedure. The logic is that what the person is looking at should provide insight into knowing what information in the environment the person is attending to.

Can we validly relate eye movements to attention? Research by Shepherd, Findlay, and Hockley (1986) specifically addressed this question. Based on their observations of eye movements in visual search situations, they concluded that while it is possible to give attention to a feature in the environment without moving the eyes to focus on that feature, it is not possible to make an eye movement without a corresponding shift in attention. Thus, while it may be possible to underestimate what is being attended to in a visual selective attention situation by using eye movement recordings, it is likely that a good estimate of what in the environment is being attended to by a person can be obtained through these recordings.

Feature integration theory. One of the more popular answers to questions about how certain cues in the environment are selected by a performer as a result of visual search strategies comes from the **feature integration theory** of visual attention proposed by Anne Treisman (Treisman & Gelade, 1980; Treisman, 1988). This view indicates that during visual search, we initially group stimuli together according to their unique features, such as color, shape, or movement. This grouping occurs automatically and does not demand attention. These groups of features form "maps" related to the different values of each feature, such as a color map would identify the various colors in the observed scene, while a shape map would indicate which shapes are observed. These maps become the basis for further search processes when the task demands that specific cues must be identified. Attention is required for further processing and must be directed to selecting specific features of interest. This selection occurs by focusing the "attentional spotlight" on the master map of all features. Attention can be directed over a wide or narrow area, and it appears that the spotlight can be split to cover different map areas. If the task is to search for a target having a certain distinct feature, then the target will "pop-out" as a result of this search process because the feature is distinct among the groupings of features. Thus, the more distinctive the feature identifying the target of the visual search, the more quickly the person can identify and locate the target. If the distinctive feature is a part of several cues in the array, the search slows as each cue is assessed in terms of how its characteristics match those of the target.

Thus, in terms of performing motor skills where visual selective attention is required, the key to successful selection of information from the environment is the *distinctiveness* of the features most relevant to performing the skill. In the following sections of this discussion, we will consider why certain features are selected in specific skill performance situations and what contributes to determining the likelihood of attending to the most appropriate features.

Selective Attention and Limited Capacity

In Concept 4.1, we considered Kahneman's (1973) model of attention. In that model selective attention plays a very important role because the limited capacity must not be exceeded. As a result, certain activities must be selected for the available capacity to be allocated in such a way that the system is not overloaded. Accordingly, Kahneman indicated that certain factors will influence the allocation policy for distributing the available capacity to certain activities. In this section, we will consider two of those policies in more detail to see how Kahneman's model can help us better understand what influences our selection of the information to which we will direct attention in the performance of motor skills.

Enduring disposition rules. The first factor presented by Kahneman that influences the selection of information for the allocation of attention capacity is called *enduring dispositions.* Kahneman indicated that these are what can be considered as "rules of involuntary attention." That is, some things characteristically attract our attention regardless of our intentions.

There are several such "rules." The first is that *unexpected stimuli attract our attention.* You can see this in your own daily experiences. When concentrating on your professor during a lecture, haven't you been distracted by a classmate sneezing or dropping some books on the floor? You switched your attention from the professor to the noise, thus altering your attention capacity allocation policy. This rule helps explain why a golfer needs a quiet crowd when hitting a ball, whereas a baseball batter performs very well with a noisy crowd. To the golfer, noise in the crowd will attract his or her attention because it is uncharacteristic of the way in which golf is played. As a result the noise represents unexpected stimuli, which tends to be distracting. To the baseball player, crowd noise is a common experience, not a distraction.

A second enduring disposition rule is that *we tend "naturally" to direct attention to visual in-*

formation rather than to some other sensory modality. This point fits nicely with the discussion in Concept 3.2 that considered vision as the predominant sensory system. The typically observed predominance is an enduring disposition for attention allocation. As Posner (1978) has indicated, we really do not know why this attention bias toward vision exists.

The effect of this rule of visual attention bias is that in situations where performers should be allocating attention to sensory information from sources other than vision, the tendency will be to ignore those other sources unless instructed to do so. For example, beginning typists and pianists must practice not watching their fingers while typing or playing. Children must be instructed not to watch their hands dribbling a ball if they are going to effectively move while dribbling. In each of these situations, the "natural" tendency is for the individuals to allocate attention capacity to visual information that comes from a source other than where it should for effective performance. Instruction and practice for doing otherwise becomes critical for overcoming this enduring disposition.

Third, *we typically allocate attention to the most meaningful information* when confronted with a choice of stimuli. An example of this was seen in the cocktail party phenomenon. A person's name is very meaningful to him or her, and as a result, when heard in a crowded room, a person's attention will be directed to where the name was spoken.

Donald Norman (1968) actually developed a model of selective attention based on this notion of meaningfulness (see Figure 4.2–1). Rather than using the word *meaningfulness,* however, Norman used the term *pertinence*. In his **pertinence model,** Norman maintains that all signals that arrive at the sensory receptors pass through a stage of analysis performed by the early physiological processes. Based on this analysis, certain information is stored concerning each signal. But all signals excite their stored representations in memory; that is, they activate what has been placed in memory from previous experiences. However, only the in-

formation that the system considers to be the most *pertinent,* based on expectations and perceptual processes, is selected for further processing. Thus, the pertinence model implies that we only select that information from the environment we consider to be the most pertinent, or relevant, to the situation. Here the need to consider the meaning of the available information is critically important. If the pertinence model accurately describes how we selectively attend to information in the environment, then the importance of previous experience and instruction concerning essential cues becomes critical for instructors of motor skills.

While there are other enduring disposition rules that could be considered, these three provide sufficient support for the principle that attention capacity is allocated according to "natural" distractions. Because of this, it is essential that the second factor influencing allocation be given an important role in the attention allocation process.

Momentary intentions. Kahneman indicated that we allocate attention to those things we have been instructed to attend to or that we have, through practice or experience, learned to attend to. These are considered to be *momentary intentions*. That is, in a given situation, we allocate attention to sources of information that we might not otherwise consider. One way of viewing this allocation factor is that it takes into account our natural tendencies to attend to certain types of information and provides a means of overcoming those tendencies. As such, this factor provides the basis for establishing the need for effective instruction to beginning students in motor skills where they may be confused about the appropriate stimuli to which they should direct their attention.

An interesting point is that we seem to be capable of very quickly redirecting our allocation of attention from one source of information to another. This process, known as *attention switching,* can be both an advantage and a disadvantage in different performance situations. The advantage occurs in activities that demand rapid decision making that must be made from a variety of

FIGURE 4.2-1
Information-flow diagram
illustrating Norman's
"Pertinence Theory" of
selective attention.

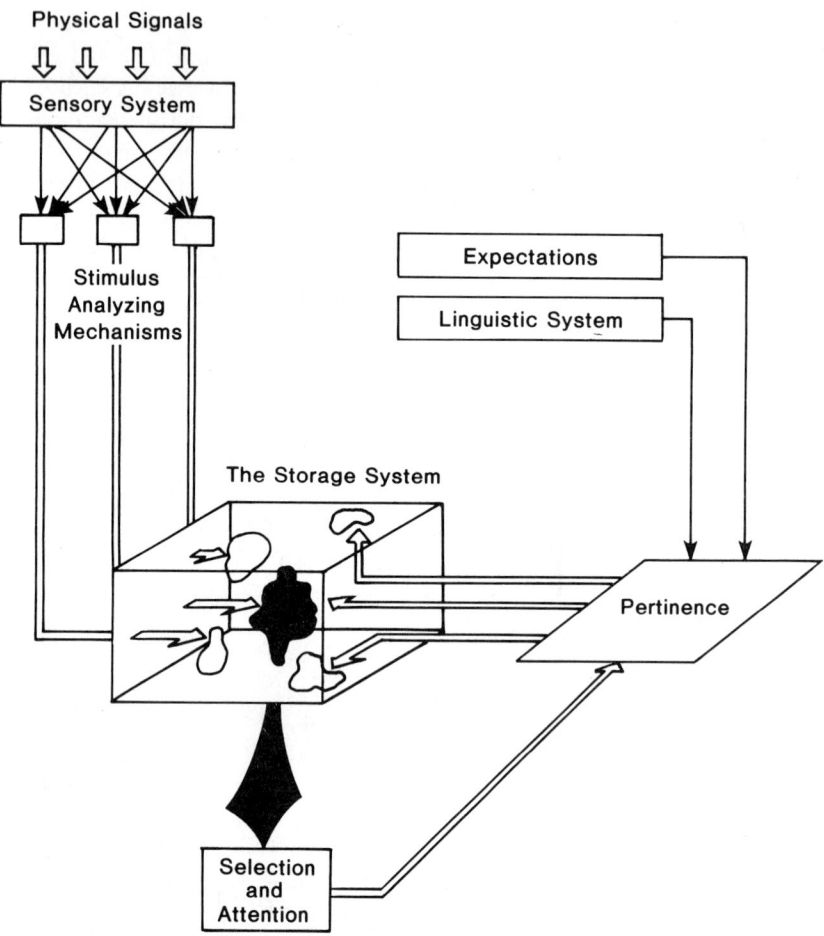

sources of information. The quarterback in football must determine if a primary receiver is open; if not, he must find another receiver. In the meantime, the quarterback must be making certain that he is not about to be tackled or kept from delivering a pass. He uses both visual and auditory sensory modalities to receive this information. All of this activity must happen in the course of a few seconds. To effectively carry out these activities, the player must rapidly switch attention from one source of information to another. This switching occurs within the same sensory modality as well as between different modalities.

Attention switching can be a disadvantage in activities that require a rapid, accurate series of movements, as in closed skills such as typing, piano playing, or dancing. In those skills, a certain degree of attention switching may be helpful, as we considered in the discussion of Concept 4.1. However, it will be to the advantage of the performer to maintain attention directed at a primary source of information for extended periods of time. If the pianist is constantly switching visual attention from the written music to the hands and keys, it will be difficult to maintain the precise timing structure required by the piece being played.

Selective Attention and Learning

There are two points to consider in relating selective attention to motor skill learning. First, we must ask whether or not the learner must give conscious attention to cues in the environment for learning to occur. Second, we must address changes in selective attention characteristics as a person progresses along the learning continuum from the novice to the skilled stages of learning.

Is conscious attention to environmental cues necessary for learning? In Concept 4.1 the point was made that the term *attention* does not necessarily indicate that conscious awareness is characteristic of attention processes. This point is also important to consider in selecting information from the environment to allow an appropriate action to occur. It is evident from research that we select information from the environment that enables us to make correct responses without being consciously aware of that information. A good example of this can be seen in an experiment reported by Richard Pew (1974) in which people improved in performing a tracking skill without being aware of an important characteristic of the stimulus pattern they were tracking.

In Pew's experiment, subjects sat before an oscilloscope and observed a target cursor move for 60 seconds in a very complex waveform pattern. The subject's task was to move a joystick in such a way to move his own cursor so that it stayed as close to the target cursor as possible. This task was practiced for 24 trials on each of 16 days. The interesting feature of the pattern produced by the target cursor was that the first and third 20-second segments of the pattern were randomly generated patterns on every trial. However, the middle 20-second segment was always the same for each trial. For learning purposes, you would expect that selecting this relevant feature of the waveform pattern would be related to improving performance on this portion of the task. In fact, you would

probably expect that because this characteristic could be selected, subjects would do better on this segment of the task than on the other two segments. The results indicated that, in fact, the subjects did perform the middle segment better by the end of practice than the other two segments. But what is important for our present discussion is that the subjects were not consciously aware that the middle segment was the same on every trial. The relevant information was obviously selected by the subject's processing system to enable performance on that segment of the task to be greater than that of the other two segments, but this selection was an unconscious process.

The results found by Pew were recently replicated in experiments in which the repeated segment was in the middle of the three segments (Magill & Hall, 1989), as Pew had done, and in the first of the three segments (Magill, Schoenfelder-Zohdi, & Hall, 1990). The results of this latter experiment are shown in Figure 4.2–2 and illustrate the degree of superior performance by subjects on the repeated segment of the tracking pattern compared to the random pattern segments. Again, no subjects in either of these experiments reported that they were aware that a segment of the patterns they tracked was repeated on every practice trial.

Another example of the unconscious selection of appropriate environmental stimuli was reported by Nissen and Bullemer (1987). In that experiment, subjects performed a serial RT task on a microcomputer. On each trial, an asterisk appeared on the computer monitor at one of four locations indicating that one of 3, 5, 7, and 9 digit keys on the keyboard should be depressed. The stimuli appeared one by one every 500 msec for a 10–trial sequence. Subjects performed a total of 8 blocks of 100 trials each. One group of subjects received a repeating sequence on each set of their 10 trials in the 100–trial block. The second group of subjects received a 10–trial sequence that was

FIGURE 4.2-2 Results of the experiment by Magill et al., showing performance on a 60-second tracking task where the first 20 seconds (segment A) was repeated on every practice trial, whereas the second and third 20 seconds (segments B and C) were random on every trial.

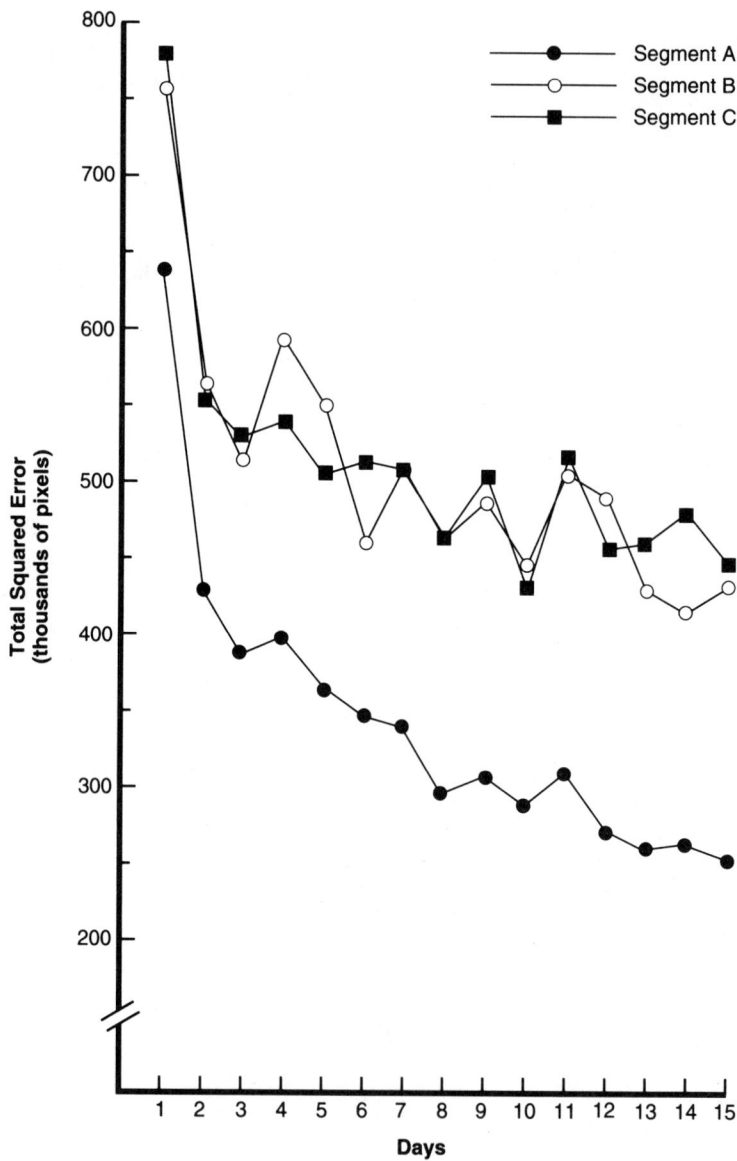

randomly determined for the 100–trial block. The results showed (see Figure 4.2–3) the subjects who performed the repeated sequence improved RT much more than the group who received the random sequences. In fact, the randomly presented sequence group did not show much improvement at all over the 800 total trials. But what is even more revealing with regard to selective at-

tention is that when questioned, *none* of the subjects in the repeated sequence group said they noticed a sequence.

Such experiments reveal an important characteristic of the selection process that is involved in attending to appropriate environmental information so that a correct response can be made. That is, this selection process can occur without

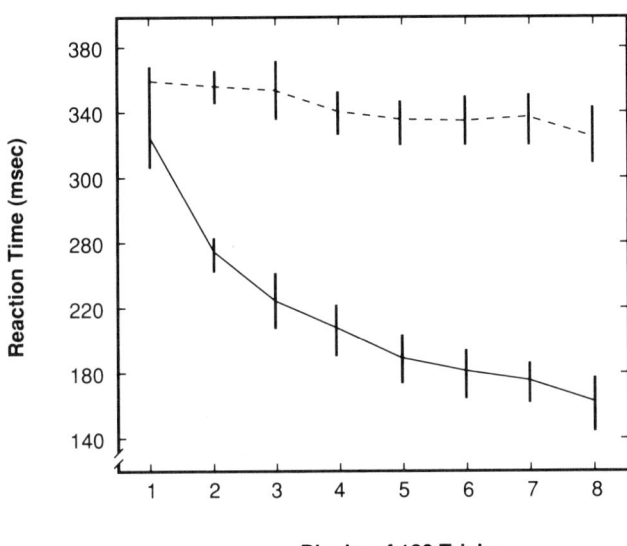

FIGURE 4.2-3 Results from experiment 1 by Nissen and Bullemer showing RT effects from practicing a serial RT task in 10-trial sequences that were either the same sequence (------) or random sequences (------) for sets of ten 10-trial sequences. The vertical bars represent standard errors.

conscious awareness. When a person attends to the appropriate stimuli, the information from that stimuli that is relevant for performance of the response will be selected and appropriately used by the motor control system. Thus, the key is directing people to attend to the appropriate stimuli and to let the processing system take over from there. It does not appear necessary for people to be consciously aware of what features characterize that stimulus information.

Selective attention and the stages of learning.

In Concept 2.2 you were introduced to several changes that occur as a result of practicing a motor skill and progressing along the learning stages continuum. One of those changes discussed occurred in visual selective attention characteristics. The results of the study by Abernethy and Russell (1987) showed that one of the things that changes across the learning stages of badminton skills is the direction of visual attention so that reliable information used to make a response can be extracted as early in the opponent's action as possible. The results of the Vickers (1988) experiment indicated that as novice gymnasts progress to the expert stage, they learn to determine which

part of the body provides the most useful information for evaluating a performance. Thus, the evidence from these two experiments fits well within the points that have been emphasized in this discussion. That is, as people learn skills, they learn to select the most relevant features for successful performance of the skill. (See Abernethy, 1988, for a more detailed review and discussion of research supporting this conclusion.)

As such, the empirical evidence from visual search studies provides strong support for what Gentile (1972) emphasized as an important part of the learning process in her model of learning stages that was discussed in Concept 2.2. Recall that she stated that the discrimination of relevant from non-relevant stimuli from the environment and the selection of relevant stimuli to control action were critical components of learning skills. The few examples of research evidence we have considered indicate that this process goes on very successfully as a function of learning. And, also based on the evidence that we have, it would appear that this improvement in selecting relevant environmental cues occurs with a limited amount of attention demanded of the person.

Selective Attention and Instruction

Based on the discussion to this point, we can draw several conclusions about how instruction can be effectively designed to incorporate what we know about selective attention and motor skill performance. We will consider three conclusions that have specific implications for teaching motor skills.

We are capable of attending to relevant environmental cues in the midst of many competing cues. This conclusion should first of all be a source of encouragement for instructors of motor skills and provide them with a basis of support or confidence. Most skills are taught in environments where there are many cues competing for the learner's attention. The implication for instruction here is that the learner can be taught to ignore the many non-relevant cues or distractions that will confront them in most motor skill situations. The important question of course is, How can the learner be taught to do this? The best answer to this question is to direct the learner's attention to the important cues or to the skill to be performed. Because we know that we have a limited attention capacity, it is possible to effectively "fill" that capacity by directing attention to relevant cues. Or, to look at this another way, attention focus can be narrowed to focus only on specific cues in the environment. The effect is to block out what would be distracting cues or influences in the environment. And in situations where the relevant cues are not readily identifiable, attending to performing the skill as successfully as possible will enable the learner to take advantage of the power of the selective attention processes that appear to successfully select from the available cues the relevant ones for controlling the intended action. Because this selection process can occur without the need for conscious attention directed toward the relevant cues, instruction can direct the person to attend to performing the task well, without directing attention to specific cues.

The learner will attend to the cues that are most meaningful or pertinent to him or her. This conclusion indicates that learning can be facilitated by providing the learner with instruction about *which* cues are important. For example, the child needs instruction about where to concentrate his or her visual attention on an oncoming ball so it can be caught. The racquetball player should be told which cues to concentrate on when receiving a serve. Thus, this instruction is especially helpful for beginners because they need to be oriented to where to direct their attention. It is also worth noting that this instruction will benefit people who are in rehabilitation situations where previously well-learned skills, such as walking, drinking from a cup, or buttoning a shirt, must be re-learned. In rehabilitation settings, attention must be directed to important cues because conscious thought about such effort was not characteristic of performing those skills prior to the need for rehabilitation due to things such as a stroke, accident, or surgery. When conscious attention is not directed toward the relevant cues in this way, it is possible that in many situations, the relevant cues will "pop out" and become meaningful as the person practices the skill and increases his or her capability for performing it well.

Distractions can and do occur but can be overcome. While we do not completely understand why we are distracted by stimuli that we are not attending to, we can identify some possible reasons that may be applicable to motor skill situations. A primary reason for the influence of distractions appears to be related to the meaningfulness of what is not attended to. Recall the cocktail party phenomenon as an example. What this indicates to the instructor is that he or she must provide the learner with ample practice in concentrating on the cues that have been learned to be the most pertinent or meaningful. Thus with practice the distractions can be overcome and eventually the number of possible distractions will decrease as the most meaningful cues are more and more reinforced in the learner. Another reason for distractions seems to be the learner's lack of confidence that the cues he or she is attending to are the most pertinent. Again, the importance of practice while directing attention to the most relevant or important cues is essential to develop the learner's confidence in attending to those cues.

Summary

An essential aspect of the process of producing a motor response is the selection of information from the environment on which the response can be based. The process of selecting certain information from the environment while ignoring other phenomena is known as selective attention. The "cocktail party phenomenon" illustrates our ability to attend to specific information in the midst of much noise or unwanted information. It also indicates how we can be distracted by information other than what we are attending to. In many motor skills, visual selective attention is critical for successful performance. Techniques for assessing visual attention have been described. Novices and experts have distinctively different visual attention characteristics in most skill performance situations. Experts have learned to focus attention on the relevant cues and they do this earlier in preparing or executing a skill than novices. Two of the factors influencing attention allocation policy presented in Kahneman's model of attention were developed in relation to how certain stimuli have a tendency to receive attention while others do not. Certain characteristics of stimuli attract attention because they receive our involuntary attention. These characteristics include being unexpected, visual, and meaningful to the individual. Attention is also directed to certain stimuli because the individual has been directed to do so or has learned to do so. It is also important to realize that learning skills are not dependent on all relevant stimuli being attended to consciously. These factors have been considered in terms of how to develop instruction based on our knowledge of selective attention principles.

Related Readings

Abernethy, B. (1988). Visual search in sport and ergonomics: Its relation to selective attention and performer expertise. *Human Performance, 1,* 205–235.

Kahneman, D. (1973). *Attention and effort.* Englewood Cliffs, NJ: Prentice-Hall. (Read chapter 1.)

Nissen, M. J., & Bullemer, P. (1987). Attentional requirements of learning: Evidence from performance measures. *Cognitive Psychology, 19,* 1–32.

Norman, D. A. (1976). *Memory and attention: An introduction to human information processing* (2nd ed.). New York: John Wiley. (Read chapter 2.)

CONCEPT 4.3

Limited attention capacity requires alertness and preparation of the movement control system to produce voluntary, coordinated movement

Key Terms

foreperiod

psychological refractory period (PRP)

Hick's Law

cost-benefit trade off

stimulus-response compatibility

complexity

anxiety

attentional focus

vigilance

Application

Undoubtedly you have heard, or even said, following a poor shot in tennis or a bad swing at a good pitch in baseball, "I wasn't ready!" These words imply that if you had been "ready," the results would have been quite different. Why is that? What is so important about getting ready for a response that makes it an essential part of successfully performing any motor skill?

In the discussion of this concept, we shall see the role played by alertness and preparation in the outcome of performing a skill. We are not talking here about the long-term preparation that occurs during the days prior to an event but to the specific preparation made by the movement control system that occurs just prior to a required response. This preparation includes the entire spectrum of motor responses: for example, when the sprinter in track gets into the blocks and prepares to explode out of them in order to get a good start; when the batter in baseball prepares for a pitch; when the golfer prepares to make a particular shot. In each case, preparation during the time immediately preceding the response is critical to the outcome of that response. In the discussion that follows, we will be concerned primarily with what occurs during preparation time that makes it such a critical part of any performance, and what influences alertness and the preparation of a response.

Discussion

Attention as Alertness and Response Preparation

An important issue in the investigation of attention is what occurs immediately prior to making a voluntary movement. This aspect of the study of attention can be found in research literature related to both alertness and signal preparation. This latter term developed from the typical experimental approach taken to study response preparation, which involved subjects responding in a predetermined fashion to a visual or auditory signal. By manipulating conditions immediately prior to the signal or by manipulating the characteristics of the signal itself, researchers were able to investigate influences on a subject's preparation to respond to a signal. In present day study of response preparation, a signal may be specified or it may be a cue in the environment that must be detected in order for an action to occur.

Thus, in this discussion, the primary focus is on preparing the motor control system to produce a required voluntary movement. An important element of this preparation is being alert to detect the appropriate cues indicating that the action should be initiated or which action should occur. Of particular interest in this discussion is what happens during the preparation time before and after the signal to respond occurs, just prior to the response. Also of interest will be the various factors that have been shown to influence alertness and the process of preparing a voluntary movement.

To study alertness and the preparation of a response, researchers have typically used reaction time (RT) experimental paradigms in their investigations. Because RT is the amount of time between the onset of a signal and the initiation of a response, RT seems a good measure on which to base inferences about response preparation. As you will see in various experiments considered in this discussion, it has been common for experimenters to investigate questions related to alertness and response preparation by observing the effect on RT of a manipulated experimental variable, such as the complexity of the movement that must be made or the number of response choices possible. The logical inference made from these manipulations is that if RT is longer under one condition than under another, then the first condition requires more preparation. By skillfully manipulating appropriate experimental variables, researchers are able to determine not only which variables influence response preparation but also what occurs during that preparation. Thus, it is important to consider RT as a measure of response preparation. Note, however, that RT can be used as a measure of other processes involved in learning and performance, which you will see in other parts of this text. However, in the context of preparing a motor response, RT provides a useful means of investigating response preparation.

The Need for Alertness and Time to Prepare a Response

An important assumption regarding the investigation of response preparation is that preparation takes time. (See Meyer, Osman, Irwin, & Yantis, 1988, for an excellent overview of the history of the use of time measure for making conclusions about human information processing activity.) If more preparation is needed in certain circumstances than in others, more time will be required to make that preparation. Thus, RT is used as a measure of response preparation. An important

question that you might ask is, On what basis is this assumption made? How do we know that preparing to make a response takes time and that this amount of time is influenced by the amount of preparation required?

You have already been introduced to some evidence supporting this assumption. In the discussion of Concept 3.3, an experiment by Henry and Rogers (1960) showed that RT increased as a function of the complexity of the rapid response. That is, when a simple response had to be made to a signal, in this case simply lifting the finger off a telegraph key, the RT was shorter than when a more complex response had to be made, such as making a three-component rapid movement. From these results, Henry and Rogers inferred that the preparation required for a rapid response to a signal is dependent on the complexity of the response that must be made.

However, two other, more basic, approaches provide a basis for the assumption that preparing for a response takes time. These will be described next.

The RT foreperiod. The time interval between a warning signal and the "go" signal is called the **foreperiod.** This time interval is important in the study of alertness and response preparation because it is when the individual initially prepares to respond. Two questions are pertinent to this interval. First, what happens to RT if there is no warning signal, thereby effectively eliminating a foreperiod? Second, what happens to RT if the length of the foreperiods vary? We will consider the evidence that exists to answer these questions and what the answers mean with respect to response preparation.

The influence on RT on the use of a warning signal was a popular topic in the first half of this century. By 1954, Teichner, in a review of RT research, concluded that the use of a warning, or "ready," signal prior to the onset of the "go" signal yields faster RTs than does the omission of such a preparatory signal. Also, for choice RT situations, the occurrence of a warning signal not only leads to faster RTs, it also leads to more accurate responses to the "go" signal.

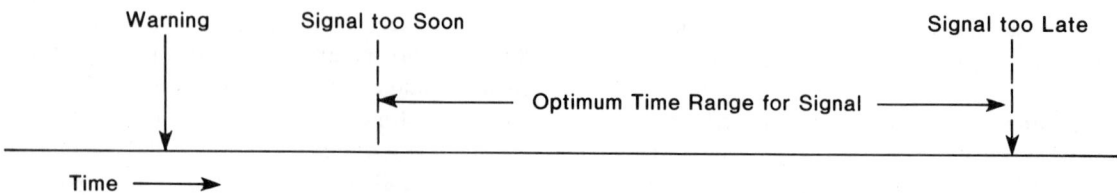

FIGURE 4.3-1   A time line showing a continuum of time for the occurrence of a response signal to follow a warning signal to ensure optimal readiness to respond. The actual amounts of time along this continuum should be considered as task-specific.

What is the benefit of the warning signal? Primarily, it alerts the individual to prepare for the "go" signal. If the warning signal is not provided, RT increases, indicating that the individual was not fully prepared to respond to the "go" signal. Thus, alertness of the individual is an important part of the preparation to respond. Without sufficient alertness, preparation will not occur as effectively and efficiently as it would otherwise. Another important alertness issue involves the effect of alertness when attention must be maintained over long periods, which will be considered later in this discussion.

The second question related to the RT foreperiod concerns foreperiod length. Is there an optimal foreperiod length that relates to optimal RT performance? This question is particularly relevant to the assumption concerning the need for time to prepare a response. Changes in RT as a function of changes in the RT foreperiod would indicate that preparation time needed to respond to a signal is indeed important. This question is also particularly relevant in many sport situations where an athlete must hold a prepared response until a signal to respond occurs, such as in a swimming or track start. Research investigating this question can be traced back to the early part of this century when, for example, Woodrow (1914) reported that for simple RT situations, maximum preparation was not reached in less than 2 sec, and was not maintained much longer than 4 sec. This 2- to 4-sec range has been generally accepted as reflecting the minimum and optimal signal preparation time. There is other evidence which indicates a 1- to 2-sec minimum.

These results indicate the need to consider the time required to prepare for a signal as a continuum where there is a minimum amount of time necessary for signal preparation as well as a maximum period of time. Between those extremes is the optimal amount of time during which the signal should occur for the best response. This continuum is presented in Figure 4.3–1. Following a warning or ready signal, if the signal to respond occurs too early, that is, before the optimal range of time, the individual will not have had sufficient time to prepare to respond. If the signal occurs after the optimal time range, the individual has been waiting too long, and his or her ability to respond is less than it would have been during the optimal time range.

The exact amounts of time that should be used on the general time line represented in Fig. 4.3–1 will vary according to the motor task associated with it. For example, a simple RT response made with a hand can be made with a shorter foreperiod than if the response is made with the foot. Also, simple RT responses can be made with a shorter foreperiod than a choice RT response. In general, however, it appears that the minimum foreperiod length is between 0.5 and 2 sec. The maximum time should be about 4 sec. Thus the optimal range of time would be from approximately 0.5 to 4 sec.

A good example of the application of this optimal time for signal preparation principle can be seen in swimming- and track-start examples mentioned earlier. In these sports, starters in the various events are instructed to adjust the time span between giving the ready signal and firing the gun

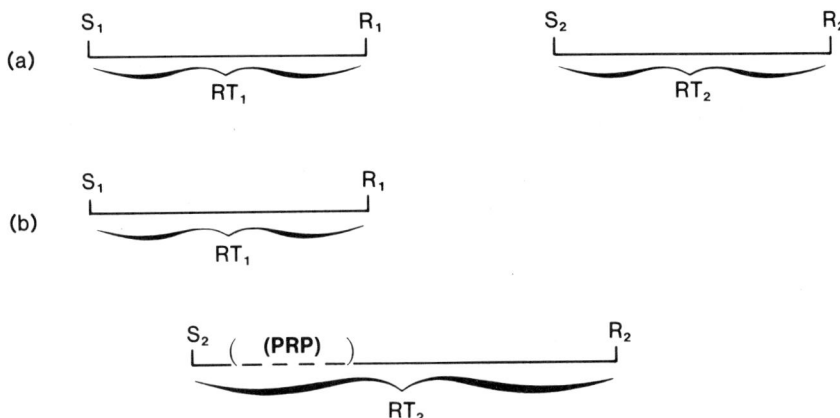

FIGURE 4.3-2 The psychological refractory period. (a) The RTs for the S_1 (light)-R_1 (button press) and the S_2 (buzzer)-R_2 (vocal response) conditions when performed separately. (b) The effect on RT for the S_2-R_2 condition when S_2 arrives during the RT interval for the S_1-R_1 condition. RT_2 is typically lengthened by the amount of time between the onset of S_2 and the completion of R_1. This extra time is shown by the dashed line and indicates the PRP.

to a range of between 1 and 3 or 4 sec. This range fits very nicely into the RT signal preparation optimal time range that we have proposed based on the research literature.

The psychological refractory period (PRP).
Another way to demonstrate that time is needed to prepare a response is by considering the **psychological refractory period (PRP)**. The term *refractory* is synonymous with the term *delay*. The PRP can be thought of as a delay period during which a planned response seems to be "put on hold" while another response is being executed. Although there are different views of why the PRP occurs (see Gottsdanker, 1979, 1980, for a review of these), there is little disagreement that the PRP demonstrates that some minimal amount of time is needed to prepare a motor response.

Figure 4.3–2 illustrates the PRP in a situation where two different responses must be made to two different signals. However, rather than the signals occurring simultaneously, one occurs just after the other. The subject in this situation is told to respond as quickly as possible to the first signal (press a button when the light goes on) and also respond as quickly as possible to the second signal

(say "bop" into the microphone when the buzzer sounds). If the response to the buzzer in this situation is compared to the response to the buzzer when another preceding response has not been required, the PRP can be seen. The RT for the buzzer signal will be longer when a response has to be made immediately prior to it than when no previous response is required. This extra time, or delay, is the PRP.

An interesting application of the value of the PRP in a sport situation involves faking. For example, suppose a basketball player is dribbling the ball and is confronted by a defensive player in a one-on-one situation. A common strategy to get around the defensive player is to use a head fake by moving the head in the opposite direction the body will go. If done properly, the defensive player will initiate a response to go in the direction the head indicates. However, upon seeing the offensive player's body actually going in the other direction, the defensive player must initiate a second response to go in the opposite direction. The advantage gained by the offensive player in this situation is the extra time, the PRP, required to initiate a second response after an initial one was already in progress.

FIGURE 4.3-3
Schematization of fractionated reaction time indicating the relationship between the EMG signal activity and the premotor and motor time intervals.

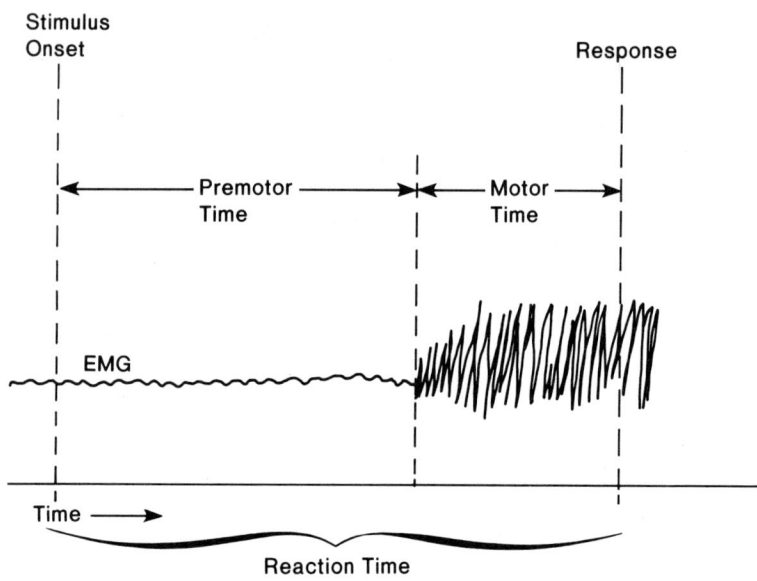

Two important characteristics of the PRP provide some additional insight into the faking example. First, the PRP will not be demonstrated if the second stimulus occurs after a period of time that is the RT for the first stimulus. For the fake, this suggests that it is important that the "real" move be made quickly after the fake has been given. If it is not, the opponent can easily prepare and initiate the appropriate response to defend the real move.

Second, the PRP will not occur if the first signal is not considered important and the subject only pays attention to the second signal. The implication for the fake should be obvious here. If the fake is not viewed by the defender as being an indication of the real move, then the fake will not be effective. The defender will simply ignore the fake and wait to respond to the real move.

Fractionating RT

One way to realize that different events occur during the preparation of a response is to *fractionate* an EMG recording of the RT interval. (You were introduced to this in Concept 1.2.) As

you can see in Figure 4.3–3, the EMG signal can be divided, or fractionated, into two distinct parts. The first part is called the *premotor time,* although it also has been referred to as electromechanical delay. Note that the EMG signal has not changed much from what it was prior to the onset of the stimulus. However, shortly after the onset of the stimulus, the EMG signal shows a rapid increase in electrical activity. This indicates that the motor neurons are firing and the muscle is preparing to contract even though no observable, physical response has yet occurred. This period of time is called the *motor time,* which is the period of increased EMG activity preceding the observable response, and begins at the point marked response.

From this fractionation researchers have inferred that the premotor time indicates perceptual or cognitive processing of the stimulus information. It seems reasonable to consider that if motor program preparation is occurring during the RT interval, as discussed in Concept 3.3, preparation would occur during this time. The motor time, on the other hand, begins the actual motor output phase of a response. During this time, the specific muscles involved in the action are firing and preparing to begin the observable movement.

Some researchers have attempted to determine if changes in RT that result as a function of various response characteristics are due primarily to changes in premotor time, motor time, or both. For example, Christina and Rose (1985) reported that the changes in RT due to increases in *response complexity,* such as those reported by Henry and Rogers (1960), were reflected in increases in premotor time. For a two-part arm movement, premotor time increased an average of 19 msec over that for a one-part arm movement, while motor time increased only 3 msec. In an experiment investigating movement *response durations,* Siegel (1986) found that while RT increased linearly as response durations increased from 150, 300, 600, to 1,200 msec, premotor time also increased linearly. Motor time, on the other hand, remained the same until the response duration became 1,200 msec, then motor time showed a slight increase. Premotor time was also shown to be responsible for RT increases due to increases in the velocity of the required movement (Sheridan, 1984). However, Carlton, Carlton, and Newell (1987) found that both premotor and motor time changes resulted from altering *force-related characteristics* of the response. Thus, certain response characteristics primarily influence the more perceptual-cognitive component of RT, whereas others affect this component as well as the more peripheral, motor component.

Thus, fractionating RT is a useful procedure for gaining insight into the locus of preparation activity. For example, for those who advocate that preparation of a response involves programming activity involving central processing, it is important to show that factors that should require more programming time influence premotor time during the RT interval. However, our current knowledge about the processes involved in response preparation is such that more research is needed, especially research involving RT fractionation so that more definitive conclusions can be made concerning what occurs during the RT interval. By developing appropriate manipulation of response and situation characteristics and then observing the influence of these manipulations on the components of RT, researchers will be able to provide more insight into response preparation activity.

Factors Influencing Response Preparation Time

As you are undoubtedly aware by now, numerous factors influence the amount of time required to prepare a response. This point has been alluded to in discussions of motor program preparation in Concept 3.3 and in the preceding section on fractionating RT. In this section, we will consider several of these factors in more detail. As you will see, factors related to characteristics of the individual, the task, and the response situation all influence the amount of time taken to prepare a response when that response must be made as rapidly as possible to a given signal. It is important to remember that although it can be demonstrated that various factors influence RT, we do not need to conclude that this influence necessarily reflects motor program preparation. Although such a conclusion has been made with regard to several of these factors, as discussed in Concept 3.3, there is some debate concerning whether or not motor program preparation must be inferred from changes in RT. (See Carlton, Carlton, & Newell, 1987, and Kelso, 1984b, for discussions about these differing views.)

However, regardless of what the RT changes represent in terms of processes causing such changes, it is important to be aware of factors that alter the amount of time required to prepare a response. It should be apparent from the discussion thus far that knowledge of these factors has implications for theoretical issues related to the preparation of a motor response. However, such knowledge also has important implications for practical applications. For example, if you know that a particular factor can increase the RT associated with making a response, then it may be possible to appropriately alter the situation to enable the person to respond more quickly than he or she might if the situation had not been altered. What follows, then, is a discussion of several factors that influence the amount of time needed to prepare to make a motor response to a signal.

Reaction time vs. movement time set.

Throughout this discussion, many of the response situations involve a goal of moving as fast as possible when the signal to move occurs. In these situations, there are two important components of the total response, the RT and the movement time (MT). Because the amount of time taken to produce these two components is essentially independent (an important point that will be discussed in Concept 6.2), it is possible to influence RT by consciously attending either to reacting to the signal as fast as possible or to moving as fast as possible. These two different response strategies have been called a *sensory set* and a *motor set,* respectively.

The first evidence to show that having either a sensory or a motor set would differentially influence RT was offered by Henry (1961). However, because Henry's results were based on the subjects' opinions of what their set was for a particular trial, Christina (1973) sought to replicate these results by imposing on subjects a sensory or a motor set. The task required the subject to respond as quickly as possible to a buzzer by moving the index finger of the right hand to four different response keys that were positioned at different locations on a response panel. The sensory set group was told to focus attention on the sound of the buzzer but to move off the response key as fast as possible. The motor set group was told to focus on moving as quickly as possible. Results showed that RT was affected; the sensory set group showed a 20–msec faster RT than the motor set group. Interestingly, MT for the two groups was not statistically different. Thus, focusing attention on the reaction signal and allowing the movement to

happen naturally shortened the preparation time required and did not penalize movement speed. Results showed the overall response time was faster for the sensory set group.

An obvious application of Christina's results is in sport situations where a rapid movement must be made in response to a signal, as in track or swimming. But do these results generalize to these nonlaboratory situations? To investigate this question, Jongsma, Elliott, and Lee (1987) compared sensory and motor set for a sprint start in track. They also considered the influence of experience. Half the subjects had at least 8 years of sprinting experience and half had only a 6-week track class at a university. To measure RT, a pressure-sensitive switch was embedded in the rear foot starting block. MT was measured as the time from release of this switch until a photoelectric light beam was broken 1.5 meters from the starting line. Subjects were given 10 trials on which they were to use their normal start, 10 trials with a sensory set, and 10 trials with a motor set.

Results of this experiment showed that for both novices and experienced sprinters, RT was fastest for the sensory set condition. The novices had a 292-msec RT for their preferred set, a 308-msec RT for the motor set, and a 285-msec RT for the sensory set. Thus, there was a 7-msec advantage for the sensory set over their preferred set, and a 23-msec advantage over the motor set. For the experienced sprinters, the preferred set yielded a 259-msec RT, while the motor set had a 261-msec RT and the sensory set had a 252-msec RT. Again, the advantage of the sensory set was small; it was only 7 msec and 9 msec faster than the motor and preferred set, respectively. Although these times were not statistically different, they are worth noting, however, because the set time differences for the novices are in line with those reported by Christina. The smaller differences observed for the experienced sprinters are a good example of the effect of practice on response preparation, which will be discussed later.

The number of stimulus-response choices. One of the characteristics of the task to be performed that will influence response preparation is the number of decision alternatives, or choices, that are possible before the required response is known. For example, a racquetball player must prepare to respond to a variety of possible serves, whereas the swimmer must prepare to respond to only one signal to go. As these examples suggest, the preparation demands for motor skills vary as the number of possible responses that can be made in response to the stimulus varies.

In the discussion of Concept 1.2, you saw that RT increases according to the number of stimulus or response choices. The fastest RTs occur in a simple RT situation, where there is only one stimulus and one response. RT slows down when more than one stimulus and more than one response are possible, as in the choice RT situation. This demonstrates how the response preparation demand increases as the amount of information that must be processed to make a response increases.

The RT increase in a choice situation is such a stable effect that a law, i.e., a reliable prediction, has been developed to predict the RT when the number of stimulus response choices is known. This law, known as **Hick's Law** (Hick, 1952), states that RT will increase logarithmically as the number of stimulus-response choices increases. The equation that describes this law is $RT = K \log_2 (N + 1)$, where K is a constant, which is simple RT in most cases, and N equals the number of possible choices. This means that RT increases linearly as the number of stimulus-choice alternatives increases. The magnitude of this increase can be mathematically predicted by applying Hick's equation.

The $\log_2$ function comes from ascribing the RT increase to the increase in the information transmitted by the possible choices, rather than to only the number of choice alternatives. $\log_2$ is used because it relates to a *bit* in information theory, which refers to a yes/no choice between two alternatives. In a 1-bit decision, there are two alternatives, there are four alternatives in a 2-bit

decision, a 3-bit decision involves eight choices, and so on. Thus, the number of bits indicates the least number of "yes/no" decisions that could be made to solve the problem created by the number of choices involved. For example, if there were eight choices possible in a situation, the first decision would be based on the answer to "Is the correct choice in this half of the possible choices?" Regardless if the answer is yes or no, you now have reduced the possible choices to four. You would then ask the same question again in reference to one-half of these remaining possible choices to make the second decision. This answer reduces the possible choices to two. For the third decision, you ask the question that will give you the correct choice, "Is it this one?" Again, regardless of whether the answer is yes or no, you will know the correct choice. In this way, you have determined the correct choice out of a possible eight-choice set with only three yes/no questions, hence a 3-bit decision situation.

Relating the choice RT situation to information theory was an important part of Hick's work. Previously, the increase in RT was considered relative only to the number of stimulus alternatives. By relating the choice situation to information theory, Hick expanded the application of this law to variables other than the number of choices. For example, the law also is valid when the number of alternatives are held constant but probabilities of either response occurring on a given trial are varied. For example, in an experiment by Fitts, Peterson, and Wolpe (1963), a nine-choice RT situation was used in which one stimulus was designated as occurring more frequently (with a .94 probability) than the other eight. The results showed that for the frequently occurring stimulus, RT averaged 280 msec while the others averaged 450 msec. We will address this probability influence on RT later in this discussion.

One of the applications of Hick's Law to sport skills can be related to situations in which an individual has several options of what to do, depending on what occurs in a situation. For example, suppose a football quarterback is running an option play and has the choice of handing off to a back, keeping the ball and running, or running and pitching out. In this situation, there are three response alternatives. How can the situation be structured to reduce the total possible stimulus conditions? If the quarterback is not given very specific "keys" to watch for in the defense, there will be an extremely large number of possible choices on which he can base his response. This will result in the need for greatly increased preparation time, which will result in little chance for success for the play. The implication for the coach is to tell the quarterback what specific information to look for and to make the response accordingly.

The predictability of the stimulus. Many times in sport we hear the comment that a player "telegraphed" a move. By this, the speaker means that the responding player had a lot of time to prepare an appropriate response because the other player let his or her response be known in advance of its actual occurrence. This often occurs in baseball when a pitcher "telegraphs" a pitch by only throwing a certain pitch with a unique motion. It can also occur in other sports where one player gains an advantage by increased preparation time and another has had very little preparation time.

As you saw in the discussion of anticipation timing in Concept 3.2, the more predictable a stimulus, the faster and more accurately a person can make a response. This increase in accuracy is undoubtedly related to having more time to make fewer decisions about the response than would otherwise be possible. Our baseball example fits well here. If a ball is pitched at 90 mph, it will take approximately 0.4 sec to reach the plate. To be successful, the batter typically has 0.15 sec of this time to start a swing and get the bat to make contact with the ball. This allows only 0.25 sec for decision making about whether or not to swing and, if the decision is to swing, what swing should be made. Of that 0.25 sec, probably only 0.1 to 0.15 sec can realistically be allotted to conscious de-

cision making. The obvious advantage of being able early in the pitch to know what the ball will do during its flight is that the batter will have more time to make the appropriate decisions necessary to hit the ball.

Research that has demonstrated the relationship between the predictability of a stimulus and response preparation time and accuracy has typically followed a choice-RT arrangement in which the subjects are provided advance information about which stimulus will appear. This experimental procedure, popularized by the work of David Rosenbaum (1980), is called the *precuing technique*. One of the results of this procedure has been to demonstrate the benefit gained in RT by receiving any amount of advance information about the upcoming response.

A discussion of the precuing technique by Rosenbaum (1983) reveals some of the history, rationale, procedures, and inferences that are possible using this experimental technique. We will concern ourselves only with the basic procedures used and how these procedures yield results that we can use to determine the role of advance information in aiding a response. Figure 4.3–4 illustrates the response panel used in the experiments by Rosenbaum. The squares in the center are the "home" buttons for the subject's two index fingers. The circles represent the target buttons. The response to be made contained three dimensions: the *arm* to move (left or right); the *direction* to move (away or toward the body); and the *extent* of the movement (short or long). The subject observed a monitor. When a colored dot appeared, the subject was required to move the correct arm as rapidly as possible from the home button to the target that was marked with the corresponding colored dot shown on the monitor. Prior to the signal to move, that is, the appearance of the colored dot on the screen, the subject could receive advance information (the precue) that indicated something about the upcoming response. The subject could receive a precue about none, one, two, or all three of the dimensions of the response.

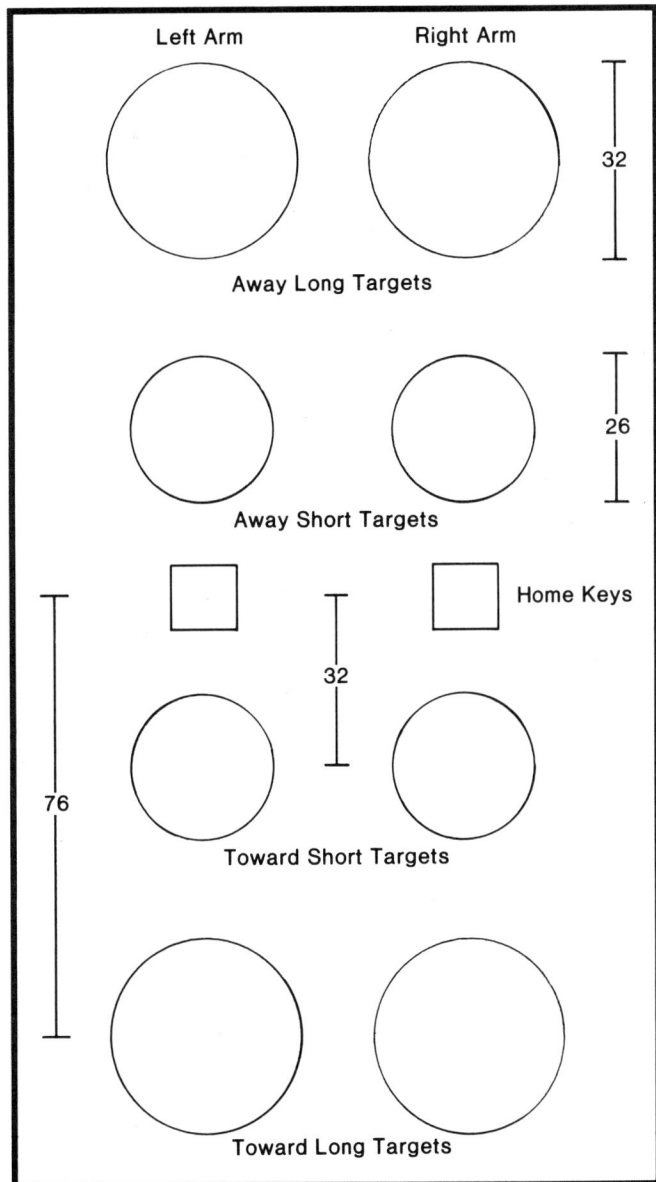

FIGURE 4.3-4   Response panel used in the Rosenbaum precuing experiments.

FIGURE 4.3-5 The effects of the number of response dimensions precued for a three-dimension task (arm, direction, extent) as reported by Rosenbaum.

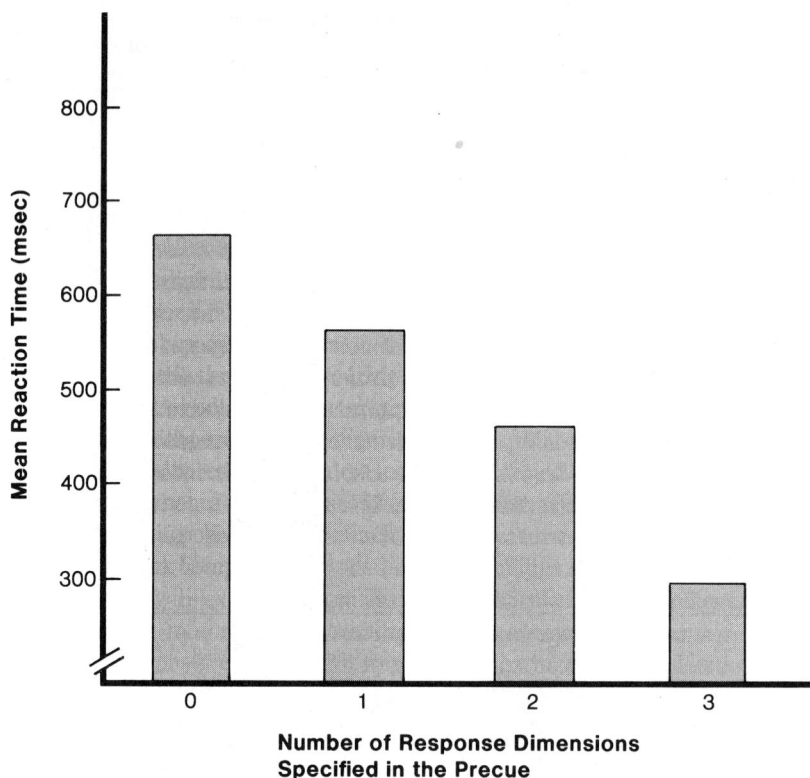

Number of Response Dimensions Specified in the Precue

The results of this precuing procedure are presented in Figure 4.3–5. As you might expect, the fastest RT occurred when all three dimensions were precued. This should be no surprise because the three-choice RT situation was reduced to a simple RT situation. Similarly, as the number of precued dimensions was decreased, the RT increased. The benefit of the precue information was to allow the subjects to prepare the precued dimension(s) in advance of the "go" signal and then only have to prepare the remaining dimensions after the "go" signal.

An interesting effect can be seen in research studies where advance information is provided, but may be inaccurate. If, for example, in the task used in the Rosenbaum study, the subject had been given the precue "right arm" and the response signal actually indicated "left arm," what would the result have been? Typically, the result will

depend on the *probability* of the advance information being correct. If the precue has only a 50–50 chance of being correct, the performer will ignore it and respond as if no precue had been given. However, if there is an 80% chance that the precue will be correct, the performer will *bias* his or her response to make the response indicated by the precue.

What will happen when the performer biases a response according to the precue and the response signal requires the opposite response? In other words, what is the price of preparing the wrong response? Figure 4.3–6 illustrates the answer to that question. What you see are the results from an experiment by Larish and Stelmach (1982) where subjects were required to make a rapid movement with the correct hand from a home key to one of two targets 40 cm away. Advance information was provided about which target would be

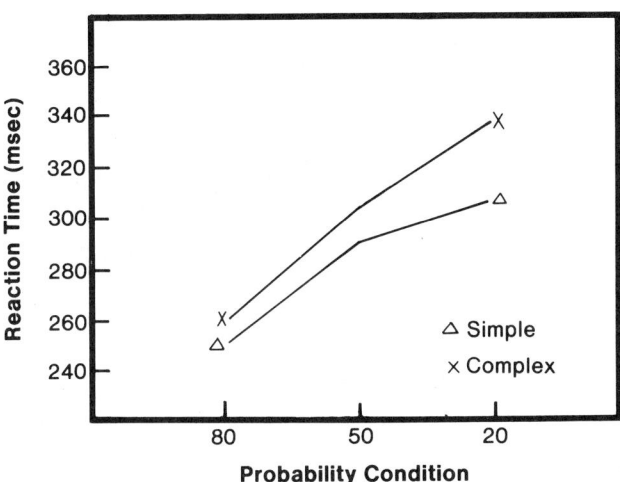

FIGURE 4.3-6 Results from the experiment by Larish and Stelmach showing the effects on RT of different probabilities of making a response for two different tasks.

the response target. However, this information was correct only 20%, 50%, or 80% of the time. Figure 4.3–6 shows the **cost-benefit tradeoff** associated with this situation. When there was a 50–50 chance (50% correct condition) of the precue's being correct, subjects responded as if the task were a two-choice RT task. In other words, they basically ignored the advance information. However, in the 80–20 condition, subjects obviously biased their response to move in the direction of the precued direction. When they were correct, there was a benefit; their RTs were *faster* than if they had not biased their response. However, if they were wrong (the 20% case), there was a cost paid because their RT was *slower* than in the 50-50 condition.

In many physical activities, we find ourselves biasing our responses by expecting to have to produce one particular response rather than some other possible one. For example, if a basketball player knows that the player he or she is defending goes to the right to make a shot only on rare occasions, the defensive player will undoubtedly bias his or her anticipated movement by "cheating" to defend moves to the left. In racquet sports, players who consistently hit to one side of the court will find their opponents "cheating" to that side. In these examples, the players have found that an advantage can be gained by "playing

the percentages" and biasing their expectancies. If they are right, the appropriate response can be made faster than otherwise would be possible. However, this is done with the possibility of being wrong. In this case, the appropriate response will take longer to initiate than if no biasing had occurred.

Stimulus-response compatibility. Another factor that will influence the amount of preparation time in a reaction time task concerns the relationship between the stimulus and response choices. The study of what is termed **stimulus-response compatibility** has a long history that dates back to World War II (see Proctor & Reeve, 1990). This extensive study has shown consistent evidence supporting the influence of the arrangement relationship of a stimulus and the response that must be made to it. We will examine this relationship and its influence on preparing the appropriate response in this discussion.

The rule of thumb here is that RT will be faster as the stimulus-response relationship becomes more compatible; conversely, RT will be slower as this relationship becomes less compatible. A highly compatible situation would be one where the stimulus indicator on a panel and the response mechanism are part of the same device. For example, if a button is to be depressed when it lights up, the stimulus and response mechanisms are highly compatible and RTs will be faster than if the stimulus is a light in a different location than the response device.

The spatial arrangement relationship between the stimulus and response devices is the most typical way of considering stimulus-response compatibility. Here, for example, consider a three-choice situation in which illumination of one of three lights indicates that one of three buttons should be depressed. If the lights and buttons are arranged horizontally, this situation is more compatible than if the lights are vertical and the buttons are horizontal. Also, if both lights and buttons are arranged horizontally and both relate to each other so that the first light to the left corresponds to a response for the left-most button, this situation is more compatible than if the far right button was the response for the far left light. In each of these situations, the more compatible relationship would lead to faster RTs than the less compatible situation. Also, as compatibility decreases, the number of choice errors will increase (see Fitts & Seeger, 1953).

In terms of the relationship between stimulus-response compatibility and Hick's Law, it has been shown that when the stimulus and response are highly compatible, such as being a part of the same mechanism, Hick's Law will not apply. In fact, Fitts and Posner (1967) reported after reviewing several studies concerning this issue, that anything tending to decrease the spatial compatibility between the stimulus and its corresponding response will increase the slope of the Hick's Law relationship between number of alternatives and RT. Hick, for example, used lights as stimuli and key presses for responses and provided support for the lawful relationship, whereas Leonard (1959) had the response key vibrate as the stimulus and found no increase in RT as the number of choices increased.

To account for the effect of stimulus-response compatibility on RT, Zelaznik and Franz (1990) argued that when stimulus-response compatibility

is low, as in the precue situation, RT increases are due to response selection problems. On the other hand, when stimulus-response compatibility is high, response selection processing is minimal and any RT changes reflect motoric processes related to preparing the selected response. By making this distinction, Zelaznik and Franz provide a means of examining which aspects of the response preparation process are influenced by variations in arrangements of stimulus and response components of a motor skill.

The stimulus-response compatibility influence on response preparation is an important one when the design of equipment or presentation of instructions is provided. For example, when you give instructions, especially if you use visual aids or demonstration, consider how compatible what you show the student is with the required response. The more translation that must be made from what is seen to what must be done, the more preparation time will be required to make the response. And, in the process, especially with a beginner, there is an increased possibility of errors being made as the translation may be incorrect.

Response complexity. You were introduced to the effect of movement response complexity in Concept 3.3 when the experiment by Henry and Rogers (1960) was discussed in connection with the motor program concept. Recall that Henry and Rogers showed RT increased from 165 msec for a simple finger lift from a telegraph key response to 199 msec for a situation requiring a movement from the key to grab a ball, and to 212 msec for a three-part movement. Thus, as the response required more component parts, the RT, or amount of preparation time, increased. Numerous other experiments have confirmed these findings since that time (e.g., Anson, 1982; Christina & Rose, 1985; Fischman, 1984; Glencross, 1973).

Of particular interest in the results on the effect of movement complexity on RT has been determining if, in fact, the key factor is the number of parts involved in the movement response. This question bears consideration if you think about the characteristics of two different complex responses. The more complex response may have more component parts to it, but it will also require more time to carry out. Also, the more complex response may require the person to move a greater total distance, and there may be a host of other possible differences as well. To address this issue and to test the Henry and Rogers conclusion that **complexity** is based on the number of parts to the movement, Christina and colleagues (Christina, Fischman, Vercruyssen, & Anson, 1982; Christina, Fischman, Lambert, & Moore, 1985; Fischman, 1985) have carried out a series of experiments in which various parameters of the movement responses have been manipulated, in addition to the number of parts. As a result of these manipulations the key variable in the RT increase in the Henry and Rogers task was the number of parts to the movement, as Henry and Rogers contended.

Practice. One of the most effective means of reducing the amount of time required to prepare a motor response is by extended practice of the response. For example, Norrie (1967) had subjects practice a three-part rapid arm movement response that involved two changes of direction. She found that only 50 trials of practice reduced the RT approximately 32 msec, from an average of 252 msec on the first 10 trials to an average of 220 msec on the last 10 trials.

Practice also can eliminate the effect of many factors discussed so far that affect response preparation time. For example, it has been consistently shown that the influence of the number of stimulus choices described by Hick's Law can be reduced by practice. Mowbray (Mowbray, 1960; Mowbray & Rhoades, 1959) has reported that the RT for a four-choice situation can be reduced to the RT for a two-choice situation after extensive practice. In fact, the effect of practice becomes even more pronounced as the number of choice alternatives increases (see Teichner & Krebs, 1974). Also, the effects of stimulus-response incompatibility on RT can be reduced by practicing the incompatible condition to the point that the RT becomes comparable to that of an unpracticed compatible situation (see Duncan, 1977).

Thus, it appears that practice is an important factor in influencing response preparation time. What does practice do that reduces this time demand? One possibility is that it reduces uncertainty in situations where much preparation time is due to translating unfamiliar stimuli or unfamiliar stimulus-response relationships. This possibility seems especially likely in the stimulus-response compatibility situation. By practicing, the person can overcome the preparation demands caused by the translation or confusion effects that were a part of the task initially. Another benefit of practice is that programming requirements are reduced as the response becomes better organized into larger coordinative structures. Because much of early practice involves developing the appropriate coordination of muscle, joint, and limb action, preparation time demands are greater than later in practice after coordination demands are reduced.

Arousal and Motor Skill Performance

In addition to factors that influence the time needed to prepare a voluntary movement, there are factors that also influence the quality of performance. One of these factors for motor skill learning and performance is arousal. The word *arousal* is synonymous with such words as *activate, awaken, alert,* or *excite.* When used to refer to performing motor skills, arousal relates to the activation levels of the emotional, mental, and physiological systems involved in producing the action. Levels of arousal before and during the performance of a skill have a profound effect on both the preparation of the upcoming movement and the quality of the movement that is produced. We will examine two very important aspects of the relationship between arousal and physical performance. One is the level of arousal of the individual at the time of the performance with specific

FIGURE 4.3-7
Diagram illustrating the relative predictions of the inverted-U and drive theories of arousal for motor skill performance.

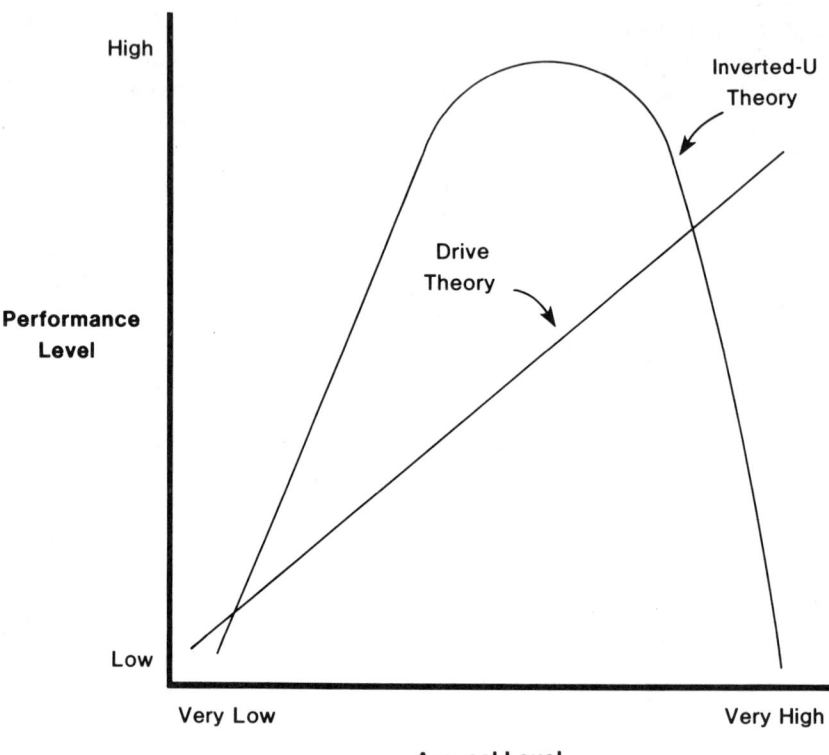

reference to anxiety and performance. The second is the type of skill to be performed and the situation in which it will be performed. It will become evident that these conditions cannot be considered separately if the effects of arousal on the learning or performance of motor skills is to be understood.

The arousal level of the performer. Two theories have emerged over the years as the most prominent in attempting to explain the relationship between arousal and motor performance. *Drive theory,* developed by Hull (1943) and promoted by Spence (1958), maintains that the relationship is a linear one, that is, as arousal increases, performance increases proportionately. Thus, a low degree of arousal would result in a low performance level, whereas a high arousal level would yield a high performance level. One of the drawbacks of this theory is its inability to accurately predict effects in motor tasks. Rainer Martens, who must be credited as the individual

primarily responsible for the development of contemporary understanding of the relationship between arousal and motor performance, reviewed many tests of the drive theory (Martens, 1971, 1972). His review indicates a lack of support for the drive theory explanation.

Alternative to this is the *inverted-U hypothesis.,* which can be traced back to research by Yerkes and Dodson (1908). This hypothesis postulates that the relationship between arousal and motor performance is in the form of an inverted U, sometimes referred to as the Yerkes-Dodson Law. According to this relationship, both too low and too high levels of arousal result in similar low performance, while a moderate level of arousal should yield high performance. (Figure 4.3–7 diagrams the differences between the drive theory and the inverted-U theory.) Although there have been some recent arguments in the research literature concerning how well the inverted-U hypothesis characterizes the arousal-motor skill performance relationship (see Neiss, 1988; Anderson, 1990, for examples of the two points of view), this hypothesis has a high degree of acceptance among scholars who study motor skill learning and performance.

Arousal level and the skill being performed. An important feature of relating the inverted-U effect to performance is the skill being performed. If you think about the various motor skills that can be performed, just from an intuitive perspective it does not seem logical to expect that different levels of arousal of a performer should result in similar effects for all types of skills. For example, if a person was experiencing a high degree of arousal prior to carrying out the tasks required of a football quarterback, would you expect this player's performance levels to be as high as those of a defensive tackle who was in a similar high emotional state? Compare the types of responses required of a ballet performer and of a weight lifter. Would the same levels of arousal yield similar results for both? These examples indicate an important aspect of the relationship between arousal and physical performance. That is, the type of skill or task to be performed must be taken into account.

Before relating how the type of skill to be performed influences the *optimal* arousal level that would produce optimal performance, consider how the arousal level of a person could influence both the preparation and execution of a motor skill, according to the inverted-U theory. If we relate the preparation of a voluntary complex movement to preparing a generalized motor program and the execution of the resulting movement to running that program, the movement parameters about the action being performed should be considered. These parameters must be appropriately determined and added to the generalized motor program during the response preparation time. Given this preparation process, it is possible to see how the arousal state of the individual is a critical factor. Remember that in Kahneman's theory of attention, levels of arousal that are too low or too high reduce the individual's capability to receive and effectively use information necessary to perform a skill as optimally as possible. Optimal levels of arousal allow a person to process information necessary to apply the appropriate parameter values to the motor program so that the intended action can be prepared and executed successfully.

Because the actual optimal level of arousal for a given skill can be related to the quantity of parameter values that must be assigned to the generalized motor program, it follows that the optimal level of arousal would vary according to specific characteristics of the skill being performed. For skills that are very complex, that is, that have many component parts, such as the quarterback's role in carrying out an option play, the optimal level of arousal is lower than for a less complex task, such as the defensive tackle's task in stopping a running back coming through the line. The important point for this discussion is that if the preparation of a response and execution of a skill is to be optimally successful, then the arousal level of the individual must be optimal for the skill to be performed. We will elaborate on the skill characteristic issue later in this discussion when the situation in which the skill is performed is considered.

Trait and State Anxiety

Anxiety is a more specifically defined psychological construct than arousal. In general, **anxiety** is a heightened level of *psychological arousal* that produces feelings of discomfort, both psychologically and physically. For our purposes, anxiety should be considered in terms of being a trait or state characteristic. *Trait anxiety* is similar to a personality characteristic. It is a person's general predisposition to perceive a situation as threatening or non-threatening. A person who is characterized by a high level of trait anxiety would tend to perceive more situations as threatening than would a person who is low on the trait anxiety scale. *State anxiety,* on the other hand, defines how the individual responds to a particular situation. That is, it is the emotional state of an individual who experiences feelings of apprehension, tension, nervousness, worry, or fear.

TABLE 4.3-1.   Sample Statements from the Sport Competition Anxiety Test (SCAT)

DIRECTIONS: Below are some statements about how persons feel when they compete in sports and games. Read each statement and decide if *you* HARDLY EVER, or SOMETIMES, or OFTEN feel this way when you compete in sports and games. If your choice is HARDLY EVER, blacken the square labeled A, if your choice is SOMETIMES, blacken the square labeled B, and if your choice is OFTEN, blacken the square labeled C. There are no right or wrong answers. Do not spend too much time on any one statement. Remember to choose the word that describes how you *usually* feel when competing in sports and games.

	Hardly Ever	Sometimes	Often
Competing against others is socially enjoyable.	☐A	☐B	☐C
Before I compete I feel uneasy.	☐A	☐B	☐C
Before I compete I worry about not performing well.	☐A	☐B	☐C
I am a good sportsman when I compete.	☐A	☐B	☐C
When I compete I worry about making mistakes.	☐A	☐B	☐C
Before I compete I am calm.	☐A	☐B	☐C
Before I compete I get a queasy feeling in my stomach.	☐A	☐B	☐C
I get nervous waiting to start the game.	☐A	☐B	☐C

Table 4.3–1. From Martens, R. Sport competition anxiety test. Champaign, Ill.: *Human Kinetics,* 1977. Reprinted by permission of the publisher.

Thus, state anxiety is closely allied to the concept of arousal. Although arousal is a continuum of emotional conditions ranging from sleep to intense excitement, state anxiety is a form of arousal that is produced by the perception of danger. State anxiety is to be considered as a negative effect; high levels are very unpleasant for the individual. The same cannot be said for high levels of activation.

This distinction between trait anxiety and state anxiety was developed as a result of the work of Charles Spielberger (1966). He provided a useful analogy to assist in distinguishing between trait and state anxiety. State anxiety is to trait anxiety as kinetic energy is to potential energy. State anxiety is similar to kinetic energy, that is energy in motion, while trait anxiety is similar to potential energy, or energy available for action when the appropriate stimulus appears.

Measuring anxiety.   Trait anxiety has customarily been measured by paper-pencil tests such as the Taylor Manifest Anxiety Scale (MAS) and Spielberger's State-Trait Anxiety Inventory (STAI). A test that has been developed specifically to determine trait anxiety for sport situations is the Sport Competition Anxiety Test (SCAT), which was developed by Martens (1977);

it follows the theoretical approach espoused by Spielberger. Each of these tests is a questionnaire that includes simple statements about how an individual generally feels in a particular situation. The person taking the test marks an appropriate space, indicating that the feeling occurs often, sometimes, or hardly ever. Examples of the statements from the SCAT appear in Table 4.3–1.

Information about an individual's trait anxiety could be useful in trying to predict the types of situations in which a high state anxiety reaction might occur. However, the indiscriminate use of the STAI or SCAT is not recommended for physical activity groups. This procedure would be of too limited practical value to justify the time spent in testing. Problems in the proper interpretation of test results also favor a more limited use of these instruments. In fact, researchers and clinicians who have been trained in the use of these tests should be the ones who use them.

State anxiety assessment can be made in a variety of ways. Because an increase in state anxiety results in increased physiological responses, monitoring the heart rate, blood pressure, or brain wave activity (EEG) can provide state anxiety information. However, such tests would not be very practical for teachers and coaches. Observation of

TABLE 4.3-2. Sample Statements from the State Anxiety Questionnaire Used with the SCAT

DIRECTIONS: A number of statements which people have used to describe themselves are given below. Read each statement and then circle the appropriate number to the right of the statement to indicate how you *feel* right now, that is, at this moment. There are no right or wrong answers. Do not spend too much time on any one statement but give the answer which seems to describe your present feelings best.

	1	2	3	4
I feel at ease.	Not at all	Somewhat	Moderately so	Very much so
	1	2	3	4
I feel nervous.	Not at all	Somewhat	Moderately so	Very much so
	1	2	3	4
I am relaxed.	Not at all	Somewhat	Moderately so	Very much so
	1	2	3	4
I am tense.	Not at all	Somewhat	Moderately so	Very much so
	1	2	3	4
I feel over-excited and rattled.	Not at all	Somewhat	Moderately so	Very much so

Table 4.3–2. From Martens, R. Sport competition anxiety test. Champaign, Ill.: *Human Kinetics,* 1977. Reprinted by permission of the publisher.

certain characteristics of the individual can also provide state anxiety information. Thus, increased levels of state anxiety are generally associated with increased sweating of the palms of the hands, tension, and nervousness.

If a more objective measure of state anxiety is desired than observation can provide, it may be better to administer some of the available paperpencil tests, which are simpler to administer than physiological tests. Both the STAI and the SCAT include a state anxiety questionnaire that can be quickly and easily administered. Table 4.3–2 includes a sample of the statements found in the state anxiety portion of the SCAT.

Information concerning an individual's state anxiety is helpful in determining what needs to be done for a person in a given situation. If the state anxiety level is too high, procedures can be implemented to calm the individual. If the individual shows too low a level of anxiety, or arousal, then the individual needs to be stimulated or aroused somewhat, to prepare him or her better for the task at hand. Again, these tests, as well as the associated techniques for altering anxiety levels, should only be used after adequate professional training or with proper professional supervision.

Levels of anxiety and the performance situation. The interrelationship between trait and state anxiety must be taken into account in relating anxiety to motor performance. This is due to the nature of both trait and state anxiety. Because trait anxiety is a predisposition of an individual to find a situation threatening or not, how that person responds to any given situation must be related to state anxiety. In general, a person characterized by high trait anxiety will respond to more situations with a high degree of state anxiety than will the low trait anxiety person. This is not to say that a low trait anxiety person will never show a high level of state anxiety. What is important to understand is that the number of situations that result in a high level of state anxiety are much greater for the high trait anxiety person. Thus, when we are concerned with anxiety as it relates to a situation, the level of state anxiety is the primary focus.

Recent investigations of the relationship between anxiety and motor performance indicate that the levels of state anxiety a person will exhibit are not related only to the trait anxiety characteristic of the individual. The trait anxiety characteristic also appears to interact with two very important situational variables, the *importance of the situation to the individual* and the *uncertainty of the outcome of the situation.* Any attempt to determine whether a person with a given level of trait anxiety will find that a particular situation will lead to a high level of state anxiety must consider these two variables.

With regard to *the importance of the situation,* the general rule of thumb is that the more importance an individual ascribes to a situation, the more likely he or she is to develop high levels of state anxiety. Of course, a high trait anxiety person would tend to consider more situations important to him or her than would a low trait anxiety person. To some individuals, a "friendly" game of racquetball becomes a very important event, while to others the same match would not appear as very important. The tension on the court of the "high importance" person can almost be felt by others on the court. An athletic event that has been given a large amount of media coverage acquires a great deal of importance to the participants as well as the fans. Similar importance effects can be observed with patients involved in rehabilitation activities. The more importance ascribed to the activity by the patient, the greater is the likelihood of the patient exhibiting high levels of state anxiety during therapy sessions.

The *degree of uncertainty of the outcome of an event* can be seen in a number of different motor skill performance situations. For example, uncertainty of outcome increases in a sport competition situation when opponents are closely matched. In a dance performance, the uncertainty increases when the dancer is not certain how his or her performance will be received by the crowd. Therapy patients find the uncertainty of the outcome increased when they are not sure whether they will be able to do the exercises the therapists describes that are to be done during a session. You can visualize other situations in which the uncertainty of the outcome is relatively high. This uncertainty is reduced when there is any indication that the probability of the outcome is in one direction or the other. As uncertainty about the outcome in-

creases, the expected level of state anxiety also rises. Conversely, the more likely it is that the outcome will be one way, the lower the expected level of state anxiety.

Anxiety and the skill being performed. Recall that in the discussion of the relationship between the inverted-U theory of arousal and motor skill performance that the skill being performed was established as an important variable influencing the optimal level of arousal. A similar relationship also exists for anxiety as well. The two characteristics of motor skills—*difficulty and complexity*—are important here. Because complexity concerns the number and intricacy of the components of a skill, it seems quite reasonable that the complexity of a skill is more related to the effects of anxiety on performance than is the difficulty of the skill. For example, it could be argued that a defensive tackle's position in football is as difficult as that of the quarterback. However, in terms of complexity, the quarterback's task is much more complex. With respect to anxiety levels, then, it could be predicted that a defensive tackle would exhibit better performance at much higher levels of anxiety than would a quarterback. Although, in neither case should those levels be excessively high. Or consider a different skill performance situation. If a patient in rehabilitation is working on picking up a filled cup of liquid and taking a drink, the degree of complexity is greater than learning to walk with a walker. Although both are difficult skills for the patient, there is a distinct difference between these skills in the number of component parts and how intricately related those parts are.

With performers at the same high level of anxiety, a skill that is highly complex will not be performed as well as one that is low on the complexity scale. The golfer who is at the high end of the state anxiety scale while putting will undoubtedly make a poor putt. On the other hand, it would be very advantageous for a power lifter's anxiety located toward the high end of the state anxiety scale.

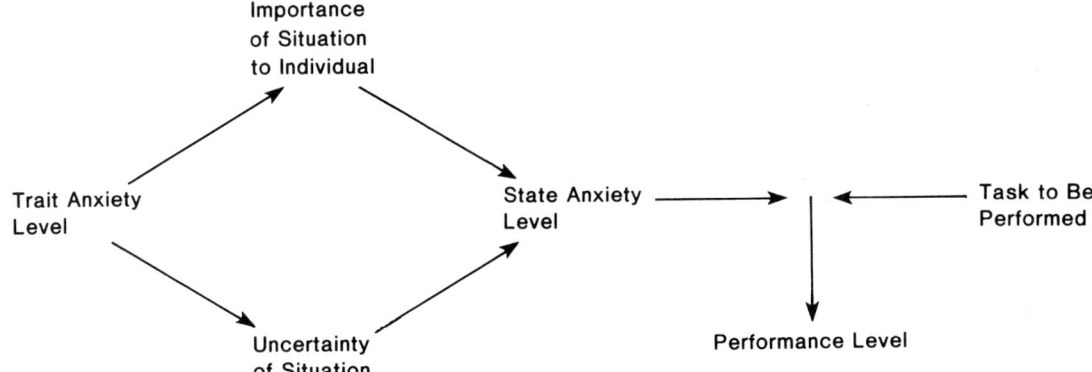

FIGURE 4.3-8   The interrelationship of individual and situation variables related to anxiety and performance.

Pulling the variables together.   The variables related to the anxiety and performance relationship can be divided into two categories. One involves the individual while the other involves the situation. The *individual variables* are the levels of trait and state anxiety of the individual. These individual variables interact with the three *situation variables,* which are the importance of the situation to the individual, the uncertainty of the situation, and the task or motor skill to be performed. Figure 4.3–8 depicts these variables as they interrelate to influence performance.

As the importance and uncertainty of the situation increase for any level of trait anxiety, the level of state anxiety is also likely to increase. State anxiety is related in an inverse manner to the complexity of the task to be performed. Thus, higher levels of state anxiety should be associated with tasks characterized toward the lower end of the complexity scale. When these variables are considered in terms of the aforementioned interrelationships, the teacher or coach is better able to prepare the individual for optimum performance.

Focusing Attention

An attention control feature that is closely related to the issue of arousal and performance, and influences both the preparation and execution of a motor skill, is what is known as **attentional focus** (Nideffer, 1976). The basis for considering this

feature comes from the views that attention can be considered in terms of both "width" and "direction of focus" (Wachtel, 1967), and that extreme levels of arousal or anxiety reduces attention capacity (Kahneman, 1973). People have the ability to broaden or narrow their attention and to direct their attention in specific situations. In performance situations characterized as high-stress, the need to focus attention becomes critical for successful performance because attention capacity is reduced and the focus narrows. The assumption is that in these situations, attention focus skills can be learned so that the performer will be maximally attentive to relevant environmental cues or aspects of performance, and that this focusing will benefit the preparation and execution of the skill.

Consider, for example, a person who is having difficulty learning to serve in tennis. This person may be thinking about the lack of good serves he or she has had during class. This is an example of an inappropriate attention focus and can lead to increased anxiety, which in turn can lead to increasingly poorer performance rather than improvement. Or, this person may be distracted by irrelevant environmental cues that do not allow the person to attend to the relevant cues that are vital for successful serving. When preparing to perform a serve, this person should focus attention on one specific aspect of the skill, such as tossing the ball well, and not think about anything else. By narrowing the focus of attention to this one important performance cue, the individual has decreased the likelihood of being overly anxious and has increased the likelihood that attention will be directed to a relevant cue that will benefit performance.

By focusing attention in an appropriate manner, the motor control system is sufficiently alerted to prepare a response and preparation is more likely to occur appropriately because the selection of environmental and control system information is being allowed to occur without distraction or interference. The information processing system can optimally operate because attention capacity has not been exceeded. This is especially important because excessively high levels of anxiety can create a reduced attention capacity. As a result of focusing attention on important cues or features of the skill, an appropriate capacity level is maintained to deal with what demands attention in the performance of the skill.

An example of research support for the benefit of using a type of attentional focus routine to prepare for performing a motor skill can be seen in a study with golfers by Boutcher and Crews (1987). Because the results were more clear-cut with the female than the male golfers, we will limit the discussion of that study to the results of the females. One group of university varsity golfers was given a specific attention focusing routine to use before putting while the other group was told to use their regular preparation routine. The specific routine related to concentrating on certain cues or actions in preparation for the putt, such as the number of glances at the hole or the number of practice putting strokes taken. Results showed that the female golfers using the focusing routine increased the number of putts holed, from 5.6 on the pretest to 7.3 on the posttest, while the no-routine group actually did a little worse from pretest (5.0) to posttest (4.0). Also, the amount of error for missed putts on the posttest was 6.2 inches less for the group who had used the attention focusing routine.

It is important to point out that narrowing attention focus is not always the most appropriate way to focus attention in motor skill performance situations. The type of focus that is best is related to the selective attention demands of the situation. For example, if the situation requires rapid scanning of the environment to select relevant cues from many irrelevant cues, a broad focus of attention is more appropriate. A sport skill application would be the attention focus requirements of a soccer player who must scan the field in front of him or her to make decisions about whether to dribble, pass, or shoot the ball. Those decisions are under time stress and therefore require rapid cue selection for the decision making process. In addition to attention focus needing to be narrow or broad, it can also be external or internal. That is, attention focus may need to be directed to cues in the environment or to internal thoughts, plans, or problem solving activities. Nideffer (1976) has argued that the broad and narrow focus and the external and internal directions of focus interact to establish four types of attention focus situations in sport performance. According to Nideffer, the successful performer is one who can shift from one type of focus to another as the situation changes and demands a different type of focus.

Various attempts have been made to provide attention focus training for athletes. The techniques incorporated in these training programs have similar characteristics. An example of a currently popular program is one developed by Nideffer (1986). It comprises several procedures that begin with providing the athlete training in the different types of attention focus that are demanded of situations. Then skills are developed in shifting attention focus from one type of focus to another. Training is provided in dealing with high arousal situations and learning to relax and focus attention appropriately. The degree of success of these programs is continually being assessed by researchers. However, there appears to be sufficient evidence to support the benefit of such training programs.

Attention focus considerations should not only be confined to sport contexts, although most of the evidence and information about focusing attention and performance is related to sport. It is easy to think of attention focus requirements in any physical activity. For example, the pianist must learn to focus attention to the music that has been memorized and to the manner in which he or she will play that music. Any concert performance is a high stress situation and leads to increased anxiety. As a result, appropriate attention focusing is essential for effective performance. In physical therapy settings, patients are typically experiencing high degrees of anxiety as they engage in rehabilitation regimens. Attention focusing is important for these individuals so that they can overcome the effects of the anxiety and optimally perform their routines.

Maintaining Alertness

Earlier you saw that for a given response there is an amount of time between the "ready" and "go" signals after which a person will not be at optimal readiness to respond to the "go" signal. Although this situation represents a problem of maintaining response preparation, there is another preparation maintenance problem to consider. This problem concerns the situation in which a person must respond quickly and accurately to stimuli that occur very infrequently during extended periods. This specific preparation maintenance situation is called **vigilance** in the research literature and is probably more accurately a case of maintaining alertness to detect stimuli, rather than a case of maintaining the preparation of a response. If attention is considered in terms of conscious awareness, then vigilance situations involve maintaining concentration over an extended period of time. In vigilance situations, an appropriate action must be taken when the cue to act has been detected. The problem, however, is to detect the cue. To do this, the person must maintain alertness, or concentration, to know when the required action must be made.

Examples of vigilance situations are relatively common in a variety of motor skill performance contexts. A common example can be seen in a factory setting in which a worker must detect a defective product and remove it from the assembly line. Driving a car along an uncrowded freeway becomes a vigilance task if a person drives for an extended time. Engaging in a repetitive motor skill drill can become a vigilance task, especially if the person has been instructed to detect and correct a specific error that occurs rather infrequently during the drill. Being a lifeguard at a pool or beach can be a vigilance problem because there are very infrequent situations requiring a response during a long shift on duty. Medical personnel are often required to work long hours and still be able to correctly identify symptoms of health problems and perform surgical techniques requiring precise motor skill control. Sport settings involve a number of vigilance situations, such as a baseball outfielder who must maintain alertness throughout an inning in the field but who may have only one ball hit his or her way, despite the many pitches thrown. Given these many situations in which vigilance maintenance is essential for successful performance of a skill, any discussion of attention factors influencing motor skill performance would be incomplete without considering the factors that influence vigilance decrements and how these decrements can be reduced.

Evidence for vigilance decrements. Research on vigilance developed during World War II and shortly thereafter. The need for this research became apparent when it was common to have radar observers work for several hours at a time. During their shift, workers had to maintain attention so that any important signal on the radar screen was reported. Researchers wanted to know how effectively radar observers could perform their task over such an extended period of time. The research has not only provided practical information to aid in establishing productive working practices for jobs requiring long periods of attention maintenance, but it has also provided useful

FIGURE 4.3-9 Results of the experiment by Wilkinson showing the effect of sleep deprivation on the performance of a serial reaction-time task performed for a period of 30 minutes.

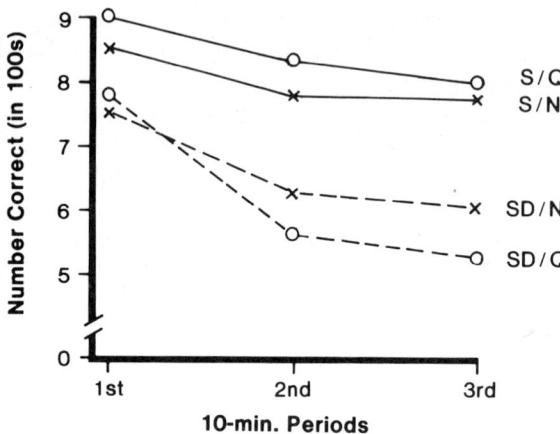

information that helps us understand human information-processing characteristics.

Most of the vigilance experiments followed similar procedures. Subjects were required to watch something similar to a radar screen. At rare intervals, a certain designated signal appeared. The subject's task was to report when a signal was noticed. The first of these vigilance studies was conducted by a British psychologist, N. H. Mackworth, during World War II (see Mackworth, 1956). The British military was primarily interested in problems associated with detecting submarines by radar from an airplane. In this study, the task involved watching a pointer moving around a clock face in one-second jumps that would sometimes make double jumps, about 24 per hour. These double jumps were to be reported by the subjects. Mackworth's study determined that during a two-hour work interval, the subjects' ability to detect the jumps markedly decreased each half hour.

Other vigilance studies have attempted to determine what factors affect the ability to maintain attention. One example is a study by Wilkinson (1963). A primary concern in this study was the effect of lack of sleep, or sleep deprivation, on a task requiring attention over a long period of time (see Figure 4.3–9). The assignment was a serial reaction time task, where the subject was required to tap a series of targets in a certain order as specified by a series of lights. Five lights defined the

series, and they were programmed to appear in various orders. This task was performed for 30 minutes by each subject. Subjects were either awake for 32 hours prior to the experiment, or they had normal sleep during that time. During the experiment, they were in conditions of either a low, constant "white" noise, like soft radio static, or quiet. Results showed that the most errors were committed by subjects who had been deprived of sleep and who performed the experiment in the quiet situation (SD/Q). Subjects who had had normal sleep and performed in the quiet situation S/Q had the fewest errors by the end of the 30-minute testing period. It is interesting to note in Figure 4.3–9 that the quiet experimental condition produced both the most and fewest errors by the end of the testing period. But with sleep deprivation, noise helped, whereas with normal sleep, the noise hindered performance.

Accounting for vigilance decrement. What do experiments like those we have just considered tell us about why people experience a loss in alertness over time? If that loss is a function of the amount of continuous time spent concentrating on a task, then perhaps we can suggest possible ways to increase our ability to maintain attention.

Several years ago, Donald Broadbent (1958) reviewed some theories that he called "theories of vigilance decrement." Some of these seem appropriate to our discussion. One theory suggests that attention loss occurs because the surroundings are monotonous. In such a setting, the person's entire level of nervous activity may be lower. The theory seems quite applicable to what happens in many instructional settings. The instructor may have set up a drill that after a short period of time becomes rather monotonous and boring to many students. Their attentiveness to instruction in the drill, or their application of such instruction to their own needs, is greatly reduced in this situation.

Another theory postulates that poor performance will occur when attention must be maintained in a setting where a signal is very infrequent, because the individual's general state of readiness has deteriorated over the time of inactivity. Such could be the case of the doubles partner in tennis who has had very few balls to return during the course of a point. What typically happens in this case is that when a ball does come toward this player, she is not as prepared to make the shot as she might otherwise have been had she been actively involved.

An interesting experiment by Eason, Beardshall, and Jaffee (1965) provided physiological evidence that an important part of vigilance decrement could be attributed to a reduction in the individual's state of readiness or arousal. Subjects were required to attend to a flashing light and report when it stayed on longer than its normal 0.5 second. The light flashed every 3 seconds and would stay on for 0.8 second 10% of the time. Subjects were given prior training to discriminate these two lengths of time. A session lasted for 1 hour, during which heart rate, neck muscle tension, and skin conductance were monitored. As expected, results indicated that vigilance performance decreased over the hour as correct detections declined from almost 90% during the first 10 minutes, to approximately 75% during the second 10 minutes, to nearly 60% over the next 30 minutes, and finally to approximately 50% during the final 10 minutes. Skin conductance followed a decrease that essentially mirrored the detection performance. Heart rate showed no change while neck tension showed a steady increase over the 1-hour session. The skin conductance decrease was con-

sidered indicative of an increased calming and drowsiness state over the session, for which the nervous system attempted to compensate by increasing muscle activity in the neck. Thus, these physiological data support the view that decline of vigilance is due to a reduction in the arousal or readiness state of the individual.

Suggestions to aid the maintenance of alertness. If we are aware that a task demands maintaining alertness for a rather long period of time, during which there will probably be infrequent opportunities for action, we can begin to help the performer of that task. Because the baseball outfielder offers a good example of a maintenance of attention problem in sports, let's begin with that situation. What can be done to help the player maintain an optimum state of readiness during an entire inning when there is typically very little activity? One suggestion is to keep the player's mind active in observing each pitch by having the player think, "What will I do with the ball if it is hit to me?" Then, at each pitch, the fielder will prepare for the necessary response. Between pitches he or she should relax for a short time, then again prepare for the next pitch. In this way, the problem of maintaining attention is solved by making each pitch a signal preparation concern.

We also used the example of the soccer, field hockey, ice hockey, or lacrosse goalie who encounters attention maintenance problems. A good suggestion for this situation would be for the coach or players on the bench to periodically yell words of encouragement or instructions directed specifically to the goalie. These words should be clear and precise so that the goalie is aware of them, and thus is "rescued" from any attention wandering that he or she may have indulged in.

Another very real attention maintenance situation occurs with physical and occupational therapists. Therapy patients are required to perform rather repetitive, monotonous, yet important exercises. A helpful suggestion applicable to this situation is based on an observation made by Mackworth in his early radar vigilance studies. He noticed that efficiency of performance could be maintained over a rather extended period of time when the subjects were given verbal knowledge of results after each of the signals to be detected had appeared. For the therapy situation, similar reports of results of the patient's performance could be furnished in such a way to motivate the patient to keep working. Also, frequent rest pauses and changes in the task being performed have also been shown to be effective in reducing attention decrements.

One additional suggestion is that the student's instructional environment should never be permitted to become monotonous or boring. Drills should be limited in time to such a degree that they do not cease to be effective. The handball student who is told only to "keep practicing that serve" for an entire class period will probably lose attention rather rapidly. By the end of the class period, little will be learned by the constant repetition after the time when attention began to diminish.

Maintenance of attention is vital to good performance or for effective instruction in any motor skill. It is very important for teachers to be aware of these situations and to attempt actively to use some procedure that may help students stay attentive to the task being performed. The suggestions made in this section are but a few that can be tried.

compatibility of spatial arrangement of the stimulus and the response, the complexity of the response, and the amount of practice the individual has had with the task. Two factors were discussed that influence both the preparation and execution of motor skills. One was arousal which requires an optimal level for optimal skill performance. Anxiety, a specific form of arousal, can be identified as trait and state types. Trait anxiety is a person's disposition to perceive a situation as threatening or non-threatening. State anxiety reflects how the individual responds to a particular situation. Various means of measuring these types of anxiety are available. The appropriate arousal or anxiety level for optimal performance of a skill must be determined according to the complexity of the skill. The other factor related to influencing both the preparation and execution of skills is focusing attention, which becomes an especially critical performance factor in situations characterized as highly stressful. Several types of attention focus are demanded in skill performance situations. Another important aspect of attention as alertness is the maintenance of alertness to detect a signal to respond over an extended time, especially when there are infrequent signals. In these vigilance situations, alertness declines as a function of time, probably due to monotony and a reduction of appropriate levels of readiness or arousal.

Summary

An important part of the concept of attention relates to alertness and response preparation. It is clear from research related to the benefit of a warning signal in a reaction time task and related to the RT foreperiod that a certain degree of alertness is required for optimal response performance, as is a minimum amount of time to prepare the response. The RT interval is an important measure of response preparation time. RT can be increased or decreased as a function of a number of factors related to the individual, the task, and the situation. Several of these factors have been discussed, such as the number of stimulus-response choices, the predictability of the stimulus, the

Related Readings

Anderson, K. J. (1990). Arousal and the inverted-U hypothesis: A critique of Neiss's "Reconceptualizing arousal." *Psychological Bulletin, 107,* 96–100.

Gottsdanker, R. (1980). The ubiquitous role of preparation. In G. E. Stelmach & J. Requin (Eds.), *Tutorials in motor behavior* (pp. 355–371). Amsterdam: North-Holland.

Hancock, P. A., & Warm, J. S. (1989). A dynamic model of stress and sustained attention. *Human Factors, 31,* 519–537.

Kelso, J. A. S. (1984). Report of panel 3: Preparatory processes. Considerations from a theory of movement. In E. Donchin (Ed.), *Cognitive Psychophysiology* (pp. 201–214). Hillsdale, NJ: Erlbaum.

Landers, D. M. (1981). The arousal-performance relationship revisited. *Research Quarterly for Exercise and Sport, 51,* 77–90.

Landers, D. M., Qi, W. M., & Courtet, P. (1985). Peripheral narrowing among experienced and inexperienced rifle shooters under low- and high-stress conditions. *Research Quarterly for Exercise and Sport, 56,* 122–130.

Meyer, D. E., Osman, A. M., Irwin, D. E., & Yantis, S. (1988). Modern mental chronometry. *Biological Psychology, 26,* 3–67.

Proctor, R. W., & Reeve, T. G. (1990). Research on stimulus-response compatibility: Toward a comprehensive account. In R. W. Proctor & T. G. Reeve (Eds.), *Stimulus-response compatibility: An integrated perspective* (pp. 483–494). Amsterdam: Elsevier Science Publishers.

Rosenbaum, D. A. (1983). The movement precuing technique: Assumptions, applications, and extensions. In R. A. Magill (Ed.), *Memory and control of action* (pp. 231–274). Amsterdam: North-Holland.

□

STUDY QUESTIONS FOR CHAPTER 4
(Attention)

1. What is meant by using the term *attention* to indicate we have a limited capacity to process information? What different types of theories have been proposed to account for this notion of limited processing capacity?

2. In Kahneman's model of attention, what four factors influence how we allocate attention in a performance situation? Give an example of how each factor can influence motor skill performance.

3. How are dual-task procedures used to investigate the role of attention in performing motor skills? What are some advantages and disadvantages of using this experimental approach?

4. Why do attention demands associated with performing skills decrease as a person practices and becomes more expert at performing the skill? Give an example of how this phenomenon can be illustrated.

5. How can your knowledge about attention as limited capacity be used to assist you in designing effective instructional procedures for teaching motor skills? Give an example.

6. What is meant by the term *selective attention*? How does the "cocktail party phenomenon" demonstrate two characteristics of selective attention?

7. Must the process of selective attention be conscious? Give an example where selective attention of appropriate information goes on unconsciously. Indicate how we know that this information was attended to unconsciously.

8. Describe two ways that researchers have demonstrated that there is a need for alertness and time to prepare a motor response.

9. Identify three factors that can influence the amount of time taken to prepare a motor response. Indicate why each factor affects preparation time.

10. Why is Hick's Law known as a "law"? Describe how Hick's Law relates to the issue of response preparation.

11. What is the "cost-benefit trade off" involved in the amount of time required to prepare a response when the probability of a specific signal occurring is 80–20? Describe a situation where under certain conditions it would be best to prepare for the 80% likely signal and under other conditions it would be better to prepare for a 50–50 likelihood of a signal occurring.

12. What is the difference between trait anxiety and state anxiety?

13. What do the drive theory and inverted-U hypothesis predict about the level of performance of a motor skill that can be expected for a given level of arousal or state anxiety?

14. How do individual and situation anxiety-related variables interact to influence motor skill performance levels based on an inverted-U hypothesis view of arousal and performance?

15. How does attentional focus relate to influencing anxiety so that a skill can be optimally performed? Give an example of how this could occur in a skill performance situation.

16. Describe a "vigilance" situation in motor skills. Why is this an important issue in the study of preparing a response?

MEMORY

CONCEPT 5.1
Memory consists of two functional components called working memory and long-term memory.

CONCEPT 5.2
Forgetting can be related to trace decay, interference, or inappropriate retrieval cues.

CONCEPT 5.3
The retention of information in memory is related to movement characteristics, storage and retrieval strategies, and context characteristics.

CONCEPT 5.1

Memory consists of two functional components
called working memory and long-term memory

Key Terms

memory
working
  memory
long-term
  memory

procedural
  memory
semantic
  memory
episodic
  memory

declarative
  knowledge
procedural
  knowledge

Application

Have you ever had the experience of calling an information operator to ask for a telephone number and then found out that you didn't have a pen? Hurriedly, you dialed the number as quickly as possible after the operator gave it to you. Why did you do this? "Obviously," you say, "because I would have forgotten it if I hadn't dialed right away." Do you need to do this with your home telephone number? You can quite readily recall your home number at almost any time, without any assistance.

Consider a few other memory situations. When you are at a party and you are introduced to someone, you often find it very difficult to recall that person's name, even a very short time later.

Compare that to remembering a teacher's name from your elementary school. You can probably name most of your teachers with little difficulty. Consider also the situation when you are shown how to serve a tennis ball for the first time. When you try it, you find that you have considerable difficulty in remembering all the things that are to be done to produce a successful serve. That situation differs quite drastically from your ability to hop onto a bicycle, even after you have not been on one for many years, and ride it down the street successfully.

The situations described here point out one of the important characteristics of human memory; that is, its structure involves a distinction in how permanently information is stored in memory. Information may be only temporarily stored or it may be more permanently stored. The telephone number you received from the information operator was only kept in a temporary store, whereas your home number has been kept more permanently in a long-term store. The discussion section that follows will focus on these two memory storage systems, considering *what* distinguishes them and *how* we seem to be able to transfer information from one store to the other.

Discussion

Memory plays an important role in our processing of information to produce a desired response. As you have observed in the preceding section, we are involved in memory situations almost constantly. Whether in conversation with a friend, working mathematical problems, or playing tennis, we are confronted by situations that require the use of memory to produce action.

What is memory? We often think of memory as being synonymous with the words *retention* or *remembering*. As such, most people consider the word *memory* to indicate a capacity to remember. One of our leading contemporary memory theorists, Endel Tulving (1985) stated that **memory** is the "capacity that permits organisms to benefit from their past experiences" (p. 385). Given this view of what memory is, it is not surprising that the study of human memory involves a variety of topics. In this chapter, we will look at several of these topics by discussing memory issues that are relevant to the study of motor learning.

Some Introductory Issues

Before considering the various topics to be discussed in our study of memory, it will be helpful to first clarify two issues concerning terminology that could cause confusion as you study the three concepts in this chapter.

Motor memory and verbal memory. The first issue concerns the use of two terms used frequently in this text and in the research literature related to human memory: *motor memory* and *verbal memory*. These expressions seem to imply that motor and verbal memory are separate entities. Although this issue has yet to be resolved by memory theorists, it is important for the purposes of this text to postulate a resolution to this issue. We will consider the memory for motor skills and for verbal skills as being a part of the memory system. Research evidence shows that people can have memory problems in performing certain activities that are related to verbal skills while still being able to perform certain motor activities. For example, some head injury patients have been shown to have difficulty recalling words they had just seen but had no difficulty putting together pieces of a puzzle. On the other hand, there are situations where memory functions related to performing both verbal and motor skills are impaired by an injury. This suggests then, that human memory consists of components, or modules, that are designed to deal with certain types of information. However, these modules interact in ways we currently know little about. This means that memory modules are both information specific and interactive. This arrangement allows the memory system to be adaptable to the demands of a variety of situations in which memory functions are important.

Based on this modular view of memory, it will help you to think of the terms *motor memory* and

verbal memory as signifying *memory for movement information* and *memory for verbal information.* As you study this chapter, you will see it is often difficult to separate these types of information for many skills that people learn and perform every day. As such, we will consider the study of memory as it relates to motor learning as an attempt to understand the characteristics and processes of the memory system as it is involved in learning and performing skills that fit the definition of motor skills presented in Concept 1.1. The application of this approach to our study of memory will allow us to consider research that traditionally has been classified as relevant to either verbal or motor memory and to apply that research to the specific demands of motor skill learning and performance situations.

One final point that should be noted is that the term *kinesthetic* appears throughout this chapter. *Kinesthetic* has been used in the memory literature by researchers in a way that is synonymous with the terms *motor* or *movement*. When the term kinesthetic is used in this chapter to refer to memory, it is being used because it is the term used by the particular researchers being discussed. Therefore, in this context, kinesthetic can be used interchangably with the term motor.

Retention and forgetting. The second issue concerns the meanings of two terms common to any discussion about memory. These terms, *retention* and *forgetting,* are closely related. In fact, it could be said that they are opposites. Retention refers to what we remember while forgetting refers to what we do not remember. However, a potential problem exists when we use the term forgetting. The problem is that this term can mean two different things. When we say that something has been "forgotten," we indicate that we cannot remember something. But, in terms of interpreting what this means in memory terms, this statement can mean that the information is not in memory or that the information is in memory but unretrievable at the moment.

Consider an example that illustrates this problem. Suppose you were asked a question on a test, such as "In what city is the world's tallest building located?" You remember having studied this but right now you are unable to answer the question. You say, "I forget." But does your inability to answer mean that the information is not in memory, or that you just can't retrieve it? This distinction is important if we are to understand human memory. We must know which is the case in this forgetting situation if we are to understand memory functions. To get at the meaning of "I forget" in this case, the same question could be presented in a multiple-choice format. Suppose that you are now able to select the correct answer. This would indicate that the information needed to answer the question was in fact in memory. However, you needed something to help you locate that information. Seeing the correct answer among several alternatives enabled you to remember the answer to the question. Keep this problem about the definition of forgetting in mind because it will be a recurring theme in various discussions in this chapter and in other parts of this book.

Memory Structure

Views about the structure of memory have gone through many different phases throughout the history of the study of memory, which can be traced back to the early Greek philosophers. However, one characteristic of memory structure that is now commonly accepted is that a part of memory is oriented toward events that have just occurred while a part is related to information about events in the past. This is not a new idea. In fact, in 1890, William James wrote of an "elementary" or "primary" memory that makes us aware of the "just past." He distinguished this from a "secondary memory" that is for "properly recollected objects." To primary memory, James allocated items that are lost and never brought back into consciousness; while to secondary memory, he allocated ideas or data that are never lost. Although they may have been "absent from consciousness," they are capable of being recalled.

The debate about the structure of memory has centered around how this distinction between memory for immediate things and for things in a more distant past fits into a structural arrangement in memory. Is the memory for the immediate or "just past" a special function of one unitary memory system, or is it a separate component of memory that is distinct from the component responsible for remembering information from the more distant past? You might think of this issue as attempting to describe the functional anatomy of human memory.

At present, the bulk of the evidence points to the latter of these viewpoints. That is, there are two components of memory. The evidence for this comes from two different but complementary research approaches to the study of human memory. One of these is taken by the study of cognitive psychology where inferences about the structure and function of memory is based on observing the behavior of individuals in memory situations. The other approach is that of the neuropsychologist or neurophysiologist, who is interested in explaining the structure of memory in terms of what is occurring in the nervous system during behavioral changes related to memory. Research evidence from both of these approaches provides convincing evidence that the memory system comprises at least two components that are definable by their distinct functions.

In this discussion we will limit our consideration of the structure of memory that has been developed from the perspective of the cognitive psychologist where inferences about memory structure are based on observation of human performance. Because this direction reflects the general nature of the approach presented in this book, it would be beyond the scope of this work to become involved in the discussion of the neurophysiological bases of memory.

A two-component memory model. By the late 1960s, there were several empirical studies in the research literature indicating that the structure of memory should be subdivided for information just recently presented and information well-known to the person. Several different models were developed to represent this structure. One of the most influential was presented by Atkinson and Shiffrin in 1968. Using a computer analogy, they conjectured that memory structure should be thought of as similar to computer hardware. They considered that the software that allows the computer to function are "control processes," which involve memory processes such as storage and retrieval of information, and are under the control of the person. The structural components, they concluded, comprise a sensory register, short-term store, and long-term store.

Since the time of Atkinson and Shiffrin's presentation of theory of memory structures, the primary theoretical problem has been to determine the exact nature of these structures. Some theorists claim that the structures are separate and distinct storage systems that are controlled by different laws or principles. Others visualize the structures as lying along a continuum, with each store representing a phase or stage of memory. While debate continues about memory structure, there is general agreement that this structure of memory should include different memory storage components in addition to serving a functional role for what the person does with the information in each component. Such a view bases remembering and forgetting on the characteristics of the memory component in which the information resides and on the characteristics of the processes operating in each component.

One approach that accommodates these characteristics was proposed by Baddeley and Hitch (1974; Baddeley, 1986). According to this view, memory is seen as comprising two functional components, *working memory* and *long-term memory*. Each memory component is defined in terms of its functions. While a number of different functions have been proposed, we will focus primarily on three types of processes: those that relate to putting information in memory (referred to as storage processes), getting information out of memory (referred to as retrieval processes), and functions involved in processing information residing in each component. These functions will be discussed as they relate to the topics in this discussion and in the discussions of the two concepts that follow in this chapter. Before addressing these concerns,

however, it is important to first describe the characteristics of working memory and long-term memory as the two components of the two-component model of memory structure.

Working Memory

The **working memory** should be thought of as a system that incorporates characteristics and functions traditionally associated with sensory, perceptual, attentional, and short-term memory processes that are involved in processing information. Working memory acts in all situations requiring the temporary use and storage of information and the execution of memory and response production processes.

Working memory functions. Working memory must be thought of as a place where information is stored for a short time, as well as a functionally active structure where critical information-processing activity occurs. This functional characteristic of working memory enables people to respond according to the demands of a "right now" situation. As such, working memory plays a critical role in decision-making, problem solving, movement response production and evaluation, and long-term memory function. With regard to influencing long-term memory function, working memory provides essential processing activity needed for the adequate transfer of information into long-term memory. Finally, it is important to note that an important working memory function is to serve as an *interactive workspace* where various memory processing activities can occur, such as integrating the information in working memory with information that has been retrieved from the more permanent, long-term memory.

A motor skill performance example will help illustrate the interactive workspace function of working memory. If you are a pitcher in baseball and are trying to decide which pitch to throw, it is important to integrate information about the present situation and past experiences. You need to consider who is the batter, what the current situation is in terms of score, runners on base, number of outs, and so on. And you need to integrate this information with what you know about the batter's characteristics, such as what has been successful in the past with this batter, and so on. The working memory serves as the temporary workspace to integrate all this information. Further integration of additional information will be needed to actually throw the pitch after it has been selected. The pitch selection information that was active in the workspace gets deleted and new information is brought into the workspace to deal with the new problem of performing the selected action.

Because working memory involves both storing and processing information, it is important to consider each function separately. In terms of storing information, two characteristics of working memory are essential to understand: the length of time information will remain in working memory, which is called *duration,* and the amount of information that will reside in working memory at any one time, which is called *capacity.* Each of these characteristics will be discussed in the following sections.

Duration.   Our understanding of the duration of information in working memory is relatively recent. Peterson and Peterson (1959) were the earliest to report research on this problem; their findings were simple and straightforward. They showed that we tend to lose information (i.e., forget) from working memory after about only 20 to 30 seconds. Other research followed shortly, supporting the notion of brief duration of information in working memory.

The first experiment published relating working memory to motor skills was by Adams and Dijkstra in 1966. Their experiment was quite simple in its conception. Basically, the idea was that if verbal information in working memory has a short duration, then should not movement information at this stage of memory have a similar fate? Results of their experiment indicated that movement information is also lost quite rapidly in working memory.

The procedures used by Adams and Dijkstra in this experiment are important to understand be-

cause they became the standard for many years for carrying out what was referred to as motor short-term memory research. In this experiment, subjects were blindfolded so that attention to proprioceptive cues about each movement would be encouraged. The apparatus used was a linear positioning apparatus, which involved a virtually friction-free handle that could be moved left or right along a metal rod. To begin a trial, the subject moved the handle to a place where a physical block had been placed, which designated the criterion limb position to be remembered, and then returned the handle to the starting point. Following a specified interval of time (the retention interval) the subject engaged in a recall test by moving the handle to a place that he or she estimated was the location of where he or she moved the block, which was no longer there. To score the accuracy of the subjects' response, the experimenter simply recorded how far the subjects' estimate was from the criterion limb position. The assumption here is that the degree of accuracy of this recall test reflects how well the criterion limb position is represented in working memory. The results, which are presented in Figure 5.1–1, showed that since subjects' limb positioning accuracy deteriorated as a function of the length of the retention interval, with very rapid error increase in the first 20 to 30 sec, Adams and Dijkstra concluded that working memory duration characteristics were similar for movement and verbal information.

Though many other studies followed the Adams and Dijkstra investigation, the results of those experiments generally supported the conclusion that the duration of movement information in working memory is about 20 to 30 sec. Information that is not processed further or rehearsed is lost. In the next two concepts in this chapter, we will discuss why this information is lost as well as how we can transfer the information from working memory to the more permanent long-term memory. For the present, the important thing to understand is that information in working memory remains there for a rather brief time before it begins to deteriorate and is lost from memory.

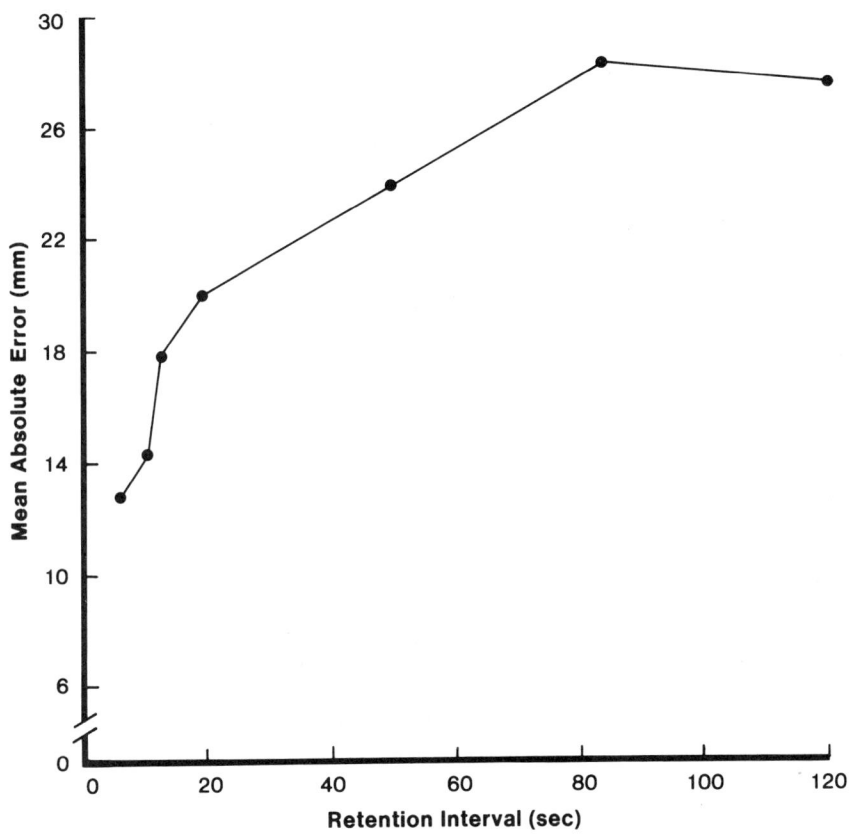

FIGURE 5.1-1
Results from the experiment by Adams and Dijkstra showing the mean absolute error for the recall of a positioning task following different lengths of retention intervals.

A different approach to assessing the duration of information in working memory involves considering the influence of information presented at one time on later performance for a task where the previously presented information should have no effect. This type of situation is common in performance settings where judges determine a performer's score, such as in gymnastics, figure skating, diving, and dance competition. A study by Ste. Marie and Lee (1991) showed that both novice and expert gymnastics judges could be biased in their judgment of a performance if the judge had seen a similar performance by that gymnast before, even though the judge was not aware of having seen the performance before. These results indicate that information can linger in working memory beyond the brief time limits described above. And this information can unin-

tentionally influence performance at a later time. Thus, assessing working memory information duration limits only on recall test performance appears to underestimate the actual duration.

Capacity. We are not only concerned with *how long* information will remain in short-term storage but also *how much* information we can accommodate. The issue of capacity in working memory was originally presented by George Miller in 1956, in an article that has become a classic in experimental psychology literature. Miller provided evidence to indicate that we have the capacity to hold about seven items (plus or minus two items) such as words or digits, in short-term storage. To increase the "size" of an item in memory involves a control process termed *organization,* which we will discuss in Concept 5.3. The larger item, or "chunk" as Miller called it, that results from the additional processing activity, enables people to recall far more than five to nine individual items at a time. However, with no practice or rehearsal of newly presented information, the capacity limit of working memory is five to nine individual items.

There does not appear to be any serious disagreement with the view that working memory has a specific capacity limit. In fact, Baddeley and Hitch proposed that working memory capacity is comparable to the attention capacity limit and characteristics that were discussed in Concept 4.1. What has been challenged is the actual capacity limit itself. For example, Chase and Ericsson (1982) argued that Miller's capacity limit is too high and that the capacity is actually only three to four items when no practice or rehearsal has been permitted. Regardless of which view is correct, the principle of a very limited working memory capacity remains. In an immediate recall situation, we can accurately recall somewhere in the range of three to nine items. Beyond this limit, errors in recall increase.

It is difficult to translate this capacity limit notion for working memory into motor skill terms. The most immediate problem is to translate an "item" into motor terms. We do not know if an item is an entire skill, a component of a skill, or a simple movement of one limb. However, there is research evidence that fits very well with the capacity limits just discussed. The following two studies provide representative examples of this evidence.

When an "item" that must be remembered is defined as a limb position in space, an experiment by Wilberg and Salmela (1973) shows capacity limits similar to those described for verbal items. In this experiment, subjects moved a joystick through a sequence of 2, 4, 6, or 8 movements. Immediately following the presentation of the movements, the subjects were asked to move through the sequence again. Results indicated that an 8-movement sequence was at the upper limits of working memory capacity.

Also, when an "item" is considered as a dance movement, there is evidence suggesting a working memory capacity limit for motor skills. For example, in an experiment by Starkes, Deakin, Lindley, and Crisp (1987), when 11-year-old "novice" and "skilled" ballet dancers were presented 8 ballet movements in an unstructured way, i.e., the movements were not a "typical" ballet sequence, the probability of recalling any one of these movements was only between 40% and 50%. This result suggests that 8 movements exceeded working memory capacity limits thereby making it difficult to recall correctly all 8 movements. However, it is important to note that when the 8 movements were a "typical" ballet sequence, the skilled dancers recalled them almost perfectly. On the other hand, the unskilled dancers had better recall for this type of sequence but it was worse than that of the skilled dancers, indicating that 8 movements still exceeded capacity. This result is in line with Miller's view that "chunking" occurs with practice. The effect was that 8 items for novices was similar to 1 item for skilled dancers. That this difference only occurred for the structured items indicates how context-specific this chunking activity is. We will consider this point in more detail in the discussion of Concept 5.3.

Processing activities. Information from the immediate past is processed in working memory so that it can be used to accomplish the goal of the problem at hand. The goal may be to remember what you have just been told or shown to do so that you can do the task. Or, you may need to use this information to solve a specific movement problem. And in both cases, you would like to remember what you did in each performance situation so that you can use your experience as a reference to help you in some future performance situation. In each case, you will involve working memory processing activities to enable you to achieve different goals.

Consider some examples of motor skill performance situations in which these different information uses could occur. Suppose your golf instructor has just given you a specific instruction to concentrate on your hand position as you swing a golf club. You must not only remember this instruction as you swing, but you must also retrieve from long-term memory the correct hand position and evaluate your present hand swing compared with the ideal. Of course, how successfully you make this comparison on your own depends on your stage of learning. But the carrying out of this verbal instruction invokes the working memory to enable you to carry it out.

Suppose you have just watched a dancer perform a sequence of dance movements and you must now perform that sequence, which is a common occurrence in instruction and dance audition situations. Working memory processing activity would be involved because you must keep in memory the visually presented sequence of movements and translate that visual information into motor performance. Involved in this translation process would be retrieving from long-term memory the movement information required to carry out the sequence.

Consider also the following example. You are a therapy patient and are given a complex puzzle to solve as quickly as possible. To solve the puzzle you must study the pieces and try to determine how the specific pieces fit together. You would continually try to match pieces as in the completed puzzle. You would try to determine an appropriate movement strategy that would allow you to put the pieces together quickly and with little error. Working memory would be actively involved in this problem-solving situation because you carried out several activities requiring several different perception, remembering, and performance characteristics that must be done virtually simultaneously.

Other information-processing activities are also the function of working memory, such as preparing the information for storage in the more permanent long-term memory. In each of the examples just described, it would be to the performer's advantage to store in some permanent way information critical to performing the task at hand. Activities that aid long-term memory storage will be described in more detail in Concept 5.3. For now it is important to be aware that working memory is more than a storage depository for newly presented information. It also serves a critical function as a workspace so that the information in working memory can be processed to solve a problem, make a decision, or transfer the information to long-term memory.

Long-Term Memory

We are calling the second component of the structure of memory *long-term memory*. As indicated earlier, **long-term memory** is a more permanent storage repository of information. It is what we typically think of when the term *memory* is mentioned. William James (1890) considered long-term memory as "memory proper." This is the component of memory that contains information about specific past events as well as our general knowledge about the world.

In terms of the *duration* of information in long-term memory, it is generally accepted that the information resides in a relatively permanent state in long-term memory. (Note however a discussion of this by Loftus, 1980; Loftus & Loftus, 1980.) Usually, "forgotten" information that is stored in long-term memory is there, but the person is having difficulty locating it. Thus, measuring forgetting and remembering in long-term memory situations can be a tricky problem and one that often cannot be satisfactorily addressed by traditional recall and recognition tests. We will come back to this important point in the discussions of Concepts 5.2 and 5.3.

With regard to the *capacity* of long-term memory, it is generally agreed that there is a relatively unlimited capacity for information in long-term memory (e.g., Chase & Ericsson, 1982). In fact, we really do not know how much information a person can store in memory. This is an issue that continually attracts research interest and is a common beginning point for developing theoretical memory models. An unlimited capacity leads to unique problems, however. For example, organization of information in memory becomes much more critical in an unlimited capacity system than in one of a limited capacity. Thus, there is a need to understand how people organize the information stored in long-term memory. This and other related issues unique to long-term memory will be discussed throughout this chapter.

In terms of information duration and capacity characteristics, it becomes obvious that long-term memory is distinct from working memory. Another distinct characteristic of long-term memory is the type of information that is stored there. In the following sections, three types of information stored in long-term memory will be discussed.

Procedural, episodic, and semantic memory. Although several proposed models describe the structure of long-term memory (see, for example, Chase & Ericsson, 1982), a model that is interesting to consider is one proposed by Endel Tulving (1985). He argued that there are at least three "systems" in long-term memory, which he termed *procedural, episodic,* and *semantic* memories. Each of these systems differs in terms of how information is acquired in the system, what information is included, how information is represented, how knowledge is expressed, and the kind of conscious awareness that characterizes the operations of the system. We will briefly consider each of these systems and how they function and differ.

Procedural memory may have the most direct relevance to long-term memory because it relates specifically to storing information about motor skills. **Procedural memory** is best described as the memory system that enables us to know "how to do" something, as opposed to enabling us to know "what to do." This distinction is readily seen in situations where you know what should be done, but you are not able to do the skill very well. For example, you may be able to describe what the elements of a dance routine are but you may not be able to actually perform them. On the other hand, just the opposite may be the case in that you are able to successfully perform a skill but you are not very successful at describing what you did that makes this performance successful.

The procedural memory system enables us to respond adaptively to the environment by carrying out learned procedures in such a way that specific action goals can be successfully achieved

in various environmental circumstances. For the performance of motor skills, procedural memory is critical because motor skill is evaluated on the basis of producing an appropriate action, rather than simply verbalizing what to do. According to Tulving, an important characteristic of procedural memory is that procedural knowledge can only be acquired through overt behavioral responses, a point commonly accepted from motor skills perspective. Information stored in procedural memory serves as a "blueprint for future action."

Semantic memory is, according to Tulving (1985), characterized by "representing states of the world that are not perceptually present" (p. 387). This means that we store in this memory system our general knowledge about the world that has developed from our many experiences. This includes specific factual knowledge, such as when Columbus discovered America or the name of the tallest building in America, as well as conceptual knowledge, such as our concepts of "dog" and "love." How information is represented in semantic memory is currently the source of much debate. The debate ranges from suggestions that all experiences are represented in some fashion in memory to suggestions that individual experiences are not represented in semantic memory, but rather, only abstractions, such as prototypes or schemas, are represented. However, to discuss this debate in any detail is beyond the scope of this text. The knowledge stored in semantic memory can be expressed various ways. You may verbally express this knowledge, or you may use typewriting or handwriting. There is no one way that semantic knowledge must be expressed.

Episodic memory consists of knowledge about personally experienced events, along with their temporal associations, in subjective time. It is this memory system that Tulving (1985) believes enables us to "mentally 'travel back' in time" (p. 387). An example here would be your memory of an important life event. You are very likely to recall this event in terms of both time and space. If you are asked the question, "Do you remember where you were when you heard about the space shuttle explosion that killed seven astronauts just after takeoff?", you would retrieve that information from episodic memory. Or, do you remember the best dance performance you ever did? Episodic memory is usually expressed in terms of remembering some experience, or episode. If you are an eyewitness to a crime, episodic memory becomes a very critical memory system if you are called to be a witness in court. And for performing motor skills, episodic memory can be the source for information to prepare you for an upcoming performance or to help you determine what you are now doing wrong that at one time you did correctly.

Distinguishing between knowing "what to do" and doing it. An important part of relating the three memory systems of long-term memory with processes underlying motor control is the distinction between knowing "what to do" and being able to successfully perform the action to accomplish that goal. Some learning theorists have argued that the information in the episodic and semantic memory systems should be considered **declarative knowledge** (e.g., Anderson, 1987). This knowledge is specified as what we are able to describe (i.e., declare) if we are asked to do so. Thus, declarative knowledge is specific to knowing "what to do" in a situation. This type of knowledge is distinct from *procedural knowledge,* which typically cannot be verbalized. As described earlier, **procedural knowledge** enables the person to know "how to do" a skill. This distinction is a useful one and will be referred to in various parts of this chapter.

One of the only experiments that has directly distinguished these two types of knowledge in a motor skill context was reported by McPherson and Thomas (1989). They classified 9- to 12-year-old boys as "expert" or "novice" tennis players based on length of playing experience and tournament play. Novices had never played in tournaments and had only 3 to 6 months playing experience. The "experts," on the other hand, had at least 2 years experience and had played in junior tournaments. These boys were clearly in an elite group for their age. The players were interviewed

after each point (something that the researchers had previously established did not disrupt the quality of performance). Players were asked to state what they had attempted to do on the previous point. When this information was later compared with what they had actually done (which was analyzed from a videotape recording), some interesting results were obtained. First, in terms of having an effective strategy or action goal, the experts knew what to do nearly all the time, whereas the novices generally never knew what to do. Second, although the experts were quite capable of demonstrating they knew what action goal to establish in a specific situation, they were not always able to accomplish it in their performance of the action. This suggests that the appropriate goal was established but there were problems in attaching the appropriate parameter values to the selected motor program. This evidence, then, supports the importance of distinguishing "what to do" from "how to do it" when discussing learning and control processes underlying complex motor skills.

In this regard, it is interesting to consider the view of the relation between declarative and procedural knowledge as proposed by Anderson (1987). He argues that early in the skill learning process, declarative knowledge predominates. That is, the "what to do" characteristics of the skill are more of what the learner knows about the skill. The person may have knowledge related to what should be done to perform a skill but the actual physical performance required to achieve the goal of the skill is not sufficient to be classified as skilled, or expert, performance. At this early learning stage, the person is learning to proceduralize declarative knowledge so that the action problem at hand can be effectively solved. That is, the beginner is trying to translate his or her knowledge of "what to do" into successfully and consistently accomplishing the goal of the skill.

This notion fits well into Gentile's (1972) model, discussed in Concept 2.1, in which she indicates that the first stage of learning is characterized by the goal of "getting the idea of the movement." The focus is on what to do and what coordinated movement pattern will enable the person to accomplish the goal of the skill. Then, as the person continues to practice and eventually becomes skillful, Anderson proposes that the knowledge about the skill is transformed from primarily declarative to primarily procedural knowledge. Here, the person can now successfully achieve the goal of the skill. And, Anderson argues, much of the verbalizable declarative knowledge of the skill drops out so that the person may find it difficult to state what he or she does to accomplish the goal of the skill without physically doing the skill or demonstrating how it should be done to indicate what he or she does. As we discussed in Chapter 4, this notion of motor skill learning involving knowledge becoming "proceduralized" to the extent that the person has difficulty verbalizing what to do is consistent with current views of automaticity.

Relating the LTM memory systems to motor control.   The question of how the systems of long-term memory relate to motor control can best be answered by considering what you must do to achieve the goal of the skill in a specific performance situation. For example, if your goal is to return a tennis serve down the line by using a forehand drive, how are these memory systems involved in accomplishing this goal? It seems that all three memory systems are involved.

To see how these systems are involved, consider first how you establish the goal of the action. You obviously see certain cues from the server and his or her action, as well as from the ball as it is served, and use these cues to help you determine that goal. You also establish your action goal, to some degree, on the basis of situational information even before the server hits the ball. For example, you may know what the server tends to do given the present score of the game and match. Although this type of specific information is available from the server, the serve, and the situation, how do you translate that information into a specific action goal for returning the serve? This is where your use of the three memory systems becomes integral. Before you set your action goal, you must retrieve infor-

mation from long-term memory to interact with currently available information to enable you to make an appropriate decision.

Episodic memory undoubtedly comes into play as you retrieve information related to specific past experiences that are similar to the one you are now in. You will use that information to provide guidance in determining what to do in the current situation. Semantic memory provides you with important information about what you have learned to do in this type of situation, thus allowing you to retrieve additional information to enable you to determine what to do. Then, procedural memory becomes the vital source for putting the action goal into motion. Now that you have determined "what to do" (i.e., based on declarative knowledge), you need to determine "how to do" this action (i.e., based on procedural knowledge) if you are to successfully perform the return.

When we consider the underlying control processes that enable you to carry out a plan to return a serve, it seems that procedural memory is the primary source of this information, although information is undoubtedly retrieved from the semantic and episodic memory systems as well before the action is finally determined and set into motion. Unfortunately, there has been no theoretical effort to relate the concept of the generalized motor programs and schemas to these three memory systems. But if we consider how the generalized motor program and schemas are proposed to function (as discussed in Concept 3.3), it is possible to relate these control mechanisms to the three memory systems.

Because the generalized motor program is essentially a type of blueprint for action, it fits very well with what Tulving describes as characteristic of procedural memory. The motor program is the memory representation of carrying out an action. However, it cannot function to allow a goal-directed response to occur without additional response-specific information (parameters). This additional information must come from the recall schema. According to Schmidt (1975), this schema is a general rule that has been developed after much practice. The schema is formed from abstracting certain pieces of information from past episodes and then synthesizing that information so that the episode-specific information is no longer represented in the schema. This suggests that the motor program and its associated schemas are a part of the procedural memory system. Thus, the process of selecting an appropriate action in a specific situation involves the episodic and semantic memory systems as the person determines what to do in this situation. Then, the information retrieved from these systems interacts with information stored in the procedural memory system as the motor program is selected and parameters chosen and finally executed to carry out the intended action.

It is important to be aware that we are not certain how the motor control system and the memory systems interact in order to produce an action in a specific situation. Nor has there been any concerted theoretical efforts to determine how this occurs. In fact, as we discussed in Chapter 3, there are some who would deny a role of memory in the control of skill. Unfortunately, part of the problem is the hesitancy to see the commonalities between cognitive and motor processes as they relate to the learning and the control of these skills. The tradition has been to consider these skills distinct, the result being theories that make little or no attempt to establish relationships between skills and their control mechanisms. If this relationship was carefully considered, it is likely that what has been previously considered two separate areas, motor control research and memory research, will be seen as more closely related (note, for example, the introduction in Magill, 1983).

Levels of Processing

A view of memory that was at one time thought to be an alternative to multi-component views of memory structure is called the *levels of processing* approach to memory. This view of memory, first proposed by Craik and Lockhart (1972), deemphasized the argument about memory structures by stressing the relationship between how information is encoded and how well that infor-

mation would be remembered. According to this view, what is most important for remembering is what the person does with information when he or she is presented it. Craik and Lockhart proposed a "hierarchy of processing stages" that would predict the strength of information in memory by determining how "deeply" the information was processed, i.e., encoded.

If the person directs attention only to the physical characteristics of the information, then the depth or level of processing is very shallow. This would be the case if you look at a word and make no attempt to determine its meaning; you only pay attention to whether the letters are in upper or lower case. On the other hand, a person can process information more deeply by associating the new word with one already known, or by determining if the word rhymes with another word on a list. The expectation of the levels of processing view would be that the shallow processing would yield poorer remembering than the deeper processing.

Rather than providing an alternative to memory structure models, the levels of processing view has provided a useful "rule of thumb" for understanding memory performance (Baddeley, 1984). Its value as a theoretical contribution to the study of memory has been questioned, although its influence in how we view memory function continues to be seen in memory research.

Summary

Memory is best viewed as consisting of two functional components, working memory and long-term memory. Working memory briefly stores information just presented as well as information that has been retrieved from long-term memory. It has a limited capacity for storing this information and this information remains in working memory for a brief amount of time. Working memory also serves an active information-processing role as it serves as a temporary interactive workspace that allows the integration of information just received with information that has been retrieved from long-term memory, so that a specific problem can be solved, or a decision can be made, or an appropriate action can be selected or evaluated. Long-term memory stores different types of information on a more permanent basis. It appears to have no real limits in terms of how much information can be stored or the length of time the information will remain there. There are three memory systems in long-term memory: procedural memory, semantic memory, and episodic memory. Each system stores a different type of information and has certain unique characteristics that distinguish it from the other systems. These memory systems can be related to motor skill performance by considering them in terms of how declarative knowledge and procedural knowledge relate to motor skill performance. And these memory systems can be related to performing a skill in a given situation by incorporating the characteristics and functions of the generalized motor program and the motor response schema

proposed by Schmidt. The relationship between what has been called memory research and motor control research has also been discussed.

Related Readings

Adams, J. A. (1983). On integration of the verbal and motor domains. In R. A. Magill (Ed.), *Memory and control of action* (pp. 3–15). Amsterdam: North-Holland.

Allard, F., & Burnett, N. (1985). Skill in sport. *Canadian Journal of Psychology, 39,* 294–312.

Baddeley, A. (1986). Editorial: Modularity, mass-action and memory. *Quarterly Journal of Experimental Psychology, 38A,* 527–533.

Ericsson, K. A. (1985). Memory skill. *Canadian Journal of Psychology, 39,* 188–231.

Magill, R. A. (1983). Preface/Introduction. In R. A. Magill (Ed.), *Memory and control of action* (pp. xi–xvi). Amsterdam: North-Holland.

Tulving, E. (1985). How many systems of memory are there? *American Psychologist, 40,* 385–398.

□

CONCEPT 5.2

Forgetting can be related to trace decay, interference,
or inappropriate retrieval cues

―――

Key Terms

encoding   retrieval   proactive
storage   recall test   interference
rehearsal   recognition   retroactive
            test   interference

Application

When we use the term *forget,* we usually indicate that we are unable to remember something. If you are asked to throw a curveball, you may respond, "I forget how to hold the ball." Why can't you remember this information? Has it been permanently lost from your memory or are you only temporarily unable to retrieve it? We use the term *forget* to imply both situations. While this distinction was introduced at the beginning of Concept 5.1, it will be considered more specifically in this concept. If we are to understand forgetting and why it occurs, then the distinction between information no longer being in memory and its being temporarily lost is an important one.

Examples of forgetting in learning and performing motor skills are many, as we have already pointed out. What is perplexing, however, are the causes of forgetting. In some situations we seem to forget information simply as a function of time. In other situations, time does not seem to be the critical factor but we forget when we must engage in some other activity either before or after we are presented the information we must remember. Sometimes neither time nor engaging in other activity is involved, and we still fail to remember all the information that has been presented.

You have probably been in a situation where someone showed you how to perform a movement skill. Suppose, for example, that you are in a be-

ginning bowling class and you are being taught the approach and release of the ball. The instructor has just told you to follow her through the steps so that you can see how to coordinate your steps with the arm movements necessary to release the ball properly. The intent of this instruction is for you to begin to get the "feel" of these movements as you practice them with the aid of a model to observe. After you go through this procedure, the instructor tells you to perform the whole skill on your own. But before you can try it, some people in the class have questions for the instructor. Finally, you can try to perform the skill on your own. For the most part you are able to do the steps and release quite well, but there are a few parts that you do not remember exactly. As a result, your performance results in the ball going off your intended course for it and you don't have the success you thought you would have. Why did you forget some of the parts when you tried to do this skill? Was it because of the time you had to wait between the instructor showing you what to do and actually being able to perform it yourself? Was it because of the interference caused by the questions from other members of the class?

According to the discussion in the first concept of this chapter, the bowling example we have just considered relates primarily to working memory. However, we must also consider forgetting as it relates to long-term memory. For example, you go to a party and someone says, "Can anyone here do the jitterbug?" You haven't done the jitterbug since you were in a dance class in high school several years ago. You say to yourself that you are not going to be the one to demonstrate it to the others. You may remember parts of the steps, but you just cannot seem to get the feel of putting the whole thing together. Finally, someone in the group gets out on the floor and shows the group how to do the jitterbug. Now that you have seen it done correctly, you are able to remember what to do and you are now able to perform the steps with little difficulty.

This dance example points to a very real problem in the study of human memory, especially in long-term storage situations. Do we ever really forget, or permanently lose, information in long-term storage? Or do we merely misplace it? If it is the latter, then recall from long-term storage becomes a retrieval problem, because the assumption is that the information is there and we just have to locate it. If it is a retrieval problem, then why does this occur and what can be done to reduce the likelihoood of its occurrence?

These few examples of forgetting information in the motor domain should provide you with some understanding of the aspect of memory we are dealing with in this concept. Forgetting is not only a very important theoretical issue in the study of human memory but also a critical, practical phenomenon. If we could determine the cause or causes of forgetting, we would be helping tremendously in the development of memory strategies that enhance remembering. And if this is possible, we should be able to incorporate this knowledge into our development of effective instruction. If we can anticipate not only *what* but *why* students forget in the process of learning motor skills, we should be able to take advantage of this knowledge and use it to our own advantage.

----------- □ -----------

Discussion

In our discussion of the structure of memory in the first concept in this chapter we indicated that information in working memory seems to remain there for a very limited amount of time. On the other hand, information in long-term memory seems to be there indefinitely. Thus, it would appear that time alone can cause forgetting information in working memory; but an inability to retrieve, or gain access to the stored information, accounts for forgetting in long-term memory. While these two conclusions seem to have empirical support, they cannot be presented as unequivocal conclusions to explain forgetting. In this discussion, some evidence will be considered relative to both working memory and long-term memory indicating that a variety of viewpoints exist to explain memory loss.

Certain terms in the discussion need to be identified and defined. **Encoding** is the transformation of information to be remembered into a form that can be stored in memory. **Storage** of information is the process of placing information in long-term memory. **Rehearsal** is a process that enables the individual to transfer information from the working memory to long-term memory. **Retrieval** involves the search through long-term memory for information that must be accessed in order to respond to the task at hand and the assessment of that information.

Assessing Remembering and Forgetting

In this discussion, the focus is on forgetting while in the discussion of the next concept, the focus is on remembering. In both discussions, it will be helpful to consider how we generally determine what or how much has been remembered or forgotten. It is important to keep in mind that when we make statements about remembering and forgetting, we make inferences based on observable behavior. We are in a similar assessment situation as the one we discussed concerning learning and performance in Concept 2.1; we make an inference about an internal event on the basis of external observations. Thus, the validity of our inference is dependent on the validity of the tests used to measure the observed behavior. In the next two sections, two categories of memory tests will be discussed to introduce you to different types of tests that are used in memory research assessing remembering and forgetting.

Explicit memory tests. When we ask people to remember something, we are asking them to consciously call something to mind. There are tests of memory that do this same type of thing. These tests are known as *explicit* memory tests. That is, they assess what a person can consciously remember. Two types of explicit memory tests that have been popular in memory research are known as recall tests and recognition tests. On the basis of the results of these tests, we are able to determine how much or what a person has consciously remembered, or, conversely, forgotten.

A **recall test** requires a person to produce a required response with few, if any, available cues or aids. This test asks the person to "recall" information that has been presented. In the verbal domain, these tests typically take the form of essay or fill-in-the-blank tests. For example, a recall test could ask, "Name the bones of the hand." In motor skills, a recall test requires the subject to produce a certain movement on command, such as "Perform the skill I just demonstrated to you", or, "Show me how you tie your shoe."

A **recognition test,** on the other hand, provides some cues or information on which to base a response. In this type of test, a person's task is to recognize the correct response by distinguishing it from several alternatives. In the verbal domain, multiple-choice or matching tests are examples of recognition tests. For example, you could be asked, "Which of these is a bone of the hand?" You are then given four alternative answers from which to choose where only one is correct. To answer the question, you need only to recognize which is the correct alternative, or which are the incorrect alternatives, to answer the question. For motor skills, recognition tests can involve having a person produce several different movements and then asking which of these is the one just demonstrated or most appropriate for a specific situation.

In terms of learning and performing motor skills, we are often confronted with both recall and recognition "tests," sometimes in the same situation. For example, if a person must climb a ladder, he or she must recall what to do and how it should be done in order to safely and effectively climb the rungs to the desired height. And a recognition test situation exists in a sport context when a football quarterback must visually inspect the defensive players to determine if their alignment is as it should be if he is to use the offensive play that has been called. Both recall and recognition tests are relevant to a baseball batter when deciding whether or not to swing at a pitch. He or she engages in a recognition test when determining if the ball is in the strike zone or not. Then, to produce the appropriate swing, the batter must recall what to do to carry out this action and then be able to recognize if the swing that has been initiated is appropriate for hitting the pitch where it is thrown. It is important to point out that recall and recognition do not necessarily demand conscious attention by the person. Accordingly, in these examples, recall and recognition activities can be occurring without the person being aware of being engaged in them.

An important benefit of recall and recognition tests is that each provides different information about what has been remembered or forgotten. It may not be possible for a person to produce a correct response on a recall test but be able to produce that response when it is one among several alternatives in a recognition test. A value of the recognition test, then, is that it enables the researcher to determine if information is actually stored in memory, but retrieval cues or aids are needed by the person in order to gain access to that information.

Recognition seems to be commonly overlooked as an important component in motor skill performance. This is undoubtedly due to the association of recognition with remembering cognitive information. However, it is often the case that the recognition of cognitive information influences motor performance. An example of this exists in the following sport situation. A linebacker in football is being praised by the press for being the leading tackler on the football team. But the reporters wonder why this is so because the player is actually smaller than is typical for a linebacker, and he is not especially fast. However, when interviewed, the player indicates that he is very quick at recognizing what play is being carried out and that gives him an advantage in getting to the right place at the right time. In this case, then, recognition plays a critical role in motor skill performance.

Implicit memory tests. Many times people have information stored in memory but it is stored in such a way that they have difficulty accessing that information so that they can respond correctly on explicit memory tests. For example, a person may be asked to describe the grammatical components of a sentence he or she is shown and be unable to do so. However, if the person were asked a question that required a sentence using the same grammatical structure, the person may be quite capable of producing that sentence. This would show that while knowledge about grammar rules that was needed to answer the explicit test was not available or accessible, knowledge about the grammar rules was in memory, but in a form that could not be brought to conscious level to be able to verbalize. Only when a person is required to use the rules in a way that did not require verbalizing the actual rules is it evident that the person had knowledge about the rules.

You saw evidence of this for motor skill performance situations in Concept 4.3 when the question about the need for conscious awareness of environmental characteristics to perform a skill was considered. In the experiments by Pew (1974) and Nissen and Bullemer (1987) described in that discussion, evidence was shown that people had the procedural knowledge of how to perform the tasks used in the experiments, but lacked declarative knowledge because they were not able to verbally describe the characteristics of the environmental stimuli that determined their responding. Thus, these experiments engaged people in a type of implicit memory test because the performance situation required them to produce an action that demonstrated they had "knowledge" of what to do but they were not able to verbally describe it.

In the motor skills memory literature, it is not common to see the distinction between explicit and implicit memory tests. Conversely, for researchers involved in studying memory related to cognitive skills, this distinction is seeing increased consideration (see Roediger, 1990, for an extensive discussion of the explicit-implicit knowledge distinction for cognitive skills). One of the reasons for not seeing this distinction related to memory for motor skills is undoutedly due to the declarative and procedural knowledge characteristics of motor skills. Some skills are distinctly procedural, such as tying a shoe. What would appear to be an explicit recall test command, such as "Show me how you tie your shoe," is actually an implicit memory test because it asks the person to perform a skill that does not require conscious attention. While most people can recall how to do this skill if given a shoe with laces, many would have trouble verbally describing what they do without the aid of the shoe or at least being able to demonstrate with their hands.

On the other hand, to test a person about his or her knowledge about what to do with a basketball in a given situation can be done in both explicit and implicit ways. An example of this was seen in the experiment by McPherson and Thomas (1989) involving young male basketball players, which was discussed in Concept 5.1. The explicit test was a paper-and-pencil test asking the players to indicate what they would do in a given situation. This information indicated declarative knowledge about what to do. However, an implicit test was also administered by observing what the players actually did in a situation to determine if they had the procedural knowledge necessary to do what they indicated should be done.

What is essential to understand, then, with regard to implicit and explicit memory tests is that both are necessary in determining what information is in memory. If forgetting or remembering is the goal of an experimental procedure, then an appropriate test needs to be developed to assess what or how much movement information has been remembered or forgotten. Explicit tests alone may lead to incomplete inferences because they can provide only a limited amount of information about remembering and forgetting.

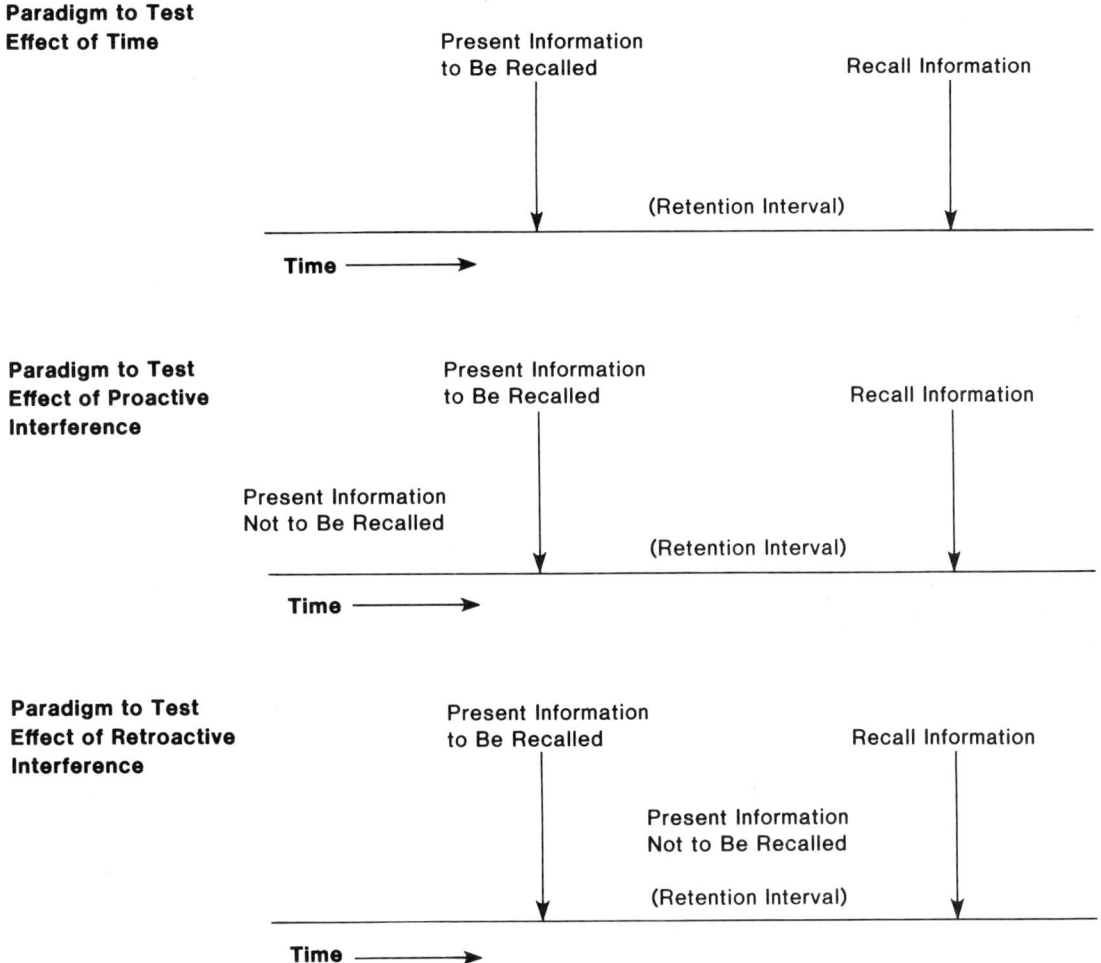

Paradigm to Test Effect of Time

Present Information to Be Recalled

Recall Information

(Retention Interval)

Time ⟶

Paradigm to Test Effect of Proactive Interference

Present Information to Be Recalled

Recall Information

Present Information Not to Be Recalled

(Retention Interval)

Time ⟶

Paradigm to Test Effect of Retroactive Interference

Present Information to Be Recalled

Recall Information

Present Information Not to Be Recalled

(Retention Interval)

Time ⟶

FIGURE 5.2-1 Time-line diagrams illustrating typical experimental paradigms used to investigate some causes of forgetting from memory.

Memory Experiment Paradigms

In discussing this concept concerning forgetting and the next concept focusing on remembering, you will see examples of experiments carried out to establish our understanding of these concepts. One thing that will help you interpret the research is understanding the experimental paradigms used by the researchers. These paradigms have been commonly used for both working memory and long-term memory investigations. Figure 5.2–1 illustrates these paradigms in simple line diagrams.

Typically, the protocol followed in memory research involves the presentation of the information to be remembered, a retention interval, and a memory test. The specific purpose of an experiment will dictate more specific procedures. For example, if the hypothesis to be tested indicates that the elapsing of time is a cause of forgetting, then the experimenter will vary the length of the retention interval. The Adams and Dijkstra (1966) study discussed in Concept 5.1 is a good example of such a paradigm. If the experiment is investigating interference as a cause for forgetting, then some activity, either cognitive or motor, is inserted either before the information to be recalled is presented or during the retention interval. When the interference occurs before the presentation of the information, we are setting up a **proactive interference** situation. If the interfering activity occurs during the retention interval, that is, after the presentation of the information, the paradigm is one investigating **retroactive interference.** Examples of research using interference paradigms will be provided as a cause of forgetting in the discussion of interference.

Trace Decay as a Cause of Forgetting

In the discussion of Concept 5.1, you were introduced to one of the earliest investigations of the effect of time on forgetting movement information held in working memory. Recall that the experiment by Adams and Dijkstra (1966) involved having blindfolded subjects move the handle of a linear positioning apparatus to a physical block, return the handle to the starting place, and then estimate the criterion location. Because the purpose of this experiment was to determine if time alone influenced forgetting, seven different retention intervals were used: 5, 10, 20, 50, 80, and 120 seconds. As you saw in Figure 5.1–1, results indicated that the amount of error the subjects made in their recall performance increased steadily as the length of the retention interval increased.

Because subjects did not engage in any activity during the retention interval, Adams and Dijkstra concluded that the memory "trace" for a movement presented only once decayed as a function of time. This meant that the memory representation for a movement deteriorated in working memory, which led to performance error. When forgetting occurs with the passing of time, the cause is generally termed *trace decay* in the memory literature. It should be noted that the term "trace" is not commonly used in contemporary memory research literature. However, it can be thought of as synonymous with what is referred to in this chapter as the representation of the movement in memory.

Few researchers have directly studied trace decay as the primary cause of forgetting as Adams and Dijkstra did. Most of our knowledge about trace decay as a cause of forgetting comes from experiments that investigated interference as a cause of forgetting, but also included a time component by involving different retention interval lengths. We will indicate those situations when we discuss interference as a cause of forgetting.

An important point to recognize about trace decay is that it can only be effectively tested as a cause of forgetting in working memory. A major problem with testing it for the long-term memory situation is the practical impossibility of maintaining a no-interference situation. For example, if you try to recall a dance routine after several years of not having performed it, you will have some initial difficulty remembering all the steps of the routine. While time is a factor, we must consider the possible interfering influences of the verbal and motor tasks you have performed since you last performed the dance routine. Hence, we observe the interaction of interference and time in the long-term memory situation. As a result, we know very little about the influence of time on forgetting information stored in long-term memory.

While time undoubtedly influences forgetting of information stored in long-term memory, it is more likely that the term forgetting refers to the misplacing of information rather than to decay or deterioration. The reason for this is based on the duration characteristic for information stored in long-term memory, which was discussed in Concept 5.1. Recall from that discussion that information is stored relatively permanently in long-term memory. Thus, forgetting becomes a retrieval problem rather than an indication of information lost from memory.

Interference

It is generally accepted that interference is a cause of forgetting. However, there seems to be only limited agreement concerning the nature of the activity that interferes with memory or when the interfering activity occurs. For our purposes, we

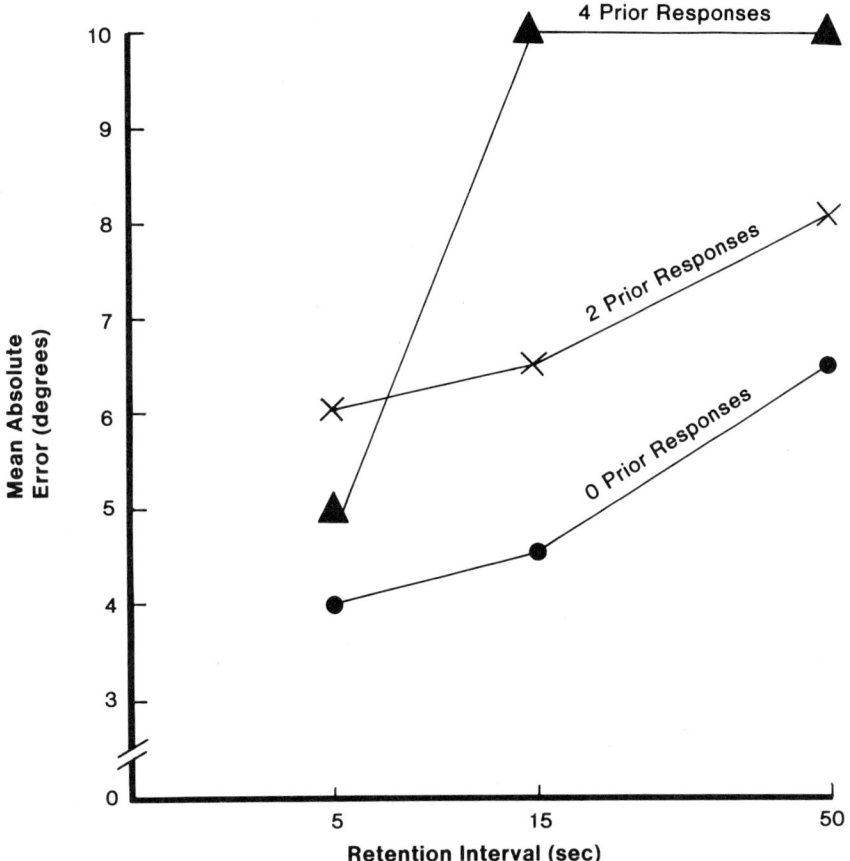

FIGURE 5.2-2
Results of an experiment by Stelmach showing proactive interference effects as a function of the amount of proactive interference activity and the length of the retention interval.

will consider the evidence that seems to support the interference theory for both working memory and long-term storage.

Proactive interference. Relatively convincing evidence suggests that proactive interference is a reason for forgetting movement information held in working memory. One of the earliest indications of this was provided in an experiment by Stelmach (1969). In his experiment, subjects were required to move to either 0, 2, or 4 locations on a curvilinear positioning task before moving to the location to be recalled. Following a retention interval of 5, 15, or 50 seconds, the subjects were asked to estimate in reverse order each of the locations they had moved to. Thus, the first location

recalled was the criterion location, or the location of interest. Results of this experiment are presented in Figure 5.2–2. Proactive interference effects can be seen rather markedly when there were 4 prior movements and a retention interval of at least 15 seconds as recall performance error is increased compared to the other time and activity conditions. Also, notice that the results of this experiment provide supporting evidence for trace decay as a cause of forgetting in working memory. This can be seen by noting that recall performance error increased as the retention interval lengthened when there were no movements preceding the criterion movement.

Several attempts have been made to explain why proactive interference affects remembering movement information. One plausible suggestion is that when the proactive interference takes the form of other movements, especially those that are similar to the criterion activity, *confusion* occurs. The individual is unable to make precisely the criterion movement because of the influence of the prior activities on the distinctiveness of the criterion movement. Whether or not verbal activity is an effective proactive interference agent does not seem to be known at this time. What evidence is available indicates that if we store the movement to be recalled as a verbal symbol, such as when we count and use a number to help recall a movement, then verbal activity can be a cause of forgetting. However, we will have to wait for more research to be published in order to better understand why proactive interference causes forgetting in working memory.

For movement information that has been transferred into long-term storage, the role of proactive interfering activities is virtually unknown. It appears that we can quite readily overcome proactive interference effects by actively rehearsing the information. This means that by active practice of a movement, we strengthen the trace for the movement in memory and thus notice few, if any, effects of proactive interference.

The appropriate view of proactive interference is that it occurs only when there is similarity between what is to be remembered and the interfering activity. This similarity seems to relate to "attribute" similarity. That is, if the information to be remembered and the interfering activity relate to the same movement attribute or characteristic, then proactive interference will build up as the number of similar movements preceding the movements to be remembered increases.

To support this viewpoint, a technique called release from proactive interference (developed by Wickens, 1970) has been used with some success. An example is a study by Leavitt, Lee, and Romanow (1980). On each trial, subjects were presented a criterion location or distance movement on a linear positioning apparatus. On the first two trials, only the criterion movement was presented and recalled. On the third and fourth trials, four additional locations or distances were presented before the criterion movement was presented. Then on the fifth trial, seven additional movements were presented prior to the criterion. If proactive interference builds up as a function of the number of preceding movements and experiences, error in recalling the criterion movement should increase accordingly. As you can see from Figure 5.2–3, proactive interference effects were in fact greater when the criterion movement was preceded by more movements. Notice, however, what happened on Trial 6. On this trial, some of the subjects had their criterion movement switched to the opposite type of movement, i.e., from a distance to a location movement or vice versa. When this occurred, there was a dramatic reduction in recall error (points E and F). Proactive interference effects were still noted for those subjects who did not have the criterion movement switched on this final trial. The important point here is that proactive interference is a specific type of interfering effect from which a person can be quickly "released."

Retroactive interference and working memory.
If an interfering activity occurs during the retention interval, we will often observe poorer retention performance than if no activity had occurred. However, rather than just any activity causing interference to the extent that retention performance is negatively affected, it seems that the degree of similarity between the interfering activity and the movement that must be remembered is an important factor. For example, in one of a series of experiments by Smyth and Pendleton (1990), subjects were shown a sequence of four movements, such as a forward bend of the head, both arms raised to shoulder level in front of the body, a bend of the knees, and left leg raised to the side. Following a retention interval, subjects were required to perform these movements, either in sequence (serial recall) or in any order (free recall). Five different retention interval characteristics were involved. These were an immediate recall condition, a 12 sec unfilled retention interval, and three 12 sec-filled intervals,

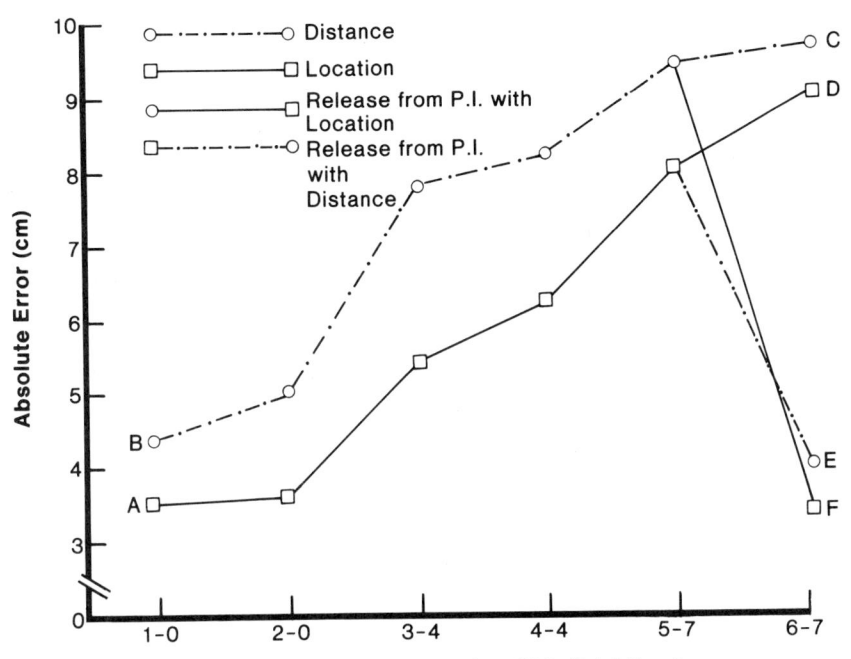

FIGURE 5.2-3
Results from the experiment by Leavitt, Lee, and Romanow showing the buildup and release from proactive interference (P.I.) as a function of the number of movements made prior to the criterion movement (second number of pair of numbers on horizontal axis) and the number of trials (first number of pair) for location and distance criterion movements. Release from P.I. occurs when a new criterion movement is experienced (points E and F on Trial 6).

during which subjects repeated movements made by the experimenter that were similar to those they had to remember, repeated pointing movements to numbers on blocks, or orally repeated words said by the experimenter. The influence of these conditions on recall performance can be seen in Figure 5.2-4. As you can see, these results showed that only when the retention interval involved subjects in reproducing movements that were similar to those they had to remember did recall performance suffer from activity in the retention interval.

Another characteristic of retroactive interference effects in working memory is one that we discussed for proactive interference. That is, activity during the retention interval causes interference that increases recall performance error only when there is a certain amount of activity. For example, Roy and Davenport (1972) showed that retroactive interference effects were evident when subjects were required to make four movements during the retention interval but not when they had to make zero or two movements. Again, the

similarity between working memory and attention capacity is seen because there appears to be a capacity limit for dealing with information to be remembered. As long as the amount of information stays within this limit, remembering is not affected. However, when that limit is exceeded, as in the Stelmach (1969) experiment showing proactive interference effects and in the Roy and Davenport (1972) experiment showing retroactive interference effects, forgetting occurs, which results in recall performance error increase.

Thus, the available research evidence indicates that retroactive interference for remembering just presented movements occurs in specific circumstances. These appear to be when the activity during the retention interval is similar to the movements that must be remembered, and when this activity and the movements to be remembered exceed working memory or attention-capacity limits.

What does our knowledge of retroactive interference in working memory tell us that is relevant to providing motor skill instruction? First of all,

FIGURE 5.2-4 Free recall results of the experiment by Smyth and Pendleton showing the retroactive interference effects of performing similar movements to those that had to be remembered. (Source: Smyth, M. M., & Pendleton, L. R. (1990). Space and movement in working memory. *Quarterly Journal of Experimental Psychology, 42A*, 291–304.)

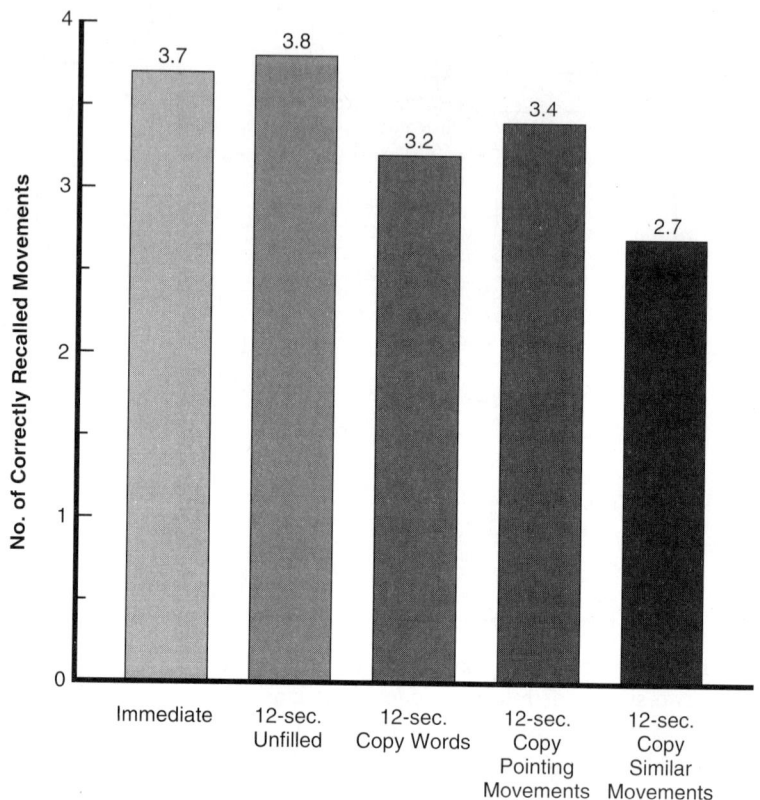

it seems clear that certain types of activities produce more interference than others. Another motor activity, especially if it is relatively similar to the one you are trying to remember, will produce more interference than less similar motor activity or verbal activity. Working memory capacity must be taken into account as well because the amount of retention interval activity appears to be a factor influencing the degree of interference that results. For instructional purposes, then, the implication is that what is done during the retention interval is important. For example, if you demonstrate a skill to a person, how well that skill is reproduced may be dependent on what that person does between the time you demonstrate the skill and when he or she attempts to perform it. It would not be advisable, for example, to show them some variations of the skill or examples of what not to do before the person has an opportunity to practice what you demonstrated.

Retroactive interference and long-term memory.
Retroactive interference effects have been found for movement information stored in long-term memory as well as in working memory. While research findings on this have been scant, there is some evidence that retroactive interference effects do occur. Methodological difficulties seem to have limited the number of research studies addressing this issue. The primary problem is that it is difficult to control subjects' activities during the retention interval, because the retention test could be a day, a week, a month, or even a year later. However, long-term forgetting characteristics of motor skills can be evaluated, even though it is difficult to assess the relative contribution of time or activity to the amount of forgetting observed. The best way to investigate the effect of retroactive interference on movement information stored in long-term memory is to look at research that has evaluated the amount of forgetting that re-

sults from very long periods of no practice. While retention interval activity is not controlled in these studies, it can be assumed that due to normal daily life activities, people engage in many different types of verbal and motor skills during the retention intervals.

It appears that retention interval length and/or activity does not have the same forgetting effects for all types of motor skills stored in long-term memory. Research evidence indicates that certain types of motor skills are remembered better over long periods than are other types of motor skills. Your own experiences may provide some support for this. You probably had very little trouble remembering how to ride a bicycle, even after not having been on one for several years. However, you did experience some difficulty in putting together the pieces of a puzzle that you had assembled quickly around the same time you learned to ride a bicycle.

The characteristic of skills that distinguishes these two situations relates to one of the classification systems discussed in Concept 1.1. That is, continuous motor skills are typically more resistant to long-term forgetting than are discrete skills, especially when the skill involves producing a series of discrete movements. This latter type of skill is sometimes referred to as a serial discrete skill or as a procedural skill. The following examples of experiments demonstrate how little forgetting occurs for continuous motor skills over long retention intervals and how much forgetting occurs for serial discrete skills.

A laboratory example of a continuous skill is the pursuit rotor. In an experiment involving this task, Bell (1950) had subjects practice for 20 one-minute trials and then return one year later for a retention test. The results of this test showed that very little forgetting occurred during the year as subjects' performance scores dropped only 29% after the one-year layoff. In fact, after only 8 trials, the subjects' scores returned to where they had been a year earlier.

Similar effects were found for another example of a continuous task called the stabilometer, a task requiring dynamic balancing. Ryan (1965) found that after only 11 trials of practice, subjects showed very little forgetting following a 3–, 6–, or 12–month retention interval. Figure 5.2–5 shows that while there was a significant decrease in performance on Trial 1 of the retention tests, after just a few trials, subjects increased their performance to a level similar to previous performance.

Compare the results from these two experiments involving continuous skills with the results of two experiments investigating long-term retention characteristics of a skill involving a series of discrete motor skills. In one experiment, Adams and Hufford (1962) trained military personnel to perform a complex bomb-toss maneuver. When the soldiers were tested on the skill 10 months later, during which time they had not performed the skill, a 95% loss in performance proficiency was found.

Another experiment involving long-term retention performance of a procedural skill was reported by Schendel and Hagman (1982), who trained soldiers to disassemble and assemble an M60 machine gun, a procedure that includes 35 discrete skills. One trial was counted when a soldier completed both the disassembly and assembly of the gun. The soldiers continued to practice this skill until they were able to perform one errorless trial. Four weeks later, during which time the soldiers did not practice, one group of soldiers had a refresher training session during which they practiced the skill as they had previously. Then, four weeks later (eight weeks later for the group that had no refresher training) a test of disassembly/assembly performance was given. The group that had the refresher training session in the middle of the retention interval showed a 57% advantage over the other group in terms of the amount of errors made on the first trial on the retention test. Thus, much forgetting occurred in this skill over an eight-week retention interval.

Several reasons have been suggested to explain why this discrete, procedural skill vs. continuous skill retention difference occurs. Adams (1987), for example, suggests that the difference is related to procedural skills having a large verbal component, which seems to deteriorate over time more

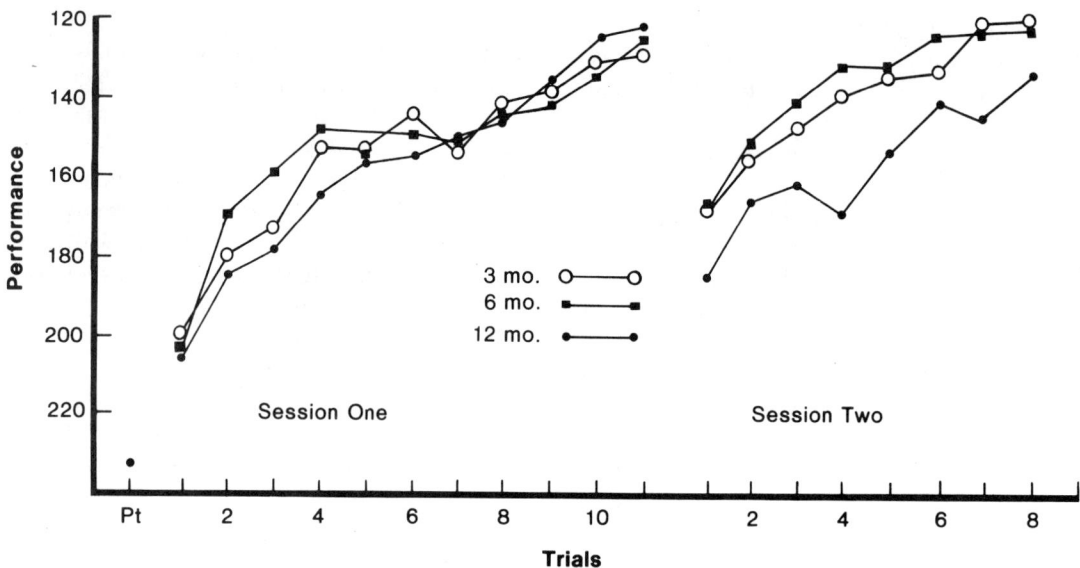

FIGURE 5.2-5 Results of the experiment by Ryan showing the performance curves for learning trials on the stabilometer (session one) and for relearning trials (session two) following either 3, 6, or 12 months of no practice.

readily than a motor component of a skill. As evidence that procedural skills have a large verbal component, Adams cites a study by Neumann and Ammons (1957) in which subjects had to learn a complex sequence of manipulating switches. Almost half of these subjects reported that they had used verbal cues to designate the locations of the switches.

Another reason less forgetting occurs for continuous skills is that they typically are practiced more than are discrete skills. This is evident if you consider what a "trial" is for these two types of skills. One trial for a discrete skill is usually one performance of the skill whereas one trial for a continuous skill is several repetitions of the skill over a period of time, such as 20 sec. Thus, 50 trials of a continuous skill yields many more practice repetitions of the skill than it does of a discrete skill.

What are the implications for motor skill instruction of this continuous skill vs. discrete, procedural skill retention difference? One implication

is that when students are taught skills in which they must learn a complex sequence of movements, such as a dance or gymnastics routine, it is important to provide additional practice after the original learning has occurred, if a test is to be given. It should not be assumed that because the student can perform the sequence correctly that he or she will remember it well enough to be tested on it at a later time. Compare this outcome to the machine gun disassembly/assembly experiment discussed earlier.

Another implication for developing effective practice is to require additional practice at the time of original practice. This extra practice should be beyond what is needed to achieve one correct performance of the sequence. The additional practice, called "overpractice" or "overlearning," appears to be very beneficial in diminishing the amount of forgetting that occurs in procedural skills over long-term retention intervals, and will be more thoroughly considered in Concept 8.2.

Inappropriate Retrieval Cues

One of the things we can learn from the results of memory tests is that the availability of retrieval cues can be important for remembering. Retrieval cues should be thought of as aids or hints that provide a useful means for finding information stored in memory. For example, you may be asked to recall the name of the world's tallest building, and you respond, "I forget." If the questioner then says that the building belongs to a large department store chain, you now have received a cue that can aid your search through memory. The availability of this cue can enable you to give the correct answer to the question. Thus, the cue provides the means of turning a forgetting situation into a remembering one.

In movement situations, we often are unable to produce the required response because we "forget" how it should be done. However, a closer inspection of this situation indicates that we simply cannot retrieve the needed information on the basis of the available cues. For example, you have been asked to throw a curveball and you find that you cannot do it. You may have "forgotten" how to correctly release the ball when you throw it, although you have remembered how to do everything else. If someone helps you remember that one aspect of the pitch, you find that you can successfully throw a curve. The problem was not that you did not have the information in memory; it was that you were unable to retrieve the stored information until you were provided a useful retrieval cue.

Role of movement context. One of the important sources of retrieval cue information for producing a movement is the context of the movement. The term *context* refers to all the characteristics and conditions relating to the performance of a movement. A consideration of the movement context is particularly helpful for investigating the role of the availability of appropriate retrieval cues for remembering movement information. For certain memory situations, the availability of the same context during the test that was available during practice is essential to the accurate recall of a movement. In such situations, requiring individuals to produce a practiced movement in a new context will lead to poorer performance because the retrieval cues needed to recall the movement correctly are not available.

An example of an experiment demonstrating this effect is one by Lee and Hirota (1980). Subjects were required to move the handle of a linear positioning apparatus to a physical stop which defined the movement distance to be remembered. On some trials, the subjects actively moved the handle to the stop and were then asked to recall that movement by either again actively moving the handle to where they thought the criterion movement ended or they were moved passively by the experimenter. On the passive recall trials, the subject would tell the experimenter when to stop moving his or her arm. On other trials, the subjects passively moved the criterion movement distance. The recall was again either active or passive. Thus, an important characteristic of the movement context was whether the movement was made actively or passively. If this aspect of the context provides important retrieval cues to aid retention performance, the results of this experiment should show that active presentation with active recall and passive presentation with passive recall conditions will result in better recall performance than the two situations in which the recall conditions were different from the presentation conditions. As you can see from the results illustrated in Figure 5.2–6, this prediction was supported. The availability of appropriate retrieval cues during the recall test was important for recall performance. When the recall test context was the same as it was during the presentation of the criterion movement, the recall error was less than when the presentation and recall contexts were different.

This experiment illustrates that inferior recall performance from which we infer forgetting can be due to the unavailability of important retrieval

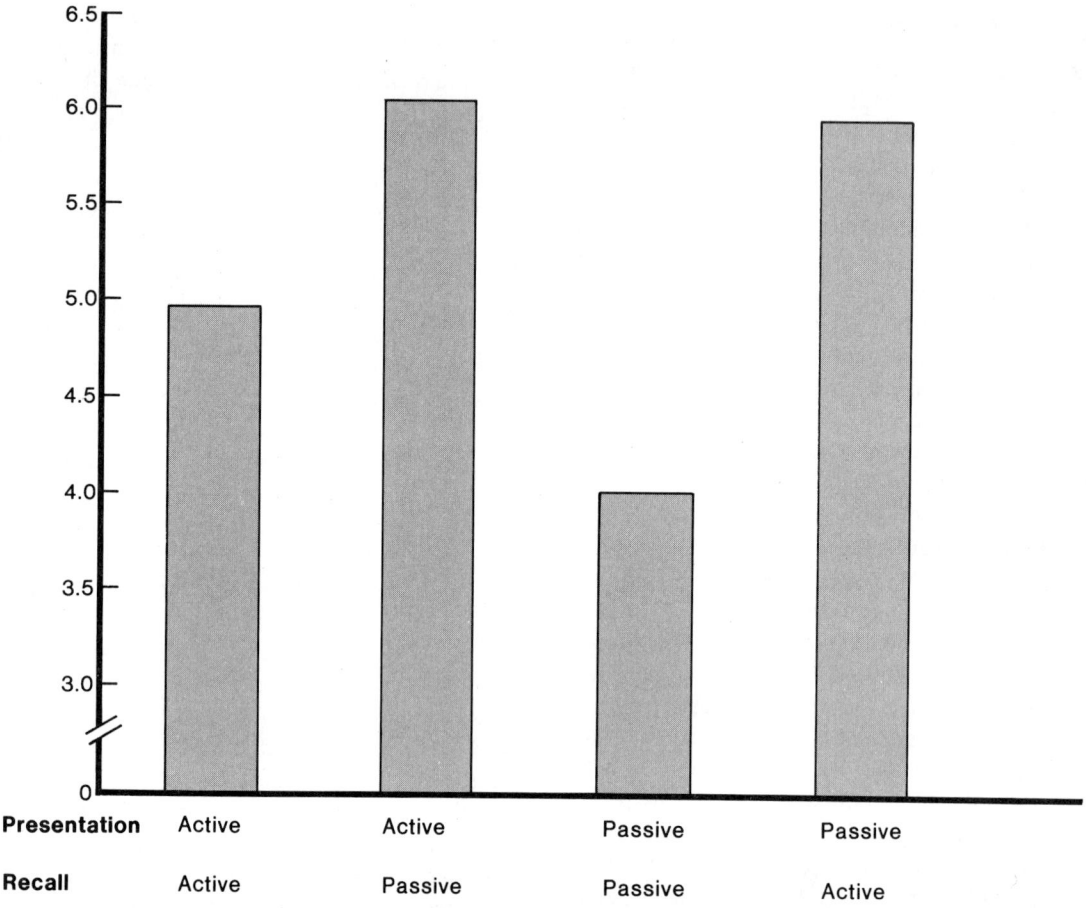

FIGURE 5.2-6   Results of the experiment by Lee and Hirota showing absolute error for recalling arm-position movements presented as either active or passive and recalled in either the same or opposite conditions.

cues. When these cues are available, retention performance is improved. This effect indicates that people encode and store in memory more than just the information they are trying to remember. Along with that information is stored context characteristics that become important cues for retrieving the stored information on a retention test. The question that remains, however, is how far this principle can be extended and under what condition it holds. We will consider this question more specifically in the discussion of the next concept. For the present, the important feature to understand is that forgetting is often the result of the

unavailability of appropriate retrieval cues. When those cues are available, remembering is enhanced.

Summary

Forgetting or loss of information is a very real problem in the study of memory. Forgetting is typically measured by determining the amount of information that a person can recall or recognize following a retention interval. Both time and activity influence forgetting in both working memory and long-term memory. The causes of forgetting related to these factors are known as trace decay, where the memory representation decays, or deteriorates as a function of time and interference, where activity causes forgetting. Interference must be considered in terms of interfering activities occurring either before (proactive interference) or after (retroactive interference) the presentation of the information. Certain types of motor skills stored in long-term memory, especially continuous skills, show little forgetting over long periods of time. Another cause of forgetting is the unavailability of appropriate retrieval cues. Here information cannot be remembered because the individual is not able to gain access to the information stored in memory. When appropriate cues are made available, an appropriate response can be made. These cues are often related to the characteristics of the context in which the movement was practiced.

Related Readings

Adams, J. A. (1987). Historical review and appraisal of research on the learning, retention, and transfer of human motor skills. *Psychological Bulletin, 101,* 41–74.

Fischman, M. G., Christina, R. W., & Vercruyssen, M. J. (1981). Retention and transfer of motor skills: A review for the practitioner. *Quest, 33,* 181–194.

Lee, T. D., & Hirota, T. T. (1980). Encoding specificity principle in motor short-term memory for movement extent. *Journal of Motor Behavior, 12,* 63–67.

Loftus, E. F., & Loftus, G. R. (1980). On the permanence of stored information in the human brain. *American Psychologist, 35,* 409–420.

Roediger, H. L. (1990). Implicit memory: Retention without remembering. *American Psychologist, 45,* 1043–1056.

CONCEPT 5.3

The retention of information in memory is related to movement characteristics, storage and retrieval strategies, and context characteristics

Key Terms

primacy-
  recency
  effect
serial-position
  effect

preselected
  movements
constrained
  movements
rote repetition

subjective
  organization
encoding
  specificity
  principle

Application

When you are given instruction on how to serve a racquetball or how to release the ball in bowling, what aspects of the movement do you remember or try to remember? How do you make yourself remember what is important for the proper execution of such skills? Do you select certain characteristics of each skill and in some way concentrate on remembering these? Do you try to combine the new instruction with past instruction and past practice experiences you have had? Do you try to think of the action you are trying to produce as being similar to some well-known action you can already perform? Each of these questions points to the importance of how movement characteristics and the strategies used to aid remembering are related to our understanding of how human memory works. These characteristics and strategies influence several different memory functions, such as the storage of information in memory, rehearsal of information, the organization of information, and how well the stored information is retrieved from memory.

Another important consideration in remembering movement information is the context characteristics related to the movement to be learned. Will practicing a skill in one environment and being tested on that skill in a different environment influence your test performance? In the following discussion, the characteristics of the practice and the test environment and their relationship will be shown to play critical roles in determining how well people perform on retention tests.

In the following discussion, then, you will be introduced to some of the factors that influence how well movement information will be remembered. Thus, rather than focusing on what causes us to forget, as we did in the previous concept, we will consider how those influences can be overcome. The result should be a more durable and accessible memory for the information being learned. One of the fringe benefits of studying these factors is that most of them can be controlled to some degree by the student or by the instructor.

Discussion

Three important factors must be taken into consideration to enhance memory performance. These are the characteristics of what must be remembered, the strategies a person uses to help him or her remember, and the context characteristics of the practice and test situations. Each factor is important to consider because memory performance can be shown to be a function of any one or combination of these factors.

The Type of Movement or Movement Characteristic

Discrete vs. continuous skills. In the discussion of Concept 5.2, you saw that continuous skills are more resistant to forgetting over a long retention interval than are discrete skills. This retention difference was stated as being especially characteristic when continuous skills are compared to skills in which a series of discrete responses must be performed in a specific order if the goal of the task is to be achieved. To briefly summarize that discussion, research examples were presented that showed continuous skills such as pursuit rotor and stabilometer performance deteriorated very little over retention intervals as long as one year. On the other hand, serial discrete skills, such as rifle or bomb assembly, suffered from dramatic performance decrements after only a few months. Based on that type of evidence, we can conclude that a significant motor skill characteristic influencing remembering is whether the skill is continuous or discrete.

Location and distance characteristics. Movement has many characteristics that we could code for storage in memory. For example, we could store the spatial position of various points of a movement, such as the beginning and the end point of a golf swing. We could also store the distance of the movement, its velocity, its force, and/or the direction of the movement. These characteristics represent specific spatial and temporal features of movement. Two of these, *location* and *distance,* have been extensively examined with regard to their codability. The logic here is that the more codable a movement characteristic is, the more easily it can be stored and retrieved. As a result, movement characteristics that are more readily encoded are remembered for longer periods of time and are more easily retrieved for a test.

Most of the research comparing location and distance characteristics of movement has used the working memory paradigms described in Figure 5.2–1. These experiments typically involve some form of limb-positioning task. To distinguish a movement's end location from its distance so that the two can be compared, the starting and/or end positions of the criterion movement must be changed for the subject's recall movement. If the end location characteristic is of interest, the recall starting position is changed. The criterion end location remains the same, thereby making the distance moved an unreliable cue to aid recall. If the distance of the movement is of primary interest, the starting and end positions must be changed for the recall test. This procedure requires the subject to remember how far the movement was and makes the location where the presentation movement ended an unreliable cue to aid recall.

Early research by Laabs (1973) demonstrated that when location and distance characteristics are separated, memory effects are markedly different. Location characteristics were found to decay very little during an empty retention interval of 20 seconds, whereas extent characteristics were influenced by decay. Activity during the retention interval was also found to have different influences on location and distance characteristics. Location was influenced by verbal counting during the retention interval, whereas distance characteristics showed no more effect for activity than for no activity during the 20-second retention interval.

Much of the research that followed essentially confirmed Laabs's findings (e.g., Diewert, 1975; Hagman, 1978), although there were conflicting findings concerning the remembering of distance information. An important breakthrough in this research was provided by Diewert and Roy (1978), who showed that when location information is a relatively reliable recall cue, subjects will use a location-type strategy to recall the movement. However, when location information is totally unreliable and only distance information will aid recall, subjects will use some non-kinesthetic strategy, such as counting, to help remember the distance of the criterion movement. Interestingly, spontaneous use of this dual strategy to aid the remembering of location and distance information has been demonstrated in children only older than nine years of age (Thomas, Thomas, Lee, Testerman, & Ashy, 1983).

Another interesting aspect of remembering location information has been pointed out by Larish and Stelmach (1982; Stelmach & Larish, 1980), who showed that subjects can more easily remember end locations of movements when they are within their own body space. For limb-positioning movements, subjects typically associate the end location of the criterion movement with a body part and use that as a cue to aid their recall performance. Other research that will be considered later suggests that subjects will also spontaneously associate the end location of limb positions with well-known objects, such as a clock face, to aid recall.

What does all this mean for teaching motor skills? One implication is that if limb positions are important for successful performance of the skill, instructional emphasis can be placed on these positions. For example, if you are teaching a beginner a golf swing, the important phases of the swing that he or she should concentrate on are critical location points in the swing. The keys could be the beginning point of the backswing or the location point of the top of the backswing. Or if a therapist is working with a patient who needs to work on flexing or extending their knee, emphasizing the position of the lower leg can help the patient remember where the last movement was or to establish a goal for future flexion attempts. If a dancer is having difficulty remembering where her arm should be during a particular sequence, a body-part cue about the location of the arm can help her remember the position more effectively.

The meaningfulness of the movement.   Another characteristic of movement information that influences remembering movements is the *meaningfulness* of the movement. A movement can be considered meaningful to an individual if that person can readily relate the movement to something already known. For example, a movement

that forms the shape of a triangle is considered more meaningful than one that makes an unfamiliar, abstract pattern. Or, if a movement is similar to one the person can do, then the new movement being learned takes on increased meaningfulness to the person.

An example of how movement meaningfulness influences remembering has been provided by Hall (1980). Subjects were presented with closed multi-dimensional movements (which can be seen in Figure 5.3–1) by means of a pantograph, a movement device that allows the subject to make the exact same arm movements as the experimenter. The memory test in this experiment was a recognition test where subjects were moved through a series of patterns and asked to indicate whether or not each pattern was the one just practiced. Results, also shown in Figure 5.3–1, indicated that recognition was highest when the presented pattern was a common geometric figure and lowest when it was a more abstract pattern. These results led Hall to develop an imagery scale for the 48 different movement patterns. On this scale, the highest values are the easiest to recognize, and the lowest values are the most difficult to recognize.

Hall's experiments, among others, suggest that certain movements have more inherent meaningfulness to people than other movements. This seems especially to be the case when the imagery value of a movement is considered. Movements that can be easily imaged appear to be inherently more meaningful to a person than those that are more difficult to image. And, the more meaningful a movement is to a person, the easier it is to remember that movement. This point is an important one to consider when providing instructions to students to help them remember how to perform a skill. We will come back to it later in this discussion when we consider strategies that increase a movement's meaningfulness.

Serial position of the movement.   There are many motor skill learning situations which involve a series of movements to be learned in a specified sequence. This can be seen, for example, when a dancer must learn a routine. Dance routines are a

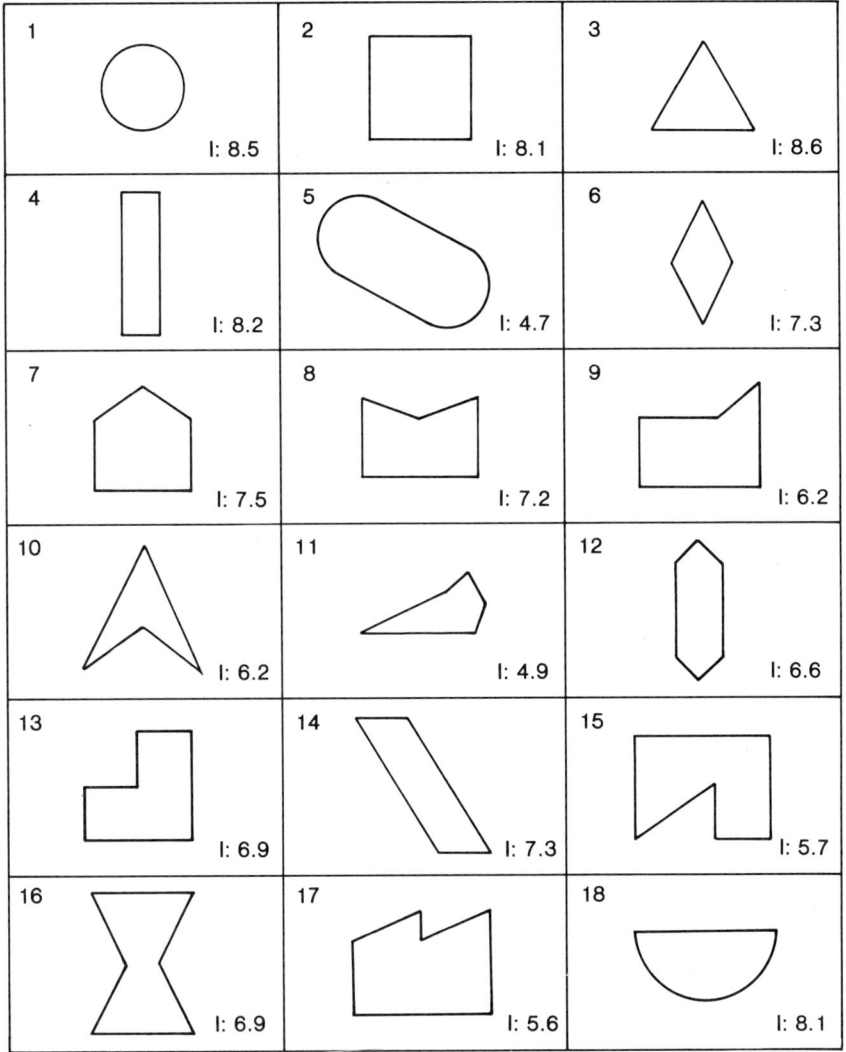

FIGURE 5.3-1
Movement patterns used in a memory experiment by Hall. The number in each top left corner is the pattern number. The number in each bottom right corner is the imagery value of the pattern. Higher numbers indicate the pattern is easier to image.

series of individual movements that are to be performed in a very specific order. The same challenge faces a gymnast. Likewise, a therapy patient who must learn to assemble parts of a piece of equipment by combining the components in a precise order so that the desired finished product will result. Hitting a golf ball, serving a tennis ball, and delivering a bowling ball are all examples of sport skills that require the performer to combine several movements in a specified arrangement. If the correct order of performing the component ac-

tions is not followed in these situations, or if certain phases are forgotten or performed improperly, the final outcome will not be the desired product. Each of these situations describes very common, practical problems that involve memory, whether the task is merely to recall a series of movements for a test, or learning a series of movements for some performance requirement.

When a series of verbal items must be recalled, one of the most consistent results obtained is termed the **primacy-recency effect,** which is sometimes referred to as the **serial-position effect.** Such as when a person recalls verbal items (words or numbers) in series. Those items that were first presented to the person and those that were presented last are usually recalled better than items in the middle of the list. Thus, the accuracy with which items on a list are recalled is a function of their position in the list. Accordingly, this typical experimental result has come to be known as the primacy- (early items on the list) recency (end items on the list) effect.

An interesting characteristic of the primacy-recency effect is that it is related to the length of the list to be recalled. Short lists of under five items typically do not show the effect but are recalled in a way that the most recent, or end-of-the-list, items are recalled best and the earliest items are recalled worst. When the list is longer than five items, then the primacy-recency effect is usually found. This list-length relationship to the primacy-recency effect could be expected based on what we know about memory capacity for working memory, as discussed in Concept 5.1.

Some memory theorists postulate that one of the things we apparently do is to rehearse actively the items on the list. To quite an extent this assumption helps to explain the primacy-recency effect. We have more time to rehearse the items presented first, hence they are recalled better. But why are the final items recalled better than the middle ones? The rehearsal explanation does not seem to predict that result. The last items on the list appear to be recalled well because of what has been termed "temporal distinctiveness." That is, the final items are distinct to us because of their location at the end of the list. Thus, we have a dual-process explanation of the primacy-recency effect. Whether or not this explains the primacy-recency effect remains to be proved. However, it seems to be a reasonable hypothesis that can be supported.

For motor skills, it had been thought that the recall of a series of movements did not follow the same laws as did the recall of a series of words. Instead, it appeared that movement series were recalled with a primacy effect only; that is, early movements were recalled best and end move-ments were recalled most poorly. However, this view changed as a result of a study by Magill and Dowell (1977) where the length-of-list relationship was applied to the motor domain. In this experiment, subjects were blindfolded and asked to move the handle on a linear positioning apparatus to a series of stops along a steel rod. The movement series consisted of either 3, 6, or 9 movements. The subjects were required to recall the movements in the same order in which they had been presented. The results can be seen in Figure 5.3–2. The linear pattern that had been traditionally considered to characterize serial recall of movements was evident only for the three-movement series. For both the six- and nine-movement series, a classic serial position curve indicating the primacy-recency effect began to appear.

Other studies in the motor domain have supported the existence of the serial-position effect for movement series and that this effect is related to the length of the movement series. For example, Wilberg and Girard (1977) showed the bowed-shaped curve with free recall and demonstrated that when the length of the movement series was beyond "memory span," i.e., greater than five to nine movements, the primacy-recency effect is readily noted.

The serial-position effect has distinct implications for motor skill instruction. Any time a skill is taught where a series of movements must be learned in a specific sequence, the serial-position effect must be taken into account. This is especially the case in the early stage of learning a skill when the learner is involved with a heavy emphasis on working memory. The following example demonstrates how the serial-position effect can be implemented in teaching motor skills.

Suppose that you are a physical education teacher who must teach a routine of floor exercises to a gymnastics class. It could be predicted from your knowledge of the serial-position effect that your class will have the most difficulty remembering what to do in the middle portions of the routine. If you demonstrate the entire routine to them, they will probably recall most readily the first and last portions of the routine. Thus, you

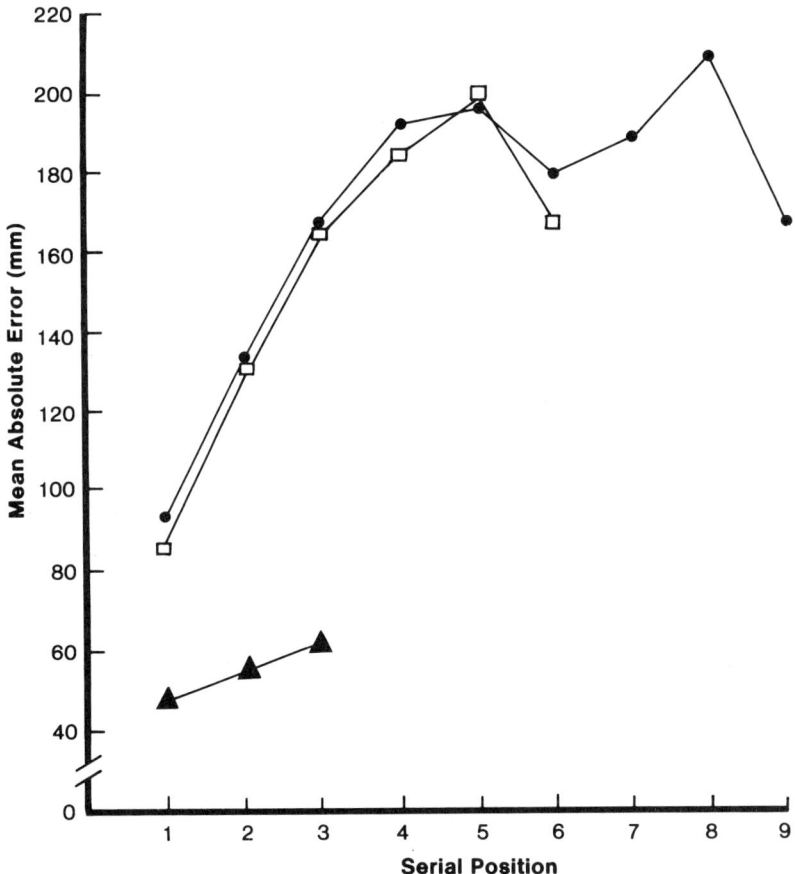

FIGURE 5.3-2 Results from the experiment by Magill and Dowell showing the serial position curves for the recall of a series of three, six, or nine movements on a linear positioning task. The triangles equal the three-movement series, the squares equal the six-movement series, and the circles equal the nine-movement series.

should be prepared to reemphasize middle portions of the routine or to encourage practice of those movements first. Another possibility is to break down the routine into smaller units, especially if the routine has several parts. Divide the routine into segments. If the segments comprise three or four movements each, then the segments can be practiced as individual units, and all units can be combined after the units are well learned. Such a procedure will help you in solving the problem posed by the primacy-recency effect. You effectively break down the whole routine into units of movements that contain a number of components well within a student's memory span. In other words, you do not overload the memory span. Dancers or pianists apply this by initially prac-

ticing segments or units to assist them in learning a new routine or piece. The entire score is broken down into manageable units for practice. As these are learned thoroughly or memorized, they are combined into larger units until the entire score is learned as one unit.

Strategy Employed

In addition to the type of movement or movement characteristic that must be remembered, the strategy used by a person to help them remember influences their memory of movements. The strategy may be one generated by the person who must remember the movement, or it may be one imposed by the experimenter or instructor. In either case, different memory strategies may have different influences on how well a movement is remembered or how much is forgotten. In this section, we will consider five strategies that may influence how well a movement is remembered.

It is important to note that any consideration of memory strategies takes into account what are known as control processes in memory. In theoretical accounts of the functioning of human memory, control processes represent the means by which we use our memories. Primarily, control processes are employed to enable us to remember information. Some of these processes are under our direct control, and therefore demand attentional resources, while other control processes are automatic, and not under our direct control. Automatic processes are assumed not to require attentional resources. Control processes involve functions such as selecting particular aspects of presented information to place in working memory, the retrieval of appropriate information from long-term memory to interact with the information in working memory, and rehearsal processes used to transfer and organize information from the working memory to long-term memory. While there are other control processes (see, for example, Hasher & Zacks, 1979; Shiffrin & Schneider, 1977), these memory operations are the foundation of this discussion on memory strategies.

Knowledge about effective memory strategies is important for people who learn skills and for those who teach skills. For those involved in instructional or rehabilitation settings, the benefit of knowing about the effectiveness of certain strategies is that it can lead to enhancing their own learning performance. Teachers, coaches, and therapists can benefit from an awareness of the effectiveness of memory strategies by being better prepared to incorporate the most effective strategies into their instructional or rehabilitative situations. Thus, this discussion of strategies will not only help you gain a better understanding of memory processes, it will also provide you with useful information to aid your own learning and teaching of motor skills.

Increasing a movement's meaningfulness. Most movements require the coordination of the body and limbs in a new way. In this respect, we could say that when you are first presented with a new motor skill, you are confronted with a movement that is more abstract than it is concrete. That is, the skill typically has little inherent "meaningfulness" to you in terms of the required organizational structure of the spatial and temporal characteristics of the limb coordination needed to perform the skill.

In this section, we will consider some ways in which you can increase the meaningfulness of the movements you are trying to learn. By doing so, you will find that it becomes easier to learn the skill as you practice it. The increased ease in learning the skill occurs to a large extent because we know that meaningful movements are remembered better than less meaningful movements, a point discussed in the preceding section. By considering this type of strategy, we are able to relate our knowledge about a characteristic of movement known to influence the memorability of a movement with a memory strategy that applies this knowledge.

One of the most commonly used strategies to increase the meaningfulness of a movement involves the use of *imagery*. Imagery as a memory strategy involves developing in your mind a picture of what a movement is like. It is best to use an image of something that is very familiar. We know that this strategy is effective because there is research evidence supporting the benefit of the use of imagery to increase the memorability of a movement.

An example of an experiment providing such evidence was reported by Hall and Buckolz (1982–83). Subjects were given 18 movement patterns from those shown earlier in Figure 5.3–2. One group of subjects was given specific instructions to develop mental images of the patterns as they were presented. Another group was simply presented with the patterns and given no instructions to image. Although the results of this experiment showed no recall difference between these two groups, it is interesting to note that post-

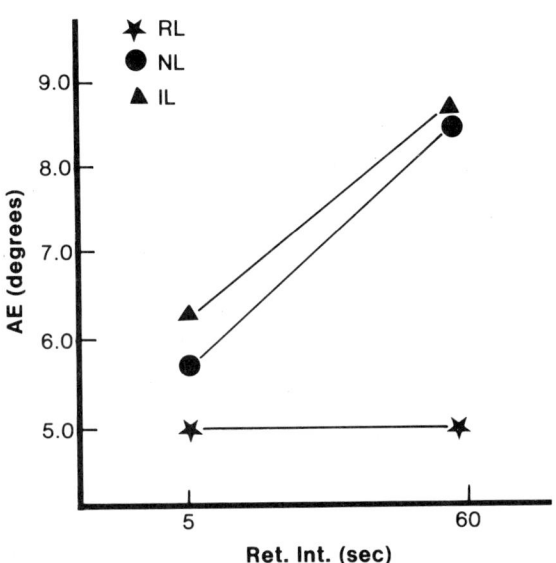

FIGURE 5.3-3 Mean absolute error computed across positions for the 5-second and 60-second retention intervals (ret. int.) for Experiment 1 by Shea. (RL = relevant label, NL = no label, IL = irrelevant label.)

experiment interviews with subjects revealed that *all* subjects in the no-instructions group spontaneously imaged when the movement patterns were presented.

We will consider other procedures related to imagery strategy in Chapter 8 in the discussion of mental practice. For the present, it is important to see that the use of mental imagery appears to be a powerful rehearsal strategy. As such, it can also be an effective instructional strategy for teachers. For example, rather than provide the complex instructions for how to coordinate the arm movements to perform a sidestroke in swimming, the instructor can provide the students with a useful image to use while practicing the stroke. The image given the students is of themselves picking an apple from a tree with one hand, bringing the apple down, and putting the apple in a basket. The remembering of the sidestroke is enhanced by changing the abstract, complex components involved in the skill into a concrete, meaningful movement.

Another effective strategy that increases the meaningfulness of a movement so that it is more accurately remembered is to attach a useful or meaningful *verbal label* to the movement, then using that label-movement association to aid the

recall of the movement. One of the earliest demonstrations of the beneficial influence of attaching verbal labels to simple movements was by John Shea (1977), who had subjects move to a stop on a semicircular positioning apparatus. When the subjects arrived at the criterion location, one group was provided with a number that corresponded to the clock-face location of the criterion location; another group received an irrelevant verbal label such as a nonsensical three-letter syllable; another group received no verbal label about the criterion location. Results, as seen in Figure 5.3–3, indicate that the group given a clock-face label showed no increase in error over a 60–second unfilled retention interval, whereas the other two groups showed a large increase in recall error.

In a subsequent experiment (Ho & Shea, 1978), the subjects given a clock-face label recalled the criterion movement better than the no-label group even after interfering activity occurred during the retention interval. Additionally, Winther and Thomas (1981) showed that when useful verbal labels are attached to positioning movements, young children's (age 7) retention performance can become equivalent to that of adults.

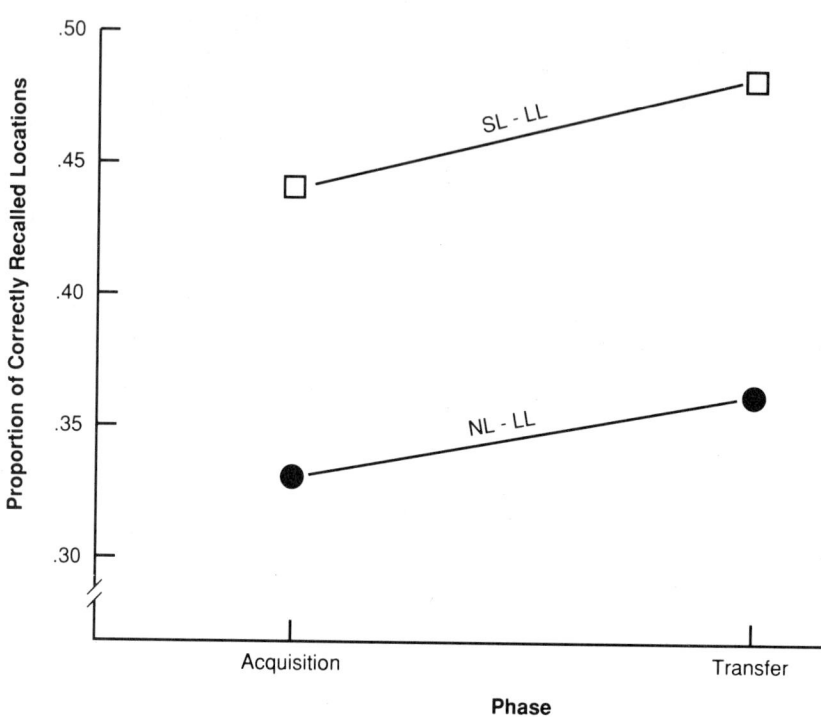

FIGURE 5.3-4 Results of Experiment 3 by Magill and Lee showing the proportion of 7 location movements recalled on each of 10 acquisition trials and the proportion of 5 location movements recalled on each trial on a transfer test. Locations were labeled as spatial (SL) or number (NL) labels during acquisition. During transfer both label condition groups performed new locations having letter labels (LL).

More recently, Magill and Lee (1987) reported the results of a series of experiments in which the meaningfulness of movements to be remembered was manipulated for a task requiring subjects to learn a series of end-location movements on a linear-positioning apparatus. On each trial of these experiments, subjects were presented with series of 12 or 7 limb-position locations. After these were presented, the subjects were asked to move to as many of the criterion locations as they could in any order they desired. One group of subjects was always provided with a more meaningful verbal label for each location (called spatial labels) that designated exact location on the apparatus, although the subjects did not know of this association. The other group of subjects was provided a less meaningful verbal label, a number from 1 to 12 or from 1 to 7, for each location (called number labels). In all three experiments, the subjects who had received the more meaningful spatial labels more accurately recalled the locations, even though they were never told what the locations

were or that the labels were related to these locations. The results of the third experiment (Figure 5.3–4) were particularly striking. After practicing the series of criterion limb locations for 10 trials, subjects were given a series of transfer trials on which both practice groups were given a series of 5 new locations, each with a letter label (from A to E). As you can see in Figure 5.3–4, the subjects who had practiced with the more meaningful spatial labels performed better on the transfer test in which new locations had new labels.

From a theoretical perspective, the use of images and verbal labels to aid the learning and control of movements poses interesting questions about the interaction of processes subserving the control of verbal and motor skills. For example, why do these strategies benefit memory for motor skills? The most probable answer is that images and labels, which are well known to us, are beneficial in that they speed up the retrieval process required to pull together the information required to perform the movement. In this way, images and labels serve as mnemonics, which are simply techniques that aid remembering. Mnemonics are commonly used to remember lists of words, such as a grocery list or the bones of the hand. Chase and Ericsson (1982) argued that mnemonics derive their power from their ability to narrow the search in long-term memory to just the information needed. If you will recall the discussion at the end of Concept 5.2 concerning the types of knowledge stored in long-term memory and how these interact so that we can perform a motor skill, this view of images and verbal labels as useful mnemonics seems quite appropriate.

Preselecting movements. In most of the memory and learning situations described thus far in this chapter, subjects were required to remember or learn movements selected by the experimenter. Would it make any difference if the movements to be remembered or learned were selected instead by the subjects? Results of investigations into this question have yielded some interesting implications for both memory theory and instructional applications.

When subjects are allowed to select their own criterion movements on which they will be tested, we call these **preselected movements.** This term is in contrast to the term **constrained movements,** which describes movements to be remembered that have been selected by the experimenter. Results of experiments comparing the recall of preselected and constrained movements have consistently shown that preselected movements are recalled more accurately. (See an excellent review of this research in an article by Kelso & Wallace, 1978.) Interestingly, this same type of effect is common in aiding remembering of words on a list, in what is called the "self-generation benefit." (See an article by Lee & Gallagher, 1981, for more information about the comparison between the preselected movement and self-generation effects.)

What causes the recall accuracy difference that has been consistently found between preselected and constrained movements? One possibility is that a preselected movement requires more attention, or central processing, by a person than is required by the constrained movement. If a person must select the movement that will later be recalled, he or she cannot just produce the criterion movement without giving it a great deal of attention. However, this is not true for the constrained movement. Thus, Kelso (1981) argued that the difference lies in the degree to which the preselected movement requires preparation. Another possibility is that preselecting a movement allows a person to more accurately encode the movement, because the person will select something that is familiar or easily associated with something familiar. From a retrieval perspective, this increase in encoding accuracy will make the preselected movement easier to recall because it would be more meaningful to the person.

What does the preselection effect mean in terms of application to motor skill instruction? One application can be made to teaching basic movement skills to elementary children. An effective technique is to allow the children to select their own movements that will accomplish the teacher's movement goal. The goal, "Can you jump over this bar in different ways?" allows the children to select their own movements to accomplish the goal, rather than trying to imitate specific movements that the teacher may have selected for them. Also, the preselection technique may be useful for aiding initial learning of a complex skill for which the person must eventually learn to perform a number of variations. For example, when teaching the volleyball serve the student will eventually want to be able to serve to any given place on the opposite court. Why not let initial practice of the serve be done by allowing the student to select his or her own target area? In doing this, the student can devote more attention resources to learning the skill without having also to try putting the ball where the teacher wants it.

Rote repetition. One effective rehearsal strategy that positively influences remembering movement information is drill-like repetition of the movement to be learned. This form of rehearsal, often referred to as **rote repetition,** involves repeating the same movements over and over again. The benefit of this type of rehearsal has been demonstrated many times in the research literature. In fact, in the study by Adams and Dijkstra (1966) referred to earlier in this chapter, it was demonstrated that rapidly increasing recall error observed in 20 seconds was dramatically reduced by increasing the number of practice repetitions of the criterion movement. Gentile and Nemetz (1978) also demonstrated this effect by showing that as the number of repetitions of a positioning movement increased, the amount of recall error decreased.

The use of rote repetition seems especially practical and effective for closed skills. Because the goal of the second stage of learning, as proposed by Gentile (1972), is to increase the accuracy and consistency of performing the movement pattern learned in the first stage, it would seem logical to expect that increasing repetitions of the exact movement pattern being learned would be an effective strategy.

The intention to remember. In all the memory experiments considered so far, subjects have always known in advance that the movements they were presented or had to practice would be later subject to a recall test. But, suppose the subjects were not told in advance? Suppose they were told that the goal of the experiment was to see how well they could move their arm to a specified location. If an unexpected recall test was given later, how well would they recall the movements made earlier? The two situations just described are known in the memory research literature as intentional vs. incidental memory situations. In addition to investigating the influence of intention to remember as an effective remembering strategy, the comparison of these two situations provides insight into the encoding of movement information processes. That is, do we only store information to which we give conscious attention, as in the case of the intentional memory situation, or do we store more information, as would be shown by good memory performance, in the incidental memory situation?

This question has received little research interest in the study of memory for movements. However, the research that has been done indicates that, in general, intention to remember leads to better remembering than no intention to remember. (See Crocker & Dickinson, 1984, for a review of this research.) Yet retention test performance in the incidental situation is typically better than if no previous experience with the test movements had occurred. In fact, some reports show incidental memory test performance to be as good as it was for the intentional situation. For example, Dickinson (1978) presented subjects with four end locations on a linear-positioning apparatus. The "intentional" group was told that they were to learn these four positions and that there would be a recall test later. The "incidental" group was told that this experiment was examining how well people could visually estimate a movement of their own hands. The results showed that for recall tests given following the 0-, 30-, and 60-second retention intervals, there were no differences between the two groups. However, after a 5-minute (600-second) retention interval, the intentional group's performance showed little forgetting whereas the incidental group showed much. Thus, the incidental group's performance showed that more information was encoded during practice than was given conscious attention. However, the incidentally encoded information did not resist the effects of time as well as did the intentionally attended information.

For more complex tasks, the intention to remember benefit is even more striking, although the performance of an incidental condition is rather striking also. For example, in a series of experiments by Crocker and Dickinson (1984), subjects performed a movement task in which they moved from a home response key to four, seven, or eleven target keys that had to be struck in a specified sequence. Subjects in the incidental condition were told to react and to move as quickly as possible to each designated target key in the sequence. In the intentional condition, subjects were told not only to move as quickly as possible to each designated key in the sequence but also that they would be tested later on how well they had learned the sequence. The results consistently showed that, regardless of sequence length, subjects who had been told of the impending recall test performed better when tested than the subjects who had not been told (the incidental group).

The investigation of intentional vs. incidental memory strategies is an important one to increase our understanding of memory processes related to encoding and storing information. Research indicates that we encode and store much more information than we are consciously aware. You will see another example supporting this conclusion in the discussion concerning the effect of practice and test contexts on memory.

One implication that the intentional vs. incidental memory research provides for instructional situations is that memory performance and skill learning can be enhanced by telling students when they begin to practice a skill that they will be tested on the skill later. The effect of this advance knowledge about a test is that students will undoubtedly increase the amount of effort given in practice, a characteristic that you will repeatedly see in this text as beneficial for memory and learning. Also, when there are specific characteristics of a skill performance situation that must be remembered for a later test, better test performance will result from telling people what these characteristics are.

Subjective organization.   A strategy frequently used by learners of large amounts of information is grouping or organizing the information into units. For example, a child learning the alphabet will generally group letters into two- to four-letter units and recite an alphabet rhyme to aid learning. If you need to learn a dialogue or a list of terms, you often will divide these long sequences into shorter, more manageable groups. In the course of practice, you find that it becomes helpful to combine these smaller groups into larger ones.

These examples of verbal organization have been well established in the research literature as effective remembering and learning strategies.

This strategy, which has been termed **subjective organization,** involves organizing information in a way that is meaningful to the individual. Other terms that have been used to describe this process are chunking, clustering, categorizing, unitizing, and grouping.

The relationship between organization and motor skill learning has not generated a large amount of research. However, insight into the benefit of organizing information to help learn it can be seen in the study by Magill and Lee (1987) described earlier. In the first experiment of this study, subjects were presented a series of 12 criterion limb-position locations on a linear-positioning apparatus on each of 12 trials of practice. The same 12 locations were presented on every trial but in a different order. The subjects were required to recall as many of the locations as they could in any order they wished. What was important was to determine whether the subjects began to ignore the presentation order of the movements and develop a consistently organized order of recall on each trial. The results showed that the subjects typically did develop some subjective organizational structure to the series of movements. Further, the subjects who demonstrated higher degrees of organization tended to have more accurate recall of the criterion movements.

One way to apply the benefit of subjective organization to motor skill learning situations is to consider the way a novice approaches the learning of a complex skill. He or she tends to consider complex motor skills as comprising many parts. As the beginner develops his or her ability to execute the skill, the number of components of the skill seems to decrease. This does not mean the structure of the skill itself has changed. Rather, the learner's view of the skill has changed. A good example is a dance or gymnastic floor exercise routine, where each of the routines is made up of many individual parts. To the beginner, a dance routine is thought of step-by-step and movement-by-movement. Beginning gymnasts think of a floor exercise as so many individual stunts. As they practice, their approach to the skills changes. They have begun to organize the routines into units or groups of movements. Three or four component parts are now considered as one. The result will be performing the entire routine with the requisite timing, rhythm, and coordination. With that result, moreover, will be the added effect of developing a more efficient means of storing the complex routine in memory.

It is interesting that skilled individuals organize information to such an extent that it appears they have an increased working memory capacity. However, it has been shown that experts have organized what they have learned so well that, in effect, they do not need to recall every item in the organizational scheme. Remember, for example, the experiment with "novice" and "expert" 11-year-old dancers by Starkes, Deakin, Lindley, & Crisp (1987) that was described in Concept 5.1. When these dancers were presented sequences of eight elements that were organized as in a ballet routine, the expert dancers recalled the routine almost perfectly, whereas the novices recalled about half of the sequence correctly. However, when the same number of elements was presented in an unstructured sequence, there was no difference between the skilled and novice dancers in terms of the number of elements they correctly recalled. This result indicates that the organizational structure of the sequence of dance movements was an important factor in determining its memorability for the experts.

As a result of much practice, long sequences of movements become organized into longer and longer units, or chunks, and become easier to incorporate into working memory when the sequence must be repeated from memory. An interesting anecdote was provided by Starkes, et al. They reported observing an adult principal national level ballet dancer being able to perform a sequence of 96 steps after having seen the sequence demonstrated one time. Thus, organization was apparently a strategy used to reduce the working memory load of this sequence and to increase the memorability of the sequence.

Because most complex motor skills have a specific organizational structure, there are a variety of ways to break up that structure for teaching or practicing the skills. Skills should not be arbitrarily broken into parts for practice. Better and more efficient learning will result from keeping together those components of a movement sequence that are interrelated and dependent on each other. For example, the motion for pitching a softball is often initially practiced by using only the underhand backswing and forward motion of the pitch. A better organizational approach would be to incorporate the forward swing of the initial part of the windup to allow the student the opportunity to understand the full structure of the movement.

Practice-Test Context Effects

An important influence on the retention of motor skills is the relationship between the context of practice and the context at the time of the test. As was discussed briefly in Concept 5.2, the context of a movement relates to both the environmental conditions in which the movement is performed as well as to characteristics related to the person performing the movement. For example, if a memory experiment is performed in a laboratory, the environmental context includes such things as the room in which the experiment is done, the experimenter, the time of day, the noise the subject can hear, the lighting, and so on. Personal context involves such things as the mood of the individual, the limb used to make the movement, the sitting or standing position of the subject, and the sensory feedback sources that are available to the subject. As you will see in this section, differences in these conditions during the time the movement to be remembered or learned is presented or practiced and during the time the movement must be recalled can influence the success of the recall performance.

The encoding specificity principle. An important point to be considered regarding the influence of movement context on remembering or learning a motor skill is how the practice and test contexts are related (Bransford, Franks, Morris, & Stein, 1979). In some situations, especially for closed

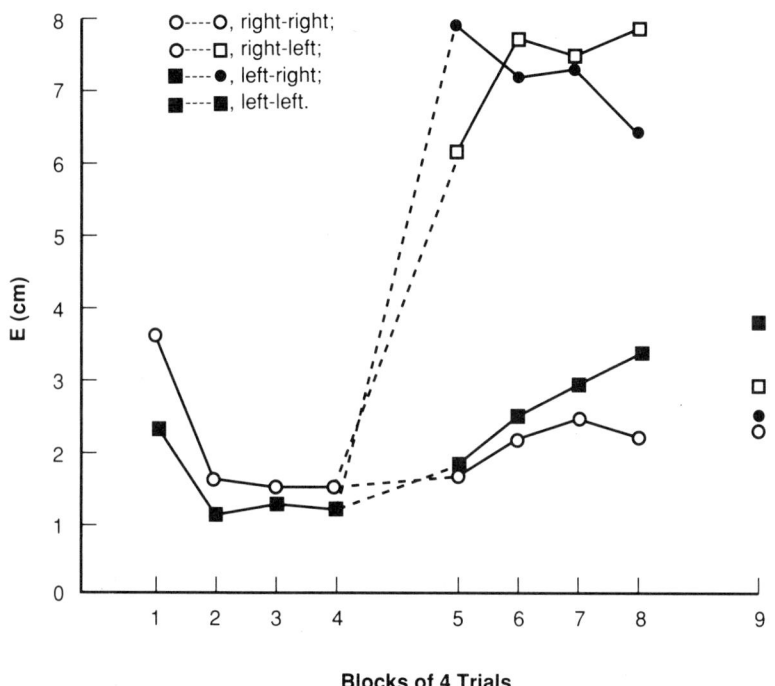

FIGURE 5.3-5 Results from Experiment 2 by Lee and Magill showing the accuracy (as measured by E) for performing a 30-cm distance movement during practice with KR (Blocks 1–4) and during a no-KR retention test (Blocks 5–8). Practice was with either the right or left arm; the retention test was with either the same or opposite arm used during practice. Block 9 shows performance when the same arm used in practice performed the movement after the retention test was completed.

skills, the test goal is essentially the same as the practice goal. That is, to shoot a free throw, you must stand in essentially the same place and shoot the ball through a hoop that is the same distance from you as it was when you practiced it. In such closed skill situations, what is known as the **encoding specificity principle** applies.

The encoding specificity principle was introduced by Tulving and Thomson (1973). According to this principle, the more the test context resembles the practice context, the better the retention performance will be. We already considered some support for this principle in the motor domain when we discussed the experiment by Lee and Hirota (1980) in Concept 5.2, in which results showed that having the same movement context available at recall was beneficial for remembering limb positioning movements.

This similarity of practice and context issue was investigated by Lee and Magill (1985) using a learning paradigm involving the same active and passive conditions as reported by Lee and Hirota (1980). A condition involving the limb used for

practice and for the test was also involved in this study. The subjects were required to practice a 30–cm limb positioning movement while blindfolded. Then, they performed test trials without any knowledge of results. In the first experiment, the results of the Lee and Hirota experiment were supported because subjects who practiced and were tested in the same active or passive movement condition performed better on the test than subjects who had to switch to a different condition on the test. In the second experiment, the same procedures were followed except that the subjects practiced with either their right or left arms. Again, test trial performance (shown in Figure 5.3–5) showed that maintaining the same movement context between the practice and the test trials led to a better test performance than switching test contexts.

One additional feature of this experiment emphasizes its relationship to the encoding specificity principle. Notice the set of results for Block 9 at the far end of Figure 5.3–5. On this final test block, all subjects were tested using the same arm used during practice. Notice what happened when the practice context was reinstated. The opposite limb transfer group showed an immediate improvement in performance and performed the movement as they had at the end of practice.

The encoding specificity principle is important for increasing our understanding of memory processes. An essential finding is that the memory representation for a movement has stored with it important sensory feedback information that is specific to the context conditions in which the movement was practiced. Evidence also supports a memorial representation for movements that have specific movement context information associated with them. Thus, the more the test, or recall, conditions match the practice, or encoding, conditions, the more accurate the test performance will be expected.

The practical implications of the encoding specificity principle seem especially relevant to remembering and learning closed skills. In a closed skill, the test context is typically stable and predictable. Because of this, practice conditions can be established that will closely mimic the test conditions. In these cases, then, the more similar the practice setting is to the test setting, the higher the probability or successful performance during the test. Consider, for example, practice for shooting free throws in a basketball game. Free throws are always either one, two, or one-and-one situations. According to the encoding specificity principle, it is essential that players have practice experiences in which these gamelike conditions prevail. This does not say that this is the only way that free throws can be practiced. However, if game performance is the test of interest, it is essential that gamelike practice be provided.

Consider also a physical therapy example where a knee joint replacement patient is working on knee joint flexion and extension. Based on the encoding specificity principle, because test conditions involve active limb movement, practice conditions should emphasize active rather than passive limb movement. Similar practice-test relationships can be established for a variety of skill practice situations.

Summary

Three different categories of factors that influence the remembering of motor skills were discussed. The first was the type of movement or movement characteristic that must be remembered or learned. Research is rather consistent in showing that continuous skills are remembered better than discrete skills, and that location information is remembered better than distance information, although some qualifications are made with each of these conclusions. Also, movements that are more inherently meaningful to the individual are remembered better than those that are not meaningful. Finally, the serial position of a movement in a sequence of movements influences how well a movement will be remembered. If the sequence involves a number of component movements close to or exceeding working capacity, the primacy-recency effect typically occurs on recall tests. The second category concerned the strategy employed by either the individual practicing the skill or the instructor. One strategy involves making movements more meaningful by engaging in imagery or verbally labeling the movements. Another strategy involves preselecting the movements that are to be remembered, because those will be remembered better than constrained movements. A third strategy that is especially effective for closed skills involves the rote repetition of movements to be remembered. Fourth, subjectively organizing complex movements into meaningful units or chunks can help reduce the memory load for remembering a long sequence of movements and enhance remembering. Finally, the intention to remember is an effective strategy. The third category related to the influence of the practice and test context characteristics. The encoding specificity principle applies to this concern and indicates that the more these context characteristics are similar during practice and during the test, the better the practiced movements will be recalled during the test.

Related Readings

Adams, J. A. (1987). Historical review and appraisal of research on the learning, retention, and transfer of human skills. *Psychological Bulletin, 101,* 41–74.

Christina, R. W., & Bjork, R. A. (1991). Optimizing long-term retention and transfer. In D. Druckman & R. Bjork (Eds.), *In the mind's eye: Enhancing human performance* (pp. 23–56). Washington, D.C.: National Academy Press.

Davies, G. (1986). Context effects in episodic memory: A review. *Cahiers de Psychologie Cognitive, 6,* 157–174.

Diewert, G. L., & Stelmach, G. E. (1978). Perceptual organization in motor learning. In G. E. Stelmach (Ed.), *Information processing in motor control and motor learning* (pp. 241–265). New York: Academic Press.

Hall, C. R., & Goss, S. (1985). Imagery research in motor learning. In D. Goodman, R. B. Wilberg, & I. M. Franks (Eds.), *Differing perspectives in motor learning, memory, and control* (pp. 139–154). Amsterdam: Elsevier Science Publishers.

Magill, R. A. (1984). Influences on remembering movement information. In W. F. Straub & J. M. Williams (Eds.), *Cognitive sport psychology* (pp. 175–188). Lansing, NY: Sport Science Associates.

■

STUDY QUESTIONS FOR CHAPTER 5

(Memory)

1. How are the terms *retention* and *forgetting* similar yet different in respect to memory issues?

2. Describe how working memory and long-term memory differ in terms of the duration and capacity of information of each of these functional components of memory.

3. Name three types of information stored in long-term memory. Identify examples of these types of information as related to motor skills.

4. Describe how declarative and procedural knowledge can be related to changes that occur from the early to the later stages of learning motor skills.

5. What is the difference between explicit and implicit memory tests? Give an example of each for a motor skill situation.

6. What are the typical experimental paradigms used to test the causes of forgetting? How does each paradigm permit the researcher to draw conclusions about a cause of forgetting?

7. Explain how trace decay, interference, and inappropriate retrieval cues can be considered causes for forgetting. Give a motor skill example of how each cause can be related to forgetting.

8. What evidence do we have that shows how resistent to forgetting motor skills are in long-term memory?

9. Describe two characteristics of motor skills that have been shown to be remembered better than others. Indicate why these characteristics may be better remembered.

10. How does the primacy-recency effect relate to recalling a series of movements? What does this effect suggest in terms of teaching skills?

11. Describe three effective strategies that can be used to help a person more effectively remember movement information. Give an example of how each of these strategies can be used in a motor skill learning situation.

12. What is meant by the "practice-test context"? How is this related to influencing how well movement information will be remembered?

13. Describe a teaching, coaching, or rehabilitation situation in which you take advantage of the "encoding specificity principle" to enhance the probability of successful "test" performance.

INDIVIDUAL DIFFERENCES

--- ☐ ---

CONCEPT 6.1
The study of individual differences has identified various
motor abilities that underlie motor skill performance.

CONCEPT 6.2
Individual difference research does not support the notion of a "general motor ability."

CONCEPT 6.3
Assessing a person's motor abilities can help predict potential for motor skill performance success.

CONCEPT 6.1

The study of individual differences has identified various
motor abilities that underlie motor skill performance

Key Terms

differential
  psychology

perceptual-
  motor
  abilities

physical
  proficiency
  abilities

psychomotor
  ability

Application

People obviously differ in how they learn and perform motor skills. One way of seeing this difference is by observing a class in which a physical activity is being taught to beginners. While most beginners' classes usually include students with some previous experience in the activity, the diversity of initial skill levels is apparent even if those individuals are not considered in the comparison. Consider for example a beginning golf class. As you observe the members of that class on the first day they are permitted to hit the ball, you will see various degrees of success and failure. Some students will spend an inordinate amount of time simply trying to make contact with the ball. At the other extreme, there will be those who seem to hit the ball rather consistently. The remainder of the class will usually be distributed somewhere along the continuum of success between those two extremes.

Parallel differences can be observed in any situation involving physical activity. People begin dance classes, driving instruction classes, physical therapy sessions, etc., with a wide variety of what is referred to in some education literature as "entry behaviors." These entry behaviors reflect the very real behavioral phenomenon that individuals differ in how they perform motor skills. These differences will also be seen as people continue in these classes; they will progress in different ways and at different rates. The impact of a particular instructional technique will not always be the same for every individual. Nor will it have the same influence on the same person during each of the stages of learning.

Several questions associated with a better understanding of the role of individual differences in motor learning arise from these examples. One important question is why people exhibit such a wide range of initial skill levels in physical activities. In the discussion that follows, this question will be addressed by attributing a large part of the differences in initial skill to differences in motor abilities. To accomplish this, we will consider what abilities are, how they have been identified, and how they relate to motor skill performance.

Discussion

Before addressing the issue of individual differences, it is important to call attention to a dramatic shift in orientation that such a discussion requires. In each of the preceding chapters, we have concentrated on what can be called the av-

erage learner. In each of the concepts, the focus of the conclusions was on how people in general are characterized by certain information processing limitations, or motor control limits, or are influenced by certain environmental features. For example, we saw that individuals can be characterized by a limited ability to store information in working memory for a short period of time. In this connection, it was suggested that this capacity can be quantified as 7 ± 2 items. However, it is important to keep in mind that this generalization is made in terms of a population average; that is, on the average, people seem to have this working memory capacity.

But what happens when we select a certain individual and try to determine how that general "rule" of memory capacity applies to him or her? This one individual may actually have a greater or lesser capacity. Does this mean the conclusion is in error? No. It simply indicates that the rule is a statement of average behavior. When it is applied at the individual level, the rule may be exactly accurate, or it may deviate somewhat. In effect, then, the rule represents a norm for behavior. In the present chapter, rather than being concerned with "average behavior," we will examine how individuals differ.

Differential Psychology

The study of individual differences in psychology has been termed **differential psychology.** This term has been used to distinguish the study of individual differences from the study of normative or average behavior. This distinction was made over thirty-five years ago in a rather straightforward manner by Lee Cronbach (1957) in his address as president of the American Psychological Association, delivered before the national convention of that organization. He entitled his presentation "The two disciplines of scientific psychology." In his talk, Cronbach proceeded to outline the apparent differences between the two approaches to the scientific investigation of human behavior, that is, experimental psychology and differential psychology. An illustrative chart highlighting these differences is presented in Figure 6.1–1. The essential points of Cronbach's statements are (1) experimental psychology is concerned with examining individuals in terms of average behavior, whereas differential psychology examines individuals in terms of how they deviate or differ from the average; (2) experimental psychology

investigates behavior by experiments that impose some manipulation of behavior and then observe group differences, whereas differential psychologists investigate behavior by observing behavior without experimental manipulations; (3) experimental psychologists attempt to minimize individual differences in their experiments, while differential psychologists seek to maximize individual differences, because these are of central interest.

Characteristically, the study of individual differences has been concerned with identifying and measuring individual abilities or traits. The study of intelligence is a prime example of this type of investigation. Study of intelligence, in turn, led to the development of the identification of the components of intelligence. This was followed by the formulation of tests to quantify an individual's level of these components, or of a general intelligence. Thus, the concept of I.Q. (intelligence quotient) emerged as a quantified indicator of intelligence. In this way, a rather abstract concept like intelligence is made somewhat concrete by putting it in the form of a meaningful number. Individuals can then be compared with some degree of objectivity.

In motor behavior, the study of individual differences has followed a similar pattern. The identification and measurement of motor abilities has been a primary focal point for investigation. Identification of motor abilities has not been an easy task; as a result, very few researchers have ventured into this area of study. Of those who have investigated human motor abilities, one of the most successful has been Edwin Fleishman (see Fleishman & Quaintance, 1984, for a complete description of this work). Fleishman's work on the identification and measurement of motor abilities has been going on for many years and must be considered as the major source of information for any scientific discussion of motor abilities.

Recall in the definition of the term ability in Concept 1.1, that *ability* refers to a capacity of the individual that is related to the performance of a variety of tasks (Fleishman, 1978, 1982). As a capacity, an ability should be seen as a relatively enduring attribute of an individual. Fleishman

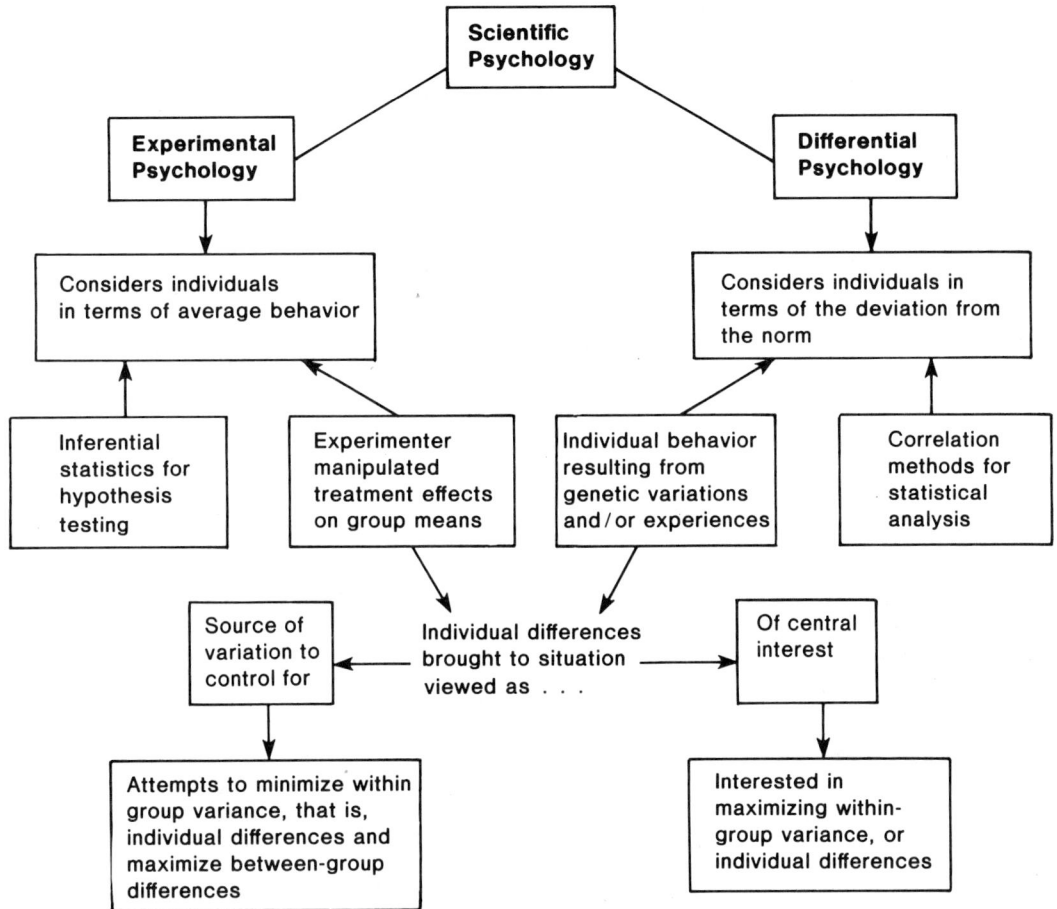

FIGURE 6.1-1 Diagram depicting the essential differences between the research approaches taken by experimental and differential psychologists.

found, for example, that the ability called spatial visualization is related to the performance of diverse tasks such as aerial navigation, blueprint reading, and dentistry. The assumption is that the skills involved in complex motor activities can be described in terms of the abilities that underlie their performance. An important step in understanding how abilities and skill performance are related is identifying these abilities and matching them with the skills involved. The approach taken by Fleishman to accomplish this has not been to identify as many abilities as possible, but to identify the fewest ability categories that relate to performing the widest variety of tasks.

Identifying Motor Abilities

Fleishman developed a "taxonomy of human perceptual-motor abilities" (Fleishman, 1972; Fleishman & Quaintance, 1984), which was based on giving extensive batteries of perceptual-motor tests to many people. The results of this testing led him to propose that there seem to be 11 identifiable and measurable **perceptual-motor abilities.** He identified these abilities as follows: (1) *multi-limb coordination,* the ability to coordinate the movement of a number of limbs simultaneously; (2) *control precision,* the ability to make highly controlled and precise muscular adjustments where larger muscle groups are involved, as in the pursuit rotor task; (3) *response orientation,* the ability to select rapidly where a response should be made, as in a choice reaction time situation; (4) *reaction time,* the ability to respond rapidly to a stimulus when it appears; (5) *speed of arm movement,* the ability to make a gross, rapid arm movement; (6) *rate control,* the ability to change speed and direction of responses with precise timing, as in following a continuously moving target; (7) *manual dexterity,* the ability to make skillful, well-directed arm-hand movements that are involved in manipulating objects under speed conditions; (8) *finger dexterity,* the ability to perform skillful, controlled manipulations of tiny objects involving primarily the fingers; (9) *arm-hand steadiness,* the ability to make precise arm-hand positioning movements where strength and speed are minimally involved; (10) *wrist, finger speed,* the ability to move the wrist and fingers rapidly, as in a tapping task; and (11) *aiming,* the ability to aim precisely at a small object in space.

In addition to perceptual-motor abilities, Fleishman also identified nine abilities that he designated as **physical proficiency abilities.** These abilities differ from the perceptual-motor abilities in that they are more generally related to athletic and gross physical performance. Typically, these abilities would be considered physical fitness abilities. The "physical proficiency abilities" identified by Fleishman are as follows: (1) *static strength,* the maximum force that can be exerted against external objects; (2) *dynamic strength,* the muscular endurance in exerting force repeatedly, as in a series of pull-ups; (3) *explosive strength,* the ability to mobilize energy effectively for bursts of muscular effort, as in a high jump; (4) *trunk strength,* the strength of the trunk muscles; (5) *extent flexibility,* the ability to flex or stretch the trunk and back muscles; (6) *dynamic flexibility,* the ability to make repeated, rapid trunk flexing movements, as in a series of toe touches; (7) *gross body coordination,* the ability to coordinate the action of several parts of the body while the body is in motion; (8) *gross body equilibrium,* the ability to maintain balance without visual cues;

(9) *stamina,* the capacity to sustain maximum effort requiring cardiovascular effort, as in a distance run.

As indicated earlier, these lists cannot be considered as exhaustive inventories of all the abilities related to motor skill performance. Remember that Fleishman wanted to identify the fewest number of abilities that would describe the tasks performed in the test battery. While he used hundreds of tasks to identify those abilities, additional types of tasks could lead to the identification of other motor abilities. For example, abilities not included in the two lists just considered include the following: *static balance,* the ability to balance on a stable surface when no locomotor movement is required; *dynamic balance,* the ability to balance on a moving surface or to balance while involved in locomotion; *visual acuity,* the ability to see clearly and precisely; *visual tracking,* the ability to visually follow a moving object; and *eye-hand* or *eye-foot coordination,* the ability to perform skills requiring vision and the precise use of the hands or feet. These are just a few of the motor abilities that were not on Fleishman's two lists. In other parts of this chapter, additional abilities will be identified.

It is important to understand that all individuals are characterized by these motor abilities. Because it is possible to measure these motor abilities, a quantifiable measure of an individual's level of each ability can be determined. People differ in the amount of each ability they possess. For this reason, motor abilities, as capacities, indicate limits that influence the person's potential for performance achievement in skills. This notion will be explored more extensively in the next section and in the remaining concepts of this chapter.

Relating Motor Abilities to Motor Skill Performance

To see where motor abilities fit into the broader issue of motor skill performance, it is helpful to consider an approach presented by Ackerman (1988). He described motor abilities as one of three categories of human abilities that relate to performing motor skills. One category is general intelligence, or general ability. Included are cognitively-oriented abilities related to memory related processes such as acquiring, storing, retrieving, combining, comparing, and using memory-based information in new contexts. The second category is perceptual speed ability. This category includes abilities associated with a person's facility for solving problems of increasing complexity and with speed of processing information that must be used to solve problems. Tests such as finding the Xs in an array of letters and transcribing symbols on a list are involved in assessing these abilities. Finally, **psychomotor ability** (i.e., motor ability) is the third category. This group of abilities, which is the focus of our discussion, is distinguished by abilities related to speed and accuracy of movements where little or no cognitive demand is required of the person. Thus, from the perspective of understanding individual differences, performance of all skills must be seen in terms of these foundational categories of abilities. However, for purposes of the present discussion, we will limit our attention to motor abilities.

The view that motor abilities are underlying, foundational components of motor skill performance is illustrated in Figure 6.1–2. This figure shows how complex motor skills can be analyzed by a process known as *task analysis* in order to identify the abilities that underlie any motor skill. For example, to serve a tennis ball successfully, certain components of that skill must be properly performed. These components are identified in the first level of analysis of the tennis serve and are represented in Figure 6.1–2 in the middle tier of the diagram. By identifying these components, it is possible to more readily identify the underlying motor abilities that are related to the successful performance of this task. These abilities are identified in the bottom tier of the diagram. Based on Fleishman's lists, these include abilities such as multi-limb coordination, control precision, speed of arm movement, rate control, aiming, static strength, etc. You could undoubtedly add others. However, these few examples should serve to illustrate the foundational role played by perceptual-motor and physical proficiency abilities in the performance of motor skills.

The value of identifying abilities. An important question at this point concerns the value of being able to identify these underlying, foundational abilities. One benefit is that this knowledge can be useful in the construction of effective elementary physical education curricula. If you were to compare the abilities underlying a large number of motor skills, you would find some very interesting similarities. For example, speed of arm movement is important for performing a wide range of throwing and batting skills. Balance is likewise a foundational ability to many different skills. From this type of information, it is possible to identify those abilities that should be the basis for establishing what foundational movement experiences should be provided for preschool and elementary school children. For example, because balance is an essential component ability required in a variety of complex skills, movement experiences must be provided that will allow the children the opportunity to develop their balance ability in a variety of movement situations.

A second benefit of identifying foundational motor abilities is that this process can allow a teacher, coach, or therapist more specifically to identify the source of problems or difficulties in a student's or patient's performances. Often an individual has difficulty learning a new skill because he or she lacks adequate experience involving the motor ability essential to the performance of that particular skill. For example, a child may be having difficulty catching a thrown ball. In addition to the probable lack of experience with this skill, the child may also have a poorly developed ability to visually track a moving object or to time a movement response to an oncoming object. An important step for the teacher is to provide specific practice experiences that emphasize these abilities related to the successful performance of a batting skill.

A third benefit of understanding the relationship between motor abilities and the performance

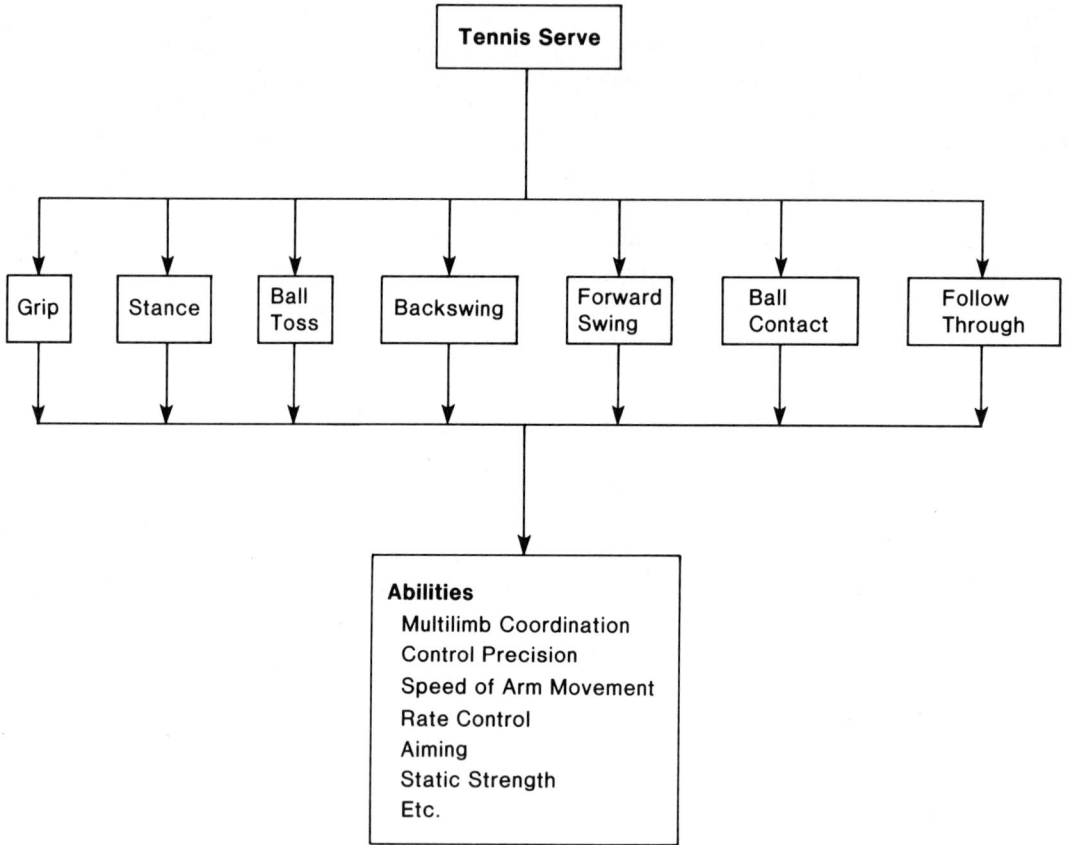

FIGURE 6.1-2 A task analysis for the tennis serve indicating the component parts of the serve and some examples of perceptual-motor abilities underlying performance of the serve.

of motor skills relates to predicting the potential for an individual to succeed in a particular skill. Because this issue will be the basis for the discussion in Concept 6.3, it will not be discussed here. At this point, know that the identification and measurement of underlying motor abilities can be a useful component in a test battery designed to determine which individuals may be best suited for certain motor activities.

The Cause of Motor Abilities

One question that is important to consider is why individuals differ from each other in terms of motor abilities. This is by no means an easy ques-

tion to answer. Attempts at responding to such questions have led to some of the most heated professional controversies of our time, such as the debate concerning the causes of intelligence, which raged during the late 1960s and early 1970s. We may assume, however, that the answer to this question can be related to one or both of two factors. One explanation postulates that the abilities are *genetically determined;* that is, individuals are born with these characteristics. The second explanation maintains that individuals develop abilities through *nongenetic factors,* such as experience, which appears to be the most predominant of the nongenetic factors.

It seems that the most satisfactory means of resolving this issue is to view the response as not being an either/or issue. Rather, the limited literature available seems to indicate that both genetics and experience are involved in the level of ability an individual possesses. The point to be investigated, then, is the relative contribution of each factor to abilities. For example, what proportion of an individual's manual dexterity ability is due to genetics and what proportion is due to experiences?

Unfortunately, there is very little empirical evidence on which to base unequivocal conclusions to this issue. Instead, we must rely on authority as the basis for our decision making. Most motor behavior theorists maintain that motor abilities are more genetically than experience determined; that is, the ultimate ability level of an individual is controlled primarily by genetic factors. However, you must be careful in what you conclude from such a statement. Do not assume from this that two individuals cannot achieve similar levels of proficiency in a physical skill because of genetically determined ability differences. Experience, or training and practice, can often compensate for a lack of certain levels of specific abilities in an activity.

Summary

Individual difference research in motor behavior is concerned with the study of perceptual-motor abilities. The first problem encountered in this study is the identification of these abilities. One approach to this identification process is to consider Fleishman's lists of perceptual-motor and physical proficiency abilities. Motor abilities are one of three categories of human abilities that underlie motor skill performance. The value of identifying foundational motor abilities can be related to developing appropriate elementary school physical education curriculum, aiding problem identification in performing motor skills, and predicting the potential for success that an individual may have in a motor skill. Most motor behavior theorists seem to agree that motor ability levels have a higher proportion of genetic determination than experiential.

Related Readings

Cronbach, L. (1957). The two disciplines of scientific psychology. *American Psychologist, 12,* 671–684.

Fleishman, E. A. (1978). Relating individual differences to the dimensions of human tasks. *Ergonomics, 21,* 1007–1019.

Fleishman, E. A. (1982). Systems for describing human tasks. *American Psychologist, 37,* 821–834.

Thomas, J. R., & Halliwell, W. (1976). Individual differences in motor skill acquisition. *Journal of Motor Behavior, 8,* 89–99.

CONCEPT 6.2

Individual difference research does not support
the notion of a "general motor ability"

Key Terms

general motor   specificity of   motor
  ability   motor   educability
  hypothesis   abilities
motor   hypothesis
  capacity

Application

Have you ever been puzzled by the person who
appears to be an "all-around athlete?" This person
seems to be proficient at whatever athletic endeavor he or she is involved in. The image of the
all-around athlete is kept alive with stories and
news features about the wide range of athletic
skills possessed by a variety of professional athletes such as Bo Jackson, Deion Sanders, Dave
Winfield, or Michael Jordan. It has been reported
that Wilt Chamberlain, an outstanding former
professional basketball player, could have been a
world-class boxer, bowler, and volleyball player
had he chosen to do so rather than to play professional basketball. We do not even have to look to
these highly successful professional athletes for
examples of the all-around athlete. Most of us have
known certain individuals with whom we went to
school or whom we knew by reputation in the
community in which we grew up. These individuals seemed to have little difficulty in achieving a
high level of success in every sport they were involved in.

A perplexing question about these all-around
athletes is why they are so good in so many different activities. Are they born with some special
"motor ability" that enables them to be successful
at all they do? Have they had an abundance of
good training and practice in a wide variety of
sports? Are they really good at everything or only
at certain sports? Do they learn more quickly than
others, or are they "naturally" better at the sports
in which they participate? These questions are the
focus of the discussion that follows. The answers
provided will give you additional insight into how
motor abilities are related to motor skill performance.

Discussion

A common way to explain the individual who
seems to excel in a wide variety of motor skills, or
the all-around athlete, is to say that he or she has
a high level of athletic or motor ability. Note that
the word *ability* is used in the singular. This is done
deliberately, for the notion that individuals possess a singular motor ability has been popular for
a long time. Such a conclusion seems to be quite
contrary to the multi-motor abilities view that we
discussed in Concept 6.1. If you thought that you
detected such a difference of views, you were right,
because for many years there has existed a continuing controversy about the existence of a general motor ability or a multitude of specific motor
abilities.

In terms of the discussion of Concept 6.1, the
question of a general motor ability versus specific
motor abilities has important relevance. There is
little doubt from the results of research considered in that discussion that a variety of motor
abilities underlie motor skill performance and that
people are characterized by a variety of motor
abilities. The question being addressed here is how
these abilities relate to one another in the same

individual. If they are highly related, then the general motor ability view represents the nature of these abilities in an individual. If, on the other hand, these abilities are relatively independent of one another, then the specificity view of motor abilities is the more valid representation.

The controversy over general motor ability versus specific motor abilities was very evident in the research literature during the 1950s and 1960s. Although the controversy has diminished in intensity since that time, the question of which view is correct has been kept alive in many tests used to evaluate motor ability and in textbooks. For example, some tests are constructed so that the end result of the test battery is the calculation of one score that will reflect an individual's "motor ability."

The General Motor Ability Hypothesis

The **general motor ability hypothesis** maintains that there exists in individuals a singular, global motor ability. The level of that ability for an individual is purported to influence the ultimate success that person can expect in any athletic endeavor or motor skill. This notion has been in existence for quite some time. The prediction of this hypothesis is that if a person is good at one motor skill, then he or she has the potential to be good at all motor skills. The reasoning behind this prediction is based on the idea that there is *one* general motor ability.

Some well-known figures in physical education such as C. H. McCloy, David Brace, and Harold Barrow were proponents of the existence of such an ability. The tests they developed purported to be of value in assessing a person's present motor ability as well as predicting the success of the individual in athletic endeavors.

McCloy (1934; McCloy & Young, 1954), for example, developed the General Motor Capacity Test as one of his general motor ability tests. He considered **motor capacity** to comprise a person's inborn, hereditary potentialities for general motor performance. The purpose of this test is to predict potential levels an individual may be expected to

attain. The application of this test, however, is not as broad as these last few statements may suggest. McCloy noted that the test is not a measure of specific skill such as football or basketball because of the specialized abilities required in those sports. The activities in which the motor capacity test can be used for predictive purposes are those requiring "motor ability of a general nature," such as track and field. Thus, the "general" nature of the test may certainly be questioned.

There has been very little evidence reported in the research literature to support the General Motor Ability Hypothesis. An excellent review of many of the studies that have been published to investigate the validity of the tests assessing such general motor ability can be found in the tests and measurements text by Johnson and Nelson (1985). One suspects that the basis for the continued existence of this hypothesis is its intuitive appeal; tests of general motor ability are appealing because they are convenient. The fact that they are unable to predict specific sport skill ability apparently has not diminished their appeal. However, the point that must not be overlooked is that the theoretical basis on which tests rest is indeed tenuous.

The Specificity of Motor Abilities Hypothesis

Because there seems to be little direct support for the general motor ability hypothesis, an alternative hypothesis has been proposed. The **specificity of motor abilities hypothesis** suggests that there are many motor abilities and that these abilities are relatively independent. Implicit is that given the level of ability in one motor ability, it would be impossible to state with any confidence what a person's ability level might be in a different motor ability. Thus, if a person exhibited a high degree of balancing ability, it would not be possible to predict what the person's reaction time might be.

Support for this specificity hypothesis was developed by designing experiments based on a common assumption. That assumption was that if motor abilities are specific and independent, then

Table 6.2-1   Results from the experiment by Drowatzky and Zuccato (1967) showing the correlations among six different tests of static and dynamic balance.

Test	1 Stork Stand	2 Diver's Stand	3 Stick Stand	4 Sideward Stand	5 Bass Stand	6 Balance Stand
1	–	0.14	−0.12	0.26	0.20	0.03
2		–	−0.12	−0.03	−0.07	−0.14
3			–	−0.04	0.22	−0.19
4				–	0.31	0.19
5					–	0.18
6						–

From J. N. Drowatzky and F. C. Zuccato, "Interrelationships Between Selected Measures of Static and Dynamic Balance," in *Research Quarterly for Exercise and Sport*, 1967, Vol. 38, pp. 509–510. Copyright © 1967 American Alliance for Health, Physical Education, Recreation, and Dance. Reprinted by permission.

the relationship between any two abilities will be very low. Thus, in the simplest of cases, the relationship between two abilities such as balance and reaction time, or between reaction time and speed of movement, or even between static balance and dynamic balance would be very low. On the basis of this hypothesis, many experiments that followed such a rationale were published during the 1960s.

By far the bulk of the research that was based on this rationale was published by Franklin Henry and many of his students at the University of California at Berkeley. An example of this investigation is a study published by Henry in 1961. Subjects were tested on two motor abilities, reaction time (RT) and speed of movement, called movement time (MT). If the specificity of motor abilities hypothesis was valid, then the relationship between these two simple motor abilities, RT and MT, should be very low. The results of this experiment yielded a correlation coefficient of 0.02, thus supporting the specificity notion.

Other studies have produced similar results that support the specificity of motor abilities theory. Bachman (1961) and Drowatzky and Zuccatto (1967) reported experiments that showed we cannot even consider balancing to be a single, comprehensive ability but rather that there are several specific types of balance. The Drowatzky and Zuccatto study is particularly interesting be-

cause the researchers had subjects perform six different balancing tasks that have been generally regarded as measures of either static or dynamic balancing ability. The results of the correlations among all the tests are reported in Table 6.2–1. Note that the highest correlation is between the sideward stand and the bass stand (0.31). Most of the correlations range between 0.12 and 0.19. On the basis of these results, it would be difficult to conclude that there exists one test that can be considered a valid measure of balancing ability. Obviously, even the ability we generally label as "balance" should be considered more specifically in terms of certain types of balance.

So far in this discussion, we have considered experiments comparing what we have designated as perceptual-motor abilities. A study by Singer (1966a) examined the relationship between two basic or fundamental motor skills, throwing and kicking. The results of this comparison indicated that even for skills such as these, the relationship between an individual's performance on one test compared to his or her performance on the other is very low.

On the basis of the few experiments that we have considered in this section, it appears that the only justified conclusion is that motor abilities are specific in nature. There seem to be many different motor abilities that are quite independent of each other.

Although theoretical arguments continue about precisely how "specific" motor abilities are, there seems to be very little controversy about the statement that people possess many motor abilities. The evidence by Fleishman, referred to in Concept 6.1, as well as that produced by Henry and his colleagues, is strongly indicative of this fact. Ironically, even McCloy admitted that sport skill abilities are numerous. Thus, the exact nature and scope of so-called "general motor ability" can be seriously questioned. The value of determining a person's general motor ability or capacity seems to be so limited that the use of such tests appears meaningless and of negligible value.

An Appropriate View of General Motor Ability

In Concept 6.1, we discussed Ackerman's (1988) view of three categories of abilities related to motor skill performance. Recall that one of those categories, psychomotor ability, implies a general motor ability. What is important to see here is that Ackerman's reference to a psychomotor ability category does not mean the same thing as what has been described as the general motor ability hypothesis. In Ackerman's terms, a general motor ability refers to the manner in which a person's test scores are characterized from the results of a battery of tests of the various motor abilities included in the psychomotor ability category. Thus, a person with a high level of general motor ability is someone who scored high on most of the tests. This does not mean that because the person scored well on one test, we should expect that person to score well on all the tests in this category.

Explaining the "All-Around Athlete"

If we go back to the question of the so-called "all-around athlete," it should be possible at this point to develop an appropriate explanation of the success this person experiences in such range of sport skills. If motor abilities are numerous and independent, then how does one person become so proficient at such a variety of sports? The answer appears to be twofold. First, we must consider the athlete and, second, the sports or activities in which he or she is successful.

According to the specificity hypothesis and the appropriate view of the notion of general motor ability, it becomes obvious that a person is characterized by a large number of abilities. Each of these abilities can be described as being somewhere along a range of low, average, and high in terms of the amount of each that characterizes the individual. Because people differ, it seems reasonable to expect that some people have a large number of abilities at an average level and other people are characterized by a majority of abilities at the high or low end of the scale. For example, one person may be at the high end of the scale for abilities such as speed of movement, balance, and manual dexterity, while another person may be at the high end of the scale for several other abilities. Therefore, it is to be expected that a person will do very well in those activities in which the underlying abilities required for successful performance match the abilities in which he or she is at the high end of the scale.

The second point to consider in explaining the all-around athlete relates to the sports skills in which this person shows prowess. It is reasonable to assume that the all-around athlete possesses high levels of the abilities that underlie the sports or activities in which that person exhibits high levels of performance. Where this person differs from the "average" individual is in the number of abilities in which he or she can be characterized as being at the high end of the scale. As a result, there are more activities in which this individual can achieve success.

In actual fact, the true all-around athlete is a rare individual. Typically, when a person shows high performance levels in a variety of sport skills, a close inspection of those skills reveals many foundational motor abilities in common. Thus it is to be expected that a person exhibiting high levels of such abilities as speed of movement, speed of reaction, agility, dynamic balance, and visual acuity will do well in activities in which those abilities are foundational to performance. If this person engages in activities in which these abilities are not as important and in which he or she possesses only average levels of the abilities that are important, then we would expect average performance. It should also be noted that people who perform a variety of activities well are people who had a wide range of movement and sport experiences as children. Thus, early movement experiences may be an important feature of many "all-around" athletes.

Motor Educability

One further issue related to the study of motor abilities is a concept that in the past has been referred to as *motor educability*. This term was developed by Brace (1927) and popularized by McCloy (1937). These men used the expression **motor educability** to refer to the "ease with which an individual learns new motor skills." The intent of the tests developed to measure motor educability is not to assess current ability or to predict future success but rather to indicate how quickly an individual will learn motor skills. Notice that here again the general motor ability notion is apparent, because the purpose is to predict ease of learning for motor skills in general.

Some tests and measurements textbooks in physical education maintain that motor educability tests are useful for the homogeneous grouping of physical education classes and as screening devices for selecting candidates to become physical education majors at the college or university level (for example, note Mathews, 1978, p. 153). In contrast, other texts (e.g., Baumgartner & Jackson, 1982) question both the validity and utility of such tests. Which of these opinions is correct? Perhaps an investigation of some of the research evidence concerning the validity of motor educability will reveal the correct answer to this question.

Two experiments that investigated the validity of motor educability tests were published by Gire and Espenschade (1942) and by Gross, Griessel, and Stull (1956). Gire and Espenschade evalu-ated the ability of the Brace, Iowa-Brace, and Johnson tests of motor educability[1] on the basis of their ability to predict the ease with which students learned basketball, volleyball, and baseball. In all cases, the correlations were low, indicating little relationship between a student's motor educability score and the ease with which he or she learned a sport skill. Gross, Griessel, and Stull (1956) compared scores on the Iowa-Brace and the Metheny revision of the Johnson tests with students' ability to learn wrestling skills. Again, correlations were quite low.

Gallagher (1970) developed his own motor educability battery for use in determining the utility of such a test to indicate how quickly college men could learn novel motor tasks. Subjects were divided into high-skilled and low-skilled groups on the basis of the test battery scores. Results indicated that those men classified as high-skilled learned only two of six novel motor tasks more quickly than did the low-skilled group.

Experiments such as these attest to the lack of validity of motor educability tests. Thus, the use of such tests would appear to be extremely questionable. The tests are not only founded on a theoretical basis that has little empirical support, they likewise appear to have very little justifiable use in a skill learning setting.

Summary

The popular notion of the "all-around athlete" leads to a conclusion that individuals possess or exhibit different levels of a general motor ability. Thus, a person possessing a high degree of such ability would be successful at whatever motor skill he or she attempted. A low level of this ability would predict just the opposite. Although there are people who are highly skilled and successful in a wide variety of sports and physical activities, the general motor ability hypothesis does not

[1]Complete descriptions of these motor educability tests may be found in most tests and measurements in physical education textbooks.

appear to be a satisfactory means of explaining the causes of that success, because this hypothesis has almost no empirical support. An alternative explanation is the specificity of motor skills hypothesis, which postulates that individuals possess many different and relatively independent motor abilities. Each person has different levels of these abilities. Thus, the all-around athlete is a person who has higher levels of the motor abilities that are most important for performance in the sports in which he or she is successful. Motor educability is a concept that relates to the "ease" with which a person will learn motor skills. Validity studies of tests of motor educability militate against the use of motor educability as a reliable concept.

Related Readings

Drowatzky, J. N., & Zuccato, F. C. (1967). Interrelationships between selected measures of static and dynamic balance. *Research Quarterly, 38,* 509–510.

Gallagher, J. D. (1970). Motor learning characteristics of low-skilled college men. *Research Quarterly, 41,* 59–67.

Henry, F. M. (1961). Reaction time-movement time correlations. *Perceptual and Motor Skills, 12,* 63–66.

Johnson, B., & Nelson, J. K. (1985). *Practical measurement for evaluation in physical education* (4th ed.). Minneapolis: Burgess.

Magill, R. A., & Powell, F. M. (1975). Is the reaction time-movement time relationship "essentially zero"? *Perceptual and Motor Skills, 41,* 720–722.

CONCEPT 6.3

Assessing a person's motor abilities can help
predict potential for motor skill performance success

Key Terms

variance   super-
 accounted   diagonal
 for   form

Application

One of the characteristics that is common among industry, sport, and the military is that people must be selected to do specific jobs requiring motor skill performance. This selection process involves *predicting* that a person selected for a job will do that job better than some other job. This predicting process also assumes that the individual selected for that job will perform it better than those not selected. If the right people are selected for the right jobs, then much time and money is saved, and the people performing the jobs are more satisfied with what they are doing. A key part of accurate prediction in these situations is developing appropriate assessments of the motor abilities of candidates for the jobs and directing people who show potential for success at specific jobs into training for those jobs.

An event that occurs every four years brings about an interesting prediction of future performance. During the Olympic games, the question of the selection and development of the best athletes in the country becomes a major issue. Certain countries appear to have well-developed selection processes while other countries appear to have less than desirable selection processes. At issue is the prediction of future success. The common view is the country that can more accurately predict, at the earliest possible age, those who will be world-class athletes will have an advantage in competitions such as the Olympic games.

Another prediction situation occurs in physical activity classes. An instructor may wish to subdivide a large class into smaller, more homogeneous groups. What is typically done is to place people who exhibit high initial performance levels into one group, people who exhibit poor initial performance levels into another group, and so on? What emerges from such a practice concerns the relationship between initial performance levels and later success in the activity. Does a person who begins an activity by performing it poorly have any chance for later success? Or, conversely, is a person who begins an activity performing it well effectively guaranteed a high level of future success?

In each situation, the issue of predicting the *potential* for success in performing a motor skill is important. In the following discussion, this issue will be considered because it relates to how a knowledge of motor abilities can *aid* in the prediction process. However, first it is important to realize that information about motor abilities is only one type that is or should be used to predict the potential for success. Keep in mind the discussions in the preceding concepts in this chapter about different types of human abilities related to motor skill performance. In general, the more ability-related information you have about a person and the more you know about the relationship of specific abilities to performance success for a particular motor skill, the greater your chances for accurate prediction. However, the assessment of motor abilities can provide a useful part of advance information about future performance potential before a person begins training to learn a specific motor skill.

Discussion

In the discussions of the preceding concepts in this chapter, you have seen that individuals are characterized by a variety of motor abilities and that each of these abilities can be described as being at a certain level if the appropriate tests are available. You have also seen that motor skills can be described in terms of the motor abilities that are required for the successful performance of the skills. In this discussion, these two points will provide the basis for establishing how information about motor abilities can be used to predict potential for success in motor skills.

It is important to be aware that what is being considered here is the prediction of a person's *potential* for future success rather than a person's actual future success. Whether or not an individual actually achieves his or her potential will depend on many factors, such as motivation, training, opportunities, etc. Thus, the use of motor abilities for prediction must be limited to making predictive evaluations about what a person's potential for success might be given the availability of the appropriate conditions to develop that potential.

Prediction Accuracy

Before considering how motor abilities information can be used for prediction purposes, it is essential to consider some of the limitations related to how accurately this prediction can be made. While the accuracy of the prediction for a particular situation will be dependent on several factors, two are particularly critical.

First, predicting the potential for success in a motor skill depends on an accurate identification and assessment of the essential abilities required to successfully perform the skill. We will refer to this skill as the target skill. The first step is to develop a task analysis for the target skill, as was discussed in Concept 6.1. Within this analysis should be the identification of the abilities that seem to underlie the successful performance of the skill. The next step is to administer to a large sample of people a battery of abilities tests iden-

tified in the task analysis. Finally, the scores on the abilities tests must be compared to the actual performance of the target skill by your sample of people, using an appropriate performance measure. You can use various statistical techniques to provide the information you are seeking. We will not discuss these because that is not the purpose here.

A statistic that is very useful in this prediction process is known as the **variance accounted for.** This simply means that a certain percentage of the statistical variance of the performance scores for the target skill is accounted for by the scores on the abilities tests. If the target skill performance variance accounted for by the tests is high (i.e., 70% or better), you can be confident that you have identified the essential abilities underlying performance of the target skill. If, on the other hand, the variance accounted for is below that percentage, then other abilities remain to be identified.

The second factor critical in the accuracy of the success prediction is the validity and reliability of the abilities tests used. If these tests are not valid and reliable measures, there is little basis on which to expect reasonable prediction accuracy of motor skill performance.

At the present time, these two factors are at the heart of problems related to accurately predicting a person's potential for future success in a motor skill. There is much work to be done in both identifying the important abilities underlying successful performance of skills and in developing valid and reliable ability tests. However, as you will see, there has been sufficient success in many situations to warrant the consideration of the use of motor abilities testing to predict future success potential.

Relating Initial and Later Achievement

One of the essential points to understand when attempting to predict potential for future skill performance achievement from levels of abilities is the relationship between performance of a skill at the early stage of practice and performance later in practice. This is important because a low relationship between early and late stages of learning indicates that the abilities underlying performance at each stage of learning may be different. On the other hand, a high relationship between stages of learning simplifies matters by allowing the identification of abilities to be made without regarding the stage of learning.

There are two ways to see how initial performance of a new skill relates to later achievement. First, observe performance of people as they practice the skill and show evidence of moving across the stages of learning from being a novice to a skilled performer. Then, correlate early performance scores with later performance scores for these people. In most cases, the correlations will be low, indicating a low relationship between initial and later achievement. A second way to see this relationship is by intercorrelating practice trials. What typically results from this procedure is that practice trials that are close to each other are more highly correlated than those farther apart. From this, the expectation is that the further practice trials are from each other, the less related they are, which again leads to the conclusion that achievement levels later in practice are poorly predicted by those early in practice. Research examples of each of these two approaches provides support for this conclusion.

An experiment by Ella Trussell (1965) provides an example of following the progress of beginners through practicing a skill and developing a degree of success in performing it. In her experiment, 40 college women practiced juggling three tennis balls for 27 practice sessions. Each session included 75 tosses. Subjects practiced during three sessions per week for nine weeks. Final success in juggling was operationally defined as the average score, which was the number of errors or dropped balls, for the last four practice periods. Figure 6.3–1 shows the performance curve for the practice sessions. Notice that the subjects improved over practice. Error scores dropped from 50 errors per 75 tosses in the first practice period to 20 errors per 75 tosses in the

final session. The second graph shows to what extent the final scores for the subjects could be predicted on the basis of the error scores for each practice period. The measure on the vertical axis is to be interpreted as indicating the probability of being correct in predicting the final score. During the first five practice sessions, we would be correct only 50% to 60% of the time in predicting final scores. This is about as good as we could do by flipping a coin. We would like to have a more meaningful prediction than this if we wish to predict ultimate performance in the learning of a motor skill. The ability to predict final scores increased as more practice sessions are observed. After 15 sessions, or 1,025 tosses, we could predict with about 85% accuracy. Performance early in practice, then, does not lead to a very accurate indication of future performance.

The second means of looking at the relationship of early to later practice performance is to consider the relationship of performance scores between any two trials. As described earlier, the common finding has been that trials that are close to each other in time are more highly correlated than trials that are further from each other. That is, Trials 2 and 3 will show a higher correlation than will Trials 2 and 20. This characteristic of the relationship between trials follows what has been called a **superdiagonal form.** This term refers to the way the trial-to-trial correlations appear on a correlation matrix where all trials are compared against each other, with the same trials located on both the vertical and the horizontal axes of the matrix. The correlation of a trial with the trial that succeeds it, such as Trials 2 and 3, will be found just above the diagonal of the matrix where a trial would be correlated with itself. According to the superdiagonal form, the highest correlations in the matrix should be found along the diagonal that is just above the main diagonal of the matrix.

An example of an experiment taking this approach is one reported by Thomas and Halliwell (1976). In this experiment, subjects learned three motor skills, the pursuit rotor, the stabilometer, and a rhythmic arm movement task. The correlation

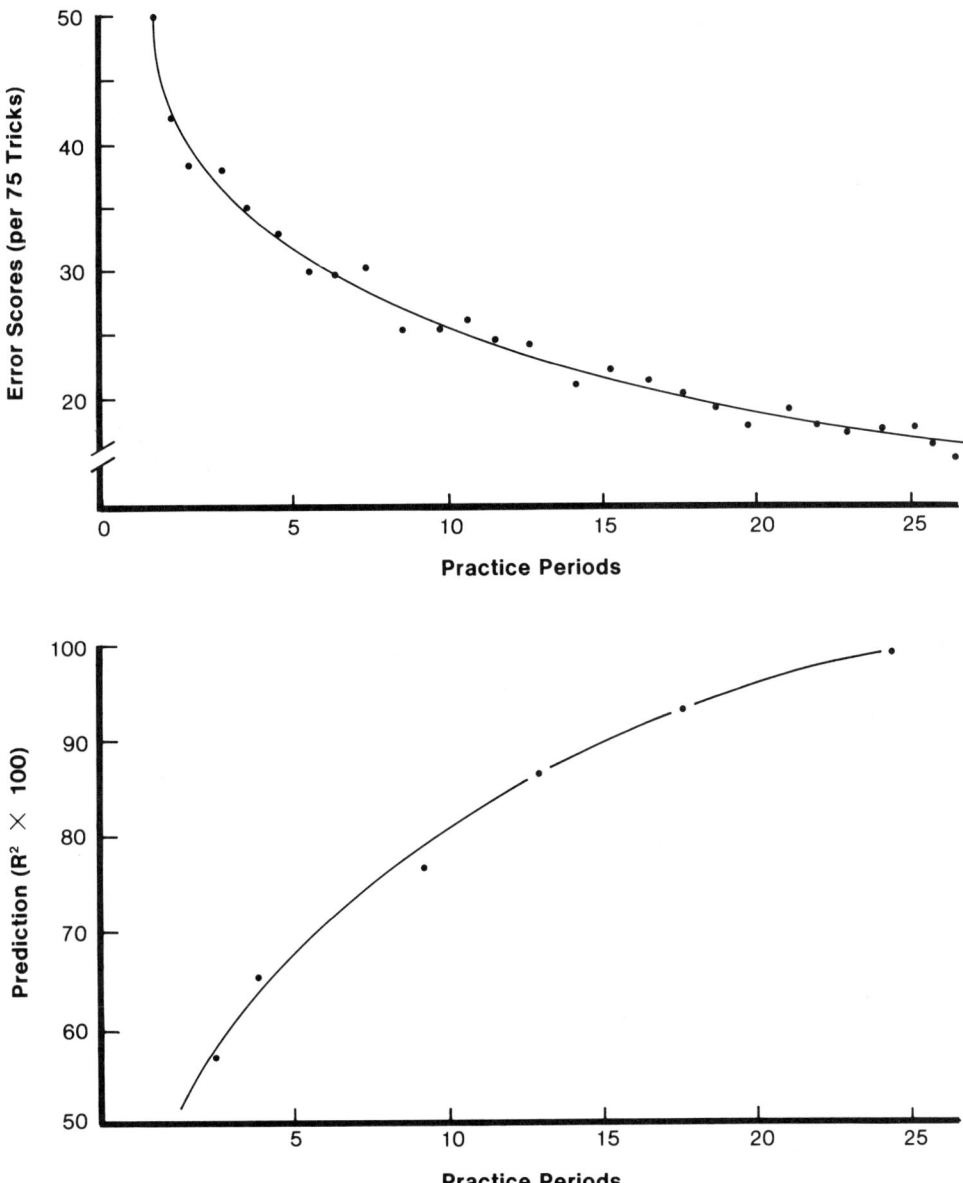

FIGURE 6.3-1 The top graph shows the performance curve from the experiment by Trussell for a juggling task. The numbers of errors are indicated for the practice periods. The bottom graph indicates the accuracy of prediction of final performance in the juggling task as a function of the amount of practice used for prediction.

Table 6.3-1   The intertrial correlation matrix from performance on a rhythmic arm movement task reported by Thomas and Halliwell (1976). The correlations are based on the spatial error scores from the task.

Trial	1	2	3	4	5	6	7	8	9	10	11	12	13	14	15
1	—	27	−.05	.33	.23	.08	.27	.15	.00	−.04	−.09	.11	−.05	.13	−.12
2		—	.63	.71	.57	.57	.64	.54	.57	.38	.54	.29	.15	.67	.25
3			—	.60	.46	.18	.56	.50	.45	.53	.48	.12	.09	.37	.24
4				—	.73	.45	.61	.62	.45	.29	.51	.15	.17	.49	.12
5					—	.37	.67	.57	.59	.32	.52	.22	.28	.52	.21
6						—	.53	.54	.50	.39	.68	.52	.41	.61	.35
7							—	.71	.67	.70	.65	.51	.57	.80	.50
8								—	.67	.67	.65	.52	.43	.59	.48
9									—	.47	.73	.54	.61	.78	.41
10										—	.56	.59	.63	.62	.64
11											—	.49	.57	.72	.62
12												—	.63	.58	.47
13													—	.71	.63
14														—	.53
15															—

From J. R. Thomas and W. Halliwell, "Individual Differences in Motor Skill Acquisition." in *Journal of Motor Behavior,* 1976, 8; 89–100. Copyright © 1976 Heldref Publications, Inc., Washington, D.C. Reprinted by permission.

matrix in Table 6.3–1 is from the results of subjects' initial 15 trials of practice on the rhythmic arm movement task. This task involved learning to move a lever held at the side of the body to a visual target in time with a metronome. Performance was scored in terms of both spatial and temporal error. As you can see in Table 6.3–1, the highest between-trial correlations for spatial error performance on the practice trials for this task are typically found along the diagonal located just above the main diagonal of the correlation matrix. (Note that if the correlations were presented on the main diagonal, they would be 1.0, because a trial would be correlated with itself.) Then, as you move to your right to compare a particular trial to other trials, the correlation between trials is generally less. For example, the correlation between Trials 4 and 5 is 0.73 while the correlation between Trials 4 and 12 drops to 0.15. As such, these results provide additional evidence that performance early in practice is a poor predictor of performance later in practice.

Accounting for poor prediction.   An important question about the common finding that early practice performance poorly predicts later achievement is, What accounts for this poor prediction? Why does it occur? Although there is some debate among individual difference psychologists (see Ackerman, 1989; Henry & Hulin, 1987, for good discussions of both sides of this debate), we will consider a prevalent view that argues that the repertoire of abilities needed to perform a skill changes as a skill has been practiced so that the abilities related to performance early in practice are not the same abilities related to performance later in practice.

Ackerman (1988) has related ability changes to skill acquisition by proposing three principles describing the abilities that account for performance in each of the three learning stages of the Fitts and Posner model, discussed in Concept 2.2. Principle 1 is that in the first stage of learning, the cognitive stage, general abilities are most critical for performance. As described in the discussion of

Concept 6.1, general abilities relate primarily to general intelligence, or cognitive ability. Principle 2 states that in the second stage of learning, the associative stage, perceptual speed ability accounts for performance. This ability relates to a person's facility for how quickly problem-solving activity can be accomplished, especially problems requiring visual search and memory use. Finally, Principle 3 indicates that in the autonomous stage of learning, the third stage, task-specific, noncognitive motor abilities predominate to allow successful performance of the skill. Speed and accuracy of performing movement components of a skill are particularly characteristic of these abilities. Specific examples of these were described in Concept 6.1. As a result, we should expect that there should be higher correlations for cognitive abilities and early skill practice than later practice. Conversely, task-specific motor abilities should yield lower correlations during early practice than later practice.

Support for this view can be found in the research by Fleishman and colleagues. A good example is an experiment by Fleishman and Hempel (1955) in which 264 subjects were given a battery of nine motor abilities tests and then practiced a complex motor skill. The task was a complex discrimination and coordination test that required the subjects to push toggle switches as quickly as possible in response to a pattern of signal lights. The complexity of this task was established by requiring a certain movement response to different patterns of signal lights. The subjects had to learn the appropriate signal light pattern and response combination as they practiced the task. It was reported that subjects were able to improve their response times during the 16 practice sessions, which consisted of 20 trials each. The average response times of the subjects improved from almost 500 msec during the first practice session to under 250 msec during the final practice session.

The results indicating the relationship between the nine abilities and the performance levels across the practice sessions are presented in Figure 6.3–2, which shows the percentage of variance accounted for by each of the nine abilities. In this graph a marked area indicates the percentage of the total variance accounted for by the particular ability. The greater the percentage of the total variance accounted for by an ability, the more important that ability is to performance of the task.

As you can see, the relationship between each ability and performance of the task is plotted across the practice sessions. During the first practice session, the spatial relations (36%), discrimination reaction time (17%), verbal comprehension (6%), and psychomotor coordination (5%) accounted for 64% of the total variance for the performance on the complex task. Now look at the right-hand side of the graph where performance during the last session of practice is considered. As you can see, the relative importance of the various abilities to task performance changed in many cases from what it was earlier in practice. The most significant abilities related to task performance were discrimination reaction time (35%), rate of arm movement (17%), spatial relations (11%), reaction time (9%), and perceptual speed (5%). Thus, early in practice, spatial relations was a very important factor in accounting for performance on the task. However, by the last practice session, its level of importance had decreased significantly (from 36% to 11%). On the other hand, reaction time and rate of arm movement were of negligible importance early in practice. However, later in practice, these abilities accounted for over 30% of the variance of the task performance. Discrimination reaction time increased from 17% to 35% over the practice sessions.

Ackerman (1988) reanalyzed these results in terms of the three principles he proposed to predict which category of abilities account for skill performance in each of the three stages of learning. He showed that, as predicted, perceptual speed ability was more correlated with performance in early practice than in later practice, and, that task-specific motor abilities, such as rate of arm movement and discrimination RT, were more correlated with performance later than earlier in practice.

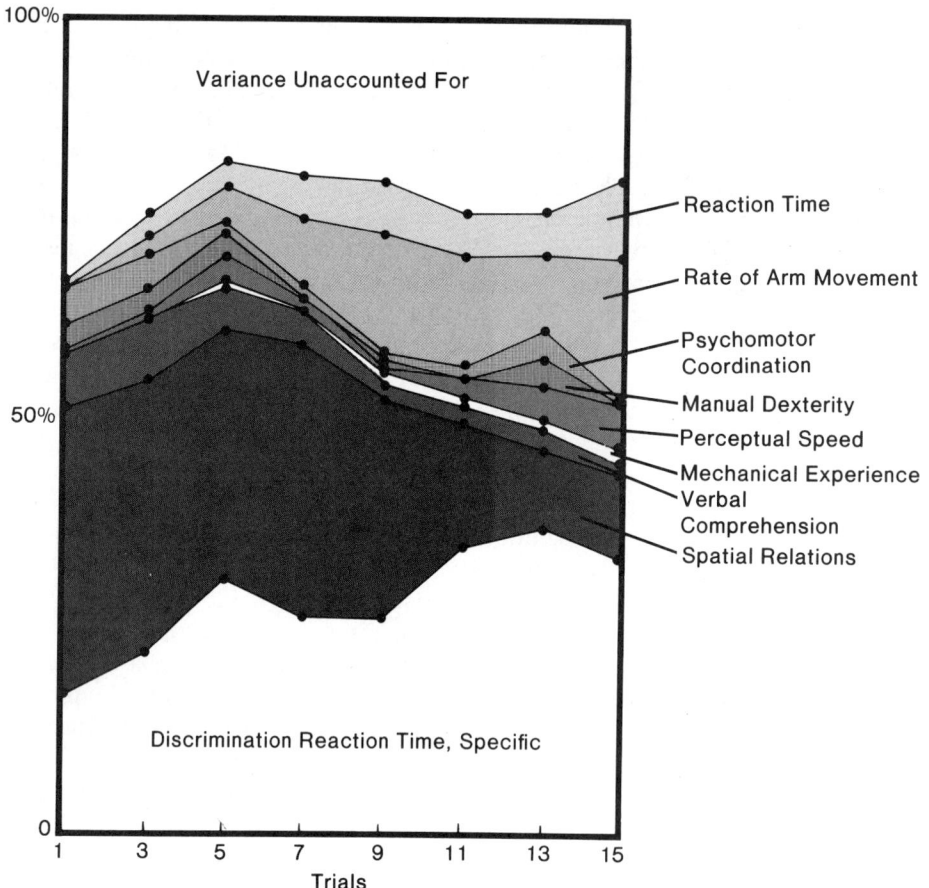

100%

Variance Unaccounted For

— Reaction Time

— Rate of Arm Movement

–Psychomotor
Coordination

–Manual Dexterity
–Perceptual Speed
–Mechanical Experience
–Verbal
Comprehension
–Spatial Relations

50%

Discrimination Reaction Time, Specific

0

1   3   5   7   9   11   13   15
Trials

FIGURE 6.3-2 Results of the experiment by Fleishman and Hempel showing the percentage of variance accounted for by different abilities at different stages of practice on a complex discrimination reaction-time task. Percentage of variance is represented by the size of the shaded areas for each ability.

The key point is that it is very difficult to predict future achievement in learning a motor skill when the prediction is based on early performance only. Abilities that account for a person's level of performance change in importance from the early stage of learning to later stages. Those abilities that are important in accounting for a person's performance score early in practice are typically not as important later in practice. However, prediction of future performance seems to improve if there is an awareness of the specific abilities that are essential to performance in the different stages of learning and if there is also an awareness of the corresponding abilities within the learner.

To the instructor of motor skills, this concept is very important. The instructor must be aware that a person may eventually perform better than initial performance indicates. To "give up" on a person because of such undependable evidence as early performance alone would be doing that person a grave injustice.

Using Abilities Tests to Predict Performance Potential

Thus far in this discussion we have considered some of the problems involved in predicting an individual's potential for success in a motor skill.

While it is obvious there are problems, there is a role for the use of abilities testing to predict motor skill performance potential. Testing abilities for the purpose of predicting future success is a part of what is known in industry as "screening." Tests developed for screening purposes are usually batteries of specific tests designed to determine the potential for success of candidates for specific jobs. We will consider three studies, one from an industrial setting, one from a military setting, and one involving a sport skill, to exemplify how this screening can be successful.

To predict pole-climbing performance for telephone company trainees, Reilly, Zedeck, and Tenopyr (1979) used a battery of 14 physical and motor ability measures such as height, weight, body density, leg strength, reaction time, arm strength, balance, and static strength. From this battery, three measures were found to successfully predict pole-climbing performance: body density, balance, and static strength. As a result, three tests could be given to training course applicants as an initial screening device to determine who should be permitted to enroll in the course. That is, a person achieving a score above a specified score on the test battery would have a 90% chance of passing the training course.

The United States Air Force has been interested in predicting success of pilot trainees since the early 1940s. The most recent effort was reported by Cox (1988), who analyzed performance of 320 prospective pilots in the Air Force Undergraduate Pilot Training Program, which lasts approximately 49 weeks. The two primary ability tests used were the Two Hand Coordination Task and the Complex Coordination Test, both of which demand coordinating movement of both hands to track moving targets on a computer screen. Based on analyzing performance on these tasks, Cox was able to significantly predict success in the training program. Cox's findings were beneficial because the Air Force loses approximately $65,000 for each trainee who does not graduate from the training program. Thus, a valid screening program that is simple and provides good prediction of success could save significant amounts of money for the Air Force.

The benefit of early prediction of success potential in industrial and military settings is obvious. People can be screened and placed into jobs for which they are best suited before too much time and money is invested in training. This same logic has been applied to the sport setting as a means of identifying people who have the greatest potential to be successful competitors in specific sports. If this is done, individuals would be more accurately channeled into those sports in which they had the greatest likelihood of being world-class performers.

An interesting example of using ability testing in a sport setting can be seen in a study by Landers, Boutcher, and Wang (1986) of individuals involved in training programs in archery. They found that certain physical, perceptual-motor and psychological characteristics accurately predicted archery performance. After administering several batteries of physical and psychological tests to 188 amateur archers, they found that individuals with greater relative leg strength, lower percentage of body fat, faster reaction times, better depth perception, greater imagery ability, more confidence, and better use of past mistakes had higher archery performance scores than other archers. In fact, the leg strength, percentage of body fat, reaction time, depth perception, and past mistakes characteristics together correctly predicted how 81% of the archers would be classified (average or above average) as archers. Clearly, certain abilities and characteristics are required for people to achieve different levels of sport performance.

Perhaps the most vocal call in the sport world for developing accurate prediction instruments is from those who see this approach benefiting the selection of world-class competitors. The appeal of such a selection process for athletes goes beyond the savings in training time and money this process represents, and it also would help ensure a greater degree of success for a country in world-class competitions. Although some success has been reported using predictive-type testing for this purpose in some countries, the process of testing and selection is complex and lengthy. And the results are not well validated. The testing process involves much more than just motor ability tests, and includes a wide range of physiological and psychological test batteries that must be carefully developed. Also, coaches and researchers must be trained not only to administer the tests, but also to carefully observe athletes at all stages of their development.

An important point must be interjected here. It is essential that developmental characteristics be taken into account in any attempts to predict potential for future success in sport, especially for pre-adolescents and adolescents. Attempts to make such predictions for these children are tenuous at best. The primary reason for this is that children mature at different rates. That is, a child of 12 may be physically more like an 8- or 9-year-old or more like a 12- or 13-year-old. (See Malina, 1984, for a good discussion of this topic.) Early maturers, those who are physically advanced for their age, may be successful because of their physical advantage rather than their skill advantage. When the late maturers, those who are physically behind for their age, catch up, the once apparent difference in skill levels often disappears. The message, then, is never to give up on a young athlete because you think he or she has no chance to ever experience success. In your role as a teacher or coach of children and youth, it is essential to provide optimum experiences and opportunities for all, not just for those who look as if they will be successful because of their current success.

Summary

Information about an individual's motor abilities can be useful in predicting his or her potential for success in various motor skills. While this information cannot be expected to lead to absolutely perfect prediction, it can be used with other information to aid in the prediction process. Predicting the potential for success depends on the accuracy of the identification of the essential abilities related to successfully performing the motor skill of interest. Also critical to the prediction process is the development and use of valid and reliable tests of motor abilities. Abilities related to performance of a skill in the early stages of learning are often different from those that are important for performance of the skill later in learning. The types of abilities related to performance can be specified according to the stage of learning, where more general cognitive abilities account for performance early in learning and more task-specific motor abilities are related to success in later stages. Predicting future success depends on identifying levels of abilities within the individual that are essential to successful task performance and on identifying those abilities within the task that relate to successful performance of the task. Screening tests for making this type of prediction have been successfully used in industrial, military, and sport settings.

Related Readings

Ackerman, P. L. (1987). Individual differences in skill learning: An integration of psychometric and information processing perspectives. *Psychological Bulletin, 102,* 3–27.

Fleishman, E. A. (1969). Abilities at different stages of practice in rotary pursuit performance. *Journal of Experimental Psychology, 60,* 162–171.

Fleishman, E. A. (1982). Systems for describing human tasks. *American Psychologist, 37,* 821–824.

Henry, R. A. & Hulin, C. L. (1987). Stability of skilled performance across time: Some generalizations and limitations on utilities. *Journal of Applied Psychology, 72,* 457–462.

Malina, R. M. (1984). Physical growth and maturation. In J. R. Thomas (Ed.), *Motor development during childhood and adolescence* (pp. 2–26). Minneapolis: Burgess.

STUDY QUESTIONS FOR CHAPTER 6

1. How does the study of individual differences differ from the study of normative or average behavior?

2. What motor abilities has Fleishman identified? What other motor abilities can you identify?

3. Describe two ways in which knowledge about minor abilities can be of value to a teacher of motor skills.

4. What seems to be the most generally accepted position concerning the cause or origin of motor abilities?

5. What is the difference between the general motor ability hypothesis and the specificity of motor abilities hypothesis? Give an example of some research that indicates which of these hypotheses is more valid.

6. How can a specificity view of motor abilities explain how a person can be an "all-around athlete"?

7. What is meant by the term motor educability? Is it a valid notion?

8. Why can knowledge of an individual's motor abilities only help in predicting that person's potential for success in a particular motor skill?

9. How successfully can eventual success in motor skill performance be predicted from how well a person performs the same skill in early practice?

10. What is the "superdiagonal form" that is characteristic of the between-practice trial relationship for many motor skills? What does this correlation pattern tell us about the relationship of early to later practice performance?

11. What are Ackerman's three principles that relate motor abilities to performance and three different stages of skill learning? How does the Fleishman and Hempel study provide support for these principles?

12. Why is cutting a 10–year-old from a sports team because of poor performance a bad policy? Consider this in terms of maturation rate differences in children and how that relates to motor skill performance success.

UNIT III

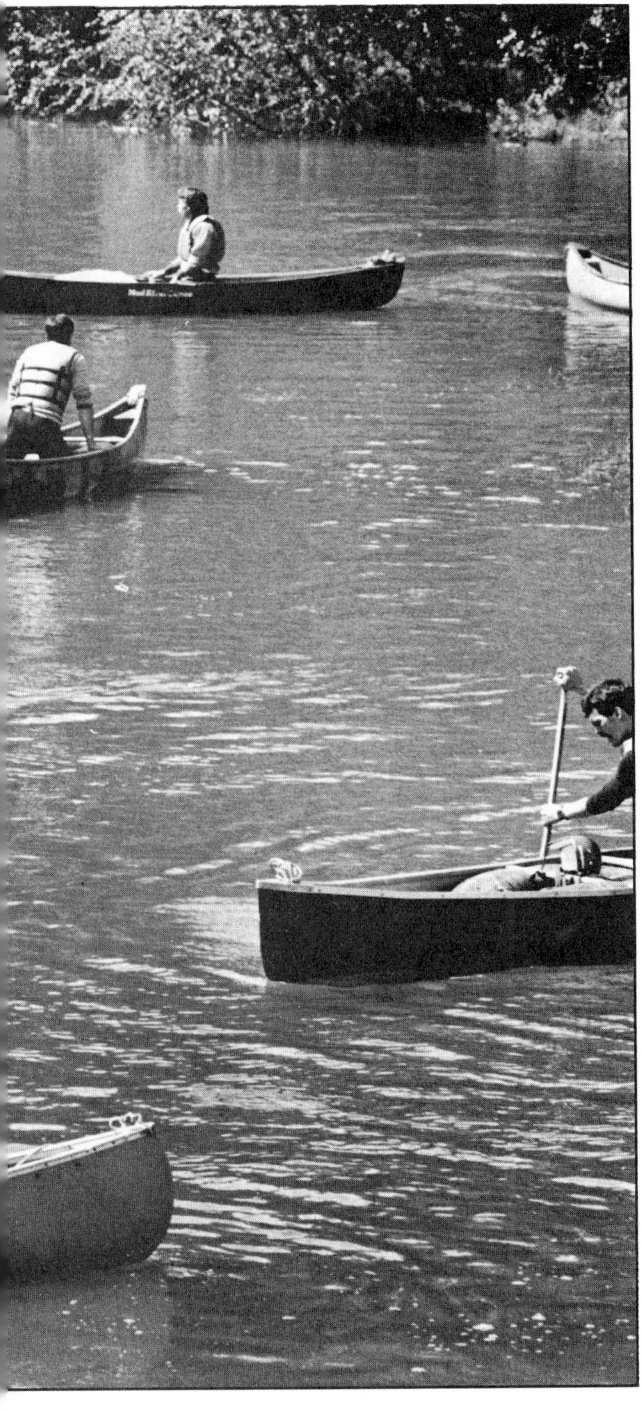

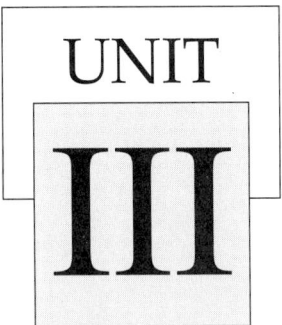

The Learning Environment

CHAPTER

7

INSTRUCTION AND AUGMENTED FEEDBACK

CONCEPT 7.1

Demonstration is an effective form of instruction for teaching motor skills.

CONCEPT 7.2

Decisions about whether to teach and practice a motor skill as a whole
or by parts can be made on the basis of the complexity and organization of the skill.

CONCEPT 7.3

Augmented feedback can improve, hinder, or have no effect on motor skill learning.

CONCEPT 7.4

Augmented feedback can be provided in a variety of ways and in different frequencies.

CONCEPT 7.5

The timing of augmented feedback relates to concurrent or terminal presentation
and to the intervals of time preceding and following terminal presentation.

CONCEPT 7.1

Demonstration is an effective form of instruction for teaching motor skills

Key Terms

modeling

observational learning

cognitive mediation theory

dynamic view of modeling

Application

If you are teaching a new skill and want to communicate to your students how this skill should be performed, what is the most likely way you would communicate this information? You would probably demonstrate the skill so that the students could see for themselves how the skill should be performed. If you couldn't demonstrate the skill yourself, you might have them watch another student in the class demonstrate the skill, or have them watch a film or videotape of someone doing the skill. In each of these situations, demonstration is the common means of communicating information about how to perform a skill. Each of these forms of demonstration is included in what is commonly referred to by learning researchers and theorists as **modeling** *or* **observational learning.** This form of instruction may be the most frequently used strategy for communicating to students how a skill should be performed.

Skills demonstration can be done in a wide range of situations. For example, a physical education teacher may demonstrate to a large class how to putt in golf. An aerobics teacher may dem-

onstrate to a class how to perform a particular sequence of skills. A baseball coach may show a player the correct form of bunting a ball. An occupational therapist may demonstrate to a patient how to button a shirt. Or a physical therapist may demonstrate to a wheelchair patient how to get from the floor into the chair. The common goal in each of these situations is to communicate how to correctly perform a skill. By demonstrating a skill, the instructor indicates that he or she believes that more information is conveyed in less time than would be required if he or she verbally explained how to perform the skill. So, whether you are teaching a large class, working with a small group, or providing individual instruction, and whether you are teaching a complex skill or a simple skill, demonstration can be used as a regular instruction strategy.

Although demonstration seems to be universally accepted as a form of instruction for teaching motor skills, numerous issues must be addressed to establish when demonstration is effective, why it is effective, and what is required to most effectively use demonstration as an instructional strategy for teaching motor skills. In the following discussion, these issues will be addressed so that you will have a more substantial basis for determining how to use demonstration more effectively in whatever motor skill instruction or training situation you may find yourself.

Discussion

While demonstration undoubtedly has been one of the most common (if not the most common) forms of providing instructions about how to perform a skill, it is ironic there is so little research related

to it. In fact, most of what we know about the use of demonstration comes from modeling research and theory related to social learning. For a number of years, social behavior researchers and theorists have considered modeling to be an important means for learning values, attitudes, and other social behaviors (e.g., Bandura, 1977, 1984). However, there has been a recent increase in interest to understand more about the role of demonstration in skill learning. One reason involves the increase in interest in the role of vision in skill learning, as was discussed in Concepts 3.2 and 4.2. Because providing demonstration of how to do a skill involves observational learning on the part of the learner, the study of modeling and skill learning has provided a means of assessing how the visual system is involved in skill learning and performance. Also, from an instruction theory perspective, because demonstration is such a common instructional strategy and so little is known about its effective implementation teaching motor skills, there has been an increased attempt to improve our understanding of how to use demonstration to teach skills and why it works so effectively. ■

The Effective Model

One of the more comprehensive reviews of modeling research related to motor skill acquisition was published by McCullagh, Weiss, and Ross (1989). They addressed a number of important questions that need to be answered if we are to understand conditions in which modeling is and is not effective, as well as why modeling facilitates motor skill learning. One of the important outcomes of research on modeling has been the finding that modeling is more effective under certain circumstances than others. This result suggests that modeling should not be used without first determining whether the instructional situation warrants its use. In the following sections, some of these circumstances will be considered to provide you with a better understanding of the use of modeling. The initial focus will be on circumstances related to the model. As you will see, the degree of effectiveness that can be achieved by the use of modeling is dependent on a number of factors related to the model, including things such as the characteristics of the model, the model's demonstration, and when the model is used.

Status of the model. One of the first things to consider when deciding about demonstrating a skill is, who should do the demonstration. It may be surprising to find that the status of who demonstrates the skill can be influential in establishing the effectiveness of the demonstration. For example, consider an experiment by Landers and Landers (1973) in which they compared skilled and unskilled models that were either the teacher or student peers. In this experiment, gradeschool children learned to climb the Bachman ladder, a free-standing ladder the subject holds and then climbs as many rungs as possible before losing balance. One group observed a skilled teacher, another group observed a skilled student peer, a third group observed an unskilled teacher, and the last group observed an unskilled peer. Results indicated that the teacher was a more effective model when skilled at performing the task. However, when the teacher could not perform the skill well, an unskilled student was the more effective model.

As you may have noticed, the Landers and Landers (1973) experiment did not include a retention or transfer test, thus limiting the potential of this study to indicate the influence of the model's status on learning. However, McCullagh (1987) reported an experiment that did include a retention test and that was designed also to look at model status. She compared the performance of college females on the Bachman ladder task. The status of the model was established by portraying the higher-status model as a gymnast/dancer who was experienced in balance-type activities. Thus, the model was considered dissimilar to the subjects. The lower-status model was described as being similar to the subjects in that she was portrayed as a college student with no particular background related to the task. However, the model for both conditions was actually the same person and performed the skill equally well for both groups of subjects. A third group did not observe a model. As you can see from the results in Figure 7.1–1, the group that saw the similar status model showed higher performance during the practice trials. Also note that both model

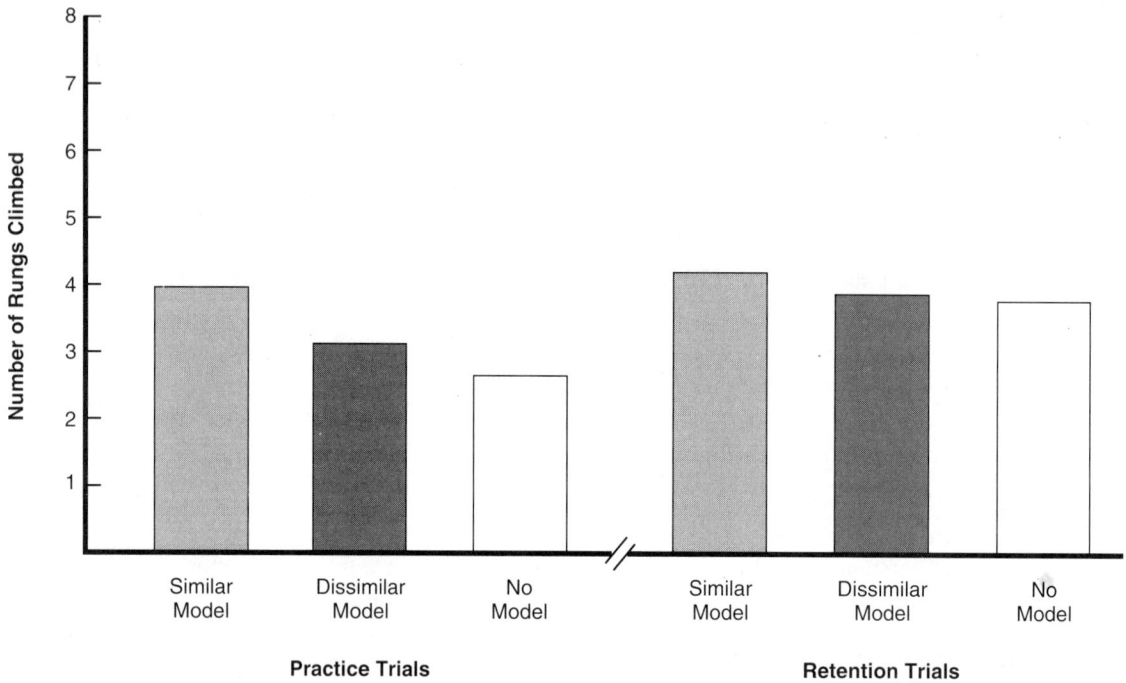

FIGURE 7.1-1   Results from the experiment by McCullagh showing the influence of a similar and a dissimilar model or no model on performing the Bachman ladder task during practice trials with KR and on retention trials without KR.

groups performed better than a control group that had not watched a model. However, the influence of the similarity of the model to the subjects did not influence learning, because all subjects performed similarly on the retention test given one minute later.

Thus, when the model is a peer of the students or is one who has a higher status, there is a temporary benefit, as shown in the results of the McCullagh experiment. Why should the model's status be expected to influence the effect of modeling on skill acquisition? Two possibilities have been suggested. First, the higher-status model may influence students to pay closer attention to the demonstration, which positively affects the amount of information students receive from the demonstration. The second possibility is that the higher-status model provides an increased motivation to perform well. The students are more motivated because of their desire to be like the person they

admire. It is also possible that both explanations are involved in the model status influence.

Correctness of the demonstration.   A common conclusion about a model's performance of the skill is that the skill should be performed correctly. Recall that in the Landers and Landers (1973) experiment there was a comparison of skilled and unskilled models and their influence on how well the subjects acquired the ladder-climbing task. The results showed that a skilled teacher as a model led to better student performance than the unskilled teacher demonstration. This seems to be common in studies that make similar model performance comparisons. In fact, as a conclusion to their review of modeling and skill acquisition research, Gould and Roberts (1982) stated that "High-status models must accurately and skillfully portray the skill" (p. 228).

Why would the more accurate demonstration lead to better learning? The most likely reason is that when the student is asked to try the skill after having seen a demonstration of it, the student typically tries to imitate as closely as possible what the model did. Research evidence supports this possibility. In an experiment by Martens, Burwitz, and Zuckerman (1976, experiment 3). Subjects observed a model perform a "shoot-the-moon" task that involved moving a ball up an incline that is formed by two metal rods held by the subject and moved back and forth to make the ball move up the incline. The score is based on where the ball falls through the rods to the base below. The experiment involved using different groups of subjects observing models performing the task using one of two strategies. One strategy, called the "creep strategy" involved moving the ball slowly up the incline. Although this strategy rarely led to high scores, it led to consistent scores on each trial. The other strategy, the "explosive strategy," involved moving the rods in such a way to rapidly propel the ball up the incline. Although this strategy led to higher scores, it also was the riskier strategy because it often led to extremely low scores as well. The results showed that the subjects typically adopted the strategy they saw used by the model they observed.

There has been an increasing interest in the effect of novices observing unskilled models practicing skills. The proposed benefit of this approach to modeling is that it discourages imitation of how a model is performing the skill because performance is not correct, and encourages the observer to engage in more active problem solving activities. Evidence for the benefit of this approach can be traced back to the 1930s (e.g., Twitmeyer, 1931), although interest in this approach never developed until some experiments by Adams (1986) were published. Since then, others have pursued the investigation of the use and benefit of observing an unskilled model learning a skill (e.g., McCullagh & Caird, 1990; Pollock & Lee, 1992; Weir & Leavitt, 1990). One of the characteristics of a learning environment in which observing an unskilled model is beneficial is when the observer

not only can watch the model but also can hear the augmented feedback given by the instructor or experimenter. Under these conditions, the observer actively engages in problem-solving activity that is beneficial for learning. The observer sees what the unskilled model does, what he or she is told is wrong with the attempt, what the model does to correct errors, and how successful he or she is on the succeeding attempts.

A very practical issue to consider is what you should do in a situation where you as the instructor cannot demonstrate the skill very well. There appear to be several options, and two of these relate to using an alternative means of providing a skilled model while the other involves using an unskilled model. To provide a skilled model for demonstrating the skill, use a film or videotape of a well-known, skilled individual performing the skill. These types of films are readily available for a variety of motor skills. The second option is to use a skilled student to demonstrate the skill. The third option is one that is not commonly used in instruction situations and its implementation appears to have exciting potential. Pairs of students can be organized, and while one student practices the skill for several trials, the other observes and listens to the feedback given by the instructor. The teacher would not have to skillfully demonstrate the skill but would need to provide accurate feedback about performance attempts by the students.

When should the model begin demonstrating?
Another decision that must be made about the use of a model is when the model should begin demonstrating a skill to best facilitate learning. This decision concerns whether to begin demonstrating the skill before practice begins or after some practice has occurred. One argument promotes demonstrating the skill before practice begins so that the students have an idea of what the skill looks like when it is performed. This approach would be in keeping with Gentile's (1972) proposal that the goal of the first stage of learning is to "get the idea of the movement." If seeing the model perform the skill before actually practicing it helps the student

get the idea of the movement, then introducing the model as early in practice as possible would be more effective.

An alternative to this approach is to allow students to first try the skill on their own after being provided with information about the goal of the movement and some basic verbal instructions about how to perform the skill. This approach emphasizes initial trial-and-error practice and may help the student to develop some initial coordination capabilities, as well as learn some movement characteristics that will not work. After some initial exploration with the skill, the model could then be introduced. The argument for the benefit of introducing the model at this time would be that the student would have a better idea of what to look for in the model's performance and would therefore benefit more by seeing the model after some practice, rather than before practicing the skill.

Although this is an interesting issue, there has been limited research, and the findings that have been reported lead to an unsettled conclusion. Two experiments illustrate this. First, consider the experiment by Landers (1975), who had subjects practice the Bachman ladder balancing task. Observation of a model was introduced in one of three ways. One group of subjects watched the model perform 4 trials of the task before practicing 30 trials. Another group saw the model perform 4 trials before practicing 15 trials and then saw the model perform 2 more trials before practicing the second set of 15 trials. Finally, the third group practiced 15 trials and then observed the model perform 4 trials, and then did the remaining 15 trials. Results showed that although observing a demonstration before practice was beneficial for learning, what was even more beneficial was to observe the model again halfway through the practice trials.

Another experiment that provides some interesting findings about when to introduce the model involves some developmental considerations. Thomas, Pierce, and Ridsdale (1977) had 7- and 9-year-old girls practice the stabilometer task. Three groups of subjects were formed for each age

level. One group, the "beginning model" group, saw the model before beginning their 12 practice trials. Another group, the "middle model" group, saw the model after practicing 6 trials and then practiced the remaining 6 trials. The third group did not observe a model. The interesting results of this experiment (Figure 7.1–2) were that introducing a model in the middle of the practice trials led to detrimental performance by the 7-year-olds, whereas it benefited the 9-year-olds. Thus, for the older children, the early opportunity to explore how to accomplish the task goal was useful practice experience.

These results suggest that introducing a model before practice begins is an appropriate use of the modeling technique. However, it is advisable to provide an opportunity for students to observe the model at other times during practice, in addition to this initial opportunity. These results also suggest that there are situations in which allowing students the opportunity to initially explore how the task can be done before introducing the model can be beneficial, especially if the students are old enough.

The frequency of demonstrating a skill. Although it is recommended that a skill be demonstrated before practicing the skill, it would also be beneficial to demonstrate the skill at various times during practice. The question that arises is, If the skill should be demonstrated during practice, how frequently? Unfortunately, there is little research that addresses this question. One recent study suggests that more frequency may be better than less frequency. An experiment by Hand and Sidaway (1992) involved subjects learning to hit plastic golf balls into a target circle using a 9-iron. Subjects performed 150 shots during 3 days of practice. One group observed a skilled model before every shot, while two other groups observed the model before every fifth shot and before every tenth shot. A fourth group did not observe a model. The results of no-KR and no modeling retention and transfer tests given one day after practice ended showed that the group that had observed the model before every trial did better than

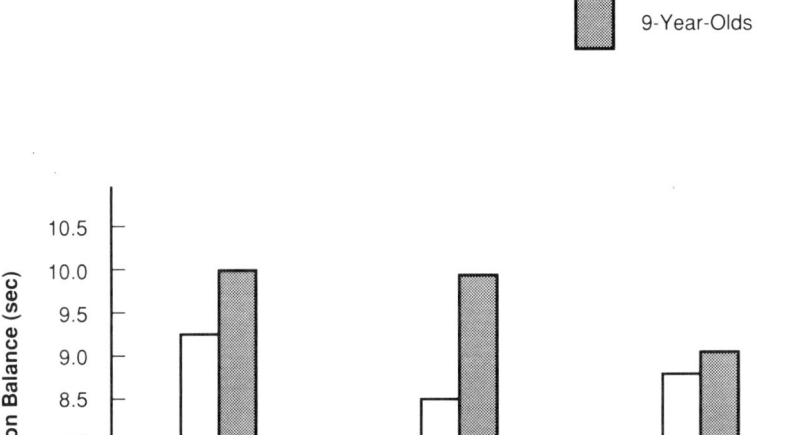

FIGURE 7.1-2 Results of the experiment by Thomas, Pierce, and Ridsdale showing the effect of having a model available at the beginning (BM) of practice, only at the middle of the practice trials (MM), or no model at all (NM), for 7- and 9-year-olds learning a stabilometer task.

all other groups on the retention test. The results of both the retention and transfer test revealed a tendency for more frequent observation of the model to yield better performance on these tests.

Modeling and the Skill Being Learned

The influence of observing a model on skill acquisition appears to depend on the skill being learned. Some experiments have reported that modeling does not lead to better learning of a skill. Others have concluded that modeling certain features of a skill is not beneficial compared with not modeling that feature of the skill. What these reports typically have in common is that the characteristics of the skill being learned may or may not lend themselves to being learned better by observing a model.

For example, the Bachman ladder task has been popular in modeling and skill acquisition research. When the performance of subjects who observed a model is compared with the performance of those who did not, results are consistent

in showing a benefit for those who observed the model. The benefit of modeling has also been reported for nonlaboratory tasks, such as a racquetball forehand (Southard & Higgins, 1987). However, there are other skills that have not shown a modeling benefit. For example, Doody, Bird, and Ross (1985) showed that observing a model perform a barrier knockdown timing task led to no better achievement of the criterion movement time than not observing a model. Also, Burwitz (1975) reported no modeling benefit for learning the pursuit rotor task. These apparently conflicting results suggest that we cannot say very much about the use of demonstration as an instruction strategy. However, there is another way to look at these results that indicates that they are not contradictory and, in fact, are quite revealing about the role of visual demonstration in skill learning. This alternative view of these results relates to the type of skill that was used in these experiments and what was being learned from observing the model. This view is discussed in the following section.

The observer perceives information about coordination. What differentiates skills in terms of how demonstration will influence how well they are learned? An answer to this question is based on what information about the performance of the skill is conveyed by a model. Scully and Newell (1985) proposed that when a person observes a model performing a skill, the visual system picks up information from the model about the coordination pattern of the skill. It is worth noting, based on our discussion in Concept 4.2, that the learner is probably not aware of what information is being selected by the visual system during this process. What is selected during the observation process appears to be information about the invariant features of the coordinated movement pattern that is being performed. These invariant features are characteristics of the skill that are the same from one performance of the skill to another, regardless of the situation in which it is performed. By observing invariant features, the learner can develop the pattern of movement required to perform the skill.

Research evidence to support the proposal that the visual system picks up the invariant features of a movement pattern comes from studies of visual perception, in which questions are addressed about how people recognize patterns they see in their world. An important principle developed from this research is that people rarely use the actual characteristics of the individual components of a pattern to make judgments about the pattern. Rather, they use relative information about how the various components relate to each other. This same principle has been shown to relate to judgments about human movement.

For example, experiments have been reported in which the goal was to determine what information people use to recognize different gait patterns. To determine if relative information about the components of movement are used, a procedure known as a point-light technique has been used. This technique involves placing a light on the joints of the model so that when the model is observed by a person, only the lights are observed and not the whole model. When the model moves,

the various lights move in a certain configuration. Research by Johansson (1973) has shown that people can accurately and quickly recognize different gait patterns under these conditions because different configurations of lights characterize the different gait patterns.

To determine what perceptual cues about gait discriminate between different kinds of gait patterns, Hoenkamp (1978) created a computer simulation of dot patterns of different gaits. He found that movement of the lower part of the body contains enough information to distinguish among major gait categories. And the most critical information for making the judgment of which gait pattern is being observed is the ratio of time duration between the forward and return swings of the lower leg. Thus, the relative time relationship between two components of gait, the forward and return swings of the lower leg, provide the information necessary for discriminating one gait pattern from another rather than any one characteristic of the gait, such as whether one foot is on the ground, or both feet are off the ground, or how the knees are acting, and so on.

What these results indicate is that when a model performing a skill is being observed, the visual system automatically detects information that is relevant for determining how to produce the coordinated movement characterizing the model's performance. In some manner, which continues to be debated, the person is able to use that information and translate it into movement commands for his or her own motor control system. The information that is detected and used may not be specific components of the actual movement but rather some relative information about how different components of the skill act in relation to each other.

Coordination vs. control characteristics of the skill. Because information vital to coordination appears to be the information a learner uses from observing a model, it seems logical to expect that demonstrating a skill would have its greatest benefit for skills where a new pattern of coordination must be learned. Recall from our discussions of

FIGURE 7.1-3 A person performing on the slalom ski simulator.

the concepts in Chapter 3 the distinction between coordination and control aspects of a complex movement. From this distinction it is possible to predict the types of skills that would benefit the most from demonstration.

One hypothesis is that the learner will benefit the most from observing skills that require the acquisition of a new pattern of coordination. Examples of this type of skill learning situation include learning to serve in tennis, learning a new dance step, and, learning to get into a wheelchair from the floor. On the other hand, when the skill involves using a previously learned pattern of coordination and requires the learning of a new control parameter characteristic, demonstrating the skill will be no more beneficial than verbal instructions. Examples of this type of learning situation include things such as learning to throw a ball at different speeds, learning to kick a ball from different distances, and learning to grasp and lift different sizes of cups.

An experiment that provides supports for this hypothesis was reported by Whiting, Bijlard, and den Brinker (1987). Subjects practiced a slalom ski simulator task that is shown in Figure 7.1–3. This simulator consists of two rigid, convex, parallel tracks on which sets a movable platform. The subject stands on the platform with both feet and is required to move the platform right and left as far as possible (55 cm to either side) with rhythmic slalom ski-like movements. Coordination and effort are required to perform this skill because the platform has rigid springs on either side that ensure the platform always returns to the center (normal) position. Thus, the subject had to learn to control moving the platform from side to side as far as possible using smooth ski-like movements, just as one would while actually skiing.

One group of subjects observed a film of a skilled model demonstrating performance of the skill during their practice sessions and the other

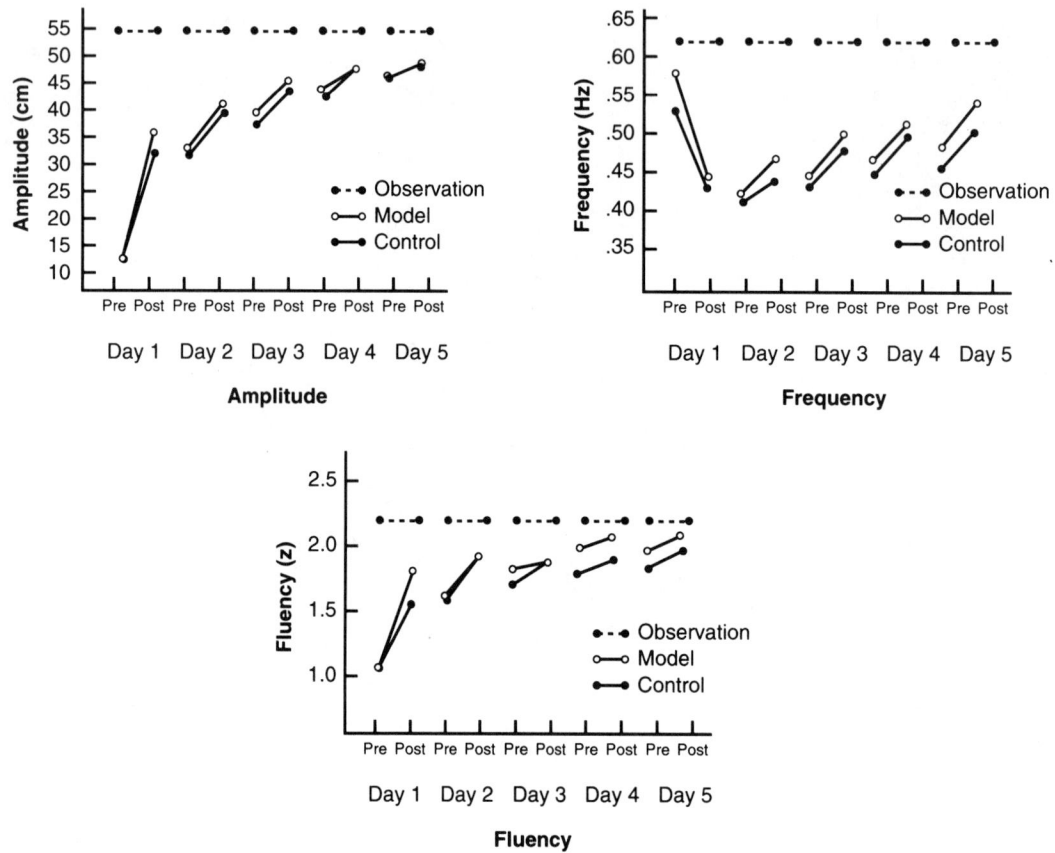

FIGURE 7.1-4   Results of the modeling experiment by Whiting, Bijlard, and den Brinker showing the effects of learning a slalom ski simulator skill with a model available to observe (model) or no model available (control). The model's performance (observation) is also shown in these graphs. The definitions of the measures amplitude, frequency, and fluency are in the text.

group saw no model. There were 5 days of practice with six 1.5-minute trials each day. Before and after the practice trials each day, the subjects were given a 1-minute test trial with no model available. The results of this experiment, which are presented in Figure 7.1–4, showed that the influence of the model on performance depended on which performance characteristic was measured. The observation of a model had no beneficial influence on performance "amplitude" (the average distance the subject moved the platform on a trial). However, for both the "frequency" (how many times the subject moved the platform side to side

on a trial) and the "fluency" (how smooth the movement was during the trial), the group that observed the model performed better than the group that did not. Also, it is interesting to note that for frequency, the benefit of observing a model was almost immediate, whereas for fluency benefit was not seen until the fourth day of practice. The authors concluded that the visual model conveyed task-related information that provided the basis for the subjects to learn to produce the pattern of body and limb movements required to effectively perform the skiing task. This conclusion is consistent with the point that the critical information a learner perceives from a model is information about the relationship of the components of a skill, which is information about the coordination of the skill.

If skills are considered in terms of whether a new pattern of coordination or a new parameter characteristic for an old pattern of coordination must be learned, then the apparent discrepant and confusing results of modeling research described earlier make more sense. That is, in experiments where skills required subjects to acquire a new pattern of movement, such as climbing the Bachman ladder, the typical results are that observing a model leads to better learning than not observing a model. However, in experiments where skills required subjects to acquire a new control parameter characteristic for an already established, or previously learned pattern of movement, such as performing the pursuit rotor task, the typical results are that there is no difference between observing and not observing a model. This suggests then that the effectiveness of demonstration is closely related to the type of skill that is being learned.

Skills benefiting from auditory modeling.
There are skills where visual demonstration is not as effective for learning as other forms of demonstration. For example, if the goal of a skill is to make a response in certain criterion movement time, then it is likely that a visual model will not convey useful information to the learner. This expectation would be consistent with the hypothesis proposed in the previous section where visual demonstration would not be expected to be effective for learning a skill where a new movement pattern was not being learned. When timing of a movement is being learned, the pattern of movement is typically well established. However, it appears that it is still possible to provide a demonstration that will benefit learning of timing. The type of demonstration that works is providing auditory information that demonstrates the achievement of the goal of the movement.

Research evidence that provides support for the benefit of auditory modeling in learning a timing goal is seen in an experiment by Doody, Bird, and Ross (1985). They had subjects practice knocking down a specified sequence of seven 10.5×7-cm barriers in a criterion movement time of 2,100 msec. One group of subjects observed a videotape of a model before each practice trial. The videotape included both the video and audio aspects of the performance. Another group saw only the video portion of the tape and received no auditory modeling information. A third group received only the audio portion of the modeled performance and never saw the task performed by the model. A control group was not given any advance information other than the goal movement time. Results indicated that during 10 acquisition trials with KR and 18 no-KR retention trials, the groups that received audio modeling did better than the visual model only and the control group. In fact, the visual model only group did not do any better than the control group. Thus, although visual modeling was not effective for learning this task, auditory modeling was. The information conveyed by the auditory model was more relevant for learning than was the information conveyed by the visual model.

A final comment. The point of this discussion about characteristics of skills and how they interact with the use of demonstration is that it appears possible that modeling will facilitate skill learning *if* the model conveys information that is critical for successful performance of the skill. This means that when the choice is made to demonstrate a skill, it is important to determine whether only visual information is to be provided or whether other perceptual information about performing the skill will also be provided. Or it may be that the skill may be learned as effectively from verbal instructions as from demonstration.

It will help to relate this point about the relationship between the use of demonstration and the skill being learned to a point made earlier in this text in the discussion of Kahneman's attention model (Concept 4.1). Recall that an important factor influencing a person's attention allocation policy is what Kahneman called "momentary intentions." This means that attention will be directed to those features of a skill that the student has been instructed to give attention. In addition to giving specific instructions, knowledge of results can also be considered as another example of a momentary intention device for directing attention to specific features of a skill. Now we see another example. One of the functions served by a model is to direct the student's attention to how the skill should be performed. If no particular instructions are provided about what to observe, the student will perceive the most salient aspects of what is observed. No conscious attention appears to be needed for this to occur. Whether what is observed will facilitate learning any more than not observing will depend on how observable the important information is.

Why Does Modeling Benefit Learning?

So far in this discussion we have considered various factors that influence the benefit of modeling for skill acquisition. However, we have yet to establish *why* learning is facilitated when all the important factors have been taken into account and are a part of the use of modeling. Although there has not been extensive theoretical development of the modeling effect, two different views of why modeling facilitates skill learning have emerged. One view is based on research related to social behavior learning, whereas the other view is related to how perception of visual information occurs.

The view that predominates current thinking about why the modeling effect occurs is one proposed by Bandura (1977, 1984), which is based on Bandura's work with modeling and social learning. This view of the modeling effect can be called the **cognitive mediation theory,** although it is also referred to as the mediation-contiguity theory and the stimulus-contiguity theory. This theory proposes that when a person observes a model, symbolic coding of what is observed occurs in memory. This means that the movement information that is observed and processed by the information processing system is translated into a symbolic memory code that forms the basis of a representation in memory. This representation is stored in memory and can be accessed by the person when performance of the skill is required. This representation then serves as a guide for the performance of the skill and as a standard for error detection and correction. The key point is that the visual information received by observing the model is transformed into a cognitive memory representation that can then be cognitively rehearsed and organized. To perform the skill, the memory representation must first be accessed and then translated into the appropriate motor control code needed to produce the body and limb movements. Thus, cognitve processing serves as a mediator between the perception of the visual information obtained from observing the model, and the action by establishing a cognitive memory representation that exists between the perception and the action.

According to Bandura, there are four subprocesses that govern learning by observation of a model. The first is the *attention process,* which determines what is observed and what information is extracted from the model act. The second subprocess is the *retention process,* which involves transforming and restructuring what is observed into symbolic codes that are stored in memory as internal models for action. Certain cognitive activities, such as rehearsal, labeling, and organization, benefit the development of this representation. The *behavior reproduction process* is the third subprocess and involves translating the memory representation of the modeled action and turning it into physical action. Successful accomplishment of this process requires the individual to possess the physical capability to perform the modeled action, otherwise, the action cannot be performed. Finally, the *motivation process* involves the incentive or motivation to perform the modeled action. This process, then, focuses on all those factors that influence a person's motivation to perform. Without this process being completed, the action will not be performed.

The second view of why modeling benefits skill acquisition is based on the direct perception view of vision proposed by Gibson (1966, 1979) and extended by Turvey (1977) to the performance of motor skills. This view has been called the **dynamic view of modeling** and has been proposed as an alternative to Bandura's theory to explain modeling effects for skill acquisition by Scully and Newell (1985). The dynamic view questions the need for a symbolic coding or the memory representation step between the observation of the modeled action and the physical performance of that action. The dynamic view argues that the visual system is capable of automatically processing visual information in such a way that it constrains the motor response system to act according to what is detected by vision. The visual system "picks up" salient information from the model that effectively constrains the body and limbs to act in specific ways. As such, information received via the visual system does not need to be transformed into a cognitive code and stored in memory, because the visual information can directly provide the basis for coordinating and controlling the various body parts required to produce the action. Thus the critical need for the observer in the early stage of learning is to be able to observe demonstrations that enable him or her to perceive the important relationships between body parts, which is termed *coordination*. Additional modeling will benefit the learner if information is perceived that allows for parameterizing the coordinated action, which means applying the appropriate values to dynamic features such as the force and kinematic elements required by the action.

There is no conclusive evidence available in the research literature that shows one of these two views of the modeling effect to be the more valid one. At present, both views appear to be viable theoretical approaches to explain why modeling benefits skill acquisition. The cognitive mediation theory has been the more prominent of the two and has received the most attention in motor skills research (see Carroll & Bandura, 1987, for a discussion of some of this research and arguments in

favor of the cognitive mediation theory). However, the dynamic view has only recently been proposed and should provide the basis for research to test its viability as an alternative explanation of the modeling effect.

Summary

Modeling is the demonstration of a skill to those who are learning it. It is a commonly used form of instruction that conveys information about how a skill should be correctly performed. Several factors influence the effectiveness of using a model on skill acquisition. Factors such as the status of the model, the correctness of the demonstration, the frequency of demonstration, and when the model is introduced can all influence the benefit that will be derived from demonstrating a skill. Also, the type of skill demonstrated is critical to the effective use of modeling. Observation of a model appears to provide essential information needed for developing the appropriate pattern of coordination necessary for performing the skill. Because of this, it seems likely that those skills requiring a new pattern of movement will benefit more from observing a demonstration than skills where a new parameter feature is being learned for an already established pattern of movement. Two theoretical viewpoints are prominent concerning why modeling benefits learning motor skills. One view is based on Bandura's social learning research and is called the cognitive mediation theory. This view argues that a memory representation is developed from the observation of a model and that this representation must be accessed prior to performing the skill. The alternative view, called the dynamic view, holds that cognitive mediation is not needed because the visual system can automatically constrain the motor system to act in accordance with what has been modeled. The effective use of modeling requires the instructor to give close attention to several factors that were discussed related to implementing modeling as a beneficial form of instruction for skill learning.

Related Readings

Carroll, W. R., & Bandura, A. (1987). Translating cognition into action: The role of visual guidance in observational learning. *Journal of Motor Behavior, 19,* 385–398.

Gould, D. R., & Roberts, G. C. (1982). Modeling and motor skill acquisition. *Quest, 33,* 214–230.

McCullagh, P., Weiss, M. R., & Ross, D. (1989). Modeling considerations in motor skill acquisition and performance: An integrated approach. In K. B. Pandolf (Ed.), *Exercise and sport science reviews* (Vol. 17, pp. 475–513). Baltimore: Williams & Wilkins.

Scully, D. M., & Newell, K. M. (1985). Observational learning and the acquisition of motor skills: Toward a visual perception perspective. *Journal of Human Movement Studies, 11,* 169–186.

Weiss, M. R., & Klint, K. A. (1987). "Show and Tell" in the gymnasium: An investigation of developmental differences in modeling and verbal rehearsal of motor skills. *Research Quarterly for Exercise and Sport, 58,* 234–241.

CONCEPT 7.2

Decisions about whether to teach and practice a motor skill as a whole or by parts can be made on the basis of the complexity and organization of the skill

Key Terms

task	segmentation	progressive-
organization	simplification	part method
fractionization		

Application

An important instructional decision you must make when you teach any motor skill is related to how the skill should be practiced. Should the skill be practiced in its entirety or should only parts of it be practiced? Practicing a skill as a whole would seem to help people get a better feel for the flow and timing of all the component movements of the skill. However, to practice the skill by parts would reduce the complexity of the skill and it would place an emphasis on performing each part correctly before putting the whole skill together. Why this decision is an important one is related to the efficiency of instruction. It is probably correct to state that practicing the skill as a whole or in parts will be effective in helping the students learn the skill. However, it is equally correct to say that either method will probably not help the student to attain the same level of competency in the same amount of time. One method will generally be more efficient than the other as a means of at-

taining competent performance. A question we will consider in the following discussion is: Will one method always be more efficient than the other, or is the efficiency of the method related to the skill being learned?

Suppose you are teaching a beginning tennis class. You are preparing to teach the serve. Most tennis instruction books break down the serve into six or seven parts that are generally presented as the grip, stance, backswing, ball toss, forward swing, ball contact, and follow-through. The decision you are faced with is whether to have the students practice all of these parts together as a whole or to practice each component or group of components separately.

The tennis serve situation also illustrates a further decision that you may have to make. If you decide to encourage practice of the serve by its parts, then which parts will the students practice separately? Will you attempt to set up drills and practice situations in which each part will be practiced separately? Will you combine some of the components to be practiced together, while requiring practice of other parts separately? On what basis will you combine parts for practice? There are many decisions to be made related to the question "How will I have my students practice the tennis serve?"

Discussion

The issue of whole vs. part practice has been a topic of discussion in the motor learning literature since the early part of this century. Unfortunately, the research generated has led to more confusion than understanding. One of the primary reasons for this confusion is the nature of the research,

which has tended to be very task-oriented in its approach to the problem. That is, the major question investigated was only whether whole or part practice was better for this task or that task. As a result, we have examples of a variety of published research studies that appear almost identical. Similar experimental designs were used to test the same basic hypotheses, which differed only in the tasks that were used. Sometimes the experiments added an experimental group by modifying part practice, such as "progressive part," or combining part and whole practice as "whole-part" or "part-whole." Some examples of the published research will serve to illustrate the point being made here. Barton (1921) compared progressive part, part, and whole practice for learning a maze. Brown (1928) compared whole, part, and whole-part practice for learning a piano score. Knapp and Dixon (1952) compared whole and part-whole practice for learning to juggle. Wickstrom (1958) compared whole and a form of progressive part practice for learning gymnastic skills.

Fortunately, some attempt was finally made at trying to organize and formulate the problem to determine a general rule that could be followed to help in resolving the whole-part practice question. James Naylor and George Briggs (1963) concluded that the issue could be resolved if two features of the task or skill in question were considered. They called these features task organization and task complexity. *Task complexity* refers to how many parts or components are in the task and the information-processing demands of the task. A highly complex task would have many components and require much attention throughout. For example, a dance routine and serving a tennis ball are highly complex tasks. A low complexity task has relatively limited attention demands and relatively few component parts. Tasks such as shooting an arrow and picking up a cup would be low in complexity. **Task organization** refers to how the components of a task are interrelated. A task in which the parts are intimately related to one another would have a high degree of organization, such as shooting a jump shot in basketball. A task in which the parts are rather independent of one another would be low in organization; this is the case in many dance routines.

Each of these features of motor skills or tasks can be regarded as being represented by a continuum of low to high. In this way, the complexity or organization of a task may be thought of as being very high or very low or somewhere in between. The precise designation along the continuum is not as important as the relative position, that is, how the task in question compares to other tasks, higher or lower.

Skill Complexity and Organization

The problem of using whole or part practice for more efficient use of practice time can be resolved largely by assessing the degree of complexity and organization that characterize the skill. If the skill is *low in complexity and high in organization,* practice of the whole skill would be the better choice. Thus, a relatively simple skill, with its component parts highly related, would be most efficiently learned by the whole practice method. Examples of this type of skill would include such skills as buttoning a button, throwing a ball, and putting a golf ball. On the other hand if the skill is *high in complexity and low in organization,* it would be learned most efficiently by the part method. For example, serving a tennis ball; reaching for, grasping, and drinking from a cup; and shifting gears on a car are skills that fit these characteristics.

The way to apply these general rules of motor skill complexity and organization to any skill-learning situation is first to consider the skill that will be practiced. Analyze the skill to identify its component parts and the extent to which those parts are interrelated. Parts of a skill where performance depends on what precedes or follows the part are higher in oganization. Then decide to which end of the complexity continuum and the organization continuum the skill is more related. Your part vs. whole practice decision can then be made on the basis of how the complexity and organization features are related. For example, consider the tennis serve discussed in the application section. We determined that the serve has approximately seven component parts. Thus, the tennis serve would most appropriately lie toward the high end of the complexity continuum. The components of a tennis serve seem to be both independent of and dependent upon one another. Thus, the serve would be somewhere in the middle of the organization continuum. Here, then, is a skill that is relatively high in complexity and moderate in organization. The practice method decision would seem to favor a modified part practice, where certain of the parts would be combined for practice and other parts would be practiced separately.

Practicing Parts of a Skill

There are several different ways that parts of a skill can be taught and practiced. In a review of training methods involving the use of part-task practice, Wightman and Lintern (1985) identified three different part-task training methods. One was called **fractionization,** which involves practicing separate components of the whole skill. A second method was called **segmentation,** which involves separating the skill into parts and then practicing the parts so that after one part is practiced, it is then practiced together with the next part, and so on. This method has also been referred to as the progressive part method. A third method of part practice is called **simplification.** This method involves reducing the difficulty of different parts of the skill. These three methods will be discussed in the following sections.

Practicing separate parts of a skill. After the decision has been made to practice certain parts of the skill separately, such as described in the tennis serve example, you must determine how that practice will take place. What parts will be practiced separately and what parts will be combined for practice? A general rule of thumb here is that those parts of the skill that are highly dependent on each other should be practiced together as a unit, but parts that are relatively independent can be practiced individually. This rule of thumb is consistent with the points made in Concept 7.1 about what is observed when a model demonstrates a skill. Recall that there are critical relationships between parts of a skill that are perceived by the observer and that become the basis for producing an action. What this means, then, is that it is possible to provide instruction or to practice components of a skill that emphasize parts that are too small. As a result, it is important that

components of the skill be taught and practiced as units that include critical relationships among parts of the skill. Some motor learning scholars have referred to these units as "natural units of coordinated activity" and emphasize the need to establish parts of a skill for instruction or practice on this basis (e.g., Holding, 1965; Newell, Carlton, Fisher, & Rutter, 1989).

If we apply this rule of thumb to the tennis serve, most would agree that the grip, stance, backswing, and toss are relatively independent, and could therefore be parts that could be practiced separately. However, because the forward swing, ball contact, and follow-through are strongly interdependent, they should always be practiced as a complete unit. If we consider non-sport skills such as reaching for, grasping, and picking up a cup to drink from it, this rule of thumb can also be applied. Because reaching and grasping research has shown that the act of grasping is closely related to the reaching phase, it would be recommended that these two parts *not* be practiced separately. However, the picking up and drinking parts of this skill are relatively independent of each other and of the reach-grasp parts and could be practiced as separate parts.

The critical part to making the decision about whether certain parts can be practiced separately or together with other parts is dependent on the instructor's knowledge of the skill itself. An analysis of a skill may appear to identify certain components as independent. However, because of the way the skill must be performed, it could be a disadvantage to practice a certain part separate from a part that precedes or follows it. There should be a natural division of the parts. If the learner practices separately certain parts of the skill that actually should be combined with other components as a unit, the end result might be that he or she will require more time to learn the skill than might otherwise be necessary.

The part method seems very helpful for the practice of trouble spots. It is helpful to know if the toss is a source of error in a student's tennis serve, because the toss is a relatively independent part of the serve and can be practiced alone. However, suppose the student is having difficulty with the follow-through. In such a case the practice should include the forward swing, ball contact, *and* follow-through as one unit. The ball toss may or may not be included, depending on whether the instructor wants to keep that variable out of the practice. A ball suspended at the proper height from a string attached to an overhanging pole could suffice to provide a ball for contact. The benefit of this type of practice is that it allows emphasis to be placed on the phase of the skill where problems occur. When the follow-through is not made properly, the cause is usually with the ball contact phase of the serve. Thus, when the three-part unit is practiced, the problem can more easily be corrected.

The progressive-part method. Although practicing individual parts can be helpful to learning a skill, difficulty can be experienced later when the part has to be put back together with the whole skill. One way to overcome this problem is to use the **progressive-part method.** This method takes advantage of the "chunking" strategy that was discussed in Chapter 4, Attention, and Chapter 5, Memory. Rather than practicing all parts separately before putting them together as the whole skill, the parts are organized according to the order in which each part occurs in performing the skill, and then the parts are progressively linked together. This means that after the first part has been practiced as an independent unit, the second part is practiced first as a separate part, and then together with the first part. Each independent part, then, progressively becomes a part of a larger part. As practice develops, the entire skill eventually becomes practiced as a whole skill. Thus, the parts are progressively "chunked" together as larger parts until the whole skill can be performed as one large "chunk."

A simple example of the progressive-part method can be seen in a commonly used approach to teach the breaststroke in swimming. The breaststroke is easily subdivided into two relatively independent parts, the leg kick and the arm

action. Because a difficult aspect of learning the breaststroke is the timing of the coordination of these two parts, it is helpful to reduce the attention demands of the whole skill by practicing each part independently first. This enables the student to allocate attention to just the limb action requirements, because each part can be learned without attending to how the two parts should be coordinated as a unit. After each part is practiced independently, the two can be put together to practice as a whole unit, with attention now directed toward the temporal and spatial coordination demands required for the arm and leg actions.

Practicing musical scores on a piano can also take advantage of the progressive-part method, as reported in an experiment by Ash and Holding (1990). They designed a musical score of 24 quarter notes played singly. These were grouped into three sets of eight notes. The first two segments were easy and the third segment was difficult. Two types of progressive-part method practice were used, which involved doing either the two easy segments and then the difficult segment or the reverse of this progression. The third method was the whole method where all segments were practiced as one unit. The influence of these methods on learning the whole score was assessed with an immediate test of the whole score after completing the practice trials and with a retention test one week later. Results, which were based on errors made, rhythmic accuracy, and rhythmic consistency, showed that the two progressive part methods were better than the whole method and that easy-to-difficult progression tended to be better for learning the score than the difficult-to-easy progression.

The distinct advantage of the progressive-part method is that it takes advantage of the benefits offered by both part and whole methods of practice. That is, the part method offers the advantage of restricting the attention demands on the individual so that specific aspects of a part of a skill can be practiced without considering how that part should be coordinated with other parts. The whole method, on the other hand, has the advantage of requiring important spatial and temporal coordination of the parts to be practiced together. In the progressive-part method, both of these qualities are combined so that attention demands of performing the skill are kept under control; the parts are progressively put together so that the important spatial and temporal coordination requirements of performing the parts as a whole can be practiced.

Reducing the difficulty of the skill. Another way to provide instruction and practice for a complex skill is to make the parts less difficult for people to perform. For example, when learning to juggle, it is possible to begin by practicing with objects that are easier to see and to catch. Scarves or bean bags are easier to juggle than are balls or clubs. Thus, an interesting way to encourage learning of juggling would be to reduce the difficulty of what must be juggled. Because the principles of juggling still must be used while learning to juggle the easier objects, it could be argued that beginning by using easier objects will enable the learner to learn juggling principles and then be able to easily transfer them to juggling with more difficult objects.

An example of an experiment that supports using easier objects first to learn to juggle was reported by Hautala (1988). He had 10- to 12-year-old boys and girls who had no previous juggling experience organized into four instructional groups. The goal for all groups was to learn to juggle three balls. One group began practicing with three "juggling balls" of three different colors. The second group began by using cube-shaped beanbags. The third group received initial instruction and practice using scarves of different colors, then switched to beanbags, and then to the juggling balls. The fourth group began with weighted scarves and then switched to the balls. All groups practiced 5 minutes per day for 14 days and then were tested for 1 minute with the juggling balls. The results, based on a catches-to-misses "juggling score" ratio, showed that the group who practiced all 14 sessions with the bean-

bags did better on the test with the balls than all the other groups. In fact, that group's juggling score was over 50% higher on the juggling test with balls than the group that practiced with the balls and the group that practiced with scarves, then beanbags, and then balls. And the beanbag practice group's test score was over 100% higher than the group that practiced with the weighted scarves and then beanbags.

These results show that certain simplification procedures work better than others. For example, practicing first with scarves was easier than with beanbags but test performance while juggling balls showed that practice with the beanbags was better than practice with the scarves. Similar effects have been shown for reducing the speed of pursuit rotor for initial practice. Leonard, Karnes, Oxendine, and Hesson (1970) showed that 45 trials of practice on the pursuit rotor at 30 rpm led to poorer performance on a test at 45 rpm than did practice at 40 rpm. Thus, when determining how to simplify a complex skill for initial practice, it is important not to think that the more simple, the better. Knowledge of the skill itself and what is required for successful performance becomes critical in the decision of how to simplify parts of the skill for practice.

Another method of simplifying parts of a skill can be seen in an experiment involving rehabilitation of gait disorders by Staum (1983). She provided musical accompaniment during the rehabilitation of a variety of patients with gait disorders to help patients control their steps as they practiced walking. One condition involved playing marches that maintained consistent tempo and had been recorded on a cassette recorder during rehabilitation sessions. Another condition involved playing rhythmic pulses produced by tapping two tone blocks together. These pulses were performed at the same tempi as the marches. The 25 children and adult subjects wore headphones to hear the music or rhythmic pulses, and were directed to step either on the first beat, on the first and third beat, or on all four beats, depending on individual ability. The results showed that after three weeks of rehabilitation, rhythmic and/or consistent walking improvement was shown for all subjects in whom arrhythmia was prevalent.

Simplifying parts of a skill can be a very useful means of helping people learn a complex motor skill. The simplification can be done by reducing the demands of the skill and thereby making the task less difficult, as in the case of initially using beanbags to practice learning to juggle balls. And skills can be simplified by providing external aids that provide specific cues for how to perform the skill, as in the case of providing a rhythmic beat cue for rehabilitating gait disorders. While there are other means to accomplish simplification, these can serve to illustrate the usefulness of this instruction and practice technique.

An Attention Approach to Part Practice

Sometimes it is not advisable or practical to physically separate the parts of a skill for practice. This, however, does not mean that parts of the whole skill cannot be practiced. It is possible to practice the whole skill while directing the person's attention to specific parts of the skill while he or she performs the skill. This approach provides the advantage of part practice, where emphasis on specific parts of the skill facilitates improvement of these parts, while at the same time provides the advantage of whole practice, in which the emphasis is on how the parts of the skill relate to each other to produce skilled performance. The key to this approach is at the instructional level. The instructor directs the learner's attention to a key part of the skill by providing specific instructions that will require attention to be directed to a particular component of the skill.

An example of a research example that used this attention-directing strategy for part practice was presented by Gopher, Weil, and Siegel (1989). Subjects learned a complex computer game, known as the Space Fortress Game, that requires an individual to master perceptual, cognitive, and motor skills as well as to acquire specific knowledge of the rules and game strategy. This game, developed for a large research project in the Cognitive Psychophysiology Laboratory at the University of Illinois, requires a person to shoot missiles at and destroy a space fortress. The missiles are fired from a movable spaceship. The player controls spaceship movement and firing by a joystick and trigger. To destroy the fortress, the player must overcome several obstacles, which include things such as the fortress rotating to face the spaceship to defend itself, the fortress being protected by mines that emerge on the screen periodically and can destroy the spaceship if it runs into one, and so on. (See Mané & Donchin, 1989, for a complete description of this computer game.)

In the experiment by Gopher, Weil, and Siegel, three groups of subjects were given instructions during the first six practice sessions that emphasized a strategy requiring them to direct attention to one specific component of the skill. One group was given instructions that emphasized attention on controlling the spaceship. A second group was given instructions that emphasized attention on handling the mines around the fortress. The third group was given spaceship control instructions for the first three practice sessions and then mine handling instructions for the next three sessions. All groups were then allowed to perform for three more sessions without any specific instructions provided. When these three groups were compared against a control group that did not have any strategic instructions provided, it was apparent that the attention directing instructions were effective. As you can see in Figure 7.2–1, the control group improved with practice but not to the extent that the three instruction groups did. And the group that received the two different strategies outperformed those that received only one.

These results provide empirical evidence that attention-directing instructions can serve to establish a part-practice type of environment while allowing the person to practice the whole skill. And these instructions are more effective than having the person practice the skill without providing such strategies. This type of part practice has not been addressed with any degree of intensity in the motor learning or teaching methods literature and clearly deserves more consideration and investigation.

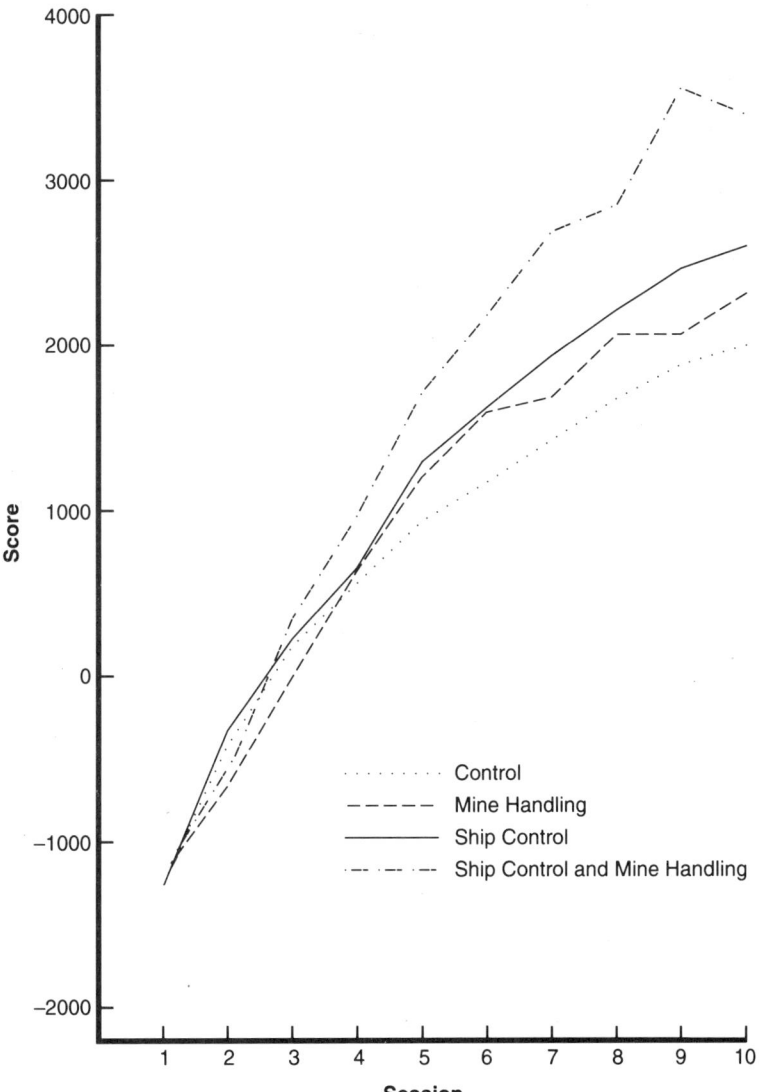

FIGURE 7.2-1   Results of the experiment by Gopher, Weil, and Siegel showing the change in performance on the computer game Space Fortress for attention-directing instructions related to specific parts of the skill.

Summary

One of the many decisions that an instructor of motor skills must make is whether the skill being taught should be practiced as a whole or in parts. This decision should be made according to the complexity and organization of the skill. Whole practice is advisable when the skill tends toward the low complexity and high organization ends of the high-low skill or task complexity and organization continua. Part practice is advisable when the skill is more closely related to the opposite ends of the two continua, that is, high in complexity and low in organization. If the decision is made to follow a part practice method, there are at least three different ways to provide part instruction and practice. One involves practicing the parts of the skill separately. If this method is used, it is important that components of a skill significantly associated or interdependent should be practiced together as a "natural unit." Parts of the skill that are relatively independent can be practiced separately. Another, more preferred part method is the progressive-part method, which takes advantage of the beneficial qualities of both the part and the whole methods and is an effective practice method for learning complex skills. The third part method involves simplifying parts of the skill for practice. If physically separating a skill into parts for practice is not practical, it is possible to encourage part practice by providing instructions that will direct the learner's attention to a specific component of the skill.

Related Readings

Holding, D. H. (1987). Concepts of training. In G. Salvendy (Ed.). *Handbook of human factors.* New York: Wiley.

Knapp, C. G., & Dixon, W. R. (1952). Learning to juggle: A study of whole and part methods. *Research Quarterly, 23,* 389–401.

Naylor, J., & Briggs, G. (1963). Effects of task complexity and task organization on the relative efficiency of part and whole training methods. *Journal of Experimental Psychology, 65,* 217–244.

Newell, K. M., Carlton, M. J., Fisher, A. T., & Rutter, B. G. (1989). Whole-part training strategies for learning the response dynamics of microprocessor driven simulators. *Acta Psychologica, 71,* 197–216.

Singer, R. N., & Dick, W. (1979). *Teaching physical education: A systems approach* (2nd ed.). Boston: Houghton-Mifflin. (Read chapters 2 and 6.)

Wightman, D. C. & Lintern, G. (1985). Part-task training strategies for tracking and manual control. *Human Factors, 27,* 267–283.

CONCEPT 7.3

Augmented feedback can improve, hinder, or have no effect on motor skill learning

Key Terms

augmented feedback

knowledge of results

knowledge of performance

augmented sensory feedback

Application

When you are setting out to learn a new activity, such as golf, tennis, or a new style of dance, how do you generally feel after the first few attempts? Probably you feel somewhat frustrated because you are not very successful. You have so many questions that you need to have answered before beginning the next few attempts. Remember, you are in the early phase of the cognitive stage of learning. You should have many questions about what you are doing right and what you are doing wrong.

One of the important roles played by a teacher of motor skills involves providing feedback to a student. What an instructor tells a novice golfer hitting practice balls about each hit or series of hits is very important to the development of that person's skill in playing golf. Such information can

be valuable to the learner in a number of ways. First, it can provide specific information about what he or she has been doing incorrectly, which becomes a basis for trying to make some adjustments on the next practice attempt. Second, the information provided can be a valuable form of reinforcement. This is especially noticeable when the learner has done something correctly or nearly correctly. When the instructor informs a novice about correct performance, it becomes a reinforcement. As a result, the learner will try to duplicate that performance on the next attempt. Finally, what the instructor tells the novice golfer can be valuable as a form of motivation. Learners need to know that they are improving, yet many times they are unable to detect improvement by watching their own performance. In this case the instructor becomes a vital source of motivation to help learners continue practicing.

In the following discussion, we will consider the information the instructor gives to the learner following a practice attempt. Providing this information, which we are referring to as augmented feedback, will thus appear as one of the most important functions that an instructor of motor skills performs for the learner.

Discussion

When a person performs a motor skill, there are several sources from which information can be obtained about the outcome of the response or about what caused the outcome. One of these sources of information, discussed in Chapter 3, is the person's own sensory feedback system. This information source comes into play, for example, when the person sees where the golf ball he or she just

hit has landed or feels what the swing was like that produced that outcome. The second source of information is when another person observes the skill and the observer provides information about the outcome of the response or its cause. For beginning learners of a motor skill, the observer is often the instructor. These two sources of information, one internal and one external to the person performing the skill, are important for skill learning to occur.

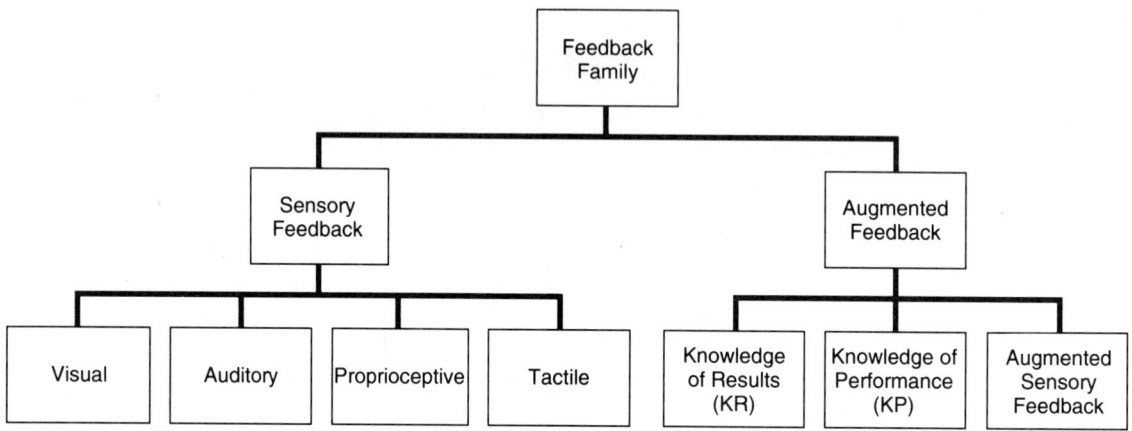

FIGURE 7.3-1   Diagram illustrating the different types of feedback in the feedback family that are related to learning and performing motor skills.

The Feedback Family

In the study of motor learning and human performance, a great deal of effort has been directed toward the study of feedback. One of the unfortunate results of this long history of study has been the creation of a variety of terms related to feedback that, at times, can cause misunderstanding about how one term relates to or differs from another. The term *feedback* should be viewed as a general term that refers to information that comes from a source and goes to a mechanism that uses the information to make error corrections. As you saw in Concept 3.1, when feedback is related to controlling movement, it is considered to be information that occurs as a result of movement.

Several types of feedback have been identified. Figure 7.3–1 demonstrates the relationship among the various types in a family of feedback. As you can see, the two principle forms of feedback are sensory and augmented feedback. When feedback comes from the person's own sensory/perceptual system, we refer to this type of feedback as sensory feedback, which was the basis for the discussion in Concept 3.2. In our present discussion, the focus shifts to the side of the family where the feedback comes from external sources and is augmented. In motor learning, augmented feedback refers to information that is "enhanced" in some way and is "fed back" to the individual during and/or after a movement.

Defining Augmented Feedback

For this textbook, the term **augmented feedback** is used to refer to any form of externally presented feedback that enhances sensory feedback and is provided to an individual or group of individuals. For example, when a golf student is told that his or her shot went too far to the right, the teacher enhances the student's visual feedback by verbally telling the student the outcome of the shot. In some situations, this additional information augments sensory feedback that the person can readily detect on his or her own. The golf example just given describes such a case. Or it can provide information that the person may not be able to detect using his or her sensory system. An example of this would occur in the golf example if the student was hitting the ball over a hill and could not see where it went. The verbal information about where the ball landed would be augmented sensory feedback by providing information that is not detectable otherwise. Augmenting sensory feedback can also be done non-verbally. For example, if a physical therapist is helping an amputee learn to use an artificial limb, the proprioceptive feedback needed by the patient to control this limb may not be apparent to the patient. To augment the proprioceptive information, the therapist may use computer monitors that show EMG traces to the patient so that he or she can know when the appropriate muscles are functioning.

It is important to note that the term augmented feedback is being used in this book to include several different types of augmented feedback commonly used in the motor learning research literature. These can be seen in Figure 7.3–1, where each has been referred to by different terms. It is important to note that when a specific type of augmented feedback is being discussed, the term appropriate to that type of feedback will be used.

One type of augmented feedback is **knowledge of results,** which is commonly referred to as *KR.* KR is externally presented information about the *outcome* of a movement. An example of KR occurs when a person shoots an arrow at a target and a person or machine indicates the score of that shot. Also, the information may be error related, such as telling the archer, "The shot was in the blue at 9 o'clock." The second type of augmented feedback is **knowledge of performance,** which is known as *KP.* KP is information about the *movement characteristics* that led to the outcome of a movement. It is important to note that KP can be presented in several different forms. The most common means of providing KP is *verbally,* such as in the archery situation just described where the archer could be told that he or she pulled the bow to the left at the release of the arrow. KP can also be provided by showing the person a *videotape* of his or her performance. And, KP can be presented *graphically,* such as a golfer being shown the movement kinematics of his or her golf swing. The third type is **augmented sensory feedback** in which an external device is used to enhance sensory feedback. In the archery example, sensory feedback would be augmented if a sound device indicated to the archer when the arrow was correctly aimed or when the bow was being held in a steady position. Typically, KR and KP are presented after a response is made (i.e., terminally) while augmented sensory feedback is provided while the movement is in progress (i.e., concurrently). However, it is possible to give KP concurrently and augmented sensory feedback terminally.

There seems little doubt that augmented feedback plays a critical role in the process of learning motor skills. As a learning variable that the instructor can directly manipulate, it becomes especially important to understand augmented feedback in terms of how and why it influences skill learning. The first point to understand is that it plays several different roles or functions in the skill-learning process. Sometimes these roles are independent of one another, whereas in other situations its functions overlap. Functionally, then, augmented feedback provides information about performance that serves to guide error correction and to motivate the individual to continue striving to achieve the goal of the skill or his or her own performance goal.

The Roles of Augmented Feedback in Skill Acquisition

The research literature indicates that augmented feedback plays two roles in the learning process. One role is to provide the learner with performance information about the success of the movement in progress or just completed and/or what must be done on a succeeding performance attempt. This information may be very general and indicate that the movement was or was not successful. Or this information may be quite specific and indicate precisely what movement errors were made or what movement corrections need to be made. In this form, augmented feedback is high in prescriptive information value and enables the learner to plan an upcoming performance attempt.

The second role played by augmented feedback is to motivate the learner to continue striving toward a goal. Although the feedback is also informational, it is a different type of information and is used in a different way than for planning an upcoming response. The feedback indicates how well the learner is doing in comparison to a performance goal that the person has established. As such, the feedback is used to engage in evaluation decisions related to continuing to strive toward that goal, or to stop and either change goals or stop performing the activity.

The motivation role of augmented feedback is not to be taken lightly. The focus of this chapter, however, is on augmented feedback as a source of information to help the learner acquire a skill by providing information that can be used to evaluate an ongoing or just completed movement or plan an upcoming response. (See Little & McCullagh, 1989; Locke, Cartledge, & Koeppel, 1968, and Adams, 1978, 1987, for more complete discussions of the motivational role of augmented feedback in skill performance.)

How Essential is Augmented Feedback for Skill Acquisition?

When a learner performs a skill during practice, is it essential that augmented external information be provided to that person to enable him or her to successfully learn the skill? A review of the augmented feedback literature indicates that the only appropriate answer to this question depends on the skill being performed. While this view is not consistent with traditional theories of motor learning (e.g., Adams, 1971; Schmidt, 1975), it is becoming increasingly apparent from the research literature that the need for augmented feedback depends on the skill being learned. In this section, four different types of effects of augmented feedback will be discussed along with a consideration of the skill characteristics that appear to be related to each of these effects.

Augmented feedback can be essential for skill acquisition.   For certain skills, it appears that the information needed to determine the appropriateness of a movement cannot adequately be detected or used by a learner and therefore must be augmented in some way. For example, if a person is learning to throw a ball at a target as accurately as possible but cannot see the target, important information that is needed to determine the appropriateness of a throw is not directly available to that person. Thus, some form of augmented feedback would be necessary for learning

this skill. Or if a person is learning to throw a ball at a certain rate of speed, and due to lack of experience was not able to determine the rate of speed of a throw, feedback would need to be augmented. For skills or skill learning situations such as these, augmented feedback appears to be critical for skill acquisition to occur.

Examples of research evidence supporting the need for augmented feedback in these situations can be seen throughout the motor learning literature. Consider first the situation where the learner does not have available critical sensory feedback information. If movements cannot be seen, such as while trying to draw a line of a certain length (e.g., Trowbridge & Cason, 1932), or while trying to move a lever to a criterion location (e.g., Bilodeau, Bilodeau, & Schumsky, 1959), then augmented feedback in the form of KR has been shown to be essential for learning. The results of the experiment by Bilodeau, Bilodeau, and Schumsky (1959) are presented in Figure 7.3–2 to illustrate this effect. In this experiment, KR was or was not provided on all the practice trials, or it was withdrawn after 2 or 6 trials. As you can see from the results, practice performance improved as a function of the number of trials for which KR was provided.

In the two research examples just cited, KR was verbal information about the accuracy of the response. KR served to augment visual feedback that was not available to the subjects. KR thereby provided a means for making the response outcome versus task goal comparison needed to plan and perform succeeding responses during practice. If KR were not available in these situations, such a comparison would be difficult if not impossible, and learning would not occur.

A different type of situation occurs when all the sensory feedback systems are available to the learner, but the learner is not capable of using the information to determine the adequacy of a response. Such a situation is typically characteristic of beginning learners. An example of this in the research literature was reported by Newell (1974). Subjects learned to make a 24 cm lever movement in 150 msec. Although they could see their arms,

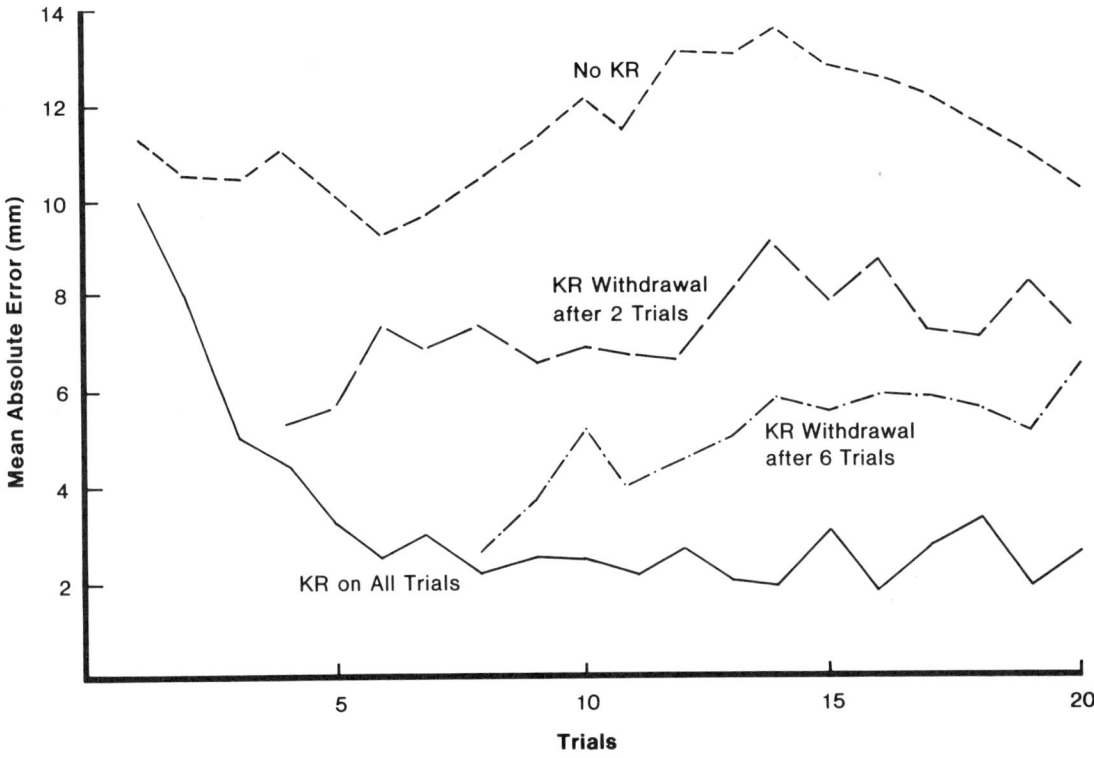

FIGURE 7.3-2   Results of the experiment by Bilodeau, Bilodeau, and Schumsky showing the effect of KR on the learning of a simple positioning task.

the lever, and the target, the subjects did not have a referent for comparing the actual speed of their own movement response with the 150 msec goal. The results of this experiment, presented in Figure 7.3–3, show that subjects who received KR about the accuracy of their responses for 52 or 75 trials learned the skill very well, whereas those who received KR for only 2 trials showed no improvement and actually performed worse with practice. Thus, augmented feedback was necessary to help the learner establish a referent for 150 msec that could be used to compare the appropriateness of any practice attempt. After that referent was established, which occurred between 32 and 52 trials of practice with KR, the subjects no longer needed KR and effectively used the available sensory information to make the comparison between the outcome of the movement and the goal of the task. Thus, by providing sufficient amount of practice

with KR when KR was needed to learn the skill enabled subjects to develop their own error detection and correction capabilities so that they no longer needed augmented feedback to perform the skill correctly.

Augmented feedback may not be needed for skill acquisition.   Some motor skills inherently provide sufficient sensory feedback so that augmenting feedback for the learner is not necessary. For such skills, the learner can obtain the information needed to determine the appropriateness of his or her movement and compare the outcome and/or movements of the just-performed response with the goal of the task. Augmented feedback for these skills becomes information that is redundant with information available in the environment, and is therefore not needed to learn the skill.

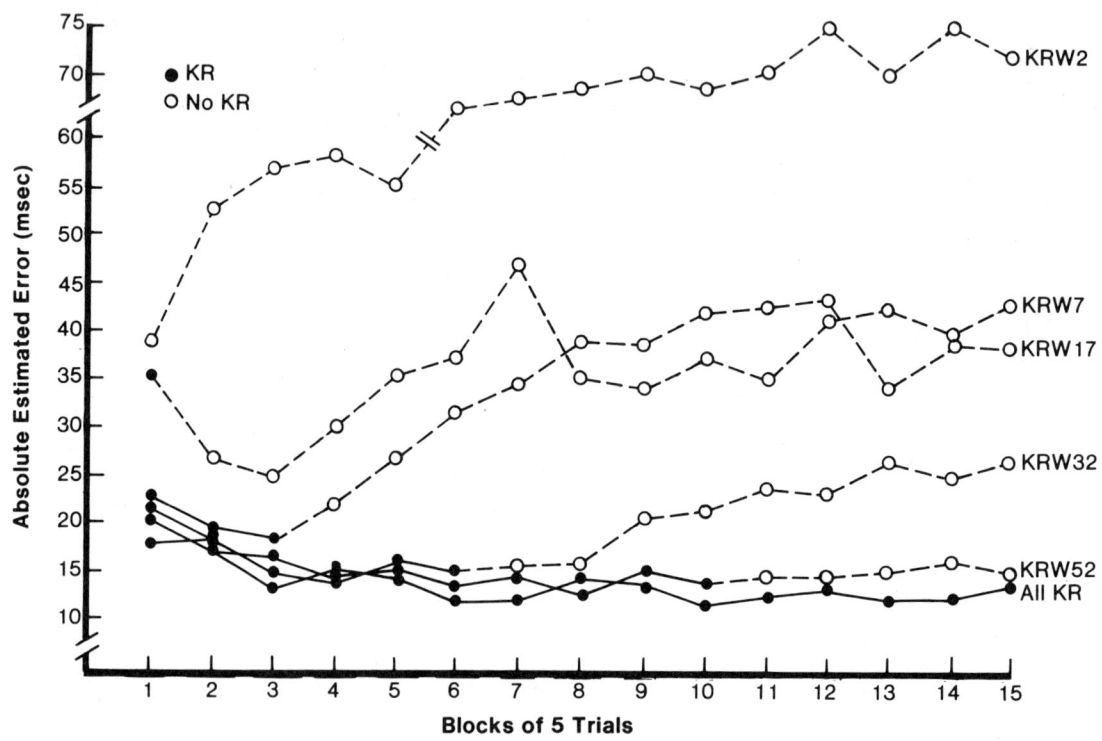

FIGURE 7.3-3　Results of the experiment by Newell showing the performance curves for groups who had KR withdrawn at various points of the 75 trials to learn to make a linear movement in 150 msec. The open circles indicate blocks of trials during which no KR was given; the closed circles show blocks of trials with KR. The numbers following the KRW indicate the trial on which KR was withdrawn.

A research example of augmented feedback redundancy was reported recently for KR by Magill, Chamberlin, and Hall (1991). Subjects learned a coincidence-anticipation skill that simulated striking a moving object, such as batting a pitched baseball or hitting a moving tennis ball. Ball movement was simulated as a series of sequentially lighting LEDs on a 281 cm long trackway. The subject faced the trackway at eye level with the LEDs lighting from the subject's left to right. Directly in front of the subject's eyes was the target LED. There was a small wooden barrier directly under the target that the subject was to knock down with a hand-held bat coincident with the lighting of the target. KR was given as the number of msec the barrier was knocked down

before or after the target lighted. Four experiments were completed in which subjects made the striking response to either one or three trackway speeds during the practice sessions. Results of these experiments indicated that all subjects significantly improved their anticipation performance during practice, regardless of the feedback condition. More importantly, receiving KR during the practice trials did not lead to better learning than practice without KR, which was determined by evaluating retention performance of the practiced speeds one day later and transfer performance for new trackway speeds.

Motor skills that do not need augmented feedback during practice have at least one important identifiable characteristic. There is some detectable external referent in the environment that a learner can use to determine the correctness of a movement response either while the response is in progress, such as in a tracking task, or at the completion of the response, as in the anticipation timing task. For the anticipation timing task, the target and other LEDs were the external referents. The learner could see when the barrier was contacted in comparison to when the target lighted, which enabled him or her to see the relationship between his or her own movements and the goal of those movements. It is important to note here that the learner may *not* consciously be aware of this relationship. The sensory system and the motor control system appear to operate in these situations in a way that does not demand the person's awareness of the environmental characteristics. Thus, to enhance these characteristics by providing augmented feedback does not influence learning the skill.

An interesting result from investigating the use of verbal feedback by physical education teachers is relevant here. In such studies, the consistent result has been low correlations for the relationship between teacher feedback and student achievement (e.g., Eghan, 1988; Pieron, 1982; Silverman, Tyson, & Krampitz, 1991; Silverman, Tyson, & Morford, 1988). This finding suggests that the amount and quality of teacher feedback is not the critical variable that it has been thought to be for improving the skill of beginners in sport skills class settings. Whether this phenomenon is limited to teaching in class settings, to the specific skills being taught, or to other instructional variables, such as amount of practice or teacher demonstration, awaits further research. However, these results do question the traditional view that motor skills cannot be learned without augmented feedback (see Magill, 1991, for a further discussion of this issue).

Augmented feedback can be a hindrance to skill acquisition. Augmenting feedback for certain motor skills during practice appears to make the learner dependent on the availability of that feedback. As a result, performance deteriorates when the augmented information is removed. In fact, in some situations, not only does performance deteriorate when augmented feedback is withdrawn, the transfer performance is no better than for subjects who practiced without augmented feedback. This effect seems to be prevalent in situations where augmented sensory feedback is presented while the person is carrying out the movement.

For example, Annett (1959) had subjects learn to produce a specified amount of force either by depressing a movable plunger or pressing against a fixed metal bar. Augmented feedback was provided concurrently in different ways. One type of feedback showed the force produced graphically on an oscilloscope. Another type of feedback involved illuminating a neon indicator when the force being exerted was within a certain range of the criterion force. Augmented feedback was also provided terminally, which means it was given after the person completed the movement. This type of augmented feedback was given either verbally as the amount of force exerted or by allowing the subject to see the oscilloscope reading after the subject indicated that he had made his response. In both the concurrent and terminal augmented feedback conditions, performance deteriorated when transfer performance required subjects to produce the force without augmented feedback. However, transfer performance for the group trained with concurrent augmented feedback deteriorated immediately and the amount error became very large. The group that had been trained with terminal augmented feedback showed a gradual decrement in performance when augmented feedback was no longer available.

The most prevalent hypothesis proposed to explain the deterioration effect in the absence of augmented feedback is that when sensory feedback intrinsic to the task itself is minimal or difficult to interpret, learners will substitute concurrently provided augmented feedback for task intrinsic feedback and therefore become dependent on the augmented feedback to perform the skill. They do not learn the sensory feedback characteristics associated with performing the skill because they have learned to perform the skill on the basis of the augmented feedback (e.g., Adams, 1964; Lintern, Roscoe, & Sivier, 1990).

Cases of performance deterioration during transfer have also been found in studies investigating the question of the optimal frequency for providing terminal KR. For example, Winstein and Schmidt (1990) had subjects practice for two days (almost 200 trials) a single limb lever movement to produce a complex wave-form pattern. They reported results indicating that subjects who received KR after every practice trial performed the practiced skill without KR at a level that was essentially the same as they had performed the skill during the first 24 trials of practice. The researchers accounted for these results by proposing that subjects became dependent on KR when it was available after every trial. This dependence led subjects to need the KR information to successfully perform the skill. When KR was not available during the transfer trials, performance deteriorated.

Proteau and his colleagues (Proteau, Marteniuk, Girouard, & Dugas, 1987; Proteau & Cournoyer, 1990) have taken this notion of dependence one step further and have argued that the augmented feedback becomes a part of the memory representation that develops during practice. Thus, when subjects are required to perform the skill in a situation where no augmented feedback is provided, the memory representation is not adequate for performing the skill successfully.

Augmented feedback can enhance skill acquisition. There are some motor skills that can be learned without augmented feedback provided during practice but that will be learned more quickly or at a higher level if augmented feedback

is provided during practice. In this case, the augmented feedback is neither essential nor redundant but *enhances* learning. An example of a skill that is influenced in this way can be seen in an experiment reported by Stelmach (1970). Subjects learned a 3-segment arm movement that required them to move their hand 28 cm forward from a response key to hit a piece of rubber tubing, then back to the response key near the start position, and finally forward again to hit a response key. The goal of the movement was to do it as quickly as possible. Augmented feedback was KR, which was given as the movement time for the entire 3-segment movement. Results, presented in Figure 7.3–4, showed that a group that did not receive KR improved during the practice trials, which indicated learning was occurring. However, the group that received KR improved more rapidly and reached a higher level of performance than the group that did not get KR. Similar results were reported by Newell, Quinn, Sparrow, and Walter (1983) for a task having the same move-as-fast-as-you-can goal. Without KR, subjects showed improvement only to a certain level and then showed no further improvement, whereas subjects who received KR continued to show improvement during practice.

An interesting experiment using a sport skill that demonstrated the enhancement benefit of augmented feedback was reported by Wallace and Hagman (1979). Beginners in basketball learned to make a one-hand set-shot with the nondominant hand while they were 3.03 m from the basket and 45 degrees to the left side of the basket. Two types of augmented feedback were used in this experiment. One group of subjects received KP by being told performance error information about their stance and limb movement during each shot. Another group did not receive KP but were given verbal encouragement after each shot, such as "Good shot," "You can do it," "Try harder next time," and so on. The results are presented in

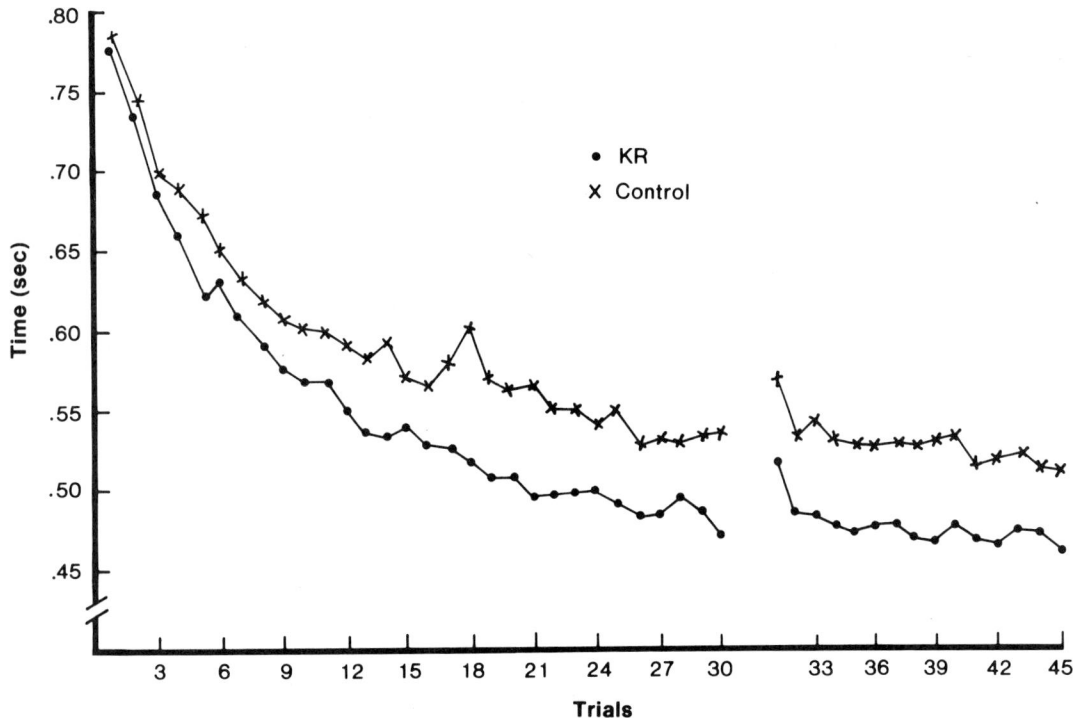

FIGURE 7.3-4 Results of the experiment by Stelmach showing mean performance times for groups with or without KR as a function of practice.

Figure 7.3–5. After 25 practice attempts, both groups were performing similarly. However, beyond that point the verbal encouragement group showed no further improvement while the group receiving KP continued to improve. This trend continued for the 25 retention trials on which no KP or verbal encouragement was given.

To perform the type of task used in the experiments just described, subjects seemed to be able to determine to a limited degree the amount of success they had in achieving the task goal on a given trial, especially during the early practice trials. As a result, they could improve their performance without KR about the movement times, in the Stelmach (1970) and Newell et al (1983) experiments, and without KP about shooting stance and limb movements in the Wallace and Hagler (1979) experiment. However, at a particular point in practice, this improvement stopped. It seems that KR and KP added information to the available sensory feedback to enable subjects to improve beyond that point. In some way, which is not well understood, the augmented feedback increased learners' capability to compare present and past movements in such a way that they could more effectively plan an upcoming movement and therefore continue to improve beyond what they could have without augmented feedback.

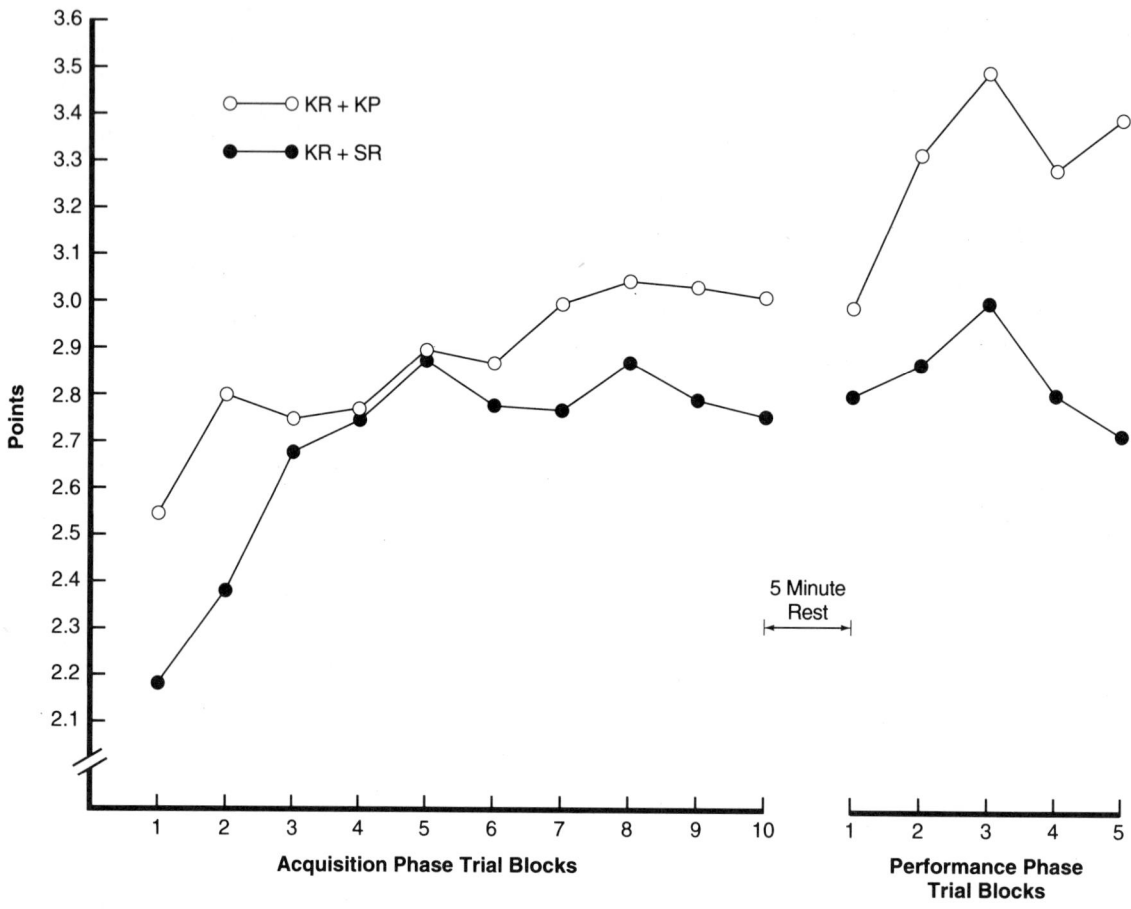

FIGURE 7.3-5   Results of the experiment by Wallace and Hagler showing the benefit of KR + KP for learning a basketball shooting skill.

Summary

Conclusions about the need for augmented feedback must be considered incorrect when those conclusions state that motor skill learning cannot occur without some form of augmented feedback (e.g., Adams, 1971; Bilodeau, 1969; Schmidt, 1975). Research evidence has been considered in this section that demonstrated four different effects of the presence of augmented feedback during motor skill training. This evidence has shown that augmented feedback can be essential, not essential, detrimental, and an enhancement for learning skills. The effect varies according to the skill being learned. What remains to be determined from future research are the skill characteristics and/or skill learning conditions that relate specifically to each of these four effects. Some hypotheses concerning these characteristics and conditions have been proposed. It appears that when the performance of the skill provides the performer with sensory feedback that can effectively be interpreted by the performer so that the performance can be evaluated, augmented feedback is not necessary. Sensory feedback can be from the environmental characteristics of the performance context or from the movements involved in the skill itself. However, when this type of interpretable sensory feedback is not available, some form of augmented feedback is beneficial. The exact type that is needed and how or when it should be provided appears to be related to the skill being performed. Situations exist in which the learner can become dependent on augmented feedback will be hindered by augmented feedback.

Related Readings

Adams, J. A. (1987). Historical review and appraisal of research on the learning, retention, and transfer of human motor skills. *Psychological Bulletin, 101,* 41–74. (Read the sections on KR: pp. 43–44, 48–49, 61–62.)

Bilodeau, I. M. (1966). Information feedback. In E. A. Bilodeau (Ed.), *Acquisition of Skill* (pp. 255–296). New York: Academic Press.

Holding, D. H. (1965). *Principles of training.* Oxford: Pergamon. (Read chapter 2.)

Salmoni, A. W., Schmidt, R. A., & Walter, C. B. (1984). Knowledge of results and motor learning: A review and critical reappraisal. *Psychological Bulletin, 95,* 355–386.

CONCEPT 7.4

Augmented feedback can be provided in a variety
of ways and in different amounts of frequencies

Key Terms

qualitative augmented feedback

quantitative augmented feedback

absolute frequency

relative frequency

fading technique

guidance hypothesis

summary KR

Application

Suppose that you are learning the golf swing and it is the second or third day of your lessons. After you have made a few practice swings, your instructor says, "You are not hitting the ball correctly." What would be your reaction? And how much help would that comment be in improving your swing? Let us carry this example one step further. This time your instructor tells you, "You are not keeping your head down long enough, your grip is too tight, your right hand is under the club too much, your backswing is too fast, you are not shifting your weight properly, and your follow through is too short." What would be your reaction this time? Obviously both examples are extremes, but they lead to a discussion of how much information should be presented to the learner as augmented feedback. At one end of the continuum, you have the problem of not enough information, while at the other end you have an equally perplexing problem of too much information. Are these "problems" real for the learner in terms of acquiring a skill? How should the characteristics as well as the amount of information change as performance becomes more skilled?

Suppose your instructor provides just the right amount of information each time, but he or she gives augmented feedback after *every* swing you make. Is this an optimal learning situation? Could it be that too much information is provided if augmented feedback is given too frequently? Suppose that it is. How often, then, should augmented feedback be given to lead to the best possible learning of the skill?

Consider also that in the situations described so far, the augmented feedback has been verbal. Are there other ways the instructor could provide feedback that would be more beneficial for you? What about other methods of giving augmented feedback, such as videotape or computer-generated graphic representations of a performance? How effective are these methods?

Each of the questions raised in this section concerns a basic issue that confronts providers of motor skill instruction, which is the need to provide adequate information to benefit the learner. As these questions are addressed in the following discussion, compare the answers provided with your own experiences and intuitive responses. The answers not only help us better understand motor skill learning processes but also provide useful practical information for the instructor.

Discussion

The discussion in Concept 7.3 indicated that augmented feedback can be any of several different types of information. In this concept, the focus shifts to the information provided by augmented feedback. Of primary interest is how the characteristics and the rates of presentation of feedback influence skill learning. Augmented feedback, in its various forms, can range from very general information to very specific information about a person's movement. It can also be presented to the person in different ways, such as verbally, or by videotape or computer-generated graphics. And augmented feedback can be based on different characteristics of the person's performance, such as the errors related to the outcome of the performance, or the characteristics of the movements that produced the outcome. Augmented feedback can also cover the correctly performed parts of the movement rather than the errors that were made. Closely related to these concerns is how frequently augmented feedback should be presented. Each of these issues is addressed in the discussion of this concept.

Before addressing these issues, it is interesting to point out that investigations of the characteristics of physical education teachers illustrates the relevance of the issues addressed in this concept for people who teach motor skills. This evidence consistently shows that teachers provide various types of augmented feedback and present the feedback with varying degrees of frequency for students in a class. For example, in one of the earliest studies of feedback characteristics of physical education teachers, Fishman and Tobey (1978) observed teachers in 81 classes. They found that KP was provided to the students 94% of the time, while KR was given 6% of the time. These forms of augmented feedback were intended to provide students with an appraisal of the performance 53% of the time and to provide instruction about how to improve performance on the next attempt 41% of the time. And 5% of the time the teachers used augmented feedback to praise or criticize performance. Thus, it seems that it is common practice for instructors of motor skills to vary the type and intent of augmented information that is given. Fishman and Tobey also found that augmented feedback was given at a rate of just over one instance per minute for 35 min classes. However, the actual amount of feedback across the classes ranged from a low of 1 to a high of 297, with the median at 47. This means that some students received several feedback statements each day while others received very few. In no case did any student receive feedback after every practice attempt. These findings are important to keep in mind as you consider the discussion of the issues that follow and relate them to your own motor skill instruction situation.

The Content of Augmented Feedback

Two general points, which can guide decisions about determining the appropriate characteristics for augmented feedback, are important to establish as introductory considerations for the discussion that follows.

The first point is to understand that when augmented feedback is given about a specific part of a movement, it serves to direct the person's attention to that part. Recall in our discussion of Kahneman's model of attention in Concept 4.1 that an important feature of attention is the need to appropriately allocate attention capacity so that a skill can be performed correctly. One factor Kahneman proposed as influential in determining how attention capacity is allocated is what he calls "momentary intentions." In many respects, augmented feedback serves as a type of momentary intention because it directs, i.e., allocates, the individual's attention to a particular feature of the movement. Sometimes the augmented feedback is too general to direct the allocation of attention in a useful way. However, when specific enough information is given, augmented feedback serves an important attention-directing function. That is, if the information is sufficiently meaningful, it helps the person allocate attention capacity in an appropriate way so that a performance characteristic can be corrected or performed again just as it was performed.

A second point that must be considered in determining the content of augmented feedback is to establish which part or parts of the performance should receive directed attention. If augmented feedback serves to direct attention to certain aspects of performing a skill, it is important to direct the attention to the parts that, if improved, will significantly improve performance of the entire skill. For example, suppose you are teaching a child to throw a ball at a target. Also suppose this child is making many errors, which is typical of beginners. The child may be looking at his or her hand, stepping with the wrong foot, releasing the ball awkwardly, or not rotating the trunk. Probably the most fundamental error is not looking at the target. This, then is the error about which you should provide feedback, because it is the part of the skill to which you want the child to direct his or her attention; it is the part of the skill that, if corrected, will have an immediate, significant, positive influence on performance. By correcting this error, the child will undoubtedly also correct many of the other errors that may have characterized his or her performance.

Interesting experimental support for these two points comes from an article by den Brinker, Stabler, Whiting, and van Wieringen, (1986) of Free University in Amsterdam. Subjects in this experiment were required to learn to perform on the slalom ski simulator described in Concept 7.1 and shown in Figure 7.1–3. In this experiment, subjects were provided one of three types of KP. One type was in terms of the amplitude, or distance, of platform movement. The second type of KP was about the frequency, or tempo, of their movement of the platform. (They were told there was an optimum frequency [0.67 Hz] for performing this skill.) The third type was about the fluency of their movements, which was to be interpreted in terms of smoothness, or absence of jerk. Fluency KP was the difference between achieved fluency and what was considered perfect fluency. Each of these three types of KP was given to a different group of subjects in the experiment. All subjects practiced the

ski simulation task for four days, with six 1.5-minute trials each day. A test trial was given daily before and after the practice trials, during which the subjects were filmed.

The results indicated that early in practice, the type of KP provided influenced the performance measure related to that feature of performing the skill more than any of the other types. For example, early in practice the frequency KP group performed better than the other two groups on the frequency measure of performance. Thus, KP served to direct attention to that feature of the skill relevant to the KP. This directed attention led to more initial improvement of that feature of the skill than of any other feature. However, another important result showed that the different types of KP were related to performance in different ways as practice proceeded over the four days. In the last day of practice, the fluency KP group reached amplitudes that were similar to those achieved by the amplitude KP group, while the amplitude KP group achieved as close to the perfect frequency value as did the fluency KP group. Also, the amplitude KP and the frequency KP groups performed with more fluency on the fourth day than did the fluency KP group. What these results show is that from the third day until the end of training, amplitude KP led to the best performance on all three measures.

Therefore, both points about determining the content of augmented feedback are supported by the results of this experiment. First, when augmented feedback is given about specific performance characteristics early in practice, you can expect the person's attention to be directed toward that characteristic. You can also expect that characteristic to show the greatest improvment early in practice. Second, there are certain performance characteristics about which augmented feedback should be given in preference to others. The reason for this is that attention directed to that specific feature will allow development of performance of not only that feature, but also of certain other features.

Qualitative vs. quantitative information. Augmented feedback can be qualitative, or quantitative, or both. Whether augmented feedback is **qualitative** or **quantitative** depends on how specific, or precise the information given to the learner is. For example, a person learning a serve in tennis could be told about a particular serve that it was "good," or "long;" or could be told "You made contact with the ball too far in front of you;" or; a bell could ring when the serve is good. In each of these situations, the augmented feedback conveys information about the quality of the serve. On the other hand, the person could be told "The serve was 6 cm too long," or "You made contact with the ball 10 cm too far in front of you;" or the person could be presented with precise displays of the kinematic characteristics of his or her serving motion. In each of these situations, the information is quantitative and therefore more precise than the qualitative feedback described.

How do these two levels of precision of augmented feedback influence skill learning? While the research investigating this question typically has been directed at KR, it seems reasonable that the results can be generalized to other forms of augmented feedback as well. Investigations of the influence of augmented feedback have a very long history in motor learning research. Traditionally, results have indicated the superiority of quantitative over qualitative KR for skill learning. These results have been reported for learning laboratory tasks as well as for learning sport skills.

A good example of KR precision research involving sport skills is an experiment by Smoll (1972). Subjects learned to roll a duckpin bowling ball at 70% of each person's maximum velocity, with KR provided after each practice attempt in one of three ways. One group received qualitative KR in the form of statements indicating that a roll was "too fast," "too slow," or "correct." One of two quantitative KR groups was told how many tenths of a second the roll was in error of the goal velocity, while the other quantitative KR group

was given error information in hundredths of a second. Results, which can be seen in Figure 7.4–1, show that the two quantitative groups performed better during practice than the qualitative group, and that there was no difference between the two quantitative groups. Thus, while quantitative information was more beneficial, the more precise hundredth of a second level KR was not more beneficial than the less precise tenth of a second level KR.

A problem that has typified most of the research investigating the KR precision issue was pointed out in an excellent review of the KR literature by Salmoni, Schmidt, and Walter (1984). The conclusion that quantitative KR is better for learning must be considered as tentative. Retention or transfer tests were not provided to determine the influence of qualitative vs. quantitative KR on learning, as opposed to immediate performance in the presence of the respective types of KR. Two experiments that did include no-KR retention tests were reported by Reeve and Magill (1981) and by Magill and Wood (1986). Although both investigations showed results favoring quantitative over qualitative KR, they also supported a view of the precision effect that previously had not been considered. That is, the question of KR precision should not be viewed simply as qualitative vs. quantitative. It is important also to consider the stage of learning or the amount of practice of the learner.

The experiment by Magill and Wood (1986) is a good illustration of the relationship between the precision of augmented feedback and the stage of learning of the learner. Subjects in this experiment learned to move an arm through a series of wooden barriers to produce a specific six-segment movement pattern. Each segment had its own criterion movement time that had to be learned. Following each of 120 practice trials, subjects were given either qualitative KR for each segment (i.e., "too fast," "too slow," or "correct") or quantitative KR for each segment (i.e., the number of msec

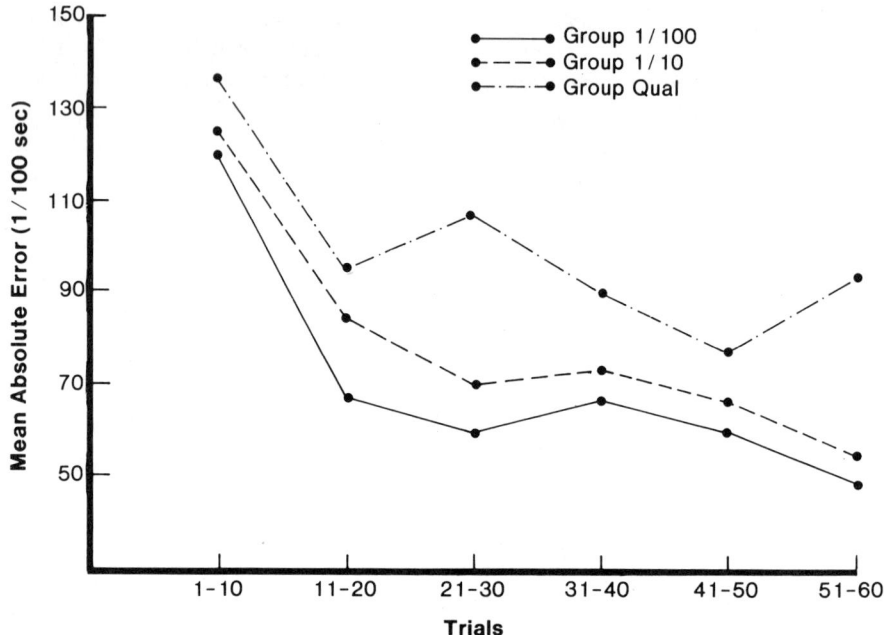

FIGURE 7.4-1   Results of the experiment by Smoll showing the effects of three levels of precision of KR on learning to roll a duckpin bowling ball at 70% of the subject's own maximum velocity.

too fast or too slow). The results are presented in Figure 7.4–2. These results indicate that during the first 60 trials, there was no difference between the two levels of KR precision. That is, during the first stage of learning, even those subjects who received the quantitatively more precise KR were undoubtedly operating only on the qualitative information of each KR statement. However, during the final 60 trials and on the 20 no-KR retention trials, the quantitative KR condition yielded better performance, which indicated a shift in the attention of the subjects to the quantitative information the KR provided.

Results such as these indicate that a certain degree of quantitatively precise augmented feedback is beneficial only after the learner has experienced a sufficient amount of practice so that he or she can effectively use more precise information. Prior to that time, the learner needs less

precise, i.e., more general, information about performance errors. In the Magill and Wood experiment, it seems that the first thing subjects needed to establish in practice was what was meant by the terms "too fast" or "too slow" and how these terms related to their movements. Only after this meaning was established could the subjects use the specific quantitative information provided about their movement.

What this demonstrates is that more precise augmented feedback is not necessarily better for facilitating learning. The degree of precision of the information must match the capability of the learner to make effective use of that information. For a beginner learning a new skill, there will be a limited benefit from receiving augmented feedback that provides information more specific than he or she is capable of using. While telling a beginning tennis student he or she "Contacted the

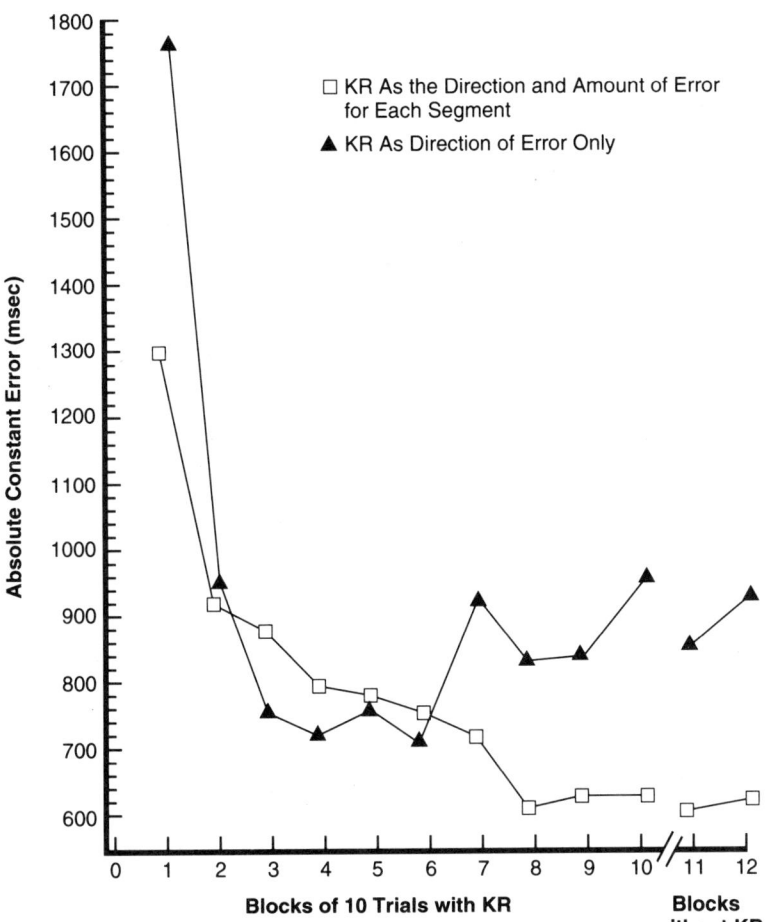

FIGURE 7.4-2 Absolute constant error scores during practice with KR (Blocks 1–10) and without KR (Blocks 11–12) on a six-segment timing pattern in the experiment by Magill and Wood.

serve 10 cm too far in front" of them is quantitatively more specific, it probably communicates no more than the qualitative information in that statement, that they "Contacted the ball too far in front." Another point that seems particularly relevant concerns the use of highly sophisticated movement analysis information for providing augmented feedback to beginners. The benefit of providing such precise information must be evaluated in terms of the person's capability of translating that information into action terms that will enable him or her to make needed corrections in the future.

Augmented feedback based on errors vs. correct performance. An important concern for determining which information to present as augmented feedback is whether the information should be related to the errors being made during the performance or to those aspects of the performance that have been done correctly. Unfortunately, this has not been investigated very intensely; the few studies that have addressed this question were done in the 1950s and 1960s using tracking types of tasks. However, the results of these studies are reasonably consistent and have implications for learning theory and skill instruction.

The most informative studies have used the rotary pursuit task in which subjects must maintain stylus contact on a rotating target for as long as possible. The size and shape of the target depends on the piece of equipment used, although some pursuit rotors permit several different target sizes and shapes. Augmented feedback can be provided for this task in a variety of ways. Both error and correct performance information can be given either concurrently or terminally. Error information can be provided as concurrent augmented sensory feedback by providing an auditory signal indicating when the stylus is off-target, or it can be provided as terminal KR by telling the subject how much time he or she was off-target. Correct performance information can be provided in similar ways by making the augmented sensory feedback or the terminal KR relate to on-target rather than off-target performance.

A representative example of an experiment investigating the on-target vs. off-target feedback issue for learning the rotary pursuit task was reported by Gordon and Gottlieb (1967). Subjects practiced for 33 trials with one of three augmented feedback conditions. One group received visual augmented sensory feedback in the form of a yellow light that illuminated the entire rotary pursuit apparatus when they were on-target. The second group saw the same light when they were off-target. The third group was a control group and received no augmented feedback. Results for both the practice trials and 9 transfer trials without augmented feedback showed that the two augmented feedback groups performed better than the group having no augmented feedback. Also the off-target feedback condition led to slightly better learning than the on-target feedback condition.

The results from research on whether augmented feedback should be error-based or based on correct performance consistently demonstrate that error-based augmented feedback is beneficial and typically leads to better learning than augmented feedback based on correct movement. Thus, the research evidence supports the hypothesis proposed by Annett (1959). Repeating a precise response is not sufficient to produce learning, but the addition of experience with error-based feedback is needed for skill acquisition for tasks that benefit from augmented feedback. And, as Lintern and Roscoe (1980) argued, on-target augmented feedback, when it augments relatively obscure sensory feedback from the task itself, may create a strong dependency on the on-target augmented information, which will lead to poor performance when the augmented feedback is withdrawn.

It is interesting to note that the issue of whether augmented feedback should be based on errors or correct performance is one of importance in pedagogy texts also. One interesting approach to dealing with how to best address this problem in an instructional setting was proposed by Siedentop (1983). He suggested that instructors give a combination of error and correct performance feedback during practice sessions. In fact, he specified that the best combination ratio would be 4 error-based augmented feedback statements to 1 correct performance-based statement. Whether this type of combination is best for skill learning must await experimental study because there is no published empirical evidence supporting such conclusions. However, if the functions of augmented feedback discussed in Concept 7.3 are taken into account, it seems that such a combination provides a way to involve the functions of error correction and motivation to continue practicing in the same situation.

Augmented feedback based on performance bandwidths. Closely related to the question of whether to provide augmented feedback based on correct performance or errors in a performance is the question of how much of an error should be made before augmented feedback is given. This question has distinct practical appeal because it undoubtedly reflects what occurs in actual teaching or coaching situations, especially when large groups are involved in a class. Because augmented feedback cannot be given for every error made by students, it seems reasonable to provide feedback only for those errors that are large enough to warrant attention. This practice suggests that the instructor establishes a performance-based bandwidth that provides a criterion for when augmented feedback will or will not be given. If the student is performing within the tolerance limits of the bandwidth, augmented feedback will not be given. But if an error is made that is outside that performance bandwidth, feedback will be given.

An experiment that illustrates the effectiveness of basing augmented feedback on a performance-based bandwidth criterion is one reported by Sherwood (1988). He had subjects practice a rapid elbow flexion task with a goal to make the movement in 200 msec. One group received KR about their movement time error after every trial regardless of the amount of error, i.e., a 0% bandwidth. Two other groups received KR only when their error exceeded bandwidths of 5% and 10% of the 200 msec goal movement time. The results of a no-KR retention test showed that the 10% bandwidth condition resulted in the least amount of variable movement times (i.e., variable error) while the 0% condition resulted in the most variable error. These results, which were replicated by Lee, White, and Carnahan (1990), support the point discussed earlier in this chapter that error information is not always needed to learn a skill and can, in fact, negatively influence learning. And as will be discussed in a later section, providing augmented feedback based on performance bandwidths appears to be an effective means of determining an appropriate frequency for providing augmented feedback to individuals in practice settings.

Erroneous augmented feedback when augmented feedback is not needed. In an earlier section of this chapter, situations were described where motor skill learning could occur without augmented feedback. In those situations, augmented feedback was redundant with available sensory feedback and did not lead to better learning. But in those redundancy situations, a question arises about whether the augmented feedback is ignored or used in some way by the learner. One way to address this question is to consider the influence of erroneous augmented feedback. If augmented feedback is ignored because it is not needed to learn the skill, erroneous information should also be ignored and sensory feedback would be the information source. This approach was described recently by Buekers, Magill, and Hall (1992). They reported two experiments in which subjects practiced an anticipation timing task similar to the one described earlier in the experiments by Magill, Chamberlin, and Hall (1991). Experiment 2 will serve as an illustrative example of addressing this issue.

Subjects practiced the anticipation timing skill for 75 trials. For three groups, KR was given after every trial. KR was the correct direction and amount of timing error for one group, and was incorrect error information for another group. For the second group, KR indicated that the subjects struck the barrier 100 msec later than they actually did. A third group received correct KR for the first 50 trials and then received the incorrect KR for the last 25 trials. A fourth group did not receive any KR. Following the practice trials, all subjects performed the same task without KR one day and one week later. Notice two things about the results of this experiment, which are presented in Figure 7.4–3. First, further evidence was found showing that KR was not needed to learn the skill. Second, the results indicated that KR is used by subjects when it is available to them. The erroneous KR information led subjects to perform according to the KR rather than according to the feedback intrinsic to the task itself. This effect was seen even for the group that had received correct KR for the first 50 trials and then was switched to the erroneous information. After the switch, this group began performing similar to the group that had received the incorrect KR for all the practice trials. This erroneous information not only influenced performance when the incorrect KR was provided, it also influenced retention performance one day and one week later when no KR was provided.

When augmented feedback is presented to beginning learners when it is not needed for learning the skill, the role played of the feedback appears

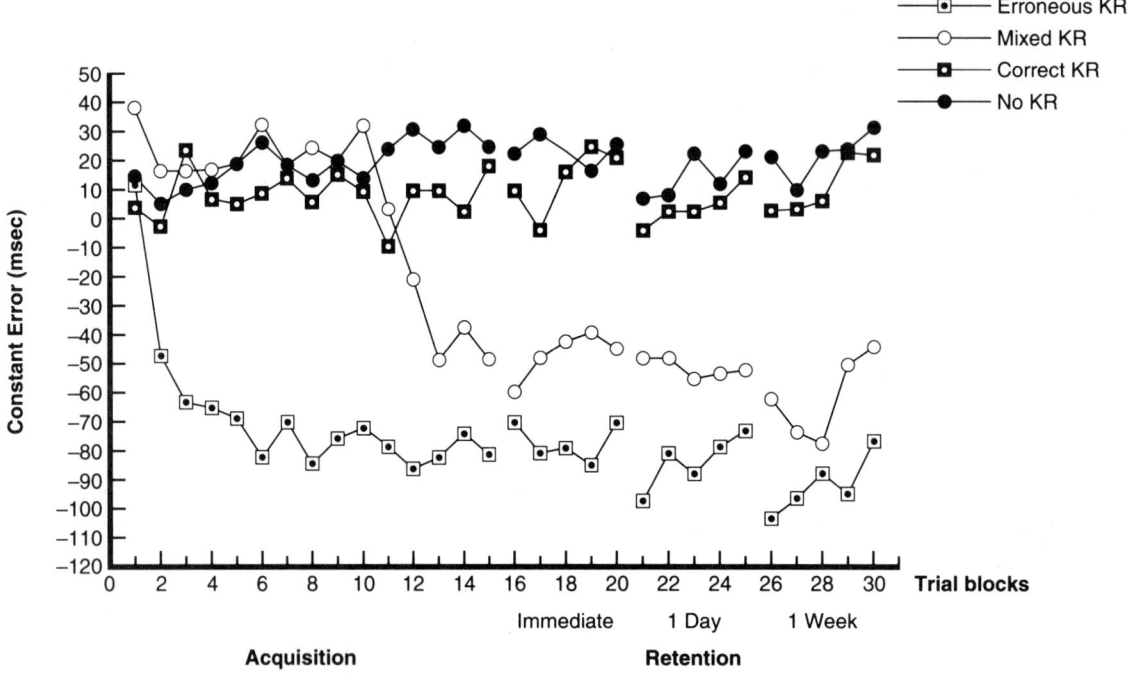

FIGURE 7.4-3 Results of the experiment by Buekers, et al., showing the effects of erroneous KR compared to no KR, and correct KR for learning an anticipation timing skill. Note that the mixed KR group received correct KR for their first 50 trials and then received erroneous KR for their last 25 practice trials.

to depend on whether it agrees or is in conflict with the information the person has derived intrinsically through the sensory system. If there is conflict, the conflict is resolved in favor of the augmented feedback. Because beginners are not certain how to use or interpret their own sensory feedback, the externally presented augmented feedback becomes a critical source of information for making movement adjustments on future trials.

This influence of augmented feedback suggests that instructors need to be certain that the information they provide as augmented feedback is appropriate and establishes a means of interpreting sensory feedback. Performance can then eventually be carried out without the need for augmented feedback by the instructor. Beginning learners are of particular concern because they will ignore what their own sensory feedback is telling them, even though it is correct, and adjust movements on the basis of what the instructor tells them, even though it may be incorrect.

Verbal knowledge of performance as augmented feedback. Most of this discussion thus far has been based on using KR as augmented feedback. Although most of the conclusions from that research is relevant to verbal KP, it is worth looking at some of the research that has used verbal KP in its investigations. One of the unique concerns about using verbal KP is what to tell the learner about his or her performance. Because there are usually many parts of the performance about which information can be given, it is important to determine how to select which parts should be the basis for KP for a given practice trial. This is a distinct characteristic difference between KP and KR. Because KR is performance outcome-based, there is usually no difficulty in determining what information to give, apart from the concerns addressed in the preceding sections. If a basketball shot missed the rim, the outcome of the performance limits the number of options an instructor has about what to tell the person as KR. However, if KP is to be provided, the decision must be made about which aspect of the performance that led to the shot being missed should be told to the person.

The first thing that must be done to determine what KP to give is to perform a skill analysis of the skill being practiced. This means that the various component parts of the skill must be identified. Then the parts must be organized in terms on their importance for performing the skill correctly. The most important part should be listed first, followed by the second most important and so on. To determine which part is most important decide which part of the skill absolutely must be done properly for the entire skill to be performed correctly? For example, if you are performing a relatively simple task like throwing a ball at a target, it would appear that the most critical component is watching the target. Regardless if all other parts of the skill are done correctly, there is a very low chance that the skill would be performed correctly if the person did not look at the target. In this case, then, looking at the target would be the first part of the skill on the skill analysis priority list. This means, then, that if that part of the skill were to be done incorrectly, regardless of what other parts are being done incorrectly, the KP given should be about this part of the skill.

A good example of prioritizing components of a skill can be seen in an experiment by Magill and Schoenfelder-Zohdi (1992). The skill learned by the subjects was a rhythmic gymnastics rope skill. In this skill, subjects had to begin by holding the rope with both knots at the ends of the rope in one hand. Then they were to circle the rope two times forward in the sagittal plane. At the end of the second circle, they were to let one knot go and allow the rope to go to full extension, hitting the floor, while at the same time they were to do a half turn, so they would be facing the opposite direction of their starting position. As the rope came back to them, they were to catch the knot at the end of the rope. This complex skill has many component parts. Because one of the variables investigated in this experiment was KP, a priority list of KP statements had to be developed so that an appropriate statement could be given after each trial. The skill analysis indicated that at least 35

KP statements were needed. These are presented in Table 7.4–1 in the priority order that was used for the experiment. During the experiment, a subject who was to receive KP after a trial was given one statement from this list. That statement was selected by the experimenter as the most critical error of all that were made to be corrected on the next trial.

One final point is important to make about verbal KP. The KP statements in the Magill and Schoenfelder-Zohdi experiment prescribed to subjects how to correct the error that was identified as the most critical for that trial. In research analyzing teacher behavior, this type of KP is called "prescriptive" feedback. Less informative would be what is called "descriptive" feedback, in which the KP statement simply describes the error that was made rather than providing directions for correcting the error. Hence, the prescriptive KP statement, "Circle the rope 2 times" would be "You did not circle the rope the correct number of times" if it were a descriptive KP statement. According to studies like the one by Fishman and Tobey (1978) described earlier in this discussion, teachers give both types of KP in about the same proportions.

Which type of KP would better facilitate learning? The answer to this, although there is no empirical evidence on which to base an answer, would seem to relate to the stage of learning of the individual practicing the skill. A beginner would not be helped very much by a descriptive statement. While such a statement would identify the error made, the beginner would not have sufficient knowledge to determine how to correct the error. Recall that in Adams' (1971) description of the stages of learning, error detection capability develops before error correction capability. The beginner needs KP information that not only detects the error but also provides information about how to correct that error. Thus, the prescriptive KP statement would appear to be more appropriate for the beginner. The more advanced person, on the other hand, would have the knowledge to correct the error. Because of that capability, a descriptive KP statement would be sufficient for him or her.

Table 7.4-1   Priority List of KP Statements for a Rhythmic Gymnastics Rope Skill

Priority	KP Statement
1	Hold both knots in one hand
2	Circle rope 2 times
3	Circle rope forward
4	Move arm away from your body
5	Circle rope in the sagittal plane
6	Circle rope slower
7	Circle rope faster
8	Make a half-turn
9	Do not turn your body to the left
10	Turn your feet
11	Turn earlier
12	Turn later
13	Do no turn too much
14	Do not twist your body
15	Do not turn abruptly
16	Let the knot go earlier
17	Let the knot go later
18	Do not let go of the other knot
19	Move your arm down when letting knot go
20	The rope should hit the floor
21	Do not hit the rope so hard on floor
22	Do not interrupt the motion of rope
23	Move your arm to your right
24	Move your arm to the side of your body
25	Move your arm to shoulder height
26	Let the rope slide far enough
27	Keep your arm straight
28	Pull the rope downward
29	Pull the rope back earlier
30	Pull the rope back later
31	Pull the rope back stronger
32	Pull the rope back weaker
33	Do not grab the middle of the rope
34	Guide the rope better
35	Try to catch the knot
36	That was correct

From R. A. Magill & B. Schoenfelder-Zohdi, "A Visual Model and Knowledge of Performance as Sources of Information for Learning a Complex Skill." Copyright © 1991 R. A. Magill and B. Schoenfelder-Zohdi. Reprinted by permission of the author.

Videotape as augmented feedback.   While there seems to be little doubt that the most common means of providing augmented feedback to students is verbal (e.g., Eghan, 1988; Fischman & Tobey, 1978), there are other means of presenting KP information. There is an increasing use of videotape as a means of presenting augmented feedback as videotape equipment becomes less expensive and more readily available to the general public as well as to teachers, coaches, and therapists. Unfortunately, we know very little about the use of videotape as a means of providing augmented feedback. In fact, the only extensive review of the research literature was published by Rothstein and Arnold (1976).

In the Rothstein and Arnold review, over 50 studies were considered that involved 18 different sport activities, including archery, badminton, bowling, gymnastics, skiing, swimming, and volleyball. In most of these studies, the students were beginners, although there were a few studies that included intermediate- and advanced-level performers. Although there were generally mixed results about the effectiveness of videotape as a method of providing augmented feedback, two points were clear. First, while the type of activity was not a critical factor in determining the effectiveness of videotape, the skill level of the student was a critical factor. Beginners needed the aid of an instructor to point out information from the videotape replay. Advanced or intermediate performers did not appear to need instructor aid as much as did beginners. Second, videotape replays were most effective when used for at least five weeks. In those studies in which videotape was used less than this amount of time, the researchers typically found replays to be an ineffective form of augmented feedback to aid learning.

It is also apparent that certain types of information related to skill performance are transmitted to the learner better than other types. An example of this was reported in a study by Selder and Del Rolan (1979) in which 12- and 13-year-old girls were learning to perform a balance beam routine. A control group received only verbal feedback about their performance on each trial. Each girl was given a checklist to use for critically analyzing her own performance on the basis of the verbal feedback they received. Another group of girls observed videotape replays of their performances. These girls were told to use the checklist as a means of determining what to observe on the videotape and for evaluating their own performances. At the end of 4 weeks of practice there were no differences between the two groups' performances of the practiced routine. However, as you can see in Figure 7.4–4, at the end of 6 weeks of practice, the videotape group scored significantly higher than the verbal feedback group. What was more revealing, however, was that the videotape group scored significantly higher on only four of the eight factors making up the total score. These factors were precision, execution, amplitude, and orientation and direction. There was no difference for rhythm, elegance, coordination, and lightness of jumping and tumbling. Thus, it appears that the use of videotape will benefit correction of those aspects of a performance that can be readily observed and corrected on the basis of visual information. Other factors, not as readily discernible, appear to be difficult to translate from the visual input to the motor output modes and may need to be augmented by verbal information.

Graphic kinematic representations as augmented feedback. With the advent of personal computers and software capable of doing sophisticated kinematic analysis of movement, it has become increasingly more common to find instructors who provide students with graphic kinematic representations about their performances as a form of feedback. As with videotape, it is im-

portant to determine the effectiveness of this means of providing augmented feedback and to establish guidelines for implementing its use. Unfortunately, there is very little empirical evidence that provides definitive answers to these concerns. In this section, we will consider two experiments that can provide some insight. (For additional information about graphic kinematic representations used as augmented feedback in motor skill learning, see Schmidt & Young, 1991.)

One of the earliest studies to present evidence that kinematic representations of movement can be effective as augmented feedback for enhancing skill learning was reported by Lindahl (1945). In this study, which concerned the training of machine operators in industry, workers had to be trained to precisely and quickly cut thin discs of tungsten with a machine that required fast, accurate, and rhythmic coordination of the hands and feet. Typical training for this job was by trial and error. However, Lindahl developed an alternative training method that was based on providing augmented feedback. He provided the workers with a paper tracing of the pattern they produced by the foot during the cutting of the tungsten discs. The foot movement was used for this feedback because it had been identified as the most critical component of this complex task. An example of recordings for the correct foot action for these cuttings is presented at the top of Figure 7.4–5. The trainees were presented with charts illustrating the correct foot action and were periodically shown the results of their own foot movement as augmented feedback.

The bottom portion of Figure 7.4–5 shows the production performance of the trainees who used the augmented feedback compared to that of workers who had been trained using the factory's traditional trial-and-error method. The trainees achieved production performance levels in eleven weeks that had taken other trainees five months

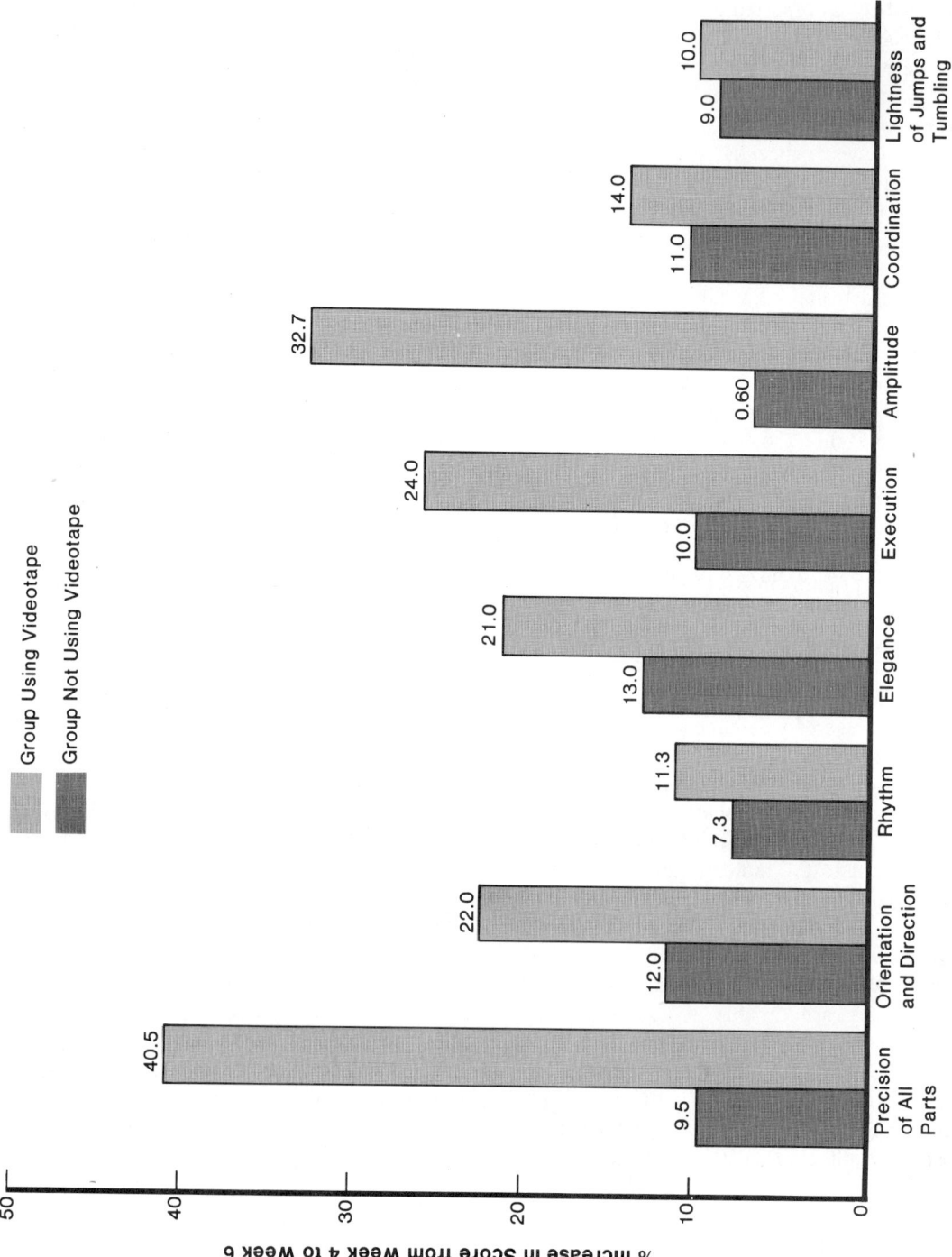

FIGURE 7.4-4   Results of the experiment by Selder and Del Rolan showing the percentage increase in scores of a group using videotape and a group not using videotape.

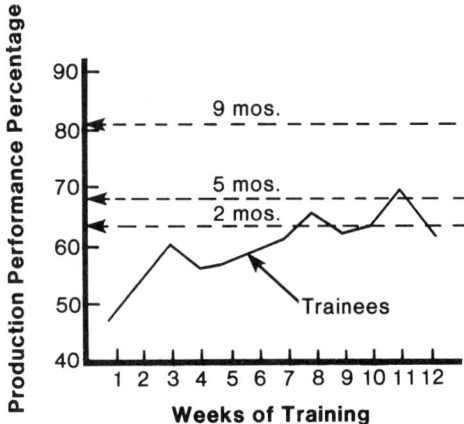

FIGURE 7.4-5 The upper panel illustrates the foot action required by the machine operator to produce an acceptable disc cut in the experiment by Lindahl. The graph at the bottom indicates the production performance achieved by the trainees using graphic information during 12 weeks of training. The dashed lines indicate the levels of performance achieved by other workers after 2, 5, and 9 months of experience.

to achieve. Additionally, the trainees reduced their percentage of broken cutting wheels to almost zero in twelve weeks, a level not achieved by those trained with the traditional method in less than nine months. Thus, the use of a graphic kinematic representation as feedback was not only effective in helping workers to achieve desired performance levels, it helped them achieve those levels in significantly less time.

Additional support for the effectiveness of this method of providing augmented feedback was provided in a laboratory setting by Newell, Quinn, Sparrow, and Walter (1983), which was an extension of an earlier experiment by Hatze (1976). In the second experiment of this study, subjects practiced moving a lever as fast as possible to a target. Three types of KR conditions were used. One group of subjects was verbally given their movement time as KR. A second group was shown a graphic display on a computer monitor of their movement velocity-time trace as KR, while a third group received no KR. The results of this exper-

iment can be seen in Figure 7.4–6. The graphic kinematic representation form of KR led to the best performance, followed by the verbal KR condition, and then the no-KR condition. It is interesting to note here that the no-KR condition showed improvement for the first 25 trials but then performance reached a steady state without further improvement while the two KR conditions continued to show improvement. For this skill, the graphic presentation of movement velocity led to better overall performance than verbal KR. The difference between the types of KR became more pronounced as practice continued.

The study of the use and benefit of kinematic representations as a means of providing augmented feedback needs more attention by researchers. As the use of computers and movement analysis systems become more commonplace, the possibility of using information derived from these systems will increase, along the need to know how to more effectively use the systems to enhance skill learning and performance.

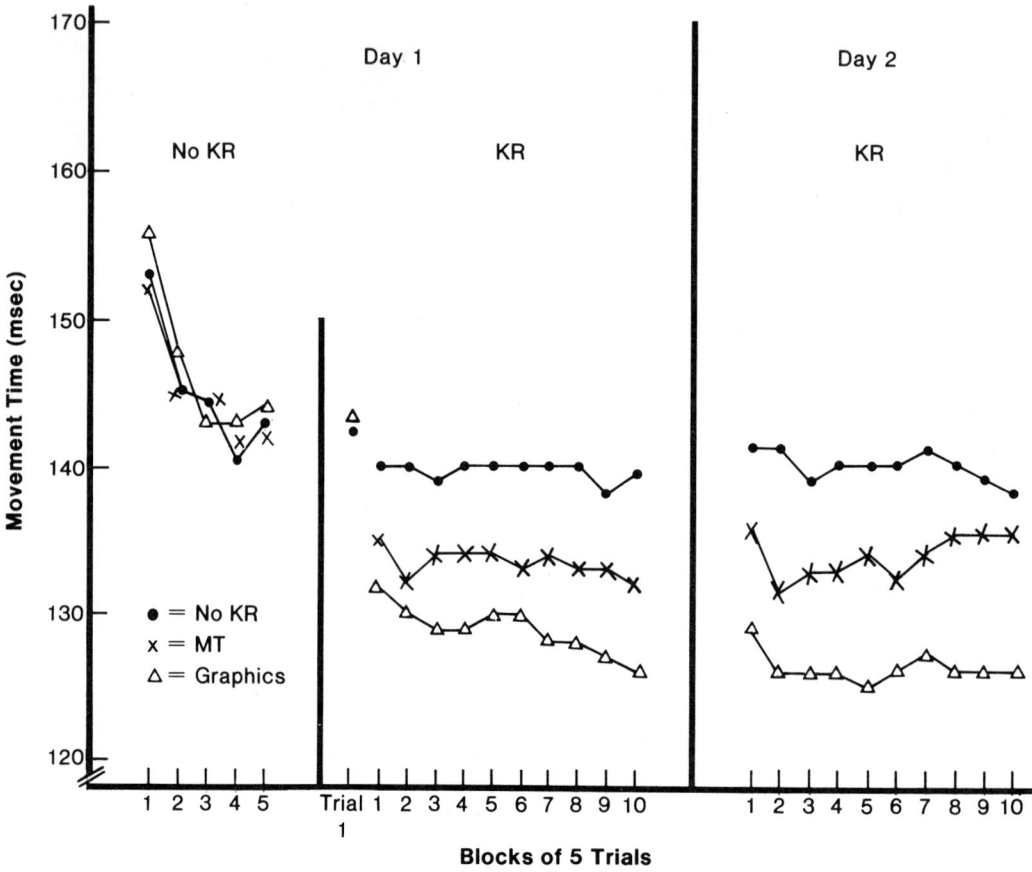

FIGURE 7.4-6 Results of the experiment by Newell et al., showing mean movement time as a function of KR condition and practice over trial blocks and days.

Guidelines for Giving Augmented Feedback

In each of the preceding sections of this discussion, several different issues were discussed in which different types of information were considered in relation to their influence on skill learning. From an application to instruction perspective, the problem at this point is how to determine what information to give to a person as augmented feedback. Based on the discussion so far, some distinct guidelines can be suggested.

1. The person must be capable of using the information presented. Recall that more specific or precise augmented feedback is not necessarily better. Less precise information appears to be more useful by novices, whereas more precise information is more useful as skill learning progresses.

2. Augmented feedback based on errors leads to better learning than when it is based on doing something correctly. However, because augmented feedback enables a person to improve by providing error correction information, it also motivates a person to continue practicing the skill. These two important functions suggest that perhaps augmented feedback based on errors and on correct aspects of a skill should both be provided during practice sessions.

3. Presenting augmented feedback that is based on errors made outside a performance bandwidth can be an effective way of facilitating skill learning. One of the benefits of this is that it provides a way to begin with less precise feedback and move to more precise feedback as the person progresses through the learning stages.

4. Selecting the appropriate part of a performance for KP should be based on the most critical error made during that performance. This critical error should be identified on the basis of a prioritized list of components of the skill, where the most critical component is listed first.

5. Prescriptive KP is better for novices while descriptive KP is more appropriate for skilled performers. Novices need information to help them detect as well as correct errors. Experts, when they make errors that they seem to have difficulty correcting, usually only need information that helps them detect their error.

6. Videotape can be a useful means of presenting augmented feedback. However, novices will have the same problems using videotape to help them detect and correct errors as they would have using verbal augmented feedback.

7. Computer generated descriptions of the kinematics of a performance can be helpful to facilitate skill learning. However, this form of augmented feedback seems to be more effective when it is presented to more advanced performers rather than to novices.

Frequency of Presenting Augmented Feedback

Closely related to the issue of the content of augmented feedback is the question of how frequently augmented feedback should be given to a person. This frequency question has been investigated in the research literature primarily as it relates to KR. In this section, three issues will be discussed. The first concerns whether absolute or relative frequency is important, and if so, what frequency would be optimal for learning. The second part of this discussion considers the relationship between KR frequency and providing KR on the basis of performance bandwidths. The last section addresses the question of whether KR can be given in summary form and be effective for learning.

Absolute vs. relative KR frequency. The term **absolute frequency** refers to giving KR a specific number of trials during practice, whereas the term **relative frequency** refers to the percentage of trials on which KR is given. For example, if a person were to practice a skill for 80 trials, and a person received KR on 20 of them, the absolute frequency would be 20 while the relative frequency would be 25%. The traditional conclusion in motor learning has been that the greater the frequency of KR, the better the learning will be that results. Bilodeau and Bilodeau (1958a), for example, held absolute frequency constant while allowing relative frequency to vary among four groups learning a simple lever pulling task. Because the results showed no differences among the relative frequencies, the researchers argued that the critical variable for learning motor skills is the absolute frequency of KR. That is, learning will increase as a function of the number of exposures a learner has to KR. This view argues that receiving KR is essential for learning and that the learner will not benefit from practice trials where KR is not provided.

However, results from experiments where absolute frequency has been permitted to vary, and where a learning test was included in the experiment (which was not in the Bilodeau and Bilodeau experiment) have argued against the conclusion that absolute frequency of KR is the critical factor for learning. In these experiments (e.g., Annett, 1959; Ho & Shea, 1978; Winstein & Schmidt, 1990, Experiment 1) reduced KR frequency did not produce either detrimental or beneficial learning effects. Because relative and absolute frequency covaried in these experiments, and all conditions had the same number of practice trials, support for an absolute KR frequency view could not be established.

***The benefit of not giving augmented feedback on
every trial.*** Evidence has been accumulating
over the past few years indicating that earlier views
about the optimal frequency for giving augmented feedback were not correct. It is becoming
increasingly clear that 100% frequency is not necessary, nor desirable to establish an optimal
learning condition. The case against the traditional view began primarily as a result of the article by Salmoni, Schmidt, and Walter (1984) in
which they reviewed the KR literature in terms of
conclusions that could be made from experiments
involving and not involving tests of learning. They
found that the conclusion that the need for 100%
frequency was based on experiments in which no
tests of learning were provided. Hence, the results
could be due to 100% frequency being performance artifact rather than a learning effect.

Although several research studies provided
support for the view that augmented feedback does
not need to be presented after every trial to facilitate learning, one by Winstein and Schmidt
(1990) provides the most insight into this issue.
The approach they took was to systematically
expand the number of trials on which KR was *not*
provided during practice. To consider this procedure another way, they systematically reduced the
frequency of KR during practice from 100% to
25%, which yielded an average KR frequency of
50% for the practice sessions. A brief description
of Experiment 2 will illustrate their procedure and
results.

Subjects practiced producing the complex
movement pattern shown in the top panel of Figure
7.4–7 by moving a lever on a tabletop to manipulate a cursor on a computer monitor. During the
192 practice trials (96 trials for each of two days),
subjects received KR after either 100% or 50% of
the trials. For the 50% condition, a **fading technique** was used where the KR was systematically
reduced in frequency by providing KR after each
of the first 22 trials of each day, then 8 trials of
no KR, then KR for 8, 7, 4, 3, 2, and 2 trials for
each of the remaining 8–trial blocks each day. The
results of this procedure are presented in the
bottom panel of Figure 7.4–7. Based on the results

of a retention test given one day later where no
KR was presented on any trials, subjects who had
experienced the "faded" 50% KR frequency condition performed better than those who had received KR after every trial during practice (the
100% condition). In fact, subjects in the 100%
condition performed their retention test trials at a
level resembling their performance early on the
first day of practice.

It seems that for skills where augmented feedback benefits learning, optimal learning does not
depend on receiving augmented feedback after
every practice trial. Research has been consistent
in demonstrating that when KR is provided on
fewer than 100% of the practice trials, learning is
as good as or better than when KR was provided
on 100% of the practice trials. What remains to
be determined is whether or not there exists an
optimal KR frequency to optimize skill learning.
It is doubtful that one frequency would be found
to be "best" for learning all skills. However, empirical evidence must be provided before even this
speculative generalization can be supported.

Theoretical implications of the frequency effect.
The finding that learning does not depend on 100%
frequency, and, in fact, can actually be hindered
in some cases when KR is given after every practice trial, has important theoretical implications
for skill learning. The theoretical importance is
that motor learning theory needs to establish why
KR frequency of less than 100% would be better
for learning than KR after every trial.

One possible reason is that KR given after ever
trial eventually leads to an attention or working-
memory capacity "overload." After several trials,
the cumulative effect of the information received
by the individual establishes a condition where
there is more information available than the person
can handle.

Another possibility is that giving KR on every
trial leads to engaging the learner in a fundamen-
tally different type of learning processing than
when KR is not given on every trial. A view that
promotes this reasoning is advocated by Schmidt
and his colleagues (e.g., Salmoni, Schmidt, &

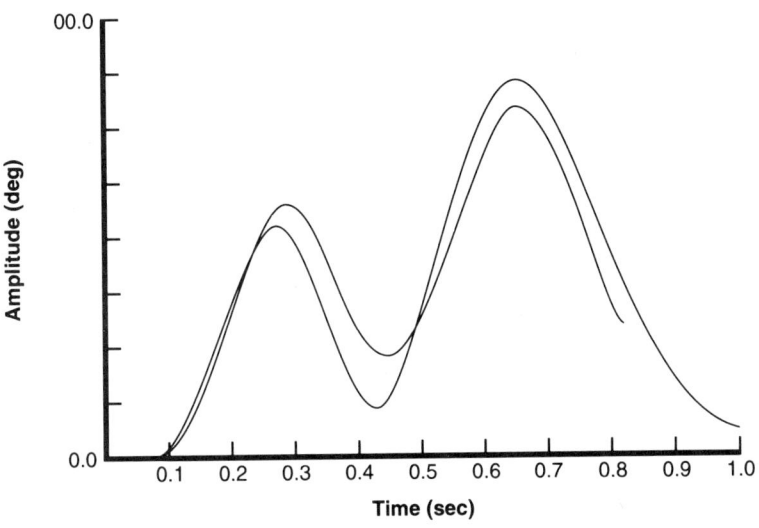

RMS Error = 9.36

FIGURE 7.4-7 The top panel shows the goal movement pattern used in the Winstein and Schmidt experiment. A sample of one subject's attempt to produce this pattern is superimposed. The RMS Error score is shown as the subject saw it. Note the goal pattern was for .80 sec while the subject produced a 1.0-sec pattern. The bottom panel shows the results of this experiment for the 100% KR and 50% KR frequency groups, where the 50% group had KR frequency "faded" from 100% to 0%.

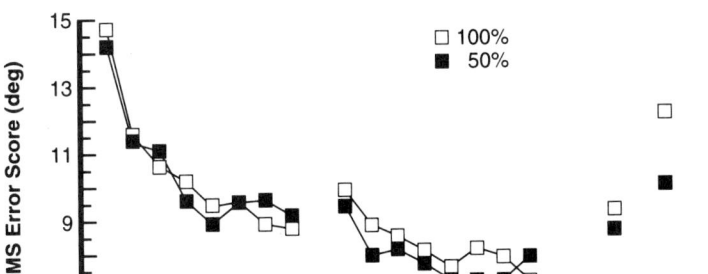

Walter, 1984; Schmidt, 1988; Winstein & Schmidt, 1990) and is called the **guidance hypothesis.** According to this view, if the learner receives KR on every trial, i.e., 100% frequency, then the KR will be used as an effective "guide" that enables the learner to perform the movement correctly. The negative part of this process is that by

using KR in this way, the learner develops a dependency on the availability of KR such that when the skill must be performed without KR, performance will be poorer than if KR were provided. In effect, to provide KR on every trial is to provide a crutch for the learner that becomes essential for performing the skill. If KR is removed, it is like removing the crutch and performance suffers. On the other hand, when KR is provided less frequently during practice, the learner engages in more beneficial learning processes during practice such as problem solving activities on the trials where no KR is given. Under these conditions, the learner does not become dependent on the availability of KR and can therefore perform the skill well, even in the absence of KR. Whether the guidance hypothesis describes the relationship between skill learning processes and the frequency of KR depends on much needed empirical tests of the hypothesis.

Practical implications of the frequency effect. An important practical implication of the finding that less than 100% frequency leads to learning as well as 100% frequency, or even better in some cases, is that it reduces the demand on the instructor to provide feedback all the time. It is comforting to the instructor to realize that he or she will not be causing a person harm by not giving feedback after every practice attempt. In fact, harm could actually result from giving feedback after every practice attempt. It is interesting that sport pedagogy research has shown that teachers and coaches of sport skills do not provide feedback with 100% frequency. In fact, in group practice situations, feedback typically is provided about one or two times per minute, with the same student rarely receiving more than a few feedback statements throughout a class session or practice period (e.g., see Eghan, 1988; Fishman & Tobey, 1978; Silverman, Tyson, & Krampitz, 1991).

When the question is asked concerning how often augmented feedback should be provided, it is important not to ignore the role of augmented feedback as a source of motivation to achieve a goal. While externally presented error correction information is not needed after every trial, it may be beneficial to provide feedback that serves a different purpose on some intervening trials. As Mosston (1981) has indicated in his text on

teaching effectiveness, it is important that the teacher provide feedback in the forms of "corrective statements," which identify error and how to correct it; "value statements," which project a value or feeling about the previous performance; and, "neutral statements," which provide factual information about the performance but do not correct or judge. Taken from this perspective, the question of augmented feedback frequency becomes one of effectively integrating the various types of information that can be provided by augmented feedback.

Frequency of augmented feedback and performance-based bandwidths. In an earlier section of this discussion, the issue of basing augmented feedback on performance-based bandwidth criteria was considered. Recall that evidence was presented indicating that learning can be enhanced by providing augmented feedback only when performance is *not* within a pre-established tolerance limit, or bandwidth. If the bandwidth issue is considered along with the frequency of giving augmented feedback, it is possible to see an interesting relationship. That is, if augmented feedback is based on a performance bandwidth, feedback will be provided with less frequency than when feedback is given regardless of the magnitude of the performance error. This relationship was initially addressed by Lee, White, and Carnahan (1990) and directly investigated in a follow-up experiment by Lee and Carnahan (1990).

In the Lee and Carnahan experiment, subjects in the 5% and 10% bandwidth conditions were yoked with subjects who received KR on the same trials on which the bandwidth subjects received KR. Thus, the use of yoked subjects controlled for frequency of KR because they received KR on a frequency basis rather than on a performance criterion basis. If the bandwidth effect is essentially a frequency effect, then subjects should perform similarly in the yoked bandwidth and frequency conditions. Subjects practiced for 60 trials a two-segment limb movement task that had a goal movement time of 500 msec. Results showed that the bandwidth-based KR conditions led to better retention performance than the yoked frequency KR conditions. Thus, the effect of performance-based bandwidth criterion for giving KR appears to be the result of more than simple frequency effects. Lee and Carnahan proposed that the bandwidth effect is due to combining KR with what the motor control system is capable of doing. That is, early in practice, the system is not capable of correcting errors with the precision required if errors must be corrected within a 5% or 10% tolerance limit. Thus, the bandwidth-based KR delivery allows the control system to adapt to the demands of the task and develop appropriate error correction processes needed to perform the skill correctly and to stabilize performance from one trial to the next.

From an applied perspective, the bandwidth procedure provides an interesting means of individualizing the systematic reduction of the frequency of augmented feedback for students. If, as suggested by the results discussed earlier of Winstein and Schmidt (1990), weaning individuals from the need for augmented feedback is beneficial for learning, then providing augmented feedback on the basis of performance-based bandwidths naturally reduces the frequency with which augmented feedback is given. Because the bandwidth is related to individual performance, the "weaning" process becomes one that is specific to the performance of each individual.

Summary KR.   Another way to reduce the frequency of KR while providing the same amount of information as if KR were given after every trial is to provide a summary of KR after a certain number of trials during practice. For example, suppose that a person is practicing a shooting skill where he or she cannot see the target because of the distance involved. Efficiency of practice could be increased if that person did not need to receive KR after each shot but could receive KR about each shot after every 10 shots. The question here is, however, How would this influence learning? Because the frequency of KR research has been reasonably consistent in showing that reduced KR frequency does not hinder learning, could learning actually be enhanced by reducing frequency while at the same time providing the same amount of information as if it were given 100% of the time during practice?

An experiment by Schmidt, Young, Swinnen, and Shapiro (1989) effectively demonstrates a current view about providing KR in summary form during practice. In this experiment, which was a replication and extension of an earlier study by Lavery (1962), subjects practiced moving a lever along a trackway to achieve a goal movement time. During the 90 trials of practice, KR was presented to subjects as a graphical representation on a piece of paper. One group received this KR after every trial, the other three groups received a summary of their performances after 5, 10, or 15 trials. The results of this experiment can be seen in Figure 7.4–8. As you can see, the results showed little differences among the groups during practice or on a retention test given 10 min after practice. However, on a retention test given 2 days later, the group that had received KR after every trial performed the worst while the group who had summary KR every 15 trials performed the best.

The summary KR benefit has been considered to be related to factors similar to the frequency of KR benefit. That is, during the no-KR practice trials, subjects engage in beneficial cognitive processing that is not characteristic of subjects who receive KR after every trial. This processing is speculated to involve working memory effort related to comparing sensory feedback information with KR, which results in developing a memory representation that does not depend on the presence of KR for retrieval. Thus, in both summary and frequency of KR experimental situations, subjects may in effect operate on KR in a similar

FIGURE 7.4-8   Results of the experiment by Schmidt, et al., showing the effects of learning a timing movement with different summary KR conditions. (Sum 1 = KR after every trial; Sum 5 = KR for 5 trials presented every 5 trials, etc.)

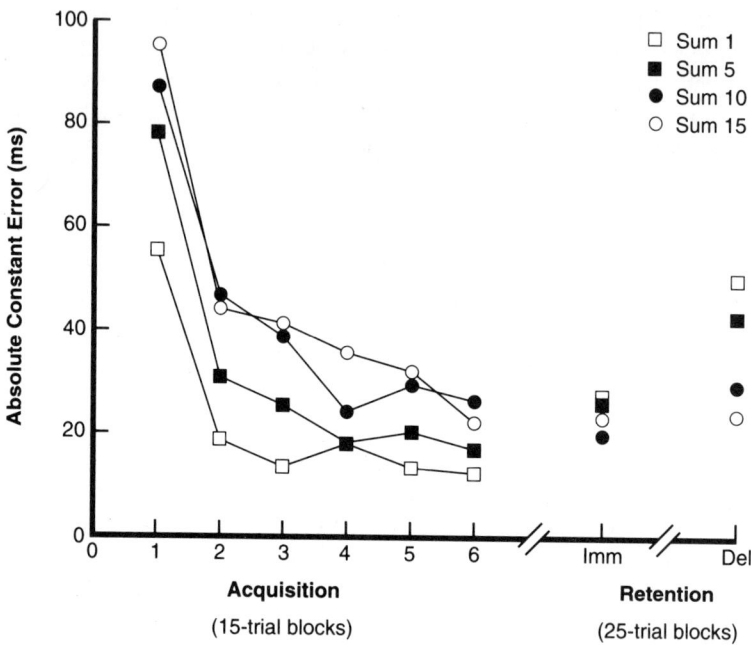

way. KR is used by subjects to compare their own sensory feedback-based performance and to update their developing memory representation of the skill being learned. If this is so, then in the summary conditions where more trials are summarized than can be effectively stored in working memory, subjects are probably not attending to the complete summary, but either to the general trend of their performance over the summarized trials or only to the most recent trials provided. If the latter is what occurs, the summary condition becomes essentially the same as the frequency of KR experimental condition, a point made from the results of an experiment by Sidaway, Moore, & Schoenfelder-Zohdi (1991).

Summary

Because augmented feedback is such an important part of skill learning, it is important to understand what information should be provided to facilitate learning and how often that information should be given. Three points are important for determining what augmented feedback informa-

tion should be given. First, the precision of the information should be determined. Augmented feedback can be either too precise or too general to aid learning. Second, the content of the augmented feedback should be determined. To determine the content of augmented feedback, it is essential to understand that augmented feedback serves to direct attention to certain parts of the skill and that it is important to use augmented feedback to direct attention to the most important part of the skill that is to be improved on the next trial. Third, the form of presenting augmented feedback should be established. While verbal augmented feedback is the most common means, alternative methods, such as videotape replay, graphic representations of movement kinematics, or augmenting sensory feedback can be used effectively. With regard to augmented feedback frequency, it seems that augmented feedback should not be provided on every trial. Thus, there are many questions that the instructor of motor skills must answer before augmented feedback can be confidently provided to students to most effectively facilitate learning.

Related Readings

Keefe, F. J., & Surwit, R. S. (1978). Electromyographic feedback: Behavioral treatment of neuromuscular disorders. *Journal of Behavioral Medicine, 1,* 13–25.

Lindahl, L. G. (1945). Movement analysis as in industrial training method. *Journal of Applied Psychology, 29,* 420–436.

Newell, K. M., & McGinnis, P. M. (1985). Kinematic information feedback for skilled performance. *Human Learning, 4,* 39–56.

Newell, K. M., Quinn, J. T., Sparrow, W. A., & Walter, C. B. (1983). Kinematic information feedback for learning a rapid arm movement. *Human Movement Science, 2,* 255–269.

Rothstein, A. L., & Arnold, R. K. (1976). Bridging the gap: Application of research on videotape feedback and bowling. *Motor Skills: Theory into Practice, 1,* 36–61.

Salmoni, A. W., Schmidt, R. A., & Walter, C. B. (1984). Knowledge of results and motor learning: A review and critical reappraisal. *Psychological Bulletin, 95,* 355–386. (Read the section on precision of KR.)

CONCEPT 7.5

The timing of augmented feedback relates to concurrent or terminal
presentation and to the intervals of time preceding
and following terminal presentation

Key Terms

concurrent
  augmented
  feedback
terminal
  augmented
  feedback

biofeedback
KR-Delay
  Interval

subjective
  error
  estimate
Post-KR
  Interval

Applications

Two important issues related to the timing of augmented feedback are whether it should be presented concurrently or terminally, and how time and activity during intervals preceding and following the presentation of augmented feedback affect it.

When you are learning to play golf you could receive augmented feedback at several different times. Feedback could be given while you swing, which is known as concurrent feedback, or it could be given after you have hit the ball, which is known as terminal feedback. If you receive feedback after you hit the ball, three time intervals become important to you. First, there is the time interval from

when you have finished hitting the ball until your instructor tells you what you did wrong or right. The second is the time that elapses from the instructor's giving you that information until you are allowed or able to hit another ball. Finally, there is the entire time period from hitting one practice ball and hitting another ball. These three periods of time are important to you because it is during these intervals that you have the opportunity to use the information you have received both from your own feedback systems and from augmented feedback.

Some very important practical questions must be considered in relation to these timing issues of providing augmented feedback. For example, does it matter if the feedback is given during or after a movement is completed? Does it matter how long a person must wait to get augmented feedback after completing a movement? How important is the amount of time between completing the movement and when the next movement is made? What will be the effect of doing something else during one of those intervals? These questions will provide the basis for the discussion in the following section.

Discussion

Two key issues relate to the timing aspects of augmented feedback. The first is whether it is better to give augmented feedback while the person is practicing, which is known as **concurrent augmented feedback,** or to give it at the end of a practice attempt, which is known as **terminal augmented feedback.** The other issue relates to terminally given augmented feedback. There are

two intervals of time created between the end of one practice attempt and the beginning of the next when augmented feedback is given after a practice attempt. These two intervals are illustrated in Figure 7.5–1. The interval of time between the end of a practice attempt and the giving of augmented feedback is typically referred to as the KR-Delay Interval. The interval that follows the augmented feedback and the beginning of the next practice

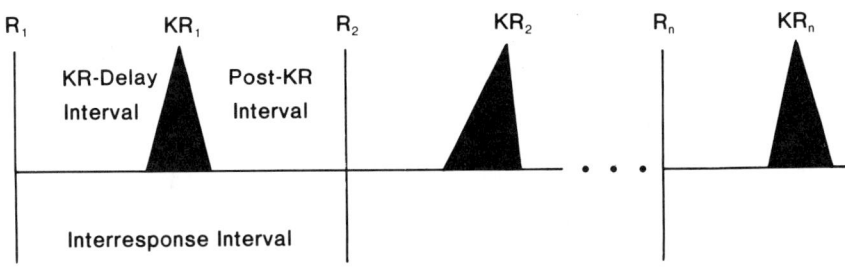

FIGURE 7.5-1
Intervals of time related to KR during the acquisition of a skill.

trial is the Post-KR Interval. Note that the terminology used to describe these two intervals is based on the traditional labels used to identify them. The use of the term KR shows that historically, the research investigating these intervals has focused on the use of KR as augmented feedback. However, these intervals are also relevant to the other forms of augmented feedback as well.

Concurrent Augmented Feedback

When augmented feedback is given concurrently with performing a skill, it is usually in the form of augmented sensory feedback. Two types are most common. One involves enhancing the feedback available in the environment and is called augmented environmental feedback. Examples of this type include having a buzzer sound when a target is hit or having a light go on when a response is off-target. The other type, popularly known as **biofeedback,** involves providing information about physiological processes through the use of instrumentation. Thus, sensory feedback can be augmented by providing an external source of information. Two examples of biofeedback that relate to motor skill learning are having a buzzer sound along with an electromyographic (EMG) signal from a muscle group, and augmenting the heartbeat so the person can hear each beat.

Augmented environmental feedback. There is evidence of two types of effects when augmented environmental feedback is provided after a skill is performed. One is that initial performance is very good, but then performance asymptotes and can

actually decline on transfer trials where the augmented feedback is removed (e.g., Annett, 1959, 1970; Fox & Levy, 1969; Patrick & Mutlusoy, 1982). In these situations, it appears that learners direct their attention away from the critical sensory feedback related to the movement being made and direct it toward the augmented feedback so that it becomes a crutch and therefore necessary for future performance (e.g., Karlin & Mortimer, 1963; Lintern & Roscoe, 1980).

The other effect is that the concurrent use of augmented environmental feedback can be an effective training device. Examples of this effect have been reported by Lintern and his colleagues in work related to the training of flight skills for airplane pilots (e.g., Lintern, 1980; Lintern, Roscoe, Koonce, & Segal, 1990; Lintern, Roscoe, & Sivier, 1990). In those experiments, augmented environmental feedback was provided by instrumentation on the control panel of the aircraft. Specific benefits of visual augmentation of feedback have been reported for training pilots in landing and bombing skills. It is worth noting that in these studies, Lintern and his colleagues also found situations where augmenting feedback is of no benefit and can actually hinder performance. They argue (Lintern, Roscoe, & Sivier, 1990) that learning with augmented feedback will benefit to the extent that the feedback sensitizes the learner to properties or relationships in the task that specify how the system being learned can be controlled.

Another perspective on the type of effect to expect from using concurrent augmented environmental feedback has been provided by Annett

(1959, 1969, 1970). He hypothesized that there is probably a maximum amount of value in augmented feedback, which can be related to the informativeness of feedback instrinsic to the task itself. If the task instrinsic feedback is high, such that the skill could actually be learned without augmented feedback, then to augment this feedback and provide it concurrently while performing can lead to improved learning, and does not establish dependence on the augmented feedback. On the other hand, when the task intrinsic feedback is low, providing augmented sensory feedback concurrently appears to develop a dependency on the augmented feedback. In this latter case, there appears to be a tendency for people to become dependent on the augmented feedback and not try to discover the critical feedback that their own sensory system is receiving while performing the task.

Biofeedback. The most commonly used form of biofeedback in motor skill learning research has been EMG biofeedback. Most of what we know about the effect of EMG biofeedback on skill learning comes from research done in rehabilitation settings. The typical results of this work show beneficial effects (see Inglis, Campbell, & Donald, 1976; Leiper, Miller, Lang, & Herman, 1981; Sandweiss & Wolf, 1985; Wolf, 1983, for examples and reviews of research on biofeedback related to motor skill rehabilitation).

This research can be illustrated by an example of a study reported by Mulder and Hulstijn (1985). In this experiment, subjects practiced a movement that required the abduction of the big toe while keeping the other toes of the foot from moving. While this may seem to be a strange task, the researchers argued that the task required subjects to control a specific muscle group to enable the action to occur, which was common to many motor skills people must learn. Five different feedback conditions were compared. One condition allowed normal proprioceptive feedback, but subjects could not see their foot and received no verbal feedback about their performance. Another condition involved proprioceptive and visual

feedback where subjects could see their foot but received no verbal feedback. The third condition provided subjects with proprioceptive, visual, and tactile feedback where they could see their foot and also received tactile feedback from a force meter, but received no verbal feedback. Two additional groups received augmented sensory feedback in the form of biofeedback. These groups saw either an EMG signal or a force meter display in addition to normal proprioceptive and visual feedback. Results showed that the two augmented biofeedback groups performed better than the nonaugmented groups on each of the two days of training. However, it is important to note that, as in many other biofeedback studies, tests of learning were not provided. As a result, we can only speculate about the effects on learning, that is, whether the observed effects were temporary performance or long-lasting learning effects.

Another form of biofeedback that has been used in motor learning research can be seen in an experiment reported by Daniels and Landers (1981) involving rifle shooting training. They presented augmented heartbeat information auditorially to subjects during their shooting performance. The goal of using this feedback was to assist subjects in learning to squeeze the rifle trigger between heartbeats, which had been established as a characteristic of elite shooters. Results indicated that the use of biofeedback facilitated acquisition of this important shooting skill and led to improved shooting scores.

Concurrent vs. terminal augmented feedback. Because both concurrent and terminal augmented feedback have been considered in this discussion, it will be helpful to consider how these two presentation timing characteristics for augmented feedback compare. The most useful basis for comparison comes from research in which both types of augmented feedback have been considered in the same experimental setting. Research in which this comparison has been made has typically considered augmented environmental feedback where a mechanical device was used to signify some performance characteristic, such as being on- or off-target. Some examples of these types of experiments were discussed earlier in this discussion. The experiments described earlier that were reported by Goldstein and Rittenhouse (1954) and by Annett (1959) provided evidence that terminal feedback for two different types of tasks led to better learning than did concurrent feedback. This result is typical of the research comparing concurrently and terminally presented augmented feedback.

The KR-Delay Interval

The interval of time between the completion of a movement and the presentation of augmented feedback traditionally has been, termed the **KR-Delay Interval,** although it also has been called the information feedback (IF) delay interval. This time interval has led to much confusion in its relationship to learning. For example, Ammons (1958) proposed that lengthening the KR-Delay Interval would lead to poorer learning because the information value of the KR would diminish over time. On the other hand, Adams (1971) concluded that the delay of KR has little or no effect on skill learning. Since the time of these two conclusions, researchers have provided a clearer picture of the actual influence of various manipulations that can be associated with this interval.

To appropriately discuss this interval, it will be best to consider two variables that are commonly manipulated in investigations of the role of the KR-Delay Interval on skill learning. These two variables are time, or variations in the length of the interval, and activity, which involves investigating cognitive and motor activity during the interval.

The length of the KR-Delay Interval. One outcome of early research involving the KR-Delay Interval was that distinct contrasts were evident between human and animal learning (see Adams, 1987). Human research established that KR was more than a reward, because KR had informational value that humans used to solve problems, such as to learn a skill. And it became evident that the effect of delaying KR in human skill learning led to different results than occurred when rewards were delayed in animal learning. Whereas animal learning studies showed that delaying reward led to decreased learning (e.g. Roberts, 1930), human skill learning studies showed that delaying KR did not influence learning. Perhaps the most striking example of this latter finding is a study by Bilodeau and Bilodeau (1958b). They reported five experiments in which they used tasks such as lever positioning and micrometer dial turning. The KR-Delay Interval varied from a few seconds to seven days. The consistent results in all of these experiments was that KR delays, even up to one week, did not affect the learning of those skills.

While delaying the presentation of KR does not appear to affect skill learning, there does seem to be a minimum amount of time that must pass before KR is given. A recent study by Swinnen, Schmidt, Nicholson, and Shapiro (1990), showed evidence that giving KR too soon after a movement was completed had a negative effect on learning. Two experiments involved learning a task in which subjects moved a lever through a two-reversal movement to achieve a specific movement time goal (Experiment 1), and learning a coincident timing task where subjects had to move a lever, coincident in time with the appearance of a target light, that passed by the light with the appropriate rate of speed (Experiment 2). In each experiment, KR was given "instantaneously," which meant the subjects saw their score immediately upon the completion of the required movement, or KR was delayed for 8 sec after completing the movement in Experiment 1 or for 3.2 sec in Experiment 2. The results of these two experiments can be seen in Figure 7.5–2. In both experiments, the two KR-delay conditions were not different from each other at the end of the practice trials but were significantly different on retention tests given 10 min later and 2 days later (Experiment 1) and 10 min, 2 days, and 4 months later (Experiment 2).

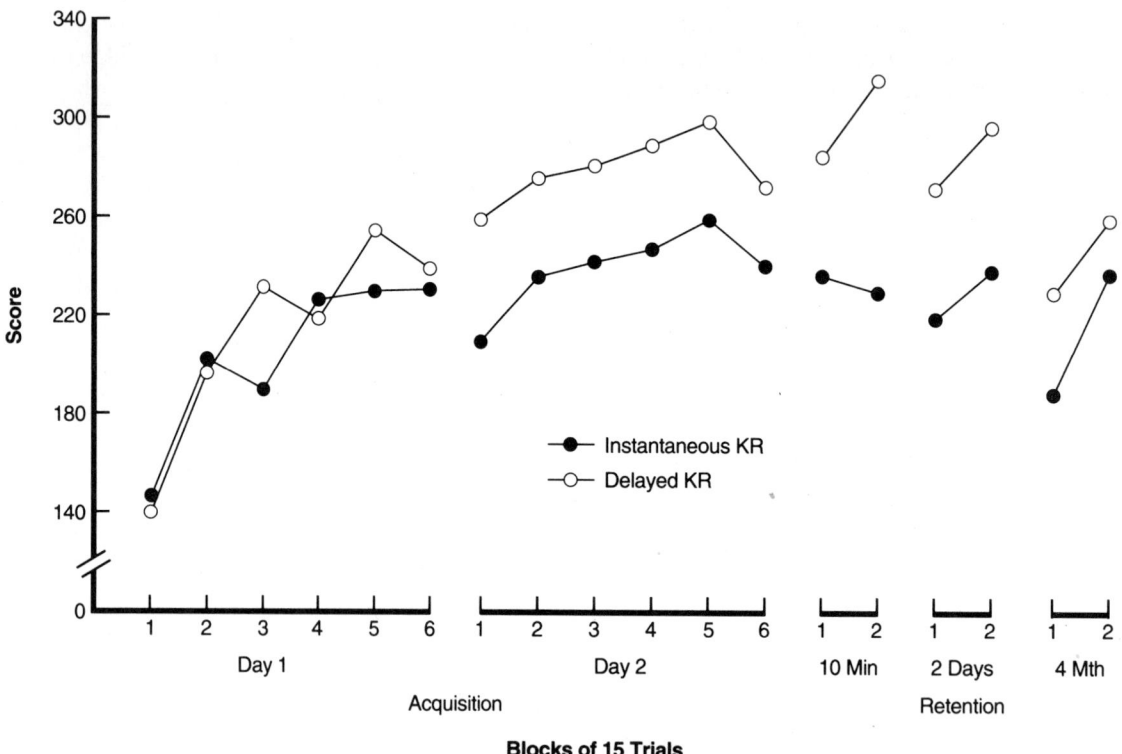

FIGURE 7.5-2   Results of an experiment by Swinnen, et al., showing the effect of instantaneous KR compared to delayed KR for learning an anticipation timing task that required accurate timing and force production.

The authors proposed that the degrading of learning that resulted from providing KR too soon after the completion of a movement was due to the need for learners to engage in the subjective analysis of response-produced feedback, which is essential for developing appropriate error detection capabilities. This poorly developed capability was not evident until retention tests were given in which subjects had to respond without KR and therefore had to rely on their own error detection capabilities to respond. Delaying KR by only a few seconds appeared to be sufficient to enable subjects to develop this capability, whereas providing KR immediately after completing a movement hindered the development of this capability.

Activity during the KR-Delay Interval.   The evidence that has accumulated from the research of the effects of activity during the KR-Delay Interval has provided a variety of results. In some cases, activity has no effect on skill learning, while in other cases, activity has been shown to both hinder and benefit learning. Rather than establish a confusing state of affairs, these different results have provided insight into the learning processes in which a learner engages during the KR-Delay Interval, and they have provided distinct implications for developing effective instructional strategies.

The most common effect of activity during the KR-Delay Interval on skill learning is that it has

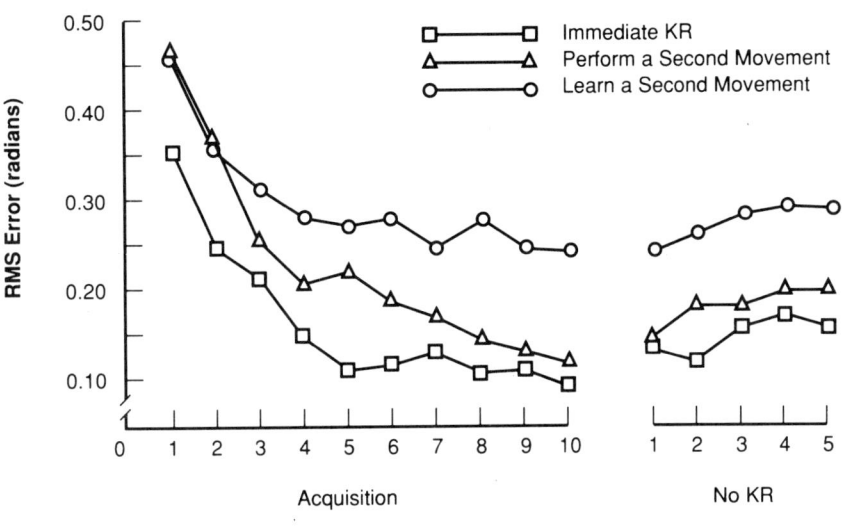

FIGURE 7.5-3
Results from the experiment by Marteniuk showing the interference effects of learning another complex movement during the KR-delay Interval.

---

no influence on learning. Experiments investigating the activity effect have demonstrated this result for over twenty years (e.g., Bilodeau, 1969; Boulter, 1964; Marteniuk, 1986). The experiment by Marteniuk will serve as an appropriate example of the research yielding this conclusion. Subjects practiced a complex lever movement that required them to move a lever to produce a specific sine-wave-like pattern that had both spatial and temporal goals. A control group received KR within a few seconds after completing the movement and engaged in no activity during the KR-Delay Interval. Another group had a 40-sec KR-Delay Interval, but did not engage in any activity during the interval. The third group also had a 40-sec KR-Delay Interval, but engaged in a lever movement task in which the subjects attempted to reproduce a movement pattern that the experimenter had just performed. The results of this experiment indicated that during acquisition trials and on a no-KR retention test given 10-min later, there were no differences among the groups.

Another effect of activity during the KR-Delay Interval is that it *hinders learning.* An example of

an experiment demonstrating this effect is one that was a part of the study by Marteniuk (1986) referred to in the preceding paragraph. Marteniuk reasoned that the activity of reproducing a movement pattern during the KR-Delay Interval did not interfere with learning because the activity did not demand the same type of learning processes as did learning the lever movement task. He hypothesized that if the KR-Delay Interval activity were to interfere with learning, it would have to interfere with the same learning processes as those required by the primary task being learned. Therefore, in two follow-up experiments Marteniuk added a condition in which subjects had to learn another skill during the KR-Delay Interval. In one experiment, the skill was another lever movement skill, while in the other experiment, the skill was a cognitive skill that was a number-guessing task. Results of the experiment in which subjects either learned another movement or simply repeated a movement made by the experimenter are presented in Figure 7.5–3. The results of this experiment resemble those of the one in which the number learning task was involved. In

FIGURE 7.5-4 Results of the experiment by Hogan and Yanowitz showing the effects of having subjects guess (Estimate) or not guess (No Estimate) their error after each response and before receiving KR for trials when KR was present or withdrawn.

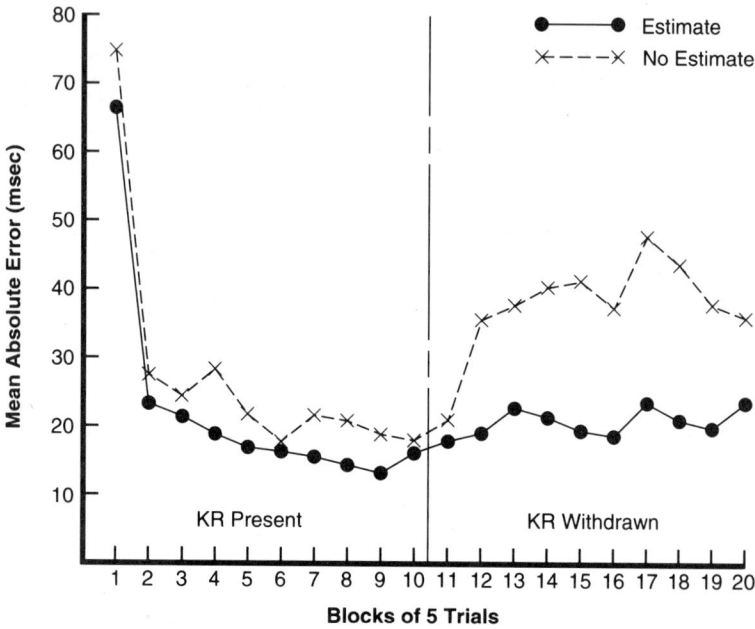

both experiments the results indicated that learning another skill during the KR-Delay Interval interfered with learning the primary skill. This interference effect has also been reported by Shea and Upton (1976), in which subjects engaged in short-term memory tasks during the KR-Delay Interval, and by Swinnen (1990) in two experiments in which subjects were required to estimate the movement time error of the experimenter's lever movement performed during the KR-Delay Interval.

Finally, results of some experiments indicate that certain activities during the KR-Delay Interval can actually *benefit learning*. The first evidence of this beneficial activity effect was reported by Hogan and Yanowitz (1978). Subjects practiced a task where the goal was to move a handle along a trackway a specified distance of 47 cm in 200 msec. One group did not engage in any activity before receiving KR while a second group was required to give a **subjective error estimation,** which is a verbal estimate of their own error for each trial before receiving KR for that trial. The results of this experiment can be seen in Figure

7.5–4. Although there were no differences between groups at the end of the 50 trials of practice, the group that had engaged in the error estimation activity during the KR-Delay Interval performed significantly better on retention trials where no KR was provided. These same error estimation benefits have been reported in two experiments by Swinnen (1990).

What do these different effects of activity in the KR-Delay Interval reveal about learning processes that occur during this interval of time? Swinnen (1990; Swinnen et al., 1990) has argued that the learner is actively engaged in processing movement information and in detection of errors during the KR-Delay Interval. He bases this argument on the experiment mentioned earlier that replicated the one by Hogan and Yanowitz (1978). However, Swinnen extended their experiment by adding a group of subjects that had to guess the experimenter's error during the KR-Delay Interval. In this situation, the experimenter made a movement after the subject finished his or her movement. Before receiving KR about his or her own movement, the subject had to estimate the

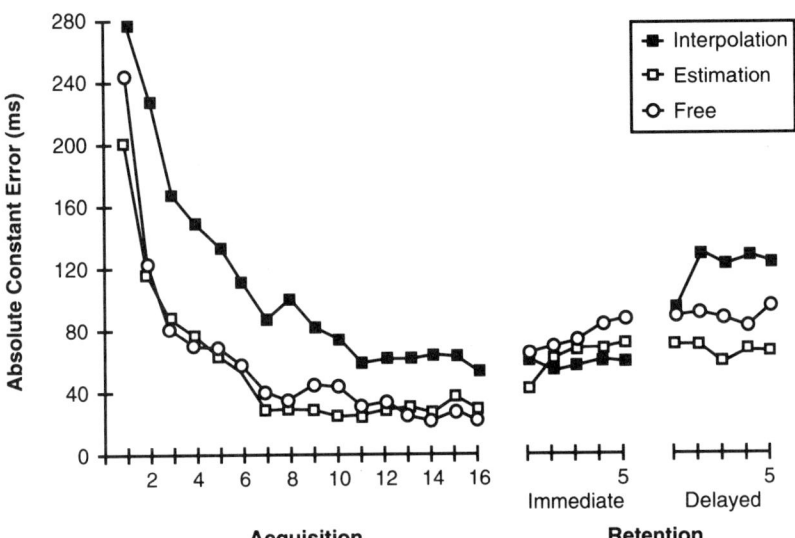

FIGURE 7.5-5 Results from the experiment by Swinnen showing the influence of estimating the experimenter's movement error (interpolation group) and of estimating the subject's own error (estimation group) during the KR-delay Interval compared with no activity during the interval (free group).

experimenter's error. As you can see in the results of this experiment shown in Figure 7.5–5, this estimation did not lead to learning the skill as well as when the subjects estimated their own error. However, it was better than not estimating error at all during the KR-Delay Interval.

Thus, there is evidence that during the KR-Delay Interval, learners are involved in self-generated error estimation activities that may benefit future performance. If the evidence described earlier is viewed from this perspective, the three different effects of activity during the KR-Delay Interval would be expected. When learners are encouraged to engage in this type of error-detection activity, as occurred in the experiments by Hogan and Yanowitz (1976) and Swinnen (1990), the learner's error detection capability is enhanced, which benefits learning. However, if learners are engaged in activity that does not permit such self-generation of error estimation, as would appear to have occurred in the experiments by Marteniuk (1986), Shea and Upton (1978), and Swinnen, et al. (1990) where attention-demanding activity was required during the KR-Delay Interval, then learning is hindered. Finally, if the activity engaged in during the KR-Delay

Interval is not attention demanding to the degree that the learner can still engage in appropriate error-estimation processing, then learning will not be influenced by the KR-Delay Interval activity, which was demonstrated in the experiments by Marteniuk (1986) and others.

For instructional purposes the most significant implication of these results is that students can be engaged in activity that will benefit them after they complete a movement and before they receive augmented feedback from a teacher or coach. This activity should require them to actively attempt to determine what they did wrong on that particular trial. They should try to answer the question, "What do you think you did wrong?" before they are told what they did wrong. Based on the research evidence, this type of activity will have a positive influence on skill learning because it forces the learner to subjectively evaluate his or her own sensory feedback in relation to the response that was just made.

The Post-KR Interval

The interval of time between the presentation of augmented feedback and the beginning of the next trial, or practice attempt, is commonly called the

Post-KR Interval. This interval of time became the focus of research interest after research and comments by the Bilodeaus (e.g., Bilodeau & Bilodeau, 1958b; Bilodeau, 1969) and Adams (1971) that this interval may be the most important interval of time during skill acquisition. The basis for this view is that the Post-KR Interval represents the period of time during which the learner has both his or her own sensory feedback and the externally provided augmented feedback. He or she must use this information to develop a plan of action for the next trial. Accordingly, the amount of time available for the processing and the activity that may occur concurrently with this processing became the variables of interest for research about the Post-KR Interval.

The length of the Post-KR Interval. The expectations of how the length of the Post-KR Interval would influence skill learning are similar to those discussed earlier for the KR-Delay Interval. That is, there would appear to be an optimal range of time during which the next trial should occur after KR is given. If the next trial occurs too soon after KR, the important processing activities would not have sufficient time to be carried out. Or, if the next trial is delayed for too long after KR is given, some forgetting will occur and the next response will not be as good as it would have been otherwise. This reasoning seems logical, and indeed has been stated before by others (e.g., Adams, 1971).

What is interesting is that the only empirical support for these expectations relates to the "too early" end of the time continuum just described. This evidence was reported by Weinberg, Guy, and Tupper (1964) who demonstrated that for learning a limb positioning movement, a 1-sec Post-KR Interval led to poorer acquisition than did a 5-, 10-, or 20-sec interval. None of these latter three interval lengths revealed any differences. A similar finding that indicated the need for a minimum Post-KR Interval length was reported by Rogers (1974). It is interesting to note that Gallagher and Thomas (1980) reported similar results for children.

Thus, similar to the KR-Delay Interval, there appears to be a minimum amount of time needed to engage in the learning processes required during the KR-Delay Interval if optimal learning is to be achieved. What is not known, and will await further research, is how this minimum amount of time changes as a function of the skill being learned or as a function of the stage of learning of the learner.

With respect to the other end of the optimum range of time for the next trial to begin following KR being given, there is no evidence indicating that too long a delay will hinder learning. An example of the type of research addressing this question was reported by Magill (1977) who compared Post-KR Interval lengths of 10- and 60-sec for subjects learning three limb positions on a curvilinear positioning device. Results showed no differences between the two interval lengths.

Activity during the Post-KR Interval. The effect of engaging in activity in the Post-KR Interval is similar to what was seen for the KR-Delay Interval. Depending on the kind of activity, activity can interfere with learning, benefit learning, or have no influence on learning. An interesting feature of these effects is that they are not in line with traditional predictions of the effect of activity during the Post-KR Interval. Earlier views of KR (e.g., Adams, 1971; Bilodeau, 1969; Newell, 1976) typically expected that because so many important information processing activities occurred during this interval, engaging in other activity during this time would interfere with learning. But more recent evidence has shown that this is only one of three effects that can occur.

That activity during the Post-KR Interval has *no effect on skill learning* has clearly been the most common finding. An example of this result is seen in an experiment reported by Lee and Magill (1983). Subjects practiced making an arm movement through a series of three small wooden barriers in 1050 msec. During the Post-KR Interval, one group engaged in a motor activity of learning the same movement in 1350 msec, one group engaged in a cognitive activity involving number guessing, and a third group did not do any

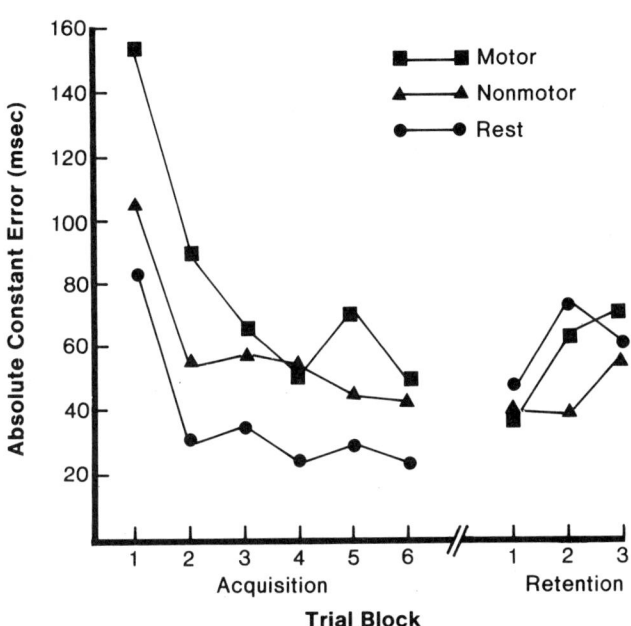

FIGURE 7.5-6 Results of the experiment by Lee and Magill showing acquisition and retention performance for absolute constant error (|CE|) as a function of activity during the post-KR interval. Retention performance is without KR.

activity. As can be seen from the results presented in Figure 7.5–6, at the end of the practice trials the two activity groups showed poorer performance than the non-activity group. However, on a no-KR retention test, the three groups did not differ from each other.

Results indicating that activity during the Post-KR Interval *hinders learning* have been reported by several researchers (e.g., Benedetti & McCullagh, 1987; Boucher 1974; Hardy, 1983; Swinnen, 1990, Expt. 3). Of these experiments, only those by Benedetti and McCullagh (1987) and Swinnen (1990) included an appropriate test for learning. In both of these experiments, the interfering activity was a cognitive activity. Subjects in the experiment by Benedetti and McCullagh engaged in a mathematics problem-solving task, whereas subjects in the experiment by Swinnen were involved in guessing the movement time error of the experimenter's lever movement made during the Post-KR Interval.

Only one experiment has reported *beneficial learning effects* for activity in the Post-KR Interval. An experiment reported by Magill (1988) involved subjects learning to perform a two-

component movement in which each component had its own criterion movement time. One group was required to learn two additional two-component movements during the Post-KR Interval and one group was required to learn a mirror-tracing task. A third group did not engage in activity during the Post-KR Interval. Results showed different effects for retention and transfer. When subjects were asked to perform the skill on a no-KR retention test given one day after practice, there were no group differences. However, on a transfer test where subjects had to perform a new two-component task similar to the one they had learned, the two Post-KR Interval activity groups performed better than the no-activity group. These beneficial transfer effects were proposed to be due to the increased problem solving activity experience during practice by the Post-KR Interval activity groups. The activity enabled them to more successfully transfer to a situation that required new problem-solving activity of a kind similar to that experienced in practice.

In terms of instructional implications, the evidence related to the Post-KR Interval suggests that it does not need to be given much direct consideration in teaching settings. Although there appears to be a minimum Post-KR Interval length, the minimum does not seem problematic when applied to the typical teaching situation. And although some activities have been found to be both detrimental and beneficial to skill learning, more evidence is needed to address the effects before instruction applications can be made with confidence.

Summary

One of the benefits of investigating issues related to the timing of providing augmented feedback is that it provides a means of addressing questions about learning processes involved between trials during practice. It seems clear from the evidence discussed in this section that attention to processing of sensory feedback critical to performing the skill is important for effective skill learning. Evidence for this was provided in studies showing the problems that can result from providing augmented feedback concurrently with performing the skill. The typical finding seems to be that this form of presentation of augmented feedback establishes a dependence on the availability of it by shifting the learners' attention away from sensory feedback related to task performance to the augmented feedback itself. Also, processing of the sensory feedback seems critical because both the KR-Delay and Post-KR Intervals can be too short to allow optimal learning. Further support of this need for processing sensory feedback was seen in experiments where subjects who estimated their own error prior to receiving KR learned the skill better than those who did not.

Related Readings

Adams, J. A. (1971). A closed-loop theory of motor learning. *Journal of Motor Behavior, 3,* 111–149. (Read pp. 132–136.)

Bilodeau, E. A., & Bilodeau, I. M. (1958). Variation of temporal intervals among critical events in five studies of knowledge of results. *Journal of Experimental Psychology, 55,* 603–612.

Lee, T. D., & Magill, R. A. (1983). Activity during the post-KR interval: Effects upon performance or learning? *Research Quarterly for Exercise and Sport, 54,* 340–345.

Salmoni, A. W., Schmidt, R. A., & Walter, C. B. (1984). Knowledge of results and motor learning: A review and critical reappraisal. *Psychological Bulletin, 95,* 355–386. (Read section on the Temporal Locus of KR, pp. 364–372.)

STUDY QUESTIONS FOR CHAPTER 7

1. What is meant by the term "modeling" as it relates to motor skill instruction? What are three important issues that must be considered when determining how to provide an effective model?

2. What are two proposed reasons why modeling benefits motor learning?

3. How can you decide whether a skill would be learned best if it were practiced as a whole or in parts? Give a motor skill example to show how these rules can be applied to a teaching situation.

4. What are three different methods of practicing skills following a part method of instruction and practice? Give a motor skill example of each.

5. What are the two types of information referred to by the terms KR and KP? Give two examples of each.

6. Describe skill learning conditions where augmented feedback would be neccesary for learning, not be necessary for learning, facilitate learning, and be a hindrance to learning.

7. Explain how a skill that was dependent of the availability of augmented feedback early in learning can be performed later in learning without augmented feedback.

8. What is meant by the "precision" of augmented feedback? What do we know about the precision of augmented feedback and learning of motor skills?

9. What two important points must be strongly considered when deciding on augmented feedback or KP content? Give an example of a motor skill situation that illustrates these two points.

10. Why is augmented feedback frequency an important issue to consider when it refers to augmented feedback in a practice situation? What seems to be the most appropriate conclusion to draw regarding the frequency with which augmented feedback should be given during learning?

11. What are two important guidelines for the effective use of videotape as a form of augmented feedback?

12. What do we currently know about the use and benefit of kinematic information as augmented feedback to help learn a motor skill? When do you think this type of information would be most helpful?

13. What is the difference between concurrent and terminal augmented feedback? Give two examples of each.

14. What are the two time intervals associated with KR and practicing a skill? Why are researchers interested in investigating these intervals?

15. What can we conclude about the effect of time and activity during the KR-Delay Interval? During the Post-KR Interval? What do these conclusions tell us about the role played by KR in learning motor skills?

CHAPTER

8

PRACTICE ORGANIZATION

CONCEPT 8.1
A variety of practice experiences is essential for learning both closed and open skills.

CONCEPT 8.2
The amount of practice affects learning, although the effect is not always proportional.

CONCEPT 8.3
The spacing or distribution of practice can affect both practice performance and learning.

CONCEPT 8.4
Practice that occurs mentally can be beneficial for learning
new motor skills and for preparing to perform a skill.

CONCEPT 8.5
Practicing while physically fatigued appears to affect performance to
a greater degree than learning, although learning can be affected.

□

CONCEPT 8.1

A variety of practice experiences is essential for learning both closed and open skills

___

Key Terms

variable
    practice

contextual
    interference

contextual
    interference
    effect

blocked
    practice

random
    practice

serial practice

Application

The purpose of practicing a skill is to learn to perform that skill in situations where you will in some way be tested. For sports skills, the test may be in the form of a skill test, game, or match. For dance, the test may be a performance before an audience or judge. In a therapy context, the test is performing the skill in your everyday environment without the aid of the therapist. Thus, an important task for any instructor of motor skills is designing and establishing practice conditions that will lead to maximum test performance.

A characteristic of practice that is important relates to the variability of practice experiences. What this means is that it is essential to have a variety of practice experiences involving variations of the skill being learned so that a person can successfully perform a skill in a variety of performance situations. However, several questions need to be answered before variability of practice experiences can be effectively implemented. One of the questions concerns what type of variety of experiences needs to be included in practice. Another concerns how much variety is actually needed. Still another question concerns how to organize the variety of experiences in the practice sessions.

Open and closed skills differ with respect to how performance conditions in practice relate to conditions in a test situation. Closed skills, such as bowling or archery, can be practiced under conditions that are identical, or very similar, to those that will be faced in a test situation. On the other hand, open skills, such as hitting a pitched baseball or throwing a ball to a moving target, are always performed under conditions that are somewhat different from those during practice. As a result, it is not possible to establish practice conditions that will be exactly like those confronted in a test situation. However, the learning of both closed and open skills will benefit from experiencing practice conditions that allow the learner to perform the skill in a variety of movement conditions. It seems, then, that because of the differences between open and closed skills, the way in which variability of practice experiences should be developed will require different approaches.

In the discussion that follows, these issues will be addressed with the intent of providing some guidelines that you can use to establish effective practice conditions to take advantage of the benefit that variable experiences can provide.

□

Discussion

Some insight can be gained into the practice structure issue by considering a theoretical model of skill acquisition applied to teaching that was developed by Gentile (1972). An important concept in that presentation was the distinction between *relevant* and *non-relevant* stimuli or conditions. These terms refer to the conditions related to performing a skill that are either relevant or not relevant in establishing how the movement must be performed to achieve the desired goal of the movement. The idea behind the use of these terms should not be new to you because you studied this situation in Concepts 2.2 and 4.2. Relevant stimuli can be considered as movement-related information that must be attended to or taken into account if the goal of the movement is to be achieved. Non-relevant stimuli include all other nonrelated environmental information.

To hit a racquetball in a rally, the relevant information to be taken into account may include the opponent's position on the court, the speed of the ball, the angle and location of the rebound from the front wall, etc. If these pieces of information are not taken into account, chances of successfully returning the ball are greatly reduced. Non-relevant information, on the other hand, includes information related to who is watching, how quiet or loud the spectators are, what the opponent is wearing, the type of racquet the opponent is using, etc. These factors, while they may be indirectly related to how you perform, have little to do with establishing the characteristics of the action you will produce to carry out the intended shot.

To develop appropriate practice conditions, it is necessary to consider the characteristics of the test situation. Of particular importance is determining the likelihood of whether the relevant and non-relevant stimuli for a skill will be novel during the test. Before this can be done, however, it is first necessary to understand how the relevant stimuli differ in closed and open skills. As you should recall from the discussion of Concept 1.1, closed skills require similar responses each time a response is required. In Gentile's terms, the likelihood of change for the relevant stimuli is close to zero. The performer can predict well in advance what the conditions will be like during the execution of the response. In contrast, open skills are performed under conditions in which relevant stimuli change during the movement execution and may vary from one attempt to the next. The performer is required to make rapid modifications in his or her plan of action to match the demands of the situation. Non-relevant stimuli conditions are likely to have a degree of novelty to them for both closed and open

skills. For example, the performance setting itself may be new to the person, there may be people watching, the spectators may be noisier than experienced before, or the situation may be unique in some way.

The Benefit of Variable Practice

One of the key features of Schmidt's schema theory (Schmidt, 1975), which was discussed in Concept 3.1, was the prediction that successful performance in a novel response situation was a function of the variability of practice experience by the individual. This prediction indicates that better retention performance and novel response performance would result from practice that requires more **variable practice** experiences than fewer variable experiences. Since the publication of schema theory, a number of studies have investigated this variability of practice prediction (see Lee, Magill, & Weeks, 1985, for a review of these studies). In general, results of experiments investigating the practice variability hypothesis have provided support for the prediction. Increasing variable practice has also been shown to be beneficial for retention performance as well (Shea & Kohl, 1990).

Variable practice can be applied to both closed and open skills. However, the way in which variable practice conditions are developed will differ to some degree because of how open and closed skills differ in terms of which characteristics of a performance situation will most likely be the same or novel in a test situation. These characteristics and how the practice variability hypothesis can be applied to instruction situations for both closed and open skills are discussed in the next sections.

Variable practice and closed skills. Because the test conditions for a closed skill include relevant stimuli that are stable and relatively predictable, and non-relevant stimuli that are likely to be novel, Gentile's model indicates that two conditions are important to incorporate into the practice prior to a test of closed skills. First, practice should be under the same conditions as will prevail under the test situation. Second, the relevant stimuli should be held constant while the non-relevant stimuli should be varied in the practice conditions.

These two points are supported by what you have already studied in this text. In the discussion of the practice-test relationship in Concept 5.3, you saw that increased remembering can be expected when the practice and test conditions are as similar as possible. At that time, it was stated that in terms of motor skills, this similarity situation seems especially pertinent to closed skills. Also, in the discussion in Concept 2.3 you saw that increased transfer from practice to test can be expected when the conditions are similar. This holds especially valid for closed skills. And evidence supporting the practice variability hypothesis of Schmidt's schema theory argues in favor of these two points.

Gentile's model provides a guideline for establishing *what* needs to be varied in the practice conditions. That is, non-relevant conditions rather than relevant stimuli need to be varied in practice. Other conditions need to be as similar as possible to the test conditions to maximize the transfer effects. The problem faced by the instructor is to determine which characteristics of the skill and/or performance context to vary during practice. However, if Gentile's ideas are applied, the decision becomes much simpler.

The basketball free throw will serve as a good example. Let's establish that there are two goals for the learner in this example: the learner needs to become proficient at successfully shooting a free throw, and the learner must learn to successfully shoot free throws in a game situation. These two goals suggest the type of practice conditions that should be established. On the one hand, there is a need to practice the free throw time after time in as constant a manner as possible, using the same relevant stimuli such as hand placement, body position, etc. The goal is to learn the appropriate movement pattern that will consistently put the ball through the basket. On the other hand, to accomplish the game-related goal, it is important to incorporate game conditions into the practice routine. Two-shot free throws, one-and-one situa-

tions, and one-shot only situations must be practiced often. Similarly, the non-relevant conditions, such as crowd noise, game score, time of game, fatigue characteristics of the player, etc., must be experienced and must be varied as much as possible to match the conditions that may be confronted in a game.

From this example it is possible to see how variability of practice can be incorporated into practice conditions for closed skills. The variety of experiences must be developed around the non-relevant conditions related to performing the skill under test conditions. For closed skills, these non-relevant conditions are performance context characteristics that establish the specific conditions in which the skill must be performed. For the relevant stimuli, similarity rather than variety of trial-to-trial experiences is the key. The instructor, then, needs to determine those characteristics of the skill itself and the context in which it will be performed that can be classified as relevant and non-relevant. Then an appropriate variety of practice experiences can be established in accordance with what needs to remain as constant as possible from one practice attempt to another, and what needs to vary from one practice attempt to another.

Variable practice and open skills. The unique characteristic of open skills is that each response that must be produced is a novel one. That is, the movements that must be done have probably not been done in exactly the same way before. Certain characteristics of the performance context are unique and therefore lead to the need to make some modification of previous movements carried out to achieve the goal of the skill. For example, if you are preparing to return a serve in tennis, it is likely that certain characteristics of the ball action will be unique to the serve being performed. Thus, practice of open skills not only needs to consider the practice-test relationship, but also the changing characteristics of the performance requirements for every performance situation. In effect, each practice attempt is like a novel test of the effect of prior practice.

FIGURE 8.1-1 Results of the experiment by Wrisberg and Ragsdale showing anticipation timing performance for high and low levels of stimulus variability and response requirements (HRR = high response requirements; LRR = low response requirements).

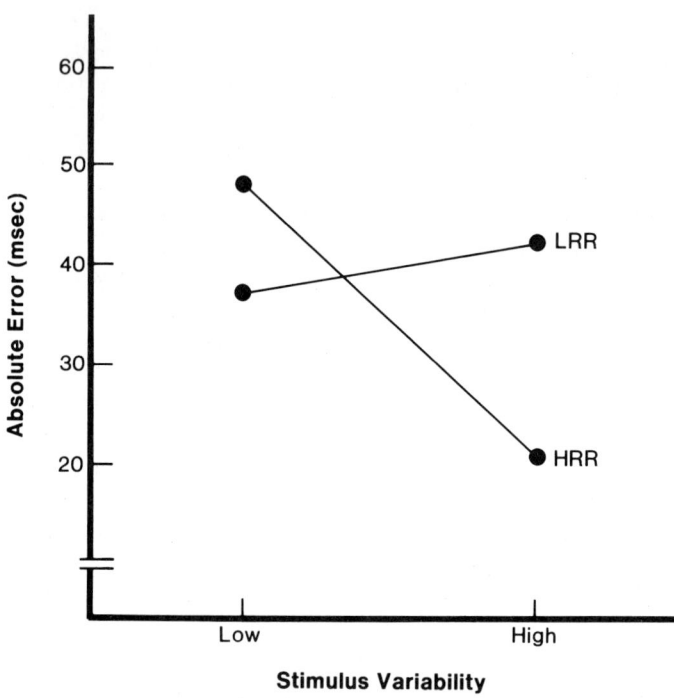

For open skills, the changing nature of the response requirements in every situation makes it essential to vary the relevant stimuli related to performing the skill. As Gentile (1972) explained, providing this type of variability during practice enables the performer to acquire the repertoire of motor patterns that match the possible responses that may be required.

The following research example will serve to support the point of the benefit of varying relevant stimuli during the practice of an open skill. In a test of Schmidt's schema theory variability of practice hypothesis, Wrisberg and Ragsdale (1979) had subjects practice an anticipation timing task. Subjects needed to depress a button to be coincident with the lighting of the last of a series of lights on a runway 29.5 cm long. Variability of relevant stimuli was developed for both stimulus and response characteristics of the task. The high stimulus-high response variability group practiced for 40 trials with stimulus velocities of 22.35, 31.29, 49.17, and 58.12 cm/sec. The high stimulus-low response variability group observed

the same 4 speeds for 40 trials but did not make an overt response. The low stimulus-high response subjects overtly responded to only one of the four speeds used for the high stimulus variability group. Finally, the low stimulus-low response group observed only one stimulus speed for 40 trials. All subjects were then required to perform in a test situation in which a novel stimulus speed of 40.23 cm/sec was encountered. Results, which are presented in Figure 8.1–1, showed that on the novel speed task, the subjects who were required to make an overt response and who had practiced the four different stimulus speeds were more accurate in responding to the novel speed. Thus, practicing making the required movement response with a variety of stimulus speeds (the relevant stimuli for this task) led to better performance with a novel stimulus speed than practicing with only one stimulus speed.

Although some studies have not found that variable practice leads to superior novel response performance (e.g., Johnson & McCabe, 1982; Zelaznik, 1977), sufficient evidence exists to give us

		Class Day					
		1	**2**	**3**	**4**	**5**	**6**
Blocked Practice	10 min 10 min 10 min	All Overhand	All Overhand	All Underhand	All Underhand	All Sidearm	All Sidearm
Random Practice	10 min 10 min 10 min	Underhand Overhand Underhand	Sidearm Underhand Overhand	Overhand Sidearm Sidearm	Underhand Overhand Overhand	Sidearm Overhand Sidearm	Underhand Underhand Sidearm
Serial Practice	10 min 10 min 10 min	Overhand Underhand Sidearm	Overhand Underhand Sidearm	Overhand Underhand Sidearm	Overhand Underhand Sidearm	Overhand Underhand Sidearm	Overhand Underhand Sidearm

FIGURE 8.1-2   A six-day unit plan demonstrating three different practice structures (blocked, random, and serial) for teaching three different throwing patterns (overhand, underhand, and sidearm). All classes are 30 minutes long and are divided into 10-minute segments. Each practice condition provides an equal amount of practice for each throwing pattern.

confidence in the variability of practice prediction. When a person is practicing a skill in which the test will be a novel response, an important requirement of the practice is that it provide a variety of experiences related to the skill being learned. As a result, a wide range of the varying relevant stimuli will be experienced. The result of this experience is enhancing the likelihood of being successful when a novel variation of the relevant stimuli is encountered.

An education application of the variable practice benefit.   An interesting application of the variability of practice component of Schmidt's (1975b) schema theory was made by Schmidt himself in an article published in 1977. He indicated that the approach taken in the typical movement education experience is well supported by the schema theory view of the benefit of practice variability. In a movement education class, students are encouraged to explore and experience a variety of ways to perform a skill. For example, students may be asked to find as many ways as possible to jump across two ropes lying on the floor to allow them to experience a variety of jumping movements. Or they may experience throwing a variety of objects at different targets using several different throwing patterns. The benefit of these types of experiences

is that they serve to help develop a strong motor recall schema that can be called upon when the students must eventually produce a novel response. As such, these movement exploration experiences provide a foundation that will serve the students well when they must learn more specific skills, such as pitching a baseball.

Organizing Variable Practice

You have seen that variability is beneficial as a characteristic for practicing both closed and open skills. For closed skill practice, the need is for variability in the non-relevant factors related to the movement. For open skills practice, the relevant as well as the non-relevant factors need to be varied. But how should variability be organized within a practice session or unit of instruction?

Suppose you are an elementary school physical education teacher and you are organizing a teaching unit on throwing for your classes. You have determined that you will devote six classes to this unit and you want the students to experience three variations of the throwing pattern: the overhand, underhand, and sidearm throws. How should these three different throws be arranged for practice during the six classes? Figure 8.1–2 shows three possible arrangements. One is to practice each throw in blocks of two days each (blocked practice). Another possibility is to practice each throw in some random arrangement with 10-minute blocks devoted to each particular pattern (random practice). Thus, each day three 10-minute blocks are experienced, although there is no specified order of occurrence for the three patterns; the only stipulation is that all three be practiced an equal amount over the course of the unit. The third arrangement, serial practice, also suggests a 10-minute block for each pattern. However, in this approach each pattern is practiced every day in the same order.

This organization problem is not unique to teaching physical education activities. It is characteristic of any situation where several variations of a skill must be practiced. In a dance setting, there could be tempo variations in a routine or other variations of particular components of a routine that must be practiced. In therapy situations, the patient may need to practice grasping objects of different sizes, weights, and shapes. Or the knee joint replacement patient may need to practice walking on different types of surfaces. The problem is the same for each of these practice situations where variations of a skill must be practiced. How should the practice of these variations be scheduled within the practice time available to facilitate learning to perform successfully in various situations?

The contextual interference approach to the scheduling question.   One way to address the question of how to best schedule variable practice is to incorporate a learning phenomenon known as the **contextual interference effect.** The term **contextual interference** was introduced by Battig (1979) to label the interference that results from practicing a task within the context of the practice situation. In some practice situations, a high degree of contextual interference can be established by having students practice several different but related skills during the same practice session. On the other hand, practicing only one skill during a practice session leads to a low contextual interference condition. Based on what you studied

in Concept 5.2 about the role of interference as an agent that induces forgetting, you might expect that a low contextual interference situation would lead to superior learning. However, Battig proposed that while the low contextual interference practice situation leads to superior practice performance, it results in much poorer retention performance than the high contextual interference situation. Thus, based on our continuing emphasis on the role of retention and transfer tests in making inferences about learning, high contextual interference practice conditions are predicted to lead to better skill acquisition.

The first test of Battig's prediction using motor skills was reported by Shea and Morgan (1979). They had subjects practice three movement patterns in which the goal was to move one arm through a series of small wooden barriers as rapidly as possible. Practice conditions were arranged so that one group practiced the three patterns following the blocked arrangement of each pattern in 18 trial blocks. A second group practiced the patterns in random arrangement so that the 18 trials of practice for each pattern were randomly distributed over the 54 total practice trials. Results supported Battig's prediction. The **blocked practice** group performed better during practice trials while the **random practice** group showed superior performance during retention trials and transfer trials where a new arrangement of barriers was introduced.

In an attempt to uncover possible reasons for these contextual interference results, Lee and Magill (1983b) added a third group to the two used by Shea and Morgan. The new group was called a **serial practice** condition. Here the 54 total practice trials were arranged so that movement pattern 1 was always followed by pattern 2, which was always followed by pattern 3. This group combined features of the blocked practice condition (perfect predictability of the upcoming pattern to be practiced) and of the random practice condition (high degree of interference between repetitions of any one pattern). The intent was to see which group the serial practice condition was more like, the blocked or the random practice.

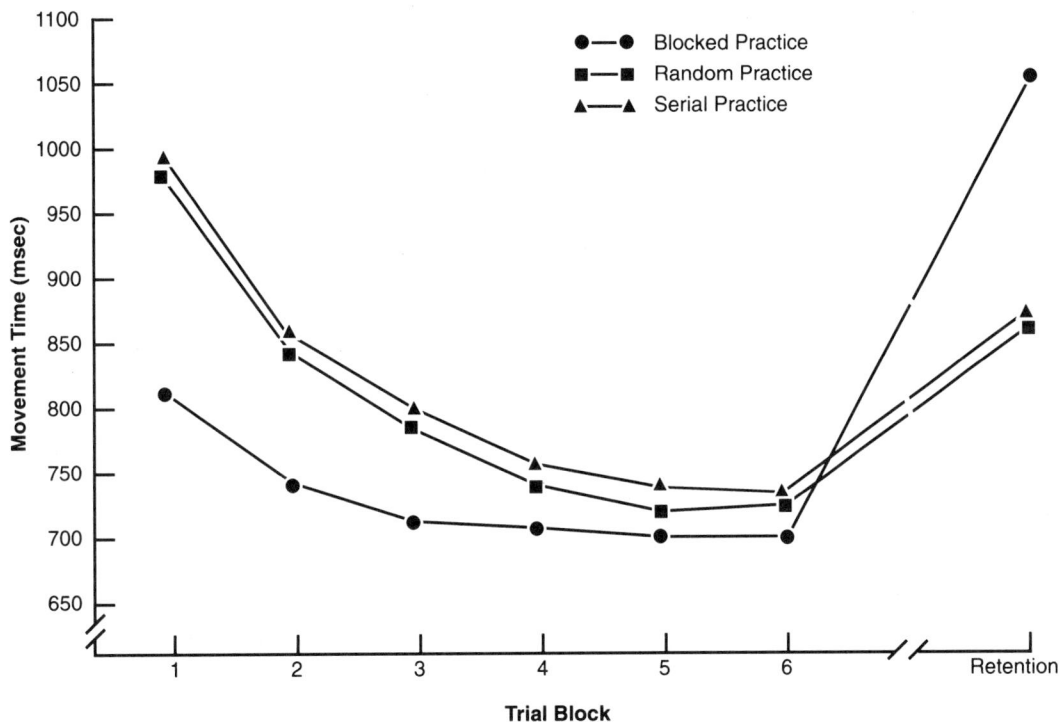

FIGURE 8.1-3 Results from the experiment by Lee and Magill showing mean movement time for completing three movement patterns using three different practice structures (blocked, random, and serial). Trial blocks (3 trials per block) 1 through 6 were with KR. The retention block was without KR.

Results, shown in Figure 8.1–3, indicated an almost exact similarity between the random and serial practice conditions during both practice performance and retention. Based on these results, Lee and Magill developed the argument that the contextual interference effect is essentially a cognitively based effect that creates a difficult practice condition in which subjects must engage in problem-solving activity each time the same pattern is practiced. As they viewed it, blocked practice allows the individual to devise and test action strategies to solve the problem of performing a movement. Interfering activity, which would necessitate the development and testing of action strategies for other movements, is eliminated. For the random and blocked conditions, the situation is just the opposite. Thus, the end result

is poorer practice performance under random and blocked practice conditions, but superior retention performance.

Perhaps the most striking negative effect of low contextual interference practice is that it prohibits the person from performing the practiced skills well in novel performance contexts. This effect is commonly seen in many contextual interference experiments. Blocked practice may lead to retention test performance under blocked conditions that is similar to that of people who practiced the skills randomly. But when switched to performing the skills under random test conditions, those who practiced according to a blocked schedule show a large decrement in retention performance (e.g., Shea, Kohl, & Indermill, 1990).

Thus, low contextual interference practice appears to develop a practice context dependency that will lead to poor test performance when a different skill variation or performance schedule context is involved. High contextual interference practice, on the other hand, appears to permit the learner to effectively adapt to novel skill variations and performance contexts.

High contextual interference schedule benefit outside the laboratory. Since the experiments by Shea and Morgan (1979) and by Lee and Magill (1983b), other experiments have been reported that demonstrate the benefit of practice schedules involving high levels of contextual interference. These benefits are for laboratory tasks other than those in which the goal is to learn to move as fast as possible through different movement patterns, or to move in specific criterion times through these patterns. An example has been reported by Del Rey, Wughalter, and Whitehurst (1982). They found that the random practice schedule was better than a blocked schedule for learning to respond to different stimulus speed variations for an anticipation timing task. Although evidence based on laboratory tasks is important for supporting the benefit of high contextual interference as a practice schedule characteristic, it does not generate enough confidence for effectively generalizing the results to skills learned outside the laboratory.

One of the more encouraging experiments that demonstrates the high contextual interference benefit for skills outside the laboratory is one reported by Goode and Magill (1986). In this experiment, they provided evidence that a random practice schedule is better than blocked practice for learning variations of a skill that likely would be taught in a physical education or recreation setting. College-aged women with no prior experience in badminton were required to practice the short, long, and drive badminton serves from the right service court. They practiced the serves three days a week for three weeks, with 36 trials in each practice session for a total of 324 trials (108 trials per serve) during the practice period. The blocked practice schedule group practiced one serve each day of each week. Thus, the schedule was actually a modification of the blocked condition used in previous studies. The random practice schedule group practiced each serve randomly in every practice session. In this condition, the experimenter told the subject which serve should be done next. On the day following these nine days of practice, all subjects were given a retention test and then a transfer test for which they were required to perform all three serves from the left service court.

As you can see from the results (Figure 8.1–4), the group that practiced with the random schedule did worse during the practice sessions, but did better on the retention and transfer tests. What is especially remarkable here is that on the transfer test, the random group showed no deterioration of performance. On the other hand, the group that had practiced in a blocked schedule was not able to adapt well to performing the serves from the left court and performed at about the same level at which they had when they had begun practicing the serves from the right court three weeks earlier.

These results, which show the benefit of high contextual interference for beginners learning serves in badminton, have recently been supported in an experiment by Wrisberg (1991) where the serves were taught in actual class settings as opposed to the more controlled experimental conditions of the Goode and Magill study. Thus, even in non-laboratory settings, a practice schedule involving high contextual interference can be seen as leading to better learning than a schedule involving low contextual interference.

The influence of the type of skill variations being learned. A review of the contextual interference effect by Magill and Hall (1990) revealed that this effect has not been found for learning variations of all skills. However, rather than this finding indicating a problem for the contextual interference effect, Magill and Hall argued that whether the effect was found or not could be related to the type of skill variations that were being

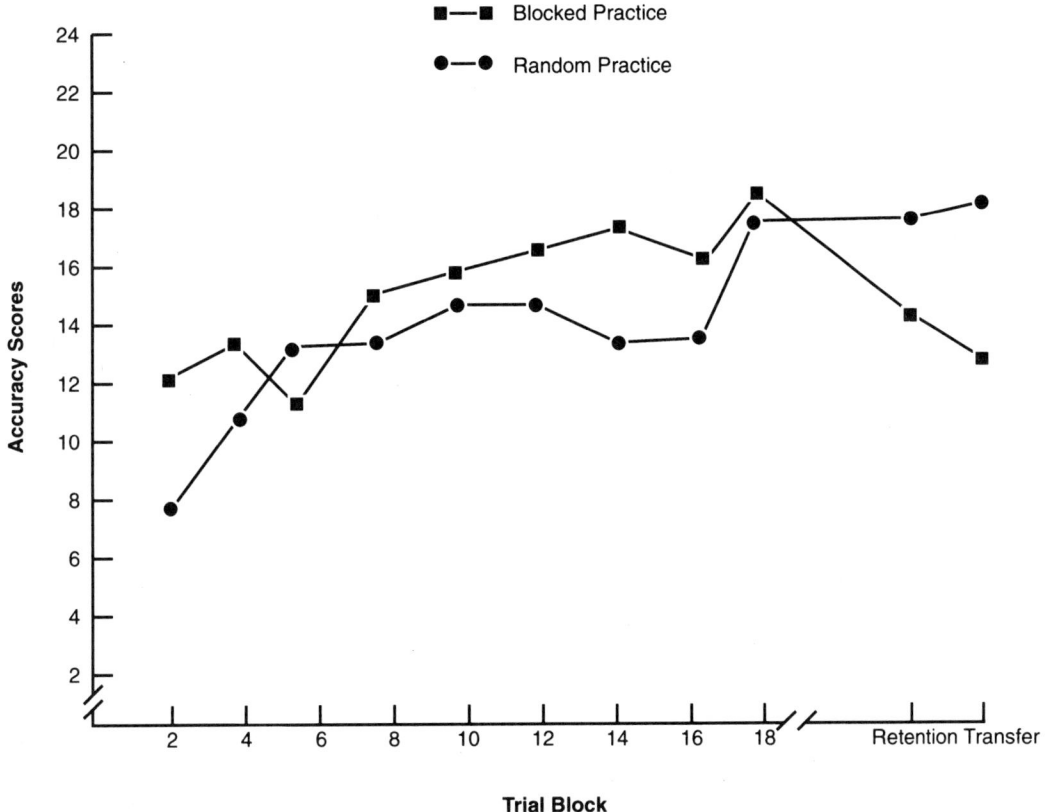

FIGURE 8.1-4   Results from the experiment by Goode and Magill showing the effects of blocked and random structured practice for three types of badminton serves on acquisition, one-day retention, and transfer.

practiced. They proposed that the type of skill variation could be related to the generalized motor program concept that was discussed in Concept 3.3.

Their hypothesis had two parts. First, if the skill variations being practiced require different motor programs, different levels of contextual interference are created by practice schedule manipulations, which in turn leads to different retention and transfer effects. That is, higher levels of contextual interference lead to better retention and transfer performance than lower levels. Second, if the skill variations being practiced involve parameter modifications of the same motor program, the contextual interference effect typically will not be found for practice schedules consisting of only

higher vs. lower levels of contextual interference. In the latter case, it could be expected that some mixed schedule, such as blocked followed by random practice, will be better than blocked or random practice only. Or, as evidence by Shea, Kohl, and Indermill (1990) has shown, random practice will be superior to blocked practice after a large number of practice trials has been experienced. They showed that 50 trials of practicing three force production levels did not produce the contextual interference effect, whereas 400 practice trials did show the effect, and then only when the blocked practice group was required to perform the retention trials in a random arrangement.

FIGURE 8.1-5 The movement patterns used in the experiment by Wood and Ging (top) and the results of random and blocked practice schedules for these patterns during acquisition and retention trials. Note numbers in patterns indicate distances in cm.

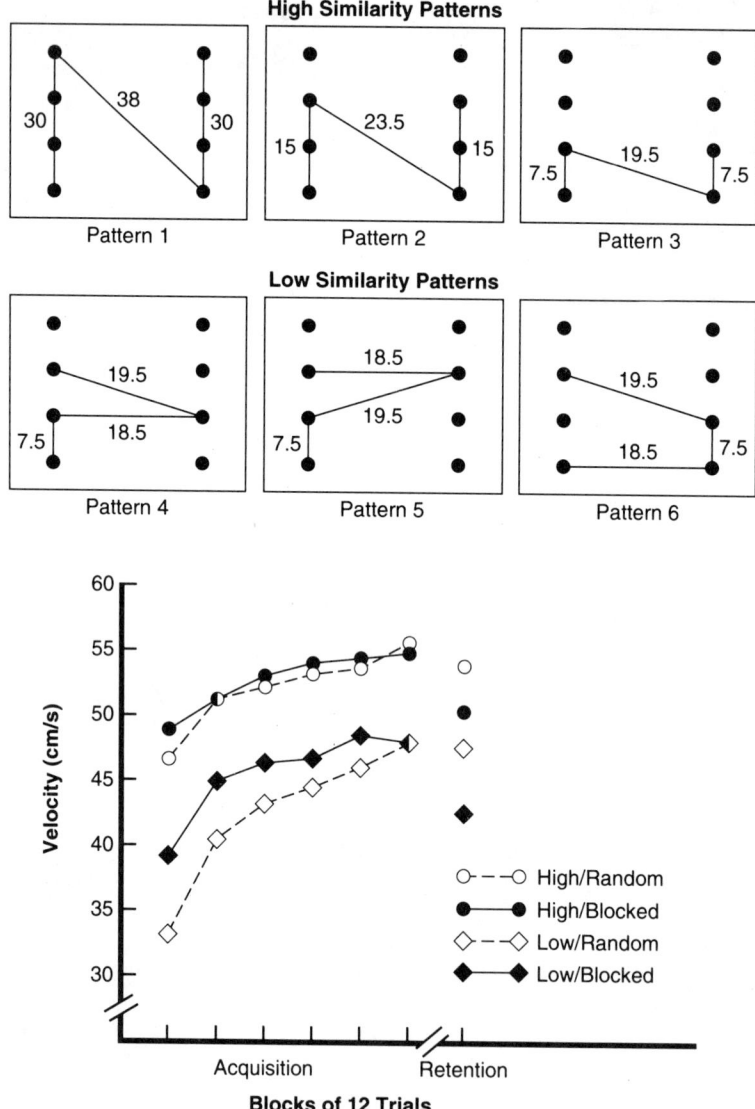

Evidence for this skill related hypothesis can be seen in an experiment by Wood and Ging (1991), who had subjects practice moving an arm as quickly as possible through a multi-segment movement pattern. One group, called the "high similarity" condition, practiced three variations of the size of a pattern that resembled the letter "N" (these patterns can be seen in Figure 8.1–5). This condition is an example of practicing skill variations that are parameter modifications of the same motor program. A second group, called the "low similarity" condition, practiced three variations of different shapes of movement patterns, thereby practicing variations of skills requiring different motor programs. Results of this experiment can be seen in Figure 8.1–5, where the velocity produced by subjects while performing the movement patterns is shown. In the graph note that the difference between random and blocked practice was statistically significant only for the "low similarity" pattern variations situation. In this case, the random practice led to better retention performance. However, there was no random vs. blocked practice schedule difference for learning the three size variations of the same movement pattern.

Why would results for random vs. blocked practice schedule comparisons be related to whether the skill variations were controlled by the same or different motor programs? Magill and Hall argued that the answer to this question concerns the difficulty of the learning situation that is created for learning the two types of skill variations. When skills variations require different motor programs to be learned, random practice schedules require the person to change motor programs from trial to trial. This involves restructuring essential composite features of the skill, such as order of events, relative timing of components, etc., in addition to modifying program parameters. On the other hand, when skill variations involve changing program parameters of the same motor program, random practice does not engage the learner in as effortful a learning situation. This is because the person must modify program parameters on each trial and not the progam itself. Thus, the random practice schedule does not generate the amount of contextual interference needed in this case to lead to the contextual interference effect.

Implementing high contextual interference practice schedules. A close observation of the different experiments considered in this discussion about the scheduling of variable practice shows that different forms of schedules have been compared. For example, Lee and Magill (1983) showed that a serial form of practice, where each of the variations as practiced in a 1–2–3 arrangement of trials, was better than blocked practice. Goode and Magill (1986) showed that a modified blocked form, where one variation was practiced for an entire day, although experienced again a week later, was not as good as random practice.

These results indicate that it is possible to invoke low and high levels of contextual interference in different ways. Random practice is not the only form of high contextual interference, and blocked practice is not the only form for invoking low contextual interference.

A practical conclusion that seems to evolve from the research is that practice conditions that allow students to experience all variations each day are superior to those that allow students to experience only one variation each day. One way of implementing practice schedules that provide more desirable variable schedules is to engage students in practicing different variations of a skill at different stations. Students are scheduled to spend a certain amount of time at each station, where one specific variation is practiced, and then move on to another station. During one class period, or practice session, all variations are experienced. Another method is to practice different variations at different times during the practice session. Again, the goal is to experience all variations in each session.

Accounting for the Contextual Interference Effect

Although there have been numerous experiments that show higher levels of contextual interference lead to better learning than lower levels, a question that remains unsolved is *why* does this effect occur? At present, two hypotheses have been proposed to account for the contextual interference effect. One, the elaboration view, has been promoted by John Shea and colleagues (Shea & Morgan, 1979; Shea & Zimny, 1983). The other, the action plan reconstruction view, has been promoted by Tim Lee and Richard Magill (Lee & Magill, 1983b, 1985). Although we will not debate these two hypotheses at length, it will be instructive to consider each briefly.

The elaboration view. In their experiment that first showed the contextual interference effect could be demonstrated in motor skill learning situations, Shea and Morgan (1979) argued that the reason could be found in the elaboration of the memory representation of the criterion skill variations that resulted from random practice. They stated that during random practice, the individual engages in more strategies as well as more different strategies than do individuals who practice in a blocked schedule. Also, because in a random practice schedule all three variations practiced are in working memory together, the person can compare and contrast each variation so that each becomes distinct from the other. The result of engaging in more and more different strategies during practice and being able to develop more distinct representations of each variation leads to the development of a memory representation for these skills that can be more readily accessed during a recall or transfer test.

The action plan reconstruction view. The alternative view from the one offered by Shea and colleagues is one forwarded by Lee and Magill that argues that the high contextual interference benefit does not necessarily enhance the elaboration of the memory trace. Rather, the key is that the benefit results from individuals being required to engage in more active processing during practice. This active processing is primarily to reconstruct an action plan on the next trial for a particular variation, because the action plan developed for the previous trial of that skill is partially or completely forgotten due to the interference created by the intervening practice trials of the other skills. This is in contrast to the blocked practice condition where the person can essentially use the same or slightly modified action plan used on the previous trial. An example from the work of Jacoby (1978), in which this view has its roots, is seen when you must add a long set of numbers. If you do this type of addition problem and then are asked to promptly do the same problem again, it is likely that you will not re-add the numbers but remember and repeat the answer. In contrast, if you were required to add several additional lists of numbers and then were given the first list again, you would probably perform the addition again because you forgot the solution to the problem.

Thus, you were required to re-solve the problem, rather than merely remember the solution.

Lee and Magill argued that the random practice condition is like the addition situation where you have forgotten much of the action plan developed for the previous trial of the task and, therefore, must re-solve the problem on the next trial in which that problem appears. On the other hand, the blocked practice schedule is like the addition problem in which the next trial follows immediately, and it is easy to remember the solution to be successful on the next trial. In the motor learning context, high contextual interference conditions require subjects to more actively engage in problem solving activity during practice. While this activity typically leads to poorer performance during practice than would be found for a low contextual interference schedule, this short-term performance deficit becomes a long-term benefit because it leads to better retention and transfer test performance.

Comparing the two views. There is much work to be done to determine which of the two hypotheses proposed to account for the contextual interference effect is correct. Based on the review of research literature that has compared these two views, Magill and Hall (1990) concluded that conclusive evidence supporting one view over the other does not exist. Both views can point to supportive empirical evidence. Rather than discussing this inconclusive work, it will be sufficient to say that much more research is needed to establish why the contextual interference effect occurs. This effect appears to be an established learning phenomenon. However, we need to know more about the conditions related to when it will occur and when it will not occur, and we need to determine why different practice schedules lead to different learning effects.

Contextual Interference and Schema Theory

An important theoretical issue related to the contextual interference effect is its relationship to Schmidt's schema theory and what each says about practice characteristics and novel response transfer success. As you will recall, Schmidt's schema theory hypothesized that more practice variability will lead to better learning than less variability. However, this theory said nothing about the scheduling of that variability during practice. Because the contextual interference effect indicates that the same amount of practice variability can lead to different learning outcomes depending on the practice schedule of the skill variations, it could be argued that the contextual interference effect provides damaging evidence for the schema theory variability of practice hypothesis.

To address this apparent conflict, Magill and Hall (1990) proposed that an inspection of the research evidence related to the schema theory practice variability hypothesis and to the contextual interference effect reveals that these two may not be in conflict. The key concerns the skill variation situations to which each refers. Schema theory discusses practice variability only in the context of variations of parameters of a generalized motor program. It does not address practicing variations of skills controlled by different motor programs. And the practice variability hypothesis predicted effects based on different amounts of variable practice. The contextual interference effect, on the other hand, relates only to those situations where the amount of variable experiences is not at issue. In contextual interference experiments, the amount of variable practice is the same for the different experimental conditions. Only the practice schedule differs.

Compare this situation to the hypothesis discussed earlier in which the contextual interference effect was predicted to occur only when skills controlled by different motor programs are practiced, whereas it would not occur when skill variations controlled by the same motor program are practiced. This latter situation appears to be related to the practice variability issue as proposed by schema theory. Thus, it seems that the contextual interference effect and the practice variability hypothesis of schema theory are not in conflict but relate to different skill learning situations.

Errors Can Benefit Learning

Another means of manipulating the variability in practice is based on the use of different practice methods that increase or decrease the amount of error a person will experience while practicing a skill. At present, there seems to be two differing views about the influence of experiencing errors during practice. One view argues that errors should be kept to a minimum so that the correct response can be experienced as often as possible. Programmed instruction approaches to learning are good examples of this view. The other view argues that errors made during practice are beneficial for the learner and, although increasing errors during practice may lead to decreased practice performance, there will be a long-term benefit in retention and transfer performance. Clearly, Schmidt's schema theory, as well as contextual interference results, favors this approach. Discovery learning or problem-solving techniques are good instructional strategy examples of the view that making errors in early practice as an important part of learning.

The typical experimental approach to investigating the benefit of errors has been to compare practice methods that will lead to different amounts of error during practice. A good example of this can be seen in an experiment reported by Edwards and Lee (1985). Two groups of subjects were required to learn to knock down a specified pattern of three small wooden barriers in a goal movement time of 1200 msec. One group, called the prompted group, was given extensive instructions about the task by means of verbal cues, tape recordings, and demonstrations. These subjects were told that if they moved according to a "ready, and, 1,2,3,4,5" count on a tape, they would complete the movement in the criterion time of 1200 msec. Each subject practiced until they could correctly do three trials in a row at 1200 msec. The second group, called the trial-and-error group, was told that the goal movement time was 1200 msec and that after each trial they would receive KR in the form of how many msec their response was

FIGURE 8.1-6 Results from the experiment by Edwards and Lee showing performance on a 1200-msec movement-time goal task during the acquisition trials and on an 1800-msec goal for the transfer task for two types of practice conditions, prompted by a tone lasting 1200 msec or practicing with KR (trial and error).

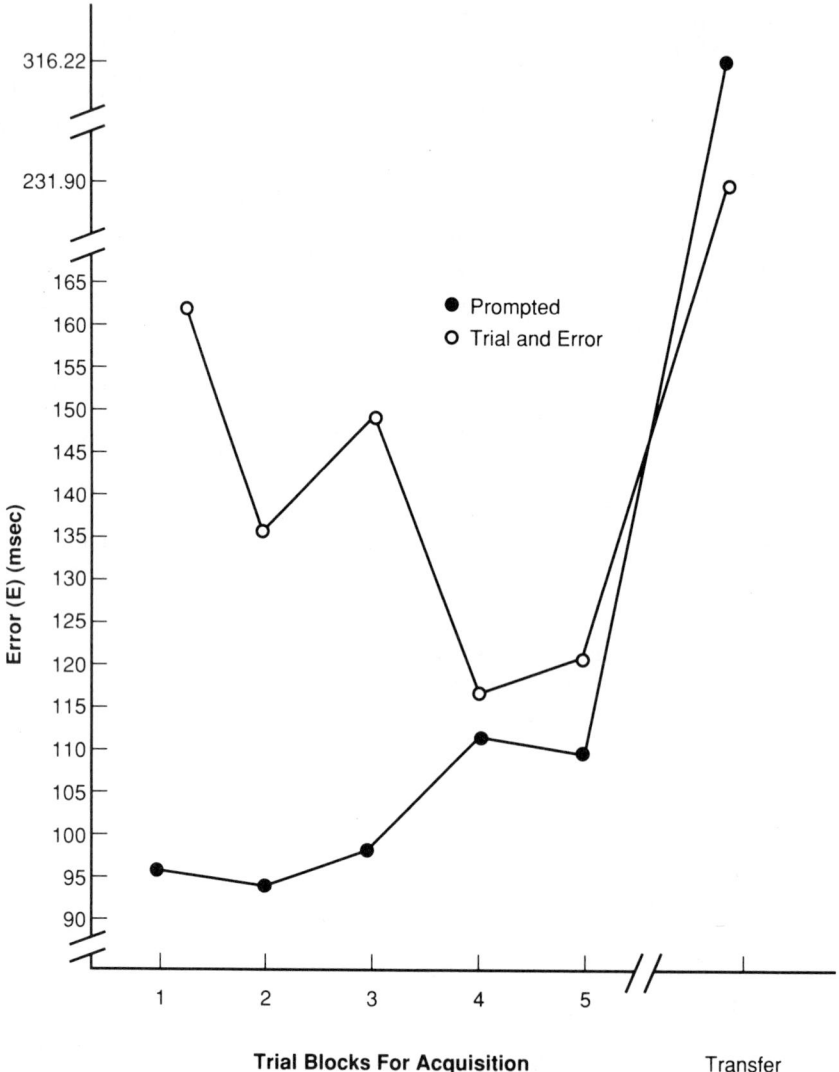

early or late of the 1200-msec goal time. Following the practice trials, there was a no-KR retention test and a transfer test. The transfer test involved performing the task in 1800 msec.

The results of this experiment, shown in Figure 8.1-6, indicated that the prompted group performed with very little error during practice. The trial-and-error group experienced much error during the first 15 trials and then performed more similarly to the prompted group by the end of the practice trials. The two groups were not different from each other on the retention test. However, what is quite revealing is that on the novel transfer test, the trial-and-error group performed the novel transfer task more accurately. Thus, experiencing less error during practice was no more beneficial for a retention test of the practiced response than was experiencing a great deal of error. And experiencing less error during practice was detrimental for transfer to a novel variation of the practiced response.

These results fit very well with the expectations of schema theory that proposes the benefit of practice variability for learning skills. The unique characteristic is that the variability is created by the type of practice strategy in which the individual engages, rather than by having different response goals practiced.

Much more research needs to be done about the question of the influence of errors during practice on the learning of motor skills. This question has had a sketchy history of research (see Singer, 1977, for a review) and has generated divergent conclusions. There is an obvious need for a more concerted effort to better understand how and why errors during practice influence learning.

Summary

A variety of experiences is an essential ingredient for practice conditions that will lead to maximal test performance. This variety should be established on the basis of non-relevant stimuli for closed skills and both non-relevant and relevant stimuli for open skills. It is important that variety be experienced by requiring subjects to perform the skill variations in all possible test conditions. Another important part of designing variable practice experiences is organizing those experiences within the practice sessions. Insight into the best type of organization has been provided by considering research on the contextual interference effect. This research has shown that increasing the variability within each practice session is preferred to practicing one variation during one session, another variation another session, and so on. The contextual interference effect is a learning phenomenon that appears to be limited to specific types of skill learning situations.

Two different views exist concerning why the contextual interference effect occurs. One view suggests that higher levels of contextual interference increase the elaborateness of the memory representation of the skills being practiced. The other view argues that the effect occurs because the action plan construction for a preceding trial for a skill must be more actively reconstructed when there have been intervening trials of a different skill. The contextual interference effect and the practice variability hypothesis of Schmidt's schema theory differ in terms of the types of skill learning situations to which each refers. Finally, the influence of different practice conditions on the amount of errors made during practice was considered as another way of looking at how variability could be manipulated during practice. Results indicate that making more errors during early practice trials benefits transfer performance.

Related Readings

Magill, R. A., & Hall, K. G. (1990). A review of the contextual interference effect in motor skill acquisition. *Human Movement Science, 9,* 241–289.

Lee, T. D., Swanson, L. R., & Hall, A. L. (1991). What is repeated in a repetition? Effects of practice conditions on motor skill acquisition. *Movement Science, American Physical Therapy Association Monograph,* 191–197.

Schmidt, R. A. (1977). Schema theory: Implications for movement education. *Motor Skills: Theory into Practice, 2,* 36–38.

Shapiro, D. C., & Schmidt, R. A. (1982). The schema theory: Recent evidence and developmental implications. In J. A. S. Kelso & J. E. Clark (Eds.), *The development of movement control and co-ordination* (pp. 113–150). New York: Wiley.

Shea, C. H., & Kohl, R. M. (1990). Specificity and variability of practice. *Research Quarterly for Exercise and Sport, 61,* 169–177.

Singer, R. N. (1977). To err or not to err: A question for the instruction of psychomotor skills. *Review of Educational Research, 47,* 479–498.

Wrisberg, C. A. (1991). A field test of the effect of contextual variety during skill acquisition. *Journal of Teaching Physical Education, 11,* 21–30.

CONCEPT 8.2

The amount of practice affects learning, although
the effect is not always proportional

Key Term

overlearning

Application

It seems reasonable to assume that the more practice a person has, the better the eventual performance will be. If a golfer wants to become a better putter, it seems only reasonable that he or she should be encouraged to spend as much time as possible on the practice putting green. The dancer who is a bit tentative in certain parts of a routine should be encouraged to spend as much time as possible going over the routine repeatedly in practice. The rehabilitation patient should be encouraged to practice the skill he or she is relearning as often as possible. Thus, when we consider the needs in each situation, it seems reasonable to accept the "more practice" approach that has been suggested. But while such an approach seems logical and will undoubtedly work, is that approach necessarily the best alternative?

When a person practices a motor skill, is it possible that he or she reaches a point of "diminishing returns" in terms of the benefits derived from the practice in proportion to the amount of time put into the practice? This "benefits vs. time" question is an important consideration that in-

structors of motor skills should not overlook when designing instruction. The amount of practice time devoted to a skill is a critical variable in any motor skill teaching situation. This is especially true because of the time limitations that are a part of all instructional settings. For a physical education teacher or dance teacher, a class can last only for a certain length of time. Or a physical therapist has a specified amount of time for a therapy session. Each of these people have time limits placed on them in terms of the number of classes or sessions they can have.

Therefore, it is paramount for all who teach motor skills to consider the time constraints that exist. This means that efficiency is critically important to the instructional process. The goal of the available instruction and practice time should include not only the most effective means of instruction or practice, but also the most efficient procedure. In other words, which form of instruction or practice will yield the greatest returns for the least expenditure of time?

The efficiency of instruction and practice methods is a principle that should not be overlooked or underestimated by instructors of motor skills. In the following discussion we will consider an important concept that can be directly applied to the development of efficient instruction.

Discussion

The question of how much practice is beneficial to assure the optimal amount of learning, while considering the time spent for benefits received, has been the focus of an area of study in learning that traditionally has been termed overlearning,

although the term should be "overpractice" or "overtraining" to be more accurately descriptive. **Overlearning** can be defined as the practice time spent beyond the amount of practice time needed to achieve a certain performance criterion. The way to implement overlearning in an instructional situation is to establish a performance criterion, determine the amount of practice time spent in attaining that criterion, then require extra practice time. The intent of the extra practice time is to help develop a memory representation of the skill that is as durable and as accessible as possible. Consider this point in relation to our earlier discussion of the storage and retrieval of information in long-term memory in Chapter 5 and of motor programs in Chapter 3. Based on this view, it could be said that the intent of the extra practice is to strengthen the generalized motor program and response schema for the skill being learned so that it can more readily be called into action when required.

The study of overlearning in motor skills has not been a popular area in recent years for motor learning research. However, there has been sufficient investigation through the years to determine that overlearning is an effective means of aiding skill learning. To help illustrate what we presently know about the benefits and implementation of the overlearning strategy as a practice procedure, two experiments will be briefly discussed. These two experiments are useful to consider because they show the effectiveness for the overlearning practice strategy for two different types of motor skill situations.

One type of motor skill that was discussed in Chapter 5 as being particularly susceptible to forgetting is what are termed *procedural skills.* These skills typically require performing a series of discrete responses, which by themselves are relatively easy to execute. However, the total task involves knowing which discrete responses to make and in what order. These types of skills are especially common in industrial and military settings. An article by Schendel and Hagman (1982) proposes that using an overlearning, or overtraining as they call it, practice strategy could be an effective way to decrease the amount of forgetting associated with procedural skills. As researchers for the U.S. Army Research Institute, they were particularly interested in improving retention following training of soldiers to assemble and disassemble an Army machine gun. This skill was of

interest because it is typically taught in a short training period and is usually characterized by a large amount of retention loss soon thereafter.

Two forms of overtraining were compared with a no-overtraining situation. The first overtraining condition required soldiers to perform 100% more trials than were necessary to achieve a performance criterion of one correct assembly/disassembly trial. The second overtraining condition also involved an additional 100% more practice trials, but these trials were administered as "refresher" training midway through the 8-week retention interval used for all subjects. Results showed that both of these overtraining groups performed better than the no-overtraining control group on the retention test, which required the soldiers to practice until they were again able to assemble and disassemble the gun correctly on a trial. However, the two overtraining groups did not differ from each other in the number of trials it took to retrain to the one correct trial criterion. The recommendation by Schendel and Hagman was to use the immediate overtraining situation because it was the more cost- and time-effective means of increasing the durability of what was learned during the original practice session. Because the trainees were already in the training session, it would save time and be less expensive to have them engage in additional practice there rather than bring them back several weeks later for a refresher training session.

In an experiment that involved learning a skill that could be considered more "motor" than the gun disassembly/assembly skill, Melnick (1971) investigated the use of overlearning for a dynamic balance skill. Two questions were of primary interest in this experiment. The first question concerned whether practice beyond what was needed to achieve a performance criterion was better than no further practice, which was a question also addressed in the Schendel and Hagman (1982) experiment. Assuming that there would be such a benefit, the second question addressed whether there was an optimal amount of extra practice that was beneficial. To investigate these questions,

TABLE 8.2-1. Results of the experiment by Melnick showing the mean scores and standard deviations at the end of practice to criterion (criterion trial) and at the end of the overlearning practice (last pretest trial) for the 4 overlearning groups for the 1-week and 1-month retention intervals.

Groups (N = 10)		Trials to Criterion	Criterion Trial Time on Balance (sec)	Last Pretest Trial Time on Balance (sec)
0% 1-wk.	M	7.7	28.72	28.72
	SD	3.80	.57	.57
0% 1-mo.	M	6.4	28.45	28.45
	SD	3.58	.30	.30
50% 1-wk.	M	7.6	28.83	29.04
	SD	2.94	.36	.83
50% 1-mo.	M	7.3	28.59	28.64
	SD	4.43	.50	.89
100% 1-wk.	M	7.5	28.81	28.18
	SD	3.38	.43	1.19
100% 1-mo.	M	6.8	28.59	28.80
	SD	3.34	.41	.92
200% 1-wk.	M	7.3	28.92	29.11
	SD	1.19	.59	.70
200% 1-mo.	M	7.1	28.80	28.60
	SD	3.15	.45	1.32

From M. J. Melnick, "Effects of Overlearning on the Retention of a Gross Motor Skill," in *Research Quarterly for Exercise and Sport,* 1971, Vol. 42, pp. 60–69. Copyright © 1971 American Alliance for Health, Physical Education, Recreation, and Dance. Reprinted by permission.

Melnick had subjects practice balancing on a stabilometer until they were able to achieve a performance criterion of 28 seconds out of 50 seconds. Following the achievement of this criterion, the subjects were then required to perform either no further trials, 50%, 100%, or 200% extra trials of practice. Then, a retention test was administered to all subjects one week later and one month later.

The results of this experiment (Table 8.2-1) indicated that the answer to the first question was as expected: the groups that had been required to engage in practice beyond what was required to achieve the 28-second performance criterion performed better on the retention tests than the group that practiced only until the criterion had been achieved. The answer to the second question was somewhat more interesting. There appeared to be a point of "diminishing returns" in terms of the amount of retention benefit gained in relation to the amount of extra practice required by the different overlearning conditions. That is, the 50%

additional practice group did as well on the retention tests as the 100% and 200% groups. So, although additional practice was beneficial, increasing the amount of additional practice beyond a certain amount was not proportionally more beneficial for improving retention performance.

This phenomenon of "diminishing returns" for the amount of practice experienced has also been demonstrated for learning skills in a physical education class. In an experiment by Goldberger and Gerney (1990), fifth-grade boys and girls practiced the two-step football punt, along with four other football tasks that were a part of the unit of instruction. One group practiced these skills according to a teacher-rotated format, where the teacher divided the class into 5 subgroups and assigned each to one of 5 stations where the skills were to be practiced for 5 min. At the end of every 5 min, students rotated to a new station. Another group of students practiced according to a learner-rotated format, where the students were provided index cards describing what was to be done at each station and then were told to use their 25 min efficiently to practice each skill. Everyone practiced like this for 2 class periods on 2 days. The next week, students were tested on the punting skill. The results showed that the two groups differed in terms of the number of practice trials for this skill but not in test performance. The learner-rotated format group actually practiced the skill an average of 7 more trials than the teacher-rotated format group. In fact, the range of the number of practice trials was notably different as well. Students in the learner-rotated format group ranged from 0 to 67 trials, whereas students in the teacher-rotated format group ranged from 0 to 87 trials. However, there was no difference between the groups in terms of amount of improvement in their punting performance scores. The additional practice time induced by the teacher-rotated format did not yield an additional skill improvement benefit.

Overlearning can lead to poor test performance.

Some recent evidence has been presented in the motor learning research literature that shows that providing many extra practice trials may also lead to negative test performance. This means that in addition to the diminishing returns effect seen for overlearning trials of practice, overlearning may also lead to learning deficits.

An example of this effect can be seen in an experiment by Shea and Kohl (1990). Subjects learned to push a handle a specified amount of force (175N). One group of subjects practiced this skill for 85 trials. Another group also practiced this skill for 85 trials, but also practiced the same skill at four other force goals (125N, 150N, 200N, and 225N) for 85 trials each, which meant a total of 285 practice trials. And one additional group practiced the 175N goal force for 285 trials. One day later, all subjects performed the 175N goal force for 10 trials. The results showed that the group that practiced the 175N goal force for 285 trials did the worst on the initial 5 trials of the retention test, whereas the group that practiced

the variable goals performed the best, and the group that practiced only 85 trials of the 175N goal was in between these two groups. These differences between these groups were even more distinct on the first retention trial. However, on the final five trials of the retention test, all three groups performed similarly. What is significant about these results is that they provide interesting evidence that there can be an amount of practice where additional practice is not only of no observable benefit for learning the skill, it can also be detrimental for performing the skill on a test given some time after practice ends.

Implementing the overlearning practice strategy.

Three points are especially worth noting in the use of overlearning as a practice strategy. First, the effective implementation of this strategy is best achieved when you know how much practice the students need to achieve a certain performance level. Thus, for skills that are practiced until a criterion level of performance must be achieved, requiring some additional practice beyond the achievement of that criterion can effectively aid learning.

Second, the amount of extra practice required should *not* be based on the notion that "more is better." Remember that there seems to be a point of diminishing returns; the amount of retention benefit gained for the extra time required to practice is not worth the extra time. And it is possible that the additional practice can lead to negative performance test results. Although this point has to be determined for your own particular situation, the experiments we considered in this discussion showed that a "safe bet" can be around 100% additional practice trials beyond the number required to achieve your specified performance criterion. Or, providing practice trials with variations of skill characteristics can be a useful means of establishing an "overpractice" type of situation.

Third, the use of requiring additional practice beyond what was needed to achieve a performance criterion seems to be a particularly useful strategy for skills that will be practiced during a specified period and will then not be performed for some time after that. For example, in the Schendel and Hagman (1982) experiment, the Army wanted the soldiers to know how to disassemble and assemble the machine gun in case a situation would arise where those procedures would be required. This skill was not something the soldiers would use everyday, but they still needed to be capable of performing the skill. Thus, the goal was to provide a practice situation that would help ensure as much as possible the durability of the capability of successfully performing the skill. This goal was achieved by requiring the soldiers to engage in 100% more practice trials than they required to correctly perform the skill one time.

The overlearning practice strategy and learning. An important aspect of the results of overlearning research is that they help to support the effectiveness of what was called in Chapter 5 "rote rehearsal" as a memory strategy. Thus it would appear that practicing a skill over and over, even though it can be performed correctly, can be a valuable form of practice to increase the permanence of the capability to perform the skill at some future time. However, it is important to be aware that a consistent conclusion from research investigating overlearning is that the amount of practice is not *the* critical variable influencing motor skill acquisition. The amount of practice invariably interacts with some other variable to influence learning. You have seen this interaction with such variables as the type of KR or the variability of practice. From this perspective, then, the typical overlearning research study indicates that a particular condition of practice is beneficial to a point. However, for continued performance improvement that is more proportionate to the time and effort given to the practice, other practice conditions must also be taken in account. This does not mean that the question of the amount of practice is unimportant. It does mean that current

views of motor learning are aware that this issue cannot be studied in isolation, but must be considered as it interacts with other important instructional variables.

Summary

The question of the time spent in practicing a motor skill versus the benefits derived from the amount of time spent in practice has been considered. The view that "more is better" does not appear to apply to motor skill learning, at least in terms of the benefits derived in relation to the amount of practice experienced. There appears to be a point of "diminishing returns" for amount of practice. While the amount of practice is an important concern for the instructor, it is more important to consider how the amount of practice interacts with other variables influencing motor skill learning. As the amount of time spent in practicing a skill increases, the value of certain conditions of practice decreases. However, the need increases for incorporating other variables into the practice routines.

Related Readings

Goldberger, M., & Gerney, P. (1990). Effects of learner use of practice time on skill acquisition of fifth grade children. *Journal of Teaching Physical Education, 10,* 84–95.

Melnick, M. J. (1971). Effects of overlearning on the retention of a gross motor skill. *Research Quarterly, 42,* 60–69.

Rubin-Rabson, G. (1941). Studies in the psychology of memorizing piano music. VIII: A comparison of three degrees of overlearning. *Journal of Experimental Psychology, 32,* 688–698.

Schmidt, R. A. (1971). Retroactive interference and level of original learning in verbal and motor tasks. *Research Quarterly, 42,* 314–326.

Shea, C. H., & Kohl, R. M. (1990). Specificity and variability of practice. *Research Quarterly for Exercise and Sport, 61,* 169–177.

CONCEPT 8.3

The spacing or distribution of practice can affect
both practice performance and learning

Key Terms

massed   distributed
  practice   practice

Application

Suppose you are a physical educator teaching a volleyball unit. In this unit, you must schedule time to practice basic skills of volleyball such as the serve, pass, set, spike, receiving serve, and so on. In addition to the practicing scheduling concerns addressed in the previous two concepts in this chapter, you are also faced with how to distribute the practice of these various skills throughout the unit. For example, should you spend entire class periods having the students practice these skills and then devote the remaining class periods of the unit to playing actual games of volleyball? Or would it be better to more widely distribute the practice time for these skills by devoting only a portion of each class period to practicing the skills and then allow students to play some games each period? Although both of these schedules would devote the same amount of practice to each skill, the difference between the two schedules is how that practice is distributed within and between the class periods. The second schedule would distribute the instruction and practice time devoted to teaching the skills over a greater number of class periods than the first schedule. Then, even if you make this decision, you must consider the scheduling problem of distributing practice within a class period itself. Is there an optimal amount of time your students should rest between practice trials, or can they simply begin another trial as soon as possible after they complete the previous trial?

This example, taken from a physical education context, illustrates two important practice scheduling decisions relevant to any other context in which motor skills are practiced. These decisions concern how to distribute the practice time available for learning a skill. The first is related to how much practice time should be spent on a particular skill in a given practice session. In order to address this problem, you must first decide whether it is best to practice the skill for a relatively short period each day, which will mean practicing it for several days, versus practicing the skill for a longer period each day, which will mean that the amount of practice time you have allocated to that skill could be accomplished in fewer days. The second scheduling concern relates to the amount of rest given between practice trials. The scheduling concern shifts from distributing practice sessions across days to distributing practice within a practice session. Both of these issues are important and must be addressed before determining how the practice schedule will be organized.

The basis for making either of these scheduling decisions is how different practice distribution schedules influence learning the skill. If learning a skill is better with a particular type of practice distribution schedule than another, then it would be clear that this schedule would be the most desirable one. However, it is always a possibility that the practice distribution schedule doesn't really influence the quality of learning that results from practice. In the discussion that follows, this practice distribution issue will be considered to provide some guidance in the scheduling decision process.

Discussion

The study of practice distribution, or the spacing of practice, has been a popular topic of research in motor learning for many years. The most popular era for this study seems to have been from the 1930s through the 1950s. Widespread attention to the topic of practice distribution appears to have been brought about by a controversy related to the amount of rest needed between practice trials to ensure an optimal learning environment. At issue was the question of whether *massed* or *distributed* practice trials provided for better learning of motor skills. Some researchers argued that distributed practice was definitely better, whereas others maintained that it really did not make much difference which spacing strategy was followed.

While this early controversy focused on practice distribution as it was related to the between-trial rest interval, it is important to understand that the study of massed versus distributed practice involves two different ways to consider the distribution of practice. These two ways were illustrated in the Application section. One way, as was the focus of the controversy described above, concerns the amount of rest allowed between practice trials. The second concerns the amount of practice during each session of practice. Involved in this issue is whether it is better to have fewer sessions or more sessions, and how much rest should be provided between sessions. Both of these practice distribution issues will be addressed in this discussion.

Defining Massed and Distributed Practice

Although there has been considerable controversy over whether massed or distributed practice schedules lead to better skill learning, there also has been considerable controversy over the definitions of the terms *massed practice* and *distributed practice*. The most problematic is finding agreement for these terms when they relate to the interval length between trials. When these terms are used to relate to distributing practice across sessions, there seems to be general agreement that the terms are used in a relative way. That is, a

massed practice schedule will have fewer practice sessions than the distributed schedule, with each massed practice session requiring more and/or longer practice. A distributed schedule, on the other hand, will distribute the same amount of practice time across more sessions, so that each session is shorter than in the massed schedule, so the sessions must be over a longer period if the same total amount of practice is to be achieved.

However, when defining these two terms in relation to the length of the intertrial interval, there is not this same general agreement about an operational definition. For example, Singer (1980) defined massed practice rather narrowly as practicing "without any intermittent pauses" (p. 419). Schmidt (1987), on the other hand, defined massed practice more broadly as practice in which "the amount of practice time in a trial is greater than the amount of rest between trials" (p. 384). Distributed practice is defined by Singer as practice periods "divided by rest intervals or intervals of alternate skill learning" (p. 379). Schmidt defined distributed practice as a situation in which "the amount of rest between trials equals or exceeds the amount of time in a trial" (p. 384).

For our purposes, we shall define **massed practice** as practice in which the amount of rest between trials is either very short or none at all so that practice is relatively continuous. **Distributed practice,** then, is practice in which the amount of rest between trials or groups of trials is relatively large. While "very short" and "relatively large" as used in these definitions are somewhat ambiguous, it is necessary to use these terms to permit the greatest amount of generalization from the massed vs. distributed practice research literature as applicable to motor skill learning situations. The precise meanings of these terms should be considered in relation to the skill and learning situation to which they are applied.

The Intertrial Interval and Practice Distribution

By far the greatest amount of research on the distribution of practice has been related to the length of the intertrial interval. This research has also led to the greatest amount of controversy over which schedule leads to better learning. It is difficult to establish a definitive answer to this question by looking at reviews of this research or at motor learning textbooks because these sources provide varying answers. For example, Ellis (1978) stated that "distributed practice facilitates the acquisition of motor skills" (p. 236). However, in another review of practice distribution research, Adams (1987) concluded that "Massed practice influences how well you perform, not how well you learn" (p. 50), indicating that although the massing of practice depresses practice performance, the amount of learning results is not affected. Thus, Adams contended that the practice distribution schedule is of little consequence for skill learning, whereas Ellis held that it is an important learning variable.

Two problems appear to underlie the controversy surrounding the issue of massed versus distributed practice and motor skill learning when the focus is on the length of the intertrial interval. The first problem is related to the issue of practice performance versus learning effects, an issue that was discussed at length in Chapter 2. What appears to be a problem is that many of the massed vs. distributed practice experiments reported in the research literature have not included retention or transfer trials. Thus, conclusions must be based on the results during practice trial performance only. The second problem is one that was pointed out by Schmidt (1975a) and further developed by Lee and Genovese (1988, 1989), which concerns the general failure to consider possible differences in the influence of the two practice distribution schedules on learning different types of skills. These researchers argue that one conclusion is warranted for results investigating continuous skills, whereas a quite different conclusion must be made when discrete skills are learned. Thus, it appears that deriving any conclusion about the effect of different practice distribution schedules on motor skill learning is dependent of research involving either continuous or discrete skills.

Massed vs. distributed practice for learning continuous skills. By far the most common type of motor skills used to investigate massed vs. distributed practice effects have been continuous skills. And the most popular continuous task has been the pursuit rotor, where the subject must keep a hand-held stylus in contact with a small disk on a rotating turntable for as long as possible. A trial is usually a specified length of time, such as 20 or 30 seconds. What makes this type of task useful for investigating the massed vs. distributed practice issue is that it is quite easy to specify massed and distributed intertrial interval lengths. Because massed practice schedules typically have few, if any, seconds of rest between trials, whereas the distributed schedules are as long or longer than the trial itself, intertrial interval lengths that are readily acceptable as distinctly massed or distributed can be established.

One of the consistent results from the research investigating the effect of these two practice schedules has been that at the end of the practice trials, subjects who practice under a massed practice schedule do much worse than those who practiced with a distributed schedule. Thus, when experiments include only practice trials and no retention or transfer trials, the conclusion is that a distributed schedule is better than a massed schedule. However, when a retention or transfer test is added, the results become less clear-cut. We will consider two experiments to illustrate this discrepancy. In both experiments there was a transfer test in which both the massed and distributed practice groups were required to perform the task under a common distributed schedule. The use of the distributed schedule as the common transfer schedule is the most interesting transfer condition because the most interesting question is, What will happen to the massed practice group after the massed condition has been removed? If the massing of practice is a performance rather than a learning variable, then removing this practice condition should enable those who practiced under this schedule to perform as those who practiced under a distributed schedule.

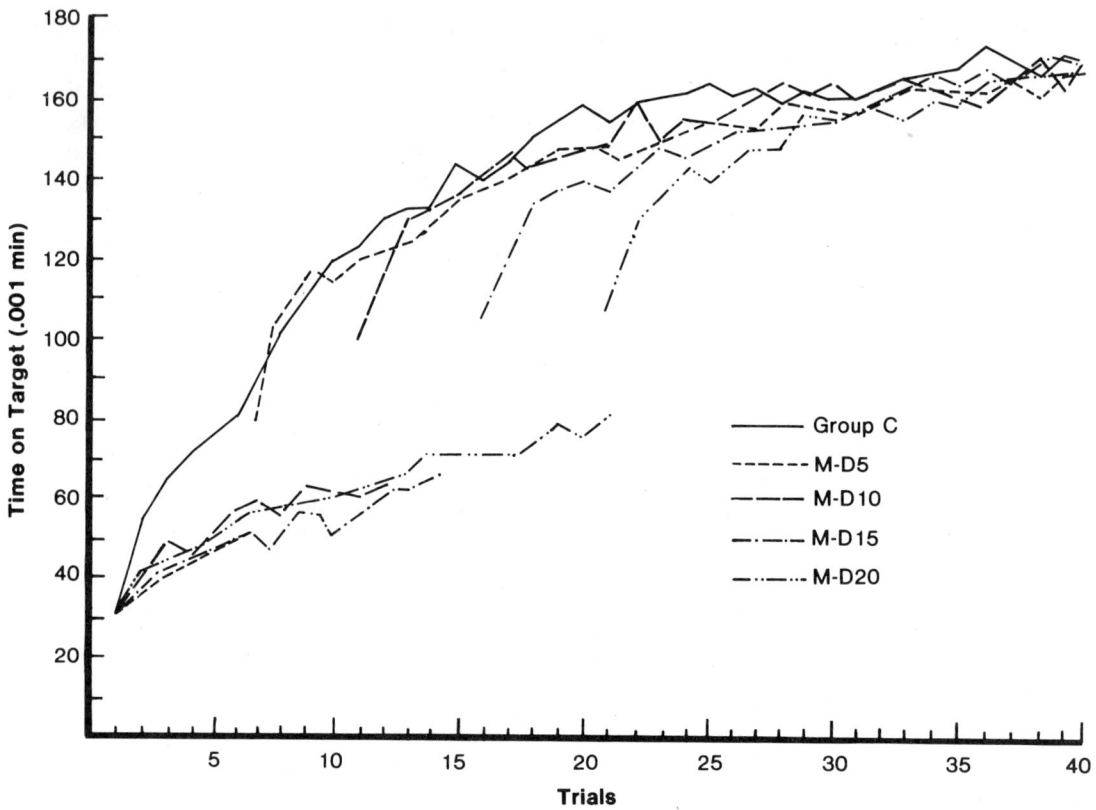

FIGURE 8.3-1 Results of the experiment by Adams and Reynolds showing rotary pursuit performance curves for the control group (Group C) and the four experimental groups who practiced under massed practice conditions for different numbers of trials before shifting to a distributed practice condition such as that of the control group.

An experiment that led to the conclusion that massing practice leads to a performance but not a learning decrement was reported by Adams and Reynolds (1954). Subjects practiced the pursuit rotor task for 40 trials and began practicing the task under a massed schedule in which they had no rest between trials. Then one group of subjects was transferred to a distributed schedule after five trials. This switch in schedule occurred following a five minute rest. A second group of subjects transferred to the distributed schedule after 10 trials, while a third group was switched after 15 trials and a fourth group after 20 trials of massed practice. A fifth group was a control group that

practiced all 40 trials in a distributed schedule. The results of this experiment are presented in Figure 8.3–1. As you can see, after being switched to a distributed schedule, all subjects showed immediate improvement and soon were performing similarly to the control group. From these results Adams and Reynolds concluded that the massing of practice only depressed practice performance and did not influence the learning of this skill.

A different conclusion was reached by Denny, Frisbey, and Weaver (1955). Subjects in their experiment practiced a pursuit rotor task for 12 trials with each trial lasting 30 seconds. The massed group had no rest between trials while the dis-

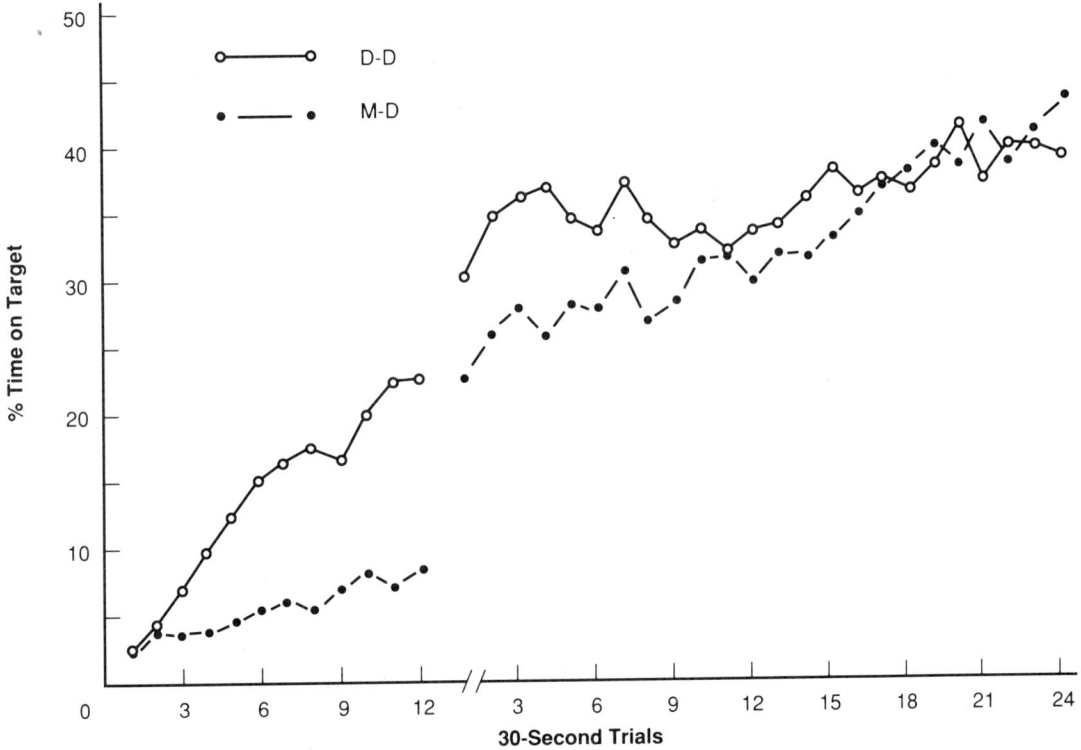

FIGURE 8.3-2 Results from the experiment by Denny, Frisbey, and Weaver showing the effects of massed and distributed practice on a pursuit rotor task. The first 12 trials are either massed (M) or distributed (D) practice conditions. The second set of 24 trials is distributed for both groups.

tributed group had a 30-second rest. Then, both groups were given a 5-minute rest and began performing 24 transfer trials with 30 seconds between trials. The results (Figure 8.3–2) showed that performance on the 12 practice trials yielded much poorer performance for the massed group than for the distributed group. And this advantage for the distributed practice group remained for the first 11 transfer trials, at which time the two groups started to perform similarly. Thus, massing practice not only depressed practice performance, it also hindered learning.

How can the apparent discrepancy between these two experiments, which represent many others showing similar differing results, be resolved? One way is to look more closely at the Adams and Reynolds (1954) results and compare them with the results of Denny et al. (1955). The results from both experiments are actually more similar than different. In both experiments, subjects eventually performed as the group that had only experienced the distributed schedule. However, in both experiments, it took the massed practice subjects several trials to catch up. In fact, in the Adams and Reynolds experiment, the more massed practice trials that were experienced, the longer it took subjects to catch up when they were transferred to the distributed schedule. In the experiment by Denny et al., it took subjects 11 trials to catch up to the distributed group after having experienced 12 practice trials with a massed schedule. In the Adams and Reynolds experiment, a similar massed practice condition, the M-D15 group took more than 15 trials to catch up to the distributed control group. Thus, it appears that the most appropriate conclusion is that for continuous skills, the distributed schedule of practice is preferable to a massed schedule, because the massing of practice not only depresses practice performance, but also negatively affects learning.

Massed vs. distributed practice for discrete skills. A problem with using discrete skills to investigate the massed vs. distributed practice issue is directly related to the definition problem discussed earlier. For example, if a massed schedule allows no rest between trials, whereas a distributed schedule involves a rest interval that is the same length as the practice trial, then two intertrial intervals will be essentially the same length, because a discrete response is typically very short. Consider for example a situation where subjects are practicing a rapid-aiming task that has a duration of approximately 150 msec. In this situation the distributed practice condition could, by definition, have a 150-msec intertrial interval. If the massed condition had no rest between trials, only 150 msec would separate the massed from the distributed practice schedules. Thus, the definition problem for the terms *massed* and *distributed* becomes important when discrete tasks are used. Probably one reason this has not troubled researchers is that discrete tasks were seldom used for investigating the massed vs. distributed practice issue. In fact, in the comprehensive review by Lee and Genovese (1988), only one study was found in the research literature in which a discrete task was used. However, the results of that one study are quite interesting and worth considering.

This single experiment was reported by Carron (1969) and involved a task that required subjects to learn to pick up a small dowel from a hole, turn it end-for-end, and reinsert it in the hole as quickly as possible. One attempt equalled one trial, which lasted on the average between 1.3 and 1.7 seconds. Carron defined massed and distributed practice conditions in a relative way. That is, the massed condition had a maximum 300-msec intertrial interval, whereas the distributed group was given 5

seconds between trials. The results of this experiment showed that, as opposed to research with continuous tasks, practice performance for this discrete task was not depressed by massed practice. And performance on a retention test two days later showed that the massed practice group actually outperformed the distributed practice group.

In an experiment that sought to further investigate Carron's (1969) results, Lee and Genovese (1989) had subjects perform a task that required them to learn to move a hand-held stylus from one 8 × 8-cm metal plate to another plate 29 cm away in a goal movement time of 500 msec. The massed practice group had 0.5 seconds between trials whereas the distributed group had 25 seconds between trials. Both groups practiced this task for 50 trials, with KR given on each trial. At the end of these practice trials, each group was split into two groups, a massed and a distributed group for performance on two retention tests, one given 10 minutes after the practice trials were completed, the other given one week later.

The results of this experiment (Figure 8.3–3) confirmed to some extent what Carron had found earlier, but added an important new dimension to those findings. First, notice that the massed practice group performed better than the distributed group at the end of the practice trials. But then, notice what happens to the groups that were formed for the retention tests. A strong practice-test context effect is seen. On the 10-minute retention test, the massed practice-massed retention group performed better than the other groups, but the massed practice-distributed retention group performed about the same as the distributed practice-distributed retention group. The distributed practice-massed retention group performed the worst and actually made more errors than at the beginning of the practice trials. Thus, the massed practice condition led to better immediate retention performance when the retention test was also performed in a massed condition. For the one week retention test, the two groups that performed the retention test under the same conditions as they practiced performed comparably and

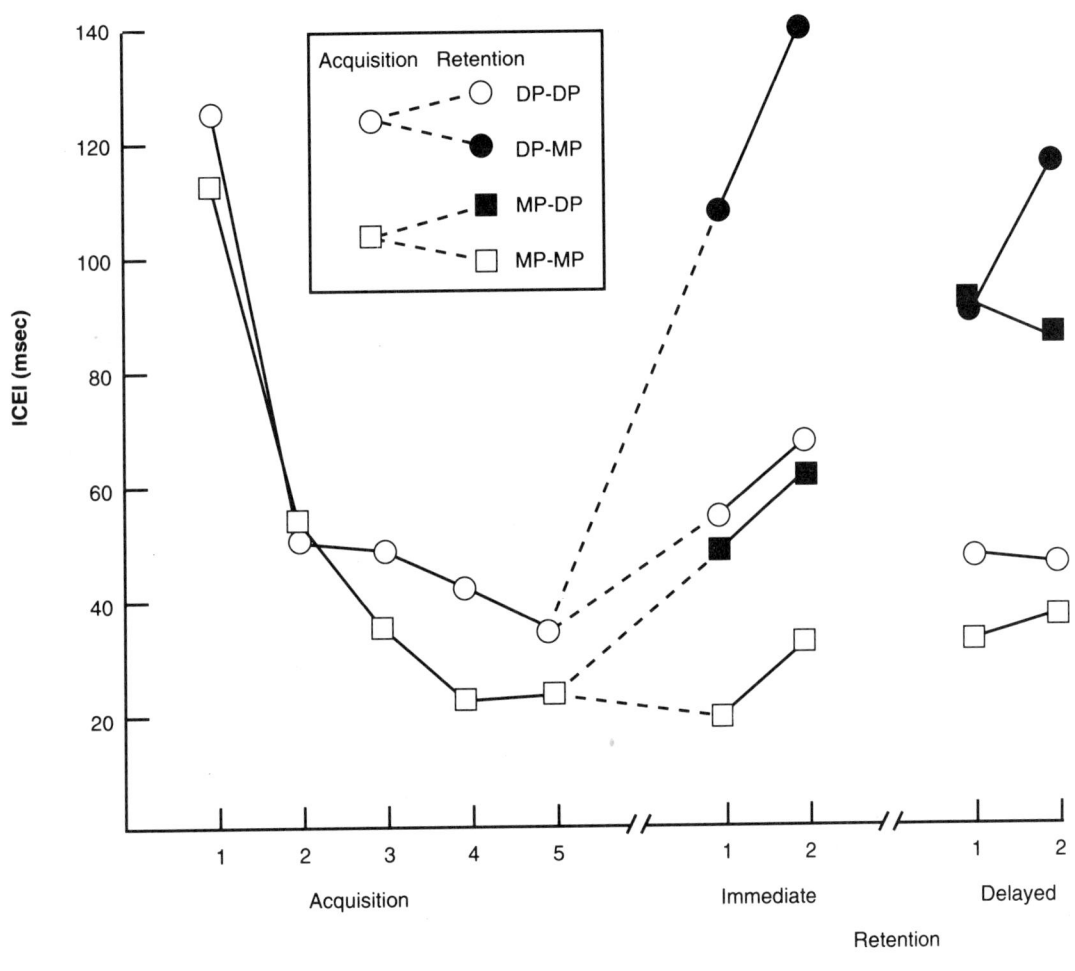

FIGURE 8.3-3 Results of the experiment by Lee and Genovese showing the effects of massed practice (MP) and distributed practice (DP) on the acquisition and retention performance for the discrete time-based tapping task. Note during retention trials, the DP and MP practice groups were subdivided into MP and DP groups.

better than both groups that were switched from their practice condition to the other condition.

Thus, it appears that massing of practice trials for discrete tasks does not hinder learning and can in fact benefit learning. However, there is a strong relationship between the practice distribution conditions during practice trials and during test trials. When the conditions are the same, the massed practice condition is advantageous for tests

that follow closely in time after the end of practice, although this advantage disappears after an extended retention interval. However, when the practice and test conditions are different, both practice distribution conditions suffer, with the distributed practice condition seemingly suffering more. These results, then, suggest that for learning discrete tasks, the more beneficial practice condition is to mass the distribution of practice trials.

Accounting for the intertrial practice distribution effects.   The question that emerges from the discussion so far is, Why does massed practice hinder the learning of a continuous task while it benefits the learning of a discrete task? One possible reason is that fatigue effects become so severe during practice of a continuous task under a massed schedule that learning, as well as practice performance, are affected, a point to be discussed more fully in Concept 8.5. For the discrete task, where fatigue is not usually a problem, the distributed condition may lead to frustration or boredom from having to wait so long between trials. Although there may be other explanations for these differences, they await further research to be validated.

Implementing intertrial massed vs. distributed schedule results.   What the results of the research we have just considered make reasonably clear is that the decision about which practice schedule to use within a practice session is not an easy one. Two important points to consider are the type of skill being taught and the type of test situation. In terms of the type of skill being taught, it seems safe to recommend that if the skill is of the continuous type, that is, if it lasts a reasonably long time and requires relatively repetitive actions, then a more distributed schedule is recommended. Thus, more gross skills like walking, swimming, and bicycling, as well as repetitive, more precision-oriented skills, such as typing or piano playing, will benefit from a more distributed between-trial schedule. Of course, the key is what constitutes the length of a trial. In most of these activities, however, a trial typically lasts several minutes. If the action required is reasonably brief, then massing practice will likely benefit. Skills such as hitting a golf ball or hitting tennis balls would not benefit from long intertrial intervals. Many industrial skills or skills being trained in an occupational therapy session fall into this category and will likely benefit from practice schedules that keep intertrial intervals short.

The Length and Distribution of Practice Sessions

Another way to consider the massed vs. distributed practice schedule issue is to consider how to distribute an allotted amount of practice time within and between practice sessions. A massed practice schedule would incorporate longer practice sessions for a few sessions, whereas a distributed schedule would spread out the same number of practice hours in shorter practice sessions across more sessions of practice. A potential problem that develops in considering this practice schedule is that many times there is little flexibility in the number of days available for practice sessions. If a teacher has only 10 days for a unit of instruction, then the practice schedule must fit that limit. Similarly, if a dancer must perform in a set number of days, then the practice schedule must adjust accordingly. Or a physical therapist may be limited in the number of hours a patient can receive therapy due to medical insurance limitations. Thus, the consideration of the distribution of practice in terms of the length of each practice session and how many sessions are held may have its limitations. However, the basic question of whether it is better to have more sessions of shorter duration or fewer sessions of longer duration remains a relevant and important question regardless of the limitations that may exist.

While there is not an abundance of research addressing the practice distribution question, the available evidence is relatively consistent in pointing to the benefit of distributed practice. The general result of experiments comparing a few long practice sessions with more and shorter sessions is that practicing skills during shorter sessions leads to better learning. A good example of this type of evidence can be seen in a study published by Baddely and Longman (1978). They investigated the issue of length and distribution of practice sessions for learning a typing task. Subjects in this experiment were postal workers who needed to be trained to use a mail sorting machine, which required operating a typewriter-like keyboard. All trainees were provided with 60 hours of practice time and practiced 5 days each week. However, this practice time was distributed in four different ways according to two lengths and two frequencies of training sessions. Two groups practiced for 1 hour in each session. One of these groups practiced for only one session each day, which resulted in a total training time of 12 weeks, while the second group had two sessions each day, thereby reducing the number of weeks in training to 6. Two other groups practiced for 2 hours in each session. One of these groups had only one session each day, while the other had two sessions per day. These latter two groups therefore had 6 weeks and 3 weeks of training, respectively. As this situation demonstrates, there are a variety of ways to distribute 60 hours of practice. The most distributed schedule required training for 12 weeks while the most massed distribution allowed training to be completed in only 3 weeks. The difference was in how long each session was and how many sessions were held each day.

Numerous performance measures were used to determine the effectiveness of the different practice schedules on learning the typing task. Two are described in Table 8.3–1. One of these was the amount of time it took the trainees to learn the keyboard. As you can see, the least amount of time to learn the keyboard was 34.9 hours, while the most amount of time was 49.7 hours. These times were required by the most distributed and the most massed schedules respectively. Thus, for learning the keyboard, keeping practice sessions short and having only one session a day led to faster learning. Another interesting measure was typing speed. The set goal was to learn to type 80 keystrokes per minute. The originally scheduled time of 60 hours for achieving this goal was attained only by the most distributed schedule group, who did it in 55 hours. All of the other groups required additional practice time. And what is most interesting is that the most massed schedule group, which practiced two 2-hour sessions each day, never did achieve this goal; they were still doing only a little better than 70 keystrokes per minute after 80 hours of practice. Retention tests were given 1, 3, and 9

TABLE 8.3-1 Results of the Baddeley and Longman experiment with practice distribution schedules for training postal workers

Practice Schedule	Number of Hours to Learn Keyboard	Number of Hours to Type 80 Keystrokes/ minute
1 hr/session— 1 session/day (12 wks. training)	34.9	55
1 hr/session— 2 sessions/day (6 wks. training)	43	75
2 hrs/session— 1 session/day (6 wks. training)	43	67
2 hrs/session— 2 sessions/day (3 wks. training)	49.7	80+

Data from A. D. Baddeley and D. J. A. Longman, "The Influence of Length and Frequency Training Session on the Rate of Learning to Type," in *Ergonomics,* 21, 1978: 627–635.

months after training had finished. After 9 months, the most massed group performed the worst on the typing speed test with the other groups performing about the same. Finally, a very revealing result was obtained from the trainees' own ratings of the training schedules. Although most preferred their own schedule, the most massed group preferred theirs the most, whereas the most distributed liked theirs the least.

The results of this experiment indicate that fitting 60 hours of training into 3 weeks, where there had to be two 2-hour practice sessions each day, was a poor practice schedule. While the most distributed schedule generally attained performance goals in the least amount of time, they did not perform any better than two of the other groups on the retention tests. Given all the results, the authors concluded that the 1-hour training sessions were more desirable than the 2-hour sessions and that one session per day was only slightly more effective than two sessions per day. However, having two 2-hour sessions each day was not a good training regime.

Other studies have reported similar distributed practice superiority effects. For example, Annett and Piech (1985) found that two 5-trial training sessions separated by one day led to better learning of a computer target shooting game than one 10-trial session. One trial involved shooting at 10 singly-presented moving targets. Learning was assessed by a performance test given one day after the end of the training session. The distributed group not only had more "hits" on the test but also had less error in the shooting attempts. Similar results were reported for the learning of word processing skills by Bouzid and Crawshaw (1987). Typists who practiced 12 skills during two sessions of 35 and 25 min each, separated by a 10-min break, required less time to learn the skills, and had fewer errors on a test than typists who practiced the skills during one 60-min session.

There are distinct implications from these studies for scheduling practice sessions for teaching motor skills. First, it is clear that practice sessions can be too long. In each experiment, the longer practice sessions consistently produced the poorest results. Second, more frequent practice sessions are preferable to fewer sessions. Again, in each experiment, groups that had more practice sessions learned the skills better than those having fewer sessions. Third, time saved in terms of the number of days of practice can be a false savings, because massing sessions too much can lead to poorer learning. Finally, the Baddely and Longman study showed that what students, trainees, or patients feel is a more desirable schedule may not be the best schedule for learning the skill. Remember, if the postal trainees had had their way, they would have chosen the schedule that got them through the training in the shortest amount of time, which ironically was the poorest schedule for learning the skill.

Summary

An important instruction decision is how to distribute the practice time that has been allotted for practicing a skill. Research investigating this issue has led to the comparison of massed and distributed schedules of practice. Two types of practice schedule concerns are relevant to this issue. One is the length of rest given between trials, the intertrial interval. Results of this research have shown that for continuous tasks, distributed schedules are generally better for learning than are massed, although the degree of difference is not a large one. However, for discrete tasks, just the opposite has been found. For these tasks, massed practice schedules are the preferred schedules. The second concern about the distribution of practice involves the length and frequency of practice sessions. Although this has not been a common problem of investigation by researchers, the evidence is consistent in showing that practice sessions can be too long and too infrequent to lead to optimal learning. Generally, skill learning occurs better when shorter and more sessions of practice are organized than when the sessions are long and there are fewer of them.

Related Readings

Adams, J. A. (1987). Historical review and appraisal of research on the learning, retention, and transfer of human motor skills. *Psychological Bulletin, 101*, 41–74.

Drowatzky, J. N. (1970). Effects of massed and distributed practice schedules upon the acquisition of pursuit rotor tracking by normal and mentally retarded subjects. *Research Quarterly, 41*, 32–38.

Lee, T. D., & Genovese, E. D. (1988). Distribution of practice in motor skill acquisition: Learning and performance effects reconsidered. *Research Quarterly for Exercise and Sport, 59*, 279–287.

Singer, R. N. (1965). Massed and distributed practice effects on the acquisition and retention of a novel basketball skill. *Research Quarterly, 36*, 68–77.

□

CONCEPT 8.4

Practice that occurs mentally can be beneficial for learning new
motor skills and for preparing to perform a skill

Key Terms

mental
practice

internal
imagery

external
imagery

imagery
ability

Application

Situations abound in which mental practice can
be applied to motor skills. These situations range
from employing mental practice to help learn a
new skill, to using it to assist in the performance
of an activity at a world-class competitive event.
Before discussing the effectiveness of mental
practice and why it seems to be so effective, a few
examples of how mental practice can be used in
motor skill situations will help to set the stage for
the discussion that follows.

A gymnast is standing beside the floor exercise
mat waiting to begin his or her routine. However,
before actually beginning that routine, the gymnast goes through the entire routine mentally, vis-
ualizing the performance of each stunt in the
routine, from beginning to end. Following this, the
gymnast steps onto the mat and begins the routine.

A physical therapy patient is having difficulty
learning how to get into her wheelchair from the
floor. After several demonstrations by the therapist and several practice attempts, the patient still
has trouble performing this skill. The therapist
tells the patient to stop practicing and to sit down
on the floor and mentally practice getting into the
chair. The patient is told to do this by imaging
herself getting into the chair perfectly 15 times in
a row. She is encouraged to go through the entire
sequence in her mind of being on the floor to actually sitting in the chair on each practice attempt. Following this procedure, the patient is then
instructed to go back to physically practicing this
skill.

A situation that is often perplexing to a novice
learner is one in which a good response is made,
but because of the nature of the activity, it would
be physically impossible to practice that response
in the same way. Golf is a good example of this
type of situation. If the golfer has just hit a beautiful drive right down the middle of the fairway,
he or she would like to be able to hit a few more
drives just to try to reproduce and reinforce the
swing that produced such a beautiful result. But
another type of practice can be used while walking
down the fairway to the ball; the golfer can mentally practice the swing that produced the drive.
As the golfer walks down the fairway, he or she
can be imaging hitting that excellent drive over
and over again.

Notice that in each of the examples, mental
practice was applied in a slightly different way in
accordance with the different goals of the mental
practice. The gymnast practiced mentally to prepare for an immediate performance of a routine
that had been practiced many times and was well
learned. The therapy patient was using mental
practice as a means to help improve a skill that
was in the process of being learned. Finally, the
golfer, although learning a new skill, was implementing the mental practice procedure to reinforce an appropriate action as an aid to an
upcoming demand to produce that action.

In the discussion that follows, these different types of situations in which mental practice can be used will be considered. Of interest in this discussion will be what research evidence indicates about the effectiveness of using mental practice and what types of mental practice are desirable. As you will see, the use of mental practice as an aid for learning and performing motor skills can be an effective means of facilitating the achievement of skill learning and performance goals.

——— □ ———

Discussion

When the term **mental practice** is used in the research literature it refers to the cognitive rehearsal of a physical skill in the absence of overt physical movements. Mental practice, as we are considering it here, is not to be confused with meditation, which generally connotes the involvement of the mind in deep thought in such a way to block out the awareness of what is happening to or around the individual. Meditation can, however, be thought of as a form of mental practice; in fact, it seems to be a potentially effective means for enhancing physical performance. For example, in a *Psychology Today* article, William Morgan (1978), a sport psychologist, reported that world-class long distance runners, such as marathoners, engage in an effective form of meditation while they run. Some runners disassociate their mental concentration from their running, while others relate their mental concentration to their running by attending to finite details of the physiological status of their bodies throughout the race.

In this discussion, we are limiting the use of the term *mental practice* to cognitive or mental rehearsal. According to this use of the term, an individual is involved in mental practice when he or she is *imaging* a skill, or part of a skill, that is actually being performed. No involvement of the body's musculature is noticed by an observer. This imaging may occur while the learner is observing another person or a film or videotape, while observing him or herself on film or videotape, or it may occur without any visual observation at all.

Two different types of imaging, or mental rehearsal, have been categorized by Mahoney and Avener (1977) as internal and external imagery. **Internal imagery** involves the individual actually approximating the real-life situation in such a way that the person actually "images being inside his/her body and experiencing those sensations which might be expected in the actual situation" (p. 137). **External imagery,** on the other hand, involves the individual viewing himself or herself from the perspective of an observer, as in watching a movie of oneself. We will not compare the efficacy of these two types of imagery conditions in this discussion. The interested reader can consult the Mahoney and Avener (1977) article or one by Hale (1982). However, be aware that these two types of imagery represent two different forms that mental rehearsal can take. Unless otherwise specified, either of these forms can be involved when mental practice is being considered.

Two Roles for Mental Practice

The study of mental practice as it relates to the learning and performance of motor skills has taken two distinct research directions over the years. These approaches have followed the patterns suggested by the different situations described in the Applications section. One of these directions has been the investigation of the role of mental practice in the *acquisition* of motor skills. Here the critical question is how effective mental practice is for a beginning learner who is in the initial stages of learning a motor skill. The example of the physical therapy patient learning to get from the floor into a wheelchair, presented in the Application section, illustrates the orientation of this type of mental practice study.

A second research direction has considered how mental practice can aid in the *performance* of a well-learned skill. Two approaches to this use of mental practice can be taken. The first was illustrated by the gymnast example presented in the Application section. Here mental practice is being used to aid in the preparation of the immediately upcoming performance. As such, mental practice can be seen as a means of response preparation, as discussed in Concept 4.3. The second use of mental practice as an aid to performance was seen in the example of the golfer mentally imaging a successful swing as he or she walks down the fairway. Here mental practice combines characteristics of both the acquisition and performance situations by providing a means of rehearsal, a memory process discussed in Concept 5.3. The memory benefit relates to both memory storage and retrieval. That is, a successful movement is rehearsed, which aids storage of that movement in memory, and retrieval from memory is facilitated by maintaining the successful movement in an activated state that aids recall when it is necessary to reproduce the swing.

Beginning as early as the 1890s, research literature is replete with mental practice studies. Several excellent reviews of this research literature have been published and should be consulted for more specific information than will be presented in this review (see Richardson, 1967a, 1967b; Corbin, 1972; Feltz & Landers, 1983; Feltz, Landers, & Becker, 1988). These reviews describe the convincing evidence that is available to support the point that mental practice is an effective strategy for aiding skill acquisition and performance preparation.

Mental Practice and Skill Acquisition

Most experiments investigating the effectiveness of mental practice in motor skill acquisition follow a similar design. Typically, one group is provided physical practice on a task; another group mentally practices the task for the same number of trials as the physical practice group; a third group is a control condition where subjects do not practice the task. Following these practice conditions, all groups perform the task on a retention test. In some experiments, a fourth condition is added that involves some combination of physical and mental practice trials.

In general, comparison of the physical, mental, and no-practice conditions indicate that physical practice is better than the other conditions. However, mental practice is typically better than no practice. This finding alone is interesting to support the effectiveness of mental practice in aiding acquisition. However, even more interesting is what happens when a physical-mental practice combination is compared to these three conditions.

Combining physical and mental practice. One of the most extensive research attempts to combine mental and physical practice is provided by an experiment by Hird, Landers, Thomas, and Horan (1991). Subjects practiced two tasks. One was a more cognitively oriented pegboard task, which required subjects to place as many round and square pegs in appropriately marked places in the pegboard as they could in 60 sec. The other was a pursuit rotor task, which involved maintaining contact with a target as it moved in a circular pattern at 45 rpm for 15 sec. There were six different practice conditions. Five of these involved differing combinations of physical and mental practice. At one extreme was 100% physical practice while at the other extreme was 100% mental practice. In between these two conditions were practice routines requiring 75% physical and 25% mental practice, 50% physical and mental practice, and 25% physical practice and 75% mental practice. The sixth condition was a control group that did other activity during the practice sessions. When combinations were used, the two kinds of practice were interspersed among the practice trials. Subjects practiced 8 trials of the pursuit rotor task and 4 trials of the pegboard task on each of 7 days. On the day before and on the day after these practice days, subjects performed a pretest and a posttest, respectively, on each task.

Results of this experiment can be seen in Figure 8.4–1. In terms of posttest performance, mental practice alone was better than no practice for both tasks, which is in keeping with other research findings. Note also that as the proportion of physical practice increased for both tasks, the level of

FIGURE 8.4-1 Results of the experiment by Hird, et al. The top graph shows the pre- and posttest results for the different practice conditions for the pegboard task. The bottom graph shows results for the pursuit rotor task.

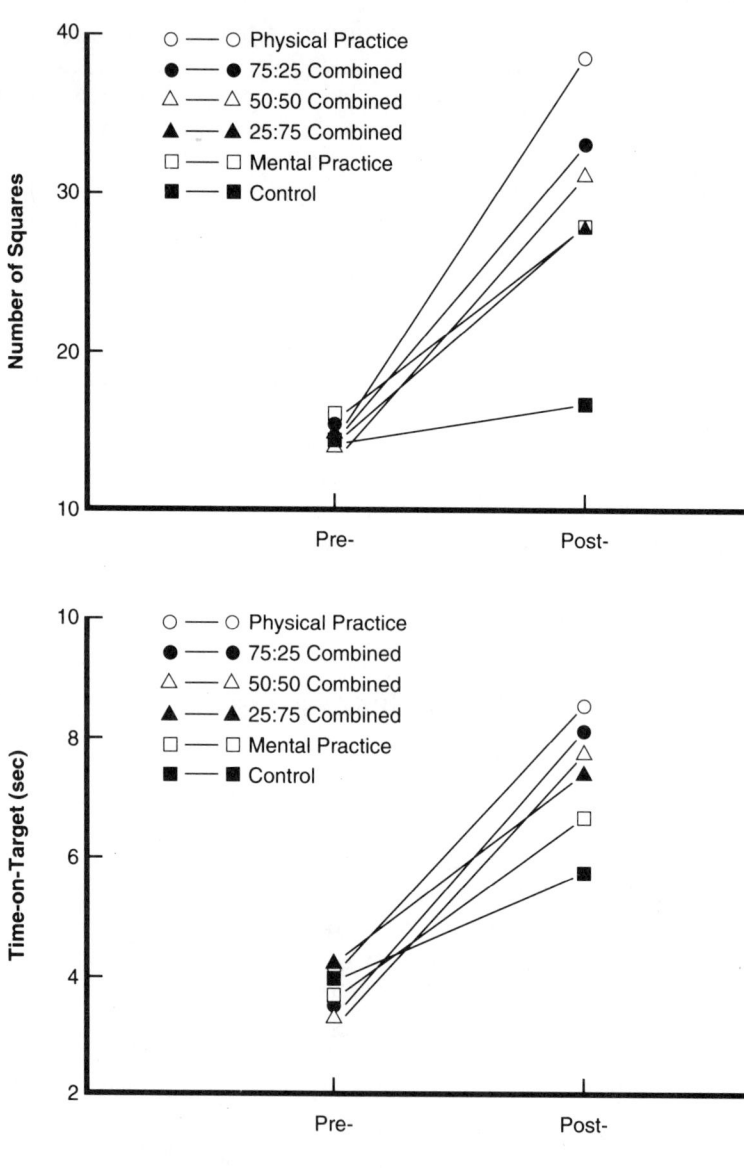

posttest performance increased. And physical practice alone was better than combinations of mental and physical practice. These differences were very small, however, especially for the pursuit rotor task when the 50% and 75% physical practice conditions are compared to the 100% physical practice condition.

The similarity in learning effects for combinations of physical and mental practice is not uncommon. In fact, some researchers have shown a combination of these types of practice to be equivalent to physical practice only. For example, in an experiment by McBride and Rothstein (1979), an open and a closed skill were compared in terms of how mental practice related to learning these different skills. In this experiment, all subjects were required to hit a solid whiffle golf ball at a 6-foot target that was 10 feet away. For the closed skill, the ball was placed on a batting tee 3 feet high. For the open skill, a 5-foot curved tube was placed at a 45° angle and balls were dropped down the tube at the rate of one every 10 seconds. Subjects used a forehand stroke with the non-dominant arm to hit the ball with a table tennis paddle. The physical practice group physically performed 40 trials. The mental practice group was given a demonstration and three physical practice trials. They then practiced 40 trials mentally, keeping a score for each hit. The physical and mental practice group alternated 10 physical, 10 mental, 10 physical, and 10 mental practice trials. The results showed that for both the open and closed skills the combination of mental and physical practice trials was superior to the mental practice and physical practice conditions for both test and retention trials. What is especially notable about these results is that the physical-mental practice group actually had only half as many physical practice trials as did the physical practice group. However, even with this much less physical practice, their retention scores were superior.

Why would a combination of mental and physical practice trials lead to learning effects that are as good as or even better than physical practice only? One answer to this question can be derived by considering some points discussed throughout this text about memory and learning processes. To be more specific, consider the need to engage in effective rehearsal strategies to ensure a durable and accessible memory representation in long-term memory. Also consider the point made in Concept 8.1 that effective problem-solving activity during practice is an important element in skill acquisition. Together, these lead to the expectation that any practice condition that encourages an effective rehearsal strategy, which includes problem-solving activity, will lead to better learning than practice conditions that do not. When mental and physical practice trials are combined, it is likely

that these conditions are in effect and therefore lead to better retention performance than physical or mental practice alone.

Mental practice benefits in rehabilitation settings. Mental practice has also been shown to be effective for learning skills in a rehabilitation setting. For example, Linden, Uhley, Smith, and Bush (1989) examined the effects of using mental practice on learning to improve walking balance by women aged 67 to 90 years. The task involved an activity course that required the women to stand on two footprints, and then walk along a simulated balance beam, which was actually a 4 in. (10.16 cm) wide strip of masking tape along the center of a carpeted walkway. This simulated balance beam was followed by a ramp that had a 4° slope. Then subjects stepped off the ramp and to a table to pick up juice and cookies. The mental practice consisted of engaging in 6 min of mentally imaging themselves walking along the simulated balance beam. The mental practice group engaged in this mental imaging activity for 8 days, while a control group spent the same amount of time sitting, playing word and memory games. Pretest and posttest performance for the simulated balance beam equilibrium task and for walking the activity course were done on the day before mental practice or the control activity began, and the day after the fourth day and the eighth day of the mental practice and control activity. These testing trials were videotaped for later analysis by the researchers.

Equilibrium and foot placement measures, used as indications of walking balance, indicated no differences between the two groups. However, when subjects were required to carry an object in each hand, the group that had engaged in mental practice showed better equilibrium characteristics. Thus, while the mental practice routine was not as successful as the researchers had hoped, it was beneficial. It is important to remember here that this experiment did not involve subjects in both mental and physical practice but was a comparison between mental practice and no practice. It is interesting to speculate about the outcome of this experiment had there also been a mental-physical practice condition similar to the ones used in the studies described earlier in this discussion. It is possible that this combination would have led to equilibrium and walking performance that was better than the mental practice only situation.

Mental practice benefits for power training. A characteristic of many motor skills is the need to generate speed over relatively short distances. Sprint events in running, bicycling, and crew are examples of skills involving this characteristic. An experiment by Van Gyn, Wenger, and Gaul (1990) has provided evidence that mental practice can be beneficial for improving power for people learning a 40-m bicycle sprint. Subjects were university students who had no experience in bicycle racing. They were given a pretest on a bicycle ergometer (stationary bicycle) to determine peak power for a 40-m sprint. Then they began three training sessions each week for 6 weeks on the bicycle ergometer to improve power performance. This training involved physical practice where maximum speed for 10 sec was required. Two groups of subjects were given imagery training where they imaged themselves performing the sprint 8 times. One of these groups did only the mental practice for the 6 weeks training period. The other imagery group did the mental practice while physically practicing on the bicycle ergometer. A third group received only the power training, while a fourth group served as a control group by receiving neither the imagery nor the power training.

The results of this experiment showed that on the posttest given at the end of the 6 week training period, only the group that received both the imagery and power training improved in their sprint time. Only the imagery training group and the imagery and power training group improved their peak power scores between the pre- and post-tests. Here again is an example of the benefit of a combination of physical and mental practice during training. The difference between the use of the mental and physical training combination in this experiment and other experiments is that they were done simultaneously rather than separately. While it would be difficult to implement such a procedure for many skills, there are skills where this integration of the two types of practice can be applied.

Mental Practice as Response Preparation

In the field of sport psychology, a popular topic of interest is the benefit of having elite athletes image themselves performing a skill prior to actually performing it. While there is ample evidence from newspaper and sport magazines that athletes make this type of preparation, there is little research evidence to determine whether this form of preparation is better than any other form. However, some evidence does suggest that mental rehearsal is an effective form of response preparation.

In a direct test of several different methods of performance preparation, Gould, Weinberg, and Jackson (1980) examined three different preparation conditions and compared them to two control conditions. One mental preparation condition was called *attentional focus*. Subjects were given specific instructions to concentrate on the feelings in the specific muscles involved in the task to prepare them for maximum performance. The second mental preparation condition was called *imagery*, which we have been considering in this discussion. Subjects were instructed to visualize themselves performing the task and setting a personal best score. The third condition was called *preparatory arousal*. In this condition, subjects were told to "psych" themselves up for maximum performance. This could be accomplished by getting mad or "pumped up" to perform as well as possible. The two control conditions involved subjects doing nothing for the 20-second preparation time or counting backwards by 7s from a four-digit number for 20 seconds.

The performance task used in this experiment was a leg-strength task in which subjects were required to exert as much power as possible with one leg on a leg-strength testing machine. Each subject was to produce a personal best score for each of four trials. A preparation interval preceded each trial during which the subjects engaged in the preparation condition assigned to their group. Results showed that the imagery and the preparatory arousal preparation conditions produced higher strength scores than the other three conditions.

The results of this study by Gould, Weinberg, and Jackson support the view that certain mental preparation strategies are better than others for producing maximum or peak performance. While imagery was not better than the arousal preparation condition, it was better than the attentional focus strategy or doing nothing at all. Because the task was an explosive strength task, it is not surprising to find that the emotional arousal strategy was effective. (Recall the discussion in Concept 4.3 about arousal level and performance as related to the type of task being performed.)

The use of mental imagery by athletes. Some insight into the use of mental imagery as an aid to performing sport skill was provided by the results of a survey by Hall, Rodgers, and Barr (1990). They administered a 37-item questionnaire to 381 male and female athletes in six sports in Canada. Results of the questionnaire indicated that the use of mental imagery is much more common as a preparation technique during competitions than during practice. This indicates that athletes see mental imagery more as a technique for enhancing performance than as an aid for learning. The researchers argue that this result shows that coaches need to instruct and remind athletes to use mental imagery in their regular practice sessions. The athletes saw mental imagery as having several benefits for competitions. It was seen as a way to keep focused on an event, as an aid in remaining self-confident about an upcoming performance, and as a means of controlling emotions and arousal level. Most of the athletes used mental imagery to image themselves winning rather than losing a competition. Most of the athletes indicated that they did not have structured sessions for using mental imagery. And, the higher the level of competition, e.g., international vs. local, the more mental imagery was used by the athletes involved.

Why Is Mental Practice Effective?

There have been various attempts at trying to explain why mental practice is effective as both a learning and a performance variable. The two most plausible explanations are a neuromuscular explanation and a cognitive explanation.

A neuromuscular explanation. The notion that mental practice benefits learning or response preparation for a neuromuscular reason can be traced to work by Jacobson (1931). When subjects were asked to visualize bending their right arm, Jacobson observed EMG activity in the ocular muscle but not in the biceps brachii. However, when subjects were asked to imagine bending the right arm or lifting a 10-pound weight, EMG activity was noted in the biceps brachii on more than 90% of the trials. Support from this type of electrical activity in the muscles of subjects asked to imagine movement has been provided many times since Jacobson's early study (e.g., Hale, 1982; Lang, et al. 1980).

Evidence such as this can give us some insight into why mental practice is an effective means of aiding skill acquisition and response preparation. You saw in earlier parts of this book the importance of sensory feedback in establishing an effective memory representation for a movement. Schmidt (1975) indicated that the sensory consequences of a movement are critical in developing a strong recall schema. Adams (1971) had earlier emphasized the importance of sensory feedback for developing a strong perceptual trace. From these viewpoints, mental practice can be seen as providing sensory information that can be used to effectively learn a skill.

And, in the discussion of response preparation in Concept 4.3, you saw that "tuning" activity precedes a response and presets the appropriate musculature for action. Because imaging an action creates electrical activity in the musculature that is involved in the movement, imaging can be considered a form of response preparation that aids in the tuning process.

FIGURE 8.4-2   Results of the experiment by Ryan and Simons showing performance on two Dial-A-Maze tasks before (T_1) and after (T_{11} and T_{12}) practice sessions in which subjects engaged in physical, mental, or no practice.

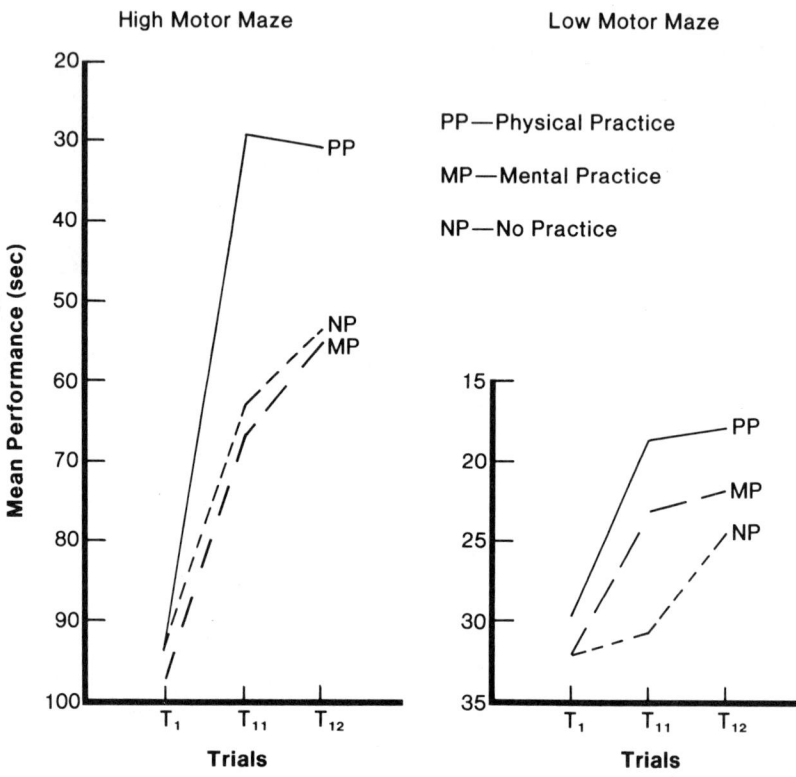

A cognitive explanation.   If you will recall the discussion in Concept 2.2, the first stage of learning motor skills is generally acknowledged to involve a high degree of cognitive activity. Much of this activity is related to questions about "what to do" with this new task. It should not be surprising, then, that mental practice can be effective practice during the first stage of learning. Mental practice can help the learner to answer some of the questions that characterize the early stage of learning, without the learner being pressured simultaneously to physically perform the skill. In the later stages of learning mental practice would seem to be beneficial in assisting the learner to consolidate strategies as well as to correct errors.

An example of some support for a cognitive basis of explanation of mental practice is an experiment by Ryan and Simons (1983). They reasoned that if mental practice is essentially a cognitive phenomenon, then learning a task that

is heavily cognitively oriented should benefit more from mental practice than a task that is more motor oriented. To test this, Ryan and Simons compared acquisition on two motor tasks, one low in motor demands and the other high in motor demands. These tasks were practiced under conditions of physical practice, mental practice, and no practice. The task, called a Dial-A-Maze, resembles a child's Etch-A-Sketch toy. A stylus is moved through a maze pattern by rotating two handles, one controlling horizontal movement, the other controlling vertical movement. The low motor demand task consisted of moving the stylus through the maze only in horizontal and vertical directions. Motor coordination demands were minimal because the two hands did not have to work together. The high motor demand task required the two hands to work together to move the stylus in a diagonal direction. The results are seen in Figure 8.4–2. Notice that as predicted the mental practice was superior to the no-practice condition for the low motor demands maze. That is, mental practice benefited the task that was heavily cognitively demanding.

Mental Practice and Imagery Ability

Although both physiological and psychological reasons have been proposed to explain why mental practice is effective for learning and performing motor skills, another issue related to the effectiveness of mental practice is worth considering. Recall that in Chapter 6 perceptual and motor abilities were identified as types of abilities related to motor skill performance. When the effectiveness of mental practice is considered, we find that another type of ability is thought to come into play: **imagery ability,** which is the ability to image an action when requested to do so. As an individual difference characteristic, this ability differentiates people in that some have great difficulty imaging a described action, whereas others can image with a high degree of vividness and control.

An interesting hypothesis has been proposed by Craig Hall (1980, 1985) concerning the relationship between imagery ability and the effectiveness of mental practice. He proposed that imagery ability is a critical variable in determining the success that can be expected to result from mental practice. That is, those individuals who have a high level of imagery ability will benefit from mental practice of motor skills, while those with a low level will not benefit as much from mental practice. A problem with testing this hypothesis has been the lack of appropriate tests of imagery ability relevant to motor skill performance (see Hall, Pongrac, & Buckolz, 1985, for a discussion of imagery ability tests). To overcome this problem, Hall and Pongrac (1983) developed the Movement Imagery Questionnaire (MIQ).

The MIQ consists of 18 action situations that a person is asked to physically perform. Then the person is asked to do either one of two mental tasks, either "form as clear and vivid a mental image as possible of the movement just performed" or, "attempt to positively feel yourself making the movement just performed without ac-

tually doing it." In this test, the first mental task is called "mental imagery" while the second mental task is called "kinesthetic imagery." After one of these mental imagery tasks has been performed, the individual is asked to rate how easy or difficult it was to do the mental task. The individual is not to rate how good or bad their performance was of the mental task, but how easy or difficult the mental task was to do. An example of two items from the MIQ, one from the visual and one from the kinesthetic imagery subscales, are presented in Figure 8.4–3. The two rating scales for each can also be seen in this figure. As you can see, specific action instructions are provided in each item. The ratings of all items in the test are tallied and an imagery score is obtained that indicates if the individual has a high or a low level of imagery ability, or is somewhere between the two extremes.

To test the hypothesis that imagery ability relates to the effectiveness of mental practice for learning a motor skill, Goss, Hall, Buckolz, and Fishburne (1986) selected individuals for participation in a mental practice experiment on the basis of their scores on the MIQ. Three categories of imagery ability individuals were selected, high visual/high kinesthetic (HH), high visual/low kinesthetic (HL), low visual/low kinesthetic (LL). These subjects practiced four complex arm movement patterns to a criterion level of performance. Before each of the practice trials, subjects were required to kinesthetically image the movement about which they were given instructions. Visual feedback, which showed the subjects their response in comparison to the criterion pattern, was provided after each trial. Two days later, all subjects returned for a retention test on the four movement patterns. During this test, no visual feedback was provided on the first three trials, but was provided for the remainder of the trials until the subjects achieved the performance criterion that was used during the acquisition trials.

The results of this experiment showed that the HH group performed the patterns to criterion in the fewest number of trials (11.0), with the HL group next (15.4), and the LL group taking the

Starting Position: Stand with your feet slightly apart and your hands at your sides.

Action: Bend down low and then jump straight up in the air as high as possible with both arms extended above your head. Land with your feet apart and lower your arms to your sides.

Mental Task: Assume the starting position. Form as clear and vivid a mental image as possible of the movement just performed. Now rate the ease/difficulty with which you were able to do this mental task.

Rating

Starting Position: Stand with your feet slightly apart and your arms at your sides.

Action: Jump upwards and rotate your entire body to the left such that in the same position in which you started. That is, rotate to the left in a complete (360°) circle.

Mental Task: Assume the standing position. Attempt to feel yourself making the movement just performed without actually doing it. Now rate the ease/difficulty with which you were able to do this mental task.

Rating

Rating Scales

Visual Imagery Scale

1	2	3	4	5	6	7
Very Easy to Picture	Easy to Picture	Somewhat Easy to Picture	Neutral (Not Easy nor Hard)	Somewhat Hard to Picture	Hard to Picture	Very Hard to Picture

Kinesthetic Imagery Scale

1	2	3	4	5	6	7
Very Easy to Feel	Easy to Feel	Somewhat Easy to Feel	Neutral (Not Easy nor Hard)	Somewhat Hard to Feel	Hard to Feel	Very Hard to Feel

FIGURE 8.4-3   A sample of two items and the rating scales from the Movement Imagery Questionnaire.

greatest number of trials to achieve criterion (23.7). During the retention phase, the three groups again showed this same order, although the differences were not as dramatic. The HH group required 6.3 trials, while the HL and LL groups required 6.7 and 9.2 trials, respectively, to reattain the performance criterion. Another interesting analysis was based on how many subjects in each group performed at least one of the movement patterns correctly during the retention test. The results of this analysis showed that again, the HH group did the best, with half of the group performing at least one pattern correctly, whereas no subjects in the LL group could do this.

The results of this experiment along with others (e.g., Hall, Buckolz, & Fishburne, 1989) indicate that there is a relationship between imagery ability and the effectiveness of mental practice. However, the results also show that individuals who are low in imagery ability can still benefit from mental practice for learning motor skills. These individuals may need to practice more than those with high imagery ability, but they will still be able to take advantage of the use of mental practice as an effective learning strategy. It is hoped more research will be done to help increase our understanding of imagery ability and its relationship to the effectiveness of mental practice for both learning and performing motor skills.

Mental Practice as an Instructional Strategy

A very practical benefit to be derived from using mental practice as a part of instruction is that it can help alleviate problems of what to do with students in a class that is too large, or does not have enough equipment, or has an injured student. Students who are waiting their turn can be instructed to practice mentally a certain number of movements or exercises. It is important, however, that the teacher be very specific, and instruct the students how the mental practice should be performed. The teacher should tell the students to imagine themselves doing the skill correctly. This

imagining can include the entire skill or a specific part of the skill that is being worked on. The teacher should instruct students to go through this procedure a specific number of times, such as five or ten mental practices. Following these guidelines for implementing mental practice, the teacher not only keeps inactive students occupied, but also provides them with an opportunity to be involved in an activity that will help them learn the skill they are practicing.

An interesting example of incorporating mental practice into a practice or performance preparation routine can be seen in some work that has come out of Robert Singer's laboratory. Singer (1986) proposed that the learning of closed motor skills could be facilitated if persons engaged in a general learning strategy. This learning strategy involves five steps, three of which involve elements of mental practice. The first step is to get ready physically, mentally, and emotionally. The second step involves mentally imaging performing the action, both visually and kinesthetically. The third step involves concentrating intensely on only one relevant cue related to the action, such as the seams of a tennis ball. The fourth step is to execute the action. Finally, the fifth step is to evaluate the performance outcome.

To test whether this general strategy could be an effective strategy for learning a specific motor skill, Singer and Suwanthada (1986) compared subjects who used this strategy with those who used more task-specific strategies and with those who were not given a strategy. The task involved underhand throwing of a dart at a rifle target that was on a wall 3 m from the subject. Following 50 practice trials with the dart throwing task, all subjects were required to perform two related tasks, a lawn dart throwing task and a type of basketball foul shooting task. The lawn dart task involved throwing a lawn dart underhand to the rifle target that was on the ground 6 m from the subject. The foul-shooting task involved shooting a soccer ball one-handed at a target attached to a basketball backboard from a distance of 4.5 m. As

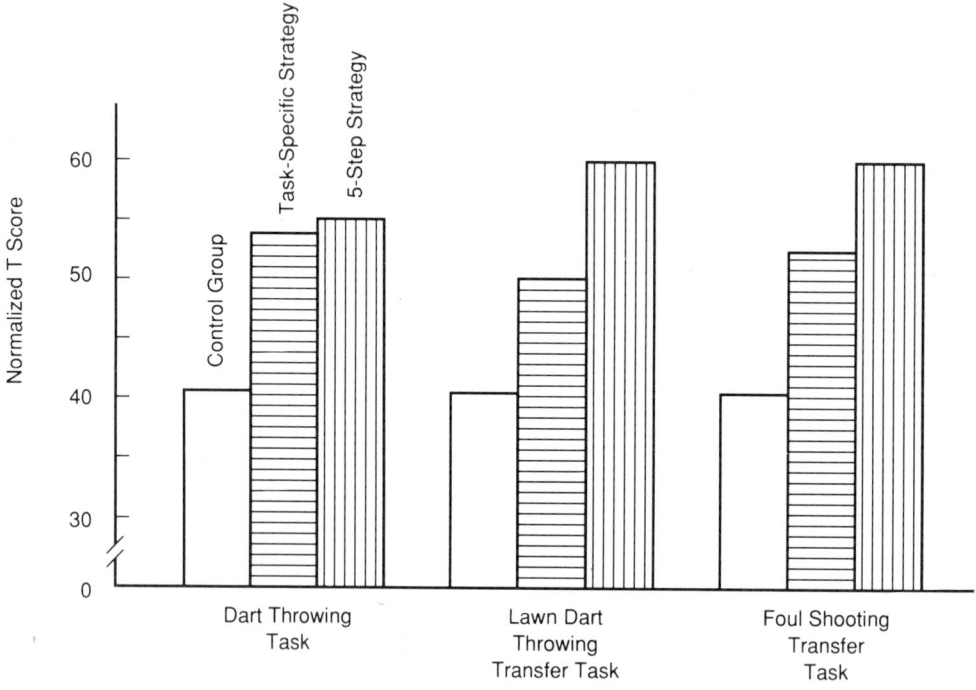

FIGURE 8.4-4   Results of the experiment by Singer and Suwanthada showing the influence of a generalized learning strategy (5-step strategy), a task-specific strategy, and no strategy for initial practice with a dart throwing task and transfer performance on a lawn dart throwing task and a foul shooting task.

you can see in Figure 8.4–4, subjects who used the five-step general strategy to practice the dart throwing task performed as well as those who used task-specific strategies. Also note that the strategy groups performed better than the no-strategy control group. However, on both transfer tasks, the subjects who had practiced the dart throwing task with the general five-step strategy performed better than the other groups. Thus, a general strategy that involved subjects in using mental practice to prepare for each practice response was an effective means to aid learning the skill for which the strategy was used, but it also was beneficial for effective transfer to related tasks.

Mental practice is by no means recommended as a panacea. It is presented, however, as a means of practice that, when used properly, can be effective in the learning and performance of motor skills. Furthermore, mental practice is not being recommended as a substitute for physical practice. But mental practice can be an effective instructional strategy, although proper implementation is critical to its effectiveness.

Summary

Mental practice is the cognitive rehearsal of a physical skill in the absence of overt, physical practice. It involves mental imagery of seeing oneself performing the actual movement. Experimental evidence has shown that mental practice can be an effective aid for learning skills as well as an effective means for preparing to perform a skill. As a practice method when skills are being learned, mental practice is best when used in combination with physical practice rather than as the sole means of practice. Explanations of why mental practice is effective in both skill acquisition and as a preparation for performance procedure relate to neuromuscular and cognitively based views. Evidence supporting both viewpoints has been discussed. The effectiveness of mental practice can be related to a person's ability to mentally image action. Mental practice can also be an effective instructional strategy when implemented as a strategy for preparing to perform a skill. The implementation of the use of mental practice requires effective planning by the teacher and use by the students.

Related Readings

Burhans, R. S., Richman, C. L., & Bergey, D. B. (1988). Mental imagery training: Effects on running speed performance. *International Journal of Sport Psychology, 19,* 26–37.

Feltz, D. L., & Landers, D. M. (1983). The effects of mental practice on motor skill learning and performance: A meta-analysis. *Journal of Sport Psychology, 5,* 25–57.

Gould, D., Weinberg, R., & Jackson, A. (1980). Mental preparation strategies, cognitions, and strength performance. *Journal of Sport Psychology, 2,* 329–335.

Hall, C. R. (1985). Individual differences in the mental practice and imagery of motor skill performance. *Canadian Journal of Applied Sport Sciences, 10,* 175–215.

Hall, C. R., Rodgers, W. M., & Barr, K. A. (1990). The use of imagery by athletes in selected sports. *The Sport Psychologist, 4,* 1–10.

Linden, C. A., Uhley, J. E., Smith, D., & Bush, M. A. (1989). The effects of mental practice on walking balance in an elderly population. *Occupational Therapy Journal of Research, 9,* 155–169.

Singer, R. N., & Cauraugh, J. H. (1985). The generalizability effect of learning strategies for categories of psychomotor skills. *Quest, 37,* 103–119.

Weinberg, R. S. (1982). The relationship of mental preparation strategies and motor performance: A review and critique. *Quest, 33,* 195–213.

□

CONCEPT 8.5

Practicing while physically fatigued appears to affect performance to a greater degree than learning, although learning can be affected

---

Key Term

threshold of
  fatigue

Application

A characteristic of most motor skills is that practicing them can be physically fatiguing. Activities such as dance, wrestling, gymnastics, swimming, many motor skill rehabilitation activities, and a host of others demand much from the participant in terms of physical energy. The person responsible for organizing and conducting the practice sessions for these activities is often confronted with the problem of what can be accomplished when the participants are fatigued. Can learning occur even though participants are fatigued? Should something new be introduced at this time, or could the time be better spent?

For example, a dance class has been practicing very hard for an entire class period. They are obviously fatigued. However, as the instructor, you feel that to maintain a time schedule, a new move-

ment should be introduced to the class before they are dismissed. Although your calendar indicates the need for you to present this new information at this time, does learning theory support it? If learning theory does not support this procedure, then you will, in effect, be wasting your time and that of your students by introducing a new movement while they are fatigued. However, if there is evidence to show that some benefit can be derived from students practicing the new movement even while fatigued, the time will not be wasted.

Situations similar to this dance class example can be proposed for a variety of motor skills in many instructional settings. Common to all these situations is the need for the instructor to know whether a person can learn while fatigued or whether practicing while fatigued is a waste of time. The concept we are considering indicates a positive response to this question. That is, learning does appear to be possible, even though an individual is fatigued. In the following discussion we shall consider this conclusion more critically to determine what it means to instructors of motor skills.

□

Discussion

The problem that we are considering is similar in nature to the problem discussed in previous sections of this book. That is, does fatigue affect learning or performance, or both? We have already considered the fatigue problem to some degree in Concept 2.1 and have set the stage for this discussion. That is, the research literature seems to indicate that fatigue has a primary

impact on inhibiting performance but not learning. This means that performance scores can be expected to be depressed during the practice in which the individual is fatigued. However, as soon as the person is given an opportunity to rest, thus reducing or eliminating the fatigue, performance during the following practice session will be similar to that of a person who had been previously practicing the skill in a nonfatigued condition.

Evidence that supports the detrimental influence of fatigue on performance is abundant. There is also ample evidence to suggest that learning is generally unaffected by fatigue. However, the research on which these conclusions are based is not without its problems, which will be discussed later. To complicate matters, an unequivocal conclusion seems impossible at this time because of some evidence indicating that learning can also be affected by fatigue.

Evidence Supporting Fatigue as a Performance Variable

A good example demonstrating that fatigue is more a performance than a learning variable is the one by Godwin and Schmidt (1971) discussed in Concept 2.1. This experiment was presented in that discussion as an example of how practice performance effects can sometimes lead to incorrect inferences about learning effects. We can briefly look at it again here to consider what it has to say about fatigue and learning.

In the Godwin and Schmidt experiment, female subjects formed two groups, a fatigued group (F) and a nonfatigued group (NF). Each subject was required to perform on the sigma task, which involves rotating a handle in a clockwise direction for one revolution until hitting a stop, then reversing the direction of the handle for one more revolution, and then finally releasing the handle and knocking down a wooden barrier 11 in. away. Subjects were scored on the total amount of time it took to complete the task, that is, movement time. Subjects in the fatigue group were required to crank a hand-crank ergometer for 2 min before every trial of the first session of the experiment, which involved 20 trials. All subjects were asked to return to the laboratory 3 days later to perform 10 more trials on the sigma task, but with no fatiguing condition. The results, which were presented in Figure 2.1–5, indicated that while the fatigued group performed the task more slowly than the nonfatigued group during day 1, they

performed as well as the nonfatigued group on the no-fatigue transfer trials on day 2 after just 2 trials.

The Godwin and Schmidt experiment is a good example of several experiments indicating that fatigue should be considered to be more of a performance variable than a learning variable. Because performance on the task being learned was impaired only for two trials on the second day of trials when there was no fatigue condition, the inference is that learning was not impaired during the practice trials that were performed while fatigued. Before determining how conclusive these results are, it will be necessary to consider an example of some other research that points to some different results.

Evidence Supporting Fatigue as a Performance and Learning Variable

A study conducted by Carron (1972) presented results indicating that fatigue could be considered as both a performance and a learning variable. In that experiment, male subjects learned the free-standing ladder, a balancing task. This task requires the subject to climb as many rungs as possible on the ladder within a certain period of time. Each time the subject begins to fall, he must begin again and continue until the practice trial is over. The performance measure is the total number of rungs climbed in a practice trial. Every subject was given 68 trials of 20 seconds each. One group of subjects was fatigued by riding a bicycle ergometer for 10 min prior to the first 18 trials. Each practice trial was also followed by 2 min of this exercise. The other group, the control group, did not exercise. This procedure was followed for 2 days, or 36 trials. On the final 2 days of 18 trials each, neither group exercised. The results of this experiment can be seen in Figure 8.5–1. The group that was physically fatigued showed poorer performance on all 4 days of the practice trials. Thus, fatigue during practice affected both performance *and* learning.

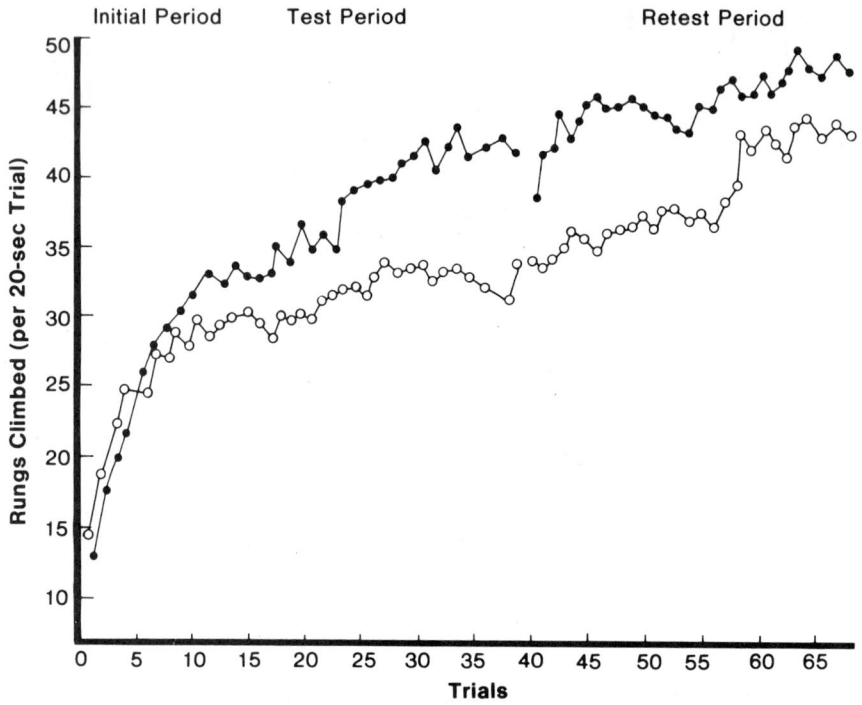

FIGURE 8.5-1 Results of the experiment by Carron showing the performance curves for the fatigued group (open circles) and nonfatigued group (closed circles) for the free-standing ladder climbing task.

The Issue Reconsidered

The two experiments that have been described in this discussion indicate quite opposite results, which leads to the obvious question of which one is correct in its findings. Unfortunately, the answer to that question is a very difficult one. The cause of that difficulty lies in the procedures followed in experiments investigating the fatigue and learning issue. The primary problem in the procedures is the absence of consideration of individual fitness levels of the subjects. In most experiments, the fatigue condition is based on having all subjects performing an exercise for a certain amount of time or to a certain heart rate. To be truly fatiguing for all subjects, it would seem that all subjects should be given exercise bouts that would be fatiguing for each person.

A second procedural problem apparent in many of these studies is that the exercise is not specific to the muscle groups used in the task being learned. In an actual teaching situation, students generally become fatigued from using muscles involved in the task being learned. It would only seem reasonable to make the conditions of the experimental situation similar in nature to those of the instructional situation.

Finally, the issue is difficult to resolve because various fatigue levels have not been adequately considered. It appears that light to moderate fatigue affects performance but has little influence on learning, while heavy or extreme fatigue affects both performance and learning. Thus, there seems to be a **threshold of fatigue** that should be used as a guideline for instructors. If fatigue levels appear to be below that threshold, practice of a new aspect of the skill will be beneficial in the long run. However, if fatigue levels are greater than the threshold, further practice would not be advisable. Unfortunately, no evidence has been provided in the research literature to suggest any valid criteria for determining such a threshold. Until such criteria are developed, instructors must use intuition and past experience to guide them in determining the amount of fatigue that their students can show before eliminating any further instruction. The threshold of fatigue must be considered as being related to the fitness level of the individual and the task or skill involved.

While the effect of fatigue on learning motor skills has been the primary concern in this discussion, one other factor must be taken into consideration. The risk of injury to a participant must outweigh all considerations of the effect that fatigue might have on learning. If even a slight amount of fatigue would increase the chances of injury, further practice would not be advisable until the student has recovered from the fatigued condition.

Summary

Physical fatigue is common to many motor skills. The instructor must decide whether or not further instruction will be beneficial to students who are obviously fatigued. Research evidence seems to indicate that light to moderate levels of fatigue will produce performance decrements while practicing in the fatigued state but will not impair learning. Extreme levels of fatigue, however, may impair both performance and learning.

Related Readings

Alderman, R. B. (1965). Influence of local fatigue on speed and accuracy in motor learning. *Research Quarterly, 36,* 131–140.

Carron, A. V. (1972). Motor performance and learning under physical fatigue. *Medicine and Science in Sports, 4,* 101–106.

Godwin, M. A., & Schmidt, R. A. (1971). Muscular fatigue and discrete motor learning. *Research Quarterly, 42,* 374–383.

□

STUDY QUESTIONS FOR CHAPTER 8

1. Why is variety of practice beneficial for learning (a) closed motor skills? (b) open motor skills? Give an example of how you would implement variety in practice for a closed and for an open skill.

2. How is contextual interference related to the variability of practice issue in motor learning?

3. How could you incorporate contextual interference into practice sessions for a skill you might teach?

4. What are two reasons that have been proposed concerning why contextual interference benefits motor skill learning?

5. Why is the issue concerning whether errors early in practice are harmful or beneficial to learning an important one for people who teach motor skills? What does the available research suggest is the more appropriate answer to this issue?

6. How is the concept of "overlearning" related to motor skill learning? Why is overlearning beneficial to learning?

7. Describe how the concept of practice distribution can be related to the intertrial interval and to the length and distribution of practice sessions. Describe a motor skill learning situation for each.

8. How do massed and distributed practice schedules influence the learning of discrete and continuous motor skills? Why do you think there is a difference in how these two schedules influence learning these skills?

9. What is "mental practice"? Describe an example of how you would implement mental practice procedures to aid (a) learning a skill, and (b) preparing to perform a skill.

10. What are two reasons why a combination of physical and mental practice trials can lead to learning a skill as effectively as an equivalent amount of physical practice trials?

11. What are three reasons proposed to explain why mental practice aids motor learning and performance?

12. When does fatigue appear to be (a) a performance variable? (b) a learning variable? Why do you think fatigue is related to learning motor skills in these two ways?

CHAPTER

9

MOTIVATING ACHIEVEMENT

CONCEPT 9.1
Setting an appropriate goal is an effective means of motivating motor skill learning and performance.

CONCEPT 9.2
Applying appropriate reinforcement techniques can facilitate motor skill learning and performance.

CONCEPT 9.1

Setting an appropriate goal is an effective means of
motivating motor skill learning and performance

Key Terms

goal setting   mastery goals   achievement
ideal goals   competitive   orientation
action goals   goals

Application

One of the problems faced by those who provide motor skill instruction is motivating people to achieve the best performance they can. While these people may want to learn the skill being taught, there may be difficulties when it comes to exerting maximum effort during practice or rehabilitation sessions. One of the ways that has been shown to help overcome this problem is the use of goal setting. This procedure involves establishing a performance goal for the person to achieve. Think about why this technique might work. How do you approach performing after you have set for yourself a specific goal to achieve in that situation compared to when you have no specific goal to work toward? Or how do you perform when you set a goal based on defeating an opponent compared to a goal based on some performance characteristic of your game?

For instance, suppose you plan to play golf on a particular afternoon. You and your opponent are fairly well matched, and you probably have in mind a goal of wanting to win the match. While winning obviously is a goal, it is a rather general goal. You could win and play very poorly or score much higher than you think you should. The goal "to win" may or may not be a goal that motivates you to perform your best. You could easily choose opponents whom you know you could defeat and thereby achieve that goal. This "win" goal also would not be very effective if you were in the process of trying to improve your game, because

achieving your goal does not provide a very specific means of evaluating your performance. How would performing with this "win" goal compare to some more performance-related goal, such as a particular score in this round, or averaging a five on all holes? Or you might set a performance-oriented goal for one aspect of your game, such as putting. Here, you could set a goal of averaging two putts per hole for the day's round. These specific performance objectives give you a definite means of evaluating your performance in terms of how you actually played as compared to what you think you should have done at this stage of your learning the game. From that evaluation, you would have a better understanding of how to improve the use of your practice time.

Goal setting, as it has been illustrated here, can be a very effective motivator for skill learning as well as for the maintenance and the intensity of motor skill performance. However, the proper use of goal setting is critical. To use the goal-setting technique incorrectly could lead to results quite opposite from those desired. In the following discussion, the approach to setting realistic goals will be considered. Also considered will be types of goal setting. The concern will be goal setting for a particular instance or performance, as in the golf example, or for a longer term situation, such as establishing goals for learning to play golf during the next year or six months. Goals are performance objectives that can be effective for motivating an individual to remain involved in a learning or performance situation. Goal setting can also be an effective method for obtaining an optimal level of performance from an individual. However, the proper use of this form of motivation requires an understanding of the complexities associated with its role in both learning and performance.

Discussion

The term **goal setting** refers to the level of performance on a task that is established for a person to achieve in the future. This future may be either very short term, as in the practice or therapy session coming up this afternoon, or it may be very long term, as the goal for the semester class or the end of the prescribed therapy period. It should be noted here that the term goal setting is a more common and popular term than *level of aspiration,* a comparable expression that also has been used in psychology literature. We will consider these terms as interchangeable.

The study of the relationship between goals and human behavior developed serious interest primarily through the work of Lewin and colleagues (1944), whose work identified two types of goals that are related to our discussion, *ideal goals* and *action goals.* **Ideal goals** are ultimate goals. They are objectives the individual desires to attain as the end result of his or her practice and participation in an activity. A young gymnast may have participation in the Olympic Games as an ultimate goal. A therapy patient may have as an ultimate goal the ability to walk without the aid of external support. An ultimate goal for a student learning ballet may be to perform in a community ballet company. Ideal or ultimate goals furnish a long-range end that provides the individual not only with an incentive to continue but also with a standard of performance against which points of achievement can be measured to provide information about what remains to be accomplished. **Action goals,** which are also referred to as momentary goals, are the "right now" goals. These objectives are associated with performance in a situation that immediately confronts the individual. The example of the golfer, presented earlier, illustrated several action goals.

From the base that goals are important for influencing behavior, Locke (1968) proposed a motivation model in which goals and setting goals were critical components. This model became very influential in directing research into the investigation of the relationship between goal setting as a motivational technique and performance. Locke's basic hypothesis was that setting specific, difficult goals would lead to better performance than setting less specific and easy goals or no goals. Strong support was subsequently reported for this hypothesis for performing a variety of laboratory, industrial, and problem solving skills (Locke, Shaw, Saari, & Latham, 1981).

Locke later applied his notions of goal setting to sport and physical activity contexts (Locke & Latham, 1985). They argued that the basic hypothesis of the Locke (1968) model should apply to these contexts as well as it had to industrial and everyday activities. Their principle proposal for sport and physical activity was that difficult and challenging goals, that are also realistic and attainable, should lead to better sport and physical activity performance than goals that are not challenging or that are unrealistic or unattainable. In fact, Locke and Latham indicated that setting goals that are unattainable would actually lead to undermining motivation and would cause performance to decrease. Evidence from the investigation of these proposals generally has supported the hypothesis that setting difficult, challenging goals is best for motivating performance, but has not supported the hypothesis that setting unrealistic, unobtainable goals will lead to decreased performance and undermine motivation. (See Weinberg, Fowler, Jackson, Bagnall, & Bruya, 1991, for an overview of this research.)

Goals and Achievement

Before discussing various concerns about the setting of goals, it is important first to explore the concept of goals and how they relate to performance in situations involving the learning of motor skills. When a person practices a skill to improve performance or performs the skill in a situation where evaluation of that performance occurs, that person is in what social psychologists call an *achievement situation,* which elicits what is called *achievement behavior.* There are many social psychologists who hold that to understand achievement behavior, it is important to understand the goals of the action in the achievement situation (e.g., Nicholls, 1984; Roberts, 1992). Once these goals are understood, it is possible to design instruction, provide feedback, and set goals that are more appropriate for facilitating learning or performance in that situation.

Mastery and competitive goals. Of the variety of achievement goals that have been identified, the two that are most related to motor skill learning and performance situations are *mastery goals* and *competitive goals* (see Roberts, 1992). It is important to note that other terms have been used to refer to these two goals. For example, some call them task-involved and ego-involved goals (e.g., Nicholls, 1984), while others call them learning and performance goals (e.g., Dweck, 1986), as well as mastery and ability goals (e.g., Ames, 1992). **Mastery goals** are those that have learning to perform the skill well as the primary focus. The person's goal is to "master" the skill. **Competitive goals,** on the other hand, are those that have demonstrating skill or a person's capability to perform the skill as the focus. The term competitive is used to describe these goals because some social comparison will be necessary to demonstrate skill level, hence a competition situation is established if such a goal is involved. Research evidence has demonstrated that a person's behavior in an achievement situation is related to the type of goal he or she has in that situation.

Which one of these two types of goals characterizes a person in an achievement situation has interesting implications not only for his or her immediate performance and perception of that performance, but also for his or her longer-term behaviors and perceptions of the situation. For example, people who approach a skill-learning situation that has a competitive goal will likely perform according to how others are performing in the class or group. Even though a person may be capable of achieving a higher level of performance, that level is not achieved because successful achievement of the competitive goal did not demand a higher level of performance than was attained. On the other hand, people with mastery

goals tend not to be concerned with how others are performing, but focus more on trying to master the skill. Thus, in competitive situations, people with mastery goals may be well satisfied with their performance, even if they lose the competition, if their mastery goal was achieved. It is interesting to note with respect to persisting in an activity, people who have competitive goals are more likely to drop out of the activity than mastery goal people. This is especially true for people who are constantly seeing themselves as performing worse than others in a group.

With respect to motor skill learning, it is interesting to note that not only can mastery or competitive goals dominate a person's approach to an achievement situation, but also a mastery or competitive environment can exist, or be created, in which the achievement situation occurs. These environments have distinct characteristics. For example, competitive situations emphasize competition among the participants with evaluation of performance based on the performance of other people rather than on the participant's performance alone. Mastery environments, on the other hand, emphasize participation in the skill and exerting effort in performing the skill with the goal to increase the capability to perform the skill. Evaluation of the performance of that particular skill is self-referenced.

It is important to set goals that are appropriate to the situation. Mastery goals are clearly preferable when it is essential that skills be improved or when evaluation is based on performance characteristics of the skill itself. In these situations, goals need to be set that reflect mastering the skill being learned. Competitive goals, on the other hand, are preferable for performance situations where evaluation of performance is based on comparisons with other people in the situation. The goals set should reflect the competitive nature of the situation. When the types of goals set for a situation are inappropriate, it becomes increasingly possible to elicit less than optimal performance as well as inappropriate perceptions of competence. However, when the goals set are consistent with the characteristics and demands of the achievement situation, chances for optimal performance are enhanced as are the likelihood of appropriate perceptions of competence.

Evidence That Goal Setting Is Effective

Before suggesting how goals should be set and what performance outcomes could be expected in return, it will be useful to consider the empirical basis for accepting the notion that goal setting is an effective means of influencing skill learning and performance. It is essential to keep the learning-performance distinction in mind. We will consider some examples of research evidence that support the efficacy of goal setting for situations in which an individual is attempting to acquire a new skill or to improve his or her skill level. On the other hand, some examples will reflect performance situations where an individual is performing a skill rather than practicing it. Both conditions have been shown to be influenced by goal setting.

Goal setting and performance. Because physical performance encompasses a wide range of motor activities, we will consider some experiments that have supported the role of goal setting in different types of motor activity situations. First, we will examine a study by Nelson (1978), which considered the motivating effects of goal setting on muscular endurance testing. Second, in a study by Burton (1989), we will observe the effects of goal setting on the performance of swimming. Third, we will discuss work by Duda, Smart, & Tappe (1989) in which effort exerted in a rehabilitation setting was investigated.

Nelson (1978) gave four groups of college men different goals to strive for in an elbow flexion strength test. These goals were an actual performance norm for the task, a fictitious norm, an attainable performance goal, or nothing. A score for each subject was the number of repetitions the load attached to a cable tensiometer could be lifted in one attempt. The load was individualized for each subject. Results showed that the three groups that were provided with an objective standard to be used as a goal (realistic or not), performed better than the control group, which was given no norms

or goals. In fact, the fictitious norm group performed better than either the realistic norm group or attainable goal group.

The study by Burton (1989) involved the use of a goal setting program with intercollegiate swimmers. Mastery goals were used as the basis for this program. Swimmers were trained to set accurate goals on the basis of personal performance standards, rather than on place-related outcomes of individual meets. Based on performance of these swimmers during a mid-season dual meet and the end of the season conference championship, the swimmers who used the goal-setting approach performed better than those who had set inaccurate goals or who had not set performance goals.

In the experiment reported by Duda, Smart, and Tappe (1989), college athletes involved in an injury-rehabilitation program were investigated. These athletes were rated in terms of their achievement motivation orientation and could be classified as having low or high mastery orientation. Based on daily ratings of the athletic trainers involved in working with these athletes, the athletes who were more oriented toward mastering the rehabilitation tasks (i.e., mastery goal oriented) tended to push themselves harder and work harder during the rehabilitation sessions. On the other hand, the athletes who were low in mastery goal orientation were observed to essentially "walk through" their exercise protocols each session. Thus, while goal setting itself was not involved in this study, the results indicate that setting mastery goals would have been expected to be positively related to rehabilitation performance.

Each of these studies supports the contention that goal setting is a very potent form of motivation that influences a person's performance of physical activities. While questions remain from studies like these about why goal setting is effective, the point is that goal setting *is* effective. Not only was the setting of a goal related to better performance than when none was set; performance was also superior when the performer knew he was exceeding the preestablished goal, even when that information was not based on actual performance.

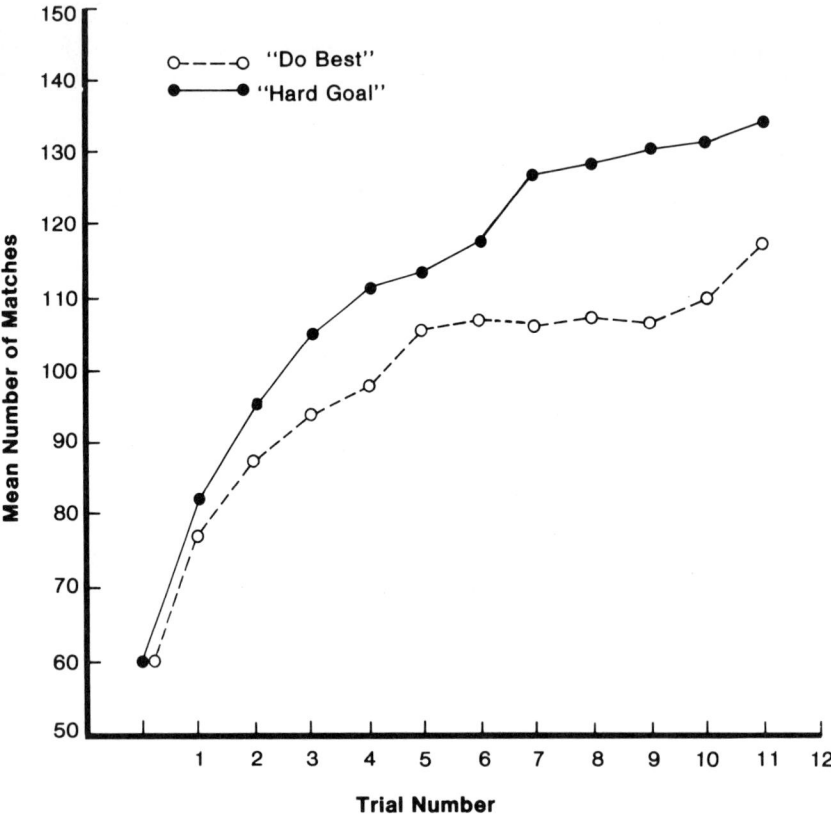

FIGURE 9.1-1 Results of the experiment by Locke and Bryan showing the performance curves for the two groups provided with different incentive goals for performing a complex motor task.

Goal setting and learning.   Support for the use of goal setting in a motor skill learning situation can be found in an often-cited study by Locke and Bryan (1966). By manipulating both hand and foot controls, subjects were required to match a set of light patterns on a display with another set of lights. The task was to match 13 different patterns in a sequence, as quickly and as frequently as possible. One group of subjects was told to "do their best" while a second group was given a specific goal to strive for. This latter goal was a score based on their previous test score. Results (Figure 9.1–1) showed that the specific goal group not only performed better overall, but also had a faster rate of improvement.

Augmented feedback and goal setting.   In the discussion of Concept 7.3 you saw that one of the functions of augmented feedback is to act as a means of motivation. In this role, augmented feedback provides information that can be an incentive for a person to try harder or to persist longer at a task. It is interesting to relate the type of augmented feedback used in this motivational role to the type of goal a person has in a situation. If a mastery goal characterizes the situation, it could be expected that any form of augmented feedback, whether it is KR, KP, or augmented sensory feedback, could serve a motivational function. Because the goal of the person is to improve performance of the skill, each form of augmented feedback gives information that can be a means for a person to compare his or her own performance with the mastery goal set for the situation. On the other hand, KR can be more closely associated with a competitive goal because outcome is the basis for ascertaining competitive goal achievement.

The difficult aspect of investigating augmented feedback as a form of motivation is distinguishing between the functions of augmented feedback as error correction information and as information that serves as an incentive to achieve a goal. For example, KR can provide the learner with information about a movement that indicates whether performance errors must be corrected. It also provides information that lets the person know how close he or she is to achieving an established goal. Further research is needed along with better developed techniques for separating these roles before we can develop our understanding of the motivational role of augmented feedback in motor skill learning and performance.

Summarizing goal-setting effects. As the evidence from the research presented in the preceding sections indicates, there is little doubt that goal setting is an effective motivation technique that influences both the learning of skills as well as the performance of skills in test situations. It is encouraging that the research on goal setting and its effects on performance have been consistent in supporting specific relationships between types of goals set or means of goal setting and performance. This research literature, from both laboratory- and field-based experiments, has been analyzed by Tubbs (1986) and can be summarized as four goal-setting characteristics that influence performance of skills in a positive way.

First, difficult goals lead to better performance than easy goals. There is strong support from a large number of studies indicating that goals should be difficult to achieve if they are to be effective. In keeping with this notion, the level of difficulty must be achievable by the individual. This condition adds a special concern for the person setting the goal, because it requires taking into account the capabilities of the individual and the potential to achieve a certain level of performance.

Second, specific goals lead to better performance than do-your-best goals or no goals. This characteristic of effective goals advances the first characteristic by establishing a requirement for the difficult goal. Not only should the goal be difficult to achieve, it should be specific in terms of what should be achieved. The experiment by Locke and Bryan (1966) is just one example of research that has supported the benefit of specific goals as an effective means of improving performance.

Third, goal setting plus performance feedback is better than goal setting alone. This characteristic fits well with our discussion of augmented feedback and goal setting. The important point is that the effect of goal setting will be enhanced by providing the individual with information about his or her performance with specific reference to how he or she is doing in terms of reaching the set goal. Also, the effect of performance feedback appears to be stronger when it is formally given by the person who set the goal. Although there is not much evidence to support this conclusion, there is sufficient evidence to suggest that this result be given consideration in performance situations. It is important to note that Tubbs indicated that the goal setting plus feedback relationship to performance is an important one that needs further research.

Fourth, participant involvement in goal setting leads to better performance than goals assigned without participant involvement. It is important to qualify this conclusion from the research literature. Tubbs noted that this conclusion could only be made when the goal level that was set was not held constant. This means that if the same goal is set by a participant involvement group and a group that does not participate in the goal setting, performance of the two groups is similar. What typically happens when participants are allowed to be involved in the goal-setting process is that they will set *higher* goals than when they are not involved and someone assigns a goal to them. Thus, in the typical case, the goal-setting level is not held constant. This is an important issue in goal setting because it relates not only to the characteristic of the goal that is set, but also to who sets the goal. Participant involvement does not mean that the participants set the goal. It means that the participants are involved in the goal-setting process with the person in charge, such as the teacher, coach, or therapist.

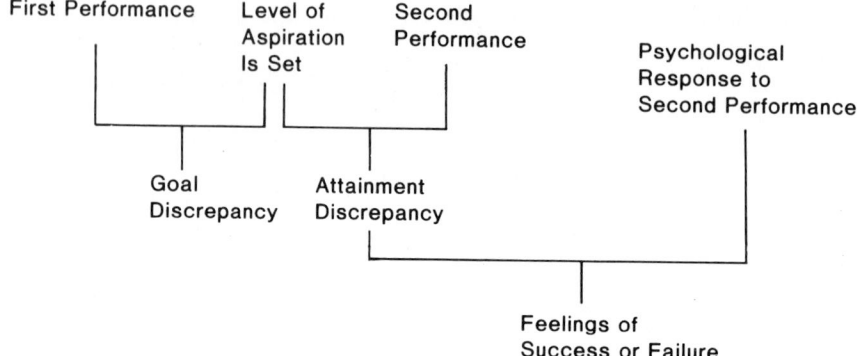

FIGURE 9.1-2   Diagram indicating the typical sequence of events and responses in a goal-setting situation.

Personal and Situational Influences in Goal Setting

In addition to the goal-setting characteristics we have just considered, there are some personal and situation-related factors that must be taken into account before establishing specific guidelines for setting realistic goals. An important individual difference characteristic is the person's **achievement orientation.** This characteristic concerns whether the person tends to approach achievement situations with a mastery or a competitive orientation, which are anchor points at each end of a continuum of achievement orientations. As you would expect, this orientation will be directly related to what kind of goal a person sets, as well as the level of that goal. This individual difference characteristic becomes especially influential when a person is permitted to set a performance goal without consulting the person in charge of the activity. Several tests for achievement orientation have been developed and are available. A popular one that assesses achievement orientation in any achievement situation is one developed by Maehr and Nicholls (1980). Sport-specific inventories have been published by Gill and Deeter (1988) and by Vealey (1986). Each of these tests provides a quantifiable measure of a person's general tendency to approach achievement situations with a more mastery or a more competitive orientation.

An important situation-related factor that interacts with the need for achievement by the individual is very powerful in its influence on goal setting. This factor, *past experiences,* related to prior successes or failures in achieving previously established goals, is intimately involved in influencing the type of goal the individual will set for the next attempt. The role of previous goal-setting experiences has been aptly illustrated by Alderman (1974), as adapted from Atkinson (1964), in a time-sequence diagram (Figure 9.1–2) in which each event is represented on a time line. The level of aspiration, or goal, is set following a given performance, noted as "first performance" in the diagram. The difference between these events can be interpreted as the "goal discrepancy," which is indicative of the individual's orientation toward success as well as his or her confidence. A goal level that was set rather low would indicate little confidence in being successful at achieving much beyond what has already been achieved. Then the next performance of the task occurs. The difference between the results of this performance and the goal represents the "attainment discrepancy." This reveals how accurate the individual was in the evaluation of his or her own ability, as well as his or her aspirations in the task. This includes the person's "feelings of success or failure" follow that evaluation, which is related to the individual's "psychological response to the second performance."

Individuals with past experiences of success in achieving goals will tend to strive harder in the future. The opposite seems true for past experiences of failure. In a basketball setting, for example, the future performance of a player who is always asked to defend someone who usually beats him or her will likely be influenced by those past experiences. The coach who permits all players to experience a degree of success as often as possible increases the likelihood that his or her players will strive for goals that represent improved performance as well as require maximum effort.

Goal-Setting Guidelines

On the basis of what has been discussed thus far, it seems that certain guidelines can be established in using goal setting as an effective means of motivating achievement in motor skill learning and performance situations. Try to apply each guideline to a situation in which you might be involved.

1. *Set goals that will enhance skill mastery.* Although there are two different types of achievement goals, it seems clear that mastery goals are preferable for the types of motor learning and performance situations under consideration in this book. The focus of our discussions is on improving skills. Performance of skills can be improved in either practice or competitive situations. Thus, mastery goals, which focus on the skill being performed rather than on comparison with other people performing the skill, will lead to the type of performance achievement we are seeking. Goals should be set on the basis of characteristics of the skill being performed by the person for whom the goal is being set, rather than on the basis of how others have performed the skill. As a result, it is important to analyze skills being taught to determine what skill characteristic goals should be set. Goals based on mastery of skills not only lead to optimal performance, but also lead to increased persistence in being involved in the activity.

2. *Set objective goals.* Goals should be in the form of a number to provide the student or performer with an objective means of evaluating his or her own performance. We have seen evidence that the statement "do your best" falls short in its effectiveness as a motivator when compared to a specific objective goal. Objective goals will be even more effective if specific time frames are established for accomplishing the goals.

3. *Set goals that are meaningful.* A goal must have meaning to the person. It will be a more effective means of motivation to tell a student that to make 6 out of 10 shots in a basketball goal-shooting task is an above average score than to simply say, "try to make 6 out of 10." The performer not only needs an objective goal to strive for, but one that is meaningful in order to provide an immediate point of reference for performance. If team-related or group-related goals are set, it is important to be certain that each member understands the specific tasks he or she is responsible for and how that task is to be carried out to enable the group to achieve the goal. Providing such an understanding enhances the meaningfulness of goals to individual group members by letting them see how their function in the group helps the group as a whole.

4. *Set goals that are attainable.* Although goals that are almost unattainable may lead to performance increases early in a performance experience, as in the Nelson (1978) study, failure to achieve those goals during a series of attempts will tend to lead to poorer performance than when realistic goals are used. Consideration must be given to the level of achievement that is desired by the individual. Some goals are attainable only through maximum effort, while others are attainable with little effort.

5. *Set goals according to individual differences.* Because both past experiences and the personality of the individual are intricately

related to the effectiveness of goal setting, the instructor must determine goals for each individual. While the coach or teacher realizes that the goal can be reached only if a maximum effort is exerted, the student or performer may not be aware of this, or may not wish to exert a maximum effort for fear of not achieving the goal.

6. *Set goals on the basis of past experiences.* Goals will fit many of these guidelines if they are established in terms of past performances. The goal should be objective, it should be meaningful to the individual, and it should be individualized. Whether or not it is attainable is up to the individual and the instructor. The instructor or coach should not just "pull a number out of the air" as a performance goal. The instructor must be alert to what the individual has done in the past, not only in terms of performance levels but in terms of the amounts of improvement associated with those performance levels.

7. *Set both short-term and long-term goals.* Although there is very little research addressing the issue of short- versus long-term goals, there is evidence indicating that the combination of these is preferable (see Tenenbaum, Pinchas, Elbaz, Bar-Eli, & Weinberg, 1991). Short-term goals provide needed immediate incentive and feedback about progress, whereas long-term goals provide an ultimate goal that becomes the focus of performance and the standard of performance on which comparisons can be made for setting and adjusting short-term goals.

Commitment to Achieving Goals

An important part of any goal-setting program or procedure is getting people to commit to achieving the goals they set. Some suggestions for increasing commitment to achieving goals has been provided by Martens (1987) and are applicable to a variety of goal-setting contexts. He provides six suggestions:

1. *Explain the benefits of setting goals and of pursuing goals systematically.* If people know why the goals are being set and why such a process will benefit them, then chances are increased that they will commit to achieving the goals they set.

2. *Do not threaten or intimidate people to set goals at a certain level.* Remember that involving the people who will be performing the skills in the goal-setting process is beneficial in enhancing the likelihood that the goals set will be achieved. This suggests that if gaining a commitment to achieve goals is important, then it is important that these people feel that they have willingly involved themselves in setting the goals to be achieved.

3. *Be highly supportive of people striving to achieve their goals.* People who feel confident about their attempts to achieve the goals they have set are more likely to set higher goals.

4. *Reward progress and attainment of goals.* If people know that their efforts to achieve goals will be acknowledged, they are more likely to commit to achieving the goals they set. Rewards can be in various forms, such as praise, encouragement, and tangible rewards.

5. *Provide regular feedback about progress in achieving goals.* Just as feedback about progress has been shown to increase the likelihood of achieving goals, it also has been shown to increase commitment to achieve goals.

6. *Help people with their plan of action for achieving goals.* If people feel they are not being left to drift in uncharted waters in their attempts to achieve the goals they have set, they are more likely to commit to achieving these goals. This feeling can be abated by help from the person directing their progress in the activity, such as a teacher, coach, trainer, or therapist.

Summary

Goal setting is a potent form of motivating achievement in both performance and learning situations. Achievement goals can be either mastery related, where the focus is on improving the skill being performed, or competition related, where the goals are based on comparison with others who are also performing the skill. In general, mastery goals are preferable for most motor learning and performance situations. Research evidence has shown that setting performance goals can yield performance that is superior to when no specific goal has been provided. The commonly used phrase "do your best" does not result in as great a performance improvement as does a specific, objective goal. Also, appropriately set and achieved goals can increase the likelihood of a person remaining involved in an activity or rehabilitation program. The goal that an individual will establish in a situation can be related to the person's achievement orientation and the individual's past experiences of success or failure in attaining goals. Specific guidelines have been presented to assist in effectively using goal setting as a means of enhancing motor skill performance and learning.

Related Readings

Duda, J. L. (1992). Motivation in sport settings: A goal perspective approach. In G. C. Roberts (Ed.), *Motivation in sport and exercise* (pp. 57–91). Champaign, IL: Human Kinetics.

Hall, H. K., & Byrne, A. T. J. (1988). Goal setting in sport: Clarifying recent anomalies. *Journal of Sport and Exercise Psychology, 10,* 184–198.

Lewthwaite, R. (1991). Motivational considerations in physical activity involvements. *Movement Science,* American Physical Therapy Association Monograph, 56–67.

Locke, E. A., Cartledge, N., & Koeppel, J. (1968). Motivational effects of knowledge of results: A goal-setting phenomenon? *Psychological Bulletin, 70,* 474–485.

Locke, E. A., Shaw, K. N., Saari, L. M., & Latham, G. P. (1981). Goal setting and task performance: 1969–1980. *Psychological Bulletin, 90,* 125–152.

Martens, R. (1987). *Coaches guide to sport psychology.* Champaign, IL: Human Kinetics Publishers. (Read chapter 10.)

Weinberg, R. S. (1982). Motivating athletes through goal setting. *Journal of Physical Education, Recreation, and Dance, 53* (9), 46–48.

CONCEPT 9.2

Applying appropriate reinforcement techniques can
facilitate motor skill learning and performance

Key Terms

law of effect	punishment	negative
reinforcement	positive	reinforcers
	reinforcers	shaping

Application

Picture yourself as an elementary school physical education teacher. The young boys and girls in your class are trying to learn to dribble a soccer ball, but it is obvious to you that most of these students are having a difficult time learning this skill. You have instructed the entire class in the proper techniques of dribbling; you have also worked with many of the students in correcting wrong techniques. Besides providing technical advice or instruction about dribbling, is there anything else you can do to facilitate the learning of this skill? One thing you can do is to praise a student individually with encouraging words whenever he or she properly performs the skill or some part of the skill. From your own experience with these children, you have undoubtedly noticed that they seem to enjoy being praised by you. Your decision, then, is to apply this praise to their performance when practicing a new and difficult skill.

Let's consider a different situation and context. It is not uncommon in athletics to find a coach who believes that he or she should not praise the players too often. Such coaches have determined that it works better, for their purposes, to constantly chide the players to do better and to improve their performance. These coaches' reaction to the good execution of some aspect of the game is to say nothing. Thus, the approach is to consistently "get on" the players, but to say nothing when something is done correctly or well. It is not that praise is never used, but that nothing is said that will be interpreted by the players as approval.

Another example of the use of reinforcement techniques is seen in providing an incentive for a varsity wrestling team. Suppose you are the coach. You have determined that the team needs to improve its ability in achieving takedowns. As an incentive to improve, you have devised a point system for the team. For every takedown a team member gets during a match, he will receive one point on a large chart you have placed in the wrestling room. At the end of the season, you will give a special award to the wrestler who has accumulated the most points for takedowns.

Consider one more situation. You are teaching a tennis class, but you are concerned that the class has not understood the full importance of the first serve. In fact, as you observe the class, you notice that the students seem to place very little emphasis on getting the first serve in-bounds. Instead, they seem to be satisfied with just "dinking" the ball over the net to start the rally going. You decide to have them play a game you call "one-serve tennis." In this game, there is no second serve; any missed first serve becomes a point for the opponent. To eliminate "dinking" and to emphasize concentration on their serving skills, you further indicate that the first serves cannot be simply "patted" over; there must be a full service motion.

In each of these four situations, a different technique was used to try to improve performance or learning. The elementary school class was being verbally praised. The coach in the second situation stopped chiding a player when something was done well. The wrestling coach provided a reward as a goal to strive for. The tennis teacher devised a game that penalized incorrect performance. Each of these situations represents a technique that can be considered under the broad heading of reinforcement. In the following discussion, you will be provided with information that should help you to determine what types of results may be expected from the use of these techniques.

———— □ ————

Discussion

When the word *reinforcement* is used, what do you think of? Rats learning to push a bar in order to get a pellet of food? Pigeons learning to bowl? Programmed instruction books? Behavior modification? Each of these situations has become rather well known in most educational circles. Much media publicity for the work of B. F. Skinner has served to popularize many of the techniques in which reinforcement has been a key concept.

The role of reinforcement in human learning received its initial impetus from the studies of animal learning by Edward Thorndike in the first third of this century. Thorndike's **law of effect** set the stage for recognizing the influence of reinforcement theory in human learning. The law of effect states that learning is related to the presence of rewards or punishments following a response. A reward serves to strengthen the response, which means increased likelihood of the response occurring again. Conversely, punishment has the effect of weakening the response or lowering the probability of the response being repeated. Thus, responses apparently are made as efforts to comply with a motive, that is, to reduce a drive or need. If a reward follows a particular response that response becomes "stronger" than any alternative response. Thus, a reward that satisfies a motive positively influences the learning of a desired response.

While other learning theorists have proposed different explanations of reinforcement in learning (such as Hull [1943] and Tolman [1932]), the individual who exerted the greatest influence on current views of reinforcement is B. F. Skinner. Skinner's view of reinforcement was not as dependent on the role of rewards; rather, he considered reinforcement to be related to an arrangement of stimulus and response conditions. The idea of *response contingency* is important here. If a particular response is the one that should be learned, the response must be contingent on the occurrence of a particular stimulus condition. Contingency, then, is a condition that stipulates that in order for a particular event to occur, it must be preceded by some other event. For example, serving an ace in tennis is contingent upon swinging the racquet. Another example would be that receiving a trophy in a golf tournament is contingent upon beating every other player's score.

Based on Skinner's view of reinforcement, the learning of a desired response will be the result of arranging the learning setting so that for the individual to receive a reinforcer, the proper response must first be made. In reinforcement theory, it is what occurs *after* a response that is important. To increase the probability of the occurrence of a desired response, a reinforcer or reinforcement should follow the desired response. The reinforcer need not be a reward. As you will see later in this discussion, a reinforcer could be *not* receiving something. To decrease the probability of a response, a punishment or penalty should follow that response.

Reinforcement and Punishment

In discussing reinforcement theory, it is important to identify and understand several terms that relate to the events that follow a desired response or to the events that are contingent on a particular behavior. **Reinforcement** is any event, action, or phenomenon that increases the probability of a response occurring again. A **punishment,** on the other hand, is any event, action, or phenomenon that decreases the probability of a response occurring again.

Reinforcers are of two types, positive and negative. **Positive reinforcers** are events that serve as reinforcers when they are *presented* to the individual when a desired response is produced. **Negative reinforcers** serve as reinforcers when they are *withdrawn* from the individual when a desired response occurs. Remember, reinforcers always serve to strengthen a desired response. From the examples that were presented in the application section, the use of verbal praise by the teacher for the children learning to dribble a soccer ball was an example of positive reinforcement for a correct response. The wrestling coach who made a special award to the wrestler who had the most takedowns during the season was also employing positive reinforcement techniques to improve behavior. Negative reinforcement was used by the coach who withdrew or stopped chiding a player when that player produced a desired response. Thus, positive reinforcement is the presentation of a desirable stimulus, while negative reinforcement is withdrawing or terminating an adverse stimulus when a desired response is produced.

Punishment should not be confused with negative reinforcement. Punishment is always an event that follows a response in order to eliminate that response. The tennis teacher who devised a new rule for tennis provides an example of using punishment in a learning situation. The response that the teacher was trying to eliminate was the students' poor first serve. The new rule the teacher devised punished the server for making a bad first serve by giving a point to the opponent.

The Nature of Reinforcers and Punishment

Reinforcers and punishment can be either *tangible* or *intangible*. A piece of candy, a trophy, and money are examples of tangible reinforcers. Tangible forms of punishment could be a paddling or an electrical shock. Intangible reinforcers would be such things as verbal praise or a smile. These are phenomena that the individual being reinforced cannot physically hold. An intangible punishment would be a scolding or a scowl from the teacher.

Another important characteristic of reinforcers and punishment is that they must be *important to or desired by the individual*. If a trophy is contingent on a certain performance and an individual is completely indifferent to being awarded a trophy, the effectiveness of the trophy as a reinforcement is greatly diminished. If the teacher does not permit a child to play in a game or activity following bad behavior by the child and participation is very important to the child, then the punishment will probably be effective. This characteristic of reinforcers or punishment is too often overlooked by teachers and coaches. In order for a reinforcer or punishment to be effective, the teacher must be certain that the chosen reinforcer or punishment is actually important to the individual.

Finally, the effectiveness of a reinforcer or punishment is dependent upon its *temporal association* with the response. That is, a reinforcement should closely follow, in time, the desired response. There should be no doubt on the part of the student that the reinforcer was for a particular response.

Using Reinforcement Techniques

Because the primary concern in this book is the learning of motor skills, reinforcement techniques relating to instructional situations will be the focus of the discussion in this section. Unfortunately, little is known about the effectiveness of punishment in a learning situation. On the other hand, much research supports reinforcement as an effective tool in facilitating learning.

Two important questions about the use of reinforcement in learning will provide the basis of this discussion. One of these relates to *when* reinforcers should be used. The second question is *how often* reinforcers should be used. Although there are no unequivocal answers to these questions, positive guidelines can be furnished to assist you in using reinforcement techniques effectively.

When should reinforcers be used? From the discussion so far, it appears that a reinforcer should only be used following a proper or correct behavior or response. To adapt this statement to a learning situation would seem to lead to a rather unrealistic conclusion. If the elementary physical education teacher waited to praise a child until the child dribbled the soccer ball correctly, there would be a strong possibility that no praise would ever be given. To resolve this problem, reinforcement theorists have developed a concept they call **shaping behavior.** This means that the role of a reinforcer is to approve and strengthen a response that is somewhat similar to the end response desired. In this way, the instructor can "shape" the behavior of the student by rewarding that student each step of the way, as he or she progresses toward the ultimate response desired. In the soccer dribbling example, the teacher should praise students who are showing responses that in some way indicate progress in learning the skill.

How often should reinforcers be used? It would not be physically or practically possible to reinforce every correct or semi-correct response of each student in a class. To solve this problem, reinforcement theorists have concluded that *partial reinforcement* can be just as effective as reinforcing every correct response. Partial reinforcement can occur in accordance with a schedule in which the reinforcement is made on the basis of some specified temporal norms. Another way to use partial reinforcement is to reinforce a student after a certain number of correct responses. The teacher should try various temporal and number-of-correct-response schedules to determine which is the most effective for his or her needs.

Summary

Reinforcement of desired behavior is an effective motivator of behavior. Reinforcement has been defined as any event, action, or phenomenon that serves to increase the probability or likelihood of a response or behavior occurring again. A reinforcer may be either positive or negative. In either case, the result is the strengthening of a desired response. A punishment is any event, action, or phenomenon that serves to decrease the probability of a behavior or response occurring again. Both reinforcers and punishment must be important to the individual and contingent on the behavior of interest, if they are to be effective. In learning situations, reinforcement should be related to responses that approximate the desired end result, in order to direct or "shape" behavior in the desired direction. Schedules of partial reinforcement, based on time or the number of correct responses, can be developed to overcome the practical problem of reinforcing each correct response.

Related Readings

Skinner, B. F. (1968). *The technology of teaching.* New York: Appleton-Century-Crofts. (Read chapter 7.)

Vallerand, R. J. (1983). The effects of differential amounts of positive verbal feedback on the intrinsic motivation of male hockey players. *Journal of Sport Psychology, 5,* 101–109.

Weinberg, R. S. (1984). The relationship between extrinsic rewards and intrinsic motivation in sport. In J. M. Silva III and R. S. Weinberg (Eds.), *Psychological foundations of sport* (pp. 177–187). Champaign, IL: Human Kinetics.

STUDY QUESTIONS FOR CHAPTER 9

1. Name two types of achievement goals and describe what characterizes each.

2. Describe an achievement situation where setting performance goals has been shown to lead to better performance than not setting goals.

3. How can goal setting be related to improving skill learning?

4. List four guidelines that should be followed to set realistic performance goals. Give a motor skill performance example for each.

5. How can different types of augmented feedback be used as a source of motivation when achieving an established performance goal is involved?

6. Describe four ways to increase the likelihood that people will commit to achieving goals they set.

7. Give an example of providing positive and negative reinforcement in a teaching situation you might be in. How does punishment differ from negative reinforcement?

8. What are three aspects of reinforcement that should be considered before applying reinforcement techniques in teaching?

GLOSSARY

Ability A general trait or capacity of an individual that is a foundational element for the performance of a variety of motor skills.

Absolute constant error (|CE|, or, ACE) The absolute value of the average constant error. A measure of the amount of (but not the direction of) response biasing.

Absolute error (AE) The unsigned deviation from the target or criterion, represents amount of error. A measure of the magnitude of response error without regard to the direction of the deviation.

Absolute frequency Refers to giving augmented feedback for a specific number of trials during practice.

Achievement orientation An individual difference characteristic related to achievement situations that indicates the person's tendency to approach a situation with a mastery or a competitive orientation.

Action A goal-directed response that consists of body and/or limb movements.

Action goals Momentary goals. Objectives a person desires to attain in a particular situation.

Anxiety A form of psychological arousal that is considered in terms of trait and state anxiety levels.

Applied research Research in which the goal is to develop knowledge that can answer an immediate and specific problem.

Arousal The general state of excitability of a person, it includes physiological, emotional, and mental systems.

Associative stage of learning The second stage of learning in the Fitts and Posner model. An intermediate stage on the learning stages continuum.

Asymmetric transfer Bilateral transfer in which there is a greater amount of transfer from one limb to another.

Attentional focus Directing attention to specific characteristics or cues in a performance situation to enhance performance by maintaining attention demands within capacity limits.

Augmented feedback Information about performing a skill that is added to sensory feedback and comes from a source external to the person performing the skill.

Augmented sensory feedback   A type of augmented feedback that involves an external device to enhance awareness of sensory feedback.

Automaticity   Implies that skills, or certain aspects of skills, can be performed without attention capacity being required.

Autonomous stage of learning   The third stage of learning in the Fitts and Posner model. The final stage on the learning continuum. Also called the automatic stage.

■

Basic research   Research in which the goal is to develop knowledge having implications for expanding theory.

Bilateral transfer   Transfer of learning that occurs between limbs.

Biofeedback   A type of augmented sensory feedback about physiological processes through the use of instrumentation.

Blocked practice   A practice schedule in which one skill is practiced repeatedly before moving on to practice another skill.

■

Capacity   The resources available to appropriately process information. The amount of effort or mental activity that can be given for processing information.

Ceiling effect   Occurs when performance score reaches a maximum level for the measure of performance.

Closed-loop control system   A system of control in which feedback is compared against a standard or reference to enable a specified action to be carried out as planned.

Closed motor skill   A skill performed in a stable or predictable environment where the performer determines when to begin the action.

Cognitive mediation theory   A theory for explaining the benefit of modeling proposing that when a person observes a model, the movement information observed is translated into a cognitive code that is stored in memory and used when the skill is performed by the observer.

Cognitive stage of learning   The first stage of learning in the Fitts and Posner model. The beginning or initial stage on the learning continuum.

Competitive goals   Performance goals that have as the focus demonstrating a person's capability to perform the skill. The performance objective is based on performing sufficiently well to outperform another person.

Complexity   Refers to how many parts or components are in a response or skill and is distinct from difficulty.

Concurrent augmented feedback   Augmented feedback that is provided while a person is performing a skill or making a movement.

Constant error (CE)   The signed $(+/-)$ deviation from the target or criterion. It represents amount and direction of error and is also a measure of response bias.

Constrained movements   Movements to be remembered are selected by the person giving the test.

Contextual interference   The interference that results from practicing a task within the context of a practice situation.

Contextual interference effect   The learning benefit resulting from practicing multiple skills in a high contextual interference practice schedule, such as random practice, compared to practicing the skills in a low contextual interference schedule, such as blocked practice.

Continuous motor skill   A skill with arbitrary beginning and end points.

Coordination   The patterning of body and limb motions relative to the patterning of environmental objects and events.

Coordinative structures   Functionally specific collectives of muscles and joints that are constrained by the nervous system to act cooperatively to produce an action.

Cost-benefit trade-off   The cost (in terms of slower RT), and benefit (in terms of faster RT) that occurs as a result of biasing the preparation of a response in favor of one of several possible responses, compared to preparing as if each possible response is equally probable.

◼

Declarative knowledge   Knowledge about "what to do" in a situation, typically verbalizable.

Degrees of freedom   The number of independent elements or components in a control system and the number of ways each component can act.

Dependent variable   The variable that is measured in an experiment, sometimes referred to as the dependent measure.

Differential psychology   The study of individual differences in psychology.

Discrete motor skill   A skill with clearly defined beginning and end points, usually requiring a simple movement.

Distributed practice   A practice schedule in which the amount of rest between trials or groups of trials is relatively large.

Dual-task procedure   An experimental procedure used in the study of attention to determine the degree of interference caused by one task when simultaneously performing another task.

Dynamic systems theory   An approach to describing the control of coordinated movement that emphasizes the role of information in the environment and the dynamical properties of the body and limbs.

Dynamic view of modeling   A theoretical view for explaining the benefit of visually observing a model. It proposes that the visual system is capable of processing the observed movement in such a way to constrain the motor response system to act accordingly so that there is no need for cognitive mediation.

◼

E (Total Error)   A composite error score of constant error and variable error. (Similar to root-mean-squared-error.)

Electromyography (EMG)   A technique for recording the electrical activity of a muscle or group of muscles.

Encoding   The transformation of information into a form that can be stored in memory.

Encoding specificity principle   A memory principle emphasizing the relationship between the practice and test context. It states that the more the test context resembles the practice context, the better the test performance will be.

Enduring dispositions   An attention-capacity allocation factor in Kahneman's model that includes situations or characteristics that seem to involuntarily demand attention, such as unexpected stimuli and meaningful information.

Episodic memory   The sub-system of long-term memory that stores and provides knowledge about personally experienced events, along with their temporal associations, in subjective time.

Error correction phase   In manual aiming movements, phase in which attempts are made to minimize error between the limb's current position and the target.

External imagery   A form of mental practice in which the person imagines viewing himself or herself performing a skill from the perspective of an observer.

◼

Fading technique   A way to decrease the frequency of augmented feedback by systematically reducing the frequency during the course of practice so that the person is effectively "weaned" from depending on its availability.

Feature integration theory   A theory to explain selective attention proposing that during visual search, we initially group stimuli together according to their unique features, such as color, shape, or movement.

Fine motor skill   A skill that requires control of the small muscles of the body to achieve the goal of the skill, and typically involves eye-hand coordination.

Fitts' Law   The law specifying the movement time for an aiming response when the distance to be moved and the target size are known. It is quantified as $MT = a + b \log_2(2W/D)$, where a and b are constants and W = target width, and D = distance from the starting point to the target.

Fixation/diversification   The second stage of learning in Gentile's model. Fixation refers to closed skills in which the movement pattern becomes refined so that it can be produced correctly, consistently, and efficiently from response to response. Diversification refers to open skills in which a large repertoire of motor patterns is developed.

Floor effect   Occurs when the performance score reaches a minimum level for the measure of performance.

Foreperiod   In a reaction time paradigm, the time interval between a warning signal and the go signal, or stimulus.

Fractionization   A part-task training method that involves practicing separate components of a whole skill.

■

General motor ability hypothesis   A hypothesis that maintains that there exists in individuals a singular, global motor ability.

Generalized motor program   The general memory representation of a class of actions that share common invariant characteristics. It provides the basis for controlling an action.

"Getting the idea of the movement"   The first stage of learning in Gentile's model, it refers to the need for the learner to establish an appropriate movement pattern to accomplish the goal of the skill.

Goal-setting   Establishing a level of performance for a skill that a person should try to achieve.

Gross motor skill   A skill involving large musculature to achieve the goal of the skill.

Guidance hypothesis   Hypothesis indicating that the role of augmented feedback in learning is that during practice, it serves to guide performance to be correct. However, if it is provided too frequently, it can cause the learner to develop a dependency on its availability and therefore perform poorly when it is not available.

■

Hick's Law   A law of human performance stating that RT will increase logarithmically as the number of stimulus-response choices increases.

■

Ideal goals   Ultimate goals. Objectives a person desires to attain as the end result of his or her practice and participation in an activity.

Identical elements theory   An explanation of positive transfer proposing that transfer is due to the degree of similarity between the component parts or characteristics of two skills or two performance situations.

Imagery ability   An individual difference characteristic that differentiates people who can image an action with a high degree of vividness and control, from people who have difficulty imaging an action.

Independent variable   The variable of interest in an experiment. The variable that is manipulated by intentionally changing its characteristics.

Index of difficulty (ID)   According to Fitts' Law, a quantitative measure of the difficulty of performing a skill involving both speed and accuracy requirements. It is calculated as the $\log_2(2W/D)$, where W = target width, and D = distance from the starting point to the target.

Initial impulse phase   In manual aiming movements, phase in which the actual movement is begun as the limb is propelled in the general direction of the target.

Internal imagery   A form of mental practice in which a person imagines being inside his or her own body, performing a skill and experiencing the sensations that are expected in the actual situation.

Intertask transfer   Transfer between tasks or skills.

Intratask transfer   Transfer occurring within the same task or skill as a result of an intervening experience.

Invariant features   A unique set of characteristics that define a generalized motor program. Fixed characteristics of a motor program that do not vary from one performance of the action to another.

■

Kinematics   The descriptions of movement without regard to force or mass. It includes displacement, velocity, and acceleration.

Knowledge of performance (KP) A type of augmented feedback that gives information about the movement characteristics that led to the outcome of the movement or skill performance.

Knowledge of results (KR) A type of augmented feedback that gives information about the outcome of a movement or skill performance.

KR-Delay Interval The interval of time between the completion of a movement and the presentation of augmented feedback.

Law Describes a stable relationship between an independent and dependent variable, and is a building block of a theory.

Law of effect Law indicating that learning is influenced by the presence of rewards or punishments following a response, where a reward serves to strengthen the response and punishment serves to weaken the response.

Learning A change in the capability of a person to perform a skill that must be inferred from a relatively permanent improvement in performance as a result of practice or experience.

Learning variable Variables that influence both performance and learning.

Limited-capacity theories Theories of attention proposing that the capability for processing information needed to perform any task or tasks is limited and cannot be exceeded if successful performance is to be achieved.

Long-term memory A memory system that provides a relatively permanent storage repository of declarative and procedural information.

Massed practice A practice schedule in which the amount of rest between trials or groups of trials is either very short or none at all so that practice is relatively continuous.

Mastery goals Performance goals that have learning to perform the skill well as the primary objective of performance.

Memory Our capacity to remember or benefit from past experiences. A component of the information processing system that stores and processes information.

Memory trace In Adams' closed-loop theory, the component that contains the necessary information to initiate a movement. It is described as a "modest motor program" that operates in an open-loop fashion.

Mental practice The cognitive rehearsal of a physical skill in the absence of overt, physical movements. It usually involves imaging oneself performing a skill.

Modeling The use of demonstration as a means of conveying information about how to perform a skill.

Momentary intentions An attention capacity allocation factor in Kahneman's model indicating temporary factors influencing attention demand, such as instructions to attend to something.

Motor capacity A person's inborn, hereditary potential for general motor performance.

Motor educability The ease with which an individual learns new motor skills.

Motor program A memory representation that stores information needed to perform motor skills. It provides the basis for giving commands to the motor system so that these skills can be performed in a way that will allow their action goals to be achieved. It has also been referred to as a generalized motor program.

Movement preparation phase In manual aiming movements, phase that begins as soon as the decision has been made to move to the target.

Movement time (MT) The interval of time between the initiation of a movement and the completion of the movement.

Multiple resource theories Theories of attention proposing that there are several information-processing mechanisms, each of which is limited in how much information can be processed simultaneously during performance and learning.

Negative reinforcer When an aversive stimulus is withdrawn if a desired response is produced, such as verbal chiding stops when a skill is performed correctly. It strengthens the probability of the desired response.

Negative transfer Performance of a skill is poorer due to prior experience than it would have been without the previous experience.

Non-relevant stimuli   Characteristics of a skill performance situation that are not relevant to determining how the skill must be performed to achieve the desired goal of the skill.

Observational learning   Learning a skill by observing a person performing the skill. See also modeling.

Open-loop control system   A control system in which all the information needed to initiate and carry out an action as planned is contained in the initial commands to the effectors.

Open motor skill   A skill that involves a changing, unpredictable environment where the environment determines when to begin the action.

Overlearning   Practice that continues beyond the amount needed to achieve a certain performance criterion.

Parameters   Features of the generalized motor program that can be varied from one performance of a skill to another. The features of a skill that must be added to the invariant features of a generalized motor program before a skill can be performed to meet the specific demands of a situation.

Percentage of transfer   A measure of the amount of transfer indicating the percentage of improvement in the transfer situation due to the previous experience.

Perceptual-motor abilities   Abilities of an individual that include such things as multi-limb coordination, manual dexterity, etc.

Perceptual trace   In Adams' closed-loop theory, the reference mechanism that is used to assess the status of a movement being made. The memory component responsible for terminating a limb positioning movement.

Performance   Observable behavior. A temporary behavioral act seen when a person performs a skill.

Performance variable   Variables that influence practice performance but not learning. Variables that typically inflate or deflate performance.

Pertinence model   A model of selective attention proposing that we only select information from the environment we consider pertinent, or relevant, to the situation.

Physical proficiency   Abilities of an individual including things such as static strength, dynamic strength, stamina, etc.

Plateau   A performance steady-state that follows regular improvement and that is followed by continued improvement.

Pool of effort   The amount of mental resources available needed to carry out activities.

Positive reinforcer   Anything that serves as a reinforcer when provided if a desired response is produced. It strengthens the desired response.

Positive transfer   When performance of a skill is increased due to prior experience beyond what it would have been without the previous experience.

Post-KR interval   The interval of time between the presentation of augmented feedback and the beginning of the next trial.

Prehension   The reaching and grasping of an object that may be stationary or moving.

Preselected movements   Movements to be remembered that are selected by the person performing a test.

Primary-recency effect   Memory effect in which items presented first and last in a series are recalled better than items in the middle of the series. Also known as the serial position effect.

Proactive interference   A cause of forgetting due to activity occurring before the presentation of the information to be remembered.

Procedural knowledge   Knowledge that enables a person to know "how to do" a skill or procedure, and is typically not verbalizable.

Procedural memory   The sub-system of long-term memory that stores and provides knowledge needed for "how to do" something.

Progressive-part method   A part-task training method that involves practicing the parts of the skill in the order in which each part occurs in performing the skill, and practicing the parts progressively together.

Psychological refractory period (PRP)   A delay period during which a planned response seems to be "put on hold" while a previously initiated response is executed.

Psychomotor ability   A category of human abilities related to speed and accuracy of movements where no or little cognitive demand is required of the person.

Punishment   Any event, action, or phenomenon that decreases the probability of a response occurring again.

■

Qualitative augmented feedback   Augmented feedback that is descriptive in nature (e.g., good, long), and indicates the quality of performance.

Quantitative augmented feedback   Augmented feedback that indicates a performance quantity, such as the amount of error made in the performance.

■

Random practice   A practice schedule in which there is no specified order of occurrence for practicing several different skills.

Reaction time (RT)   The interval of time between the onset of a signal (stimulus) and the initiation of a response.

Recall test   A memory test that requires a person to produce a required response with few, if any, available cues or aids.

Recognition test   A memory test that provides cues or information on which to base a response by requiring the person to select one of several alternative responses.

Rehearsal   A memory storage process that enables a person to transfer information from the working memory to long-term memory and enhance memorability of that information in long-term memory.

Reinforcement   Any event, action, or phenomenon that increases the probability of a response occurring again.

Relative force   The proportion of force produced by the various components of a skill during the performance of that skill.

Relative frequency   Refers to giving augmented feedback for a certain percentage of the total number of trials.

Relative timing   The proportion of time required by the various components of a skill during the performance of that skill.

Relevant stimuli   Characteristics of a skill performance situation that are relevant in determining how the skill must be performed to achieve the desired goal of the skill.

Response time   The time interval involving both reaction time and movement time; that is, from the onset of a signal (stimulus) to the completion of a response.

Retention test   A test of a practiced skill that is given following an interval of time after practice has ceased.

Retrieval   A process involving the search through memory for information that must be accessed in order to respond to the task at hand.

Retroactive interference   A cause of forgetting due to activity occurring during the retention interval.

Root-mean-squared error (RMSE)   An error measure indicating the amount of error between the displacement curve produced and the criterion displacement curve.

Rote repetition   A memory storage strategy involving repeating the same movements over and over again.

■

Savings score   A measure of the amount of transfer indicating the amount of practice time saved in learning a particular skill because of previous experience.

Schema   A rule or set of rules that serves to provide the basis for a decision. In Schmidt's schema theory, an abstract representation of rules governing movement.

Scientific method   An objective means of gathering information involving observation to provide knowledge that will allow us to describe, explain, or predict characteristics in the universe.

Segmentation   A part-task training method that involves separating the skill into parts and then practicing the parts so that after one part is practiced, it is then practiced together with the next part, and so on. (See also progressive-part method.)

Selective attention   Selecting certain information, stimuli, or cues from an array of possible alternatives.

Semantic memory   The sub-system of long-term memory that stores and provides our general knowledge about the world that has been developed from our many experiences.

Serial motor skill   A skill involving a series of discrete skills.

Serial position effect   An effect seen when a series of items must be renumbered in sequence. The first few and last few items are remembered best, whereas the middle items are remembered worst. (See also primary-recency effect.)

Serial practice   A practice schedule in which several skills are practiced in a specified and repeating order during each practice period.

Shaping   A means of encouraging correct performance by progressively providing reinforcement during practice when a part or parts of a skill are performed correctly, rather than providing reinforcement only when the entire skill is performed correctly.

Simplification   A part-task training method that involves reducing the difficulty of different parts of a skill.

Single-channel theory   Theory of attention proposing that the human is a single-channel processor of information where only one source of information can be processed at a time.

Skill   (a) An action or task that has a specific goal to achieve. (b) An indicator of quality of performance.

Specificity of motor abilities hypothesis   A hypothesis that maintains that the many motor abilities in an individual are relatively independent.

Speed-accuracy trade-off   A characteristic of motor skill performance in which speed of performing the skill is influenced by movement accuracy demands. The trade-off is that increasing speed yields decreasing accuracy and vice-versa.

State anxiety   State anxiety refers to the anxiety response a person produces in a specific situation.

Stimulus-response compatibility   A characteristic of the spatial arrangement relationship between the stimulus and response. This relationship will influence the amount of preparation time in a reaction time task involving stimulus and response choices.

Storage   The process of placing information in memory so that it can be retrieved when needed.

Subjective error estimate   The person performing a skill indicates what he or she thinks was wrong with their performance.

Subjective organization   A memory strategy involving the grouping of items into units, groups, clusters, or categories that are meaningful to the person performing the task.

Summary KR   A way to reduce the frequency of giving KR by providing the person with a summary of KR after a certain number of trials.

Superdiagonal form   Refers to the way the trial-to-trial correlations appear in a correlation matrix where all trials are correlated with each other. Trials that are closer to each other have scores more highly correlated. The correlation decreases as trials become further apart from each other.

Symmetric transfer   Bilateral transfer in which the amount of transfer is similar from one limb to another.

Task organization   Refers to how the components of a task are interrelated or interdependent where low organization indicates components are independent while high organization indicates components are highly interrelated.

Tau   Mathematical function that specifies time-to-contact with an object.

Terminal augmented feedback   Augmented feedback that is provided after a person has completed performing a skill or making a movement.

Theory   Addresses why consistently observed effects of independent on dependent variables occur, usually based on a set of facts, laws, or principles. It provides a basis for predicting effects in situations not tested experimentally.

Threshold of fatigue   A hypothetical level of fatigue where learning is not influenced by fatigue at levels below this threshold, but is influenced at levels above this threshold.

Trait anxiety   Trait anxiety refers to a person's general disposition to respond to situations with anxiety.

Transfer   The influence of having previously practiced or performed a skill or skills on the learning of a new skill.

Transfer-appropriate processing   An explanation of positive transfer proposing that transfer is due to the similarity of cognitive processing characteristics required by the two skills or two performance situations.

Transfer test   A test in which a skill must be performed that is different from the skill that was practiced or in which the practiced skill must be performed in a situation different from the practice situation.

Variable error (VE)   An error score representing the variability, or consistency, of responses by a person.

Variable practice   Practice that provides a variety of experiences for performing a skill.

Variance accounted for   The amount, as designated by a percentage, of the statistical variance of a performance score accounted for by some factor, such as an ability test score.

Vigilance   Maintaining attention in a performance situation in which the frequency of stimuli requiring a response is infrequent.

Visual search   Actively engaging vision in seeking information in the environment that will enable the performer to determine what to do in a situation.

Working memory   A functional memory system that operates to temporarily store and use just presented information. It provides a temporary workspace to integrate information retrieved from long-term memory with just presented information to make possible problem solving, decision making, and response execution. It also serves as a processing center to transfer information into long-term memory.

REFERENCES

Abernethy, B. (1986). Enhancing sports performance through clinical and experimental optometry. *Clinical & Experimental Optometry, 69*, 189–196.

Abernethy, B. (1988). Visual search in sport and ergonomics: Its relation to selective attention and performer expertise. *Human Performance, 1*, 205–235.

Abernethy, B., and Russell, D. G. (1987). Expert-novice differences in an applied selective attention task. *Journal of Sport Psychology, 9*, 326–345.

Abrams, R. A., Meyer, D. E., and Kornblum, S. (1990). Eye-hand coordination: Oculomotor control in rapid aimed limb movements. *Journal of Experimental Psychology: Human Perception and Performance, 16*, 248–267.

Ackerman, P. L. (1988). Determinants of individual differences during skill acquisition: Cognitive abilities and information processing. *Journal of Experimental Psychology: General, 117*, 288–318.

Ackerman, P. L. (1989). Within-task intercorrelations of skilled performance: Implications for predicting individual differences? (A comment on Henry & Hulin, 1987). *Journal of Applied Psychology, 74*, 360–364.

Adams, J. A. (1964). Motor skills. In P. R. Farnsworth (Ed.), *Annual review of psychology* (pp. 181–202). Palo Alto: Annual Reviews, Inc.

Adams, J. A. (1971). A closed-loop theory of motor learning. *Journal of Motor Behavior, 3*, 111–149.

Adams, J. A. (1978). Theoretical issues for knowledge of results. In G. E. Stelmach (Ed.), *Information processing in motor control and learning* (pp. 87–107). New York: Academic Press.

Adams, J. A. (1986). Use of the model's knowledge of results to increase the observer's performance. *Journal of Human Movement Studies, 12*, 89–98.

Adams, J. A. (1987). Historical review and appraisal of research on the learning, retention, and transfer of human motor skills. *Psychological Bulletin, 101*, 41–74.

Adams, J. A., and Dijkstra, S. J. (1966). Short-term memory for motor responses. *Journal of Experimental Psychology, 71*, 314–318.

Adams, J. A., and Hufford, L. E. (1962). Contributions of a part-task trainer to the learning and relearning of a time-shared flight maneuver. *Human Factors, 4*, 159–170.

Adams, J. A., and Reynolds, B. (1954). Effects of shift of distribution of practice conditions following interpolated rest. *Journal of Experimental Psychology, 47*, 32–36.

Alderman, R. B. (1974). *Psychological behavior in sport*. Philadelphia: W.B. Saunders.

Alderson, G. J. K., Sully, D. J., and Sully, H. G. (1974). An operational analysis of a one-handed catching task using high speed photography. *Journal of Motor Behavior, 6,* 217–226.

Allport, D. A. (1980). Attention and performance. In G. Claxton (Ed.), *Cognitive psychology: New directions* (pp. 112–153). London: Routledge & Kegan Paul.

Ames, C. (1992). The relationship of achievement goals to student motivation in classroom settings. In G. C. Roberts (Ed.), *Motivation in sport and exercise* (pp. 161–176). Champaign, IL: Human Kinetics.

Ammons, R. B. (1958). Le mouvement. In G. H. Steward and J. P. Steward (Eds.), *Current psychological issues* (pp. 146–183). New York: Henry Holt & Co.

Anderson, J. R. (1987). Skill acquisition: Compilation of weak-method problem solutions. *Psychological Review, 94,* 192–210.

Anderson, K. J. (1990). Arousal and the inverted-U hypothesis: A critique of Neiss's "Reconceptualizing arousal". *Psychological Bulletin, 107,* 96–100.

Annett, J. (1959). Learning a pressure under conditions of immediate and delayed knowledge of results. *Quarterly Journal of Experimental Psychology, 11,* 3–15.

Annett, J. (1969). *Feedback and human behavior.* Baltimore: Penguin.

Annett, J. (1970). The role of action feedback in the acquisition of simple motor responses. *Journal of Motor Behavior, 2,* 217–221.

Annett, J. and Piech, J. (1985). The retention of a skill following distributed training. *Programmed Learning and Educational Technology, 22,* 182–186.

Annett, J., and Sparrow, J. (1985). Transfer of training: A review of research and practical implications. *Programmed Learning and Educational Technology, 22,* 116–124.

Anson, J. G. (1982). Memory drum theory: Alternative tests and explanations for the complexity effects on simple reaction time. *Journal of Motor Behavior, 14,* 228–246.

Ash, D. W., and Holding, D. H. (1990). Backward versus forward chaining in the acquisition of a keyboard skill. *Human Factors, 32,* 139–146.

Atkinson, J. W. (1964). *An introduction to motivation.* Princeton, NJ: Van Nostrand.

Atkinson, R. C., and Shiffrin, R. M. (1968). Human memory: A proposed system and its control processes. In K. W. Spence and J. T. Spence (Eds.), *The psychology of learning and motivation: Advances in research and theory* (Vol. 2, pp. 89–197). New York: Academic Press.

Bachman, J. C. (1961). Specificity vs. generality in learning and performing two large muscle motor tasks. *Research Quarterly, 32,* 3–11.

Baddeley, A. D. (1984). The fractionation of human memory. *Psychological Medicine, 14,* 259–264.

Baddeley, A. D. (1986). *Working memory.* New York: Oxford University Press.

Baddeley, A. D., and Hitch, G. (1974). Working memory. In G. H. Bower (Ed.), *The psychology of learning and motivation: Advances in research and theory* (Vol. 8, pp. 47–89). New York: Academic Press.

Baddeley, A. D., and Longman, D. J. A. (1978). The influence of length and frequency of training session on the rate of learning to type. *Ergonomics, 21,* 627–635.

Bahill, A. T., and LaRitz, T. (1984). Why can't batters keep their eyes on the ball? *American Scientist, 72,* 249–252.

Bandura, A. (1977). Self-efficacy: Toward a unifying theory of behavioral change. *Psychological Review, 84,* 191–215.

Bandura, A. (1984). *Social foundations of thought and action.* Englewood Cliffs, NJ: Prentice-Hall.

Bartlett, F. C. (1932). *Remembering: A study in experimental and social psychology.* Cambridge: Cambridge University Press.

Barton, J. W. (1921). Smaller versus larger units in learning the maze. *Journal of Experimental Psychology, 4,* 414–424.

Battig, W. F. (1979). The flexibility of human memory. In L. S. Cermak and F. I. M. Craik (Eds.), *Levels of processing in human memory* (pp. 23–44). Hillsdale, NJ: Erlbaum.

Baumgartner, T. A., and Jackson, A. S. (1982). *Measurement for evaluation in physical education* (2nd ed.). Dubuque, IA: Wm. C. Brown.

Beaubaton, D., and Hay, L. (1986). Contribution of visual information to feedforward and feedback processes in rapid pointing movements. *Human Movement Science, 5,* 19–34.

Bell, H. M. (1950). Retention of pursuit rotor skill after one year. *Journal of Experimental Psychology, 40,* 648–649.

Benedetti, C., and McCullagh, P. (1987). Post-knowledge of results delay: Effects of interpolated activity on learning and performance. *Research Quarterly for Exercise and Sport, 58,* 375–381.

Bernstein, N. (1967). *The co-ordination and regulation of movement.* Oxford: Pergamon Press.

Bilodeau, E. A., and Bilodeau, I. M. (1958a). Variable frequency of knowledge of results and the learning of a simple skill. *Journal of Experimental Psychology, 55,* 379–383.

Bilodeau, E. A., and Bilodeau, I. M. (1958b). Variation of temporal intervals among critical events in five studies of knowledge of results. *Journal of Experimental Psychology, 55,* 603–612.

Bilodeau, E. A., and Bilodeau, I. M. (1961). Motor skills learning. *Annual Review of Psychology, 12,* 243–280.

Bilodeau, E. A., Bilodeau, I. M. and Schumsky, D. A. (1959). Some effects of introducing and withdrawing knowledge of results early and late in practice. *Journal of Experimental Psychology, 58,* 142–144.

Bilodeau, I. M. (1969). Information feedback. In E. A. Bilodeau (Ed.), *Principles of skill acquisition* (pp. 225–285). New York: Academic Press.

Bizzi, E., and Polit, A. (1979). Processes controlling visually evoked movements. *Neuropsychologia, 17,* 203–213.

Bootsma, R. J., and van Wieringen, P. C. W. (1990). Timing an attacking forehand drive in table tennis. *Journal of Experimental Psychology: Human Perception and Performance, 16,* 21–29.

Boucher, J. L. (1974). Higher processes in motor learning. *Journal of Motor Behavior, 6,* 131–137.

Boulter, L. R. (1964). Evaluations of mechanisms in delay of knowledge of results. *Canadian Journal of Psychology, 18,* 281–291.

Boutcher, S. H., and Crews, D. J. (1987). The effect of a preshot attentional routine on a well-learned skill. *International Journal of Sport Psychology, 18,* 30–39.

Bouzid, N. and Crawshaw, C. M. (1987). Massed versus distributed wordprocessor training. *Applied Ergonomics, 18,* 220–222.

Brace, D. K. (1927). *Measuring motor ability.* New York: A.S. Barnes.

Brady, J. I., Jr. (1979). Surface practice, level of manual dexterity, and performance of an assembly task. *Human Factors, 21,* 25–33.

Bransford, J. D., Franks, J. J., Morris, C. D., and Stein, B. S. (1979). Some general constraints on learning and memory research. In L. S. Cermak and F. I. M. Craik (Eds.), *Levels of processing in human memory* (pp. 331–354). Hillsdale, NJ: Erlbaum.

Broadbent, D. E. (1958). *Perception and communication.* Oxford: Pergamon Press.

Brown, R. W. (1928). A comparison of the whole, part, and combination methods for learning piano music. *Journal of Experimental Psychology, 11,* 235–247.

Bryan, W. L., and Harter, N. (1897). Studies in the physiology and psychology of the telegraphic language. *Psychological Review, 4,* 27–53.

Buekers, M. J., Magill, R. A., and Hall, K. G. (1992). The effect of erroneous knowledge of results on skill acquisition when augmented information is redundant. *Quarterly Journal of Experimental Psychology, 44A,* 105–117.

Burroughs, W. A. (1984). Visual simulation training of baseball batters. *International Journal of Sport Psychology, 15,* 117–126.

Burton, D. (1989). Winning isn't everything: Examining the impact of performance goals on collegiate swimmers' cognitions and performance. *The Sport Psychologist, 2,* 105–132.

Burwitz, L. (1975). Observational learning and motor performance. *FEPSAC Conference Proceedings,* Edinburgh, Scotland.

Carlton, L. G. (1981). Processing visual feedback information for motor control. *Journal of Experimental Psychology: Human Perception and Performance, 5,* 1019–1030.

Carlton, L. G., Carlton, M. J., and Newell, K. M. (1987). Reaction time and response dynamics. *Quarterly Journal of Experimental Psychology, 39A,* 337–360.

Carroll, W. R., and Bandura, A. (1987). Translating cognition into action: The role of visual guidance in observational learning. *Journal of Motor Behavior, 19,* 385–398.

Carron, A. V. (1969). Performance and learning in a discrete motor task under massed vs. distributed practice. *Research Quarterly, 40,* 481–489.

Carron, A. V. (1972). Motor performance and learning under physical fatigue. *Medicine and Science in Sports, 4,* 101–106.

Cavanagh, P. R., and Kram, R. (1985). The efficiency of human movement—A statement of the problem. *Medicine and Science in Sports and Exercise, 17,* 304–308.

Chase, W. G., and Ericsson, K. A. (1982). Skill and working memory. In G. H. Bower (Ed.), *The psychology of learning and motivation* (Vol. 16, pp. 1–58). New York: Academic Press.

Chase, W. G., and Simon, H. A. (1973). Perception in chess. *Cognitive Psychology, 4,* 55–81.

Cherry, E. C. (1953). Some experiments on the recognition of speech with one and with two ears. *Journal of the Acoustical Society of America, 25,* 975–979.

Christina, R. W. (1973). Influence of enforced motor and sensory sets on reaction latency and movement speed. *Research Quarterly, 44,* 483–487.

Christina, R. W. (1977). Skilled motor performance: Anticipatory timing. In B. R. Wolman (Ed.), *International encyclopedia of psychiatry, psychology, psychoanalysis, and neurology* (Vol. 10, pp. 241–245). New York: Van Nostrand Reinhold.

Christina, R. W., Barresi, J. V., and Shaffner, P. (1990). The development of response selection accuracy in a football linebacker using video training. *The Sport Psychologist, 4,* 11–17.

Christina, R. W., and Buffan, J. L. (1976). Preview and movement as determiners of timing a discrete motor response. *Journal of Motor Behavior, 8,* 101–112.

Christina, R. W., Fischman, M. G., Lambert, A. L., and Moore, J. F. (1985). Simple reaction time as a function of response complexity: Christina et al. (1982) revisited. *Research Quarterly for Exercise and Sport, 56,* 316–322.

Christina, R. W., Fischman, M. G., Vercruyssen, M. J. P., and Anson, J. G. (1982). Simple reaction time as a function of response complexity: Memory drum theory revisited. *Journal of Motor Behavior, 14,* 301–321.

Christina, R. W., and Rose, D. J. (1985). Premotor and motor response time as a function of response complexity. *Research Quarterly for Exercise and Sport, 56,* 306–315.

Cook, T. W. (1933a). Studies in cross-education. I. Mirror tracing the star-shaped maze. *Journal of Experimental Psychology, 16,* 144–160.

Cook, T. W. (1933b). Studies in cross-education. II. Further experimentation in mirror tracing the star-shaped maze. *Journal of Experimental Psychology, 16,* 670–700.

Cook, T. W. (1934). Studies in cross-education. III. Kinesthetic learning of an irregular pattern. *Journal of Experimental Psychology, 17,* 749–762.

Cook, T. W. (1935). Studies in cross-education. IV. Permanence of transfer. *Journal of Experimental Psychology, 18,* 255–266.

Cook, T. W. (1936). Studies in cross-education. V. Theoretical. *Psychological Review, 43,* 149–178.

Corbin, C. (1972). Mental practice. In W. P. Morgan (Ed.), *Ergogenic aids and muscular performance* (pp. 93–118). New York: Academic Press.

Corcos, D. M. (1984). Two-handed movement control. *Research Quarterly for Exercise and Sport, 55,* 117–122.

Cox, R. H. (1988). Utilization of psychomotor screening for USAF pilot candidates: Enhancing prediction validity. *Aviation, Space, and Environmental Medicine, 59,* 640–645.

Craik, F. I. M. (1970). The fate of primary memory items in free recall. *Journal of Verbal Learning and Verbal Behavior, 9,* 143–148.

Craik, F. I. M., and Lockhart, R. (1972). Levels of processing: A framework for memory research. *Journal of Verbal Learning and Verbal Behavior, 11,* 671–676.

Crocker, P. R. E., and Dickinson, J. (1984). Incidental psychomotor learning: The effects of number of movements, practice, and rehearsal. *Journal of Motor Behavior, 16,* 61–75.

Cronbach, L. J. (1957). The two disciplines of scientific psychology. *American Psychologist, 12,* 671–684.

Crossman, E. R. F. W., and Goodeve, P. J. (1983). Feedback control of hand movements and Fitts' Law. *Quarterly Journal of Experimental Psychology, 35A,* 251–278. (Original work published in 1963)

Damos, D., and Wickens, C. D. (1980). The identification and transfer of timesharing skills. *Acta Psychologica, 46,* 15–39.

Daniels, F. S., and Landers, D. M. (1981). Biofeedback and shooting performance: A test of disregulation and systems theory. *Journal of Sport Psychology, 3,* 271–282.

Davids, K. (1988). Developmental differences in the use of peripheral vision during catching performance. *Journal of Motor Behavior, 20,* 39–51.

Davis, R. C. (1942). The pattern of muscular action in simple voluntary movements. *Journal of Experimental Psychology, 31,* 437–466.

Del Rey, P., Wughalter, E., and Whitehurst, M. (1982). The effects of contextual interference on females with varied experience in open skills. *Research Quarterly for Exercise and Sport, 53,* 108–115.

den Brinker, B. P. L. M., Stabler, J. R. L. W., Whiting, H. T. A., and van Wieringen, P. C. (1986). The effect of manipulating knowledge of results in the learning of slalom-ski type ski movements. *Ergonomics, 29,* 31–40.

Denny, M. R., Frisbey, N., and Weaver, J., Jr. (1955). Rotary pursuit performance under alternate conditions of distributed and massed practice. *Journal of Experimental Psychology, 49,* 48–54.

Deutsch, J. A., and Deutsch, D. (1963). Attention: Some theoretical considerations. *Psychological Review, 70,* 80–90.

Dickinson, J. (1978). Retention of intentional and incidental motor learning. *Research Quarterly, 49,* 437–441.

Diewart, G. L. (1975). Retention and coding in motor short-term memory: A comparison of storage codes for distance and location information. *Journal of Motor Behavior, 7,* 183–190.

Diewart, G. L., and Roy, E. A. (1978). Coding strategy for memory of movement extent information. *Journal of Experimental Psychology: Human Learning and Memory, 4,* 666–675.

Doody, S. G., Bird, A. M., and Ross, D. (1985). The effect of auditory and visual models on acquisition of a timing task. *Human Movement Science, 4,* 271–281.

Drowatzky, J. N., and Zucatto, F. C. (1967). Interrelationships between selected measures of static and dynamic balance. *Research Quarterly, 38,* 509–510.

Duda, J., Smart, A., and Tappe, M. (1989). Personal investment in the rehabilitation of athletic injuries. *Journal of Sport and Exercise Psychology, 11,* 367–381.

Duncan, J. (1977). Response selection rules in spatial choice reaction tasks. In S. Dornic (Ed.), *Attention and performance VI* (pp. 49–61). Hillsdale, NJ: Erlbaum.

Dunham, P., Jr. (1977). Effect of practice order on the efficiency of bilateral skill acquisition. *Research Quarterly, 48,* 284–287.

Dweck, C. S. (1986). Motivational processes affecting learning. *American Psychologist, 41,* 1040–1048.

Eason, R. G., Beardshall, A., and Jaffee, S. (1965). Performance and physiological indicants of activation in a vigilance situation. *Perceptual and Motor Skills, 20,* 3–13.

Eccles, J. C. (1973). *The understanding of the brain.* New York: McGraw-Hill.

Edwards, R. V., and Lee, A. M. (1985). The relationship of cognitive style and instructional strategy to learning and transfer of motor skills. *Research Quarterly for Exercise and Sport, 56,* 286–290.

Eghan, T. (1988). *The relation of teacher feedback to student achievement.* Unpublished doctoral dissertation. Louisiana State University.

Elliott, D. (1985). Manual asymmetries in the performance of sequential movements by adolescents and adults with Down Syndrome. *American Journal of Mental Deficiency, 90,* 90–97.

Elliott, D. (1986). Continuous visual information may be important after all: A failure to replicate Thomson (1983). *Journal of Experimental Psychology: Human Perception and Performance, 12,* 388–391.

Elliott, D., and Allard, F. (1985). The utilization of visual information and feedback information during rapid pointing movements. *Quarterly Journal of Experimental Psychology, 37A,* 407–425.

Elliott, D., Calvert, R., Jaeger, M., and Jones, R. (1990). A visual representation and the control of manual aiming movements. *Journal of Motor Behavior, 22,* 327–346.

Ellis, H. C. (1978). *Fundamentals of human learning, memory, and cognition* (2nd ed.). Dubuque, IA: Wm. C. Brown.

Ells, J. G. (1973). Analysis of temporal and attentional aspects of movement control. *Journal of Experimental Psychology, 99,* 10–21.

Engle, R. W., and Buckstel, L. (1978). Memory processes among bridge players of differing experiences. *American Journal of Psychology, 91,* 673–690.

Feltz, D., and Landers, D. M. (1983). The effects of mental practice on motor skill learning and performance: A meta-analysis. *Journal of Sport Psychology, 5,* 25–57.

Feltz, D. L., Landers, D. M., and Becker, B. J. (1988). A revised meta-analysis of the mental practice literature on motor skill learning. In D. Druckman and J. Swets (Eds.), *Enhancing human performance: Issues, theories, and techniques* (pp. 1–65). Washington, D.C.: National Academy Press.

Fischman, M. G. (1984). Programming time as a function of number of movement parts and changes in movement direction. *Journal of Motor Behavior, 16,* 405–423.

Fischman, M. G., and Schneider, T. (1985). Skill level, vision, and proprioception in simple one-hand catching. *Journal of Motor Behavior, 17,* 219–229.

Fishman, S., and Tobey, C. (1978). Augmented feedback. In W. Anderson and G. Barrette (Eds.), *What's going on in gym: Descriptive studies of physical education classes* (pp. 51–62). *Motor Skills: Theory into Practice, Monograph 1.*

Fitts, P. M. (1954). The information capacity of the human motor system in controlling the amplitude of movement. *Journal of Experimental Psychology, 47,* 381–391.

Fitts, P. M., Peterson, J. R., and Wolpe, G. (1963). Cognitive aspects of information processing: II. Adjustments to stimulus redundancy. *Journal of Experimental Psychology, 65,* 425–432.

Fitts, P. M., and Posner, M. I. (1967). *Human performance.* Belmont, CA: Brooks/Cole.

Fitts, P. M., and Seeger, C. M. (1953). S-R compatibility: Spatial characteristics of stimulus and response codes. *Journal of Experimental Psychology, 46,* 199–210.

Fleishman, E. A. (1972). On the relationship between abilities, learning, and human performance. *American Psychologist, 27,* 1017–1032.

Fleishman, E. A. (1978). Relating individual differences to the dimensions of human tasks. *Ergonomics, 21,* 1007–1019.

Fleishman, E. A. (1982). Systems for describing human tasks. *American Psychologist, 37,* 821–834.

Fleishman, E. A., and Hempel, W. E. (1955). The relationship between abilities and improvement with practice in a visual discrimination reaction task. *Journal of Experimental Psychology, 49,* 301–311.

Fleishman, E. A., and Quaintance, M. K. (1984). *Taxonomies of human performance.* Orlando, FL: Academic Press.

Flowers, K. (1975). Handedness and controlled movement. *British Journal of Psychology, 66,* 39–52.

Fox, P. W., and Levy, C. M. (1969). Acquisition of a simple motor response as influenced by the presence or absence of action visual feedback. *Journal of Motor Behavior, 1,* 169–180.

Franks, I. M., and Wilberg, R. B. (1982). The generation of movement patterns during the acquisition of a pursuit tracking task. *Human Movement Science, 1,* 251–272.

French, K. E., and Thomas, J. R. (1987). The relation of knowledge development to children's basketball performance. *Journal of Sport Psychology, 9,* 15–32.

Gage, N. L. (1972). *Teacher effectiveness and teacher education: The search for a scientific basis.* Palo Alto, CA: Pacific Books.

Gallagher, J. D. (1970). Motor learning characteristics of low-skilled college men. *Research Quarterly, 41,* 59–67.

Gallagher, J. D., and Thomas, J. R. (1980). Effects of varying post-KR intervals upon children's motor performance. *Journal of Motor Behavior, 12,* 41–46.

Gentile, A. M. (1972). A working model of skill acquisition with application to teaching. *Quest,* Monograph XVII, 3–23.

Gentile, A. M. (1987). Skill acquisition: Action, movement, and neuromotor processes. In J. H. Carr, R. B. Shepherd, J. Gordon, A. M. Gentile, and J. M. Hind (Eds.), *Movement science: Foundations for physical therapy in rehabilitation* (pp. 93–154). Rockville, MD: Aspen.

Gentile, A. M., Higgins, J. R., Miller, E. A., and Rosen, B. M. (1975). The structure of motor tasks. *Mouvement, 7,* 11–28.

Gentile, A. M., and Nemetz, K. (1978). Repetition effects: A methodological issue in motor short-term memory. *Journal of Motor Behavior, 10,* 37–44.

Gentner, D. (1987). Timing of skilled motor performance: Tests of the proportional duration model. *Psychological Review, 94,* 255–276.

Gibson, J. J. (1966). *The senses considered as perceptual systems.* Boston: Houghton Mifflin.

Gibson, J. J. (1979). *The ecological approach to visual perception.* Boston: Houghton Mifflin.

Gill, D. L., and Deeter, T. E. (1988). Development of the Sport Orientation Questionnaire. *Research Quarterly for Exercise and Sport, 59,* 191–202.

Gire, E., and Espenschade, A. (1942). The relationship between measures of motor educability and learning specific motor skills. *Research Quarterly, 13,* 43–56.

Girouard, Y., Laurencelle, L., and Proteau L. (1984). On the nature of the probe reaction-time task to uncover the attentional demands of movement. *Journal of Motor Behavior, 16,* 442–459.

Gleick, J. (1987). *Chaos: Making a new science.* New York: Viking Penguin.

Glencross, D. J. (1973). Response complexity and latency of different movement patterns. *Journal of Motor Behavior, 5,* 95–104.

Godwin, M. A., and Schmidt, R. A. (1971). Muscular fatigue and discrete motor learning. *Research Quarterly, 42,* 374–383.

Goldberger, M., and Gerney, P. (1990). Effects of learner use of practice time on skill acquisition of fifth grade children. *Journal of Teaching Physical Education, 10,* 84–95.

Goldstein, M., and Rittenhouse, C. H. (1954). Knowledge of results in the acquisition of a gunnery skill. *Journal of Experimental Psychology, 48,* 187–196.

Goode, S. L., and Magill, R. A. (1986). The contextual interference effect in learning three badminton serves. *Research Quarterly for Exercise and Sport, 57,* 308–314.

Gopher, D., Weil, M., and Siegel, D. (1989). Practice under changing priorities: An approach to the training of complex skills. *Acta Psychologica, 71,* 147–177.

Gordon, N. B., and Gottlieb, M. J. (1967). Effect of supplemental visual cues on rotary pursuit. *Journal of Experimental Psychology, 75,* 566–568.

Goss, S., Hall, C., Buckolz, E., and Fishburne, G. (1986). Imagery ability and the acquisition and retention of motor skills. *Memory and Cognition, 14,* 469–477.

Gottsdanker, R. (1979). A psychological refractory period or an unprepared period? *Journal of Experimental Psychology: Human Perception and Performance, 5,* 208–215.

Gottsdanker, R. (1980). The ubiquitous role of preparation. In G. E. Stelmach and J. Requin (Eds.), *Tutorials in motor behavior* (pp. 355–371). Amsterdam: North-Holland.

Gould, D., and Roberts, G. C. (1982). Modeling and motor skill acquisition. *Quest, 33,* 214–230.

Gould, D., Weinberg, R., and Jackson, A. (1980). Mental preparation strategies, cognitions, and strength performance. *Journal of Sport Psychology, 2,* 329–335.

Goulet, C., Bard, C., and Fleury, M. (1989). Expertise differences in preparing to return a tennis serve: A visual information processing approach. *Journal of Sport & Exercise Psychology, 11,* 382–398.

Gross, E., Griessel, D. C., and Stull, G. A. (1956). Relationship between two motor educability tests, a strength test, and wrestling ability after eight weeks of instruction. *Research Quarterly, 27,* 395–402.

Hagman, J. D. (1978). Specific-cue effects of interpolated movements on distance and location retention in short-term motor memory. *Memory and Cognition, 6,* 432–437.

Hale, B. D. (1982). The effects of internal and external imagery on muscular and ocular concomitants. *Journal of Sport Psychology, 4,* 379–387.

Hall, C. R. (1980). Imagery for movement. *Journal of Human Movement Studies, 6,* 252–264.

Hall, C. R. (1985). Individual differences in the mental practice and imagery of motor skill performance. *Canadian Journal of Applied Sport Sciences, 10,* 17S–21S.

Hall, C. R., and Buckolz, E. (1982–83). Imagery and the recall of movement patterns. *Imagination, Cognition, and Personality, 2,* 251–260.

Hall, C. R., Buckolz, E., and Fishburne, G. (1989). Searching for a relationship between imagery ability and memory for movements. *Journal of Human Movement Studies, 17,* 89–100.

Hall, C. R., and Pongrac, J. (1983). *Movement Imagery Questionnaire.* London, Ontario, Canada: University of Western Ontario.

Hall, C. R., Pongrac, J., and Buckolz, E. (1985). The measurement of imagery ability. *Human Movement Science, 4,* 107–118.

Hall, C. R., Rodgers, W. M., and Barr, K. A. (1990). The use of imagery by athletes in selected sports. *The Sport Psychologist, 4,* 1–10.

Hamilton, W. (1859). *Lectures on metaphysics and logic.* Edinburgh: Blackwood.

Hand, J., and Sidaway, B. (1992). Relative frequency of modeling effects on the performance and retention of a motor skill. (Abstract) *Research Quarterly for Exercise and Sport,* Supplement to Vol. 63, Number 1, p. 57f.

Hardy, C. J. (1983). The post-knowledge of results interval: Effects of interpolated activity on cognitive information processing. *Research Quarterly for Exercise and Sport, 54,* 144–148.

Hasher, L., and Zacks, R. (1979). Automatic and effortful processes in memory. *Journal of Experimental Psychology: General, 108,* 356–388.

Hatze, H. (1976). Biomechanical aspects of successful motion optimization. In P. V. Komi (Ed.), *Biomechanics V-B* (pp. 5–12). Baltimore: University Park Press.

Hautala, R. M. (1988). Does transfer of training help children learn juggling? *Perceptual and Motor Skills, 67,* 563–567.

Helsen, W., and Pauwels, J. M. (1990). Analysis of visual search activity in solving tactical game problems. In D. Brogan (Ed.), *Visual search* (pp. 177–184). London: Taylor & Francis.

Henry, F. M. (1961). Reaction time-movement time correlations. *Perceptual and Motor Skills, 12,* 63–66.

Henry, F. M. (1974). Variable and constant performance errors with a group of individuals. *Journal of Motor Behavior, 6,* 149–154.

Henry, F. M., and Rogers, D. E. (1960). Increased response latency for complicated movements and the "memory drum" theory of neuromotor reaction. *Research Quarterly, 31,* 448–458.

Henry, R. A., and Hulin, C. L. (1987). Stability of skilled performance across time: Some generalizations and limitations on utilities. *Journal of Applied Psychology, 72,* 457–462.

Heuer, H., and Schmidt, R. A. (1988). Transfer of learning among motor patterns with different relative timing. *Journal of Experimental Psychology: Human Perception and Performance, 14,* 241–252.

Hick, W. E. (1952). On the rate of gain of information. *Quarterly Journal of Experimental Psychology, 4,* 11–26.

Hicks, R. E., Frank, J. M., and Kinsbourne, M. (1982). The locus of bimanual skill transfer. *Journal of General Psychology, 107,* 277–281.

Hicks, R. E., Gualtieri, T. C., and Schroeder, S. R. (1983). Cognitive and motor components of bilateral transfer. *American Journal of Psychology, 96,* 223–228.

Higgins, J. R. (1977). *Human movement: An integrated approach.* St. Louis: C.V. Mosby.

Higgins, J. R., and Spaeth, R. A. (1972). Relationship between consistency of movement and environmental conditions. *Quest, 17,* 61–69.

Hird, J. S., Landers, D. M., Thomas, J. R., and Horan, J. J. (1991). Physical practice is superior to mental practice in enhancing cognitive and motor task performance. *Journal of Sport & Exercise Psychology, 13,* 281–293.

Ho, L., and Shea, J. B. (1978). Levels of processing and the coding of position cues in motor short-term memory. *Journal of Motor Behavior, 10,* 113–121.

Hoenkamp, H. (1978). Perceptual cues that determine the labeling of human gait. *Journal of Human Movement Studies, 4,* 59–69.

Hogan, J., and Yanowitz, B. (1978). The role of verbal estimates of movement error in ballistic skill acquisition. *Journal of Motor Behavior, 10,* 133–138.

Holding, D. H. (1965). *The principles of training.* Oxford: Pergamon Press.

Holding, D. H. (1976). An approximate transfer surface. *Journal of Motor Behavior, 8,* 1–9.

Housner, L. D. (1981). Expert-novice knowledge structure and cognitive processing differences in badminton. (Abstract) *Psychology of motor behavior and sport-1981* (p. 1). Proceedings of the annual meeting of the North American Society for the Psychology of Sport and Physical Activity, Asilomar, CA.

Hubbard, A. W., and Seng, C. N. (1954). Visual movements of batters. *Research Quarterly, 25,* 42–57.

Hull, C. L. (1943). *Principles of behavior.* New York: Appleton-Century-Crofts.

Inglis, J., Campbell, D., and Donald, M. W. (1976). Electromyographic biofeedback and neuromuscular rehabilitation. *Canadian Journal of Behavioral Science, 8,* 299–323.

Jacobson, E. (1931). Electrical measurement of neuromuscular states during mental activities: VI. A note on mental activities concerning an amputated limb. *American Journal of Physiology, 43,* 122–125.

Jacoby, L. L. (1978). On interpreting the effects of repetitions: Solving a problem versus remembering a solution. *Journal of Verbal Learning and Verbal Behavior, 17,* 649–667.

James, W. (1890). *Principles of psychology.* New York: Holt.

Jeannerod, M. (1981). Intersegmental coordination during reaching at natural visual objects. In J. Long and A. Baddeley (Eds.), *Attention and Performance IX* (pp. 153–168). Hillsdale, NJ: Erlbaum.

Jeannerod, M. (1984). The timing of natural prehension. *Journal of Motor Behavior, 16,* 235–254.

Johansson, G. (1973). Visual perception of biological motion and a model for its analysis. *Perception and Psychophysics, 14,* 201–211.

Johnson, B., and Nelson, J. K. (1985). *Practical measurement for evaluation in physical education* (4th ed.). Minneapolis: Burgess.

Johnson, R., and McCabe, J. (1982). Schema theory: A test of the variability of practice hypothesis. *Perceptual and Motor Skills, 55,* 231–234.

Jongsma, D. M., Elliott, D., and Lee, T. D. (1987). Experience and set in the running sprint start. *Perceptual and Motor Skills, 64,* 547–550.

Kahneman, D. (1973). *Attention and effort.* Englewood Cliffs, NJ: Prentice-Hall.

Kantowitz, B. H., and Knight, J. L., Jr. (1976). Testing tapping timesharing: II. Auditory secondary task. *Acta Psychologica, 40,* 343–362.

Karlin, L., and Mortimer, R. G. (1963). Effect of verbal, visual, and auditory augmenting cues on learning a complex skill. *Journal of Experimental Psychology, 65,* 75–79.

Keele, S. W. (1968). Movement control in skilled motor performance. *Psychological Bulletin, 70,* 387–403.

Keele, S. W., Cohen, A., and Ivry, R. (1990). Motor programs: Concepts and issues. In M. Jeannerod (Ed.), *Attention and performance XIII: Motor representation and control* (pp. 77–110). Hillsdale, NJ: Erlbaum.

Keele, S. W., and Posner, M. I. (1968). Processing of visual feedback in rapid movements. *Journal of Experimental Psychology, 77,* 153–158.

Keller, F. S. (1958). The phantom plateau. *Journal of Experimental Analysis of Behavior, 1,* 1–13.

Kelso, J. A. S. (1977). Motor control mechanisms underlying human movement reproduction. *Journal of Experimental Psychology: Human Perception and Performance, 3,* 529–543.

Kelso, J. A. S. (1981). Contrasting perspectives on order and regulation in movement. In J. Long and A. Baddeley (Eds.), *Attention and performance IX* (pp. 437–457). Hillsdale: NJ: Erlbaum.

Kelso, J. A. S. (1984a). Phase transitions and critical behavior in human bimanual coordination. *American Journal of Physiology: Regulatory, Integrative, & Comparative Physiology, 15,* R1000–1004.

Kelso, J. A. S. (1984b). Report of panel 3: Preparatory processes: Considerations from a theory of movement. In E. Donchin (Ed.), *Cognitive psychophysiology* (pp. 201–214). Hillsdale, NJ: Erlbaum.

Kelso, J. A. S., and Holt, K. G. (1980). Exploring a vibratory systems analysis of human movement production. *Journal of Neurophysiology, 43,* 1183–1196.

Kelso, J. A. S., Holt, K. G., and Flatt, A. E. (1980). The role of proprioception in the perception and control of human movement: Toward a theoretical reassessment. *Perception and Psychophysics, 28,* 45–52.

Kelso, J. A. S., and Scholz, J. P. (1985). Cooperative phenomena in biological motion. In H. Haken (Ed.), *Complex systems: Operational approaches in neurobiology, physical systems, and computers* (pp. 124–149). Berlin: Springer-Verlag.

Kelso, J. A. S., Southard, D. L., and Goodman, D. (1979). On the coordination of two-handed movements. *Journal of Experimental Psychology: Human Perception and Performance, 5,* 229–238.

Kelso, J. A. S., Stelmach, G. E., and Wanamaker, W. M. (1974). Behavioral and neurological parameters of the nerve compression block. *Journal of Motor Behavior, 6,* 179–190.

Kelso, J. A. S., Tuller, B. H., Vatikiotis-Bateson, E., and Fowler, C. A. (1984). Functionally specific articulatory cooperation following jaw perturbations during speech: Evidence for coordinative structures. *Journal of Experimental Psychology: Human Perception and Performance, 10,* 812–832.

Kelso, J. A. S., and Wallace, S. A. (1978). Conscious mechanisms of control. In G. E. Stelmach (Ed.), *Information processing in motor control and learning* (pp. 79–116). New York: Academic Press.

Kelso, J. A. S., Wallace, S. A., Stelmach, G. E., and Weitz, G. A. (1975). Sensory and motor impairments in the nerve compression block. *Quarterly Journal of Experimental Psychology, 27,* 123–129.

Knapp, C. G., and Dixon, W. R. (1952). Learning to juggle: A study of whole and part methods. *Research Quarterly, 23,* 389–401.

Kohl, R. M., and Roenker, D. L. (1980). Bilateral transfer as a function of mental imagery. *Journal of Motor Behavior, 12,* 197–206.

Kolers, P. A., and Roediger, H. L., III (1984). Procedures of mind. *Journal of Verbal Learning and Verbal Behavior, 23,* 425–449.

Laabs, G. J. (1973). Retention characteristics of different reproduction cues in motor short-term memory. *Journal of Experimental Psychology, 100,* 168–177.

Landers, D. M. (1975). Observational learning of a motor skill: Temporal spacing of demonstrations and audience presence. *Journal of Motor Behavior, 7,* 281–287.

Landers, D. M., and Landers, D. M. (1973). Teacher versus peer models: Effect of model's presence and performance level on motor behavior. *Journal of Motor Behavior, 5,* 129–139.

Landers, D. M., Boutcher, S. H., and Wang, M. Q. (1986). A psychobiological study of archery performance. *Research Quarterly for Exercise and Sport, 57,* 236–244.

Lang, P. J., Kozak, M. J., Miller, G. A., Levin, D. M., and McLean, A., Jr. (1980). Emotional imagery: Conceptual structure and pattern of somato-visceral response. *Psychophysiology, 17,* 179–192.

Larish, D. D., and Stelmach, G. E. (1982). Preprogramming, programming, and reprogramming of aimed hand movements as a function of age. *Journal of Motor Behavior, 14,* 322–340.

Lashley, K. S. (1917). The accuracy of movement in the absence of excitation from the moving organ. *American Journal of Physiology, 43,* 169–194.

Lashley, K. S. (1951). The problem of serial order in behavior. In L. A. Jeffress (Ed.), *Cerebral mechanisms in behavior* (pp. 112–136). New York: John Wiley.

Laszlo, J. L. (1966). The performance of a single motor task with kinesthetic sense loss. *Quarterly Journal of Experimental Psychology, 18,* 1–8.

Laszlo, J. L. (1967). Training of fast tapping with reduction of kinesthetic, tactile, visual, and auditory sensation. *Quarterly Journal of Experimental Psychology, 19,* 344–349.

Laurent, M. & Thomson, J. A. (1988). The role of visual information in control of a constrained locomotor task. *Journal of Motor Behavior, 20,* 17–38.

Lavery, J. J. (1962). Retention of simple motor skills as a function of type of knowledge of results. *Canadian Journal of Psychology, 16,* 300–311.

Leavitt, J. L. (1979). Cognitive demands of skating and stickhandling in ice hockey. *Canadian Journal of Applied Sport Sciences, 4,* 46–55.

Leavitt, J. L., Lee, T. D., and Romanow, S. K. E. (1980). Proactive interference and movement attribute change in motor short-term memory. In C. H. Nadeau, W. R. Halliwell, K. M. Newell, and G. C. Roberts (Eds.), *Psychology of motor behavior and sport 1979* (pp. 585–593). Champaign, IL: Human Kinetics.

Lee, D. N. (1974). Visual information during locomotion. In R. B. MacLeod and H. Pick (Eds.), *Perception: Essays in honor of J. J. Gibson* (pp. 250–267). Ithaca, NY: Cornell University Press.

Lee, D. N. (1976). A theory of visual control of braking based on information about time-to-collision. *Perception, 5,* 437–459.

Lee, D. N. (1980). Visuo-motor coordination in space-time. In G. E. Stelmach and J. Requin (Eds.), *Tutorials in motor behavior* (pp. 281–295). Amsterdam: North-Holland.

Lee, D. N., Lishman, J. R., and Thomson, J. A. (1984). Regulation of gait in long jumping. *Journal of Experimental Psychology: Human Perception and Performance, 8,* 448–459.

Lee, T. D. (1988). Testing for motor learning: A focus on transfer-appropriate-processing. In O. G. Meijer & K. Roth (Eds.), *Complex motor behaviour: 'The' motor-action controversy* (pp. 210–215). Amsterdam: Elsevier Science Publishers.

Lee, T. D., and Carnahan, H. (1990). Bandwidth knowledge of results and motor learning: More than just a relative frequency effect. *Quarterly Journal of Experimental Psychology, 42A,* 777–789.

Lee, T. D., and Gallagher, J. D. (1981). A parallel between the preselection effect in psychomotor memory and the generation effect in verbal memory. *Journal of Experimental Psychology: Human Learning and Memory, 7,* 77–78.

Lee, T. D., and Genovese, E. D. (1988). Distribution of practice in motor skill acquisition: Learning and performance effects reconsidered. *Research Quarterly for Exercise and Sport, 59,* 59–65.

Lee, T. D., and Genovese, E. D. (1988). Distribution of practice in motor skill acquisition: Learning and performance effects reconsidered. *Research Quarterly for Exercise and Sport, 59,* 59–67.

Lee, T. D., and Hirota, T. T. (1980). Encoding specificity principle in motor short-term memory for movement extent. *Journal of Motor Behavior, 12,* 63–67.

Lee, T. D., and Magill, R. A. (1983a). Activity during the post-KR interval: Effects upon performance or learning. *Research Quarterly for Exercise and Sport, 54,* 340–345.

Lee, T. D., and Magill, R. A. (1983b). The locus of contextual interference in motor skill acquisition. *Journal of Experimental Psychology: Learning, Memory, and Cognition, 9,* 730–746.

Lee, T. D., and Magill, R. A. (1985). Can forgetting facilitate skill acquisition? In D. Goodman, R. B. Wilberg, and I. M. Franks (Eds.), *Differing perspectives in motor learning, memory and control* (pp. 3–22). Amsterdam: North-Holland.

Lee, T. D., Magill, R. A., and Weeks, D. J. (1985). Influence of practice schedule on testing schema theory predictions in adults. *Journal of Motor Behavior, 17,* 283–299.

Lee, T. D., and Weeks, D. J. (1987). The beneficial influence of forgetting on short-term retention of movement information. *Human Movement Science, 6,* 233–245.

Lee, T. D., White, M. A., and Carnahan, H. (1990). On the role of knowledge of results in motor learning: Exploring the guidance hypothesis. *Journal of Motor Behavior, 22,* 191–208.

Leiper, C. I., Miller, A., Lang, L., and Herman, R. (1981). Sensory feedback for head control in cerebral palsy. *Physical Therapy, 61,* 512–518.

Leonard, J. A. (1959). Tactual choice reactions: I. *Quarterly Journal of Experimental Psychology, 11,* 76–83.

Leonard, S. D., Karnes, E. W., Oxendine, J., and Hesson, J. (1970). Effects of task difficulty on transfer performance on rotary pursuit. *Perceptual and Motor Skills, 30,* 731–736.

Lewin, K., Dembo, T., Festinger, L., and Sears, P. S. (1944). Levels of aspiration. In J. M. Hunt (Ed.), *Personality and behavior disorders* (Vol. I, pp. 333–378). New York: Ronald Press.

Lindahl, L. G. (1945). Movement analysis as an industrial training method. *Journal of Applied Psychology, 29,* 420–436.

Linden, C. A., Uhley, J. E., Smith, D., and Bush, M. A. (1989). The effects of mental practice on walking balance in an elderly population. *Occupational Therapy Journal of Research, 9,* 155–169.

Lintern, G. (1980). Transfer of landing skill after training with supplementary visual cues. *Human Factors, 22,* 81–89.

Lintern, G., and Roscoe, S. N. (1980). Visual cue augmentation in contact flight simulation. In S. N. Roscoe (Ed.), *Aviation psychology* (pp. 227–238). Ames, IA: Iowa State University Press.

Lintern, G., Roscoe, S. N., Koonce, J. M., and Segal, L. D. (1990). Transfer of landing skills in beginning flight training. *Human Factors, 32,* 319–327.

Lintern, G., Roscoe, S. N., and Sivier, J., (1990). Display principles, control dynamics, and environmental factors in pilot training and transfer. *Human Factors, 32,* 299–317.

Little, W. S., and McCullagh, P. M. (1989). Motivation orientation and modeled instruction strategies: The effects on form and accuracy. *Journal of Sport and Exercise Psychology, 11,* 41–53.

Locke, E. A. (1968). Toward a theory of task motivation incentives. *Organizational Behavior and Human Performance, 3,* 157–189.

Locke, E. A., and Bryan, J. F. (1966). Cognitive aspects of psychomotor performance: The effects of performance goals on level of performance. *Journal of Applied Psychology, 50,* 286–291.

Locke, E. A., Cartledge, N., and Koeppel, J. (1968). Motivational effects of knowledge of results: A goal-setting phenomenon. *Psychological Bulletin, 70,* 474–485.

Locke, E. A., and Latham, G. P. (1985). The application of goal setting to sports. *Journal of Sport Psychology, 7,* 205–222.

Locke, E. A., Shaw, K. N., Saari, L. M., and Latham, G. P. (1981). Goal setting and task performance: 1969–1980. *Psychological Bulletin, 90,* 125–152.

Loftus, E. F. (1980). *Memory: Surprising new insights into how we remember and why we forget.* Reading, MA: Addison-Wesley.

Loftus, E. F., and Loftus, G. R. (1980). On the permanence of stored information in the human brain. *American Psychologist, 35,* 409–420.

Logan, G. D. (1982). On the ability to inhibit complex movements: A stop-signal study of typewriting. *Journal of Experimental Psychology: Human Perception and Performance, 8,* 778–792.

Logan, G. D. (1985). Skill and automaticity: Relations, implications, and future directions. *Canadian Journal of Psychology, 39,* 367–386.

Mackworth, N. H. (1956). Vigilance. *Nature, 178,* 1375–1377.

Maehr, M. L., and Nicholls, J. G. (1980). Culture and achievement motivation: A second look. In N. Warren (Ed.), *Studies in cross-cultural psychology* (pp. 221–267). New York: Academic Press.

Magill, R. A. (1977). The processing of knowledge of results for a serial motor task. *Journal of Motor Behavior, 9,* 113–118.

Magill, R. A. (1983). Preface/Introduction. In R. A. Magill (Ed.), *Memory and control of action* (pp. xi–xvi). Amsterdam: North-Holland.

Magill, R. A. (1988). Activity during the post-knowledge of results interval can benefit motor skill learning. In O. G. Meijer and K. Roth (Eds.), *Complex motor behavior: 'The' motor-action controversy* (pp. 231–246). Amsterdam: Elsevier Science Publishers.

Magill, R. A. (1991). The exaggerated role of verbal feedback in motor skill learning. (Manuscript submitted for publication).

Magill, R. A., Chamberlin, C. J., and Hall, K. G. (1991). Verbal knowledge of results as redundant information for learning an anticipation timing skill. *Human Movement Science, 10,* 485–507.

Magill, R. A., and Dowell, M. N. (1977). Serial position effects in motor short-term memory. *Journal of Motor Behavior, 9,* 319–323.

Magill, R. A., and Goode, S. (1982). The representation of limb position information in memory. (Abstract). *Psychology of motor behavior and sport-1982* (p. 43). Proceedings of the annual meeting of the North American Society for the Psychology of Sport and Physical Activity, College Park, MD.

Magill, R. A., and Hall, K. G. (1989). *Implicit and explicit learning in a complex tracking task.* Paper presented at the annual meeting of the Psychonomics Society, Atlanta, Georgia.

Magill, R. A., and Hall, K. G. (1990). A review of the contextual interference effect in motor skill acquisition. *Human Movement Science, 9,* 241–289.

Magill, R. A., and Lee, T. D. (1987). Verbal label effects on response accuracy and organization for learning limb positioning movements. *Journal of Human Movement Studies, 13,* 285–308.

Magill, R. A., and Parks, P. F. (1983). The psychophysics of kinesthesis for positioning responses: The physical stimulus-psychological response relationship. *Research Quarterly for Exercise and Sport, 54,* 346–351.

Magill, R. A., Schoenfelder-Zohdi, B., and Hall, K. G. (1990). *Further evidence for implicit learning in a complex tracking task.* Paper presented at the annual meeting of the Psychonomics Society, New Orleans, Louisiana.

Magill, R. A., and Wood, C. A. (1986). Knowledge of results precision as a learning variable in motor skill acquisition. *Research Quarterly for Exercise and Sport, 57,* 170–173.

Mahoney, M. J., and Avener, A. (1977). Psychology of the elite athlete: An exploratory study. *Cognitive Therapy and Research, 1,* 135–141.

Malina, R. M. (1984). Physical growth and maturation. In J. R. Thomas (Ed.), *Motor development during childhood and adolescence* (pp. 2–26). Minneapolis: Burgess.

Mané, A., and Donchin, E. (1989). The Space Fortress game. *Acta Psychologica, 71,* 17–22.

Mark, L. S. (1987). Eyeheight-scaled information about affordances: A study of sitting and stair climbing. *Journal of Experimental Psychology: Human Perception and Performance, 13,* 361–370.

Marteniuk, R. G. (1986). Information processes in movement learning: Capacity and structural interference. *Journal of Motor Behavior, 5,* 249–259.

Marteniuk, R. G., and Mackenzie, C. (1980). A preliminary theory of two-handed coordinated control. In G. E. Stelmach and J. Requin (Eds.), *Tutorials in motor behavior* (pp. 185–197). Amsterdam: North-Holland.

Marteniuk, R. G., and Romanow, S. K. E. (1983). Human movement organization and learning as revealed by variability of movement, use of kinematic information and Fourier analysis. In R. A. Magill (Ed.), *Memory and control of action* (pp. 167–197). Amsterdam: North-Holland.

Martens, R. (1971). Anxiety and motor behavior: A review. *Journal of Motor Behavior, 3,* 151–179.

Martens, R. (1972). Trait and state anxiety. In W. P. Morgan (Ed.), *Ergogenic aids and muscular performance* (pp. 35–66). New York: Academic Press.

Martens, R. (1977). *Sport competition anxiety test.* Champaign, IL: Human Kinetics.

Martens, R. (1987). *Coaches guide to sport psychology.* Champaign, IL: Human Kinetics.

Martens, R., Burwitz, L., and Zuckerman, J. (1976). Modeling effects on motor performance. *Research Quarterly, 47,* 277–291.

Mathews, D. K. (1978). *Measurement in physical education* (4th ed.). Philadelphia: W.B. Saunders.

McBride, E., and Rothstein, A. (1979). Mental and physical practice and the learning and retention of open and closed skills. *Perceptual and Motor Skills, 49,* 359–365.

McCloy, C. H. (1934). The measurement of general motor capacity and general motor ability. *Research Quarterly, 5,* Supplement, 46–61.

McCloy, C. H. (1937). An analytic study of the stunt type tests as a measure of motor educability. *Research Quarterly, 8,* 46–55.

McCloy, C. H., and Young, N. D. (1954). *Tests and measurements in health and physical education* (3rd ed.). New York: Appleton-Century-Crofts.

McCullagh, P. (1987). Model similarity effects on motor performance. *Journal of Sport Psychology, 9,* 249–260.

McCullagh, P., and Caird, J. K. (1990). Correct and learning models and the use of model knowledge of results in the acquisition and retention of a motor skill. *Journal of Human Movement Studies, 18,* 107–116.

McCullagh, P., Weiss, M. R., and Ross, D. (1989). Modeling considerations in motor skill acquisition and performance: An integrated approach. In K. B. Pandolf (Ed.), *Exercise and sport science reviews* (Vol. 17, pp. 475–513). Baltimore: Williams & Wilkins.

McKeithern, K. B., Reitman, J. S., Reuther, H. H., and Hirtle, S. C. (1981). Knowledge organization and skill differences in computer programmers. *Cognitive Psychology, 13,* 307–325.

McLeod, P. (1978). Does probe RT measure central processing demand? *Quarterly Journal of Experimental Psychology, 30,* 83–89.

McLeod, P. (1980). What can probe RT tell us about the attention demands of movement? In G. E. Stelmach and J. Requin (Eds.), *Tutorials in motor behavior* (pp. 579–589). Amsterdam: North-Holland.

McPherson, S. L., and Thomas, J. R. (1989). Relation of knowledge and performance in boy's tennis: Age and expertise. *Journal of Experimental Child Psychology, 48,* 190–211.

Meeuwsen, H., and Magill, R. A. (1987). The role of vision in gait control during gymnastics vaulting. In T. B. Hoshizaki, J. Salmela, & B. Petiot (Eds.), *Diagonistics, treatment, and analysis of gymnastic talent.* (pp. 137–155). Montreal: Sport Psyche Editions.

Melnick, M. J. (1971). Effects of overlearning on the retention of a gross motor skill. *Research Quarterly, 42,* 60–69.

Meyer, D. E., Abrams, R. A., Kornblum, S., Wright, C. E., and Smith, J. E. K. (1988). Optimality in human motor performance: Ideal control of rapid aimed movements. *Psychological Review, 95,* 340–370.

Meyer, D. E., Osman, A. M., Irwin, D. E., and Yantis, S. (1988). Modern mental chronometry. *Biological Psychology, 26,* 3–67.

Miller, G. A. (1956). The magical number seven plus or minus two: Some limits on our capacity for processing information. *Psychological Review, 63,* 81–97.

Miller, G. A., Galanter, E., and Pribram, K. H. (1960). *Plans and the structure of behavior.* New York: Holt, Rinehart, and Winston.

Moore, S. P. (1984). Systematic removal of visual feedback. *Journal of Human Movement Studies, 10,* 165–173.

Moore, S. P., and Marteniuk, R. G. (1986). Kinematic and electromyographic changes that occur as a function of learning a time-constrained aiming task. *Journal of Motor Behavior, 18,* 397–426.

Moray, N. (1959). Attention in dichotic listening: Affective cues and the influence of instructions. *Quarterly Journal of Experimental Psychology, 11,* 56–60.

Moray, N. (1967). Where is attention limited? A survey and a model. *Acta Psychologica, 27,* 84–92.

Morgan, W. P. (1978, April). The mind of the marathoner. *Psychology Today,* 38–45.

Morris, C. D., Bransford, J. D., and Franks, J. J. (1977). Levels of processing versus transfer appropriate processing. *Journal of Verbal Learning and Verbal Behavior, 16,* 519–533.

Mosston, M. (1981). *Teaching physical education* (2nd ed.). Columbus, OH: Merrill.

Mourant, R. R., and Rockwell, T. H. (1972). Strategies of visual search by novice and experienced drivers. *Human Factors, 14,* 325–335.

Mowbray, G. H. (1960). Choice reaction times for skilled responses. *Quarterly Journal of Experimental Psychology, 12,* 193–202.

Mowbray, G. H., and Rhoades, M. U. (1959). On the reduction of choice reaction times with practice. *Quarterly Journal of Experimental Psychology, 11,* 16–23.

Mulder, T., and Hulstijn, W. (1985). Delayed sensory feedback in the learning of a novel motor skill. *Psychological Record, 47,* 203–209.

Navon, D., and Gopher, D. (1979). On the economy of the human processing system. *Psychological Review, 86,* 214–255.

Naylor, J., and Briggs, G. (1963). Effects of task complexity and task organization on the relative efficiency of part and whole training methods. *Journal of Experimental Psychology, 65,* 217–244.

Neiss, R. (1988). Reconceptualizing arousal: Psychobiological states in motor performance. *Psychological Bulletin, 103,* 345–366.

Nelson, J. K. (1978). Motivating effects of the use of norms and goals with endurance testing. *Research Quarterly, 49,* 317–321.

Neumann, E., and Ammons, R. B. (1957). Acquisition and long-term retention of a simple serial perceptual motor skill. *Journal of Experimental Psychology, 53,* 159–161.

Newell, K. M. (1974). Knowledge of results and motor learning. *Journal of Motor Behavior, 6,* 235–244.

Newell, K. M. (1976). Knowledge of results and motor learning. In J. Keogh and R. S. Hutton (Eds.), *Exercise and sport sciences reviews* (Vol. 4, pp. 196–228). Santa Barbara, CA: Journal Publishing Affiliates.

Newell, K. M., Carlton, M. J., Fisher, A. T., and Rutter, B. G. (1989). Whole-part training strategies for learning the response dynamics of microprocessor driven simulators. *Acta Psychologica, 71,* 197–216.

Newell, K. M., Quinn, J. T., Jr., Sparrow, W. A., and Walter, C. B. (1983). Kinematic information feedback for learning a rapid arm movement. *Human Movement Science, 2,* 255–269.

Newell, K. M., and van Emmerik, R. E. A. (1989). The acquisition of coordination: Preliminary analysis of learning to write. *Human Movement Science, 8,* 17–32.

Nicholls, J. (1984). Achievement motivation: Conceptions of ability, subjective experience, task choice, and performance. *Psychological Review, 91,* 328–346.

Nideffer, R. M. (1976). *The inner athlete.* New York: Thomas Crowell.

Nideffer, R. M. (1986). Concentration and attention control training. In J. M. Williams (Ed.), *Applied sport psychology: Personal growth to peak experience* (pp. 258–259). Palo Alto, CA: Mayfield.

Nissen, M. J., and Bullemer, P. (1987). Attentional requirements of learning: Evidence from performance measures. *Cognitive Psychology, 19,* 1–32.

Norman, D. A. (1968). Toward a theory of memory and attention. *Psychological Review, 75,* 522–536.

Norman, D. A. (1969). Memory while shadowing. *Quarterly Journal of Experimental Psychology, 21,* 85–93.

Norrie, M. L. (1967). Practice effects on reaction latency for simple and complex movements. *Research Quarterly, 38,* 79–85.

Osgood, C. E. (1949). The similarity paradox in human learning: A resolution. *Psychological Review, 56,* 132–143.

Patla, A. E. (1989). In search of laws for the visual control of locomotion: Some observations. *Journal of Experimental Psychology: Human Perception and Performance, 15,* 624–628.

Patrick, J., & Mutlusoy, F. (1982). The relatiohnship between types of feedback, gain of a display and feedback precision in acquisition of a simple motor task. *Quarterly Journal of Experimental Psychology, 34A,* 171–182.

Peters, M. (1977). Simultaneous performance of two motor activities: The factor of timing. *Neuropsychologia, 15,* 461–465.

Peters, M. (1985). Performance of a rubato-like task: When two things cannot be done at the same time. *Music Perception, 2,* 471–482.

Peterson, L. R., and Peterson, M. J. (1959). Short term retention of individual verbal items. *Journal of Experimental Psychology, 58,* 193–198.

Pew, R. W. (1974). Levels of analysis in motor control. *Brain Research, 71,* 393–400.

Pieron, M. (1982). Effectiveness of teaching a psychomotor task: Study in a micro-teaching setting. In M. Pieron and J. Cheffers (Eds.), *Studying the teaching in physical education* (pp. 79–89). Liege, Belgium: Association Internationale des Superieures d'Education Physique.

Pillsbury, W. B. (1908). *Attention.* New York: Macmillan.

Polit, A., and Bizzi, E. (1978). Processes controlling arm movements in monkeys. *Science, 201,* 1235–1237.

Pollock, B. J., & Lee, T. D. (1992). Effects of the model's skill level on observational learning. *Research Quarterly for Exercise and Sport, 63,* 25–29.

Posner, M. I. (1978). *Chronometric explorations of mind.* Hillsdale, NJ: Erlbaum.

Posner, M. I., and Boies, S. J. (1969). Components of attention. *Psychological Review, 78,* 391–408.

Posner, M. I., and Keele, S. W. (1969). Attention demands of movements. *Proceedings of the 16th Congress of Applied Psychology.* Amsterdam: Swets & Zeitlinger.

Posner, M. I., Nissen, M. J., and Klein, R. (1976). Visual dominance: An information processing account of its origins and significance. *Psychological Review, 83,* 157–171.

Poulton, E. C. (1957). On prediction in skilled movements. *Psychological Bulletin, 54,* 467–478.

Proteau, L., and Cournoyer, L. (1990). Vision of the stylus in a manual aiming task: The effects of practice. *Quarterly Journal of Experimental Psychology, 42B,* 811–828.

Proteau, L., Marteniuk, R. G., Girouard, Y., and Dugas, C. (1987). On the type of information used to control and learn an aiming movement after moderate and extensive training. *Human Movement Science, 6,* 181–199.

Proctor, R., and Reeve, T. G. (Eds.). (1990). *Stimulus-response compatibility: An integrated perspective.* Amsterdam: North-Holland.

Raibert, M. (1977). *Motor control and learning by the state-space model*. Technical Report, Artificial Intelligence Laboratory, Massachusetts Institute of Technology (AI-TR-439).

Reeve, T. G. (1976). *Processing demands during the acquisition of motor skills requiring different feedback cues*. Unpublished doctoral dissertation, Texas A&M University.

Reeve, T. G., Mackey, L. J., and Fober, G. W. (1986). Visual dominance in the cross-modal kinesthetic to kinesthetic plus visual feedback condition. *Perceptual and Motor Skills, 62,* 243–252.

Reeve, T. G., and Magill, R. A. (1981). Role of components of knowledge of results information in error correction. *Research Quarterly for Exercise and Sport, 52,* 80–85.

Reeve, T. G., and Stelmach, G. E. (1982). Response feedback and movement context in retention of sequentially presented spatial information (Abstract). *Psychology of motor behavior and sport-1982* (p. 29). Proceedings of the annual meeting of the North American Society for the Psychology of Sport and Physical Activity, College Park, MD.

Reilly, R. R., Zedeck, S., and Tenopyr, M. L. (1979). Validity and fairness of physical ability tests for predicting performance in craft jobs. *Journal of Applied Psychology, 64,* 262–274.

Richardson, A. (1967a). Mental practice: A review and discussion. Part I. *Research Quarterly, 38,* 95–107.

Richardson, A. (1967b). Mental practice: A review and discussion. Part II. *Research Quarterly, 38,* 263–273.

Ripoll, H. (1988). Analysis of visual scanning patterns of volleyball players in a problem solving task. *International Journal of Sport Psychology, 19,* 9–25.

Roberts, G. C. (1992). Motivation in sport and exercise: Conceptual constraints and conceptual convergence. In G. C. Roberts (Ed.), *Motivation in sport and exercise* (pp. 3–29). Champaign, IL: Human Kinetics.

Roberts, W. H. (1930). The effect of delayed feeding on white rats in a problem cage. *Journal of Genetic Psychology, 37,* 35–38.

Roediger, H. L. (1990). Implicit memory: Retention without remembering. *American Psychologist, 45,* 1043–1056.

Rogers, C. A. (1974). Feedback precision and post-feedback interval duration. *Journal of Experimental Psychology, 102,* 604–608.

Rosenbaum, D. A. (1980). Human movement initiation: Specification of arm, direction, and extent. *Journal of Experimental Psychology: General, 109,* 444–474.

Rosenbaum, D. A. (1983). The movement precuing technique: Assumptions, applications, and extensions. In R. A. Magill (Ed.), *Memory and control of action* (pp. 251–274). Amsterdam: North-Holland.

Rosenberg, K. S., Pick, H. L., and von Hofsten, C. (1988). Role of visual information in catching. *Journal of Motor Behavior, 20,* 150–164.

Rothstein, A. L., and Arnold, R. K. (1976). Bridging the gap: Application of research on videotape feedback and bowling. *Motor Skills: Theory Into Practice, 1,* 36–61.

Roy, E. A. (1983). Manual performance asymmetries and motor control processes: Subject-generated changes in response parameters. *Human Movement Science, 2,* 271–277.

Roy, E. A., and Davenport, W. G. (1972). Factors in motor short-term memory: The interference effect of interpolated activity. *Journal of Experimental Psychology, 96,* 134–137.

Roy, E. A., and Elliott, D. (1986). Manual asymmetries in visually directed aiming. *Canadian Journal of Psychology, 40,* 109–121.

Rumelhart, D. E., and Norman, D. A. (1982). Simulating a skilled typist: A study of skilled cognitive-motor performance. *Cognitive Science, 6,* 1–36.

Ryan, E. D. (1965). Retention of stabilometer performance over extended periods of time. *Research Quarterly, 36,* 46–61.

Ryan, E. D., and Simons, J. (1983). What is learned in mental practice of motor skills? A test of the cognitive-motor hypothesis. *Journal of Sport Psychology, 5,* 419–426.

Salmoni, A. W., Schmidt, R. A., and Walter, C. B. (1984). Knowledge of results and motor learning: A review and reappraisal. *Psychological Bulletin, 95,* 355–386.

Salmoni, A. W., Sullivan, S. J., and Starkes, J. L. (1976). The attention demands of movements: A critique of the probe technique. *Journal of Motor Behavior, 8,* 161–169.

Sandweiss, J. H., & Wolf, S. L. (Eds.)(1985). *Biofeedback and sports science*. New York: Plenum.

Schendel, J. D., and Hagman, J. D. (1982). On sustaining procedural skills over a prolonged retention interval. *Journal of Applied Psychology, 67,* 605–610.

Schmidt, R. A. (1975a). *Motor skills*. New York: Harper & Row.

Schmidt, R. A. (1975b). A schema theory of discrete motor skill learning theory. *Psychological Review, 82*, 225–260.

Schmidt, R. A. (1977). Schema theory: Implications for movement education. *Motor Skills: Theory Into Practice, 2*, 36–38.

Schmidt, R. A. (1985). The search for invariance in skilled movement behavior. *Research Quarterly for Exercise and Sport, 56*, 188–200.

Schmidt, R. A. (1987). *Motor control and learning: A behavioral emphasis* (2nd ed.). Champaign, IL: Human Kinetics.

Schmidt, R. A. (1988). Motor and action perspectives on motor behavior. In O. G. Meijer and K. Roth (Eds.), *Complex motor behavior: 'The' motor-action controversy* (pp. 3–44). Amsterdam: Elsevier.

Schmidt, R. A., and White, J. L. (1972). Evidence for an error detection mechanism in motor skills: A test of Adams' closed-loop theory. *Journal of Motor Behavior, 4*, 143–153.

Schmidt, R. A., and Young, D. E. (1987). Transfer of movement control in motor skill learning. In S. M. Cormier and J. D. Hagman (Eds.), *Transfer of learning* (pp. 47–79). Orlando, FL: Academic Press.

Schmidt, R. A., and Young, D. E. (1991). Methodology and motor learning: A paradigm for kinematic feedback. *Journal of Motor Behavior, 23*, 13–24.

Schmidt, R. A., Young, D. E., Swinnen, S., and Shapiro, D. C. (1989). Summary knowledge of results for skill acquisition: Support for the guidance hypothesis. *Journal of Experimental Psychology: Learning, Memory, and Cognition, 15*, 352–359.

Schmidt, R. A., Zelaznik, H. N., Hawkins, B., Frank, J. S., and Quinn, J. T., Jr. (1979). Motor output variability: A theory for the accuracy of rapid motor acts. *Psychological Review, 86*, 415–451.

Schutz, R. W. (1977). Absolute, constant, and variable error: Problems and solutions. In D. Mood (Ed.), *Proceedings of the Colorado Measurement Symposium* (pp. 82–100). Boulder, CO: University of Colorado.

Schutz, R. W., and Roy, E. A. (1973). Absolute error: The devil in disguise. *Journal of Motor Behavior, 5*, 141–153.

Scully, D. M., and Newell, K. M. (1985). Observational learning and the acquisition of motor skills: Toward a visual perception perspective. *Journal of Human Movement Studies, 11*, 169–186.

Selder, D. J., and Del Rolan, N. (1979). Knowledge of performance, skill level and performance on the balance beam. *Canadian Journal of Applied Sport Sciences, 4*, 226–229.

Shaffer, L. H. (1976). Intention and performance. *Psychological Review, 83*, 375–393.

Shaffer, L. H. (1978). Timing in the motor programming of typing. *Quarterly Journal of Experimental Psychology, 30*, 333–345.

Shaffer, L. H. (1980). Analyzing piano performance: A study of concert pianists. In G. E. Stelmach and J. Requin (Eds.), *Tutorials in motor behavior* (pp. 443–455). Amsterdam: North-Holland.

Shaffer, L. H. (1981). Performances of Chopin, Bach, and Beethoven: Studies in motor programming. *Cognitive Psychology, 13*, 326–376.

Shaffer, L. H. (1982). Rhythm and timing in skill. *Psychological Review, 89*, 109–121.

Shank, M. D., and Haywood, K. M. (1987). Eye movements while viewing a baseball pitch. *Perceptual and Motor Skills, 64*, 1191–1197.

Shapiro, D. C., Zernicke, R. F., Gregor, R. J., and Diestel, J. D. (1981). Evidence for generalized motor programs using gait-pattern analysis. *Journal of Motor Behavior, 13*, 33–47.

Shapiro, K. L., and Raymond, J. E. (1989). Training of efficient oculomotor strategies enhances skill acquisition. *Acta Psychologica, 71*, 217–242.

Sharp, R. H., and Whiting, H. T. A. (1974). Exposure and occluded duration effects in a ball-catching skill. *Journal of Motor Behavior, 6*, 139–147.

Sharp, R. H., and Whiting, H. T. A. (1975). Information processing and eye movement behavior in a ball-catching skill. *Journal of Human Movement Studies, 1*, 124–131.

Shea, C. H., and Kohl, R. M. (1990). Specificity and variability of practice. *Research Quarterly for Exercise and Sport, 61*, 169–177.

Shea, C. H., Kohl, R., and Indermill, C. (1990). Contextual interference contributions of practice. *Acta Psychologica, 73*, 145–157.

Shea, J. B. (1977). Effects of labelling on motor short-term memory. *Journal of Experimental Psychology: Human Learning and Memory, 3*, 92–99.

Shea, J. B., and Morgan, R. L. (1979). Contextual interference effects on the acquisition, retention, and transfer of a motor skill. *Journal of Experimental Psychology: Human Learning and Memory, 5,* 179–187.

Shea, J. B., and Upton, G. (1976). The effects of skill aquisition of an interpolated motor short-term memory task during the KR-delay interval. *Journal of Motor Behavior, 8,* 277–281.

Shea, J. B., and Zimny, S. T. (1983). Context effects in memory and learning in movement information. In R. A. Magill (Ed.), *Memory and control of action* (pp. 345–366). Amsterdam: North-Holland.

Shepherd, M., Findlay, J. M., and Hockley, R. J. (1986). The relationship between eye movements and spatial attention. *Quarterly Journal of Experimental Psychology, 38A,* 475–491.

Sheridan, M. R. (1984). Response programming, response production, and fractionated reaction time. *Psychological Research, 46,* 33–47.

Sherwood, D. E. (1988). Effect of bandwidth knowledge of results on movement consistency. *Perceptual and Motor Skills, 66,* 535–542.

Shiffrin, R. M., and Schneider, W. (1977). Controlled and automatic human information processing: II. Perceptual learning, automatic attending, and a general theory. *Psychological Review, 84,* 127–190.

Sidaway, B., McNitt-Gray, J., and Davis, G. (1989). Visual timing of muscle preactivation in preparation for landing. *Ecological Psychology, 1,* 253–264.

Sidaway, B., Moore, B., and Schoenfelder-Zohdi, B. (1991). Summary and frequency of KR presentation effects on retention of a motor skill. *Research Quarterly for Exercise and Sport, 62,* 27–32.

Siedentop, D. (1983). *Developing teaching skills in physical education* (2nd ed.). Boston: Houghton Mifflin.

Siegel, D. (1986). Movement duration, fractionated reaction time, and response programming. *Research Quarterly for Exercise and Sport, 57,* 128–131.

Siipola, E. M. (1941). The relation of transfer to similarity in habit-structure. *Journal of Experimental Psychology, 28,* 9–14.

Silverman, S., Tyson, L. A., and Krampitz, J. (1991). *Teacher feedback and achievement in physical education: Interaction with student practice.* Paper presented at the annual meeting of the American Educational Research Association, Chicago, Illinois.

Silverman, S., Tyson, L. A., and Morford, L. M. (1988). Relationships of organization, time, and student achievement in physical education. *Teaching and Teacher Education, 4,* 247–257.

Simon, J. R., and Slaviero, D. P. (1975). Differential effects of a foreperiod countdown procedure on simple and choice reaction time. *Journal of Motor Behavior, 7,* 9–14.

Singer, R. N. (1966). Comparison of inter-limb skill achievement in performing a motor skill. *Research Quarterly, 37,* 406–410.

Singer, R. N. (1977). To err or not to err: A question for the instruction of psychomotor skills. *Review of Educational Research, 47,* 479–498.

Singer, R. N. (1980). *Motor learning and human performance* (3rd ed.). New York: Macmillan.

Singer, R. N. (1986). Sports performance: A five-step mental approach. *Journal of Physical Education and Recreation, 57,* 82–84.

Singer, R. N., and Dick, W. (1980). *Teaching physical education: A systems approach* (2nd ed.). Boston: Houghton Mifflin.

Singer, R. N., and Suwanthada, S. (1986). The generalizability effectiveness of a learning strategy on achievement in related closed motor skills. *Research Quarterly for Exercise and Sport, 57,* 205–214.

Skinner, B. F. (1953). *Science and human behavior.* New York: Macmillan.

Skinner, B. F. (1963). Behaviorism at fifty. *Science, 140,* 951–958.

Slater-Hammel, A. T. (1960). Reliability, accuracy, and refractoriness of a transit reaction. *Research Quarterly, 31,* 217–228.

Smith, W. M., and Bowen, K. F. (1980). The effects of delayed and displaced visual feedback on motor control. *Journal of Motor Behavior, 12,* 91–101.

Smoll, F. L. (1972). Effects of precision of information feedback upon acquisition of a motor skill. *Research Quarterly, 43,* 489–493.

Smyth, M. M., and Marriott, A. M. (1982). Vision and proprioception in simple catching. *Journal of Motor Behavior, 14,* 143–152.

Smyth, M. M., and Pendleton, L. R. (1990). Space and movement in working memory. *Quarterly Journal of Experimental Psychology, 42A,* 291–304.

Smyth, M. M., and Silvers, G. (1987). Functions of vision in the control of handwriting. *Acta Psychologica, 65,* 47–64.

Smyth, M. M., and Wing, A. (1984). *The psychology of human movement.* London: Academic Press.

Southard, D., and Higgins, T. (1987). Changing movement patterns: Effects of demonstration and practice. *Research Quarterly for Exercise and Sport, 58,* 77–80.

Sparrow, W. A. (1983). The efficiency of skilled performance. *Journal of Motor Behavior, 15,* 237–261.

Sparrow, W. A., and Irizarry-Lopez, V. M. (1987). Mechanical efficiency and metabolic cost as measures of learning a novel gross motor task. *Journal of Motor Behavior, 19,* 240–264.

Spence, K. W. (1958). A theory of emotionally based drive and its relation to performance in simple learning situations. *American Psychologist, 13,* 131–141.

Spielberger, C. D. (1966). Theory and research on anxiety. In C. D. Spielberger (Ed.), *Anxiety and behavior* (pp. 3–20). New York: Academic Press.

Spray, J. A. (1986). Absolute error revisited: An accuracy measure in disguise. *Journal of Motor Behavior, 18,* 225–238.

Starkes, J. L., Deakin, J. M., Lindley, S., and Crisp, F. (1987). Motor versus verbal recall of ballet sequences by young expert dancers. *Journal of Sport Psychology, 9,* 222–230.

Staum, M. J. (1983). Music and rhythmic stimuli in the rehabilitation of gait disorders. *Journal of Music Therapy, 20,* 69–87.

Ste.-Marie, D. M. and Lee, T. D. (1991). Prior processing effects of gymnastic judging. *Journal of Experimental Psychology: Learning, Memory, and Cognition, 17,* 126–136.

Stelmach, G. E. (1969). Prior positioning responses as a factor in short-term retention of a simple motor response. *Journal of Experimental Psychology, 81,* 523–526.

Stelmach, G. E. (1970). Learning and response consistency with augmented feedback. *Ergonomics, 13,* 421–425.

Stelmach, G. E., and Larish, D. D. (1980). Egocentric referents in human limb orientations. In G. E. Stelmach and J. Requin (Eds.), *Tutorials in motor behavior* (pp. 167–184). Amsterdam: North-Holland.

Summers, J. J. (1975). The role of timing in motor program representation. *Journal of Motor Behavior, 7,* 229–242.

Swinnen, S. P. (1990). Interpolated activities during the knowledge of results delay and post-knowledge of results interval: Effects of performance and learning. *Journal of Experimental Psychology: Learning, Memory, and Cognition, 16,* 692–705.

Swinnen, S. P., Schmidt, R. A., Nicholson, D. E., and Shapiro, D. C. (1990). Information feedback for skill acquisition: Instantaneous knowledge of results degrades learning. *Journal of Experimental Psychology: Learning, Memory, and Cognition, 16,* 706–716.

Swinnen, S. P., and Walter, C. B. (1988). Constraints in coordinating limb movements. In A. M. Colley and J. R. Beech (Eds.), *Cognition and action in skilled behavior* (pp. 127–143). Amsterdam: Elsevier.

Swinnen, S. P., Walter, C. B., Pauwels, J. M., Meugens, P. F., and Beirinckx, M. B. (1991). The dissociation of interlimb constraints. *Human Performance, 3,* 187–215.

Taub, E., and Berman, A. J. (1963). Avoidance conditioning in the absence of relevant proprioceptive and exteroceptive feedback. *Journal of Comparative and Physiological Psychology, 56,* 1012–1016.

Taub, E., and Berman, A. J. (1968). Movement and learning in the absence of sensory feedback. In S. J. Freedman (Ed.), *The neuropsychology of spatially oriented behavior* (pp. 173–192). Homewood, IL: Dorsey Press.

Taylor, H. G., and Heilman, K. M. (1980). Left-hemisphere motor dominance in righthanders. *Cortex, 16,* 587–603.

Teichner, W. H. (1954). Recent studies of simple reaction time. *Psychological Bulletin, 51,* 128–149.

Teichner, W. H., and Krebs, M. J. (1974). Laws of visual choice reaction time. *Psychological Review, 81,* 75–98.

Tenenbaum, G., Pinchas, S., Elbaz, G., Bar-Eli, M., and Weinberg, R. (1991). Effect of goal proximity and goal specificity on muscular endurance performance: A replication and extension. *Journal of Sport & Exercise Psychology, 13,* 174–187.

Thomas, J. R., and Halliwell, W. (1976). Individual differences in motor skill acquisition. *Journal of Motor Behavior, 8,* 89–100.

Thomas, J. R., Pierce, C., and Ridsdale, S. (1977). Age differences in children's ability to model motor behavior. *Research Quarterly, 48,* 592–597.

Thomas, J. R., Thomas, K. T., Lee, A. M., Testerman, E., and Ashy, M. (1983). Age differences in the use of strategy for recall of movement in a large scale environment. *Research Quarterly for Exercise and Sport, 54,* 264–272.

Thomson, J. A. (1983). Is continuous visual monitoring necessary in visually guided locomotion? *Journal of Experimental Psychology: Human Perception and Performance, 9,* 427–443.

Thorndike, E. L. (1914). *Educational psychology: Briefer course.* New York: Columbia University Press.

Titchener, E. B. (1908). *Lectures on the elementary psychology of feeling and attention.* New York: Macmillan.

Tolman, E. C. (1932). *Purposive behavior in animals and man.* New York: Appleton-Century-Crofts.

Treisman, A. (1969). Strategies and models of selective attention. *Psychological Review, 76,* 282–289.

Treisman, A. (1971). Shifting attention between the ears. *Quarterly Journal of Experimental Psychology, 23,* 157–167.

Treisman, A. (1988). Features and objects: The fourteenth Bartlett Memorial Lecture. *Quarterly Journal of Experimental Psychology, 40A,* 201–237.

Treisman, A., and Gelade, G. (1980). A feature integration theory of attention. *Cognitive Psychology, 12,* 97–136.

Trowbridge, M. H., and Cason, H. (1932). An experimental study of Thorndike's theory of learning. *Journal of General Psychology, 7,* 245–258.

Trussell, E. (1965). Prediction of success in a motor skill on the basis of early learning achievement. *Research Quarterly, 39,* 342–347.

Tubbs, M. E. (1986). Goal setting: A meta-analytic examination of the empirical evidence. *Journal of Applied Psychology, 71,* 474–483.

Tulving, E. (1985). How many memory systems are there? *American Psychologist, 40,* 385–398.

Tulving, E., and Thomson, D. M. (1973). Encoding specificity and retrieval processes in episodic memory. *Psychological Review, 80,* 352–373.

Turvey, M. T. (1977). Preliminaries to a theory of action with reference to vision. In R. Shaw and J. Bransford (Eds.), *Perceiving, acting, and knowing* (pp. 211–265). Hillsdale, NJ: Erlbaum.

Turvey, M. T. (1990). Coordination. *American Psychologist, 45,* 938–953.

Twitmeyer, E. M. (1931). Visual guidance in motor learning. *American Journal of Psychology, 43,* 165–187.

van Galen, G. P. (1991). Handwriting: Issues for a psychomotor theory. *Human Movement Science, 10,* 165–191.

Van Gyn, G. H., Wenger, H. A., and Gaul, C. A. (1990). Imagery as a method of enhancing transfer from training to performance. *Journal of Sport & Exercise Psychology, 12,* 366–375.

Vealey, R. (1986). Conceptualization of sport-confidence and competitive orientation: Preliminary investigation and instrument development. *Journal of Sport Psychology, 8,* 221–246.

Vickers, J. N. (1988). Knowledge structure of expert-novice gymnasts. *Human Movement Science, 7,* 47–72.

Viviani, P., and Terzuolo, C. (1980). Space-time invariance in learned motor skills. In G. E. Stelmach (Ed.), *Tutorials in motor behavior* (pp. 525–533). Amsterdam: North-Holland.

von Hofsten, C. (1987). Catching. In H. Heuer and A. F. Sanders (Eds.), *Perspectives on perception and action* (pp. 33–46). Hillsdale, NJ: Erlbaum.

Vorro, J., Wilson, F. R., and Dainis, A. (1978). Multivariate analysis of biomechanical profiles for the coracobrachialis and biceps brachii (caput breve) muscles in humans. *Ergonomics, 21,* 407–418.

Wachtel, P. L. (1967). Conceptions of broad or narrow attention. *Psychological Bulletin, 68,* 417–429.

Wadman, W. J., Dernier van der Gon, J. J., Geuze, R. H., and Mol, C. R. (1979). Control of fast goal-directed arm movements. *Journal of Human Movement Studies, 5,* 3–17.

Wallace, S. A. (1977). The coding of location: A test of the target hypothesis. *Journal of Motor Behavior, 9,* 157–169.

Wallace, S. A., and Hagler, R. W. (1979). Knowledge of performance and the learning of a closed motor skill. *Research Quarterly, 50,* 265–271.

Wallace, S. A., and Weeks, D. L. (1988). Temporal constraints in the control of prehensile movement. *Journal of Motor Behavior, 20,* 81–105.

Wann, J. P., and Nimmo-Smith, I. (1990). Evidence against relative timing in handwriting. *Quarterly Journal of Experimental Psychology, 42A,* 105–119.

Warren, W. H., Jr. (1987). An ecological conception of action. *European Journal of Cognitive Psychology, 7,* 199–203.

Warren, W. H., Jr., Young, D. S., and Lee, D. N. (1986). Visual control of step length during running over irregular terrain. *Journal of Experimental Psychology: Human Perception and Performance, 12,* 259–266.

Weinberg, D. R., Guy, D. E., and Tupper, R. W. (1964). Variations of post-feedback interval in simple motor learning. *Journal of Experimental Psychology, 67,* 98–99.

Weinberg, R., Fowler, C., Jackson, A., Bagnall, J., and Bruya, L. (1991). Effect of goal difficulty on motor performance: A replication across tasks and subjects. *Journal of Sport & Exercise Psychology, 13,* 160–173.

Weir, D. J., Stein, J. F., and Miall, R. C. (1989). Cues and control strategies in visually guided tracking. *Journal of Motor Behavior, 21,* 185–206.

Weir, P. L., and Leavitt, J. L. (1990). The effects of model's skill level and model's knowledge of results on the acquisition of an aiming task. *Human Movement Science, 9,* 369–383.

Weir, P. L., Mackenzie, C. L., Marteniuk, R. G., and Cargoe, S. L. (1991). Is object texture a constraint on human prehension?: Kinematic evidence. *Journal of Motor Behavior, 23,* 205–210.

Welford, A. T. (1952). The psychological refractory period and the timing of high-speed performance—a review and a theory. *British Journal of Psychology, 43,* 2–19.

Welford, A. T. (1967). Single channel operations in the brain. *Acta Psychologica, 27,* 5–22.

Welford, A. T. (1968). *Fundamentals of skill.* London: Methuen.

Whiting, H. T. A., Bijlard, M. J., and den Brinker, B. P. L. M. (1987). The effect of the availability of a dynamic model on the acquisition of a complex cyclical action. *Quarterly Journal of Experimental Psychology, 39A,* 43–59.

Whiting, H. T. A., Gill, E. B., and Stephenson, J. M. (1970). Critical time intervals for taking in-flight information in a ball-catching task. *Ergonomics, 13,* 265–272.

Whiting, H. T. A., Savelsbergh, G. J. P., and Faber, C. M. (1988). Catch questions and incomplete answers. In A. M. Colley and J. R. Beech (Eds.), *Cognition and action in skilled behavior* (pp. 257–271). Amsterdam: North-Holland.

Wickens, C. D. (1980). The structure of processing resources. In R. Nickerson (Ed.), *Attention and performance VII* (pp. 239–257). Hillsdale, NJ: Erlbaum.

Wickens, C. D. (1984). Processing resources in attention. In R. Parasuraman and D. R. Davies (Eds.), *Varieties of attention* (pp. 63–102). Orlando, FL: Academic Press.

Wickens, C. D., Sandry, D. L., and Vidulich, M. (1983). Compatibility and resource competition between modalities of input, control processing, and output: Testing a model of complex performance. *Human Factors, 25,* 227–248.

Wickens, D. D. (1970). Encoding categories of words: An empirical approach to meaning. *Psychological Review, 77,* 1–15.

Wickstrom, R. L. (1958). Comparative study of methodologies for teaching gymnastics and tumbling stunts. *Research Quarterly, 29,* 109–115.

Wightman, D. C. and Lintern, G. (1985). Part-task training strategies for tracking and manual control. *Human Factors, 27,* 267–283.

Wilberg, R. B., and Girard, N. C. (1977). A further investigation into the serial position curve for short-term motor memory. *Proceedings of the IX Canadian Psychomotor Learning and Sport Psychology Symposium* (pp. 241–247). Banff, Alberta, Canada.

Wilberg, R. B., and Salmela, J. (1973). Information load and response consistency in sequential short-term motor memory. *Perceptual and Motor Skills, 37,* 23–29.

Wilkinson, R. T. (1963). Interaction of noise with knowledge of results and sleep deprivation. *Journal of Experimental Psychology, 66,* 332–337.

Williams, J. G., and McCririe, N. (1988). Control of arm and fingers during ball catching. *Journal of Human Movement Studies, 14,* 241–247.

Winstein, C. J., and Schmidt, R. A. (1990). Reduced frequency of knowledge of results enhances motor skill learning. *Journal of Experimental Psychology: Learning, Memory, and Cognition, 16,* 677–691.

Winther, K. T., and Thomas, J. R. (1981). Developmental differences in children's labeling of movement. *Journal of Motor Behavior, 13,* 77–90.

Wolf, S. L. (1983). Electromyographic biofeedback applications to stroke patients: A critical review. *Physical Therapy, 63,* 1448–1455.

Wood, C. A., and Ging, C. A. (1991). The role of interference and task similarity on the acquisition, retention, and transfer of simple motor skills. *Research Quarterly for Exercise and Sport, 62,* 18–26.

Woodrow, H. (1914). The measurement of attention. *Psychological Monographs* (No. 76).

Woodworth, R. S., and Schlosberg, H. (1954). *Experimental psychology* (2nd ed.). New York: Holt, Rinehart, & Winston.

Wrisberg, C. A. (1991). A field test of the effect of contextual variety during skill acquisition. *Journal of Teaching Physical Education, 11,* 21–30.

Wrisberg, C. A., Hardy, C. J., and Beitel, P. A. (1982). Stimulus velocity and movement distance as determiners of movement velocity and coincident timing accuracy. *Human Factors, 24,* 599–608.

Wrisberg, C. A., and Ragsdale, M. R. (1979). Further tests of Schmidt's schema theory: Development of a schema rule for a coincident timing task. *Journal of Motor Behavior, 11,* 159–166.

Wrisberg, C. A., and Shea, C. H. (1978). Shifts in attention demands and motor program utilization during motor learning. *Journal of Motor Behavior, 10,* 149–158.

Yerkes, R. M., and Dodson, J. D. (1908). The relation of strength of stimulus to rapidity of habit-formation. *Journal of Comparative Neurology and Psychology, 18,* 459–482.

Young, D. E., Magill, R. A., Schmidt, R. A., and Shapiro, D. C. (1988). *Motor programs as control structures for reversal movements: An examination of rapid movements and unexpected perturbations.* Paper presented at the annual meeting of the North American Society for the Psychology of Sport and Physical Activity, Knoxville, Tennessee.

Zelaznik, H. N. (1977). Transfer in rapid timing tasks: An examination of the role of variability of practice. In D. M. Landers and R. W. Christina (Eds.), *Psychology of motor behavior and sport* (Vol. 1, pp. 36–43). Champaign, IL: Human Kinetics.

Zelaznik, H. N., and Franz, E. (1990). Stimulus-response compatibility and the programming of motor activity: Pitfalls and possible new directions. In R. Proctor and T. G. Reeve (Eds.), *Stimulus-response compatibility: An integrated perspective* (pp. 279–295). Amsterdam: North-Holland.

Zelaznik, H. N., Hawkins, B., and Kisselburgh, L. (1983). Rapid visual feedback processing in single-aiming movements. *Journal of Motor Behavior, 15,* 217–236.

CREDITS

Chapter One

Figures 1.1–1 and 1.1–2: Data from A. M. Gentile, J. R. Higgins, E. A. Miller, and B. M. Rosen, "The Structure of Motor Tasks." in *Mouvement,* 1975, 7:11–28. **Figure 1.2–5:** From R. G. Marteniuk and S. K. E. Romanow, "Human Movement Organization and Learning as Revealed by Variability of Movement, Use of Kinematic Information, and Fourier Analysis." in R. A. Magill, (Ed.) *Memory and Control of Action.* Copyright © 1983 Elsevier/North-Holland, Amsterdam, The Netherlands. Reprinted by permission. **Figure 1.2–6:** From I. M. Franks, R. W. Wilberg, and G. J. Fishburne, "The Generation of Movement Patterns During the Acquisition of a Pursuit Tracking Task." in *Human Movement Science,* 1982, 1:251–272. Copyright © 1982 Elsevier/North-Holland, Amsterdam, The Netherlands. Reprinted by permission. **Figure 1.2–8:** From R. M. Enoka, R. M. Miller, and E. M.

Burgess, "Below Knee Amputee Running Gait." in *American Journal of Physical Medicine and Rehabilitation,* 61, 1978:70–78. Copyright © 1978 Williams & Wilkins Company, Baltimore, Maryland. Reprinted by permission. **Figure 1.2–9:** From B. A. Kay, "The Dimensionality of Movement Trajectories and the Degrees of Freedom Problem: A Tutorial." in *Human Movement Science,* 1988, 7:343–64. Copyright © 1988 Elsevier Science Publishers BV, Amsterdam. Reprinted by permission. **Figure 1.2–10:** From Wynne Lee, in *Journal of Motor Behavior,* 1980, 12:187. Reprinted by permission.

Chapter Two

Figure 2.1–4: From R. G. Marteniuk and S. K. E. Romanow, "Human Movement Organization and Learning as Revealed by Variability of Movement, Use of Kinematic Information, and Fourier Analysis." in R. A. Magill, (Ed.) *Memory and Control of Action.* Copyright © 1983 Elsevier/North-Holland, Amsterdam, The Netherlands. Reprinted by permission. **Figure 2.1–5:** From M. A. Godwin and R. A. Schmidt, "Muscular Fatigue and Discrete Motor Learning," in *Research Quarterly for Exercise and Sport,* 1971, Vol. 42, pp. 374–383. Copyright © 1971 American Alliance for Health, Physical Education, Recreation, and Dance. Reprinted by permission. **Figure 2.1–6:** From I. M. Franks and R. B. Wilberg, "The Generation of Movement Patterns During the Acquisition of a Pursuit Tracking Task." in *Human Movement Science,* 1982, 1:251–272. Copyright © 1982 Elsevier/North-Holland, Amsterdam, The Netherlands. Reprinted by permission. **Figure 2.2–2:** From R. A. Schmidt and J. L. White, "Evidence for an Error Correction Mechanism in Motor Skills: A Test of Adams' Closed-Loop Theory." in *Journal of Motor Behavior,* 1972, 4:143–152. Copyright © 1972 Heldref Publications, Inc., Washington, DC. Reprinted by permission. **Figure 2.2–3:**

From D. Southard and T. Higgins, "Changing Movement Patterns: Effects of Demonstration and Practice," in *Research Quarterly for Exercise and Sport,* 1987, Vol. 58, pp. 77–80. Copyright © 1987 American Alliance for Health, Physical Education, Recreation, and Dance. Reprinted by permission. **Figure 2.2–4:** From K. M. Newell and R. E. A. van Emmerik, "The Acquisition of Coordination: Preliminary Analysis of Learning to Write." in *Human Movement Science,* 1989, 8:17–32. Copyright © Elsevier Science Publishers BV, Amsterdam. Reprinted by permission. **Figure 2.3–1:** From D. Holding, "An Approximate Transfer Surface." in *Journal of Motor Behavior,* 1976, 8:1–9. Copyright © 1976 Heldref Publications, Inc., Washington, DC. Reprinted by permission.

Chapter Three

Figure 3.1–3: From A. Polit and E. Bizzi, in *Journal of Neurophysiology,* 1979, 42:fig. 1, p. 184. Copyright © by The American Physiological Society, Bethesda, Maryland. Reprinted by permission. **Figure 3.1–4:** Data from J. A. S. Kelso, K. G. Holt, and A. E. Flatt, "The Role of Proprioception in the Perception and Control of Human Movement: Toward a Theoretical Reassessment." in *Perception and Psychophysics,* 1980, 28:45–52. **Figure 3.1–5:** Data from R. A. Magill and S. Goode, "The Representation of Limb Position Information in Memory." in (Abstract). *Psychology of Motor Behavior and Sport–1982,* p. 43. Proccedings of the Annual Meeting of the North American Society for the Psychology of Sport and Physical Activity, College Park, Maryland. **Figure 3.2–1:** Data from T. G. Reeve, L. J. Mackey, and G. W. Fober, "Visual Dominance in the Cross-Modal Kinesthetic to Kinesthetic plus Visual Feedback Condition." in *Perceptual and Motor Skills,* 1986, 62:243–252. **Figure 3.2–3:** From W. M. Smith and K. F.

Bowen, "The Effects of Delayed and Delayed and Displaced Visual Feedback on Motor Control." in *Journal of Motor Behavior,* 1980, 12:91–101. Copyright © 1980 Heldref Publications, Inc., Washington, DC. Reprinted by permission of the author. **Figure 3.2–4:** From M. M. Smythe and G. Silvers, "Functions of Vision in the Control of Handwriting." in *Acta Physiologica,* 1987, 65:47–64. Copyright © 1987 Elsevier Science Publishers BV, Amsterdam. Reprinted by permission. **Figure 3.2–5:** From D. N. Lee, J. R. Lishman, and J. A. Thomson, "Regulation of Gait in Long Jumping." in *Journal of Experimental Psychology: Human Perception and Performance,* 1982, 8:448–459. Copyright 1982 American Psychological Association. Reprinted by permission. **Figure 3.2–7:** From C. A. Wrisberg, C. J. Hardy, and P. A. Beitel, "Stimulus Velocity and Movement Distance as Determiners of Movement Velocity and Coincident Timing Accuracy" in *Human Factors,* 1982, 24:604. Copyright © 1982 by the Human Factors Society, Inc., and reproduced by permission. **Figure 3.2–8:** From Whiting, H. T. A. "Acquiring Ball Skills." London: G. Bell & Sons Ltd., 1969. Reprinted by permission. Bell & Hyman Ltd., London. **Figure 3.2–9:** Data from M. G. Fischman and T. Schneider, "Skill Level, Vision, and Proprioception in Simple One-Hand Catching," in *Journal of Motor Behavior,* 1985, Vol. 17, pp. 219–229. **Figure 3.3–1:** Data from F. M. Henry and D. E. Rogers, "Increased Latency for Complicated Movements and the 'Memory Drum' Theory of Neuromotor Reactions." in *Research Quarterly,* 1960, 31:448–58. **Figure 3.3–3:** Data from A. T. Slater-Hammel, "Reliability, Accuracy, and Refractoriness of a Transit Reaction." in *Research Quarterly,* 1960, 31:217–18. **Figure 3.3–5:** From D. C. Shapiro, R. F. Zernicke, R. J. Gregor, and J. D. Diestel, "Evidence for Generalized Motor Programs Using Gait-Pattern Analysis." in *Journal of Motor Behavior,* 1966, 13:33–47. Copyright

© 1966 Heldref Publications, Inc., Washington, DC. Reprinted by permission. **Figure 3.3–6:** From J. A. S. Kelso and G. Schoner, "Self-Organization of Coordinative Movement Patterns." in *Human Movement Science,* 1988, 7:27–46. Copyright © 1988 Elsevier Science Publishers BV, Amsterdam. Reprinted by permission. **Figure 3.4–2:** Data from P. Dunham, Jr., "Effect of Practice Order on the Efficiency of Bilateral Skill Acquisition." in *Research Quarterly,* 1977, 48:284–87.

Chapter Four

Figure 4.1–4: Data from M. I. Posner and S. W. Keele, "Attention Demands of Movements," in *Proceedings of the 16th Congress of Applied Psychology,* 1969. **Figure 4.1–5:** From Y. Girouard, L. Laurencelle, and L. Proteau, "On the Nature of the Probe Reaction-Time Task to Uncover the Attentional Demands of Movement." in *Journal of Motor Behavior,* 1984, 16:442–459. Copyright © 1984 Heldref Publications, Inc., Washington, DC. Reprinted by permission. **Figure 4.1–6:** From J. Leavitt, "Cognitive Demands of Skating and Stickhandling in Ice Hockey" in *Canadian Journal of Applied Sport Science,* 1979, 4:46–55. Copyright © The Canadian Journal of Applied Sport Science, Windsor, Ontario, Canada. Reprinted by permission. **Figure 4.2–1:** From D. E. Norman, *Memory and Attention,* 2d ed. Copyright © 1976 John Wiley & Sons, Inc., New York. Reprinted by permission. **Figure 4.2–2:** From R. A. Magill, B. Schoenfelder-Zohdi, and K. G. Hall, *Further Evidence for Implicit Learning in a Complex Tracking Task.* Paper presented at the annual meeting of the Psychonomics Society, New Orleans, Louisiana. Copyright © 1990 R. A. Magill. Reprinted by permission. **Figure 4.2–3:** From M. J. Nissen and P. Bullemer, "Attentional Requirement by Learning: Evidence from Performance Measures." in *Cognitive Psychology,*

Quarterly Journal of Experimental Psychology, 39A, 43–59:1987. Copyright © 1987 Quarterly Journal of Experimental Psychology, Letchworth, Herts, England. Reprinted by permission. **Figure 7.2–1:** From D. Gopher, M. Weil, and D. Siegel, "Practice Under Changing Priorities: An Approach to the Training of Complex Skills." in *Acta Physiologica,* 1989, 71:147–177. Copyright © 1989 Elsevier Science Publishers BV, Amsterdam. Reprinted by permission. **Figure 7.3–2:** From E. A. Bilodeau, I. Bilodeau, and D. A. Schumsky, "Some Effects of Introducing and Withdrawing Knowledge of Results Early and Late in Practice" in *Journal of Experimental Psychology,* 1959, Vol. 58, 142–144. Copyright © 1959 American Psychological Association. Reprinted by permission of the author. **Figure 7.3–3:** From K. M. Newell, "Knowledge of Results and Motor Learning," in *Journal of Motor Behavior,* 1974, 6:235–244. Copyright © 1974 Heldref Publications, Inc., Washington, DC. Reprinted by permission. **Figure 7.3–4:** From G. E. Stelmach, "Learning and Response Consistence with Augmented Feedback" in *Ergonomics,* 1970, 13:421–425. Copyright © 1970 Taylor & Francis Ltd., London, England. Reprinted by permission. **Figure 7.3–5:** From S. A. Wallace and R. W. Hagler, "Knowledge of Performance and the Learning of a Closed Skill." Reprinted with permission from *Research Quarterly for Exercise and Sport,* Vol. 50, 1979, a publication of the American Alliance for Health, Physical Education, Recreation and Dance, 1900 Association Drive, Reston, VA 22091. **Figure 7.4–1:** From F. L. Smoll, "Effects of Precision of Information Feedback Upon Acquisition of a Motor Skill," in *Research Quarterly for Exercise and Sport,* 1972, Vol. 43, pp. 489–493. Copyright © 1972 American Alliance for Health, Physical Education, Recreation, and Dance. Reprinted by permission. **Figure 7.4–2:** From R. A. Magill and C. Wood, "Knowledge of

Results Precision as a Learning Variable in Motor Skill Acquisition," in *Research Quarterly for Exercise and Sport,* 1986, Vol. 57, pp. 170–173. Copyright © 1986 American Alliance for Health, Physical Education, Recreation, and Dance. Reprinted by permission. **Figure 7.4–3:** From M. J. Buekers, R. A. Magill, and K. G. Hall, "The Effect of Erroneous Knowledge of Results on Skill Acquisition When Augmented Information is Redundant." in *Quarterly Journal of Experimental Psychology,* 1992, 44(A):105–117. Reprinted by permission of The Experimental Psychology Society. **Figure 7.4–4:** Data from D. J. Selder and N. Del Rolan, "Knowledge of Performance, Skill Level and Performance on the Balance Beam." in *Canadian Journal of Applied Sport Sciences,* 1979, 4:226–229. **Figure 7.4–5:** From L. G. Lindahl, "Movement Analysis as an Industrial Training Method," in *Journal of Applied Psychology,* 1945, Vol. 29:420–436. Copyright © 1945 American Psychological Association. **Figure 7.4–6:** From K. M. Newell, J. T. Quinn, W. A. Sparrow, and C. B. Walter, "Kinematic Information Feedback for Learning a Rapid Arm Movement" in *Human Movement Science,* 1983, 2:255–269. Copyright © 1983 Elsevier/North-Holland, Amsterdam, The Netherlands. Reprinted by permission. **Figure 7.4–7:** From C. J. Winstein and R. A. Schmidt, "Reduced Frequency of Knowledge of Results Enhances Motor Skill Learning."in *Journal of Experimental Psychology: Learning, Memory and Cognition,* 1990, 16:677–691. Copyright 1990 American Psychological Association. Reprinted by permission. **Figure 7.4–8:** From R. A. Schmidt, D. E. Young, S. Swinnen, and D. E. Shapiro, "Summary Knowledge of Results for Skill Acquisition: Support for the Guidance Hypothesis." in *Journal of Experimental Psychology: Learning, Memory and Cognition,* 1989, 15:352–359. Copyright 1989 American Psychological Association.

Reprinted by permission. **Figure 7.5–2:** From S. Swinnen, R. A. Schmidt, D. E. Nicholson, and D. C. Shapiro, "Information Feedback for Skill Acquisition: Instantaneous Knowledge of Results Degrades Learning." in *Journal of Experimental Psychology: Learning, Memory and Cognition,* 1990, 16:706–716. Copyright 1990 American Psychological Association. Reprinted by permission. **Figure 7.5–3:** From J. Shea and G. Upton, "The Effects of Skill Acquisition of an Interpolated Motor Short-Term Memory Task During the KR-Delay Interval." in *Journal of Motor Behavior,* 1976, 8:277–281. Copyright © 1976 Heldref Publications, Inc., Washington, DC. Reprinted by permission. **Figure 7.5–4:** From J. C. Hogan and B. A. Yanowitz, "The Role of Verbal Estimates of Movement Error in Ballistic Skill Acquisition." in *Journal of Motor Behavior,* 1978, 10:133–138. Copyright © 1978 Heldref Publications, Inc., Washington, DC. Reprinted by permission. **Figure 7.5–5:** From S. P. Swinnin, "Interpolated Activities During the Knowledge-of-Results Delay and Post-Knowledge-of-Results Interval: Effects on Performance and Learning." in *Journal of Experimental Psychology: Learning, Memory and Cognition,* 1990, 16:692–705. Copyright 1990 American Psychological Association. Reprinted by permission. **Figure 7.5–6:** From T. D. Lee and R. A. Magill, "Activity During the Post-KR Interval: Effects Upon Performance or Learning" in *Research Quarterly for Exercise and Sport,* 1983, Vol. 54, pp. 340–345. Copyright © 1983 American Alliance for Health, Physical Education, Recreation, and Dance. Reprinted by permission.

■

Chapter Eight

Figure 8.1–1: From C. Wrisberg and M. R. Ragsdale, "Further Tests of Schmidt's Schema Theory: Development of a Schema Rule for a Coincident Timing Task." in *Journal*

NAME INDEX

SUBJECT INDEX

métro 4
for AQA Vert
Cahier d'exercices
Specification A

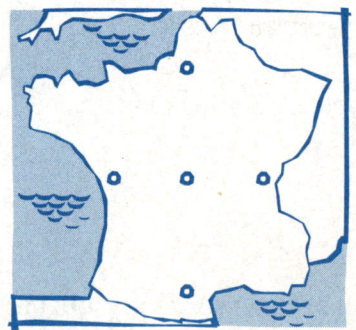

D1742315

Stéphanie Fleet

Heinemann

Heinemann Educational Publishers,
Halley Court, Jordan Hill, Oxford, OX2 8EJ

Part of Harcourt Education

Heinemann is the registered trademark of
Harcourt Education Limited

© Stéphanie Fleet 2001

First published 2001

06 05 04 03
10 9 8 7 6 5

A catalogue record is available for this book from the
British Library on request.

ISBN 0 435 37281 5

Designed and typeset by Ken Vail Graphic Design

Illustrated by Graham-Cameron Illustration (Sarah
Wimperis), Celia Hart and Sylvie Poggio Artists
Agency (James Arnold, Nick Duffy).

Printed and bound in UK by Thomson Litho Ltd

Every effort has been made to contact copyright
holders of material reproduced in this book. Any
omissions will be rectified in subsequent printings if
notice is given to the publishers.

1 *Au collège*

1 **Faites correspondre les expressions aux images.**
Match the sentences to the pictures.

1

a J'ai oublié mon cahier.

2

b Excusez-moi d'être en retard.

3

c J'ai oublié ma trousse.

4

d Je peux aller aux toilettes?

5

e Peut-on utiliser un dictionnaire?

6

f Comment dit-on 'monkey' en français?

7

g Pardon? Pouvez-vous répéter, s'il vous plaît?

8

h Je ne comprends pas.

2 **Lisez ce que Géraldine a écrit sur son trajet au collège
et complétez le résumé.**
*Read what Géraldine wrote about her journey to school and fill
the gaps in the summary.*

> Mon collège est à 4 kilomètres de chez moi. Le lundi,
> mon père me conduit en voiture parce qu'il
> commence à 9 heures. Le reste de la semaine, je
> prends ma bicyclette. C'est bon pour la forme mais
> c'est pénible quand il pleut. Le samedi matin, je
> prends le car scolaire car je passe le week-end chez
> ma grand-mère qui habite au centre-ville.

grand-mère	samedi	voiture	elle	vélo	centre-ville

Géraldine va en _____ au collège le lundi. Du mardi au vendredi,

elle y va à _____ . Le _____ elle y va en car parce qu'après

les cours _____ va au _____ chez sa _____ .

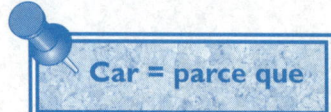

3 **Pour chacune de ces phrases, écrivez son contraire en changeant les mots soulignés.**
Write the opposite of these sentences by changing the underlined words.

Exemple: <u>Je n'aime pas</u> l'anglais car c'est <u>ennuyeux</u>.
<u>J'aime</u> l'anglais car c'est <u>intéressant</u>.

a <u>Je n'aime pas</u> les maths parce que c'est <u>inutile</u>.

_____

b <u>J'aime</u> le dessin parce que c'est <u>intéressant</u>.

_____

c <u>J'aime</u> la géographie car <u>je n'ai pas</u> beaucoup de devoirs.

_____

d <u>Je n'aime pas</u> l'histoire car la prof est <u>horrible</u>.

_____

e <u>J'aime</u> le français parce que c'est <u>facile</u>.

_____

> **Car = parce que**

> utile
> horrible
> difficile
> facile
> inutile
> intéressant
> sympa
> ennuyeux

4a **Regardez l'emploi du temps de Medhi et indiquez si les phrases sont vraies *(V)*,
fausses *(F)* ou si ce n'est pas dans le texte *(?)*.**
Look at Medhi's timetable and write V *next to the true sentences,* F *for the false ones and* ? *if it's not in the text.*

	lundi	*mardi*	*mercredi*	*jeudi*	*vendredi*	*samedi*
8–9	français	anglais	histoire-géo	physique	italien	français
9–10	français	techno	italien	informatique	étude	instruction civique
10–11	anglais	techno	français	dessin	anglais	histoire-géo
11–12	biologie	étude	français	dessin	maths	
2–3	maths	latin		musique	latin	
3–4	maths	italien		maths	EPS	
4–5	histoire-géo			latin	EPS	

a Medhi a trois heures d'étude le mardi. _____

b Il a sport le vendredi. _____

c Il mange à la cantine. _____

d Il n'a pas cours le mercredi après-midi. _____

e Il finit à quatre heures le lundi. _____

f Il étudie trois langues étrangères. _____

g Il ne va pas au collège le dimanche. _____

h Il va à deux clubs. _____

> **(heure d')étude = study period**

> The 'not in the text' sentences are a bit tricky. Whether the fact is correct or incorrect is irrelevant. What matters is: is it mentioned in the text or not? There are two 'not in the text' sentences in this exercise.

Métro 4 for AQA © Heinemann Educational 2001

4b Corrigez les phrases qui ne sont pas correctes.

Correct the wrong sentences.

_____

_____

5 *Le forum du collège*

Séverine

> Moi je trouve qu'il nous faut un nouveau gymnase et que l'équipement est dangereux, c'est nul!

Karim

> Au collège, les profs ne sont pas assez sévères. Les élèves font les imbéciles en classe. Quelle jungle!

Sélima

> Trop, c'est trop! Trois heures hier soir à mon bureau pour mes devoirs de français et je n'ai pas encore commencé mes révisions d'histoire. C'est la panique!

Marie-Thérèse

> À mon avis, il faut créer un groupe de discussion pour parler de tous les problèmes importants comme le racket, la drogue, la pression des autres, etc.

Qui dit quoi? Ecrivez le nom de la bonne personne à côté des phrases. Choisissez entre Séverine, Karim, Marie-Thérèse et Sélima.

Who says what? Write the names next to the sentences.

a Les professeurs doivent être plus stricts. _____

b On a trop de devoirs. _____

c Il faut discuter pour résoudre* certaines questions. _____

d Nos cours d'EPS ne se passent pas dans de bonnes conditions. _____

> résoudre = to resolve

6 **Lisez l'e-mail que Nico a envoyé à sa correspondante écossaise sur les vacances scolaires et dites si les phrases à la page 5 sont vraies *(V)*, fausses *(F)* ou si ce n'est pas dans le texte *(?)*.**

Read the e-mail Nico sent to his Scottish penfriend and write whether the sentences on page 5 are true (V), false (F) or not in the text (?).

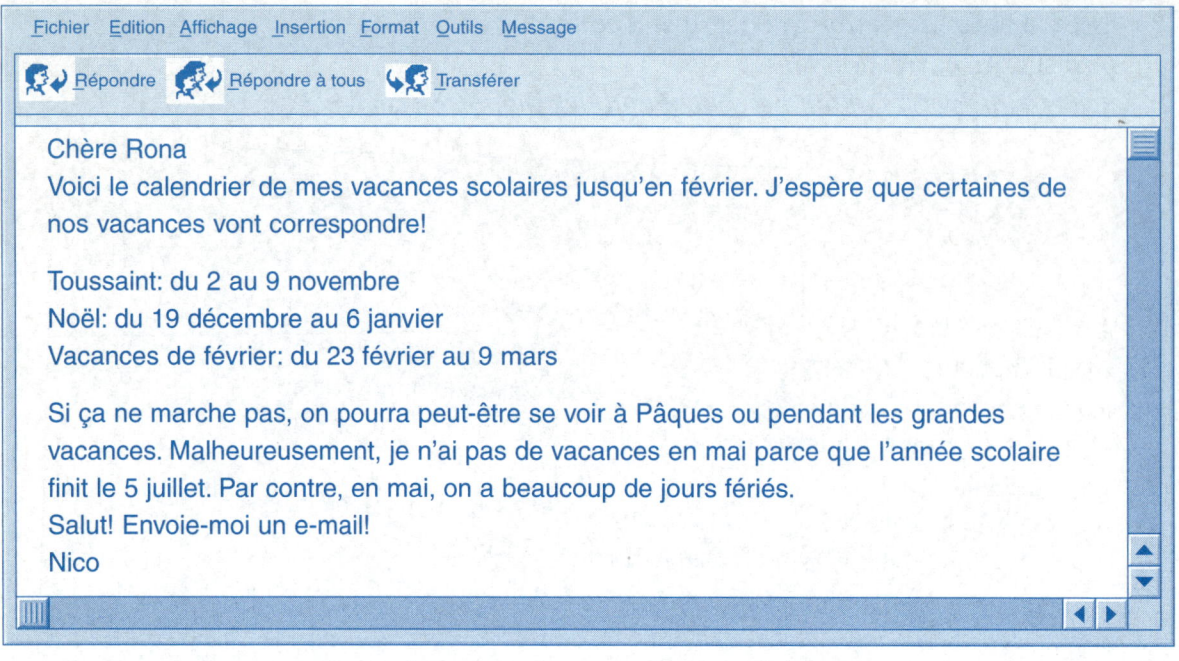

Chère Rona
Voici le calendrier de mes vacances scolaires jusqu'en février. J'espère que certaines de nos vacances vont correspondre!

Toussaint: du 2 au 9 novembre
Noël: du 19 décembre au 6 janvier
Vacances de février: du 23 février au 9 mars

Si ça ne marche pas, on pourra peut-être se voir à Pâques ou pendant les grandes vacances. Malheureusement, je n'ai pas de vacances en mai parce que l'année scolaire finit le 5 juillet. Par contre, en mai, on a beaucoup de jours fériés.
Salut! Envoie-moi un e-mail!
Nico

a   Nico a une semaine de vacances de Toussaint en novembre. _____

b   Nico a quinze jours de vacances en février. _____

c   Les vacances de Pâques durent plus de deux semaines. _____

d   Nico a une semaine en mai. _____

e   Il y a beaucoup de vacances en automne. _____

f   L'année scolaire se termine en juillet. _____

7   Que pensent ces jeunes du collège? Lisez et dites si les phrases sont positives *(P)*, négatives *(N)* ou positives et négatives *(P/N)*.
What do these young people think about school? Read the comments and say whether they are positive (P), *negative* (N) *or positive and negative* (P/N).

a   Quel travail! Tant de devoirs, c'est trop! Je préfère le weekend! _____

b   Il faut avoir de bons résultats pour trouver du travail plus tard. L'éducation est très importante. _____

c   C'est bien pour les copains mais je suis nulle en tout … C'est dur, le collège … _____

d   J'ai horreur de me lever tôt. J'aime pourtant presque tous mes cours. _____

e   Je n'ai le temps de rien faire: adieu les sorties, le sport et la rigolade! C'est affreux! _____

Métro 4 for AQA © Heinemann Educational 2001

**8a Lisez la lettre de Céline qui décrit son collège et cochez les
phrases qui correspondent.**
Read Céline's letter about her school and tick the correct sentences.

Chère Sally,

Je t'envoie quelques lignes pour te décrire mon collège. Mon C.E.S. s'appelle Arthur Rimbaud. Il y a 900 élèves (des garçons et des filles) et environ* 50 professeurs. Le collège est assez petit mais il y a beaucoup de clubs, comme le club photo ou le club théâtre. Moi, je vais au club de hand-ball le lundi. Ça, c'est passionnant! L'année prochaine je vais aller au club de théâtre avec mon amie Magali.

Pendant l'heure du déjeuner je mange à la cantine et je bavarde avec mes amis. Quelquefois je joue au football. J'adore le football.

Au collège je porte un jean, un sweat et des baskets. Je trouve ça pratique. J'aimerais porter des bijoux mais ça c'est interdit.

Le semaine dernière on a fait un voyage scolaire. On est allé à Nantes. On a fait le tour de la ville et on a visité un musée. C'etait assez intéressant.

Amitiés

Céline

*environ = *around*

1 **Le collège de Céline est**
   a pour garçons.
   b pour filles.
   c une école mixte.

2 **Il y a**
   a à peu près cinquante professeurs.
   b moins de cinquante professeurs.
   c plus de cinquante professeurs.

3 **Céline va au club**
   a de hand-ball.
   b philatélie.
   c de poésie.

4 **Céline**
   a ne mange pas à midi.
   b mange à la maison.
   c mange au collège.

5 **Céline aimerait porter**
   a un uniforme.
   b des bijoux.
   c un chapeau.

6 **La semaine dernière Céline est allée**
   a en vacances.
   b au cinéma.
   c au musée.

8b Utilisez la lettre pour écrire votre propre lettre sur votre collège.
Écrivez environ 90 mots.
Now use this letter to help you write your own about your school. Write about 90 words.

_____

_____

_____

_____

_____

_____

_____

_____

_____

_____

_____

> *Use everything you have done in class so far. Don't forget to include some opinions and use as many accurate tenses as you can. You could also use the answers to the speaking questions.*

9 Marielle a écrit ses résolutions pour sa nouvelle année scolaire. Faites correspondre les phrases en français aux phrases en anglais.
Marielle has written down her resolutions for the new school year. Match the French sentences to the English ones.

a Je vais réviser tous les soirs.	**1**	I will pass my exams.
b Je vais passer mes examens.	**2**	I will go to university.
c Je vais réussir mes examens.	**3**	I will sit my exams.
d Je vais passer les grandes vacances à l'étranger.	**4**	I will revise every night.
e Je vais aller à l'université.	**5**	I will spend the summer abroad.

10 Et vous, qu'allez-vous faire après le collège? Écrivez environ 30 mots.
What about you? What will you do after school? Write about 30 words.

_____

_____

_____

_____

_____

_____

> *Remember to use the near future: aller + the infinitive; it is much easier that way!*

Métro 4 for AQA © Heinemann Educational 2001

Grammaire

1 Choisissez le bon mot.
Choose the correct word.

masc	fem	pl
un	une	des
le	la	les
mon	ma	mes

a (Le/Les) cours commencent à huit heures et finissent à six heures.

b (Mon/Ma) matière préférée est (les/la) géographie.

c Je n'aime pas beaucoup (le/la) français ni (les/la) maths.

d Je prends (le/des) car tous (le/les) matins.

e (Mes/Mon) copains s'appellent Olivier et Franck.

f Nous mangeons (un/des) sandwichs à (la/les) cantine.

2 Aller + infinitif. Écrivez des phrases grammaticalement correctes. Puis traduisez les phrases en anglais.
'Going to'. Write sentences that are grammatically correct. Then translate the sentences into English.

a	Tu	allons	faire tes devoirs.
b	Sophie	vont	écouter son nouveau CD.
c	Je	va	aller à mon cours de français.
d	Nous	vas	aller à notre cours de géo.
e	Ils	allez	manger leurs sandwichs.
f	Jean et moi	va	aller à notre leçon de musique.
g	Elles	vont	aller à leur club de danse.
h	Marc	allons	aller à son cours de piano.
i	Agnès et toi	vais	aller à votre cours de maths.
j	On	va	manger au restaurant.

Rappel

je vais
tu vas
il va
elle va
on va
nous allons
vous allez
ils vont
elles vont

À l'oral

1   À quel collège vas-tu?

_____

2   Tu commences et tu finis à quelle heure?

_____

3   Il y a combien d'élèves et combien de professeurs?

_____

4   Quelles matières est-ce que tu fais?

_____

_____

5   Quelle est ta matière préférée et pourquoi?

_____

6   Quelles sont les qualités d'un bon professeur?

_____

7   Décris ton uniforme.

_____

_____

8   Qu'est-ce que tu penses de ton collège?

_____

9   Ce matin, comment es-tu arrivé(e) au collège?

_____

10 Qu'est-ce qu'on n'a pas le droit de faire à ton collège?

_____

_____

11 Qu'est-ce que tu vas faire après les examens?

_____

_____

12 Parle-moi du collège en France.

_____

Métro 4 for AQA © Heinemann Educational 2001

2 Chez moi

1 Vocabulaire: Remplissez les blancs dans ce tableau.

Fill in the blanks in the grid.

masculin	féminin	anglais	masculin	féminin	anglais
frère	sœur	brother/sister	demi-frère	d__-_____	
père	m___	father/mother	beau-frère	b____-_____	brother-in-law/sister-in-law
g_____	fille	boy/girl	petit ami	p_____-____	
oncle	t____	uncle/aunt	copain	c_____	boy/girl friend
g____-____	g____-____	granddad/grandmother	f ___	f ____	son/daughter
beau-père	b____-____	stepfather/stepmother	n____	nièce	
beau-fils	belle-fille		c_____	c_____	cousin

2 Remplissez cette fiche en donnant vos détails personnels.

Fill in this form with your own details.

1 Nom: _____

2 Prénom: _____

3 Date de naissance: _____

4 Domicile: _____

5 Nationalité: _____

6 Nombre de frères et sœurs: _____

7 Qualités: _____

8 Profession: _____

9 Passe-temps: _____

3a Maintenant écrivez une fiche d'identité pour une personnalité de votre choix. Vous pouvez inventer les détails!

Now fill in the form for a celebrity of your choice. You can invent some of the details!

1 Nom: _____

2 Prénom: _____

3 Date de naissance: _____

Métro 4 for AQA © Heinemann Educational 2001

4 Domicile: _____

5 Nationalité: _____

6 Nombre de frères et sœurs: _____

7 Qualités: _____

8 Profession: _____

9 Passe-temps: _____

3b Maintenant complétez le texte.
Now complete the text.

Il/Elle s'appelle _____. Il/Elle est né(e) le _____.
(nationality)

Il/Elle habite _____ et il/elle est _____. Il/Elle
                    (brothers and sisters)   (qualities)

_____.

Il/Elle est _____. Sa profession c'est _____. Ses

passe-temps sont _____ et _____.

4 Mettez les mots de chaque phrase dans le bon ordre.
Put the words in the right order.

a quatre blanches j'ai souris _____

b j'ai noirs oiseaux deux _____

c as animal un tu ? _____

d n'ai je d'animal pas _____

e perdu chien j'ai mon _____

5 Écrivez ces dates en lettres.
Write these dates in letters.

mars	avril	janvier	juillet
septembre	juin	novembre	mai
août	décembre	février	octobre

Exemple: 14/06   Le quatorze juin

a 05/02 _____

b 15/03 _____

c 01/05 _____

d 12/10 _____

e 27/07 _____

Métro 4 for AQA © Heinemann Educational 2001

6a Trouvez le sens des mots que vous ne connaissez pas dans le dictionnaire et cochez les adjectifs qui vous correspondent.
Find the meaning of the words you do not know in a dictionary and tick the adjectives that describe you.

> sympa   honnête   bavard(e)   marrant(e)   travailleur(euse)
>
> intelligent(e)   égoïste   casse-pieds   sage   poli(e)   bête   équilibré(e)

6b Écrivez maintenant environ 30 mots sur vous en utilisant les expressions suivantes.
Now write about 30 words about yourself using the following expressions.

un peu *(a little)*   plutôt *(rather)*
très *(very)*   assez *(quite)*

> *Don't forget to use the feminine form if you are female.*
> *Try to include some negative sentences (Je ne suis pas/pas du tout/pas très/ni… ni)*
> *I am not/not at all/not very/neither… nor).*

Je suis _____

_____

_____

7 Qu'est-ce qui est important pour vous chez un copain ou une copine? Classez ces mots par ordre d'importance (classez-les de 1 à 10, 1 étant le plus important).
What is important to you in a friend? Put the words in order 1 to 10 (1 being the most important).

Le copain/la copine idéal(e) est …

- intelligent(e) _____
- amusant(e) _____
- beau/belle _____

- sincère _____
- poli(e) _____
- sportif(ve) _____

- optimiste _____
- travailleur(euse) _____
- plein(e) de vie _____
- équilibré(e) _____

8 Écrivez une lettre à votre correspondant(e) français(e). Voici les questions qu'il/elle vous a posées. Pour chaque question, faites des phrases complètes.
Write a letter to your French penfriend. Here are the questions he/she asked you. For each question, answer in full sentences.

- As-tu un animal à la maison?
- Aimes-tu les animaux? Lesquels?
- Tu t'entends bien avec tes parents? (Je m'entends bien/mal avec …)
- As-tu des frères et des sœurs?
- Qui est ton/ta meilleur(e) ami(e)? Pourquoi? (Jenny est ma meilleure amie parce qu'elle est … et ….)

Métro 4 for AQA © Heinemann Educational 2001

9a Des jeunes ont écrit à un magazine pour parler de leurs problèmes. Lisez les lettres.

Four young people have written to a magazine to speak about their problems. Read the letters.

2

Chère Irma,

Moi mon problème c'est que je ne m'entends pas avec mes parents. Ils ne me comprennent pas et on se dispute toujours! Je ne peux jamais sortir. Cela m'agace!* Est-ce que je dois quitter la maison?

Alexandre

Irma, aide-moi, je t'en prie!

Ma copine m'a quitté il y a un mois. Je ne peux pas vivre sans elle!

Xavier

3

Bonjour Irma,

Voilà, mon problème c'est que j'ai trop de boutons. Je me trouve très moche et je pense que je n'aurai jamais de petit ami! Je suis désespérée.

Aide-moi!
Josiane

Chère Irma,

Au secours! Tous les ans, c'est la même chose: j'ai peur au mois de juin au moment des examens. As-tu un remède contre ceci?

Sylvie

4

*cela m'agace = ça m'agace: it annoys me

C'est qui? Écrivez le bon nom à côté de chaque phrase.
Who is it? Write the correct name beside each sentence.

A = Mes parents et moi, nous ne nous entendons pas bien. _____

B = Je suis très malheureux. _____

C = J'ai un visage horrible. _____

D = J'ai horreur des tests. _____

Pouvez-vous expliquer le problème de ces jeunes en anglais?
Can you explain these young people's problems in English?

Josiane: _____

Alexandre: _____

Xavier: _____

Sylvie: _____

9b Lisez les réponses d'Irma et trouvez à qui elles correspondent.
Read Irma's answers and find who they are for.

a Parles-en à tes profs. Pour _____

b Discutes-en avec elle. Pour _____

c Achète un bon produit en pharmacie. Pour _____

d Partir n'est pas une solution! Pour _____

Métro 4 for AQA © Heinemann Educational 2001

10 Vous avez trouvé ce message sur un site. Pouvez-vous répondre aux questions en français?

You found this message on a website. Can you answer the questions in French?
(You don't need to answer in full sentences.)

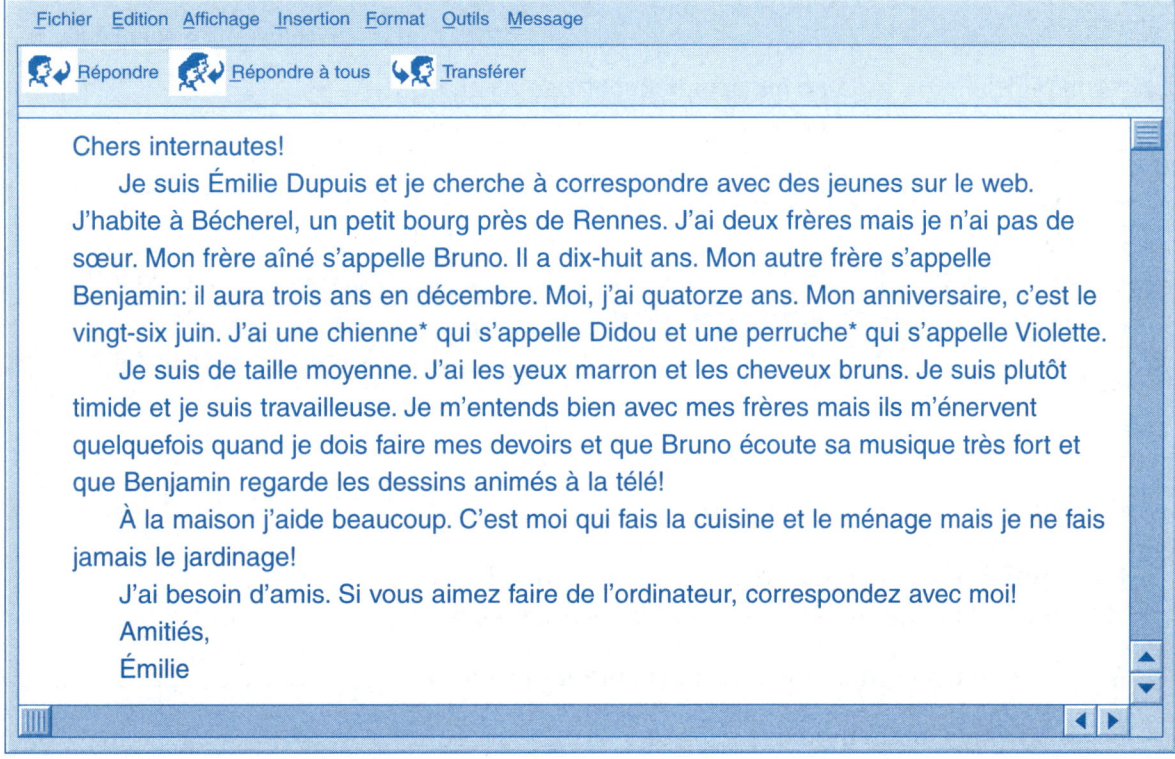

a Où habite Émilie? _____

b A-t-elle des frères ou des sœurs? _____

c A-t-elle des animaux? _____

d C'est quand son anniversaire? _____

e Comment est-elle physiquement? _____

f Quelle sorte de personne est-elle? _____

g Est-ce qu'elle s'entend bien avec ses frères? _____

h Que fait-elle pour aider à la maison? _____

chienne = (female) dog

perruche = budgerigar

Rappel

Elle a = *She has*
Elle est = *She is*
Elle fait = *She does*

11 Lisez ces lettres et remplissez la grille pour ces jeunes à la page 15.
Read these letters and fill in the grid about these young people on page 15.

> Moi, le mariage, je trouve que c'est une bonne chose. Je m'entends bien avec mes parents. Ils sont heureux et moi aussi. Il y a une bonne ambiance à la maison.
>
> Thibault

> Depuis que mes parents sont divorcés, je ne crois plus au mariage. Pour moi, c'est impossible! Mes parents sont sympa et j'habite avec mon père.
>
> Nadia

> Mes parents et moi, ce n'est pas génial … Ils critiquent toujours ce que je porte et ils m'énervent quand ils se disputent. Plus tard je ne veux pas me marier. J'aimerais vivre seule*.
>
> Martina

*seul = *alone*

> Le mariage, ça a des bons et des mauvais côtés. D'une part*, c'est positif parce que c'est une preuve* d'amour mais d'autre part* les gens peuvent changer et devenir méchants*. Mes parents sont cools et on s'entend tous bien dans la famille même si ma sœur est parfois un peu pénible!
>
> Élie

*d'une part = *on the one hand*   *preuve = *test*
*d'autre part = *on the other hand*   *méchant = *unkind*

A

Le mariage, c'est	positif ☺	négatif ☹	positif et négatif 😐
Thibault			
Nadia			
Martina			
Élie			

B

Relation avec les parents	✔ (bonne)	✗ (mauvaise)
Thibault		
Nadia		
Martina		
Élie		

12 Reliez les phrases aux images.
Link up the sentences to the pictures.

a Je déteste passer l'aspirateur.   **1**

b Débarrasser la table, ça va.   **2**

c J'ai horreur de sortir la poubelle.   **3**

d J'adore faire du jardinage.   **4**

e Je ne fais jamais les courses.   **5**

f Je lave souvent la voiture.   **6**

Métro 4 for AQA © Heinemann Educational 2001

Grammaire

1   En utilisant les verbes suivants, remplissez les blancs.
Fill in the blanks using the following verbs.

Être *(to be)*	**Avoir** *(to have)*	**Faire** *(to do)*
Je suis	J'ai	Je fais
Tu es	Tu as	Tu fais
Il/elle/on est	Il/elle/on a	Il/elle/on fait
Nous sommes	Nous avons	Nous faisons
Vous êtes	Vous avez	Vous faites
Ils/elles sont	Ils/elles ont	Ils/elles font

a Elodie _____ casse-pieds. (être)

b Mes parents _____ trois enfants. (avoir)

c Nous _____ le ménage le week-end. (faire)

d Elles _____ la vaisselle dans la cuisine. (faire)

e Tu _____ un animal? (avoir)

f Vous _____ les yeux bleus. (avoir)

g Vous _____ jolie. (être)

h Je _____ petit. (être)

i Marc _____ une barbe. (avoir)

j Je _____ mes devoirs. (faire)

2   Comment dit-on?
How do you say?

a I do _____.

b I am _____.

c I have _____.

d He does _____.

e We are _____.

f They have _____.

3   Regardez la grille ci-dessous et trouvez les bons accords.
Look at the table below and find the right agreements.

Mon père (masc sing) **est amusant.** **Ma mère** (fem sing) **est amusant<u>e</u>.**	**Mes frères** (masc pl) **sont amusant<u>s</u>.** **Mes sœurs** (fem pl) **sont amusant<u>es</u>.**

a Ma mère est _____. (grand)

b Ma tante est _____. (petit)

c Mon oncle est _____. (mince)

d Mes parents sont _____. (grand)

e Mes nièces sont _____. (équilibré)

f Mes frères sont _____. (bête)

g Ma demi-sœur est _____. (bavard)

h Mes grands-parents sont _____. (sévère)

i Ma femme est _____. (aimable)

j Mes cousines sont _____. (sage)

À l'oral

1 Comment t'appelles-tu?

_____

2 Quelle est la date de ton anniversaire?

_____

> Don't just answer 'Oui' or 'Non' – whenever possible add an explanation.

3 As-tu des frères ou des sœurs?

_____

4 Décris-le/la/les.

_____

_____

5 As-tu un animal à la maison?

_____

6 Décris-toi physiquement.

_____

7 Quelle sorte de personne es-tu?

_____

8 Décris une copine/un copain.

_____

_____

9 Explique pourquoi c'est une bonne copine/un bon copain.

_____

10 Qu'est-ce que tu fais pour aider à la maison?

_____

_____

11 Tu t'entends bien avec tes parents? Pourquoi/pourquoi pas?

_____

12 Que penses-tu du mariage?

_____

Métro 4 for AQA © Heinemann Educational 2001

3 *Temps libre*

1 Reliez les célébrités à leur passe-temps favori.
Link up the celebrities to their favourite hobby.

a	Jonathan Edwards	**1**	J'aime jouer à l'ordinateur.
b	Zinedine Zidane	**2**	J'aime la lecture.
c	Céline Dion	**3**	J'aime la pêche.
d	Le Prince Charles	**4**	J'aime l'athlétisme.
e	Pingu	**5**	J'aime le cinéma.
f	Bill Gates	**6**	J'aime la musique et chanter.
g	Tom Hanks	**7**	J'aime l'équitation.
h	William Shakespeare	**8**	J'aime jouer au football.

2 Faites un petit dessin pour chacune de ces activités.
Make a little drawing for each of these activities.

- l'équitation
- les jeux-vidéo
- la philatélie
- le patin à roulettes
- la randonnée
- la natation
- le cyclisme
- la lecture
- le footing
- la pêche

3 Lisez l'information ci-dessous et cochez les cases si la personne fait cette activité et faites une croix si elle ne la fait pas.
Read the information below and tick the boxes if the person does the activity and put a cross if he/she doesn't.

Rémi: *Moi, je fais de l'équitation tous les dimanches et je joue tous les jours aux boules avec mes amis. Je ne sors jamais en boîte mais je vais au cinéma deux fois par mois.*

Louise: Je ne vais jamais en boîte ni* au cinéma. Par contre je fais souvent de l'équitation, tous les soirs. Je joue parfois aux boules.

Édouard: *Je vais au ciné deux fois par mois, en boîte tous les samedis. J'ai horreur des boules! L'équitation, par contre, c'est un vrai plaisir.*

Barbara: Moi, je ne fais rien … Ah si: je vais au cinéma une fois par semaine!

*ni = *nor*

	Rémi	Louise	Édouard	Barbara
Équitation				
Boules				
Boîte				
Cinéma				

4 **Lisez le dépliant et répondez aux questions en français.**
Read the leaflet and answer the questions in French. (You don't need to write full sentences.)

a À quelle heure commence le match de foot? _____

b Quel jour peut-on écouter de la poésie*? _____

c Combien de sports peut-on faire cette semaine-là? _____

d Combien coûte l'entrée au match de football? _____

e Le tournoi de ping-pong est-il pour les adultes seulement? _____

*poésie = *poetry*

Lundi 18/11	**Mardi 19/11**	**Mercredi 20/11**	**Jeudi 21/11**	**Vendredi 22/11**	**Week-end du 23–24/11**
Match de football. Salle polyvalente. 14h30. 20€ l'entrée	Course de vélo. 15h00	Concours de pêche moins de 18 ans. 10h30	Tournoi de ping-pong. Toutes catégories	Séance de lecture de poèmes du monde entier. Bibliothèque municipale 17h00	Week-end de voile 200€ tout compris. Retour dimanche 20h00

5 **Lisez les dialogues suivants et remplissez les blancs ci-dessous. Quelle est leur réponse (oui ou non) et pourquoi? Suivez l'exemple.**
Read the following dialogues and fill in the gaps in the sentences below. What is their answer (yes or no) and why? Follow the example.

Exemple: *C'est Franck à l'appareil. Il y a une soirée de danse folklorique, tu viens?*
        Certainement pas! Je suis nul en danse.
        Il dit <u>non</u> parce qu'il ne sait pas <u>danser</u>.

Dialogue 1:
Allô Karine, c'est Mylène!
Ah … Salut …
Tu veux venir au tournoi de patinage ce soir?
Ben je suis malade et il fait froid là-bas…
Tant pis!

Elle dit _____ parce qu'elle _____.

> **Les raisons**
> aime sortir
> a ses devoirs à faire
> est malade
> aime bien une fille particulière

Métro 4 for AQA © Heinemann Educational 2001

Dialogue 2:

Salut, Charles! Benjamin nous invite à sa boum, super non?

Vanessa y va?

Je crois que oui …

Alors bien sûr que je viens!

Il dit _____ parce qu'il _____.

Dialogue 3:

Virginie? C'est Claire!

Ça va?

Oui, j'aimerais aller au festival de la BD. Qu'en penses-tu?

Désolée, je dois faire mes devoirs.

Elle dit _____ parce qu'elle _____.

Dialogue 4:

Amélie, tu es toujours d'accord pour aller en boîte?

Evidemment! Tu sais que j'adore sortir. On se retrouve où?

Devant l'arrêt de bus. 21 heures précises!

Elle dit _____ parce qu'elle _____.

6 **C'est à quelle heure? Écrivez l'heure en suivant le modèle.**
What time is it on? Write the times following the example.

Exemple: Deux heures quinze. 2.15

a   Six heures _____

b   Dix-neuf heures trente _____

c   Une heure et demie _____

d   Dix-sept heures cinquante _____

e   Midi moins dix _____

f   Deux heures moins le quart _____

g   Onze heures cinq _____

h   Vingt-deux heures quatorze _____

i   Quatre heures vingt-cinq _____

j   Six heures moins cinq _____

7 **Maintenant écrivez l'heure en français.**
Now write the times in French.

a   23:14 _____

b   half past eight _____

c   midday _____

d   15:45 _____

e   quarter past four _____

8 Reliez les questions aux réponses.
Match the questions to their answers.

a Qu'est-ce qu'on passe au cinéma?

b Qui sont les acteurs principaux?

c C'est en version originale?

d C'est bien?

e C'est à quelle heure la séance?

f On se retrouve où?

g Tu veux aller au cinéma?

1 Oui, c'est génial!

2 Oui. je veux bien.

3 Devant le cinéma.

4 Le film commence à 19h45.

5 *Le 5ème élément,* un film de science-fiction.

6 Bruce Willis et Milla Jovovitch.

7 Non, c'est en version française.

9 Laissez un message sur le répondeur de votre copain.
Leave a message on your friend's answering machine.

Say: Do you want to go to the cinema on Wednesday?
    The film starts at 7.30pm.
    We are meeting in front of the station at 6.00pm.

Salut, Jojo, c'est moi! _____

_____

_____

′10 Lisez ce que Nouria a écrit sur ses activités et réécrivez le passage pour vous en changeant les phrases soulignées.
Read what Nouria wrote about her hobbies and re-write the passage about yourself changing the underlined sentences.

> With 'le soir', 'le week-end' and 'pendant les vacances' use the present tense to express something you usually do. With 'hier' and 'le week-end dernier' use the perfect tense to express an action in the past.

Le soir, en général <u>je fais mes devoirs et je téléphone à mes copines</u>.

Le week-end, <u>je fais de la danse dans un club et je fais des courses avec ma mère</u>.

Pendant les vacances <u>je reste à la maison et je lis mes bandes dessinées</u>.

Hier, <u>j'ai joué du piano et j'ai fait de la cuisine</u>.

Le week-end dernier <u>je suis allée à la piscine avec ma copine Sylvie</u>.

_____

_____

_____

_____

Métro 4 for AQA © Heinemann Educational 2001

11 **Quelle est leur opinion sur le sport?**
What is their opinion on sport?

Amélie

J'adore tous les sports d'équipe sans exception.

Mon passe-temps préféré, c'est de regarder des matchs de foot; par contre jouer au foot, j'aime moins.

Yves

Flo

Ouria

Il y a un complexe sportif près de chez moi. C'est pratique pour garder la forme.

Je n'aime pas beaucoup l'exercice mais je fais quand même du footing pour ne pas grossir.

Si vous voulez mon avis, c'est fatigant et inutile.

Guillaume

	☺	😐	☹
Amélie			
Yves			
Ouria			
Guillaume			
Flo			

12a **Lisez la lettre de Victoire et cochez l'expression correspondante à la page 23.**
Read Victoire's letter and tick the correct sentence on page 23.

Chère Laura,

Merci pour ta lettre datée du 5 juin. Moi aussi je fais beaucoup de sport, on en fera ensemble quand tu viendras la semaine prochaine.

Le lundi soir je vais à mon club de hand-ball. Je suis dans la meilleure équipe* au collège et j'adore ça! Le mercredi je fais de l'aérobic; le cours dure trente-cinq minutes. Tu pourras m'accompagner, on s'y amuse bien! Le vendredi soir j'ai gymnastique. Les profs sont très sévères et exigeants, c'est dur!

Hier je suis allée à mon cours comme d'habitude. Je suis arrivée en retard et le prof était très en colère … En plus on ne peut pas bavarder, c'est barbant! Moi j'adore discuter et rire avec mes copines … Je crois que je vais changer de sport: que penses-tu du saut à l'élastique??? J'ai hâte de te voir. Téléphone-moi pour me dire à quelle heure tu arrives à la gare.

Gros bisous

Victoire

*meilleure équipe = *top team*

1 **Victoire fait du hand-ball**
  a le mercredi.
  b une fois par semaine.
  c tous les jours.

2 **Elle aime le hand-ball**
  a parce qu'elle est forte en hand-ball.
  b parce qu'elle adore le collège.
  c parce qu'elle joue le soir.

3 **Son prof de gymnastique est**
  a strict.
  b bavard.
  c barbant.

4 **Victoire est**
  a sévère.
  b paresseuse.
  c bavarde.

5 **Victoire veut**
  a changer de robe.
  b changer d'activité sportive.
  c faire du saut en hauteur.

12b Maintenant écrivez une lettre à un/une correspondant/e pour lui dire ce que vous faites pendant votre temps libre.
Now write a letter to a penfriend to tell him/her about your hobbies.

Vous devez:
● dire quels sont vos passe-temps préférés et pourquoi.
● dire quels sports vous pratiquez et quand.
● demander son opinion sur un sport. (Que penses-tu du/de la …?)

Try to include sentences in the present and the past tenses.
Le lundi: *on Mondays*
Le week-end: *at weekends*
Hier: *yesterday*
La semaine dernière: *last week*

Rappel

Present	Past
Je joue	J'ai joué
Je fais	J'ai fait
Je vais	Je suis allé(e)

Métro 4 for AQA © Heinemann Educational 2001

Grammaire

1 **Le passé composé: en utilisant les conjugaisons suivantes, traduisez les phrases.**
The perfect tense: translate the sentences using the tables below.

J'ai
Tu as
Il/elle/on a
Nous avons   regardé/joué/cuisiné/fait/lu/écouté/
Vous avez   nagé/duré/commencé/proposé/pratiqué
Ils/elles ont

Je suis
Tu es
Il/elle/on est
Nous sommes   allé/sorti/resté/venu
Vous êtes
Ils/elles sont

> *Don't forget to add the agreements to this part of the verb. Should you write: allé/allée/allés/allées? sorti/sortie/sortis/sorties?*

> *On Tuesday = mardi*

a He played football yesterday. _____ hier.

b We played basketball on Monday. _____ lundi.

c We went to the cinema. _____ au cinéma.

d I stayed at home last weekend. _____ le week-end dernier.

e Sophie and Annie came on Tuesday. _____ mardi.

f You listened to music. _____ de la musique.

g He went to a nightclub. _____ en boîte.

h The film lasted two hours. _____ deux heures.

2 **Faites deux colonnes: présent ou passé?**
Make two columns: present or past?

a Je n'aime pas nager.
b Tu veux venir au cinéma?
c J'ai fait de l'équitation.
d Je vais à la maison des jeunes.
e Elle a proposé à Simon d'aller en boîte.
f Nous avons lu un bon livre.
g J'aime faire du sport.
h J'ai fait du sport.
i J'écris des lettres.
j Je suis allé au parc d'attractions.

Présent	Passé

À l'oral

1 Quel est ton passe-temps préféré?

_____

_____

> Simple sentences are good, but try to develop your answers by giving more detailed responses.

2 Qu'est-ce que tu aimes faire le week-end?

_____

3 Quel est ton sport préféré?

_____

4 Où fais-tu ce sport?

_____

5 Quand fais-tu ce sport?

_____

6 Quelle sorte de musique aimes-tu?

_____

7 Qu'est-ce que tu aimes lire?

_____

8 Qu'est-ce que tu fais à la maison pour t'amuser?

_____

9 Qu'est-ce que tu fais avec tes amis pour t'amuser?

_____

10 Qu'est-ce que tu as fait le week-end dernier?

_____

11 Comment s'appelle le dernier film que tu as vu?

_____

12 Parle-moi de ce film.

_____

Métro 4 for AQA © Heinemann Educational 2001

4 Au boulot

1 Faites des lignes pour relier les trois: métier, dessin, location.
Draw lines to join the three: work, picture, place.

a policier		= dans un garage
b boulanger		= dans un bureau
c hôtesse de l'air		= au collège
d professeur		= dans le monde entier
e facteur		= dans une boulangerie
f infirmier		= au commissariat
g mécanicien		= à la poste
h secrétaire		= dans une ferme
i fermier		= au supermarché
j caissier		= dans un hôpital

2 Lisez l'information suivante et répondez aux questions.
Read the following information and answer the questions.

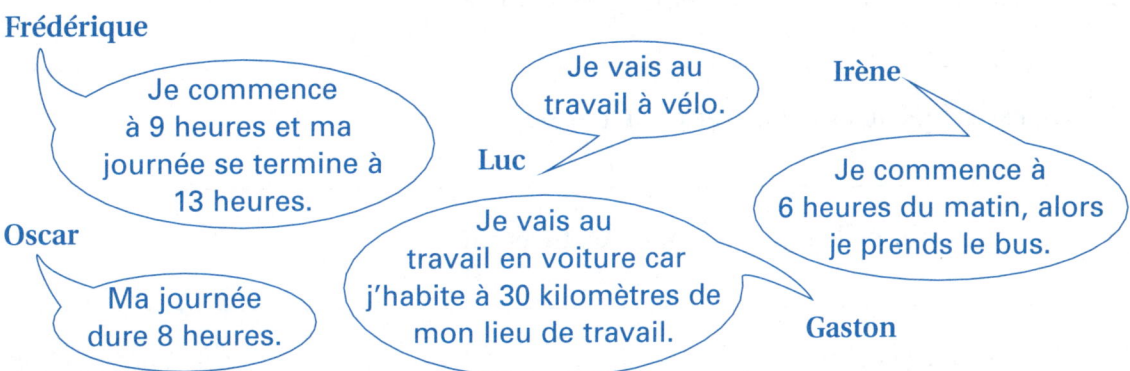

Frédérique
Je commence à 9 heures et ma journée se termine à 13 heures.

Luc
Je vais au travail à vélo.

Irène
Je commence à 6 heures du matin, alors je prends le bus.

Oscar
Ma journée dure 8 heures.

Gaston
Je vais au travail en voiture car j'habite à 30 kilomètres de mon lieu de travail.

Who …	Name
1 travels to work by bike?	
2 has a long journey to work?	
3 finishes at one o'clock?	
4 starts early?	
5 has a long day at work?	

3 **Christian en a marre!**
Voici la lettre qu'il a écrite à son patron pour lui annoncer sa démission. Pouvez-vous répondre aux questions en anglais?
Christian is fed up! Here is the letter he wrote to his boss to announce his resignation. Can you answer the questions in English?

balayer = to sweep

Cher Monsieur Dujardin,

Je vous écris pour vous annoncer ma démission à partir du 1er juillet de cette année. J'ai été très déçu par beaucoup de choses: le travail de serveur dans votre café est vraiment trop compliqué! Je dois servir les clients, laver et débarrasser les tables, donner l'addition, balayer*, faire la vaisselle, réparer le juke-box, jouer aux cartes et au baby-foot avec les clients et tout ça en même temps! En plus, c'est mal payé (cinq euros de l'heure, c'est ridicule!) et vous n'êtes jamais content!

Le café est à six kilomètres de chez moi et, à pied, c'est fatigant.

Je vous prie d'agréer, Monsieur, l'expression de mes sentiments distingués.

Christian Leduc

a When will Christian stop working? (1) _____

b What was his position? (1) _____

c Give five of the tasks he had to do. (5) _____

_____

_____

d What does he say about his pay? (1) _____

e What does he say about his boss? (1) _____

f How does he get to work? (1) _____

4 **En observant les réponses, trouvez les mots manquants dans les questions.**
Looking at the answers, find the missing words in the questions.

où	pourquoi	quand	combien	quelles	quel	comment	que

a _____ job as-tu? Je vends des journaux.

b _____ gagnes-tu? Je gagne €7 par heure.

c _____ travailles-tu? Je travaille dans une maison de la presse.

d _____ travailles-tu? Je travaille pour gagner de l'argent.

e _____ vas-tu à ton travail? J'y vais en bus.

f _____ sont tes heures de travail? Je travaille de 8h30 à 17h00.

g _____ prends-tu tes vacances? Je les prends en général en juillet.

h _____ penses-tu de ton travail? C'est fatigant mais passionnant.

Métro 4 for AQA © Heinemann Educational 2001

5 **Lisez la lettre de Samuel et trouvez les bonnes réponses ci-dessous.**
Read Samuel's letter and find the right answers beneath.

> Salut Jon,
>
>   Comment vas-tu? Moi, bof … Je suis énervé* parce que j'ai trop de devoirs à l'école. Je viens de terminer mon stage en entreprise, c'était génial! J'ai travaillé à la poste de ma ville. Je devais trier le courrier, répondre au téléphone et aider le facteur dans sa tournée. Distribuer les lettres, ça c'est amusant! Surtout que j'adore le vélo! Plus tard j'aimerais être facteur, pas pharmacien comme mes parents. J'aime travailler en plein air et j'aime le contact avec les gens.
>
>   En ce moment j'ai un petit job le week-end. Je fais du baby-sitting pour ma sœur le samedi soir. Elle a deux garçons qui sont très agréables. Je m'occupe d'eux de 18h à 23h. Je leur donne à manger et je leur lis une histoire au lit. Je gagne €5 par heure. Avec cet argent, je m'achète des timbres rares pour ma collection. Et toi, comment se passe ton stage en ce moment?
>
>   Écris-moi vite!
>
>   Samuel

*énervé = *annoyed*

1 Samuel est énervé à cause
a de son stage.
b de son travail au collège.
c de l'entreprise du stage.

2 Pendant son stage, Samuel devait
a aider le facteur à distribuer les lettres.
b travailler au guichet.
c téléphoner aux clients.

3 Le père de Samuel travaille
a dans une pharmacie.
b à la poste.
c en plein air.

4 Les deux passe-temps de Samuel sont
a la philatélie et le cyclisme.
b le vélo et la musique.
c les courses et la lecture.

5 Ses neveux sont
a amusants.
b méchants.
c sympa.

6 **Lisez les annonces suivantes et imaginez que vous avez plus de 18 ans. Écrivez une lettre de candidature selon le modèle à la page 29 (n'oubliez pas d'inclure votre CV).**
Read the following adverts. Imagine that you are over 18. Write an application letter following the example on page 29 (don't forget to include your CV).

ÉCOLE DE FORMATION CONTINUE

RECHERCHE
Professeur d'anglais

Contacter: EFC
Nantes
Tel: 02 35 58 69 46

Famille française aimerait recevoir pour un an

Jeune fille ou garçon au-pair
pour garder petite fille de 18 mois.

Écrire à: Julie et Franck Berg.
Tel: 01 36 47 69 45

VINS BORDELAIS
Établissements Médrac & Frères

Recherchent

Représentant
Régions sud/sud-ouest et région parisienne

Écrire aux: Vins Bordelais
Rue de la Haute Cloche
33000 Bordeaux

CURRICULUM VITAE

Nom:	Dusquesnois
Prénoms:	Christophe Pierre
Date de naissance:	18/12/1980
Nationalité:	française
Adresse:	20 rue des Marais
	59200 Tourcoing
Éducation:	Lycée Faidherbe, Lille
Matières étudiées:	maths, français, philosophie, anglais,
	histoire-géographie, allemand, économie
Expérience:	stage en entreprise, juin 2000
Loisirs:	équitation et lecture

Cher Monsieur/Chère Madame,

J'ai lu votre annonce avec grand intérêt au sujet du poste de (serveur). J'ai (19 ans) et je m'appelle (Christophe Dusquesnois). Je suis de nationalité (française). Je pense que je serais la personne idéale pour cet emploi car je suis (travailleur, agréable et organisé). J'aime (travailler avec les autres). J'ai déjà fait un stage (dans un restaurant). C'était (intéressant et motivant). Mes horaires étaient (de 9h à 17h). Je devais (servir les clients et préparer les sandwichs).

Veuillez trouver ci-joint mon CV.

Je vous prie d'agréer, Monsieur/Madame, l'expression de mes sentiments distingués.

Christophe Dusquesnois

7 Lisez le message et dites si les phrases sont vraies *(V)*, fausses *(F)* ou
si ce n'est pas dans le texte *(?)*.
Read the message and say if the sentences are true (V), *false* (F) *or not in the text* (?).

Facsimilé

À l'intention de Monsieur Lhermitte

Pouvez-vous s'il vous plaît me contacter? C'est assez urgent: nous devons
discuter du nouveau contrat avec une entreprise canadienne.
Voici mes différentes coordonnées:
Numéro personnel: 01 55 87 90 31
Numéro du bureau: 01 48 72 50 12
Numéro de portable: 06 99 36 19 35
Fax: 01 48 72 50 67
E-mail: jnasier@wanadoo.fr

---

a L'entreprise voudrait travailler avec le Canada. _____

b Le numéro de travail de Jacques Nasier est 01 48 72 50 12. _____

c Jacques Nasier est chef d'entreprise. _____

d On peut contacter Jacques Nasier sur deux autres numéros quand il n'est pas au
bureau. _____   .

8 Reliez les synonymes ou les expressions équivalentes.
Find the equivalents.

a	travail	**1**	Ne raccrochez pas.
b	passe-temps	**2**	Quand?
c	matière	**3**	compagnie
d	entreprise	**4**	retéléphoner
e	à l'appareil	**5**	métier
f	Ne quittez pas.	**6**	Qui est à l'appareil?
g	C'est de la part de qui?	**7**	policier
h	À quelle heure?	**8**	au téléphone
i	agent de police	**9**	loisir
j	rappeler	**10**	sujet

9 Stéphane a téléphoné à une radio locale pour discuter de son problème. Lisez ce qu'il a dit et répondez aux questions en anglais.

Stéphane phoned a local radio station to talk about his problem. Read what he said and answer the questions in English.

☎ Chers auditeurs, mon problème, c'est que je ne supporte plus la pression de mes études. Je fais des études de médecine et j'étudie depuis cinq ans. Mes parents veulent que je devienne docteur mais moi j'en ai assez* des examens tous les ans! En fait j'aurais bien aimé travailler dans le secteur du tourisme car j'adore les vacances et aller à l'étranger. Moi, ça ne m'intéresse pas de gagner de l'argent.

a How long has Stéphane been studying for? (1) _____

b What do his parents want him to be? (1) _____

c Why would he have liked to study tourism? (2) _____

_____

d What does he say he is not interested in? (1) _____

*j'en ai assez = *I've had enough*

10 Écrivez une lettre d'environ 90 mots à un copain/une copine en expliquant les points suivants:

Write a friend a letter of around 90 words including the following information:

- ce que vous voulez faire plus tard comme métier et pourquoi
- si vous voulez quitter le collège après les examens et pourquoi
- si vous aimeriez travailler à l'étranger – pourquoi?/pourquoi pas?

Je voudrais travailler	dehors/en plein air/à l'intérieur.
	dans un bureau/magasin/hôpital, etc.
	dans l'informatique/le commerce, etc.

… parce que je voudrais travailler avec les enfants/animaux/gens/ordinateurs, etc.

Je voudrais être coiffeur(euse)/maçon, etc.

Je voudrais quitter le collège parce que je voudrais gagner de l'argent.

Je (ne) voudrais (pas) travailler à l'étranger, etc.

… parce que je veux faire l'expérience d'un autre pays …

Métro 4 for AQA © Heinemann Educational 2001

Grammaire

1 **Ajoutez les bons mots et traduisez les phrases en anglais.**
Add the correct words and translate the sentences into English.

> **Le conditionnel**
> There are two ways of saying 'would like' = with aimer (to like) and with vouloir (to want).
>
> | vouloir | aimer |
> | --- | --- |
> | Je voudrais | J'aimerais |
> | Tu voudrais | Tu aimerais |
> | Il/elle/on voudrait | Il/elle/on aimerait |
> | Nous voudrions | Nous aimerions |
> | Vous voudriez | Vous aimeriez |
> | Ils/elles voudraient | Ils/elles aimeraient |

a Nous <u>voudrions</u> devenir médecins. (vouloir)

b Elle _____ être factrice. (aimer)

c Tu _____ travailler dans le secteur de l'alimentation. (vouloir)

d Vous _____ gagner beaucoup d'argent. (vouloir)

e Ils _____ voyager après les examens. (aimer)

2 **C'est quoi: présent, passé, futur ou conditionnel?**
What is it: present, past, future or conditional?

> Remember how the future tense is formed:
> **Je regarderai** (*I will watch*)
> **Tu regarderas**
> **Il/elle/on regardera**
> **Nous regarderons**
> **Vous regarderez**
> **Ils/elles regarderont**

a Je travaille dans un hôtel.
b Nous travaillerons dans un bureau.
c J'aimerais continuer mes études.
d J'ai réparé des voitures.
e Je vais au travail à vélo.
f Tu gagneras beaucoup d'argent.

3 **Faites attention aux verbes irréguliers. Apprenez ces conjugaisons et traduisez les phrases en français.**
Beware of irregular verbs! Learn the following forms and translate the sentences into French.

Aller *(to go)*	**Avoir** *(to have)*	**Être** *(to be)*
J'irai *(I will go)*	J'aurai *(I will have)*	Je serai *(I will be)*
Tu iras	Tu auras	Tu seras
Il/elle/on ira	Il/elle/on aura	Il/elle/on sera
Nous irons	Nous aurons	Nous serons
Vous irez	Vous aurez	Vous serez
Ils/elles iront	Ils/elles auront	Ils/elles seront

a They will have a job. _____ un emploi
b She will go by boat. _____ en bateau.
c I will be a pilot. _____ pilote.
d You will be a mechanic. _____ mécanicien.

À l'oral

For questions 1, 2, 3 and 9 use the present tense; for questions 4, 5, 6 and 7, use the perfect and imperfect tenses; for questions 8, 11 and 12, use the conditional; for question 10, use the near future (je vais + verb in the infinitive).

1 Que font tes parents?

_____

2 Tu as un job?

_____

3 Tu reçois de l'argent de poche?

_____

4 As-tu déjà fait un stage?

_____

5 Quelles étaient tes heures de travail?

_____

6 Qu'est-ce que tu as fait pendant ton stage?

_____

7 Comment étaient tes patrons?

_____

8 Quel métier aimerais-tu faire plus tard?

_____

9 Le chômage est-ce un problème dans ta région?

_____

10 Tu vas travailler pendant les grandes vacances?

_____

11 Aimerais-tu travailler à l'étranger?

_____

12 Tu voudrais te marier plus tard?

_____

5 Ma ville

1 Placez les bonnes villes et les bons symboles sur la carte.
Place the correct towns and symbols on the map.

1

2

3

4

5

a La ville au nord s'appelle Mignonbourg.

b La ville à l'est s'appelle Salleville.

c La ville au sud s'appelle Chezmoi.

d La ville à l'ouest s'appelle Polluville.

e La ville au centre, la capitale, s'appelle Proprette.

f Le château se situe à Chezmoi.

g Le magasin est à Polluville.

h La gare est à Proprette.

i Le syndicat d'initiative est à Mignonbourg.

j La piscine se situe à Salleville.

2 **Trouvez les images correspondantes.**
Find the matching pictures.

1 J'habite une maison au centre-ville.

2 Je vis dans un HLM dans la banlieue.

3 Nous habitons une ferme à la campagne.

4 Elles vivent dans un appartement dans la capitale.

5 Je vis dans une maisonnette dans un village.

6 J'habite dans une caravane près du collège.

7 J'habite sur une île sur la côte.

8 Il habite dans un village à la montagne.

9 Vous habitez dans une maison individuelle dans la banlieue.

10 Tu vis dans une maison mitoyenne au bord de la mer.

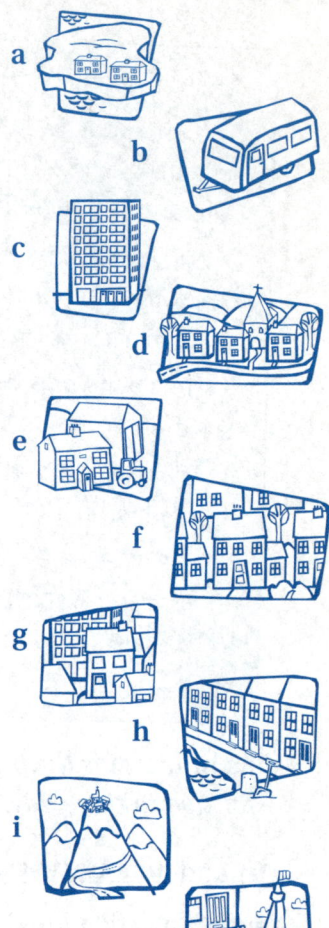

3 **Remplissez les blancs.**
Fill in the gaps.

> petits   Écosse   capitale   port   touristique
> nord   pays de Galles   jolie   historique

a Londres est la _____ de l'Angleterre. C'est une ville

extrêmement _____.

b Newcastle est une ville au _____ et Douvres est un

_____ au sud du pays.

c York est une _____ ville _____.

d En Angleterre il y a beaucoup de _____ villages pittoresques.

e Cardiff est au _____ et Glasgow en _____.

Métro 4 for AQA © Heinemann Educational 2001

4   **Lisez la lettre d'Arnaud et choisissez les bons mots.**
Read Arnaud's letter and choose the correct words.

> Chère Samia,
>
>   Merci pour ta lettre. Perpignan est très jolie. J'aimerais bien accepter ton invitation mais le train, c'est trop cher! Comme promis, je vais te décrire la ville du nord de la France où j'habite pour ton projet de géographie.
>
>   Lille se situe au nord, pas loin de la Belgique. C'est une grande métropole. Sa rivière s'appelle la Deûle. Il y a beaucoup de monuments historiques comme le Beffroi ou la Citadelle. Ce que j'aime le plus, c'est la vieille ville.
>
>   Je n'aime pas beaucoup la campagne environnante. Le centre-ville est super avec des rues piétonnes, des cinémas et plein de magasins!
>
>   Bientôt nous allons fêter la Saint-Nicolas, le 6 décembre. Il y a deux mois, le premier lundi de septembre, c'était la braderie*. Je me suis bien amusé! La braderie a duré 3 jours et 2 nuits!
>
>   À très bientôt!
>
>   Bisous
>
>   Arnaud

* La braderie *is the biggest car-boot sale in Europe. Lille is at a standstill for two to three days! It is regarded as one of the biggest local festivals.*

Arnaud (habite/voyage) à Lille, dans le (nord/sud) de la France. Lille est tout près de la (France/Belgique). Il y a (un/une) rivière qui s'appelle la Deûle. Le Beffroi et la Citadelle sont des (monuments/hôtels) de Lille. L'endroit (préféré/visité) d'Arnaud, c'est la vieille ville (historique/industrielle) il n'aime pas beaucoup la campagne environnante. À Lille on peut faire beaucoup de (sport/choses). Les deux fêtes mentionnées par Arnaud sont (Noël/la Saint-Nicolas) et (la braderie/Pâques).

5   **C'est où ?**
Where is it?

a	On peut y voir de nouveaux films.	**1**	la patinoire
b	On peut y acheter des choses pas chères.	**2**	le centre de recyclage
c	On peut y faire des courses.	**3**	le cinéma
d	On peut aller à la messe là.	**4**	la gare routière
e	On peut y jeter ses vieilles bouteilles.	**5**	le jardin public
f	On peut y trouver des autobus.	**6**	le marché
g	On peut y faire du patin à glace.	**7**	l'hypermarché
h	On peut y voir un match de foot.	**8**	le syndicat d'initiative
i	On peut y avoir des renseignements.	**9**	l'église
j	On peut s'y promener.	**10**	le stade

6 **À votre avis ces phrases sont-elles positives *(P)* ou négatives *(N)*?**
In your opinion, are these sentences positive (P) *or negative* (N)*?*

a À la campagne, c'est calme. _____

b Les villes sont souvent polluées. _____

c Il y a beaucoup d'embouteillages en ville. _____

d Il n'y a pas grand chose à faire à la campagne. _____

e On peut faire beaucoup de choses en ville. _____

f Il y a beaucoup de bruit en ville. _____

g Les rues sont sales en ville. _____

h Les oiseaux chantent plus à la campagne. _____

i Il y a plus de transports en commun en ville. _____

j On habite près de chez ses copains en ville. _____

7 **Remplissez la grille.**
Fill in the table.

Anne-Marie
Ma ville est très polluée à cause des voitures, des camions et des bus.

Zoé
J'habite un petit village. Il n'y a pas de bruit, c'est tranquille.

Boris
À Paris, il y a beaucoup de déchets par terre, c'est assez sale*.

Lise
À la campagne, on respire mieux, c'est moins pollué.

Iris
Moi ce que j'aime bien, c'est de voir des biches, des lapins et des oiseaux quand je me promène.

*sale = *dirty*

Who ...	Name
1 thinks there is too much litter in his/her town?	
2 lives in a quiet place?	
3 enjoys seeing the wildlife?	
4 thinks the air quality is better in the countryside?	
5 thinks transport is a problem in his/her town?	

8 **Écrivez un paragraphe sur là où vous habitez. Commencez vos phrases avec les expressions à la page 38.**
Write a paragraph about where you live. Begin your sentences with the phrases on page 38.

Métro 4 for AQA © Heinemann Educational 2001

J'habite _____.

C'est (un/une)(petit(e)/grand(e))(ville/village) (au nord/au sud/à l'ouest/à l'est)
(de l'Angleterre/de l'Écosse/du pays de Galles/de l'Irlande).

Il y a _____.

Il n'y a pas de _____.

Les avantages sont (que/qu') _____

_____.

Les inconvénients sont (que/qu') _____

_____.

9a **Complétez ces phrases en écrivant soit 'on protège l'environnement', soit 'on détruit l'environnement', puis traduisez les phrases en anglais.**
Finish off these sentences by writing either 'you protect the environment' or 'you destroy the environment', then translate them into English.

Exemple: En triant les déchets dans différentes poubelles, on protège l'environnement.

You protect the environment by sorting rubbish into separate bins.

a En jetant des déchets par terre, _____.

b En jetant des déchets au centre de recyclage, _____.

c En utilisant des bombes aérosol, _____.

d En conduisant en voiture, _____.

e En achetant du papier recyclé, _____.

f En faisant du vélo, _____.

g En construisant des autoroutes, _____.

h En plantant un arbre, _____.

i En utilisant beaucoup de sachets en plastique, _____.

j En éteignant la lumière quand on quitte une pièce, _____.

9b **Maintenant écrivez un petit paragraphe d'environ 30 mots sur l'environnement en français.**
Now write a paragraph of 30 words on the environment in French.

Dites:
- comment l'environnement est dans votre ville.
- comment on peut protéger l'environnement.

> **Use as many sentences from exercises 6, 7, 8, and 9 as you can.**

Métro 4 for AQA © Heinemann Educational 2001

Grammaire

1 Faites des phrases selon l'exemple.
Make sentences following the example.

Exemple:    ✓  ✗

Il y a une gare et des magasins. **Il n'y a pas de** bibliothèque.

a ✓ ✗ _____

_____

b ✓ ✗ _____

_____

c ✓ ✗ _____

_____

2 Mettez les adjectifs à la bonne place.
Put the adjectives in the right place.

> vieux hanté* petite
> longues blanche

*hanté = *haunted*

a J'habite dans une _____ maison _____ .

b Le _____ château est _____ .

c J'aime les _____ promenades.

> la maison (fem)
> le château (masc)
> les promenades (fem pl)

3 Écrivez *plus* ou *moins* aux bons endroits.
Write plus *(more) or* moins *(less) in the right places.*

a Les États-Unis sont _____ grands que la France. = *The United States is bigger than France.*

b Calais est _____ loin que Marseille. = *Calais is not as far as Marseille.*

c Le vélo, c'est _____ polluant! *Bikes do not pollute as much!*

4 Complétez ces phrases avec ne/n'aucun(e).
Complete these phrases with ne/n'aucun(e) *(no, not any).*

a Il _____ y a _____ magasin (masc) dans ce village. = *There is no shop in this village.*

b Il _____ célèbre _____ fête (fem). = *He does not celebrate any festivals.*

Métro 4 for AQA © Heinemann Educational 2001

À l'oral

> You will achieve a better grade if you expand your answers, using conjunctions such as car *(because)*, alors/donc *(so)*, mais *(but)* or tandis que *(while)*.

1 Où habites-tu?

_____

2 C'est où exactement?

_____

3 C'est à la campagne ou à la ville?

_____

4 Il y a combien d'habitants?

_____

5 Ta ville est jumelée avec une autre ville en Europe?

_____

6 Qu'est-ce qu'on peut faire là où tu habites?

_____

_____

7 Peux-tu décrire là où tu habites?

_____

_____

8 Quels sont ses avantages?

_____

9 Quels sont ses inconvénients?

_____

10 Qu'est-ce qu'il y aurait dans ta ville idéale?

_____

11 Aimerais-tu déménager? Pourquoi?

_____

12 Tu fais quelque chose pour la préservation de l'environnement?

_____

6 Aux magasins

1 Ça s'achète où?
Where do you buy this?

a du pain
b des gâteaux
c des légumes
d de la viande
e des timbres
f du parfum
g des cigarettes
h du saucisson
i des comprimés
j des bonbons

1 à la charcuterie
2 à l'épicerie
3 au tabac
4 à la parfumerie
5 à la confiserie
6 à la boulangerie
7 à la boucherie
8 à la pharmacie
9 à la poste
10 à la pâtisserie

2 C'est combien? Écrivez ces prix en mots.
How much is it? Write these prices in words.

Exemple: €25 = vingt-cinq euros
€13,20 = treize euros vingt
£3 = trois livres

a €2,70 _____

b €56,25 _____

c €150 _____

d £602 _____

e £90 _____

3 Vous organisez une boum. Écrivez une liste de ce qu'il faut acheter – au moins dix choses.
You are organising a party. Write a list of what you need to buy – at least ten things.

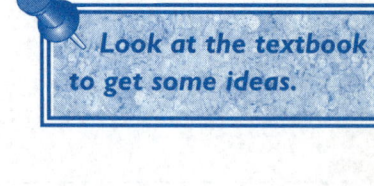

Look at the textbook to get some ideas.

_____

_____

_____

_____

_____

_____

_____

Métro 4 for AQA © Heinemann Educational 2001

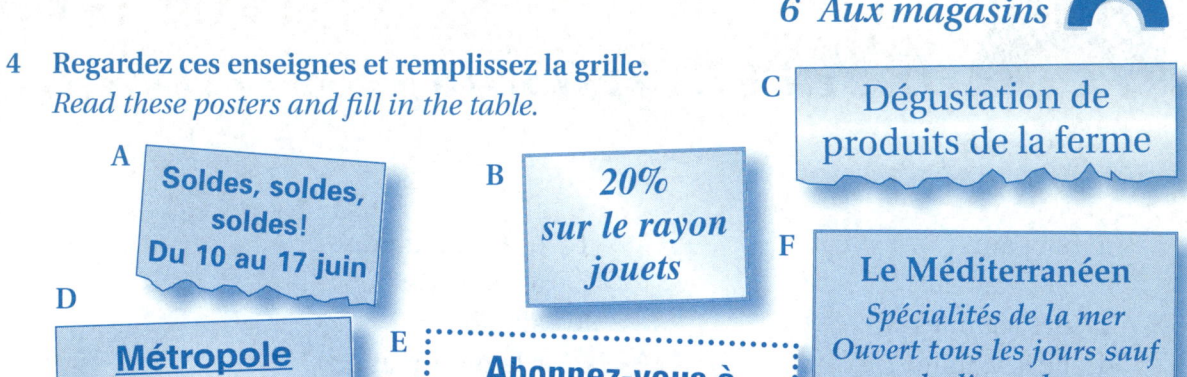

4 Regardez ces enseignes et remplissez la grille.
Read these posters and fill in the table.

A Soldes, soldes, soldes! Du 10 au 17 juin

B 20% sur le rayon jouets

C Dégustation de produits de la ferme

D **Métropole** **Grande surface** **Ouverte 7/7** **9h–23h**

E Abonnez-vous à *Ouistiti*, pour les jeunes de 10 à 15 ans

F Le Méditerranéen *Spécialités de la mer* *Ouvert tous les jours sauf le dimanche*

Which poster …	Écrivez A, B, C, D, E ou F.
1 tells you about a discount on toys?	
2 advertises a supermarket?	
3 invites you to subscribe to a magazine?	
4 offers a tasting session?	
5 is for a restaurant?	
6 announces a sale period?	

5 Écrivez ce qu'il y a dans le panier.
List what there is in the basket.

un litre de jus d'orange _____

_____

_____

_____

_____

_____

un paquet de

une boîte de

une bouteille de

une tranche de

500g de

Métro 4 for AQA © Heinemann Educational 2001

6 Vous avez reçu un texto de votre père sur votre portable: que devez-vous acheter?
Écrivez la liste en anglais.
You have received a text message from your dad: what do you have to buy? Write the list in English.

> N'OUBLIE PAS LES
> COURSES
> 2 BOUT. VIN BLANC/
> BISCUITS/ BŒUF/
> CÉRÉALES/CAFÉ/BIÈRE/
> 3 BAGUETTES/ POMMES
> DE TERRE/ CERISES/
> HARICOTS VERTS
> BISOUS PAPA

_____

_____

_____

_____

_____

_____

_____

7 Au rayon des vêtements. Mettez la conversation dans l'ordre.
In the clothes department. Put the conversation in the right order.

a En 45. _____

b Je peux vous aider, Monsieur? _____

c Elles me vont. Merci! C'est combien? _____

d Au revoir. _____

e Elles sont jolies mais trop petites. _____

f En quelle taille? _____

g Et celles-là? _____

h Voilà, Madame. Au revoir! _____

i Que pensez-vous de celles-ci? _____

j Je voudrais une paire de chaussures, s'il vous plaît. _____

k Cinquante euros. _____

8 Lisez ces publicités et remplissez la grille en anglais.
Read these adverts and fill in the grid in English.

sandales en cuir bleu marine, du 36 au 41 €50

gants violets en laine, du S au XL €18

pull noir en soie, du 1 au 3 €65

pantalon blanc en coton, du 36 au 42 €40

chemisier en viscose beige, du 40 au 46 **cent euros**

item	material	colour	sizes available	price

Métro 4 for AQA © Heinemann Educational 2001

9 **Répondez aux questions en anglais.**
Answer the questions in English.

chic *votre nouveau magasin* 9 rue Gambetta

Ouvert du lundi au samedi de 9h à 19h

Sous-sol
Parking pour 300 voitures
Rez-de-chaussée
Alimentation
Electro-ménager
1ᵉʳ étage (ascenseur disponible)
Confection hommes/femmes/enfants
Jouets
Librairie/carterie
2ᵉᵐᵉ étage
Rayon musique
Service clientèle

a Where is the car park? (1) _____

b Which floor should you go to if you want a refund? (1) _____

c Where is the food section? (1) _____

d Which departments can you find on the first floor? (3) _____

_____

e What are the opening and closing times? (2) _____

_____

f What day is the shop shut? (1) _____

g What is available for shoppers on the first floor? (1) _____

10 **À la poste. Qui parle? Le client ou l'employé? Écrivez C ou E à côté des phrases.**
Read these sentences taken from a dialogue at the post office. Who's speaking? The customer or the employee? Write C or E next to the sentences.

a Je désire envoyer ce paquet en Écosse, s'il vous plaît. _____

b 5 timbres pour les États-Unis, ça fait €4, s'il vous plaît. _____

c Une télécarte, s'il vous plaît. _____

d Il est possible de changer des chèques de voyage ici? _____

e L'euro est à combien, s'il vous plaît? _____

f Non, désolé, je n'ai pas de monnaie pour la cabine téléphonique. _____

g Servez-vous du minitel sur votre droite – vous trouverez toutes les informations nécessaires. _____

h C'est combien un timbre pour l'Angleterre? _____

11 **Lisez l'e-mail de Raphaëlle et cochez les cinq phrases correctes.**
Read Raphaëlle's e-mail and tick the five correct sentences.

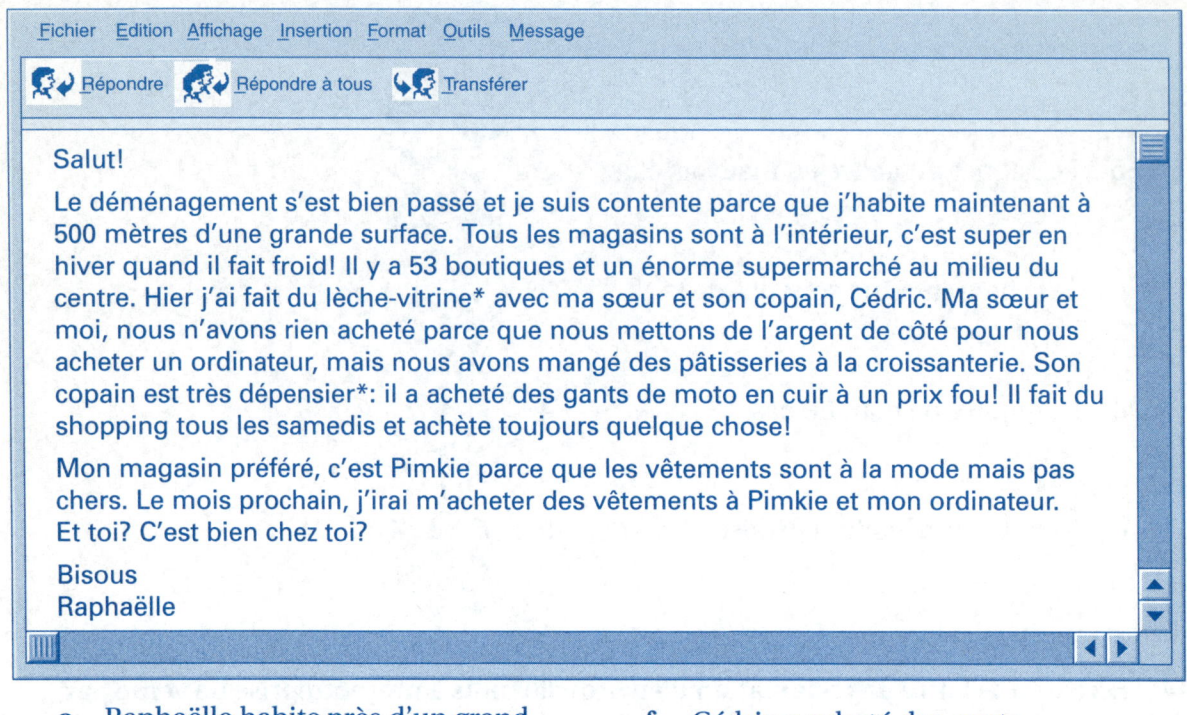

Fichier Edition Affichage Insertion Format Outils Message

Répondre   Répondre à tous   Transférer

Salut!

Le déménagement s'est bien passé et je suis contente parce que j'habite maintenant à 500 mètres d'une grande surface. Tous les magasins sont à l'intérieur, c'est super en hiver quand il fait froid! Il y a 53 boutiques et un énorme supermarché au milieu du centre. Hier j'ai fait du lèche-vitrine* avec ma sœur et son copain, Cédric. Ma sœur et moi, nous n'avons rien acheté parce que nous mettons de l'argent de côté pour nous acheter un ordinateur, mais nous avons mangé des pâtisseries à la croissanterie. Son copain est très dépensier*: il a acheté des gants de moto en cuir à un prix fou! Il fait du shopping tous les samedis et achète toujours quelque chose!

Mon magasin préféré, c'est Pimkie parce que les vêtements sont à la mode mais pas chers. Le mois prochain, j'irai m'acheter des vêtements à Pimkie et mon ordinateur. Et toi? C'est bien chez toi?

Bisous
Raphaëlle

a Raphaëlle habite près d'un grand hypermarché. _____

b Il faut faire ses achats à l'extérieur. _____

c Sa sœur a un petit ami. _____

d Hier, elles ont dépensé beaucoup d'argent. _____

e Cédric fait du shopping tous les mois. _____

f Cédric a acheté des gants. _____

g Raphaëlle aime les vêtements bon marché. _____

h Sa sœur et son copain économisent. _____

i Raphaëlle veut acheter un ordinateur. _____

*lèche-vitrine = *window shopping*   *dépensier = *extravagant*

12 **Lisez ce que Fatima pense du shopping et remplissez les blancs avec les bonnes expressions trouvées ci-dessous. Attention: il y a plus de mots que de blancs.**
Read what Fatima thinks about shopping and fill in the blanks with the correct expressions below. Be careful: there are more words than blanks.

Pour moi, le shopping, c'est comme une drogue. Je fais des courses tous les samedis et je dépense tout mon argent de poche. J'achète beaucoup de CD et de vêtements. J'aime les grands magasins parce que c'est moins cher.

> semaine   préfère
> cher   de poche
> adore   achète
> dépense
> acheter   déteste

Fatima _____ faire du shopping. Elle fait des courses une fois par

_____. Elle aime _____ des CD et des vêtements. Elle

_____ les grands magasins.

Métro 4 for AQA © Heinemann Educational 2001

13 Qu'est-ce qui ne va pas? Reliez les images aux problèmes.
What's wrong? Link the pictures to the problems.

a	Cette chemise est sale.	**1**	
b	Le paquet est arrivé en mauvais état.	**2**	
c	Les chaussures ne sont pas de la même pointure.	**3**	
d	La montre ne marche pas.	**4**	
e	La nourriture était mauvaise.	**5**	

14 Écrivez une lettre de réclamation d'environ 80 mots à une entreprise de vente par correspondance en essayant d'inclure les expressions ci-dessous.
Write a letter of complaint of about 80 words to a mail-order company. Try to include some of the sentences below.

J'ai le regret de vous informer que … = *I am sorry to tell you that …*
Ce n'est pas la bonne taille/couleur. = *It's not the right size/colour.*
… ne marche pas. = *… doesn't work.*
… est cassé(e). = *… is broken.*
… est sale. = *… is dirty.*
Pouvez-vous me rembourser?/ remplacer … ? = *Can you reimburse me?/replace … ?*
J'espère que vous réglerez ce problème dès que possible. = *I hope you will deal with this problem as soon as possible.*

Grammaire

1 **Trouvez le bon adjectif dans la colonne d'en face.**
Find the correct adjective.

> Ask yourself if the word is:
> – feminine/masculine?
> – singular/plural?

a	Un short	violette
b	Une chemise	gris
c	Des chaussettes	bleu
d	Des manteaux	vertes

2 **Trouvez les expressions correspondantes.**
Match the French expressions to the English ones.

To translate 'this' and 'these', use:
ce + masculine singular / *cette* + feminine singular /
cet + singular word that starts with a vowel or a silent 'h' /
ces + plural.

> un pull/une cravate/
> une chaussette/un
> anorak/une écharpe

To translate 'this one here' or 'these here', use:
celui-ci + masc/sing word / *celle-ci* + fem/sing word /
ceux-ci + masc/plural word / *celles-ci* + fem/plural word.

a	ce pull	**1**	this yellow one (scarf)
b	cette cravate	**2**	these ties
c	celle-ci, la jaune!	**3**	this yellow one (anorak)
d	celui-là, le jaune!	**4**	these jumpers
e	ces cravates	**5**	this jumper
f	ces pulls	**6**	these blue ones (socks)
g	celles-ci, les bleues!	**7**	these blue ones (jumpers)
h	ceux-ci, les bleus!	**8**	this tie

3 **Remplissez les blancs avec la bonne expression.**
Fill in the gaps with the correct expression.

> les plus frais   le moins cher   la plus efficace
> les plus sucrés   les plus confortables

a Achetez la crème _____ !

b Mangez les bonbons _____ !

c Si vous n'avez pas d'argent, prenez _____ !

d Choisissez les fruits _____ !

e Portez les vêtements _____ !

Rappel

le/la/les plus + *adjective* =
the most

le pullover le plus cher
the most expensive pullover
la pomme la plus grande
the biggest apple
les chaussures les plus
confortables
the most comfortable shoes
le pantalon le moins cher
the cheapest trousers

Métro 4 for AQA © Heinemann Educational 2001

À l'oral

1 Qu'est-ce qu'il y a comme magasins près de chez toi?

_____

_____

> You do not have to tell the truth! Answer 'yes' whenever possible and include plenty of verbs and opinions.

2 Quel est ton magasin préféré et pourquoi?

_____

3 Tu préfères les petits magasins ou les grandes surfaces?

_____

4 Est-ce que tu aimes faire les courses?

_____

5 Avec qui fais-tu tes courses?

_____

6 As-tu fait du shopping récemment? Qu'est-ce que tu as acheté?

_____

7 Vas-tu faire du shopping le week-end prochain? Qu'est-ce que tu vas acheter?

_____

8 As-tu déjà eu une expérience négative dans un magasin? Si oui, pourquoi?

_____

9 Qu'est-ce que tu aimes porter?

_____

_____

10 Quelle est ta couleur préférée?

_____

11 Combien d'argent de poche as-tu par semaine?

_____

12 Comment dépenses-tu ton argent de poche?

_____

_____

7 *En vacances*

1 **Reliez le pays à sa capitale.**
Link up the country with its capital.

a	la France	**1**	Washington DC
b	l'Angleterre	**2**	Amsterdam
c	le Danemark	**3**	Rome
d	la Grèce	**4**	Berlin
e	les États-Unis	**5**	Berne
f	l'Italie	**6**	Paris
g	l'Allemagne	**7**	Madrid
h	l'Espagne	**8**	Londres
i	la Suisse	**9**	Copenhague
j	les Pays-Bas	**10**	Athènes

2 **De quelle nationalité sont-ils? Répondez suivant l'exemple.**
What nationality are they? Answer following the example.

> *Adjectives of nationality don't start with a capital letter. Don't forget the feminine endings.*

Exemple: Il est né en Allemagne. = Il est allemand.
Elle est née en Allemagne. = Elle est allemande.

a Il est né en France. = _____

b Il est né en Angleterre. = _____

c Elle est née en Espagne. = _____

d Il est né au Portugal. = _____

e Elle est née en Amérique. = _____

> italien espagnol
> français portugais
> anglais
> suisse
> grec américain

3 **C'est quel symbole?**
Find the correct picture.

a Il neigera. ☐

b Il fera beau. ☐

c Il fera du vent. ☐

d Il y aura du brouillard. ☐

e Il pleuvra. ☐

1

2

3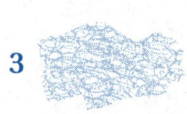

4

5

Métro 4 for AQA © Heinemann Educational 2001

4 Regardez la carte de France et répondez aux questions en français.

Look at the map of France and answer the questions in French.

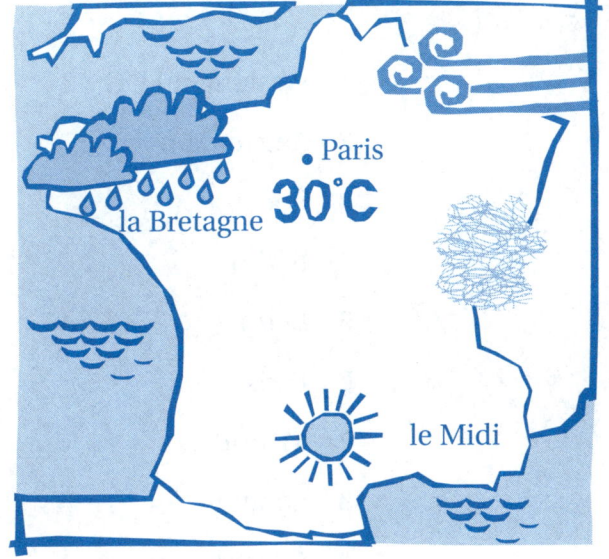

Il fait	chaud/froid.
	beau/mauvais.
	du vent.
	du brouillard.
Il	pleut/neige.

a Quel temps fait-il dans le nord? _____

b Quel temps fait-il dans le Midi? _____

c Quel temps fait-il en Bretagne? _____

d Quel temps fait-il dans l'est? _____

e Quel temps fait-il dans la capitale? _____

5a Lisez la carte postale de Hugo et dites si les phrases à la page 51 sont vraies (V), fausses (F) ou si ce n'est pas dans le texte(?).

Read Hugo's postcard and decide whether the sentences on page 51 are true (V), false (F) or not in the text(?).

Chère Mamie,

Je suis arrivé en <u>Allemagne</u> il y a <u>une semaine</u>. La ville où je suis est très <u>jolie</u>. <u>Freudenstadt</u> est dans la <u>Forêt-Noire au sud du pays</u>. Il <u>neige souvent</u>. Je porte des <u>gants</u> tous les jours!

Cette semaine, <u>j'ai fait du ski et j'ai fait des promenades dans la région</u>. <u>Je t'ai acheté des petits souvenirs</u>. Je loge <u>chez mon correspondant</u>. C'est très confortable. Je m'amuse bien ici.

À bientôt!
Hugo

Mme Éloise Degas

32 rue Fromager

13160 Châteaurenard

France

a   Hugo est en Allemagne depuis sept jours. _____

b   La ville est belle. _____

c   Freudenstadt se situe à l'est. _____

d   Il fait froid. _____

e   Il porte un chapeau en laine. _____

f   Hugo a fait des sports nautiques. _____

g   Il a fait des courses. _____

h   Hugo aimerait retourner en Allemagne l'année prochaine. _____

5b   **Écrivez une carte postale similaire en changeant les mots soulignés.**
Write a similar postcard changing the underlined words.

6   **Lisez le paragraphe qu'Élise a écrit sur ses vacances et répondez aux questions en anglais.**
Read the paragraph Élise wrote about her holidays and answer the questions in English.

MES VACANCES AUX ÉTATS-UNIS

L'année dernière, je suis allée en Amérique avec mes parents. Nous avons logé dans un hôtel en Floride et nous avons passé une journée à Disneyland. C'était super! Nous avons mangé des hot-dogs et des glaces toute la journée. L'hôtel était très agréable avec vue sur la mer. J'ai dormi dans une chambre avec un lit pour deux personnes: une vraie princesse! Le seul problème, c'était que le petit déjeuner était servi trop tôt: à six heures trente du matin! Il a fait environ trente degrés toute la semaine: quelle chaleur! J'ai bien aimé mes vacances et j'aimerais y retourner avec mes copines quand je serai plus grande.

Rappel

J'ai fait/joué/visité
Je suis allé(e)

---

a   Where did she go last year? (1) _____

b   How long did she stay there for? (1) _____

c   What did she eat there? (2) _____
_____

d   Give two reasons why she liked the hotel. (2) _____
_____

e   What didn't she like there? (1) _____

f   What was the weather like? (1) _____

g   When and with whom is she is hoping to go back some day? (2) _____
_____

Métro 4 for AQA © Heinemann Educational 2001

7 **Lisez cet extrait tiré d'une brochure touristique et dites si les phrases sont vraies (V), fausses (F) ou si ce n'est pas dans le texte (?).**
Read this extract from a holiday brochure and say if the sentences are true (V), false (F) or not in the text (?).

Soleil Vacances!

Vous voulez faire la fête? Voici ce qu'on vous propose cette année.

✴ Allez en Andalousie pour la Semaine Sainte, spectacles, processions: l'Espagne dans toute sa splendeur.

✴ Si vous voulez faire la fête toute la nuit, restez en France! Le Carnaval de Nice, avec ses masques et magnifiques déguisements vous rappellera le Carnaval de Venise.

✴ Ce sont les Gilles, ces gentils bouffons qui donneront à vos enfants des oranges et des bonbons au Carnaval de Binche en Belgique.

✴ Vous entendrez toutes sortes de musique au Printemps de Bourges, venez-y nombreux.

✴ Si vous êtes amateur de théâtre, venez au festival d'Avignon.

✴ Pour les amateurs de musique, nous organisons un voyage au Canada à l'occasion du festival de jazz de Montréal.

✴ Vous êtes amateur de bière? Ne manquez pas la Bierfest de Munich!

a Au Carnaval de Binche les Gilles donnent des fruits aux enfants. _____

b Le festival de Montréal est un festival de musique classique. _____

c On peut boire beaucoup d'alcool au festival de Munich. _____

d Le festival de Nice est seulement pour les adultes. _____

e Le festival espagnol est un festival religieux. _____

f Si on aime l'art dramatique, on peut aller à Avignon. _____

g Le festival de Bourges se passe en hiver. _____

8a Lisez cette brochure et trouvez:
Read this brochure and find:
- *3 tourist attractions*
- *4 sports you can do*
- *2 specialities*

Bienvenue à Bavay, cité antique vieille de 2000 ans!

Bavay est le plus grand site gallo-romain au nord de Paris. Cette petite ville se situe dans le département du Nord à environ quatre-vingts kilomètres de Lille.

À voir:
■ Le musée archéologique et le site.
■ Le musée de la bataille de Malplaquet du 11/09/1709. Cette bataille a eu lieu entre les Français d'un côté et les Anglais et les Espagnols de l'autre.
■ Le beffroi et l'hôtel de ville datant du XVIIème siècle et de style espagnol.

Sports et loisirs:
Il y a deux salles de sport et un stade. Vous pouvez pratiquer le football, le tennis, le tir à l'arc ou encore la gymnastique et la danse.

Spécialités:
Bavay doit sa renommée à ses célèbres bonbons 'les chiques'. La bière 'La Bavaisienne' est aussi très appréciée.

8b Trouvez les cinq phrases correctes.

Find the five correct sentences.

Exemple: Bavay est une ville du nord de la France.	✓
a Bavay est une ville touristique et industrielle.	
b Ce sont les Romains qui ont créé le site.	
c Bavay est dans la banlieue parisienne.	
d Lille est à environ 80 kilomètres de Bavay.	
e La bataille de Malplaquet a eu lieu en septembre.	
f Les Français se sont battus contre les Anglais et les Espagnols dans cette bataille.	
g Le beffroi est typiquement français.	
h On peut pratiquer la natation à Bavay.	
i Il y deux grandes spécialités bavaisiennes.	
j 'Les chiques' sont des femmes à la mode.	

9 Vous écrivez à un hôtel pour réserver une chambre. Complétez la lettre en écrivant les détails manquants.

You are writing to a hotel to reserve a room. Finish this letter by adding the missing details.

Cher Monsieur,

Je voudrais réserver une chambre pour 🧍🧍 _____

_____ avec 🛏 _____ et

🚿 _____ .

Nous voudrions rester du 📅(Août 3) _____ au

📅(Août 10) _____ .

Ma femme est handicapée: y-a-t-il un 🪟 _____ ?

Les 🐕 _____ sont-ils admis?

À quelle heure est le 🍽 _____ ?

Je vous prie d'agréer, Monsieur, l'expression de mes sentiments distingués.

Edmond Tristan

Métro 4 for AQA © Heinemann Educational 2001

10 Qui dit quoi? Reliez les phrases aux images.

Who says what? Link up the sentences to the pictures.

a   Les serviettes étaient sales.   **1**

b   La douche ne marchait pas.   **2**

c   Il faisait froid dans les chambres.   **3**

d   Il y avait trop de bruit.   **4**

e   Il n'y avait pas de savon.   **5**

11 Utilisez ce modèle pour écrire une lettre à un hôtel en vous plaignant des choses suivantes:

Use this model to write a letter complaining about the following things:

- The bathroom was dirty.
- There wasn't any soap.
- The television wasn't working.

Cher Monsieur/Chère Madame,

Je vous écris pour vous dire que j'ai été très déçu par mon séjour dans votre hôtel. Premièrement, la chambre était sale et désordonnée. Ensuite, il n'y avait pas de serviettes dans la salle de bains. Finalement, l'ascenseur ne marchait pas! J'espère que vous lirez ma lettre avec intérêt et que vous agirez en conséquence.

Je vous prie d'agréer, Monsieur/Madame, l'expression de mes sentiments distingués.

Grammaire

1 **Trouvez le bon début. Écrivez *à/au/aux/en* devant ces endroits.**
Find the correct beginning. Write à/au/aux/en *in front of these places.*

Exemple: En Belgique

a _____ France (f)
b _____ Portugal (m)
c _____ États-Unis (pl)
d _____ Italie (f)
e _____ Paris

f _____ Grande-Bretagne (f)
g _____ Espagne (f)
h _____ Écosse (f)
i _____ Londres
j _____ Allemagne (f)

2 **Le passé composé avec l'auxiliaire *être*. Traduisez les phrases ci-dessous:**
The perfect tense with the être *auxiliary. Translate the sentences below:*

With the following verbs in the perfect tense, you must use the auxiliary *être* (to be):

naître *(to be born)*
arriver *(to arrive)*
venir *(to come)*
revenir *(to come back)*
devenir *(to become)*

partir *(to leave)*
entrer *(to go in)*
retourner *(to go back)*
mourir *(to die)*
sortir *(to go out)*

aller *(to go)*
rester *(to stay)*
tomber *(to fall)*
descendre *(to go down)*
monter *(to go up)*

je **suis**	nous **sommes**		*Don't forget the agreements*
tu **es**	vous **êtes**	+ past participle	*Exemple:* je suis arrivé(**e**)
il/elle/on **est**	ils/elles **sont**		nous sommes parti**s**

We (*nous/masc*) arrived = <u>Nous sommes arrivés</u>

I (*je/masc*) became = _____

They (*elles*) came back = _____

I (*je/fem*) went out = _____

She went down = _____

He fell = _____

They (*ils*) went = _____

We (*nous/fem*) went up = _____

You (*tu/masc*) went in = _____

I (*je/fem*) stayed = _____

3 **C'est quel temps: passé composé, imparfait, présent ou futur?**
Which tense is it: perfect, imperfect, present or future?

a Il fait beau. <u>présent</u>
b Il a neigé. _____
c Il y aura des nuages. _____
d Il neigera. _____
e Il fait mauvais. _____

f Il fera froid. _____
g Il pleuvait. _____
h Il fait du brouillard. _____
i Il pleut. _____
j Il a fait chaud. _____

Métro 4 for AQA © Heinemann Educational 2001

À l'oral

1 Où aimes-tu passer tes vacances normalement?

_____

2 Tu préfères aller à l'étranger ou rester en Grande-Bretagne?

_____

3 Où es-tu allé(e) l'année dernière?

_____

4 Comment as-tu voyagé?

_____

5 Avec qui es-tu allé(e)?

_____

6 Qu'est ce que tu as fait?

_____

_____

7 Quel temps faisait-il?

_____

8 C'était bien?

_____

9 Où aimerais-tu aller l'année prochaine?

_____

10 As-tu déjà logé dans un hôtel? Si oui, était-ce une expérience positive ou négative?

_____

_____

11 Es-tu déjà allé(e) en France?

_____

12 Connais-tu une spécialité française?

_____

8 Bienvenue en France!

1 **Trouvez ce que l'on pourrait dire à ces gens.**
Find the right things to say to these people.

a J'ai quinze ans aujourd'hui.

b Je vais prendre le bateau.

c Je pars en vacances.

d Je vais chez mon correspondant français.

e J'ai un examen.

f Je vais me coucher car je suis fatiguée.

g C'est le 31 décembre, il est minuit!

h C'est ma fête aujourd'hui.

i C'est le 24 décembre.

j On est vendredi soir.

1 Bonnes vacances!

2 Bonne année!

3 Bonne fête!

4 Bon anniversaire!

5 Bon week-end!

6 Bonne chance!

7 Bon voyage!

8 Bon séjour!

9 Bonne nuit!

10 Joyeux Noël!

2 **Lisez ce dialogue et remplissez le résumé avec les mots de la grille. Attention: il y a plus de mots que de trous.**
Read this dialogue and fill in the blanks in the summary using the words in the box.
Be careful: there are more words than blanks.

Madame Jacquemin:	*Bonjour, Jonathan. As-tu fait bon voyage?*
Jonathan:	Oui, merci. La mer était calme. C'est très gentil de votre part de me recevoir. Je vous ai apporté un petit cadeau.
Madame Jacquemin:	*Oh merci! Tu est gentil.*
Corentin:	*Bonjour, Jonathan. Je suis Corentin, ton correspondant.*
Jonathan:	Enchanté.
Corentin:	*Et voici mes frères, Jules et Emmanuel.*
Jonathan:	Salut!
Corentin:	*Veux-tu boire quelque chose?*
Madame Jacquemin:	*Ou bien manger quelque chose?*
Jonathan:	Non merci, je n'ai ni faim ni soif. Je voudrais plutôt me reposer.
Madame Jacquemin:	*Alors, suis-moi, je vais te montrer ta chambre.*

> français   anglais   boisson   journée   voyager
> manger   fatigué   boire   au lit   mes   ses   les

Corentin est le correspondant _____ de Jonathan. Corentin présente

_____ deux frères et demande à Jonathan s'il veut une _____, mais

comme Jonathan est _____ , il préfère aller _____ .

Métro 4 for AQA © Heinemann Educational 2001

3 **Trouvez les expressions correspondantes.**
Find the corresponding expressions.

> *If you look for key words, you should find this easy! Once you have worked this out, remember to use these expressions in your pieces of work or presentations to show you have a good knowledge of the vocabulary encountered in this topic.*

a   maison à six chambres

b   maison avec bâtiments extérieurs

c   appartement de luxe avec ascenseur

d   maison non-mitoyenne de banlieue

e   immeuble de banlieue

f   pavillon avec grand jardin

g   ferme rénovée

h   maison de campagne

1   renovated farm

2   block of flats in the suburbs

3   bungalow with big garden

4   luxury flat with lift

5   country house

6   house with outbuildings

7   six-bedroom house

8   detached house in the suburbs

4 **Décrivez en 70 mots votre maison et votre chambre en vous aidant du texte ci-dessous.**
Describe your house and your room in 70 words using the text below to help you.

Je vais te décrire ma maison. J'habite à <u>Savigny</u>, près de <u>Paris</u>. J'habite <u>au 7 avenue Georges Pompidou</u>. Dans ma maison, il y a <u>sept</u> pièces. En bas, il y a <u>le salon, la cuisine, la salle à manger</u>. En haut, <u>les toilettes, la salle de bains et deux chambres</u>. Ma pièce préférée, c'est ma chambre. Les rideaux sont violets et les murs sont jaunes. Dans ma chambre, il y a <u>un bureau, un ordinateur et une grande armoire blanche</u>. Il n'y a pas de <u>télévision</u>. Je partage ma chambre avec mon frère. C'est super parce qu'on s'entend bien.

5 **Ces choses vont dans quelle pièce?**
Which rooms do these things go in?

lit	fauteuil	lavabo	armoire	cuisinière à gaz
ordinateur	réveil	lave-vaisselle	canapé	machine à laver
frigo	placard	douche	bureau	chaîne stéréo
four à micro-ondes				

chambre	cuisine	salon	salle de bains

6 Logique ou illogique? Cochez les phrases logiques et faites une croix
pour les phrases illogiques.
*Are these sentences logical or illogical? Tick the logical sentences and
put a cross next to the illogical ones.*

a La voiture est dans le garage. _____

b Le canapé est dans la cuisine. _____

c Le lit est dans la chambre. _____

d Le lave-vaisselle est dans la salle de bains. _____

e Le vin est dans la cave. _____

f Le fauteuil est dans le salon. _____

g La table est dans la salle à manger. _____

h Les toilettes sont dans la salle de bains. _____

i Le four à micro-ondes est dans les W-C. _____

7 Lisez la lettre d'Hervé et dites si les phrases suivantes sont vraies (V), fausses (F)
ou si ce n'est pas dans le texte (?).
Read Hervé's letter and say if the sentences below are true (V), false (F) or not in the text (?).

a Hervé est chez son correspondant. _____

b Selon Hervé, les jardins sont plus petits en France. _____

c La famille Moore mange en regardant la télé. _____

d Hervé ne porte pas d'uniforme. _____

e Hervé aime le pain. _____

f Hervé déteste son séjour en Angleterre. _____

Salut Papa et Maman!

L'Angleterre, c'est super et la ville où je suis est intéressante. La maison de
mon correspondant, Neil Moore, est typiquement anglaise. Je trouve que les
jardins sont généralement plus petits ici qu'en France.

Des fois on mange dans le salon en regardant la télé; en France on mange dans
la salle à manger. Le soir, on mange vers 6 heures alors qu'en France, on mange
vers 8 heures. Le pain est souvent coupé en tranches: pas de baguette chez la
famille Moore! Le matin, Neil met son uniforme. Moi, je garde mon vieux jean et
mes baskets!

Vous voyez, c'est différent ici et j'aime plutôt ça! Il y a une chose que je déteste,
c'est de voyager en voiture à gauche! J'ai tout le temps peur d'avoir un accident!!!

À bientôt,

Hervé

Métro 4 for AQA © Heinemann Educational 2001

8 **Des fêtes en France: lisez le paragraphe et répondez aux questions en anglais.**
Celebrations in France: read the paragraph and answer the questions in English.

le repas – *the meal*	les huîtres – *oysters*	la dinde – *turkey*
une bûche – *a Yule log*	les souliers – *shoes*	une couronne – *crown*
la fève – *a little charm hidden in the cake*	le Roi/la Reine – *the King/Queen*	la pâte d'amande – *marzipan*

Noël se fête le soir du vingt-quatre décembre. C'est une fête très familiale. Toute la famille se réunit autour d'un grand repas. On mange généralement des huîtres en hors-d'œuvre, de la dinde et des légumes et une bûche au chocolat comme dessert. On boit beaucoup de champagne! Un peu plus tard le Père Noël passe: il met des cadeaux dans les souliers près de la cheminée. À minuit, on va à l'église à la messe de minuit. Dans la maison on trouve beaucoup de décorations comme la crèche ou l'arbre de Noël.

La galette des rois est un gâteau à la pâte d'amande ou aux pommes que l'on mange à l'Épiphanie. Dans la galette il y a une fève (c'est à dire un petit personnage symbolisant la religion catholique). Celui ou celle qui a la fève dans sa part de gâteau est le Roi ou la Reine et doit choisir son mari ou sa femme. Les deux personnes doivent alors porter une couronne.

a When is Christmas normally celebrated? (1) _____

b Are many friends invited? (1) _____

c What do most people eat and drink? (2) _____

d What happens at midnight? (1) _____

e Give two types of decorations. (2) _____

f What is the 'galette' usually made of? (2) _____

g What happens if you find the charm in it? (1) _____

9 **Reliez les titres aux types de films ou d'émissions.**
Link the titles to the types of films or programmes.

a	Les Simpsons	**1**	un film d'horreur
b	Le Journal de 20 heures	**2**	une émission de sport
c	Nos Amis les Animaux	**3**	un feuilleton
d	Titanic	**4**	les informations
e	Vendredi 13	**5**	un jeu télévisé
f	Inspecteur Morse	**6**	un dessin animé
g	Le Top 50	**7**	une série policière
h	Football: France–Angleterre	**8**	un film d'amour
i	Questions pour un Champion	**9**	une émission de musique
j	Neighbours, série australienne	**10**	un documentaire

10   **Lisez les descriptions et écrivez le titre du film ou de l'émission.**
Read the descriptions and write the title of the film or programme.

> Digimon   Stade 2   Astérix et Obélix   Friends
> Elizabeth   Hit machine   Jurassic Park

a   C'est un film américain avec des dinosaures. _____

b   C'est une série humoristique qui dépeint la vie de six bons copains. _____

c   C'est un dessin animé japonais. _____

d   C'est un film historique qui raconte l'histoire d'une reine d'Angleterre. _____

e   C'est une émission de sport qui passe le dimanche. _____

f   C'est une émission de musique où l'on passe des vidéo-clips. _____

g   C'est un film français. C'est l'histoire d'un petit village gaulois qui se bat
contre les Romains. _____

11   **Donnez votre opinion sur les choses suivantes. Écrivez des phrases complètes.**
Give your opinion of the following things. Write in complete sentences.

> *Try to include as many of these key expressions as you can:*
> *ça m'intéresse/ça ne m'intéresse pas*
> *j'aime/je n'aime pas les personnages (the characters)*
> *je trouve ça bête/stupide/ridicule/nul/ débile/ennuyeux*
> *(I find it silly/stupid/ridiculous/rubbish/daft/boring)*
> *je trouve ça chouette/bien/marrant (great/good/funny)*
> *ça vaut la peine/ça ne vaut pas la peine (it's worth it/not worth it)*
> *Don't forget to justify your answers (parce que/car …).*

a   Eastenders =
b   Match of the Day =
c   La télévision =
d   La publicité =
e   Les magazines de mode =

12   **Lisez cette conversation au restaurant et cochez les 4 images à la page 62 qui correspondent à l'histoire.**
Read this conversation at the restaurant and tick the 4 pictures on page 62 that correspond to the story.

Madame Lepoint:	*Garçon!*
Le serveur:	Oui. Je peux vous aider?
Madame Lepoint:	*La carte, s'il vous plaît!*
Le serveur:	Voici, Madame.

Quelques minutes plus tard …

Le serveur:	Vous avez choisi?
Monsieur Lepoint:	*Oui, comme entrée, je voudrais une soupe de poissons. Comme plat principal, une sole meunière et comme dessert, une glace au café.*
Le serveur:	Très bien. Et pour vous, Madame?
Madame Lepoint:	*Comme hors-d'oeuvre, je voudrais du foie gras, après, des tomates farcies et comme dessert une tarte aux framboises.*
Le serveur:	C'est noté. Et comme boisson?
Monsieur Lepoint:	*Une bouteille de vin rouge, s'il vous plaît.*

Quelques minutes plus tard …

Madame Lepoint:	*Garçon!*
Le serveur:	Oui, Madame?
Madame Lepoint:	*Je n'ai pas de cuillère. Mon mari n'a pas de verre et la soupe est froide!*
Le serveur:	Oh, je suis désolé! Je m'en charge tout de suite!

Métro 4 for AQA © Heinemann Educational 2001

Grammaire

1 Rappel: Écrivez les adjectifs possessifs corrects dans les blancs.
Revision: Write the correct possessive adjectives in the gaps.

	+ masculine word	+ feminine word	+ plural
my	**mon**	**ma**	**mes**
your (informal)	**ton**	**ta**	**tes**
his or her	**son**	**sa**	**ses**
our	**notre**	**notre**	**nos**
your (formal/many)	**votre**	**votre**	**vos**
their	**leur**	**leur**	**leurs**

a J'aime _____ chambre. (my)

b Tu aimes _____ chambre? (your)

c Elle lit _____ livre. (her)

d Monsieur et Madame Gybot n'aiment pas _____ maison. (their)

e Sonia et Raphaël écoutent _____ CD préférés. (their)

f Madame Joseph, _____ déjeuner est servi. (your)

g Anne a seize ans. _____ frère a quatorze ans. (her)

h J'aime regarder la télé. _____ émission préférée, c'est Eastenders. (my)

> *Possessive adjectives agree with the noun they describe. When the noun starts with a vowel or a silent 'h', use the masculine form.*

2 Remplissez les blancs en choisissant *le/la/l'* or *les*.
Fill in the blanks choosing the right pronoun.

Exemple: il regarde **un film** = il <u>le</u> regarde
   *he watches **a film** = he watches **it***
   il regarde ***des films*** = il <u>les</u> regarde
   *he watches **films** = he watches **them***

a Il préfère **les émissions** sportives = il _____ préfère.

b Il mange **une pomme** = il _____ mange.

c Il adore **sa maison** = il _____ adore.

d Mon correspondant montre **sa chambre** = il _____ montre.

e Tu accroches **tes posters** au mur = tu _____ accroches.

Métro 4 for AQA © Heinemann Educational 2001

À l'oral

> *Where possible, give a reason for your answer. When you're asked to describe something, give two details instead of just one.*

1 Où habites-tu exactement?

_____

_____

2 Est-ce que tu habites dans une maison ou un appartement?

_____

3 Tu as un jardin?

_____

4 Il y a combien de pièces chez toi?

_____

5 Quelle est ta pièce préférée? Pourquoi?

_____

6 Comment est ta chambre?

_____

_____

7 De quelle couleur sont les murs?

_____

8 Qu'est-ce qu'il y a dans ta chambre?

_____

_____

9 Est-ce que tu partages ta chambre?

_____

10 Est-ce que tu as une télé dans ta chambre?

_____

11 Qu'est-ce que tu aimes regarder à la télé? Pourquoi?

_____

_____

12 Et au cinéma, quelle sorte de films aimes-tu? Pourquoi?

_____

9 *En bonne forme*

1 Regardez cet homme et écrivez les phrases pour décrire son état.
Look at this man and write sentences to describe his aches and pains.

Il a mal	au	nez/genou/ventre/bras
	à la	gorge/tête
	à l'	oreille
	aux	pieds/jambes

Il a mal:

a _____

b _____

c _____

d _____

e _____

f _____

g _____

h _____

i _____

2 Lisez la conversation téléphonique et écrivez une conversation similaire.
Read the telephone conversation and write a similar conversation. Here are the details: an earache; appointment on Tuesday at 4pm.

☎ Bonjour. Virginie Tartemps au téléphone. J'ai mal <u>à la tête</u>. Je voudrais un rendez-vous, s'il vous plaît.

☎ Oui, <u>lundi à dix heures quarante-cinq</u>, ça vous va?

☎ Très bien, merci!

3 Mettez ces expressions dans l'ordre chronologique.
Put these expressions in chronological order.

a Je me lave. _____

b Je prends mon dîner. _____

c Je me couche. _____

d Je me lève. _____

e Je fais mes devoirs. _____

f Je me réveille. _____

g Je vais au collège. _____

h Je rentre du collège. _____

i Je prends mon goûter. _____

j Je regarde un peu la télé avant de me coucher. _____

Métro 4 for AQA © Heinemann Educational 2001

4 Regardez ces affiches et répondez aux questions en anglais.

Look at these posters and answer the questions in English.

Glaces: choix de 10 parfums	Dégustation de cidre du pays	Fermeture hebdomadaire du café: le lundi	Plat du jour: moules/frites

a   What does the poster about ice-creams say? _____

b   Why is cider mentioned? _____

c   What happens on a Monday? _____

d   What is the dish of the day? _____

5 C'est bon ou mauvais pour la santé? Mettez les mots dans la bonne colonne.

Is it good or bad for your health? Put the words in the right column.

le chocolat 5 kg de saucisses le lait la crème l'alcool les biscuits	les légumes les pommes les céréales l'eau les bonbons le tabac

Bon pour la santé		Mauvais pour la santé	

6 Soulignez en rouge 3 viandes, en bleu 3 légumes et en noir 3 fruits.

Underline 3 types of meat in red, 3 vegetables in blue and 3 types of fruit in black.

veau   pomme   potage   ananas   bœuf   champignon   chou citron   confiture   fromage   jambon   petits pois

7 Ces personnes parlent de la nourriture. Écrivez dans la grille à la page 67 en anglais ce qu'elles aiment et ce qu'elles n'aiment pas.

These people are talking about food. Fill in the grid on page 67 about their likes and dislikes in English.

a   Je déteste les légumes mais je suis un grand mangeur de viande.

b   J'aime les fruits mais le potage, pas tellement.

c   Je mange beaucoup de choses sucrées. Les légumes, je n'aime pas ça.

d   Le midi je mange toujours un sandwich car j'ai horreur de la nourriture de la cantine.

e   Le fast-food, non merci! Je préfère la nourriture traditionnelle.

f   Je ne bois que de l'eau. L'alcool, c'est mauvais pour la santé.

g   Je préfère les boissons chaudes aux boissons froides.

h   Je ne vais jamais au restaurant. J'aime manger ce que j'ai cuisiné moi-même.

Métro 4 for AQA © Heinemann Educational 2001

	Likes	Dislikes
a		
b		
c		
d		
e		
f		
g		
h		

8 Vrai ou faux ? *Is it true or false?*

a   Les oranges sont sources de vitamine C.   _____

b   Le chocolat est bon pour le ventre.   _____

c   Les bonbons sont bons pour les dents.   _____

d   L'eau est bonne pour la santé.   _____

e   Le poisson est un produit laitier.   _____

f   Les légumes sont bons pour les pieds.   _____

g   Il y a beaucoup de calories dans une portion de frites.   _____

h   Les carottes donnent de beaux yeux bleus.   _____

i   Les céréales sont sources de fibres.   _____

j   Le beurre fait grossir.   _____

9 Vous écrivez dans votre journal. Il faut mentionner les points suivants:
You are writing in your diary. Include the following points:

● ce que vous faites pour garder la forme (Je fais du vélo, Je joue au tennis …)
● ce que vous mangez pour garder la forme (Je mange du/de la/des …)
● ce qu'il ne faut pas faire si vous voulez garder la forme (Il ne faut pas manger/boire trop de …)

10 Trouvez les bonnes images.
Find the matching pictures.

a   J'ai mal à l'oreille.

b   Je suis malade.

c   J'ai froid.

d   J'ai faim.

e   Je suis fatiguée.

f   Je suis en forme.

g   Je fais un régime pour perdre du poids.

h   J'ai un coup de soleil.

1    2    3

4   5    6

7   8

Métro 4 for AQA © Heinemann Educational 2001

11 **Comment se sont-ils fait mal? Trouvez les images correspondantes.**
How did they hurt themselves? Find the matching pictures.

a Il s'est blessé en coupant du pain.

 **1**

b Il a perdu sa dent en mangeant un bonbon au caramel.

 **2**

c Je me suis foulé la cheville en faisant du sport.

 **3**

d Elle s'est brûlée en repassant.

 **4**

e Tu t'es cassée le bras en skiant.

 **5**

12 **Lisez ces deux lettres et remplissez les blancs dans le résumé en anglais à la page 69.**
Read the letter and fill in the gaps in the English summary on page 69.

Je m'inquiète pour ma copine Lydia, qui fume jusqu'à vingt cigarettes par jour. Sa chambre et ses vêtements sentent mauvais. Elle a les doigts et les dents jaunes. En plus, elle a une petite sœur de deux ans et c'est mauvais cet air impur pour une petite fille.

Le tabac coûte très cher et Lydia n'a pas beaucoup d'argent. En plus le tabac c'est dangereux, non? On peut attraper le cancer du poumon, c'est horrible!

Lydia pense que ça la calme. Pourtant ça l'énerve. Elle pense aussi que ça lui donne confiance en elle et qu'elle aura plus de petits copains. Moi je pense que les garçons n'aiment pas les filles qui fument!
Que puis-je faire pour l'aider?
Camille

À mon avis Jean-Pierre est anorexique. Il ne mange absolument rien de sucré et refuse toujours les sucreries comme le chocolat et les bonbons. Le problème, c'est qu'il refuse aussi le poisson et la viande. Hier il a mangé une carotte et une poire, c'est tout! Comme boisson, pas de coca ou de limonade, seulement de l'eau! La semaine dernière, c'était mon anniversaire et il a mangé une part de gâteau. J'étais content mais en fait il est allé dans la salle de bains et il a vomi! C'est terrible! Quand je lui en ai parlé, il a dit que l'anorexie c'était une maladie pour les filles. Qu'en pensez-vous?
Cyril

Métro 4 for AQA © Heinemann Educational 2001

CAMILLE is worried because her friend Lydia smokes up to _____ cigarettes

a day. Both her _____ and her clothes smell. This is not healthy for her

_____ -year-old _____ . Smoking is _____ according

to Camille, but Lydia does not care as she thinks smoking will make her more confident

and help her find more boyfriends. According to Camille, boys _____

_____ .

CYRIL is worried because he thinks his friend Jean-Pierre is _____ . He always

refuses to eat food such as _____ or _____ but also

_____ or meat. The only thing he drinks is _____ . Jean-Pierre

does not believe he is ill as he says it is an illness that only _____ suffer from.

13 **Lisez les opinions suivantes et dites si elles sont positives, négatives ou positives et négatives.**
Read the following opinions and say whether they are positive, negative or positive and negative.

Héloïse

Maud

Moi, je regarde toujours Santé à la Une parce que les reportages sont d'actualité et intéressants.

Santé magazine, c'est bien mais ça rend les gens un peu complexés parfois.

Annie

Je trouve les reality-shows qui passent à la télé le matin tout à fait ridicules. Les problèmes psychologiques des autres ne m'intéressent pas du tout.

Régis

Francis

L'émission de cuisine de Maïté? Je la trouve trop vulgaire …

Le lundi matin, je ne rate* jamais les nouvelles recettes données à la radio: comme ça, j'impressionne toute la famille.

*rater = *to miss*

	Positif ☺	Négatif ☹	Positif et négatif 😐
Héloïse			
Maud			
Régis			
Francis			
Annie			

Métro 4 for AQA © Heinemann Educational 2001

Grammaire

1 Choisissez le bon mot pour ces phrases.
Choose the correct word for these sentences.

a   J'ai mal _____ main.

b   J'ai mal _____ pieds.

c   J'ai mal _____ jambe.

d   J'ai mal _____ genou.

e   J'ai mal _____ estomac.

> *In French you say 'I have an ache at the hand'.*
> *Remember! Use au + a masc/sing word; à la + a fem/sing word; à l' + a word starting with a vowel or silent 'h'; aux + plural word.*

2 Mettez le bon pronom réfléchi.
Write the correct reflexive pronoun.

a   Je _____ lave.

b   Il _____ lève.

c   Nous _____ regardons dans le miroir.

d   Elles _____ habillent.

e   Vous _____ couchez.

f   Elles _____ brossent les dents.

g   Je _____ repose.

h   Il _____ est fait mal.

i   Tu _____ es levé tard.

j   Nous _____ sommes couchés à 10h00.

> *Je me lave = I wash (myself)*
> *Tu te laves = you wash (yourself)*
> *Il/elle se lave = he/she washes*
> *(himself/herself)*
> *Nous nous lavons = we wash*
> *(ourselves)*
> *Vous vous lavez = you wash*
> *(yourselves)*
> *Ils/elles se lavent = they wash*
> *(themselves)*

> *Be careful! In front of a vowel or a silent 'h', me becomes m', te becomes t' and se becomes s'.*

3 Expressions avec *avoir*: traduisez ces phrases en français.
Translate these sentences into French using expressions with avoir *(to have).*

> *These are the verbs used, although not in this order:*
> *avoir peur/avoir faim/avoir envie/ avoir mal/avoir soif/ avoir raison/avoir froid/avoir tort/avoir chaud/avoir + age.*

j'ai   tu as   il/elle a   nous avons
vous avez   ils/elles ont

a   I am hot. _____

b   He is cold. _____

c   She is eighteen. _____

d   We are hungry. _____

e   They are thirsty. _____

f   You are in pain. (use *vous*) _____

g   You are right. (use *tu*) _____

h   He is wrong. _____

i   I am frightened. _____

j   We feel like … _____

À l'oral

1 Comment ça va aujourd'hui?

_____

2 À quelle heure te lèves-tu normalement?

_____

3 À quelle heure t'es tu levé(e) aujourd'hui?

_____

4 À quelle heure prends-tu le petit déjeuner?

_____

5 Qu'est-ce que tu manges normalement?

_____

_____

6 Où manges-tu à midi?

_____

7 Quel est ton repas préféré et pourquoi?

_____

8 Qu'est-ce que tu n'aimes pas manger ou boire?

_____

9 Est-ce que tu penses que la nourriture de la cantine est bonne pour la santé? Pourquoi?

_____

10 Tu aimes manger au restaurant? Pourquoi?

_____

11 Qu'est-ce que tu fais pour garder la forme?

_____

_____

12 Trouves-tu les émissions sur la santé intéressantes?

_____

Métro 4 for AQA © Heinemann Educational 2001

10 Le transport

1 **Faites des phrases en mentionnant 8 moyens de transport et 8 endroits que l'on trouve en ville. Faites attention à l'orthographe et à la grammaire.**
Write sentences mentioning 8 means of transport and 8 places in town. Pay attention to spelling and grammar.

Exemple: *Je vais **en voiture** à la mairie.*

1 _____ 5 _____

2 _____ 6 _____

3 _____ 7 _____

4 _____ 8 _____

2 **Lisez la conversation suivante et dites si les phrases sont vraies ou fausses.**
Read the following conversation and say if the sentences are true or false.

Pardon, Madame, pour aller à l'hôtel de ville, s'il vous plaît?
C'est assez difficile … Ce n'est pas tout près.
Il y a un bus qui y va?
Oui, le numéro 73.
Vous savez où est l'arrêt d'autobus?
Oui, c'est au bout de la rue, sur votre gauche.
Je vous remercie, Madame.
Je vous en prie.

a L'hôtel de ville est assez loin.
_____

b On peut y aller en bus.
_____

c L'arrêt est à trois kilomètres.
_____

3 **Dessinez les symboles ci-dessous à côté de l'expression correcte.**
Draw the following symbols next to the correct expression.

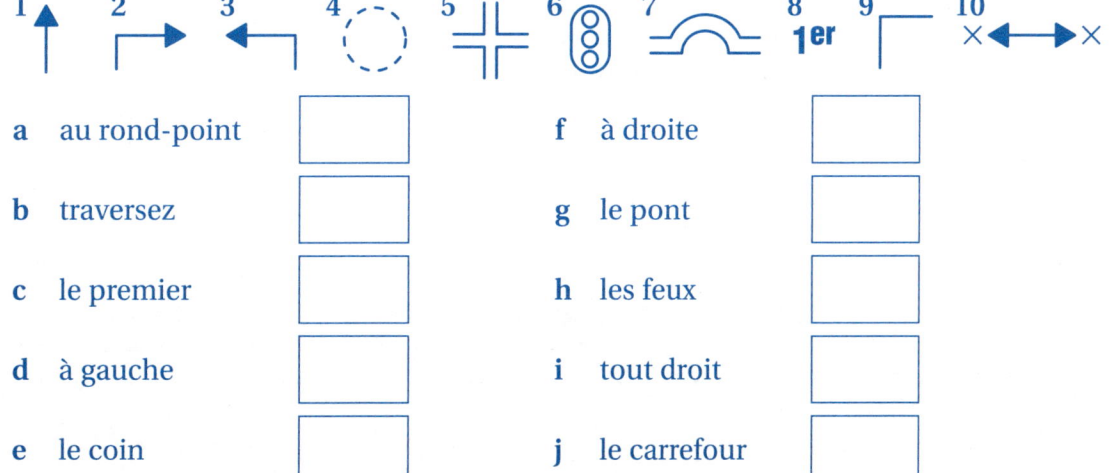

a au rond-point ☐   **f** à droite ☐

b traversez ☐   **g** le pont ☐

c le premier ☐   **h** les feux ☐

d à gauche ☐   **i** tout droit ☐

e le coin ☐   **j** le carrefour ☐

4   **Trouvez le bon verbe.**
    Find the correct verb.

a	tournez	**1**	cross
b	montez	**2**	take
c	allez	**3**	go past
d	traversez	**4**	go
e	descendez	**5**	turn
f	prenez	**6**	go up
g	marchez pendant	**7**	stop
h	continuez	**8**	go down
i	arrêtez-vous	**9**	walk for
j	passez devant	**10**	continue

5   **Lisez ces instructions et dites à quel dessin elles se réfèrent: a, b ou c?**
    Read these instructions and say what set of symbols they refer to: a, b or c?

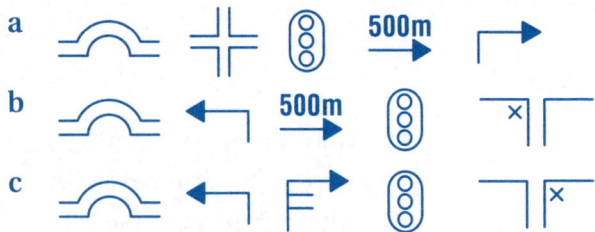

1   Pour aller chez Pauline, passez sur le pont, prenez la première rue à gauche puis marchez pendant cinq cents mètres jusqu'aux feux. La maison est au coin à gauche.

2   La maison de David? Passez par le pont. Ce n'est pas loin. Allez jusqu'au carrefour. Descendez jusqu'aux feux. C'est à cinq cents mètres sur la droite.

3   Pour venir chez moi, c'est facile. Passez par le pont. Tournez à gauche puis prenez la troisième rue à droite. Allez jusqu'aux feux. C'est sur le coin à droite.

6   **Maintenant faites votre propre explication. Utilisez les dessins suivants.**
    Now write your own explanation using the following drawings.

Pour aller chez ... _____

_____

_____

_____

_____

Métro 4 for AQA © Heinemann Educational 2001

7 Lisez l'article de journal et dites si les phrases sont vraies (V), fausses (F) ou si ce n'est pas dans le texte(?).

Read the newspaper article and say if the sentences are true (V), false (F) or not in the text(?).

> Un cycliste a été renversé hier soir vers dix-sept heures sur la route d'Annecy. Nicolas Drance roulait sans lumières quand Fabienne Jolie l'a percuté. Le jeune garçon de quatorze ans est hospitalisé. Il est blessé au bras. Sa jambe droite est cassée. Mlle Jolie a été traitée pour état de choc.

a Nicolas faisait du vélo au moment de l'accident. _____

b Fabienne roulait trop vite. _____

c Nicolas a été transporté à l'hôpital. _____

d Fabienne a été blessée. _____

8 À la gare. Qu'est-ce qu'on fait là?

At the station. What do you do in these places?

a la salle d'attente
b le buffet
c le composteur automatique
d la cabine téléphonique
e le quai
f le kiosque
g la consigne
h le guichet
i l'entrée
j la sortie

1 on y achète un sandwich
2 on y achète un magazine
3 on y achète un billet
4 on arrive par là
5 on quitte la gare par là
6 on laisse ses bagages là
7 on attend là
8 on y téléphone
9 on composte son billet là
10 on attend le train là

9 Dans le métro: Mettez les phrases dans le bon ordre pour faire un dialogue logique.

Put the sentences in the correct order to make a dialogue.

a Prenez la ligne 6 (Nation Charles de Gaulle/Etoile) jusque Bir Hakeim.
b Non, mademoiselle, c'est direct.
c Je voudrais aussi une carte de Paris.
d Oui, voilà. Ça fait 10 euros.

e Pour aller à la Tour Eiffel, s'il vous plaît?
f Voilà. C'est gratuit.
g Je peux avoir un carnet*, s'il vous plaît?
h Est-ce qu'il faut changer?

carnet = a book of 10 tickets

_____

_____

_____

_____

10 **Écrivez le nom des salles dans le plan.**
Label this map in French.

À l'aéroport

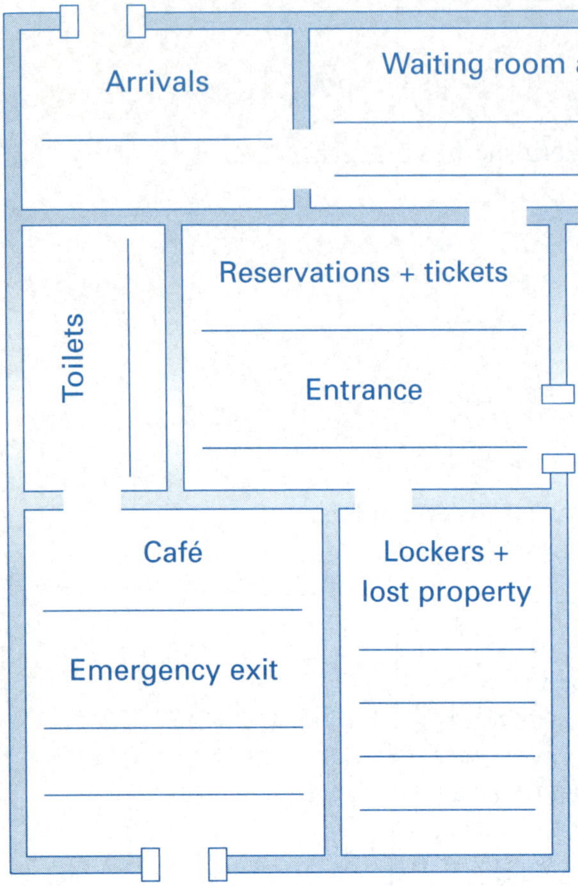

Arrivals

Waiting room area

Departures

Reservations + tickets

Toilets

Entrance

Café

Lockers + lost property

Emergency exit

> Arrivals = *arrivées*
> Departures = *départs*
> You will find most of the words you need in activity 7: don't forget that you need to build up a good knowledge of French vocabulary to be successful in the exam. Learn all these words as soon as you come across them and don't forget to transfer them from topic to topic and from skill to skill (i.e. you might use these words again in the topic of holidays or in another skill such as listening).

11 **Lisez ce dialogue et dites si les phrases sont vraies (V), fausses (F) ou si ce n'est pas dans le texte (?).**
Read this dialogue and say if the sentences are true (V), false (F) or not in the text (?).

Bonjour, Madame. Le train à destination de Paris part à quelle heure?
Le 9473 part à dix-sept heures vingt-huit, Monsieur.
Et le prochain?
Il y a des trains toutes les quarante-cinq minutes.
Je voudrais un aller-retour Nantes–Paris, s'il vous plaît.
En première ou en deuxième classe?
En deuxième classe.
Fumeurs ou non-fumeurs?
Non-fumeurs.
Oui, ça fait 56€, s'il vous plaît.
Je peux payer par carte de crédit?
Bien sûr, Monsieur.
Le train part de quel quai?
Quai treize.

Métro 4 for AQA © Heinemann Educational 2001

Il y a un distributeur de boissons par ici?
Non, mais il y a un café dans la salle d'attente.
Il y a un buffet dans le train?
Oui, Monsieur.
Merci bien!
Je vous en prie. Bon voyage!

a On peut prendre le train toutes les demi-heures. _____

b Le voyageur veut un aller simple. _____

c Il est italien. _____

d Il ne fume probablement pas. _____

e On peut payer par carte de crédit. _____

f Le train part du quai 3. _____

g Il y a des toilettes dans la salle d'attente. _____

h Le voyageur a probablement soif. _____

12 **Lisez la carte postale et répondez aux questions en anglais.**
Read the postcard and answer the questions in English.

Cher Papa,

Me voici enfin arrivée à Lyon après un voyage très difficile. J'ai eu plein de problèmes: à Paris, j'ai oublié de composter mon billet parce que je bavardais avec une copine. Je suis très distraite, tu sais! J'ai dû payer un supplément.

Après, le train a pris du retard en route. Je suis arrivée une demi-heure en retard à Lyon!

Il y avait trop de monde dans le train et j'ai laissé ma place à une vieille dame. Je suis restée debout pendant tout le trajet et maintenant j'ai mal aux jambes!

Mes bagages étaient trop lourds (30 kilos!) et j'ai aussi très mal au bras et aux épaules …

Bref, tout va mal! En plus, tu me manques mon petit Papa chéri!

Téléphone-moi vite!

   Gros bisous

   Manon

Monsieur Crouet

7 avenue Du Croquet

33 000 Bordeaux

> In a reading comprehension, always check how many points are allocated to each question and answer accordingly (see qu.g).

a Where is Manon now? (1) _____

b What did she forget to do in Paris? (1) _____

c Why? (1) _____

d What were the consequences? (1) _____

e How late was the train when it eventually arrived? (1) _____

f Who did she give her seat to? (1) _____

g Where does Manon hurt? (3) _____

h How would you define her mood: excited/angry/feeling sorry for herself? (1)

_____

13 **Réécrivez les phrases en utilisant *y*.**
Write the sentences again replacing the places with y.

a Je vais au cinéma. = _J'y vais._____

b Je travaille à la banque. = _____

c Pour aller à l'aéroport? = _____

d Je mange à la cantine. = _____

e Je descends à la gare. = _____

f J'habite à York. = _____

> **Y stands for 'there'.**
> **Je travaille au supermarché.**
> **= J'y travaille.**
> **I work in the supermarket.**
> **= I work there.**
> **The y goes before the verb.**
> **Because y is treated as a vowel, the je becomes j'.**

14 **Lisez cette carte postale et écrivez votre propre carte postale en changeant les détails soulignés.**
Read this postcard and write your own, changing the underlined expressions.

Chers parents,

Me voici à Lyon où il pleut. J'ai voyagé en avion. C'était super. Le voyage a duré deux heures.

Je loge dans un hôtel. Ça se trouve dans un carrefour en plein centre-ville.

C'est très bien ici!

À bientôt!

Karim

Monsieur et Madame Saïd

Le Champ Mignon

75005 Paris

Métro 4 for AQA © Heinemann Educational 2001

15 Écrivez environ 30 mots.

Rappel

Je vais …
à pied/vélo
en bus/voiture

- Dites comment vous allez en ville.
- Dites combien de temps le trajet dure.
- Décrivez votre ville. (C'est une petite/grande ville touristique/industrielle, etc.)

_____

_____

_____

_____

_____

_____

16 Des collégiens ont créé des slogans pour protéger l'environnement. Trouvez l'image qui correspond à chaque slogan.
Some students have written their own slogans to protect the environment. Match the pictures to the slogans.

a

Mort au bruit
Silence la nuit

b
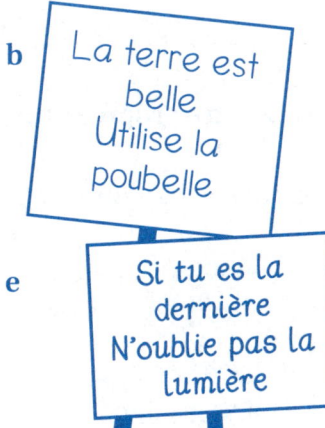
La terre est belle
Utilise la poubelle

c

I love le vélo

d
Do ré mi fa sol
À bas les bombes aérosol

e
Si tu es la dernière
N'oublie pas la lumière

f
Recycle le papier
T'auras plus de forêts

1

2

3

4

5

6

Grammaire

1 Remplissez les trous avec la bonne expression en utilisant les mots en italique.
Complete the sentences using the words in italic.

adverb	comparative: plus *(more)*/ moins *(less)*/aussi *(as)*	superlative: le plus *(the most)*/ le moins *(the least)*
vite	*moins vite*	*le moins vite*
souvent	*plus souvent*	*le plus souvent*
bruyamment	*plus bruyamment*	
régulièrement	*aussi régulièrement*	

a La moto est passée devant nous _____ que la voiture. (The motorbike drove past us more loudly than the car.)

b Les bus passent _____ pendant la semaine que le dimanche. (Buses come more often during the week than on Sundays.)

c Je prends le bus _____ . (I take the bus most often.)

d On voyage _____ à pied qu'à vélo. (It is slower to travel on foot than by bike.)

e C'est à pied qu'on avance _____ . (You make the slowest progress on foot.)

f Je vais en ville _____ que ma mère. (I go to town as regularly as my mother.)

2 Choisissez un mot parmi les mots ci-dessous: faites attention à la grammaire! Pouvez-vous ensuite traduire les phrases en anglais?
Choose one word from those below: check your grammar! Can you then translate the sentences into English?

quai train numéro heure classe circulation

> **quel** goes with a word that is masc/sing;
> **quelle** goes with a word that is fem/sing;
> **quels** goes with a word that is masc/pl;
> **quelles** goes with a word that is fem/pl.

a Quelle _____ est-il? = _____

b Le train part de quel _____ ? = _____

c Quelle _____ ! = _____

d Vous prenez quel _____ ? = _____

e C'est en quelle _____ ? = _____

f Quel est le _____ du quai? = _____

Métro 4 for AQA © Heinemann Educational 2001

À l'oral

Add reasons, explanations or descriptions to short answers.

1 Comment vas-tu au collège le matin?

_____

_____

2 Tu habites loin du collège?

_____

3 Quand tu vas faire les magasins, comment y vas-tu?

_____

4 Est-ce que tu aimes faire des promenades à pied?

_____

5 Quel est ton moyen de transport préféré et pourquoi?

_____

6 As-tu déjà pris l'avion?

_____

7 Où es-tu allée l'année dernière pendant les vacances?

_____

8 Comment le voyage s'est-il passé?

_____

9 Que penses-tu des transports en commun là où tu habites?

_____

10 Que penses-tu de la circulation en ville?

_____

11 Quel est le plus grand problème de pollution selon toi et pourquoi?

_____

12 Qu'est-ce qu'on peut faire pour améliorer notre environnement?

_____

Métro 4 for AQA © Heinemann Educational 2001

ISBN 0 435 37281 5

9 780435 372811 >

À l'oral